P9-DCX-504

BRITISH WRITERS

BRITISH WRITERS

Edited under the auspices of the British Council

IAN SCOTT-KILVERT

General Editor

VOLUME IV

WILLIAM WORDSWORTH

TO

ROBERT BROWNING

CHARLES SCRIBNER'S SONS / NEW YORK

Library of Congress Cataloging in Publication Data (Revised)

Main entry under title:

British writers.

Includes bibliographies and index.
CONTENTS: v. 1. William Langland to the English
Bible.—v. 2. Thomas Middleton to George Farquhar.
—v. 3. Daniel Defoe to the Gothic Novel.
—v. 4. William Wordsworth to Robert Browning.
1. English literature—History and criticism.
2. English literature—Bio-bibliography. 3. Authors,
English—Biography. I. Scott-Kilvert, Ian. II. Great
Britain. British Council.
PR85.B688   820'.9   78-23483   AACR1
ISBN 0-684-15798-5 (v. 1)   ISBN 0-684-16408-6 (v. 3)
ISBN 0-684-16407-8 (v. 2)   ISBN 0-684-16635-6 (v. 4)

Editorial Staff

List of Subjects in Volume IV

Introduction

British Writers is designed as a work of reference to complement *American Writers*, the eight-volume set of literary biographies of authors past and present, which was first published in 1974. In the same way as its American counterpart, which first appeared in the form of individual pamphlets published by the University of Minnesota Press, the British collection originates from a series of separate articles entitled *Writers and Their Work*. This series was initiated by the British Council in 1950 as a part of its worldwide program to support the teaching of English language and literature, an activity carried on both in the English-speaking world and in many countries in which English is not the mother tongue.

The articles are intended to appeal to a wide readership, including students in secondary and advanced education, teachers, librarians, scholars, editors, and critics, as well as the general public. Their purpose is to provide an introduction to the work of writers who have made a significant contribution to English literature, to stimulate the reader's enjoyment of the text, and to give students the means to pursue the subject further. The series begins in the fourteenth century and extends to the present day, and is printed in chronological order according to the date of the subject's birth. The articles are far from conforming to a fixed pattern, but speaking generally each begins with a short biographical section, the main body of the text being devoted to a survey of the subject's principal writings and an assessment of the work as a whole. Each article is equipped with a selected bibliography that records the subject's writings in chronological order, in the form both of collected editions and of separate works, including modern and paperback editions. The bibliography concludes with a list of biographical and critical publications, including both books and articles, to guide the reader who is interested in further

research. In the case of authors such as Chaucer or Shakespeare, whose writings have inspired extensive criticism and commentary, the critical section is further subdivided and provides a useful record of the new fields of research that have developed over the past hundred years.

British Writers is not conceived as an encyclopedia of literature, nor is it a series of articles planned so comprehensively as to include every writer of historical importance. Its character is rather that of a critical anthology posssessing both the virtues and the limitations of such a grouping. It offers neither the schematized form of the encyclopedia nor the completeness of design of the literary history. On the other hand it is limited neither by the impersonality of the one nor the uniformity of the other. Since each contributor speaks with only one voice out of many, he is principally concerned with explaining his subject as fully as possible rather than with establishing an order of merit or making "placing" comparisons (since each contributor might well "place" differently). The prime task is one of presentation and exposition rather than of assigning critical praise or censure. The contributors to the first volume consist of distinguished literary scholars and critics—later volumes include contributions by poets, novelists, historians, and biographers. Each writes as an enthusiast for his subject, and each sets out to explain what are the qualities that make an author worth reading.

The expression "romantic movement" has come to be accepted over the last century as a description of the main stream of English literature roughly between the years 1780 and 1830. The word "romantic," used as a critical and historical label—especially in contrast to "classical"—first became current in Germany through the lectures of A. W. Schlegel (translated into English in 1815), but in England it kept for a long time its earlier meanings of "legendary," "highly-colored," or "exaggerated." A romance signified a composition written simply to entertain. The leading English poets of the time never referred to themselves or to each other as writers of "romantic verse." The critics sometimes used the word pejoratively, but not as a label for any contemporary school of writing. Rather than rehearse the dispute—still unresolved—as to the meaning of "romantic" in this context, and whether such a "movement" ever existed in England, it may be more useful to describe the special qualities, themes, and influences which undoubtedly distinguished the literature of that period, and which, while arguably "romantic," were also extremely diverse and sometimes mutually contradictory.

The most pervasive general phenomenon, perhaps, was the impulse to assert the independence of the individual and the importance of a freer and fuller expression of emotional experience: this required a challenge to the repressive authority of established society, so as to loosen its grip upon conformity of taste and manners. This inclination is reflected not only in the literature but in the art and music of the period and in its fashions and decoration besides. It shows itself in the appeal of these arts to the emotions of fear and of awe, and in the willingness of writers and artists to explore the supernatural, the irrational, dreams, hallucinations, and the world of the subconscious.

In the introduction to volume III it was remarked that during the last quarter of the eighteenth century, a number of poets—in the first place Burns and Blake—turned their attention to the experiences of the poor and unlettered, the submerged majority who lived beyond the pale of prosperous urban society. Such poets now handled material that to their Augustan predecessors would have appeared "low" or "mean." "Humble and rustic life was generally chosen," writes Wordsworth in his preface of 1800 to *Lyrical Ballads*, "because in that condition the essential passions of the heart find a better soil in which they can flourish."

This choice of a different "soil" marks a radical change in the relationship between the poet and his audience. Of course by no means all the poets fixed their view upon the experiences of the poor: it might be directed to the world of childhood, as elsewhere in Wordsworth and in Blake, or to a world peopled by supernatural presences as in Coleridge, or a world of ideal beauty, as in Keats. But in rejecting the convention of a range of perennial themes accepted by polite

society as fit material for poetry, the poet ceases to address an audience of known expectations and moves toward a "one to one" relationship with the reader. For his part the poet withdraws into a more rarefied atmosphere of reading, reverie, travel, or communion with nature, and in the resulting ode, ballad, tale, lyric, or poetic autobiography he offers a private world, as in "The Ancient Mariner" or "The Eve of St. Agnes," sustained only by the intensity of his imagination: the reader, to gain access, must surrender *his* preconceptions as to the proper subject matter for poetry. Through the same process the writer becomes a more isolated figure, no longer part courtier, soldier, statesman, or cleric, but a prophet or visionary whose function in society depends as never before upon his individual powers of imaginative or intellectual creation.

A separate but very widespread characteristic of the period was its fondness for the imaginative reconstruction of the past, the luring of the reader's interest away from the present. This had originated in the admiration of scholars such as Gray and Percy for the epics and ballads of more primitive cultures and in the predilection of Walpole and his successors for historical settings, with their accompanying aura of mystery and terror: it is also revealed in a renewed appetite for classical and medieval legend. Such reconstructions find their expression most conspicuously in the fiction of Scott and the Gothic novelists, but also in the poems of Coleridge, Byron, Shelley, and Keats, and later in those of Tennyson and Browning. It is a notable paradox of the age that although its writers were keenly aware of the rapidly changing present that surrounded them, they were also strongly impelled to turn their imagination toward the past, to explore territories that were at once strange and familiar.

Historically, the literature of the period is the product of two sharply distinct age groups. The generation of Wordsworth, Coleridge, Southey, and Scott was in its teens when the French Revolution began, and at first hailed it with hope and joy, emotions soon to be offset by disillusion, fear, and the call of patriotism. For the second generation, which includes Byron, Shelley, and Keats, the revolution was already a historical fact, and by the time of their early manhood the fear of invasion and subjugation such as the rest of Europe had experienced, had vanished. Youthful idealism was now focused upon the problems of peace, the sufferings of the industrial and rural poor at home or of the oppressed subjects of the Holy Alliance and the Ottoman Empire abroad. For Wordsworth, Coleridge, and Southey, the church was still a vital part of the social fabric: their successors, notably Byron, Shelly, and Leigh Hunt, regarded official religion as a mere extension of reactionary government, the priest as an obsequious auxiliary of the king. The poetry of Wordsworth and the "Lakers" is deeply rooted in the local pieties of English country life. It deals, in Hazlitt's words, with household truths, events, and emotions that are common to all, and makes its appeal through the intensification of familiar experience. The poetry of Byron, Shelley, and Keats travels through far wider realms, not only in physical or spiritual location but also in its handling of ideological argument, ethical conflict, aesthetic ideals. It is the younger generation whom Continental critics regard as the English counterparts of the romantic school in Europe, seeing them as poets who broke traditional molds to create new, internationally shared ideals of justice, freedom, love, and beauty.

The appearance of *Lyrical Ballads* has often been hailed as the first major landmark of a new era in English literature. But this impression owes quite a lot to hindsight. Certainly the authors not only announced a new approach to poetry—"to throw over incidents taken from common life a certain colouring of the imagination, whereby ordinary things should be presented in an unusual aspect . . . and to make these situations interesting by tracing in them the primary laws of our nature"—they also offered a working model. Yet superficially, at least, as Robert Mayo has shown, the readers of the magazines of that time would not have found anything very unusual in the subject matter, diction, or metrical forms of the collection. Tales recounting the sufferings of country folk such as Goody Blake or Simon Lee, pastorals and rural sketches, meditative blank verse such as "Tintern Abbey," and ballads written in an antique vocabulary were all familiar features of the poetic fashions of the 1790's, as were the stock figures of female vagrants, old and impoverished peasants, and other victims of circumstance, while many minor poets were also striving to create a simpler diction.

The first reception of *Lyrical Ballads* was not unfavorable. Besides this, we have Coleridge's tribute to Wordsworth's poems of an even earlier date— "seldom, if ever, was the emergence of a poetic genius above the literary horizon more evidently announced," and we know that Hazlitt at twenty and De Quincey at fourteen became instant admirers of his verse. But Wordsworth's preface of 1800 asserting that his diction represented "a selection of language really used by men" proved an infinitely controversial claim. The preface and Wordsworth's subsequent writings were seen by many critics as upholding a bogus primitivism. "None but savages have submitted to eat acorns after corn has been found" argued one reviewer, and with a few honorable exceptions it required another twenty-five years for Wordsworth's stature to be recognized. "The Ancient Mariner" bewildered many early readers, and was described as "a rhapsody of unintelligible wildness and incoherence." "Christabel" and "Kubla Khan," although not published until 1816, suffered a similar fate. Shelley and Keats were likewise savaged by their early reviewers; only the poems of Byron won instant popularity.

In retrospect, however, not only was *Lyrical Ballads* the only important new production of the 1790's but, apart from Wordsworth's own work, very little else of distinction appeared for the next fifteen years. The solitary exceptions were *Childe Harold* and the Turkish tales, the verse thrillers with which Byron followed up the spectacular success of *Harold*. The downfall of Napoleon marks the turning point: the next decade witnessed the publication of almost all the major works of the so-called romantic era. The preceding lean years may be accounted for partly by the rigors of the censorship, but much more by the fact that the hearts and minds of the nation were engrossed in the struggle for survival.

In short, the true originality of *Lyrical Ballads* lay in the substance rather than the subject matter of the poetry, and in the execution of certain poems, above all "Tintern Abbey" and "The Ancient Mariner." The effect of Wordsworth's less well-known poems in the collection is admirably summed up in J. R. Watson's phrase, "a poetry the texture of which allows no escape." He stresses the skill with which Wordsworth varies his language according to the needs of each poem, and concludes that the language of *Lyrical Ballads* should be viewed as a whole: we should beware of regarding "Tintern Abbey" as the true voice of Wordsworth, and writing off the simpler style of the tales. The main part of the essay is devoted to *The Prelude*, in which the author finds some important points of resemblance to *Paradise Lost*. Although *The Prelude* is ostensibly an autobiography, it deals with the loss of the paradise of childhood, and in some respects raises the autobiographical genre to the level of epic.

While Wordsworth's contribution to *Lyrical Ballads* was so to present everyday occurrences that the reader could see them with new eyes, Coleridge undertook to provide "incidents and agents in part supernatural." Yet he was himself a most sensitive and minute observer of his surroundings, and the power of his poetry to evoke mysterious and unseen presences owes a great deal to the subtlety and delicacy of his descriptions of nature. But his great period of poetic creation was so short, and his opium addiction had become in his thirties so conspicuously damaging, that he quickly came to be regarded as a brilliant failure, and this impression has proved hard to dispel. Raymond Brett's essay challenges this view and points out that although Coleridge's later career was very different from its meteoric beginning, he possessed unexpected powers of recovery. Besides describing the unique combination of poetic and philosophic insight that distinguishes his literary criticism, the essay also surveys his writings on politics and on religion.

Byron, the eldest of the second wave of poets, is said to have been told by a craniologist that "everything in this skull has its opposite developed in great force"—an eccentric but nonetheless apt summary of his position now as the mocker, now as the incarnation of the spirit of the age. An avowed enemy of much of the new poetry, he created in his first satire, *English Bards and Scotch Reviewers,* a fresh Dunciad for the contemporary literary scene. But then his *Childe Harold* turned out to appeal to just that appetite for romance that its hero had partly been designed to burlesque. In *Harold* and in the Turkish tales, Byron offered what neither Scott nor the Gothic novelists could provide—actuality. Here was an author who was not working from the library, but had actually rubbed shoulders with Mediterranean corsairs, Albanian banditti, and Oriental despots. Thus he himself came to be regarded as living embodiment of the formula for the romantic hero, a passionate, misanthropic, aristocratic, uninhibited outcast. His subsequent career with its catalog of amorous adventures, defiance of convention, and championing of oppressed nationalities became the international model for the rebellious artist.

Malcolm Kelsall's essay explains how Byron's early upbringing and domestic circumstances isolated him from his class, but also required him to live,

unlike any of his poetic contemporaries, as a man of the world, constantly in action and in the public eye, and how he utilized such experience as the raw material for his poetry. In this context it is worth noting how his European reputation depends very largely upon *Childe Harold,* the narrative poems, and the dramas, all these compositions being written in a relatively direct and simple diction, which can be appreciated, unlike some of the finest poetry of his contemporaries, without a native grasp of the English language. In England, Byron would not be ranked as a major poet were it not for his mature satirical writings, and the essay pays due tribute to his final development as a comic poet in *Beppo, The Vision of Judgment,* and *Don Juan.*

In one of his letters from Italy, Shelley wrote, "I always seek in what I see the manifestation of something beyond the present and tangible object," a remark that throws some light on the prominence of elemental forces, winds, tempests, lightnings, volcanoes, clouds, avalanches, and earthquakes in his imagery. More than any other of his fellow poets he pictures life as a process of cosmic change on a gigantic scale. His poetry has been conspicuously successful in driving critics to excesses of praise or censure. Geoffrey Matthews notes these violent fluctuations of opinion and discusses the charge of elusiveness that is often leveled against his writings. He warns us that Shelley's deceptively fluent verse often conceals real complexity, and urges that his language requires close and patient study if the symbolic vocabulary he often uses is to be understood.

Shelley creates, it has been said, a poetry of *process* or *becoming;* Keats a poetry of *being.* *Endymion,* Keats's first long poem, proclaims the purpose that was to dominate his poetic career, the quest for beauty as the highest expression of reality and the richest source of happiness for mankind. He was supremely well equipped to describe the apprehension of beauty through the senses and, perhaps for this very reason, sharply aware of its transitory nature in the mortal world. Miriam Allott's essay draws attention to the counterpoise between vision and awakening that characterizes so much of Keats's finest poetry, the necessity to accept the transience of youth, beauty, and love, and to do so without destroying order and harmony: in three of the great odes, she traces a curve of feeling that at first carries the poet into an ideal world, and then returns him to what is actual and inescapable.

The half-century under review, whatever label

may be attached to it, certainly marks one of the great periods of change and experiment in English poetry—in language, meter, rhythm, and in the invention of new lyrical and narrative structures. Wordsworth formulated a statement concerning poetic diction, but both he and his successors often practiced something quite different. Coleridge's greatest poems are far removed from the language of conversation. Byron, despite his traditionalist approach, showed himself a pioneer in the introduction of colloquial language and the extension of satirical vocabulary. Keats created a diction that by the time of the odes had attained a sensuous richness and complexity to rival Shakespeare's: yet both he and Shelley in their last unfinished poems, *The Fall of Hyperion* and *The Triumph of Life*, were moving toward a stronger and barer diction that possesses a natural and in no way artificial simplicity. It has been well said that the exact intention of these poets could not be formulated in advance: they used the language not as a tool, but rather as a medium, and submitted their purposes to it.

The two major novelists of the period, Sir Walter Scott and Jane Austen, provide an extreme contrast both in the form and the content of their writing. From his earliest boyhood Scott had been steeped in the ballads and chronicles of border raids and Jacobite adventures. In his methods of composition, Ian Jack reminds us, he recoiled from the labor of shaping a tale with a regular plot; and fiction, as he practiced it, imposed no restrictions in respect of design or material. The essay stresses the importance of his use of the vernacular in expressing the rich variety of the Scottish character and finds that the novels rise to greatness in the speeches of characters such as Dandy Dinmont, Meg Merrilees, and Edie Ochiltree, whom Scott endows with a full measure of their native eloquence. In this respect his power to create a panoramic view of society at the great moments of Scottish history has been compared to Shakespeare's achievement in his English history plays.

Jane Austen's writing stems from a very different tradition—the portrayal of the tempo and character of ordinary everyday existence, by no means lacking in drama, but never larger than life. Her literary ancestors are Defoe, Richardson, Crabbe, and Fanny Burney, but to their achievements she added an economy of form and a perfection of artistry that have never been surpassed in the English novel. Jane Austen has on occasion been censured as the chron-

icler of an enclosed middle-class world, preoccupied with local and domestic concerns, and oblivious of the great events, changes, and sufferings of her times: why did she not apply her undoubted gifts to a larger canvas? In rebutting this criticism, Brian Southam points to the powerfully satirical character of her novels and argues that in capturing the limited vision of the gentry, she exposes its essentially self-centered nature. He claims convincingly that she succeeded in liberating the novel from its servile function as an instrument of cultural self-flattery.

Charles Lamb was justly praised in the nineteenth century as the discoverer of many neglected Elizabethan and Jacobean dramatists, and he was one of the earliest reviewers to perceive the greatness of Wordsworth. But his criticism is for modern taste too desultory, too reliant on charm, and too short on intellectual muscle, and interest has shifted to his letters and his role as a personal friend and literary ally of Wordsworth, Coleridge, Hazlitt, and Keats. Edmund Blunden's essay creates an attractive portrait of Lamb's personality, which is enriched by Blunden's knowledge of Christ's Hospital, the school at which he, like his subject, was educated.

Hazlitt's standing has also suffered in modern times, and especially since the writing of literary criticism passed from the free-lance essayist to the professional academic. He has been disparaged as a mere literary journalist and condemned for his lack of scholarship, his fondness for resounding generalizations, his incapacity for sustained reasoning, and his weakness as a theoretical critic; and certainly there are too many essays in which his personality is tiresomely interposed between reader and subject. Yet how many of his detractors can be credited with the infectious exuberance that animates the best of his prose, or with his capacity to do justice to authors with whom he is out of sympathy, such as Burke or Scott? Above all, his essays hold our interest for his eloquent firsthand judgments on his contemporaries. It is the biographical approach that dominates his writings, and Raymond Brett's study warns us at the outset that Hazlitt constantly presents ideas as an expression of personality. This method is seen at its best in *The Spirit of the Age*, where his biographical and critical insights are balanced so as to create a group of contemporary portraits of unmatched brilliance and authority.

De Quincey has fared better at the hands of modern commentators. His autobiographical *Confessions of an English Opium-Eater* ranks as a minor classic, which could scarcely be said of Hazlitt's *Liber Amoris,* and the best of his criticism is of a kind that is far more congenial to the modern approach. His fascination with psychology and with the relation between mind and body is also of perennial interest, and his gifts as a descriptive writer lift his prose at moments to heights that are comparable to the intensity of imagination shown by the contemporary poets. He wrote a great deal that has proved to be ephemeral, and Hugh Sykes Davies puts his finger on the secret of his lasting appeal when he says that De Quincey is most readable in those writings that most involved his own experience. He lays special emphasis on De Quincey's originality as one of the very few critics who have written with authority on prose composition and prose rhythm.

Carlyle was born in the same year as Keats; Hood, Disraeli, and Macaulay only a few years later. But the difference in outlook between Shelley and Keats, who died young, in the years immediately following Waterloo, and those who began to write after 1825 is unmistakable. All were keenly aware of the evils of poverty and inhumanity, but while Shelley and Keats wrote of the harsh world in terms of political or aesthetic ideals

Where but to think is to be full of sorrow

their immediate successors were acquainted in detail with factory conditions, bread riots, and the reform of the franchise. Carlyle wrote in prose and had little or no gift for versification, but his criticism of society is really couched in poetic terms, the poetry of an Old Testament prophet. His first major success, *Sartor Resartus,* describes his youthful progress, manifestly thrilling to his early readers, to the Everlasting No, the discarding of a whole wardrobe of hitherto accepted values and the creation of a new spiritual and intellectual vesture (largely self-made). Still more influential was *The French Revolution,* a history likewise forged out of poetic images. Carlyle depicts the revolution from a Calvinist standpoint, as a divine judgment on a corrupt system, which not even a far more just or adaptable ancien régime could have averted. Many of Carlyle's ideas, his doctrine of hero-worship, his slogan "no work—no recompense," his views on democracy and on color have been found repugnant by later generations. Ian Campbell's essay acknowledges these barriers to appreciation of his thinking, but reminds us both of Carlyle's originality and of his powerful influence

upon most of his contemporaries. His judgment as early as 1829 that the era then unfolding was above all a *mechanical* age, not only in its working habits but in its thinking, was extraordinarily farsighted.

The lessons that Carlyle drew from the French Revolution were profoundly pessimistic. Macaulay, who also essayed a study of the past on the grand scale in the hope of interpreting present and future, arrived at different conclusions. When he championed the continuity and flexibility of the English political system, the threat of revolution was real, and it was an urgent task to defend a more moderate alternative than the French solution. Posterity has criticized him partly because the Whig view of history undoubtedly oversimplified the pattern of events, partly because the experience of the twentieth century has made his doctrine of inevitable progress appear at once implausible and complacent. Kenneth Young's essay illuminates the many-sided nature of Macaulay's gifts, as debater and administrator, as well as historian, literary critic, and poet. He makes a thorough assessment of the *History of England* and finds that contemporary scholarship has swung back to some extent in Macaulay's favor.

In two of his most ambitious novels, *Coningsby* and *Sybil,* Disraeli anticipated Macaulay with an even more simplified interpretation of English history—the Tory picture. This was designed to illustrate the new concept of Tory democracy, an ideal conceived in the 1840's for an alliance between a reformed aristocracy and the working classes to curb the power of the rising class of industrial entrepreneurs. Disraeli at times echoes Carlyle in attacking the mechanization of contemporary life, and here his thinking has affinities with that of Burke and Coleridge, who had argued against Bentham and the utilitarians that society resembles a living organism rather than a machine. Disraeli's fiction as a whole offers an extraordinary mélange of ingredients— high society life ("the silver fork novel," in Hazlitt's phrase) documentation of social conditions, sentimental melodrama, political theorizing, thinly disguised portraits of contemporary celebrities. Paul Bloomfield's essay contends that although the novels contain incongruous elements that a natural artist would have rejected, they do possess and artistic coherence and can still hold the reader through their wit, their intellectual vitality, and their interest as a historical record.

Tennyson and Browning lived on until the last years of the century, and a considerable part of their poetry must properly be regarded as Victorian. But both were deeply influenced by their immediate predecessors, especially by Shelley and Keats; and, editorially at least, there is a case for departing from a strict chronological arrangement, so as to survey their work with that of the other five major poets in volume IV and group the work of the major nineteenth-century novelists in volume V. At the beginning of his essay, Brian Southam remarks that Tennyson dominated his age as no English poet had done before him. In consequence the reaction that duly set in against the Victorians proved disproportionately damaging to his reputation: thus the modern critic is now challenged by the fact that there is no commonly accepted view of his achievement. The essay pays special attention to "The Lady of Shalott" as embodying Tennyson's personal myth of the artist's isolation and of his "magic of creation"—the Tennysonian analogue of Coleridge's "Kubla Khan." It goes on to suggest that Tennyson felt himself in duty bound to counterbalance his interior nature as the poet of Shalott with a poetry that was more securely distanced and possessed of a more optimistic vision, and that compositions such as "Locksley Hall" and *The Princess* bear witness to the intensity of this struggle.

When Tennyson published his *Poems* (1842) he was at once hailed, at the age of thirty-three, as the leading poet of his generation. Browning encountered a harder struggle, and even after publishing some of his best work, such as *Men and Women* (1855), he had to wait another decade for recognition. Philip Drew describes the remarkable diversity of Browning's poetry, the exuberant freedom of his language, and his resource in exploring unusual themes and situations, and gives particular prominence to the monologue, the form of which Browning became the acknowledged master. He discusses how Browning handles the monologue, not merely as a brilliant display of ventriloquism, but as an exercise to involve the reader in active discrimination between truth and falsehood, in answering Browning's insistent question

What say you to the right or wrong of that?

He concludes that in spite of important differences between Browning's conception of poetry and that of his modern successors, when we look at the Victorian age, "his is the face that is turned most openly towards our own."

The series was founded by Laurence Brander, then director or publications, at the British Council. The first editor was T. O. Beachcroft, himself a distinguished writer of short stories. His successors were the late Bonamy Dobree, formerly Professor of English Literature at the University of Leeds; Geoffrey Bullough, Professor Emeritus of English Literature, King's College, London, and author of *The Narrative and Dramatic Sources of Shakespeare;* and since 1970 the present writer. To these founders and predecessors *British Writers* is deeply indebted for the design of the series, the planning of its scope, and the distinction of their editorship, and I personally for many years of friendship and advice, and invaluable experience, generously shared.

—Ian Scott-Kilvert

Chronological Table

1770 Boston Massacre
Edmund Burke's *Thoughts on the Cause of the Present Discontents*
Oliver Goldsmith's *The Deserted Village*
Death of Thomas Chatterton
William Wordsworth born

1771 Arkwright's first spinning mill founded
Deaths of Thomas Gray and Tobias Smollett
Walter Scott born

1772 Samuel Taylor Coleridge born

1773 Boston Tea Party
Goldsmith's *She Stoops to Conquer*
Johann Wolfgang von Goethe's *Götz von Berlichingen*

1774 The first Continental Congress meets in Philadelphia
Goethe's *Sorrows of Young Werther*
Death of Oliver Goldsmith
Robert Southey born

1775 Burke's speech on American taxation
American War of Independence begins with the battles of Lexington and Concord
Samuel Johnson's *Journey to the Western Islands of Scotland*
Richard Brinsley Sheridan's *The Rivals* and *The Duenna*
Beaumarchais's *Le Barbier de Séville*
James Watt and Matthew Boulton begin building steam engines in England
Jane Austen born
Charles Lamb born
Walter Savage Landor born
Matthew Lewis born

1776 American Declaration of Independence
Edward Gibbon's *Decline and Fall of the Roman Empire* (1776–1788)
Adam Smith's *Inquiry into the Nature & Causes of the Wealth of Nations*
Thomas Paine's *Common Sense*
Death of David Hume

1777 Maurice Morgann's *Essay on the Dramatic Character of Sir John Falstaff*
Sheridan's *The School for Scandal* first performed (published 1780)
General Burgoyne surrenders at Saratoga

1778 The American colonies allied with France
Britain and France at war
Captain James Cook discovers Hawaii
Death of William Pitt, first earl of Chatham
Deaths of Jean Jacques Rousseau and Voltaire
William Hazlitt born

1779 Johnson's *Prefaces to the Works of the English Poets* (1779–1781); reissued in 1781 as *The Lives of the Most Eminent English Poets*
Sheridan's *The Critic*
Samuel Crompton invents the spinning mule
Death of David Garrick

1780 The Gordon Riots in London

1781 Charles Cornwallis surrenders at Yorktown
Immanuel Kant's *Critique of Pure Reason*
Friedrich von Schiller's *Die Räuber*

1782 William Cowper's "The Journey of John Gilpin" published in the *Public Advertiser*
Pierre de Laclos's *Les Liaisons dangereuses*
Rousseau's *Confessions* published posthumously

1783 American War of Independence ended by the Definitive Treaty of Peace, signed at Paris

William Blake's *Poetical Sketches*

George Crabbe's *The Village*

William Pitt the younger becomes prime minister

Henri Beyle (Stendhal) born

1784 Beaumarchais's *Le Mariage de Figaro* first performed (published 1785)

Death of Samuel Johnson

1785 Warren Hastings returns to England from India

James Boswell's *The Journey of a Tour of the Hebrides, with Samuel Johnson, LL.D.*

Cowper's *The Task*

Edmund Cartwright invents the power loom

Thomas De Quincey born

Thomas Love Peacock born

1786 William Beckford's *Vathek* published in English (originally written in French in 1782)

Robert Burns's *Poems Chiefly in the Scottish Dialect*

Wolfgang Amadeus Mozart's *The Marriage of Figaro*

Death of Frederick the Great

1787 The Committee for the Abolition of the Slave Trade founded in England

The Constitutional Convention meets at Philadelphia; the Constitution is signed

1788 The trial of Hastings begins on charges of corruption of the government in India

The Estates-General of France summoned

U. S. Constitution is ratified

George Washington elected president of the United States

Giovanni Casanova's *Histoire de ma fuite* (first manuscript of his memoirs)

The *Daily Universal Register* becomes the *Times* (London)

George Gordon, Lord Byron born

1789 The Estates-General meets at Versailles

The National Assembly (Assemblée Nationale) convened

The fall of the Bastille marks the beginning of the French Revolution

The National Assembly draws up the Declaration of Rights of Man and of the Citizen

First U. S. Congress meets in New York

Blake's *Songs of Innocence*

Jeremy Bentham's *Introduction to the Principles of Morals and Legislation* introduces the theory of utilitarianism

Gilbert White's *Natural History of Selborne*

1790 Congress sets permanent capital city site on the Potomac River

First U. S. Census

Burke's *Reflections on the Revolution in France*

Blake's *The Marriage of Heaven and Hell*

Edmund Malone's edition of Shakespeare

Death of Benjamin Franklin

1791 French royal family's flight from Paris and capture at Varennes; imprisonment in the Tuileries

Bill of Rights is ratified

Paine's *The Rights of Man* (1791–1792)

Boswell's *The Life of Johnson*

Burns's *Tam o'Shanter*

The *Observer* founded

1792 The Prussians invade France and are repulsed at Valmy

September massacres

The National Convention declares royalty abolished in France

Washington reelected

New York Stock Exchange opens

Mary Wollstonecraft's *Vindication of the Rights of Women*

William Bligh's voyage to the South Sea in H.M.S. *Bounty*

Percy Bysshe Shelley born

1793 Trial and execution of Louis XVI and Marie Antoinette

France declares war against England

The Committee of Public Safety (Comité de Salut Public) established

Eli Whitney devises the cotton gin

William Godwin's *An Enquiry Concerning Political Justice*

Blake's *Visions of the Daughters of Albion and America*

Wordsworth's *An Evening Walk* and *Descriptive Sketches*

1794 Execution of Georges Danton and Maximilien de Robespierre

CHRONOLOGICAL TABLE

Paine's *The Age of Reason* (1794–1796)

Blake's *Songs of Experience*

Ann Radcliffe's *The Mysteries of Udolpho*

Death of Edward Gibbon

1795 The government of the Directory established (1795–1799)

Hastings acquitted

Landor's *Poems*

Death of James Boswell

John Keats born

Thomas Carlyle born

1796 Napoleon Bonaparte takes command in Italy

Matthew Lewis' *The Monk*

John Adams elected president

Death of Robert Burns

1797 The peace of Campo Formio: extinction of the Venetian Republic

X. Y. Z. Affair

Mutinies in the Royal Navy at Spithead and the Nore

Blake's *Vala, Or the Four Zoas* (first version)

Deaths of Edmund Burke, Mary Wollstonecraft, and Horace Walpole

1798 Napoleon invades Egypt

Horatio Nelson wins the battle of the Nile

Wordsworth's and Coleridge's *Lyrical Ballads*

Landor's *Gebir*

Thomas Malthus' *Essay on the Principle of Population*

1799 Napoleon becomes first consul

Pitt introduces first income tax in Great Britain

Sheridan's *Pizarro*

Honoré de Balzac born

Thomas Hood born

Alexander Pushkin born

1800 Thomas Jefferson defeats John Adams for the presidency

Alessandro Volta produces electricity from a cell

Library of Congress established

Death of William Cowper

Thomas Babington Macaulay born

1801 First census taken in England

1802 The Treaty of Amiens marks the end of the French Revolutionary War

The *Edinburgh Review* founded

1803 England's war with France renewed

The Louisiana Purchase

Robert Fulton propels a boat by steam power on the Seine

1804 Napoleon crowned emperor of the French

Jefferson reelected

Blake's *Milton* (1804–1808) and *Jerusalem*

The Code Napoleon promulgated in France

Beethoven's "Eroica" Symphony

Schiller's *Wilhelm Tell*

Benjamin Disraeli born

1805 Napoleon plans the invasion of England

Battle of Trafalgar

Battle of Austerlitz

Beethoven's *Fidelio* produced for the first time

Scott's *Lay of the Last Minstrel*

1806 Scott's *Marmion*

Death of William Pitt

Death of Charles James Fox

Elizabeth Barrett born

1807 France invades Portugal

Aaron Burr tried for treason and acquitted

Byron's *Hours of Idleness*

Charles and Mary Lamb's *Tales from Shakespeare*

Thomas Moore's *Irish Melodies*

Wordsworth's *Ode on the Intimations of Immortality*

1808 National uprising in Spain against the French invasion

The Peninsular War begins

James Madison elected president

Covent Garden theater burned down

Goethe's *Faust*, part I

Beethoven's Fifth Symphony completed

Lamb's *Specimens of English Dramatic Poets*

1809 Drury Lane theater burned down and rebuilt

The *Quarterly Review* founded

Byron's *English Bards and Scotch Reviewers*

Byron sails for the Mediterranean

Goya's *Los Desastres de la Guerra* (1809–1814)

Alfred Tennyson born
Edward FitzGerald born

1810 Crabbe's *The Borough*
Scott's *The Lady of the Lake*
Elizabeth Gaskell born

1811 The Regency of George IV (1811–1820)
Luddite Riots begin
Coleridge's *Lectures on Shakespeare* (1811–1814)
Jane Austen's *Sense and Sensibility*
Shelley's *The Necessity of Atheism*
John Constable's *Dedham Vale*
William Makepeace Thackeray born

1812 Napoleon invades Russia; captures and retreats from Moscow
U. S. declares war against England
Henry Bell's steamship *Comet* is launched on the Clyde river
Madison reelected
Byron's *Childe Harold*, cantos I–II
The Brothers Grimm's *Fairy Tales* (1812–1815)
Hegel's *Science of Logic*
Robert Browning born
Charles Dickens born

1813 Wellington wins the battle of Vitoria and enters France
Jane Austen's *Pride and Prejudice*
Byron's *The Giaour* and *The Bride of Abydos*
Shelley's *Queen Mab*
Southey's *Life of Nelson*

1814 Napoleon abdicates and is exiled to Elba; Bourbon restoration with Louis XVIII
Treaty of Ghent ends the war between Britain and U. S.
Jane Austen's *Mansfield Park*
Byron's *The Corsair* and *Lara*
Scott's *Waverley*
Wordsworth's *The Excursion*

1815 Napoleon returns to France (the Hundred Days); is defeated at Waterloo and exiled to St. Helena
U.S.S. *Fulton*, the first steam warship, built
Scott's *Guy Mannering*
Schlegel's *Lectures on Dramatic Art and Literature* translated
Wordsworth's *The White Doe of Rylstone*

Anthony Trollope born

1816 Byron leaves England permanently
The Elgin Marbles exhibited in the British Museum
James Monroe elected president
Jane Austen's *Emma*
Byron's *Childe Harold*, canto III
Coleridge's *Christabel. Kubla Khan: A Vision. The Pains of Sleep*
Benjamin Constant's *Adolphe*
Goethe's *Italienische Reise*
Peacock's *Headlong Hall*
Scott's *The Antiquary*
Shelley's *Alastor*
Rossini's *Il Barbiere di Siviglia*
Death of Richard Brinsley Sheridan
Charlotte Brontë born

1817 *Blackwood's Edinburgh* magazine founded
Jane Austen's *Northanger Abbey* and *Persuasion*
Byron's *Manfred*
Coleridge's *Biographia Literaria*
Hazlitt's *The Characters of Shakespeare's Plays* and *The Round Table*
Keats's *Poems*
Peacock's *Melincourt*
David Ricardo's *Principles of Political Economy and Taxation*
Death of Jane Austen
Death of Mme. de Staël
Branwell Brontë born
Henry David Thoreau born

1818 Byron's *Childe Harold*, canto IV, and *Beppo*
Hazlitt's *Lectures on the English Poets*
Keats's *Endymion*
Peacock's *Nightmare Abbey*
Scott's *Rob Roy* and *The Heart of Midlothian*
Shelley's *The Revolt of Islam*
Mary Shelley's *Frankenstein*
Emily Brontë born
Karl Marx born
Ivan Sergeyevich Turgenev born

1819 The *Savannah* becomes the first steamship to cross the Atlantic (in 26 days)
Peterloo massacre in Manchester
Byron's *Don Juan* (1819–1824) and *Mazeppa*
Crabbe's *Tales of the Hall*

CHRONOLOGICAL TABLE

Géricault's *Raft of the Medusa*

Hazlitt's *Lectures on the English Comic Writers*

Arthur Schopenhauer's *Die Welt als Wille und Vorstellung (The World as Will and Idea)*

Scott's *The Bride of Lammermoor* and *A Legend of Montrose*

Shelley's *The Cenci,* "The Masque of Anarchy," and "Ode to the West Wind"

Wordsworth's *Peter Bell*

Queen Victoria born

George Eliot born

1820–1830 Reign of George IV

1820 Trial of Queen Caroline

Cato Street Conspiracy suppressed; Arthur Thistlewood hanged

Monroe reelected

Missouri Compromise

The *London* magazine founded

Keats's *Lamia, Isabella, The Eve of St. Agnes, and Other Poems*

Hazlitt's *Lectures Chiefly on the Dramatic Literature of the Age of Elizabeth*

Charles Maturin's *Melmoth the Wanderer*

Scott's *Ivanhoe* and *The Monastery*

Shelley's *Prometheus Unbound*

Anne Brontë born

1821 Greek War of Independence begins

Liberia founded as a colony for freed slaves

Byron's *Cain, Marino Faliero, The Two Foscari,* and *Sardanapalus*

Hazlitt's *Table Talk* (1821–1822)

Scott's *Kenilworth*

Shelley's *Adonais* and *Epipsychidion*

Death of John Keats

Death of Napoleon

Charles Baudelaire born

Feodor Dostoyevsky born

Gustave Flaubert born

1822 The Massacres of Chios (Greeks rebel against Turkish rule)

Byron's *The Vision of Judgment*

De Quincey's *Confessions of an English Opium-Eater*

Peacock's *Maid Marian*

Scott's *Peveril of the Peak*

Shelley's *Hellas*

Death of Percy Bysshe Shelley

Matthew Arnold born

1823 Monroe Doctrine proclaimed

Byron's *The Age of Bronze* and *The Island*

Lamb's *Essays of Elia*

Scott's *Quentin Durward*

1824 The National Gallery opened in London

John Quincy Adams elected president

The *Westminster Review* founded

Beethoven's Ninth Symphony first performed

James Hogg's *The Private Memoirs and Confessions of a Justified Sinner*

Landor's *Imaginary Conversations* (1824–1829)

Scott's *Redgauntlet*

Death of George Gordon, Lord Byron

1825 Inauguration of steam-powered passenger and freight service on the Stockton and Darlington railway

Bolivia and Brazil become independent

Alessandro Manzoni's *I Promessi Sposi* (1825–1826)

1826 André-Marie Ampère's *Mémoire sur la théorie mathématique des phénomènes électrodynamiques*

James Fenimore Cooper's *The Last of the Mohicans*

Disraeli's *Vivian Grey* (1826–1827)

Scott's *Woodstock*

1827 The battle of Navarino ensures the independence of Greece

Josef Ressel obtains patent for the screw propeller for steamships

Heinrich Heine's *Buch der Lieder*

Death of William Blake

1828 Andrew Jackson elected president

Henrik Ibsen born

George Meredith born

Dante Gabriel Rossetti born

Leo Tolstoy born

1829 The Catholic Emancipation Act

Robert Peel establishes the metropolitan police force

Greek independence recognized by Turkey

Balzac begins *La Comédie humaine* (1829–1848)

Peacock's *The Misfortunes of Elphin*

CHRONOLOGICAL TABLE

J. M. W. Turner's *Ulysses Deriding Polyphemus*

1830–1837 Reign of William IV

1830 Charles X of France abdicates and is succeeded by Louis-Philippe

The Liverpool–Manchester railway opened

Tennyson's *Poems, Chiefly Lyrical*

Death of William Hazlitt

Christina Rossetti born

1831 Michael Faraday discovers electromagnetic induction

Charles Darwin's voyage on H. M. S. *Beagle* begins (1831–1836)

The Barbizon school of artists' first exhibition

Nat Turner slave revolt crushed in Virginia

Peacock's *Crotchet Castle*

Stendhal's *Le Rouge et le noir*

Edward Trelawny's *The Adventures of a Younger Son*

1832 The first Reform Bill

Samuel Morse invents the telegraph

Jackson reelected

Disraeli's *Contarini Fleming*

Goethe's *Faust*, part II

Tennyson's *Poems, Chiefly Lyrical*, including "The Lotus-Eaters" and "The Lady of Shalott"

Death of Johann Wolfgang von Goethe

Death of Sir Walter Scott

Lewis Carroll born

1833 Robert Browning's *Pauline*

John Keble launches the Oxford Movement

The Factory Act

American Anti-Slavery Society founded

Lamb's *Last Essays of Elia*

Carlyle's *Sartor Resartus* (1833–1834)

Pushkin's *Eugene Onegin*

Mendelssohn's Italian Symphony first performed

1834 Abolition of slavery in the British Empire

Louis Braille's alphabet for the blind

The Factory Act

Balzac's *Le Père Goriot*

Nikolai Gogol's *Dead Souls*, part I (1834–1842)

Death of Samuel Taylor Coleridge

Death of Charles Lamb

William Morris born

1835 Hans Christian Andersen's *Fairy Tales* (1st series)

Robert Browning's *Paracelsus*

Alexis de Tocqueville's *De la Démocratie en Amérique* (1835–1840)

1836 Texas becomes independent from Mexico and U. S. recognizes Republic of Texas

Martin Van Buren elected president

Dickens' *Sketches by Boz* (1836–1837)

Landor's *Pericles and Aspasia*

1837–1901 Reign of Queen Victoria

1837 Isaac Pitman publishes his system of shorthand

Carlyle's *The French Revolution*

Dickens' *Oliver Twist* (1837–1838) and *Pickwick Papers*

Disraeli's *Venetia* and *Henrietta Temple*

Algernon Charles Swinburne born

1838 Chartist movement in England

Elizabeth Barrett Browning's *The Seraphim and Other Poems*

Dickens' *Nicholas Nickleby* (1838–1839)

1839 Louis Daguerre perfects process for producing an image on a silver-coated copper plate

Faraday's *Experimental Researches in Electricity* (1839–1855)

First Chartist riots

Opium War between Great Britain and China

Carlyle's *Chartism*

Stendhal's *La Chartreuse de Parme*

1840 Canadian Act of Union

Queen Victoria marries Prince Albert

Charles Barry begins construction of the Houses of Parliament (1840–1852)

William Henry Harrison elected president

Robert Browning's *Sordello*

Richard Henry Dana's *Two Years Before the Mast*

Thomas Hardy born

1841 New Zealand proclaimed a British colony

James Clark Ross discovers the Antarctic continent

Punch founded

New York Tribune founded

John Tyler succeeds to the presidency after the death of Harrison

Carlyle's *Heroes and Hero-Worship*

Dickens' *The Old Curiosity Shop*

Ralph Waldo Emerson's *Essays, First Series*

Henry Wadsworth Longfellow's *Ballads and Other Poems*

Edgar Allan Poe's "The Murders in the Rue Morgue"

1842 Chartist riots

Income tax revived in Great Britain

The Mines Act, forbidding work underground by women or by children under ten

Charles Edward Mudie's Lending Library founded in London

Dickens visits America

Robert Browning's *Dramatic Lyrics*

Gogol's *Dead Souls*, part II (1842–1852)

Macaulay's *Lays of Ancient Rome*

Tennyson's *Poems*, including "Morte d'Arthur," "St. Simeon Stylites," and "Ulysses"

Wordsworth's *Poems*

1843 Marc Isambard Brunel's Thames tunnel opened

The *Economist* founded

Carlyle's *Past and Present*

Dickens' *A Christmas Carol*

Kierkegaard's *Either/Or*

John Stuart Mill's *Logic*

Macaulay's *Critical and Historical Essays*

John Ruskin's *Modern Painters* (1843–1860)

Wagner's *The Flying Dutchman* performed in Dresden

1844 Rochdale Society of Equitable Pioneers, one of the first consumers' cooperatives, founded by twenty-eight Lancashire weavers

James K. Polk elected president

Elizabeth Barrett Browning's *Poems*, including *The Cry of the Children*

Dickens' *Martin Chuzzlewit*

Disraeli's *Coningsby*

Dumas's *The Three Musketeers*

Turner's *Rain, Steam and Speed*

Gerard Manley Hopkins born

1845 The great potato famine in Ireland begins (1845–1849)

Disraeli's *Sybil*

Poe's *The Raven and Other Poems*

Wagner's *Tannhaüser* performed in Dresden

Death of Thomas Hood

1846 Repeal of the Corn Laws

Mexican War (1846–1848)

The *Daily News* founded (edited by Dickens the first three weeks)

Elias Howe's sewing machine patented

Standard gauge railway introduced in Britain

Balzac's *La Cousine Bette*

The Brontës' pseudonymous *Poems by Currer, Ellis and Acton Bell*

Edward Lear's *Book of Nonsense*

Herman Melville's *Typee*

1847 The California gold rush begins

The Mormons, led by Brigham Young, found Salt Lake City

The Ten Hours Factory Act

James Simpson uses chloroform as an anaesthetic

Anne Brontë's *Agnes Grey*

Charlotte Brontë's *Jane Eyre*

Emily Brontë's *Wuthering Heights*

Emerson's *Poems*

Tennyson's *The Princess*

Balzac's *Le Cousin Pons*

1848 The year of revolutions in France, Germany, Italy, Hungary, Poland

Marx and Engels issue *The Communist Manifesto*

The Chartist Petition

The Pre-Raphaelite Brotherhood founded

Zachary Taylor elected president

Anne Brontë's *The Tenant of Wildfell Hall*

Dickens' *Dombey and Son*

Elizabeth Gaskell's *Mary Barton*

Macaulay's *History of England* (1848–1861)

Mill's *Principles of Political Economy*

Thackeray's *Vanity Fair*

Death of Emily Brontë

1849 Bedford College for women founded

Arnold's *The Strayed Reveller*

Charlotte Brontë's *Shirley*

CHRONOLOGICAL TABLE

Ruskin's *The Seven Lamps of Architecture*

Death of Anne Brontë

1850 The Public Libraries Act

First submarine telegraph cable laid between Dover and Calais

Millard Fillmore succeeds to the presidency after the death of Taylor

Elizabeth Barrett Browning's *Sonnets from the Portuguese*

Carlyle's *Latter-Day Pamphlets*

Dickens' *Household Words* (1850–1859) and *David Copperfield*

Nathaniel Hawthorne's *The Scarlet Letter*

Charles Kingsley's *Alton Locke*

The Pre-Raphaelites publish the *Germ*

Tennyson's *In Memoriam*

Thackeray's *The History of Pendennis*

Wordsworth's *The Prelude*

Death of William Wordsworth

Guy de Maupassant born

Robert Louis Stevenson born

1851 The Great Exhibition opens at the Crystal Palace in Hyde Park

Louis Napoleon seizes power in France

Gold strike in Victoria incites Australian gold rush

Herman Melville's *Moby Dick*

Meredith's *Poems*

Ruskin's *The Stones of Venice* (1851–1853)

Verdi's *Rigoletto* produced at Venice

1852 The Second Empire proclaimed with Napoleon III as emperor

The Niagara Falls Bridge constructed

David Livingstone begins to explore the Zambezi (1852–1856)

Franklin Pierce elected president

Arnold's *Empedocles on Etna*

Harriet Beecher Stowe's *Uncle Tom's Cabin*

Thackeray's *The History of Henry Esmond, Esq.*

1853 Crimean War (1853–1856)

Arnold's *Poems*, including "The Scholar Gypsy" and "Sohrab & Rustum"

Charlotte Brontë's *Villette*

Elizabeth Gaskell's *Cranford* and *Ruth*

Hawthorne's *Tanglewood Tales for Girls and Boys*

Verdi's *Il Trovatore* and *La Traviata*

1854 Frederick D. Maurice's Working Men's College founded in London with more than 130 pupils

Abraham Gesner manufactures kerosene

Battle of Balaklava

Dickens' *Hard Times*

Theodor Mommsen's *History of Rome* (1854–1856)

Tennyson's "The Charge of the Light Brigade"

Thoreau's *Walden*

Florence Nightingale in the Crimea (1854–1856)

Oscar Wilde born

1855 David Livingstone discovers the Victoria Falls

Robert Browning's *Men and Women*

Elizabeth Gaskell's *North and South*

Tennyson's *Maud*

Thackeray's *The Newcomes*

Trollope's *The Warden*

Death of Charlotte Brontë

1856 The Treaty of Paris ends the Crimean War

Henry Bessemer's steel process invented

James Buchanan elected president

Flaubert's *Madame Bovary* (1856; new edition in book form, 1857)

Sigmund Freud born

George Bernard Shaw born

1857 The Indian Mutiny begins; crushed in 1858

The *Atlantic Monthly* founded

Dred Scott decision, involving legal status of slaves

The Matrimonial Causes Act

Baudelaire's *Les Fleurs du mal*

Charlotte Brontë's *The Professor*

Elizabeth Barrett Browning's *Aurora Leigh*

Dickens' *Little Dorritt*

Thomas Hughes's *Tom Brown's School Days*

Trollope's *Barchester Towers*

1858 Carlyle's *History of Frederick the Great* (1858–1865)

Arthur Hugh Clough's *Amours de Voyage* first published

George Eliot's *Scenes of Clerical Life*

CHRONOLOGICAL TABLE

Morris' *The Defence of Guinevere*

Trollope's *Dr. Thorne*

1859 John Brown raids Harper's Ferry and is executed

Edwin Drake drills the first oil well in Pennsylvania

Charles Darwin's *The Origin of Species*

Dickens' *A Tale of Two Cities*

George Eliot's *Adam Bede*

FitzGerald's *The Rubaiyat of Omar Khayyám*

Meredith's *The Ordeal of Richard Feverel*

Mill's *On Liberty*

Samuel Smiles's *Self-Help*

Tennyson's *Idylls of the King*

Death of Thomas De Quincey

Death of Thomas Babington Macaulay

1860 Giuseppe Garibaldi's "Thousand" liberate Sicily and Naples

Abraham Lincoln elected president

The *Cornhill* magazine founded with Thackeray as editor

William Wilkie Collins' *The Woman in White*

George Eliot's *The Mill on the Floss*

1861 American Civil War begins

Victor Emmanuel of Sardinia proclaimed king of Italy

Louis Pasteur presents the germ theory of disease

Arnold's *Lectures on Translating Homer*

Dickens' *Great Expectations*

George Eliot's *Silas Marner*

Meredith's *Evan Harrington*

Francis Turner Palgrave's *The Golden Treasury*

Trollope's *Framley Parsonage*

Peacock's *Gryll Grange*

Death of Prince Albert

Death of Elizabeth Barrett Browning

Death of Arthur Hugh Clough

1862 George Eliot's *Romola*

Victor Hugo's *Les Misérables*

Meredith's *Modern Love*

Christina Rossetti's *Goblin Market*

Ruskin's *Unto This Last*

Trollope's *Orley Farm*

Turgenev's *Fathers and Sons*

1863 Thomas Huxley's *Man's Place in Nature*

Lincoln's Gettysburg Address

Emancipation Proclamation

Ernest Renan's *La Vie de Jésus*

Berlioz' *Les Troyens* produced in Paris

Tolstoy's *War and Peace* (1863–1869)

Death of William Makepeace Thackeray

1864 The Geneva Red Cross Convention signed by twelve nations

Robert Browning's *Dramatis Personae*

John Henry Newman's *Apologia pro vita sua*

Tennyson's *Enoch Arden*

Trollope's *The Small House at Allington*

Death of Walter Savage Landor

1865 Assassination of Lincoln; Andrew Johnson succeeds to the presidency

American Civil War ends

13th Amendment abolishes slavery in the United States

Arnold's *Essays in Criticism* (1st series)

Carroll's *Alice's Adventures in Wonderland*

Dickens' *Our Mutual Friend*

Meredith's *Rhoda Fleming*

A. C. Swinburne's *Atalanta in Calydon*

Wagner's *Tristan und Isolde* first produced in Munich

Death of Elizabeth Gaskell

1866 Alfred Nobel invents dynamite

Austria at war with Prussia

First successful transatlantic telegraph cable laid

Dostoyevsky's *Crime and Punishment*

George Eliot's *Felix Holt the Radical*

Elizabeth Gaskell's *Wives and Daughters*

Ibsen's *Brand*

Swinburne's *Poems and Ballads*

Death of Thomas Love Peacock

1867 The second Reform Bill

Arnold's *New Poems*

Walter Bagehot's *The English Constitution*

Carlyle's *Shooting Niagara*

Marx's *Das Kapital* (vol. I)

Ibsen's *Peer Gynt*

Trollope's *The Last Chronicle of Barset*

Verdi's *Don Carlos* produced in Paris

1868 Gladstone becomes prime minister (1868–1874)

Johnson impeached by House of Representatives; acquitted by Senate
Ulysses S. Grant elected president
Robert Browning's *The Ring and the Book* (1868–1869)
Collins' *The Moonstone*
Wagner's *Die Meistersinger* produced in Munich

1869 The Suez Canal opened
Arnold's *Culture and Anarchy*
Flaubert's *L'Education sentimentale* (dated 1870)
Mill's *The Subjection of Women*
Trollope's *Phineas Finn*
Wagner's *Rheingold* produced in Munich

1870 The Franco-Prussian War begins
The Elementary Education Act establishes schools under the aegis of local boards
Heinrich Schliemann begins to excavate Troy
Dickens' *Edwin Drood*
Disraeli's *Lothair*
Morris' *The Earthly Paradise*
Dante Gabriel Rossetti's *Poems*
Death of Charles Dickens
Lenin born

1871 The Paris Commune
The Treaty of Frankfurt ends the Franco-Prussian war
Trade unions legalized
Newnham College, Cambridge, founded for women students
Carroll's *Through the Looking Glass*
Darwin's *The Descent of Man*
Meredith's *The Adventures of Harry Richmond*
Swinburne's *Songs Before Sunrise*
Verdi's *Aida* produced at Cairo

1872 Samuel Butler's *Erewhon*
George Eliot's *Middlemarch*
Grant reelected
Hardy's *Under the Greenwood Tree*

1873 E. Remington and Sons begin manufacturing typewriters
Arnold's *Literature and Dogma*
Mill's *Autobiography*
Walter Horatio Pater's *Studies in the History of the Renaissance*
Trollope's *The Eustace Diamonds*

1874 Disraeli becomes prime minister
Hardy's *Far from the Madding Crowd*
James Thomson's *The City of Dreadful Night*

1875 Britain buys Suez Canal shares
Tolstoy's *Anna Karenina*
Trollope's *The Way We Live Now*
Bizet's *Carmen* produced in Paris

1876 George Eliot's *Daniel Deronda*
Henry James's *Roderick Hudson*
Meredith's *Beauchamp's Career*
Trollope's *The Prime Minister*
Wagner's *Götterdämmerung* and *Siegfried* produced at Bayreuth

1877 Russia and Turkey at war
Edison invents the phonograph record
Rutherford B. Hayes elected president after Electoral Commission awards him disputed votes
Ibsen's *Pillars of Society*
Emile Zola's *L'Assommoir*

1878 The Congress of Berlin ends the Russo-Turkish War
Earliest electric street lighting in London
Hardy's *The Return of the Native*
Swinburne's *Poems and Ballads: Second Series*

1879 Gladstone's Midlothian campaign
The London telephone exchange built
Robert Browning's *Dramatic Idyls*
Ibsen's *A Doll's House*

1880 Gladstone's second term as prime minister (1880–1885)
James A. Garfield elected president
Robert Browning's *Dramatic Idyls Second Series*
Disraeli's *Endymion*
Dostoyevsky's *The Brothers Karamazov*
Hardy's *The Trumpet-Major*

1881 Garfield assassinated; Chester A. Arthur succeeds to the presidency
Death of Thomas Carlyle
Death of Benjamin Disraeli

1882 Triple Alliance formed between German empire, Austrian empire, and Italy

1883 Death of Edward FitzGerald
1889 Death of Robert Browning
1892 Death of Alfred Tennyson

List of Contributors

MIRIAM ALLOTT. Andrew Bradley Professor of Modern English Literature, University of Liverpool (1974–). Publications include *The Complete Poems of John Keats*, Longman's Annotated English Poets series; *The Complete Poems of Matthew Arnold* (second edition), Longman's Annotated English Poets series; *Matthew Arnold: Selected Poems and Prose*; *Essays on Shelley*; and essays on the romantic poets and on nineteenth- and twentieth-century fiction. **John Keats.**

PAUL BLOOMFIELD. Former Literary Editor, the *Listener* and *Time and Tide*; Cantor Lecture on William Morris, Royal Society of Arts. Publications include *Uncommon People*; *William Morris*; and *Edward Gibbon Wakefield*. **Benjamin Disraeli.**

EDMUND BLUNDEN, CBE, MC. Professor of English Literature, University of Tokyo (1924–1927); Fellow and Tutor in English Literature, Merton College, University of Oxford (1931–1943); Professor of English Literature, University of Hong Kong (1955–1965); Honorary Member, the Academy of Japan. Publications include *Undertones of War* (autobiography); *Poems 1914–1930*; *Poems 1930–1940*; *After the Bombing* (poems); *Leigh Hunt*; *Charles Lamb and His Contemporaries*; and editions of *Christopher Smart*; *William Collins*; *John Clare*; *John Keats*; *Percy Bysshe Shelley*; and *Wilfred Owen*. **Charles Lamb.**

LAURENCE BRANDER, OBE. Lecturer in English, University of Lucknow (1927–1939); BBC Representative, New Delhi (1942–1945); Director, Publications Department, the British Council (1948–1962). Publications include *George Orwell; Somerset Maugham; E. M. Forster: A Critical Study*; and *Aldous Huxley: A Critical Study*. **Thomas Hood.**

RAYMOND LAURENCE BRETT. G. F. Grant Professor of English Literature, University of Hull (1952–).

Publications include *The Third Earl of Shaftesbury; Reason and Imagination; An Introduction to English Studies*; and editions of *Poems of Faith and Doubt: The Victorian Age; S. T. Coleridge*; and *Barclay Fox's Journal*. **Samuel Taylor Coleridge; William Hazlitt.**

IAN CAMPBELL. Lecturer in English Literature, University of Edinburgh (1967–). Publications include *Thomas Carlyle; Kailyard*; and editions of *Carlyle: Reminiscences and Essays; Essays on Nineteenth-Century Scottish Fiction*. Associate Editor of Duke-Edinburgh edition of *The Collected Letters of Thomas and Jane Welsh Carlyle* (1970–). **Thomas Carlyle.**

GEOFFREY DOUGLAS CARNALL. Reader in English Literature, University of Edinburgh (1969–). Publications include *Robert Southey and His Age*. Edited and completed the late John Butt's *Mid-Eighteenth Century*, vol. VIII of the *Oxford History of English Literature*. **Robert Southey.**

PHILIP DREW. Professor of English, University of Glasgow (1977–). Publications include *Robert Browning: A Collection of Critical Essays; The Poetry of Browning: A Critical Introduction*; and *The Meaning of Freedom*. **Robert Browning.**

SIR GEORGE ROSTREVOR HAMILTON, FRSL. Publications include *The Making; Epigrams; The Sober War* (poetry); *Poetry and Contemplation; The Tell-Tale Article; The English Verse Epigram* (criticism); and the anthologies *The Soul of Wit; The Latin Portrait; The Greek Portrait*; and *Wit's Looking-Glass*. **Walter Savage Landor.**

ALETHEA HAYTER, OBE, FRSL. Representative and Cultural Attaché, the British Council, Belgium and

Luxembourg (1967–1971). Publications include *Mrs. Browning: A Poet's Work and Its Setting; A Sultry Month: Scenes of London Literary Life in 1846; Elizabeth Barrett Browning; Opium and the Romantic Imagination; A Voyage in Vain: Coleridge's Journey to Malta in 1804; Horatio's Version* (drama); and editions of Thomas De Quincey's *Confessions of an Opium-Eater;* C. R. Maturin's *Melmoth the Wanderer;* and *FitzGerald to His Friends: Selected Letters of Edward FitzGerald.* **Elizabeth Barrett Browning.**

IAN ROBERT JAMES JACK. Reader in English Poetry, University of Cambridge (1973–1976); Professor of English, University of Cambridge (1976–   ). Publications include *Augustan Satire; English Literature, 1815–1832,* vol. X of the *Oxford History of English Literature; Keats and the Mirror of Art; Browning's Major Poetry;* and editions of Laurence Sterne's *A Sentimental Journey* and *The Poetical Works of Robert Browning,* Oxford English Texts series. General Editor of the Clarendon edition of the Brontë novels. **Sir Walter Scott.**

MALCOLM MILES KELSALL. Professor of English, University College, Cardiff (1975–   ). Publications include *Christopher Marlowe;* and editions of Sarah Fielding's *Adventures of David Simple,* Oxford English Novels series; Thomas Otway's *Venice Preserv'd;* William Congreve's *Love For Love* and *The Way of the World;* J. M. Synge's *The Playboy of the Western World;* and essays on Byron. **George Gordon, Lord Byron.**

GEOFFREY MAURICE MATTHEWS. Reader in English Literature, University of Reading (1966–   ). Publications include *John Keats,* the Critical Heritage series; *Shelley: Selected Poems and Prose;* and the entry on Shelley in the *New Cambridge Bibliography of English Literature.* **Percy Bysshe Shelley.**

JOANNA RICHARDSON, FRSL. Publications include *Fanny Brawne; Théophile Gautier: His Life and Times; Princess Mathilde; Verlaine; Victor Hugo; Zola; Keats and His Circle.* Edited *FitzGerald: Selected Works,* Reynard Library edition. Translated *Baudelaire; Verlaine,* Penguin Poets series;

Henri Gautier's *Mademoiselle de Maupin,* Penguin Classics series. **Edward FitzGerald.**

BRIAN CHARLES SOUTHAM. Formerly Lecturer in English, Westfield College, University of London; Managing Director, the Athlone Press, London. Publications include *Jane Austen's Literary Manuscripts; A Student's Guide to the Selected Poems of T. S. Eliot.* Edited *Jane Austen: The Critical Heritage.* Editions of the novels of Jane Austen, including *Sir Charles Grandison.* General Editor of *The Critical Heritage Series.* **Jane Austen; Alfred Tennyson.**

JOHN INNES MACKINTOSH STEWART. Reader in English Literature, University of Oxford (1969–1973). Publications include *Eight Modern Writers,* vol. XII of the *Oxford History of English Literature; Character and Motive in Shakespeare;* and books on Conrad, Hardy, and Kipling. **Thomas Love Peacock.**

HUGH SYKES DAVIES. Lecturer in English Literature, University of Cambridge (1936–1967); Director of Studies in English, St. John's College (1936–1965). Publications include *The Poets and Their Critics;* and articles on Lucretius, Layamon, Swift, Wordsworth, and surrealism. Other publications are *Petron,* a sequence of prose poems, and three novels. **Thomas De Quincey.**

JOHN RICHARD WATSON. Professor of English, University of Durham (1978–   ). Publications include *Picturesque Landscape and English Romantic Poetry.* Editions of the works of Robert Browning; and (with N. P. Messenger) *Men and Women: A Case-Book; Victorian Poetry.* Coeditor of *Augustan Worlds: Essays in Honour of A. R. Humphreys.* **William Wordsworth.**

KENNETH YOUNG, FRSL. Former Editor, the *Yorkshire Post;* and Political and Literary Adviser, Beaverbrook Newspapers. Publications include *Dryden* (criticism); *Balfour; Baldwin* (biography); *The Greek Passion; Chapel* (history). Editor of the *Journals and Letters of Sir Robert Bruce Lockhart.* **Thomas Babington Macaulay.**

BRITISH WRITERS

WILLIAM WORDSWORTH

(1770-1850)

J. R. Watson

LIFE

IN his great autobiographical poem, *The Prelude*, Wordsworth tells the story of his early years; but it is important to remember that the truth was more complex than the poem suggests. *The Prelude*, like all poems, selects its own imaginative material from the experience on which it is based; and many of Wordsworth's poems are founded on his own life and his interpretation of it. To understand his poetry fully, we need to know something of Wordsworth's life, in more detail than we do with other poets whose imaginations are not so intricately connected to their own experience.

William Wordsworth was born at Cockermouth, Cumberland, on 7 April 1770, the second child of John and Ann Wordsworth. John Wordsworth was an attorney, the "agent" of Sir James Lowther, for whom he acted in legal and political matters. The Wordsworth children were born in a substantial house in Cockermouth, where the family lived until 1778; but in March of that year Ann Wordsworth died, and the family was split up. William's beloved sister Dorothy (born 25 December 1771) was sent to live at Halifax with her mother's cousin, and the boys were sent to school at Hawkshead. Fortunately they were well educated there and well cared for: they lived in a cottage with an old lady named Ann Tyson, who took in school boarders and who seems to have given them the right amount of affection and freedom. The impression conveyed by *The Prelude* is one of extraordinary energy and activity, but also of normality; he played games, both indoor and outdoor, with a natural exuberance and enthusiasm.

On 30 December 1783, when William was thirteen, his father died; years later he remembered the boyish anticipation of going home for the Christmas holidays and the sadness that followed. The house at Cockermouth had to be given up, and from then on the boys spent their holidays either with their uncle at Whitehaven or, more frequently, at Penrith with their maternal grandparents, the Cooksons, and their uncle, Christopher Crackanthorpe Cookson. There the boys were patronized and made to feel dependent, and William was rebellious: it is clear that his childhood was by no means as uniformly happy as *The Prelude* suggests, and it is of Hawkshead and not Penrith that the poet writes when he looks back to the happiness of the early years.

In October 1787, the young Wordsworth left the Lake District for the first time, to become an undergraduate at St. John's College, Cambridge. Although there were other boys from Hawkshead there, and he was in many ways contented, he was also uneasy in his mind and restless; just how restless may be seen from the marvelous fourth book of *The Prelude*, when he describes the joy of returning to Hawkshead for his first summer vacation. The most spectacular evidence of his unease came two years later, in the long vacation of 1790, when he and his friend Robert Jones undertook a strenuous walking tour through France and Switzerland. By then he had given up any intention of getting an honors degree, and his leaving Cambridge at a time when he might have been preparing for examinations was a snub to the academic life. The tour itself, which gave rise to *Descriptive Sketches* and later to the sixth book of *The Prelude*, was one of the great imaginative experiences of Wordsworth's life.

It was followed by an unsettled period: after graduating from Cambridge without honors in January 1791, he lived in London for some months before spending the summer in Wales, revisiting Cambridge, and then leaving for France in November.

His motive for visiting France was probably to learn the language: the results were very different. First, in a country that was experiencing a revolution he received his early political education, partly from his own observation and partly from his friendship with Michel de Beaupuy. Beaupuy was an unusual man, an army officer who was isolated from his fellow officers as a consequence of his revolutionary sympathies. Beaupuy's politics were simple and humane: he was against corruption and poverty, and looked forward to a time when men would live in liberty and brotherhood and the world would be a better place. Second, Wordsworth met Annette Vallon, the daughter of a deceased surgeon of Blois; they became lovers, and she became pregnant.

Thus, in a little over a year, Wordsworth had experienced a remarkable political and sexual awakening. Moreover, it was a time of great events: during his time in France the attack on the Tuileries, the September massacres, the abolition of the monarchy, and the split between the moderate Girondins (some of whom Wordsworth knew) and the Jacobins heralded the trial and execution of the king (21 January 1793) and the Terror. By late December 1792, however, Wordsworth had returned to England; his child, Anne-Caroline, was born and baptized on 15 December.

The following year, 1793, was of considerable importance to Wordsworth in several ways. In the first place, it saw the first publication of any of Wordsworth's poems: *An Evening Walk* and *Descriptive Sketches* appeared on 29 January. Three days later, France declared war on England, and England responded by declaring war on France on 11 February. Wordsworth's response, as he tells us in *The Prelude*, was painfully confused: his natural patriotism conflicted with his hope for the Revolution, and he must also have been disturbed by the separation from Annette and the child. Some of his anger is found in the "Letter to the Bishop of Llandaff," an unpublished reply to a sermon on *The Wisdom and Goodness of God in Having Made Both Rich and Poor*: the bishop's appendix to the sermon criticized the French and complacently preferred the British constitution and British justice. Wordsworth's reply demonstrates his impatience with what he called "the baleful influence of aristocracy and nobility upon human happiness and virtue" (p. 46) and his use of a classic argument for the revolutionary use of force:

. . . a time of revolution is not the season of true Liberty. Alas! the obstinacy & perversion of men is such that she is too often obliged to borrow the very arms of despotism to overthrow him, and in order to reign in peace must establish herself by violence.[1]

(I.33)

The "Letter" shows clearly Wordsworth's hatred of inherited rank and wealth, of rich clergy, and of the British system of justice (from which he and his brothers and sisters had suffered: after the death of their father, Lowther, now Lord Lonsdale, refused to pay for the work that he had done, and a long and inconclusive lawsuit followed).

It was at this moment that a friend, William Calvert, proposed a tour of the west of England, traveling in a small cart called a "whiskey": they began on the Isle of Wight, where Wordsworth's anger was probably further inflamed by the sight of the English fleet preparing for war. From there they set out across Salisbury Plain: an accident occurred to the whiskey, and Calvert took the horse, leaving Wordsworth to walk. Salisbury Plain was a desolate part of the country, and his solitude must have seemed to the young poet to be emblematic of his isolation and lonely frustration: he walked northward, past Stonehenge, having frightening visions (*The Prelude*, book XII, 1805 text) of ancient Britons engaged in savage war and human sacrifice. From there he traveled northwest, to Tintern Abbey and up the Wye valley to his friend Robert Jones in north Wales. The journey was remembered by him with a peculiar vividness: fifty years later he told Isabella Fenwick that it "left on my mind imaginative impressions the force of which I have felt to this day" (*Poetical Works*, I.330).[2] From it came experiences that represent two seminal themes of Wordsworth's poetry: his King Lear-like awareness of the houseless poverty of the outcasts of society, and his vivid appreciation of the beauty of a scene like that a few miles above Tintern Abbey. Meanwhile we may gain some insight into the kind of young man he appeared to be, if we realize that a tinker (who later became Peter Bell in the poem of that name) thought he might be a murderer. He had no doubt been sleeping rough and probably looked unkempt and farouche.

To the following months and years belong a variety of experiences, but none so significant as this remarkable journey on foot. Later in 1793, Wordsworth probably revisited France in secret, supposedly fleeing from Paris when his life was in danger; in 1794 he spent a happy few weeks with his sister Dorothy at Keswick; later in the year he stayed with a friend, Raisley Calvert (brother of William), being his companion during a terminal illness. Calvert died

---

[1] All prose quotations are from W. J. B. Owen and J. W. Smyser, eds., *The Prose Works of William Wordsworth*, 3 vols. (Oxford, 1974). References are to volume and page numbers.

[2] *The Poetical Works of William Wordsworth*, revised edition by E. de Selincourt and H. Darbishire, 5 vols. (Oxford, 1952–1959).

in January 1795, leaving Wordsworth a legacy that enabled him to live independently though simply. He returned to London, where he furthered his acquaintance with the radical political philosopher William Godwin, and in September he accepted the offer of a house in Dorset called Racedown (between Crewkerne and Lyme Regis) from some Bristol friends. There he and Dorothy settled down, and he began to recover from the upheavals of the previous years. He wrote much of the second version of a poem on the Salisbury Plain experience and a verse drama, *The Borderers*; though the main benefit of these years was a steady growth in the belief in his own powers. This was given a powerful boost by the developing acquaintance with Samuel Taylor Coleridge, whom Wordsworth had first met in 1794 and subsequently corresponded with. Coleridge visited Racedown in June 1797, leaping over a gate and bounding across a field in his eagerness to arrive. They read their poems to each other, with mutual delight; by mid-July, after Coleridge had brought William and Dorothy back with him to Nether Stowey (in North Somerset), they had moved into Alfoxden House nearby. There followed a year of buoyant spirits and happy activity, walking, writing, and preparing the *Lyrical Ballads* (1798). The final poem, "Lines Composed a Few Miles Above Tintern Abbey," was added in July after a short walking tour with Dorothy, in which they revisited the landscape that Wordsworth had seen in 1793; its confident tone of sustained and assured thankfulness indicates Wordsworth's joy at finding his imagination working at full stretch after the troublesome years that followed his return from France.

Throughout these years, it is difficult to overemphasize the importance of Dorothy Wordsworth's love and care: she continued to have faith in her brother and his poetry, and her vivid appreciation of nature (recorded in her journals) was an inspiration to both Wordsworth and Coleridge. The three left for Germany in September 1798, in the same month that saw the appearance of *Lyrical Ballads*. The plan was to settle near a university town, learn German, and attend lectures. They split up, to avoid speaking English all the time, and the Wordsworths settled in Goslar, during an unusually severe winter: deprived of books and company, William began to write again, composing some of the "Lucy" poems and the first parts of what was later to be book I of *The Prelude*. They left Goslar in February 1799, and after a short walking tour in Germany returned to England in the spring. In December 1799, they finally came to rest in the Lake District, in the cottage at Grasmere that is now called Dove Cottage. Except for occasional short periods or visits, Wordsworth lived in the Lake District for the rest of his life, at first at Grasmere and (after 1813) at Rydal, the next village.

The first years at Grasmere were years of great happiness, for Wordsworth seems to have felt a very deep sense of homecoming (which is expressed in "Home at Grasmere," a poem that remained unpublished at his death). In October 1802 he married Mary Hutchinson, after a brief visit to France to see Annette and the nine-year-old Anne-Caroline; he had known Mary Hutchinson and her family since childhood and stayed with them at their farm at Sockburn-on-Tees after returning from Germany. Meanwhile, Coleridge had settled at Keswick, thirteen miles away, though he was unhappy with his wife and often in poor spirits. He left Keswick for Malta in January 1804, and although the friends met again, there was never the same creative interchange and intimacy that had taken place in 1797–1798. Before leaving, however, Coleridge had introduced Wordsworth to Sir George Beaumont, a wealthy patron and connoisseur, who became a benefactor and friend until his death in 1827: it was to Beaumont that Wordsworth turned for support during the greatest crisis of his adult life, the death of his brother John at sea in February 1805.

The death of John Wordsworth, followed by the growth of the friendship with Sir George and Lady Beaumont, herald the later years of Wordsworth's life. They were, perhaps inevitably, less exciting than before: in 1813 he became distributor of stamps for Westmorland, a post that carried with it a commission on the sale of stamps, which amounted to some £400 a year, although clerks and other officials had to be paid out of this. Nevertheless, the post marked a significant change in Wordsworth's status and way of life; similarly, the friendship with Beaumont was with a man who was, unlike Coleridge, conventional and conservative in every way. We can only speculate on the reasons why Wordsworth wrote so little good poetry after 1807; but his increasingly respectable life, and the loss of Coleridge's stimulus, may have been partly responsible.

Apart from some Scottish and Continental tours, Wordsworth remained at Rydal Mount from 1813 to his death on 23 April 1850. In his later years, he was revered and honored: the University of Durham gave him an honorary degree in 1838, and Oxford followed in 1839; in 1843, on the death of Southey, he became poet laureate. His later years were clouded by the protracted illness of his sister, Dorothy, and by the death of his beloved daughter Dora in 1847; but he had the satisfaction of seeing his poems grow in popularity, and his fame spread through the English-speaking world. His faith that his poetry "must sooner or later work its way into the hearts and minds of the people"[3] had been fully justified.

EARLY POEMS

IN 1843, Wordsworth said that "no change has taken place in my manner for the last forty-five years." This dates Wordsworth's mature style at 1798, with the publication of *Lyrical Ballads*, and suggests that in the earlier poems he had failed to find his own individual voice. At first sight this seems to be the case: *An Evening Walk* and *Descriptive Sketches* (1793) are written in heroic couplets and contain many borrowings and influences from eighteenth-century poets; while another major poem of these years, the Salisbury Plain poem (in two versions), is written in Spenserian stanzas, another popular eighteenth-century form. In other respects, too, they seem conventional, with titles, diction, and description following the eighteenth-century patterns. They were later revised extensively by Wordsworth, and they are best read in the 1793 text, which is printed in many editions. There the reader can see the dominance of the contemporary style:

> —Then Quiet led me up the huddling rill,
> Bright'ning with water-breaks the sombrous gill;
> To where, while thick above the branches close,
> In dark-brown bason its wild waves repose,
> Inverted shrubs, and moss of darkest green,
> Cling from the rocks, with pale wood-weeds between;
> Save that, atop, the subtle sunbeams shine,
> On wither'd briars that o'er the craggs recline;
> Sole light admitted here, a small cascade,
> Illumes with sparkling foam the twilight shade.
> Beyond, along the visto of the brook,
> Where antique roots its bustling path o'erlook,
> The eye reposes on a secret bridge
> Half grey, half shagg'd with ivy to its ridge.
> (*An Evening Walk*, 71–84)

Here the reader notices immediately the personification of "Quiet," the use of words like "sombrous," "illumes," and "visto," the use of inversion, with a latinate postponement of the main verb, and the use of a Latin participial construction, "Sole light admitted here," to make an adjectival phrase. All these disappear in later versions, which suggests that Wordsworth himself came to regard them as blemishes on the poem. Yet the early poetry is not so unoriginal as it looks. It was *Descriptive Sketches* that first drew Coleridge's attention to Wordsworth, as he tells us in *Biographia Literaria*:

In the form, style, and manner of the whole poem, and in the structure of the particular lines and periods, there is an harshness and acerbity connected and combined with words and images all a-glow, which might recall those products of the vegetable world, where gorgeous blossoms rise out of the hard and thorny rind and shell, within which the rich fruit was elaborating. The language was not only peculiar and strong, but at times knotty and contorted, as by its own impatient strength; while the novelty and struggling crowd of images, acting in conjunction with the difficulties of the style, demanded always a greater closeness of attention, than poetry, (at all events, than descriptive poetry) has a right to claim.[4]

(I.56)

What Coleridge is describing here is a kind of individual voice, powerful and original, which he had detected: and it is true that the verse is full of energy, bursting out of the heroic couplets as a child outgrows its clothes. The subject matter, too, seems too big for the form of these poems: *An Evening Walk*, for instance, is principally about a landscape seen during the course of an afternoon, but it also contains a section in the middle that describes a destitute mother and her starving children. Similarly, *Descriptive Sketches*, which is about Wordsworth's tour of the Alps in 1790, contains a great diversity of material including descriptions of the mountain scenery, reflections on the lot of the Swiss and of mankind in general, and a prophecy of liberty. Both poems look two ways, in fact, to nature and to man, and in this we can see the beginnings of Wordsworth's continuous later concern with the interaction of the two. In these early poems they exist side by side, uncomfortably juxtaposed; in the later

[3]Mary Moorman, *William Wordsworth: A Biography*, vol. II: *The Later Years 1803-1850* (Oxford, 1965), p. 544.

[4]All references to *Biographia Literaria* are to the J. Shawcross edition (Oxford, 1907).

poetry there is a creative interaction, so that Wordsworth can portray himself.

> On Man, on Nature, and on Human Life,
> Musing in solitude. . . .
> (preface to *The Excursion*, 1–2)

The introduction of man and human life here is not just a tautology: Wordsworth surveys man, and nature, but also the larger significance that arises from the interaction between the two, between man and the world around him; he is to investigate the nature and purpose of human life, its good and evil, its joy and sorrow. These things are latent in *An Evening Walk* and *Descriptive Sketches:* both are filled with images of the beauty and sublimity of nature, but they are also conscious that mankind, besides having such enjoyments, often has to suffer hardship and misery.

Descriptive Sketches, which was written during Wordsworth's residence in France in 1792, contains a good deal of explicit political suggestion. The "Salisbury Plain" poems carry this further. They are different versions of the same poem, which ends up in the *Poetical Works*, somewhat toned down, as "Guilt and Sorrow," though part of it was published in the *Lyrical Ballads* under the title of "The Female Vagrant." The first Salisbury Plain poem draws its inspiration from Wordsworth's solitary wanderings in 1793 and his angry state of mind at the time: the first version ends with an impassioned plea for revolution and a new order:

> Heroes of Truth pursue your march, uptear
> Th'Oppressor's dungeon from its deepest base;
> High o'er the towers of Pride undaunted rear
> Resistless in your might the herculean mace
> Of Reason; let foul Error's monster race
> Dragged from their dens start at the light with pain
> And die; pursue your toils, till not a trace
> Be left on earth of Superstition's reign,
> Save that eternal pile which frowns on Sarum's plain.
> (541–549)

The story of the poem concerns a good-hearted sailor (the first stanzas of the second version show him helping an aged soldier) who has been forced into the navy by a press-gang and dismissed without reward. In his anger he robs and kills a traveler, and now wanders homeless across the plain. In a ruined building he meets a woman, the female vagrant, who relates her story: her father was forced to leave his home by a rapacious landowner, and her husband joined the army to provide for the family; they followed the army to America, where the husband and children all died; and the woman was then shipped back to England. On the following morning the sailor and the vagrant continue their journey, pacifying an angry father who is beating his child, until they meet a dying woman, who turns out to be the sailor's wife; her death affects the sailor so deeply that he gives himself up to justice and is hanged.

In the later published version, entitled "Guilt and Sorrow," the sailor is deemed to have suffered enough; in the earlier (second) version, Wordsworth drives home the message of the poem with a remorseless and fixed anger. The female vagrant is one victim of a society that allows the rich to deprive the poor of their livelihood, and in which there is no alternative to poverty but enlistment in the army. The poor and helpless, however benevolent and well disposed, are cast out to fend for themselves, while old soldiers and sailors are thrown on the scrap heap. The sailor is an example of a man who is driven to desperation by the treatment he has received; even more bitter, perhaps, is the way in which at the end, he is surrounded by complacent people who bring him to justice; like the judge in Camus's *L'Etranger*, they make no attempt to understand him. After his death, as he swings in chains on a gibbet, a fair is set up beneath, in a final macabre touch. Meanwhile, the housewife who cares for the dying woman in her last hours stands out as a type of the Good Samaritan, and we are also allowed to see the deep humanity of the sailor and the female vagrant. The sustained anger of the poem is matched only by the poet's admiration for those who can preserve their natural benevolence and kindness in the face of such adversity.

In the years following 1793 this relationship between individual behavior and the creation of the good society was clearly much in Wordsworth's mind, particularly in view of the later course of the French Revolution. The motives of the Revolution had been so good, and its outcome so disastrous (especially, Wordsworth thought, under Robespierre), that some explanation was desirable. This Wordsworth attempted to supply in *The Borderers*, the other major work of these years. The complicated plot of this tragedy in verse is conducted to a point at which a good man, Marmaduke, is persuaded to leave an old blind man to die in a bleak wasteland; Marmaduke has been deceived by Oswald, who had committed a similar crime many years before, after being manipulated by others. Marmaduke's motives are correct; he is a benevolent man who ends the play in remorse and penitence. Oswald, on the other hand, is driven by his crime to renounce remorse, to see in himself a terrible freedom from normal principles of benevolence and restraint. This is the freedom that he urges upon Marmaduke, and it was such a freedom that Wordsworth saw a man like Robespierre exercising. "Let us suppose," says Wordsworth, describing Oswald in the preface of *The Borderers*, "a young man of great intellectual powers, yet without any solid principles of genuine benevolence" (*Prose Works*, I.76). His action shows "the dangerous use which may be made of reason when a man has committed a great crime" (*ibid.*, p. 79). The note to *The Borderers* connects this clearly with the experience in France, for Wordsworth writes that "sin and crime are apt to start from their very opposite qualities," and that he had seen this "while the revolution was rapidly advancing to its extreme of wickedness" (*Poetical Works,* I.342).

When Coleridge heard Wordsworth read *The Borderers* he described it as "absolutely wonderful" (*Poetical Works*, I.344); he praised the work for its "*profound* touches of the human heart," seeing in it what later critics have come to recognize as a primary interest of Wordsworth's, the concern with the human heart, traditionally the seat of the affections and the organ of shared feeling between man and man. The concern for the human heart, and for what Wordsworth describes in the preface as "the primary laws of our nature," is brilliantly expressed in *Lyrical Ballads*. In *The Borderers* it is tangled up with a complicated plot and an undramatic scenario; in *Lyrical Ballads* it is produced in a marvelous series of spare, taut narrative poems, interwoven with concrete expressions of Wordsworth's own belief and ending with the triumphant "Tintern Abbey."

LYRICAL BALLADS

COLERIDGE described Wordsworth's part in *Lyrical Ballads* in his *Biographia Literaria*. While his own energies were to be directed toward the supernatural, Wordsworth

was to propose to himself as his object, to give the charm of novelty to things of every day, and to excite a feeling analogous to the supernatural, by awakening the mind's at-

tention from the lethargy of custom, and directing it to the loveliness and the wonders of the world before us; an inexhaustible treasure, but for which, in consequence of the film of familiarity and selfish solicitude we have eyes, yet see not, ears that hear not, and hearts that neither feel nor understand.

(II.6)

It will be seen that Wordsworth's role was to present the ordinary so that the reader would see it with new eyes; as he said himself about "The Thorn": "Cannot I by some invention do as much to make this Thorn permanently an impressive object as the storm has made it to my eyes at this moment?" (*Poetical Works*, II.511). The result is that *Lyrical Ballads* contains many poems that are concerned with simple people in ordinary surroundings, who have problems that are common, sometimes universal: old age, poverty, pregnancy and betrayal, cold, bereavement. Their stories are narrated in a style that is simple and direct, influenced by the street ballads in its dramatic abruptness. This style has sometimes been seen as unsuccessful, as Wordsworth's theory running away with his practice, yet its awkward simplicity is often peculiarly effective. Wordsworth writes a poetry the texture of which allows no escape, which is perhaps why it has been disliked: the lines shock the reader into a recognition of the suffering and the happiness of his fellow human beings, and there is no delicate transfusion of life into art, but, rather, a direct rendering of life into something more tactless and immediate than art. In its spirit it resembles Marianne Moore's poem "Poetry":

> I, too, dislike it: there are things that are important
>> beyond all this fiddle.

And yet, paradoxically, Wordsworth's is a highly functioning poetic art, in the sense described by Marianne Moore in her last verse:

> . . . if you demand on the one hand,
>> the raw material of poetry in
>>> all its rawness and
>>>> that which is on the other hand
>>>>> genuine, then you are interested in poetry.

Wordsworth certainly presents the raw material in all its rawness, in a way that, for many, commands respect; if he leaves himself open to the jeers of the cynic or the skeptic, this is a price he is willing to pay, for the greatest poets have always been vulnerable in this way. So we have Simon Lee's thick ankles, and the little pond in "The Thorn," which is three feet long and two feet wide, and poor Betty in "The Idiot Boy," "in a sad distemper." Not only is there a distinct rawness in these lines, but there is also "that which is on the other hand/genuine," the respect for the figures who appear in the poems, a respect that comes from love. Wordsworth is well aware of the danger of becoming a voyeur of human suffering: in "The Thorn," for instance, he introduces just such a figure, a retired sea captain who has too little to occupy his time, so that he becomes endlessly curious about his neighbors, and especially about the plight of one of them. We are presented, therefore, with a poem that is at once a narrative and a dramatic monologue; other examples of the sophistication of Wordsworth's art are found in "The Idiot Boy," where the diction creates its own rhetorical and rhythmical patterns, and "Simon Lee," where the colloquial simplicities of the earlier verses give way to a final quotation that requires the reader to think, sharply and suddenly, to penetrate beneath the conventional complaint of man's ingratitude to something more profound and more pathetic.

It is this respect for his fellow creatures, and this craft, that are the distinguishing marks of *Lyrical Ballads*: they are poems that challenge our very ideas about the nature of poetry and that also confound our expectations in other ways. If we accommodate ourselves to the rhetoric of "The Idiot Boy," we are surprised by the ritual game of "Expostulation and Reply" and "The Tables Turned," in which Matthew and William play out a game of statement and counterstatement. If we become accustomed to the simplicity of the ballad style, both in narrative poems and in reflective ones, we are surprised by the majestic reflections of "Lines Composed a Few Miles Above Tintern Abbey." This final poem, the last in the 1798 collection, is written in the eighteenth-century meditative blank-verse style, but with such individuality, originality, and organization as to make it a fitting conclusion to the volume; it should be seen not as the one success in a curious collection but as the open statement of what is explicit or implicit in so many of the other poems, a wonderful openness to feeling and experience. In the preface to *Lyrical Ballads*, published in the second edition (1800), Wordsworth writes of the poet that he is

a man speaking to men: a man, it is true, endowed with more lively sensibility, more enthusiasm and tenderness, who has a greater knowledge of human nature, and a more comprehensive soul, than are supposed to be common among mankind; a man pleased with his own passions and volitions, and who rejoices more than other men in the spirit of life that is in him; delighting to contemplate similar volitions and passions as manifested in the goings-on of the Universe, and habitually impelled to create them where he does not find them.

(*Poetical Works*, II.393)

The importance of this definition is not only in its splendid statement of a shared humanity between the poet and others; it is also concerned with the character of the poet as enthusiast, who is able to express his joy at being alive and finding himself in a world that is full of the same kind of passion and life. To be thus aware of the joy of the world is to be aware also of its variety and complexity, its pain as well as its joy; and Wordsworth is a great tragic poet as well as one who celebrates the happiness of man. He sees the pain of old age, the miseries of poverty, the tragicomedy of idiocy. The extraordinary feature of *Lyrical Ballads* is that they carry everywhere the evidence of the poet's love for life, for his fellow human beings, for those who are oppressed by society, for his sister, for the natural world around him. This energetic love of life is, in Wordsworth's eyes, evidence of a full humanity; in the preface he describes a poet as "singing a song in which all human beings join with him" (*Poetical Works*, II.396).

The fundamental conception of the poet as human being, sharing in the joys and sorrows of all mankind with a more than common enthusiasm, has tended to become obscured in the preface by Wordsworth's statements about poetic language. The principal object of *Lyrical Ballads* was, he said,

to choose incidents and situations from common life, and to relate or describe them, throughout, as far as was possible in a selection of language really used by men, and, at the same time, to throw over them a certain colouring of imagination, whereby ordinary things should be presented to the mind in an unusual aspect. . . .

(*ibid.*, II.386)

The phrase "a selection of language really used by men," and a similar one from the first paragraph, "a selection of the real language of men in a state of vivid sensation," have caused many problems to critics of Wordsworth, from Coleridge onward, who have wanted to know what is meant by "a selection" or by "real" language; other difficulties have been posed by those who have solemnly taken Wordsworth to task for what follows:

Humble and rustic life was generally chosen, because, in that condition, the essential passions of the heart find a better soil in which they can attain their maturity, are less under restraint, and speak a plainer and more emphatic language; because in that condition of life our elementary feelings co-exist in a state of greater simplicity, and consequently, may be more accurately contemplated, and more forcibly communicated; because the manners of rural life germinate from those elementary feelings, and, from the necessary character of rural occupations, are more easily comprehended, and are more durable; and, lastly, because in that condition the passions of men are incorporated with the beautiful and permanent forms of nature.

(*ibid.*, II.386–387)

We may disagree with Wordsworth about the need to choose humble and rustic life (although there are clear sociological indications that he may have been right), but his motives are clear and creditable: they are concerned with "the essential patterns of the heart," "elementary feelings," and "the passions of men" which are "incorporated with the beautiful and permanent forms of nature." His theory of language (partly set out in the appendix to the preface) is that primitive poets, although using a language of extraordinary occasions, spoke a language "which, though unusual, was still the language of men." In the course of time, the unusual became mistaken for the reality, so that diction became "daily more and more corrupt, thrusting out of sight the plain humanities of nature by a motley masquerade of tricks, quaintnesses, hieroglyphics, and enigmas" (*Poetical Works*, II.406). It is clear that Wordsworth was attempting to return to what he saw as a correct simplicity and directness, and that the choice of humble and rustic life, together with a predilection for ordinary language, is connected with this. The poetic results show how unprejudiced Wordsworth was about the matter, and how the actual language of his poetry varied according to the needs of the poem in question: the language of "Simon Lee" is very different from that of "We Are Seven," and the impassioned blank verse of "Tintern Abbey" is very different from the austere simplicities of "Michael." In every case the aim is to provide "little falsehood of description" and ideas "expressed in language fitted to their respective importance." So we have the hymnlike utterances of "To My Sister":

And from the blessed power that rolls
About, below, above,
We'll frame the measure of our souls:
They shall be tuned to love.

(33–36)

or the nursery rhyme cadences of "We Are Seven":

I met a little cottage Girl,
She was eight years old, she said;
Her hair was thick with many a curl
That clustered round her head.

(5–8)

The deliberate simplicity of this latter verse is characteristic of some of the shorter poems in *Lyrical Ballads*: critics have often found them naive and oversimple, but Wordsworth was not stupid and clearly had a specific effect in mind, an effect that may not seem as mature or complex as "Tintern Abbey" but that has an equal importance for an understanding of Wordsworth. He is a poet who is capable of writing with an amazing directness and hard sense, yet he is also capable of writing a poetry that has deeper and more elusive meanings.

As an example of the first kind, we may take "Simon Lee." It is a poem that underwent a number of changes after its first publication in 1798, but for convenience I shall take the version that appears in the Oxford Standard Authors edition, by Hutchinson. There the poem begins with a description of Simon Lee as a young man:

In the sweet shire of Cardigan,
Not far from pleasant Ivor-hall
An old Man dwells, a little man, —
'Tis said he once was tall.
Full five-and-thirty years he lived
A running huntsman merry;
And still the centre of his cheek
Is red as a ripe cherry.

(1–8)

Here the jingle of the rhythm, and the feminine rhyme at the end, encourage a curious jauntiness, an attention such as one gives to a straightforward, cheerful, and undemanding narrative: such a register is even clearer in the 1798 version of the second four lines:

Of years he has upon his back
No doubt, a burthen weighty;
He says he is three score and ten,
But others say he's eighty.

where the random guessing about Simon's age suggests the trivial and simple. In the reworked version of the poem, the first three verses, describing Simon in the past, continue this mood. They describe him as a huntsman in his prime, running, hallooing, and pushing himself to the limit of his endurance. Then comes the change, heralded by a phrase borrowed from Wordsworth's favorite, John Milton:

> But, oh the heavy change!—bereft
> Of health, strength, friends, and kindred, see!
> (25–26)

The same deliberate simplicity is carried on in the following stanzas, which describe the aged and feeble man: it is as though a primitive painter had produced a diptych entitled "Youth" and "Age." Now the reader is given the facts with a hard matter-of-factness:

> And he is lean and he is sick;
> His body, dwindled and awry,
> Rests upon ankles swoln and thick;
> His legs are thin and dry.
> (33–36)

After this, however, comes a surprise, as the poet himself enters the poem, with a direct address to the reader:

> My gentle Reader, I perceive
> How patiently you've waited,
> And now I fear that you expect
> Some tale will be related.
>
> O Reader! had you in your mind
> Such stores as silent thought can bring,
> O gentle Reader! you would find
> A tale in every thing.
> What more I have to say is short,
> And you must kindly take it:
> It is no tale; but, should you think,
> Perhaps a tale you'll make it.
> (61–72)

Here the style seems to be the same, with the same insistent meter and feminine rhyme; the idea behind these lines, too, seems to be of the same order of simplicity as the earlier descriptive passages, and the continual addressing of the reader has a jocular effect. But beneath the simple words, especially "tale" and "think," there lie considerable reverberations. The point of these verses, which contain the central analysis of how to consider Simon Lee and others like him, is that they emphasize the fact that Simon Lee *is*: he is a sad spectacle, an old man past his prime, living on in poverty and unable to perform the simplest task. There is ample matter for the feeling heart to consider here, and there will be no tale, for there should be none: we are contemplating old age, and there will be no escape into a story to take our minds off it. There is, as the poem's subtitle tells us, "an incident," but that is all: however, if we *think*, we can make much of that incident, that is, if we have hearts that feel, eyes that perceive, and minds that understand; if, in other words, we *think* about the plight of the elderly, we shall find a deep significance in the trivial incident that follows. It is a significance that is simple because it is universal, containing within itself the awareness of human life as brief, transitory, and often painful. So although it is no story, it contains a deep and inescapable truth:

> It is no tale; but, should you think,
> Perhaps a tale you'll make it.

The poem is given a final twist, as the traditional complaint against ingratitude is exploited to make something even more pathetic:

> —I've heard of hearts unkind, kind deeds
> With coldness still returning;
> Alas! the gratitude of men
> Hath oftener left me mourning.
> (93–96)

There are times, it appears, when gratitude is actually worse than ingratitude: from the simplicity of the earlier verses the reader is now faced with a paradox, for the poet grieves more for the pathetic condition of Simon Lee (which makes him weep for the simplest kind of help) than for the usual ingratitude.

If "Simon Lee" moves from simplicity to a sudden complexity, surprising the reader by its final turn, the movement of "Tintern Abbey" is much more deliberate, and the poem modulates with consummate skill between different registers of simplicity and complexity. It is a poem that moves between the outer world of nature and the inner world of the mind in a way that beautifully suggests the interaction between the two. There is not space enough here to provide a full examination of the poem, but the way in which its reflective moments alternate with descriptions of the actual landscape is a feature that stands out, although it is most subtly and sensitively accomplished. The poem begins with the river Wye, bounded by its steep and lofty banks, with the pastoral farms and hedgerows, and the quiet sky; at the end the poem comes to rest in the same landscape, with a sense of having gone out and returned that is artistically very satisfying. Between the beginning and end, intertwining with the descriptions of landscape, is the exploration of the poet's mind and heart, and his expressions of confidence and love for his sister and the influence of nature upon her. The poem witnesses to his own experience and his trust that the same blessing will be hers.

The poem is dated "July 13 1798," and records a visit to the Wye some five years after the memorable walk of 1793. It records the effect of the landscape on the poet's mind as he remembered it, an effect that is both moral and mystical. The movement of the verse here is characteristic of a certain kind of Wordsworthian blank verse, which begins with a fairly straightforward idea, which it then expands; this leads to a further idea, or a further development, as one moment, or one insight, gives rise to another. The paragraph rises and falls, only to rise higher; the first statements of an idea are taken up and expanded a few lines later ("that blessed mood, . . . that serene and blessed mood"); moments of insight that the reader thinks have been described are suddenly taken up again:

> . . . These beauteous forms,
> Through a long absence, have not been to me
> As is a landscape to a blind man's eye:
> But oft, in lonely rooms, and 'mid the din
> Of towns and cities, I have owed to them,
> In hours of weariness, sensations sweet,
> Felt in the blood, and felt along the heart;
> And passing even into my purer mind,
> With tranquil restoration:—feelings too
> Of unremembered pleasure: such, perhaps,
> As have no slight or trivial influence
> On that best portion of a good man's life,
> His little, nameless, unremembered acts
> Of kindness and of love. Nor less, I trust,
> To them I may have owed another gift,
> Of aspect more sublime; that blessed mood,
> In which the burthen of the mystery,
> In which the heavy and the weary weight
> Of all this unintelligible world,
> Is lightened:—that serene and blessed mood,
> In which the affections gently lead us on,—
> Until, the breath of this corporeal frame
> And even the motion of our human blood

> Almost suspended, we are laid asleep
> In body, and become a living soul:
> While with an eye made quiet by the power
> Of harmony, and the deep power of joy,
> We see into the life of things.
>
> (22–49)

The same process is found in the great central passage describing the loss and gain of Wordsworth's imaginative development: if he has lost the dizzy rapture of his first coming to the Wye valley, he has gained a maturity that allows him both to learn and to feel. In this passage the second verb echoes the first, heralding a stronger and more assured statement of an inspiration ("For I have learned. . . . And I have felt"). The central section is in three parts, rising, declaiming, and descending, with the middle part ("a sense sublime . . .") containing a great enveloping conception of the whole of nature as interfused with spirit and movement, with a life that is found in the mind of man and in the external world:

> . . . For I have learned
> To look on nature, not as in the hour
> Of thoughtless youth; but hearing often-times
> The still, sad music of humanity,
> Nor harsh nor grating, though of ample power
> To chasten and subdue. And I have felt
> A presence that disturbs me with the joy
> Of elevated thoughts; a sense sublime
> Of something far more deeply interfused,
> Whose dwelling is the light of setting suns,
> And the round ocean and the living air,
> And the blue sky, and in the mind of man:
> A motion and a spirit, that impels
> All thinking things, all objects of all thought,
> And rolls through all things. . . .
>
> (88–102)

It is tempting to see the impassioned blank verse of "Tintern Abbey" as the true voice of Wordsworth, regarding "Simon Lee" or "We Are Seven" as unfortunate applications of a theory of simple language. This is the theory of Wordsworth as the poet of "two voices," which takes its name from J. K. Stephen's parody of Wordsworth's own sonnet:

> Two voices are there: one is of the deep;
> It learns the storm-cloud's thunderous melody,
> Now roars, now murmurs with the changing sea,
> Now bird-like pipes, now closes soft in sleep:
> And one is of an old half-witted sheep
> Which bleats articulate monotony,

And indicates that two and one are three,
That grass is green, lakes damp, and mountains steep:
And, Wordsworth, both are thine. . . .

This is a sensible and witty view to take, but it ignores so much of the idiosyncrasy that makes Wordsworth himself and no other: it neglects to observe the way in which Wordsworth clung tenaciously to the very lines that seem most ludicrous to modern readers. When his friend Henry Crabb Robinson told Wordsworth that he did not dare to read these lines aloud, the poet replied, "They ought to be liked." For us to write them off is to make Wordsworth into our own poet, the poet of "Tintern Abbey" and the other meditative or narrative blank verse poems. We would be truer to the spirit of the poet himself if we took *Lyrical Ballads* as a whole and observed it with the spirit that Wordsworth himself had in a letter he wrote in 1802. A young correspondent, John Wilson, had written to him, praising *Lyrical Ballads* but querying the suitability of "The Idiot Boy," which he thought not so likely to please. Wordsworth's reply (7 June 1802) was "please whom? or what?"

I answer, human nature, as it has been and ever will be. But where are we to find the best measure of this? I answer, from within; by stripping our own hearts naked, and by looking out of ourselves towards men who lead the simplest lives most according to nature men who have never known false refinements, wayward and artificial desires, false criticisms, effeminate habits of thinking and feeling, or who, having known these things, have outgrown them. [5]

And if this is the ideal, the poet is to point to it by leading men toward the good, rather than by reflecting the wishes and feelings of the majority of men:

You have given me praise for having reflected faithfully in my poems the feelings of human nature. I would fain hope that I have done so. But a great Poet ought to do more than this he ought to a certain degree to rectify men's feelings, to give them new compositions of feeling, to render their feelings more sane pure and permanent. In short, more consonant to nature, that is, to eternal nature, and the great moving spirit of things. He ought to travel before men occasionally as well as at their sides.

(*ibid.*)

[5]From E. de Selincourt, ed., *Letters of William and Dorothy Wordsworth, The Early Years, 1787-1805*, revised by C. L. Shaver (London, 1967), p. 355.

THE PRELUDE

THE first attempts at *The Prelude* are found in a small notebook, known as MS.JJ, which Wordsworth used in Germany during the autumn of 1798. By 1799 a two-part *Prelude* of nearly 1,000 lines was complete; this became an almost completed five-book poem, taking the account through the Cambridge years and into the dedication to poetry that is now in book IV. In 1804 and 1805 Wordsworth added the later books on London, the French Revolution, his despair at its outcome and at the war, and his developing confidence in himself as a poet through the help of Dorothy and Coleridge. The result is the 1805 text, which is the complete poem in thirteen books; this was revised and altered later, with the tenth book divided into two, so that the first publication of the poem in 1850 contained fourteen books. The 1850 text is in some ways more polished, and it contains some fine observations; but the 1805 text (which will be used here) is usually preferred for its freshness and its revelation of Wordsworth's mind at this time.

The Prelude is an extraordinary poem, both in conception and execution, principally because it is epic, history, and autobiography. It is a poem about a single person, a child growing up in the Lake District in the 1770's and 1780's and a young man experiencing the university and the French Revolution; yet it is also much more than this. It contains wonderfully vivid descriptions of the experiences of childhood, but they are contained and given significance by the structure and form of the poem. Basically the poem's experience is one of loss and gain: the loss of the intense childhood experiences and a corresponding gain in maturity and insight. But that experience of loss and gain is set in an epic pattern. In *Paradise Lost*, Milton had written a new kind of epic, as the opening to his book IX shows; Wordsworth, too, is writing a new kind of epic, challenging the traditional concepts of what heroic action consists of. In book III he claims that childhood itself is heroic:

. . . Of genius, power
Creation and divinity itself
I have been speaking, for my theme has been
What passed within me. Not of outward things
Done visibly for other minds, words, signs,
Symbols or actions, but of my own heart
Have I been speaking, and my youthful mind.
O Heavens! how awful is the might of souls,
And what they do within themselves while yet

The yoke of earth is new to them, the world
Nothing but a wild field where they were sown.
This is, in truth, heroic argument,
And genuine prowess, which I wished to touch
With hand however weak, but in the main
It lies far hidden from the reach of words.

(III.171–185)

The suggestion that the poem's subject is "Not of outward things" recalls Milton's determination not to write about wars and battles,

. . . the better fortitude
Of Patience and Heroic Martyrdom
Unsung. . . .

(*Paradise Lost*, IX.31–33)

Wordsworth carries Milton's innovation a stage further, with an epic treatment of material that is traditionally not associated with the epic; in so doing he claims an epic significance for the growth of a mind, and particularly (as in this case) the growth of a poet's mind. That he had *Paradise Lost* in mind is suggested by an echo at the very beginning of *The Prelude*, where Wordsworth writes

The earth is all before me—with a heart
Joyous, nor scared at its own liberty,
I look about, and should the guide I chuse
Be nothing better than a wandering cloud,
I cannot miss my way. . . .

(I.15–19)

This takes up the final image of *Paradise Lost*, when Adam and Eve leave Paradise:

The World was all before them, where to choose
Thir place of rest, and Providence thir guide

(XII.646–647)

Where *Paradise Lost* ends, *The Prelude* begins: Milton shows us Adam and Eve at the beginning of human history, faced with the choice of free will and guided by the providence of God; Wordsworth shows us a man in time, able to choose and confident of his ability to use his freedom. In *The Prelude* liberty has replaced the theologians' conception of free will, and the wandering cloud has replaced the workings of Divine Providence: Wordsworth is writing his epic on his own terms of natural goodness and human freedom. What the child does with that freedom is the subject of the early books of *The Prelude*;

how the young man survives the pressure of events and retains his imaginative power is the continuation. The whole conception is daring: it is, said Wordsworth, "a thing unprecedented in literary history that a man should talk so much about himself" (letter to Sir George Beaumont, 1 May 1805). He is, in effect, writing an individual *Paradise Lost*, a poem that sees the life of an obscure country boy in the northwest of England as its own kind of significant progress, its own kind of movement from innocence to experience, from paradise to the world outside. Wordsworth makes the reference to *Paradise Lost* clear in a passage of Miltonic pastiche in *The Prelude* (VIII.119–143), a long paragraph of exotic vocabulary and latinate syntax including a description of Gehol's gardens "for delight/of the Tartarian Dynasty composed" and the Great Wall of China, "that mighty Wall, not fabulous, /(China's stupendous mound!)."

Immediately afterward, Wordsworth swings into his own comparison:

But lovelier far than this the paradise
Where I was reared, in Nature's primitive gifts
Favored no less, and more to every sense
Delicious, seeing that the sun and sky,
The elements, and seasons in their change,
Do find their dearest fellow-labourer there
The heart of man—a district on all sides
The fragrance breathing of humanity,
Man free, man working for himself, with choice
Of time, and place, and object; by his wants,
His comforts, native occupations, cares,
Conducted on to individual ends
Or social, and still followed by a train,
Unwooed, unthought-of even: simplicity,
And beauty, and inevitable grace.

(VIII.144–158)

The curious sliding movement of the syntax here is not very common in Wordsworth; but although the elements occur in apposition, they allow a characteristic accumulation of different effects, so that paradise appeals to the senses and to the heart of man, and is a place that encourages the best side of man: man free to work as he wishes and to live in harmony with himself and his fellow men. The sense of living as a member of a community is very important in *The Prelude*: it underlies the happiness of the early years and the early enthusiasms of the French Revolution, while the lack of an organic community was one of the features of London. It is described by

Wordsworth at the beginning of book VII in one of those homely observations that he does so well:

> . . . Above all, one thought
> Baffled my understanding, how men lived
> Even next-door neighbours, as we say, yet still
> Strangers, and knowing not each other's names.
> (VII.117–120)

The Prelude describes this vital sense of a community in a number of ways. The child himself is part of it and knows his school friends, the villagers, and the landscape with a delighted familiarity. There are many instances of this, but perhaps the most vivid is the opening of book IV, where Wordsworth describes the feelings of a university student coming home for the long vacation. He bounds down the hill, shouting for the old ferryman, who greets him; he walks on a few miles to Hawkshead, where he sees the familiar church; he is welcomed, with tears of joy, by Ann Tyson and walks around the village with her, greeting everybody. He sees the old rooms, the old garden, the boxed-in stream; he takes his place at the well-loved table and sleeps in his accustomed bed. The whole first section of book IV is a most beautiful re-creation of the emotions of coming home to a well-known landscape and a well-loved community; it looks back, of course, to the scenes of books I and II, especially to the passages that describe the children playing together, skating, or playing cards with the battered and dirty pack (the cards themselves cherished like old soldiers), or rowing or riding. It looks forward, too, to the hopes for the French Revolution as the beginning of the new Jerusalem:

> For, born in a poor district, and which yet
> Retaineth more of ancient homeliness,
> Manners erect, and frank simplicity,
> Than any other nook of English land,
> It was my fortune scarcely to have seen
> Through the whole tenor of my schoolday time
> The face of one, who, whether boy or man,
> Was vested with attention or respect
> Through claims of wealth or blood; . . .
>
> . . .
>
> . . . It could not be
> But that one tutored thus, who had been formed
> To thought and moral feeling in the way
> This story hath described, should look with awe
> Upon the faculties of man, receive
> Gladly the highest promises, and hail

> As best the government of equal rights
> And individual worth. . . .
> (IX.217–226; 242–249)

The Prelude, then, is an epic that deals with the loss of paradise; it is Wordsworth's childhood seen as myth, in that he has constructed around his own experience a reading of events that corresponds to the paradise myth. We know that he was not happy at Penrith, and we can only guess at the effect of his mother's death when he was eight and his father's when he was thirteen. Both of these are referred to in *The Prelude*, but not until books V and XI respectively, and there is nothing in the early books to suggest unhappiness and bereavement. There is fear, but that is accepted—indeed, welcomed—as part of the educative ministry of nature:

> Fair seed-time had my soul, and I grew up
> Fostered alike by beauty and by fear
> (I.305–306)

But the individual development through beauty and fear is supported by the sense that the individual is part of the community. He can be himself, but he can also be one of a number, as the skating episode shows. The pronouns shift from singular to plural in a way that conveys the mixture of individual impression and communal feeling:

> . . . All shod with steel
> We hissed along the polished ice in games
> Confederate, imitative of the chace
> And woodland pleasures, the resounding horn,
> The pack loud bellowing, and the hunted hare.
> So through the darkness and the cold we flew,
> And not a voice was idle. With the din,
> Meanwhile, the precipices rang aloud;
> The leafless trees and every icy crag
> Tinkled like iron; while the distant hills
> Into the tumult sent an alien sound
> Of melancholy, not unnoticed; while the stars,
> Eastward, were sparkling clear, and in the west
> The orange sky of evening died away.
>
> Not seldom from the uproar I retired
> Into a silent bay, or sportively
> Glanced sideway, leaving the tumultuous throng,
> To cut across the image of a star
> That gleamed upon the ice. And oftentimes
> When we had given our bodies to the wind,
> And all the shadowy banks on either side
> Came sweeping through the darkness, spinning still
> The rapid line of motion, then at once

Have I, reclining back upon my heels,
Stopped short—yet still the solitary cliffs
Wheeled by me, even as if the earth had rolled
With visible motion her diurnal round.
Behind me did they stretch in solemn train,
Feebler and feebler, and I stood and watched
Till all was tranquil as a dreamless sleep.

(I.460–489)

In this brilliant passage, with its wonderful re-creation of the movement and sound of skating, and of a Lake District winter twilight, the child is sharing in the experience and in the delight of the game with the others. Yet he is also able to retire "into a silent bay," and to perceive the way the earth seems to move, at a sudden stop. Like the poet of the preface to *Lyrical Ballads*, he is a child speaking to (or for) children, yet also a child endowed with more lively sensibility, rejoicing more than others in the spirit of life that is in him. The joyful energy of this passage is one of its most obvious characteristics, tempered as it is with a solemn awareness of the beauty and majesty of the earth. *The Prelude* as a whole is a striking combination of these qualities of individual energy and delight, with an equally important sense that the mind of the poet is, in many ways, a representative mind. It is aware, as we have seen, of the importance of the community; and the poem is also concerned with a major historical event, the French Revolution, an event of which the hopes and disappointments dominated the romantic movement. In the books on France, Wordsworth is recording the fact that he was present at the Revolution's various stages: when he first landed in France, on 13 July 1790, he and Robert Jones saw "benevolence and blessedness / Spread like a fragrance everywhere, like Spring" (VI.368–369). He had the enthusiasm and optimism of youth:

Bliss was it in that dawn to be alive,
But to be young was very heaven! . . .

(X.692–693)

and this optimism was based upon observations, upon conversations with Beaupuy, upon a direct experience of a nation struggling to find its new liberty. In book X, Wordsworth relates, with a painful authenticity, how he was torn in sympathy when prayers for an English victory were offered in church, and how his attitudes to the Revolution changed as the French became "oppressors in their

turn" (X.791). He describes how he studied the problem relentlessly,

. . . endlessly perplexed
With impulse, motive, right and wrong, the ground
Of moral obligation—what the rule,
And what the sanction—till, demanding proof,
And seeking it in every thing, I lost
All feeling of conviction, and, in fine,
Sick, wearied out with contrarieties,
Yielded up moral questions in despair. . . .

(X.893–900)

Book X of *The Prelude* is a most impressive record of a sensitive mind in confrontation with the great political events of the day: not only the French Revolution and the war, but the campaign for the abolition of the slave trade (X.202–226). He saw revolution become madness, and the rise and fall of Robespierre, with all the intense involvement of a contemporary; he remembered exactly where he was when he heard of the death of Robespierre, crossing Ulverston sands after visiting the grave of his beloved schoolmaster, William Taylor, at Cartmel. The scene (X.466–566), with the smooth sands of the Leven estuary in the foreground and the Lake District mountains in the background, is one of the most vividly pictorialized in *The Prelude*; the moment when the passing traveler told him that Robespierre was dead is sharpened by the poet's awareness of his surroundings and his feelings. It is no accident, of course, that the death of Robespierre is told to Wordsworth just after he had been thinking of the death of Taylor: the one famous and tyrannical, the other obscure and benevolent. In ways such as this, *The Prelude* is a record of what it was like to live through those years, to be a child at Hawkshead, a young man at Cambridge, a spectator in London, and an enthusiast in France.

Above all, however, these roles or stages were seen by Wordsworth in *The Prelude* as part of the growth of a poet's mind (the poem's alternative title). And if the poem is about the paradise myth, with the child growing up in the good community, and about history, with the child and young man responding to historical and social conditions around him, it is also about the development of a very special and very gifted man. Once again, it is possible to see Wordsworth referring back to Milton, who saw the role of the poet as a prophet or inspired teacher. In *Il Penseroso* the poet longs for the learning and wisdom of old age:

Till old experience do attain
To something like Prophetic strain.
(173–174)

and in *Paradise Lost* he remembers other figures who have suffered the same fate as himself, the loss of sight—

So were I equal'd with them in renown,
Blind *Thamyris* and blind *Maeonides*,
And *Tiresias* and *Phineus* Prophets old.
(III.34–36)

Wordsworth, too, uses the word "Prophet"; and in some ways the whole of *The Prelude* can be seen as moving toward the final paragraph, in which he sees himself and Coleridge as engaged in the teaching of mankind:

Prophets of Nature, we to them will speak
A lasting inspiration, sanctified
By reason and by truth; what we have loved
Others will love, and we may teach them how:
Instruct them how the mind of man becomes
A thousand times more beautiful than the earth
On which he dwells, above this frame of things
(Which, 'mid all revolutions in the hopes
And fears of men, doth still remain unchanged)
In beauty exalted, as it is itself
Of substance and of fabric more divine.
(XIII.442–452)

It is toward this end, with the poet as a responsible member of society and an inspired teacher, that so much of *The Prelude* has been moving. The range of experience that contributes to this is considerable, including the childhood episodes, education, books, and the sublime experiences that remain in the memory long after they have passed. Wordsworth calls them "spots of time" in a crucial passage:

There are in our existence spots of time,
Which with distinct preeminence retain
A renovating virtue, whence, depressed
By false opinion and contentious thought,
Or aught of heavier or more deadly weight
In trivial occupations and the round
Of ordinary intercourse, our minds
Are nourished and invisibly repaired—
A virtue, by which pleasure is enhanced,
That penetrates, enables us to mount
When high, more high, and lifts us up when fallen.
(XI.257–267)

Such moments, he goes on to say, are "scattered everywhere" (XI.274), though they may be most conspicuous in childhood; he gives an example of two episodes that are vividly remembered, being lost and finding himself beneath a murderer's gibbet, and waiting for the horses to take him home just before his father's death. In both cases there is a mysterious intensity about the episode, a moment of perception that remains with extraordinary sharpness. In the first, the child, regaining the path, sees

A naked pool that lay beneath the hills,
The beacon on the summit, and more near,
A girl who bore a pitcher on her head
And seemed with difficult steps to force her way
Against the blowing wind. . . .
(XI.303–307)

The poet recalls how he later revisited the spot and remembered the earlier occasion:

. . . So feeling comes in aid
Of feeling, and diversity of strength
Attends us, if but once we have been strong.
(XI.325–327)

We recognize this as one of Wordsworth's complex states, in which "feeling comes in aid / Of feeling." He is not clear exactly why the force of the episode is so great, but he knows that it is: the greatness of man is mysterious and deep, and it is by the exploration of such episodes that we come to understand and acknowledge it. As a child, the poet was lost; as an adult, looking back, he now says:

I am lost, but see
In simple childhood something of the base
On which thy greatness stands—but this I feel,
That from thyself it is that thou must give,
Else never canst receive. . . .
(XI.329–333)

The sentiment is reminiscent of Coleridge's "we receive but what we give" (from the "Letter to Sara Hutchinson"), and it indicates something of the interacting relationship between the mind and the external world that was so important to both poets. In their most confident moments, both poets felt a great union between man and nature, a profound interaction, or what Wordsworth describes as a "consummation" between the human mind and the natural world. Sometimes this comes at unexpected moments, as it does in the second "spot of time" in book XI. This describes the poet and his brothers waiting for the horses to take them home at Christmastime: through the misty day he waited beside a stone wall, with a single sheep and a hawthorn tree for company (it is remarkable how often single trees or lonely people and animals occur in Wordsworth). He had been so impatient to get home, the poet records, and then ten days later his father died; he saw himself tritely as punished for his impatience, though clearly this is not the point of the passage. The long wait in the mist and rain, the strange company of sheep and tree (in his impatience he had left his brothers further down the pass), these constituents of the moment remained with him as a testimony to his imaginative grasp of a situation:

> And afterwards the wind and sleety rain,
> And all the business of the elements,
> The single sheep, and the one blasted tree,
> And the bleak music of that old stone wall,
> The noise of wood and water, and the mist
> Which on the line of each of those two roads
> Advanced in such indisputable shapes—
> All these were spectacles and sounds to which
> I often would repair, and thence would drink
> As at a fountain. . . .
>
> (XI.375–384)

In this description we notice not only the emphasis on the particular objects (the wind, the rain, the single sheep, the blasted tree) but an emphasis on what Wordsworth elsewhere calls the "goings-on" of the physical world. He animates the dreariness with unobtrusive life: "all the business of the elements," "the bleak music of that old stone wall," "The noise of wood and water," the mist that "Advanced in such indisputable shapes," all these suggest a mind that goes out to the universe and responds to what it is doing—a mind that apprehends the "business," hears the "music," and sees the shapes of the mist. Wordsworth is here celebrating not the power of nature, but the power of the imagination and the memory.

The same can be said of two other great passages in *The Prelude* that are concerned with the growth of the inspired prophet-poet. The first is the crossing of the Alps section in book VI (494 and following). Once again, as in the "spots of time" moments of book XI, there is a loss of direction, a momentary sense of failure, an unfulfilled expectation; as in those "spots of time," the failure and loss, the

mistaken hope, are suddenly transformed into an awareness of the power of the imagination. In book VI, it is addressed directly, in a startling apostrophe that erupts into the verse:

> Imagination!—lifting up itself
> Before the eye and progress of my song
> Like an unfathered vapour, here that power,
> In all the might of its endowments, came
> Athwart me. I was lost as in a cloud,
> Halted without a struggle to break through,
> And now, recovering, to my soul I say
> 'I recognize thy glory'. In such strength
> Of usurpation, in such visitings
> Of awful promise, when the light of sense
> Goes out in flashes that have shewn to us
> The invisible world, doth greatness make abode,
> There harbours whether we be young or old.
> Our destiny, our nature, and our home,
> Is with infinitude—and only there;
> With hope it is, hope that can never die,
> Effort, and expectation, and desire,
> And something evermore about to be.
>
> (VI.525–542)

Here the imagination itself is like a vapor or mist; the poet seems overcome by it, lost in it as he was on the Alpine path. But he suddenly sees the power of the imagination, not in the fact but in the promise, not in the material world but in the glimpse of something higher and beyond. As he sees this he becomes aware of the sheer power of an imagination that can so transcend its material circumstances as to become conscious of its activity. Similarly, in the "climbing of Snowdon" passage from the final book of *The Prelude*, the poet describes a night climb from Bethgelert through the mist, until suddenly he and his companions came out of the mist into the moonlight. They found themselves surrounded by a sea of mist, out of which the Welsh hills lifted their peaks and over which the moon looked down "in single glory." So strong is the impression of the mist as a sea that Wordsworth has to describe it as moving eventually

> Into the sea, the real sea. . . .
> (XIII.49)

The fact that Wordsworth has to describe it as "the real sea" is a testimony of how powerful his imagination has become. Before, the real world existed, and the imagination erupted from it; now the imagination seems to be supreme, and the real world has to be admitted. Between the mountain and the shore is a chasm, a fracture in the mist:

> A deep and gloomy breathing-place through which
> Mounted the roar of waters, torrents, streams
> Innumerable, roaring with one voice.
>
> (XIII.57–59)

The stupendous natural vision is one that Wordsworth sees as an emblem of the power of the mind; only with such a powerful landscape can he begin to say what the mind is capable of doing:

> ... it appeared to me
> The perfect image of a mighty mind,
> Of one that feeds upon infinity,
> That is exalted by an under-presence,
> The sense of God, or whatsoe'er is dim
> Or vast in its own being—above all,
> One function of such mind had Nature there
> Exhibited by putting forth, and that
> With circumstance most awful and sublime:
> That domination which she oftentimes
> Exerts upon the outward face of things,
> So moulds them, and endues, abstracts, combines,
> Or by abrupt and unhabitual influence
> Doth make one object so impress itself
> Upon all others, and pervades them so,
> That even the grossest minds must see and hear,
> And cannot chuse but feel. . . .
>
> (XIII.68–84)

The imaginative minds are ever on the watch, building up greatness from the least suggestion, or from failure, or from ordinary expectations that have come to grief. This, the poet concludes, "this alone is genuine liberty" (XIII.122); the ability of the mind to transcend its surroundings, to become aware, even when it is least expected, of the strength of the imagination. For often it surprises, and surprise is a favorite idea of Wordsworth's. Moments come upon the imagination with strange suddenness: as the child rows a stolen boat out from the shore at Patterdale, he is astonished and terrified to see the mountain coming after him; as the child who is hooting to the owls (V.389 and following) fails to get a response, he is suddenly aware of something else:

> Then sometimes in that silence, while he hung
> Listening, a gentle shock of mild surprize
> Has carried far into his heart the voice

> Of mountain torrents; or the visible scene
> Would enter unawares into his mind
> With all its solemn imagery, its rocks,
> Its woods, and that uncertain heaven, received
> Into the bosom of the steady lake.
>
> (V.406–413)

Here the mind receives, but it receives because it is a mind that can give. The boy of Winander hooting to the owls is contrasted throughout book V with the fact-getting, well-behaved, unnatural child; the boy, who died young, was one of those with whom Wordsworth played:

> A race of real children, not too wise,
> Too learned, or too good, but wanton, fresh,
> And bandied up and down by love and hate;
> Fierce, moody, patient, venturous, modest, shy,
> Mad at their sports like withered leaves in winds;
> Though doing wrong and suffering, and full oft
> Bending beneath our life's mysterious weight
> Of pain and fear, yet still in happiness
> Not yielding to the happiest upon earth.
>
> (V.436–444)

And so, as so often with Wordsworth, the greatest sublimity is linked with the celebration of the ordinary; and to pursue the development of the prophet-poet, and the great creative imagination, is to be reminded that they are rooted in an ordinary childhood. It is all wonderfully simple, yet wonderfully mysterious and profound:

> Oh mystery of man, from what a depth
> Proceed thy honours! I am lost, but see
> In simple childhood something of the base
> On which thy greatness stands—. . .
>
> (XI.328–331)

and the greatness of *The Prelude* is that it does succeed in testifying to the power of the imagination while being firmly rooted in human experience.

SHORTER POEMS AFTER 1798

THE sheer ordinariness that is an essential part of Wordsworth is continued in the poems written after *Lyrical Ballads*; yet it is an ordinariness transformed, as in *The Prelude*, by an imaginative balance that seems to achieve just the right adjustment between the subject matter and its transformation.

In the "Lucy" poems, for instance, most of which were written in Germany during the winter of 1798–1799, Wordsworth writes of the death of a young girl who is an embodiment of all the natural forces of simplicity and grace. In one poem she is a "flower" and "sportive as the fawn"; she lives in the poet's memory as an ideal figure who has died while she is still in a fresh and youthful state of communion with nature. In the greatest of these poems, "A Slumber Did My Spirit Seal," she is first an ideal, almost spiritual creature and then a dead girl; yet even then she is reunited with nature in a way that seems appropriate and that turns her death into a fitting reunion with the world of which she was a part. She is both girl and nature form, shaped and molded by a force outside her; the poet sees her for a time, and loves her, only to lose her. Thus the "Lucy" poems are both elegies for a loved one and something more, a perception of an ideal and an indication of the transience of natural innocence. In his description of *Lyrical Ballads* in *Biographia Literaria*, Coleridge wrote of "the two cardinal points of poetry":

. . . the power of exciting the sympathy of the reader by a faithful adherence to the truth of nature, and the power of giving the interest of novelty by the modifying colors of imagination.

(II.5)

This is a remarkable insight into the working of Wordsworth's shorter poems: they are true to nature, that is, to a visible and recognizable external world, and yet that world is given a significance that it normally lacks. The significance is given to it by the perceiving mind, which allows the thing or person to be seen more vividly and yet as something more than its material self. So the sheepfold in "Michael" remains a sheepfold but becomes a symbol of all the unfulfilled hopes of the shepherd's life, and of more than that: it is a symbol and not an allegorical representation of something. So it has a life of its own: it exists in the eye of the passerby as he walks up the path beside Green-head Ghyll, and it has a history that sums up the whole life and fate of Michael and his family. They are simple, frugal people, who prefer to remain on the land rather than sell it to pay off the indemnity; Michael's work is with the elements, among the fields and hills, and he is summoned to work by the winds. His feelings, too, are elementary passions of the kind that Wordsworth saw as existing among rustic folk: his tenderness for his son and his love of the land on which he

has worked all his life. The laying of the cornerstone of the sheepfold, done by Luke at his request, is an act of faith and hope: the sheepfold becomes a covenant between the father and the son but also, in its way, an act of defiance against the destructiveness of the monetary and city world. Michael and Luke are forced to separate, and Luke comes to grief: Michael continues to go to the sheepfold, but he is unable to finish it, although he continues to work at it. The celebrated line

And never lifted up a single stone
(466)

has tended to make the reader forget that in fact Michael did continue to work at the sheepfold for seven years after Luke's downfall. Michael is a man of determination and perseverance; his life has been one of industrious labor, and the downfall of Luke does not alter this. But he has no heart to continue at times when the grief is too great; the sheepfold is an emblem of his purpose in life, the construction of something that will survive for Luke, as he hoped that the patrimonial fields would pass to him. Instead, in the city, Luke

. . . gave himself
To evil courses: ignominy and shame
Fell on him, so that he was driven at last
To seek a hiding-place beyond the seas.
(444–447)

In this poem, the sheepfold and the cottage are the foreground, and the city is far away; Luke's downfall is portrayed with a brisk absence of detail, whereas Michael's speeches are recorded verbatim. It is a masterly use of perspective to emphasize the quality of life and the destruction that comes into it from outside; as we know from *The Prelude*, Wordsworth had a particular admiration for shepherds, and "Michael" is a narrative poem that records the way in which the shepherd and his wife seem hardly to understand other ways. They are touchingly naive about Luke's departure, and presumably about life and conditions in the city; yet their naiveté is associated throughout with love. Michael loves the land and has an abiding love for Luke. He promises the boy that

". . . whatever fate
Befall thee, I shall love thee to the last,
And bear thy memory with me to the grave."
(415–417)

So too, after the brief account of Luke's fall, comes the resounding line

> There is a comfort in the strength of love;
> (448)

which indicates the contrary movements of love and despair that exist within Michael: he is a man who has experienced a lifetime of love, in his work and its surroundings, in the domestic happiness of his frugal home, in his land, and in the tenderness of his relationship with his son. When the last of these is broken the others remain; as so often in Wordsworth, the figures who are bereft of human relationships retain a strange and lonely dignity that comes from an affinity with nature. Michael is deeply moving because he represents every aging father with an only child in whom his hopes are centered; he is also awesome in his ability to go on loving. He is a man for whom the reader feels not tragic pity and fear but a mixture of pity and admiration.

The same is true of other solitaries in Wordsworth, most notably the leech-gatherer in "Resolution and Independence." If "Michael" is written in an austere and stately blank verse (for although the meter is the same, the language is quite different from the impassioned diction of "Tintern Abbey"), "Resolution and Independence" is written in stanza form, with a peculiar and very effective diction. It is metrically very formal, with an alexandrine at the end of each stanza, and the diction is often archaic, with a biblical cadence and rhythm:

> Motionless as a cloud the old Man stood,
> That heareth not the loud winds when they call;
> And moveth all together, if it move at all.
> (75–77)

The use of subjunctives ("if it move") and the older forms of the verb (heareth, moveth) are linked with rhythms that echo biblical ones ("consider the lilies of the field, how they grow": "That heareth not the loud winds when they call"). The result is a poem that describes an encounter with a poor old man in formal and stately terms, so that the old man himself is given dignity. In Dorothy Wordsworth's journal, he appears as "an old man almost double":

He had on a coat, thrown over his shoulders, above his waistcoat and coat. Under this he carried a bundle, and had an apron on and a night-cap. . . . His trade was to gather leeches, but now leeches are scarce, and he had not strength for it. He lived by begging. . . .

(3 October 1800)

When Wordsworth wrote "Resolution and Independence" some eighteen months later (in the productive spring of 1802), any of these details that might make the old man seem ludicrous were carefully removed. He enters the poem now at a moment when the poet is gloomily contemplating his own future: it is a brilliant fresh morning after rain, yet the poet feels uncertain about the fate of fellow poets and his own failure to provide; like the grasshopper in the fable, his whole life has been lived "in pleasant thought, / As if life's business were a summer mood" (36–37). Instead of being made to regret this by the hardworking ant, however, he meets the leech-gatherer, whose appearance is preceded by words such as "grace":

> Now, whether it were by peculiar grace,
> A leading from above, a something given,
> Yet it befell that, in this lonely place,
> When I with these untoward thoughts had striven,
> Beside a pool bare to the eye of heaven
> I saw a Man before me unawares:
> The oldest man he seemed that ever wore grey hairs.
> (50–56)

The great simplicities of Wordsworth's poetry appear to wonderful effect in a line like "I saw a Man . . . ," especially as Wordsworth goes on to qualify this:

> As a huge stone is sometimes seen to lie
> Couched on the bald top of an eminence;
> Wonder to all who do the same espy,
> By what means it could thither come, and whence;
> So that it seems a thing endued with sense:
> Like a sea-beast crawled forth, that on a shelf
> Of rock or sand reposeth, there to sun itself. . . .
> (57–63)

Here the old man is likened to a stone and to a strange sea beast; or, to complicate the process, he could be said to be likened to a stone that itself is like a sea beast. Either way, here is a strange combination of inanimate and animate, as though the old man is half immobile and insensate, and half strangely alive. It is interesting, too, to see how the rhythm of the line unobtrusively emphasizes the strangeness of the old man. He is like a stone "Couched on the bald top of an eminence," where the words "bald top" give two strong syllables in the middle of the line. Without the word "bald," the line would be regularly dactylic, with three feet:

> /   x x / x x / x x
> Couched on the top of an eminence

With "bald," it becomes strangely out of joint, especially when followed by the trochaic "Wonder" in the following line. But Wordsworth unerringly brings the reader back to the reality in the following line:

> Such seemed this Man, . . .

which echoes "I saw a Man" and allows all the strangeness of the earlier verse to be clamped between the two occurrences of "Man." The man's humanity is asserted, even, it might be said, his basic humanity: he is Man, old and unaccommodated, and the poet's meeting with him has something of the meeting of the sophisticated with the elementary or primitive. The old man's physical condition is miserable: he is bent double with age, and like the stone *cum* sea beast, he seems "not all alive nor dead." Yet he returns a courteous answer to the poet's greeting, and replies to his inquiry "what are you doing?" The poet describes him thus:

> Ere he replied, a flash of mild surprise
> Broke from the sable orbs of his yet-vivid eyes.
>
> His words came feebly, from a feeble chest,
> But each in solemn order followed each,
> With something of a lofty utterance drest—
> (90–94)

The understated skill of Wordsworth's verse is brilliantly demonstrated here, in the contrast between the rhetorical and poetic language of the first two and the last two lines here, and the strong simplicity of the middle line. In the first two lines the diction ("sable orbs," "yet-vivid eyes") might have come from Milton; so might the image of words following each other dressed in their lofty utterance. In the center is the line full of effort, with the repetition of "feebly, . . . feeble," the alliteration of which suggests a difficulty in breathing or speaking freely. The contrast embodies the whole sense of strangeness that is found within the poem, the coexistence of an internal state that does not match the external conditions. The poet is miserable on a beautiful morning;

the decrepit man is firm in his courage and his optimism. As he describes his condition to the poet (and it is noticeable that in this version he is no longer begging) the poet becomes curiously abstracted; it is as though the individual situation becomes lost in its wider implications.

> The old Man still stood talking by my side;
> But now his voice to me was like a stream
> Scarce heard; nor word from word could I divide;
> And the whole body of the Man did seem
> Like one whom I had met with in a dream;
> Or like a man from some far region sent,
> To give me human strength, by apt admonishment.
> (106–112)

The idea of the old man as having been sent "from some far region" links up with the earlier description of him as "a something given"; he seems to be both natural and in some way supernatural. He comes to bring the poet human strength, yet in the last verse the poet turns to God:

> "God," said I, "be my help and stay secure;
> I'll think of the Leech-gatherer on the lonely moor!"
> (139–140)

The leech-gatherer seems to stand for something, or rather to be something, above and beyond the customary experience and certainly above the worldly cares of the poet. It would be a great mistake to see him as an allegory of some kind of religious presence, but he is clearly an indication of something outside the poet, a strength and a resolution that contrasts forcibly with the poet's own failure to keep a serene mind. The leech-gatherer, in fact, embodies qualities that Wordsworth signally admired: an independence and a serenity that freed him from financial and other worldly responsibilities; this liberty is, for Wordsworth, a true freedom from anxiety, and it is connected with other freedoms that he celebrates in his poetry.

Politically, a love of freedom made him a supporter of the French Revolution, and later a fervent patriot; in social terms he admired societies like the one he had known in his youth, where men seemed to be independent and not bound together in a master-slave relationship; and in personal terms, he sought a freedom from anxiety, a freedom that does not seek to avoid misfortune but that comes from having the resources to bear it. Meanwhile, the relationship between this ideal freedom and the actual world of man continues to exercise Wordsworth; the ideal world is found in many forms, especially associated with nature and childhood, and the poet's delight in it is found in many of the poems written in these years, especially in the spring of 1802. Many of these poems, "The Tinker," "To a Butterfly," "Among All Lovely Things My Love Had Been," "To the Small Celandine," celebrate happiness and freedom, while others are aware of the forces that destroy these things. "The Sailor's Mother" is one, and the "Ode. Intimations of Immortality from Recollections of Early Childhood" is another. The great Ode, as it is sometimes called, balances a marvelous recapturing of the child's innocence and closeness to nature with an awareness of the later perception of an adult; the poet laments the inevitable process of growing into adulthood, embraced so enthusiastically by the child who acts grown-up parts, and yet the Ode is informed by a mature and responsible understanding that this process is necessary. A Neoplatonic sense of a reality elsewhere is joined to the memory of the child's experience, and through it our life on earth is seen to be an absence from a home in God. Yet the life on earth has its own precious moments, and not only in childhood:

> The thought of our past years in me doth breed
> Perpetual benediction. . . .
>
> (137–138)

The benediction comes not just from the memory of delight and liberty, but from something more elusive and profound:

> . . . those obstinate questionings
> Of sense and outward things,
> Fallings from us, vanishings;
> Blank misgivings of a Creature
> Moving about in worlds not realised,
> High instincts before which our mortal Nature
> Did tremble like a guilty Thing surprised. . . .
>
> (145–151)

With this praise for the mysterious and marvelous, there is another source of comfort, in the strength that the adult gains through contemplating life in all its confusion and limitations:

> In the primal sympathy
> Which having been must ever be;
> In the soothing thoughts that spring

> Out of human suffering;
> In the faith that looks through death,
> In years that bring the philosophic mind.
>
> (185–190)

The great Ode is a key poem in the understanding of the complexity of Wordsworth's beliefs. It contains, without fracturing into different pieces, the joy in childhood and liberty, the unity of this with the rejoicing natural world, and the sense, too, of the mature understanding of the role of man in the created world. The child is a prophet; the man can only remember, and understand, but his view of life involves an accommodation with things as they are that is a gain to compensate for the loss of the childhood vision.

Wordsworth's belief in the faith that looks through death was tested to the uttermost in February 1805, when his favorite brother, John, was drowned at sea. In his grief the poet turned to a favorite subject, the daisy, the "unassuming Common-place / Of Nature," which he saw as sleeping and waking upon the sailor's grave; even here there is a comfort from the simple things of nature. But in a greater poem, "Elegiac Stanzas, Suggested by a Picture of Peele Castle, in a Storm, Painted by Sir George Beaumont," Wordsworth chronicled a change. He had stayed near Peele Castle in fine weather, in 1794; now he saw Beaumont's picture, which showed it in a very different condition: a ruined tower beaten by the waves (the painting also contained a ship going down offshore, which would have reminded Wordsworth of his brother's death). The stormy sea he now sees as the true reflector of the condition of life, and the idea of a world governed by fine weather has disappeared:

> A power is gone, which nothing can restore;
> A deep distress hath humanised my Soul.
>
> (35–36)

As so often with Wordsworth, loss is turned into gain, and he sees himself as becoming more human and less likely to idealize in his bereavement. Certainly his poetry, from this time on, becomes less elusive and imaginative: even "Peele Castle" has an allegorical construction that is uncomfortably schematic—fine weather contrasted with bad weather, the castle standing against the storms of life, the sense of a "before" and "after" scene. It is saved by its austere diction and its stern sense of mourning tempered by hope:

WILLIAM WORDSWORTH

Farewell, farewell the heart that lives alone,
Housed in a dream, at distance from the Kind!
Such happiness, wherever it be known,
Is to be pitied; for 'tis surely blind.

But welcome fortitude, and patient cheer,
And frequent sights of what is to be borne!
Such sights, or worse, as are before me here. —
Not without hope we suffer and we mourn.

(53–60)

SONNETS, THE EXCURSION, AND LATER POEMS

THE "Elegiac Stanzas," "Resolution and Independence," the "Immortality Ode," and many of Wordsworth's best-known shorter poems (such as "The Solitary Reaper" and "I Wandered Lonely as a Cloud") were published in *Poems, in Two Volumes* in 1807. This volume also contains some of Wordsworth's finest sonnets, a form in which he delighted. Once again his great master was Milton, and both poets use the same Italianate form, reveling in its compression and the artistic demands of its rhyme scheme. "Nuns fret not at their convent's narrow room," wrote Wordsworth, and he seems to have relished the discipline required to produce a good sonnet. Among the sonnets are some of the best patriotic poetry ever written, which links a love of England with qualities of spiritual nobility, as in "Milton! thou shouldst be living at this hour." The arresting first line is a feature of Wordsworth's sonnets: "Earth has not anything to show more fair" is perhaps the best-known example, but there are others, such as "Once did She hold the gorgeous east in fee" (another sonnet on a political subject, the extinction of the Venetian republic by Napoleon) and "It is a beauteous evening, calm and free." In this last example, the sonnet continues with a literally breathtaking image

The holy time is quiet as a Nun
Breathless with adoration; . . .
(2–3)

and then, as so often, Wordsworth anchors the image in straightforward natural description—

. . . the broad sun
Is sinking down in its tranquillity;
(3–4)

—only to invite the imagination to work again by the use of figurative language:

The gentleness of heaven broods o'er the Sea:
Listen! the mighty Being is awake,
And doth with his eternal motion make
A sound like thunder—everlastingly.
(5–8)

It is not clear to whom the word "Listen!" is addressed. Its introduction here gives it a general sense, as though anyone on a calm evening might, by listening, hear the workings of a mighty Being. But it then acquires a particular meaning, as Wordsworth turns to address his French daughter:

Dear Child! dear Girl! that walkest with me here,
If thou appear untouched by solemn thought,
Thy nature is not therefore less divine:
Thou liest in Abraham's bosom all the year;
And worship'st at the Temple's inner shrine,
God being with thee when we know it not.
(9–14)

There is a very delicate change of mood here, from the impersonal to the personal, with an equalizing movement from the ordinary to the sacred. A further balancing is found between the tender and the reflective as the poet notes the distance between the child's unconscious communion with heaven and her conscious ordinariness. The difference between the child's apparent state, walking on the sands with a mind "untouched by solemn thought," and her actual state is underlined by the biblical formality of the last lines, which apply to the child in a mysterious and remote, yet authoritative way. Yet throughout the grand reflections is the memory of "Dear Child! dear Girl!," the outburst of genuine feeling that is so much a part of Wordsworth's poetry.

Not all the sonnets are successful: some are plainly tedious, and others are mistakenly pretentious. The long series of *Ecclesiastical Sonnets*, written at the suggestion of Sir George Beaumont, has the air of a dull exercise. At their best, however, the sonnets have the same kind of forceful austerity that Wordsworth admired in Milton, and the characteristic blend of homely tenderness and lofty sentiment.

In the later sonnets something of the magic goes out of Wordsworth's poetry. It is difficult to say what it is, but the ideas that seemed so powerful now become commonplace. The same can be said of *The Excursion* (1814), with the exception of book I, and that is better read in its earlier version as "The Ruined Cottage" (written 1797–1798). There it is a moving story of the decline of a family and the ruin of their lives and hopes by sickness and economic recession (in some respects a return to the preoccupations of the Salisbury Plain poems). In *The Excursion* it is still very fine, though to some tastes the Christian conclusion is false and trite. The central figure of Margaret, the last human tenant of the ruined cottage (last human tenant as opposed to the natural creatures who later take up their abode there), is drawn with a sustained economy and gravity: she is

> . . . a Woman of a steady mind
> Tender and deep in her excess of love;
> (I.513–514)

while her husband is "Frugal, affectionate, sober, and withal / keenly industrious." A succession of calamities (bad harvests, war, and illness), however, causes him to lose his work and sense of purpose, and he finally leaves to join the army. Margaret has to part with her elder child to a kind farmer; the younger child dies; and she is left alone, waiting for the return that never comes. Her love and loyalty prevent her from leaving the cottage, and from having any other hope in life; her continued disappointment leads to her sickness and death.

Her story is told by a central figure in *The Excursion*, the Wanderer (in the earliest version, the Pedlar), who is one of those ideal Wordsworth characters who has given up a regular and settled employment for something that is freer and more haphazard. He has no interest in what Wordsworth called "getting and spending"; he is a traveling and solitary man, who possesses a tranquil and steady mind. The result is that his energies are not directed to his own problems:

> . . . and, by nature tuned
> And constant disposition of his thoughts
> To sympathy with man, he was alive
> To all that was enjoyed where'er he went,
> And all that was endured; for, in himself
> Happy, and quiet in his cheerfulness,
> He had no painful pressure from without
> That made him turn aside from wretchedness
> With coward fears. He could *afford* to suffer
> With those whom he saw suffer. . . .
> (I.362–371)

The Wanderer is an ideal figure, who is contrasted in the poem with the Solitary, a man who has ex-perienced the hopes and miseries of the French Revolution, and whose personal sufferings have made him misanthropic. A third character, the Pastor, is perhaps the most important of all: he dominates the latter part of the poem with his practical Christian wisdom, and the final book ends with a delightful scene of the Pastor and his family. This forms an obvious contrast to the first book of the poem: from the ruined family to the happy and prosperous one is a journey that involves a full acceptance and understanding of human misery, together with an ability to remain optimistic and benevolent. Both the Wanderer, in his solitude and peripatetic life, and the Pastor, who stands for the settled family life, are able to bring comfort to others and remain at peace with themselves.

The Excursion is thus an extended illustration of different ways of approaching the central problems of human life—the failure of hopes, the loss of loved ones, the doubtful consolations of religion. In its counseling of orthodox Christian belief, *The Excursion* looks toward the work of the later Wordsworth, and indeed the poet's orthodoxy may be one reason why his later poetry is not informed by the same intense conviction as the earlier poetry that expresses his sense of natural power. It is this awareness of the power of natural life and its relation to the mind of man that Wordsworth conveys so well: it is a power beside which the preoccupation of man with material things seems idle, and it is a power whose essential optimism is a counterbalance to the very real suffering and misery of men. If men were to behave with this power as their guide, there would be less misery, for human unhappiness often comes from a failure of society to provide properly for its members. Instead, there would be

> . . . a better time,
> More wise desires, and simpler manners. . . .
> (103–104)

These lines come from the preface to *The Excursion*, originally part of a longer poem entitled "Home at Grasmere." In it we see a summary of many of Wordsworth's most deeply held beliefs. As so often, Milton is in the background as Wordsworth thinks of the earthly paradise. He knows that he (like Milton visiting Hell) will have to travel

> . . . near the tribes
> And fellowships of men, and see ill sights

Of madding passions mutually inflamed;
Must hear Humanity in fields and groves
Pipe solitary anguish; or must hang
Brooding above the fierce confederate storm
Of sorrow, barricadoed evermore
Within the walls of cities— . . .

(73–80)

But he also intends to celebrate the beauties of paradise, not just as a concept or an idea, but as an actual possibility:

. . . Paradise, and groves
Elysian, Fortunate Fields—like those of old
Sought in the Atlantic Main—why should they be
A history only of departed things,
Or a mere fiction of what never was?
For the discerning intellect of Man,
When wedded to this goodly universe
In love and holy passion, shall find these
A simple produce of the common day.

(47–55)

The last beautiful line, with its utter simplicity (and the language really used by men), emphasizes the way in which Wordsworth regarded the universe that he found all around him. It was a world that contained its full share of human misery, but that had the power of being transformed by the human mind. In that process, the poet had his full part to play, and that is why Wordsworth always thought of himself as a teacher. The poet as he described him in the preface to *Lyrical Ballads* is many things, but above all

He is the rock of defence for human nature; an upholder and preserver, carrying everywhere with him relationship and love.

(*Poetical Works*, II.396)

SELECTED BIBLIOGRAPHY

I. Bibliography. L. Cooper, *A Condordance to the Poems of William Wordsworth* (London, 1911); T. J. Wise, *A Bibliography of the Writings in Prose and Verse of William Wordsworth* (London, 1916); T. J. Wise, *Two Lake Poets: A Catalogue of Printed Books, Manuscripts etc., by Wordsworth and Coleridge* (London, 1927); J. V. Logan, *Wordsworthian Criticism: A Guide and Bibliography* (Columbus, Ohio, 1947); *Catalogue of the Library at Dove Cottage* (London, 1948); G. H. Henley, comp., *The Cornell Wordsworth Collection* (London, 1957); E. F. Henley and D. H. Stam, *Wordsworthian Criticism 1945–1964: An Annotated Bibliography* (New York, 1965); D. H. Stam, *Wordsworthian Criticism 1964–1973: An Annotated Bibliography, Including Additions to Wordsworthian Criticism 1945–1964* (New York, 1974).

II. Collected Works. *Poems, Including Lyrical Ballads*, 2 vols. (London, 1915), the first collected ed.; *Miscellaneous Poems*, 4 vols. (London, 1820–1827), 5 vols. (London, 1832), 6 vols. (London, 1836–1846), 7 vols. (London, 1849–1850); *The Poems* (London, 1845); *The Poetical Works*, 6 vols. (London, 1857), with I. Fenwick's notes; T. Hutchinson, ed., *The Poetical Works* (London, 1895), rev. by E. de Selincourt (London, 1950), the Oxford Standard Authors series, also in Oxford Paperback (London, 1969); E. de Selincourt and H. Darbishire, eds., *The Poetical Works*, 5 vols. (Oxford, 1940–1949; rev. ed., 1952–1959); W. J. B. Owen and J. W. Smyser, eds., *The Prose Works of William Wordsworth*, 3 vols. (Oxford, 1974); J. O. Hayden, ed., *William Wordsworth: The Poems*, 2 vols. (Harmondsworth, 1977), does not include *The Prelude*; S. Parrish, ed., *The Cornell Wordsworth* (Ithaca, N.Y.–Hassocks, Sussex, 1975–   ): S. Gill, ed., *The Salisbury Plain Poems* (1975); S. Parrish, ed., *The Prelude, 1798–99* (1977); B. Darlington, ed., *Home at Grasmere* (1977); J. Butler, ed., *The Ruined Cottage and The Pedlar* (1979).

III. Selected Works. M. Arnold, ed., *Poems of Wordsworth* (London, 1879); T. Hutchinson, ed., *Poems in Two Volumes* (London, 1897), from the original ed. of 1807, edited by H. Darbishire (London, 1914), and rev. ed. (London, 1952); J. Butt, ed., *Wordsworth. Selected Poetry and Prose* (London, 1964); G. H. Hartman, ed., *William Wordsworth: Selected Poetry and Prose* (New York, 1969); R. S. Thomas, ed., *A Choice of Wordsworth's Verse* (London, 1971); W. J. B. Owen, ed., *Wordsworth's Literary Criticism* (London, 1974); W. Davies, ed., *William Wordsworth: Selected Poems* (London, 1975).

IV. Separate Works. *An Evening Walk* (London, 1793), verse; *Descriptive Sketches* (London, 1793), verse; *Lyrical Ballads, with a Few Other Poems* (Bristol, 1798), also in R. L. Brett and A. R. Jones, eds. (London, 1965), W. J. B. Owen, ed. (London, 1967), and Scolar Press facs. ed. (London, 1971); *Lyrical Ballads, with Other Poems*, 2 vols. (London, 1800), also in D. Roper, ed., *Lyrical Ballads, 1805* (London, 1968); *Poems, in Two Volumes* (London, 1807), also in H. Darbishire, ed. (London, 1914); *Concerning the Relations of Great Britain, Spain, and Portugal to Each Other, and to the Common Enemy at This Crisis, and Specifically as Affected by the Convention of Cintra* (London, 1809), prose; *The Excursion, Being a Portion of "The Recluse"* (London, 1814), verse; *The White Doe of Rylstone* (London, 1815), verse, also in Scolar Press facs. ed. (London, 1971); *Thanksgiving Ode, 18 January 1816* (London, 1816); *Peter Bell, a Tale in Verse* (London, 1819); *The Waggoner* (London, 1819), verse; *The River Duddon, a Series of Sonnets* (London, 1820); *Memorials of* a Tour on the Continent (London, 1822), verse; Ecclesiastical Sketches (London, 1822), verse; A Description of the Scenery of the Lakes in the North of England; Originally Published with Select Views in Cumberland, Westmorland, etc., by the Rev. J. Wilkinson (London, 1822), prose; Yarrow Revisited, and Other Poems (London, 1835); A Guide Through the District of the Lakes in the North of England (London, 1835), prose, also in E. de Selincourt, ed. (London, 1906); The Sonnets of William Wordsworth (London, 1838); Poems Chiefly of Early and Late Years; Including the Borderers a Tragedy (London, 1842); Ode on the Installation of His Royal Highness Prince Albert as Chancellor of the University of Cambridge (London, 1847); The Prelude or Growth of a Poet's Mind; An Autobiographical Poem (London, 1850)—the standard ed. is that of E. de Selincourt, edited from the MSS with intro. and notes (London, 1926), rev. by H. Darbishire, Oxford English Texts (London, 1959); 1805 text, E. de Selincourt, ed., rev. by S. Gill (London, 1970); 1805 and 1850 texts, J. C. Maxwell, ed. (Harmondsworth, 1971); 1799, 1805, and 1850 texts, J. Wordsworth, M. H. Abrams, and S. Gill, eds. (New York, 1979); E. de Selincourt, ed., Journals of Dorothy Wordsworth, 2 vols. (London, 1941), also M. Moorman, ed. (London, 1971).

V. LETTERS. W. Knight, ed. Letters of the Wordsworth Family, 3 vols. (London, 1907); L. N. Broughton, ed., Wordsworth and Reed: The Poet's Correspondence with His American Editor: 1836–50 (London, 1933); E. de Selincourt, ed., Letters of William and Dorothy Wordsworth, 6 vols. (Oxford, 1935–1939), rev. ed. in progress: The Early Years, 1787–1805, rev. by C. L. Shaver (London, 1967), The Middle Years, Part 1, 1806–1811, rev. by M. Moorman (London, 1969), The Middle Years, Part 2, 1812–1820, rev. by M. Moorman and A. G. Hill (London, 1970), The Later Years, Part 1, 1821–1828, A. G. Hill, ed. (London, 1978); L. N. Broughton, ed., Some Letters of the Wordsworth Family (Ithaca, N. Y., 1942); P. Wayne, ed., Letters of William Wordsworth (London, 1954), in the World's Classics ed.; M. E. Burton, ed., The Letters of Mary Wordsworth, 1800–1855 (Oxford, 1958); C. H. Ketcham, ed., The Letters of John Wordsworth (Ithaca, N. Y., 1969).

VI. BIOGRAPHICAL AND CRITICAL STUDIES. S. T. Coleridge, Biographia Literaria (London, 1817)—there is a valuable modern ed., J. Shawcross, ed. (Oxford, 1907), also G. Watson, ed. (London, 1971); W. Hazlitt, Lectures on the English Poets (London, 1818); W. S. Landor, Imaginary Conversations of Literary Men and Statesmen, vol. I (London, 1824); W. Hazlitt, The Spirit of the Age (London, 1825); T. De Quincey, "Literary and Lake Reminiscences," in Tait's magazine (1834, 1839)—see also D. Masson, ed., Collected Writings of De Quincey (London, 1889–1890); J. Cottle, Early Recollections (London, 1837); J. Ruskin, Modern Painters (London, 1840–1860); C. Wordsworth, Memoirs of William Wordsworth, 2 vols. (London, 1851); J. Wilson, Recreations of Christopher North, vol. II (London, 1854); W. Knight, ed., Transactions of the Words-

worth Society (1882–1887); M. Arnold, Essays in Criticism, 2nd ser. (London, 1888); H. D. Rawnsley, Literary Associations of the Lakes (London, 1894); E. Legouis, La jeunesse de William Wordsworth (Paris, 1896), trans. by J. W. Matthews as The Early Life of William Wordsworth (London, 1897); W. Pater, Appreciations (London, 1899).

W. Raleigh, Wordsworth (London, 1903); A. C. Bradley, English Poetry and German Philosophy in the Age of Wordsworth (London, 1909); A. C. Bradley, Oxford Lectures on Poetry (London, 1909); E. J. Morley, ed., Blake, Coleridge, Wordsworth, etc.: Selections from the Remains of Henry Crabb Robinson (London, 1922); E. Legouis, William Wordsworth and Annette Vallon (London, 1922); H. W. Garrod, Wordsworth: Lectures and Essays (London, 1923); H. Read, Wordsworth (London, 1930; rev. ed., 1948); E. de Selincourt, Dorothy Wordsworth: A Biography (London, 1933); P. Burra, Wordsworth (London, 1936); E. L. Griggs, ed., Wordsworth and Coleridge: Studies in Honour of George McLean Harper (Princeton, N. J., 1939); J. D. Wilson, Leslie Stephen and Matthew Arnold as Critics of Wordsworth (London, 1939); G. W. Meyer, Wordsworth's Formative Years (Ann Arbor, Mich., 1943); J. C. Smith, A Study of Wordsworth (London, 1944); N. P. Stallknecht, Strange Seas of Thought: Studies in Wordsworth's Philosophy of Man and Nature (Durham, N. C., 1945); E. de Selincourt, Wordsworthian and Other Studies (London, 1947); N. Nicholson, Wordsworth: An Introduction and a Selection (London, 1949).

H. Darbishire, The Poet Wordsworth (London, 1950)—Clark Lectures (1949), Oxford Paperback (1966); Wordsworth at Cambridge: A Record of the Commemoration Held at St. John's College, Cambridge (London, 1950)—contains a detailed survey of Wordsworth portraits; G. T. Dunklin, ed., Wordsworth: Centenary Studies (Princeton, N. J., 1950); L. Abercrombie, The Art of Wordsworth (London, 1952); H. M. Margoliouth, Wordsworth and Coleridge (London, 1953); J. Jones, The Egotistical Sublime: A History of Wordsworth's Imagination (London, 1954); F. W. Bateson, Wordsworth: A Re-Interpretation (London, 1954; rev. ed., 1956); M. Moorman, William Wordsworth: A Biography, 2 vols. (Oxford, 1957–1965), reprinted in Oxford Paperback (London, 1968); B. R. Schneider, Wordsworth's Cambridge Education (London, 1957); K. Coburn, ed., The Notebooks of Samuel Taylor Coleridge, 2 vols. (London, 1957); F. M. Todd, Politics and the Poet: A Study of Wordsworth (London, 1957); Z. S. Fink, ed., The Early Wordsworthian Milieu (London, 1958)—a notebook of Christopher Wordsworth, with a few entries by William Wordsworth; D. Ferry, The Limits of Mortality: An Essay on Wordsworth's Major Poems (Middletown, Conn., 1959); F. Blanshard, Portraits of Wordsworth (London, 1959).

J. F. Danby, The Simple Wordsworth: Studies in the Poems, 1797–1807 (London, 1960); C. C. Clarke, Romantic Paradox: An Essay on the Poetry of Wordsworth (London, 1963); H. Lindenberger, *On Wordsworth's Prelude* (London, 1963); J. F. Danby, *William Wordsworth: The Prelude and Other Poems* (London, 1963); D. Perkins, *Wordsworth and the Poetry of Sincerity* (Cambridge, Mass., 1964); G. H. Hartman, *Wordsworth's Poetry, 1787-1814* (New Haven, Conn., 1964), contains a good critical bibliography; A. King, *Wordsworth and the Artist's Vision* (London, 1966); C. Salvesen, *The Landscape of Memory* (London, 1966); G. B. Groom, *The Unity of Wordsworth's Poetry* (London, 1966); M. L. Reed, *Wordsworth: The Chronology of the Early Years 1770-1779* (London–Cambridge, Mass., 1967); M. Rader, *Wordsworth. A Philosophical Approach* (Oxford, 1967); F. E. Halliday, *Wordsworth and His World* (London, 1969), with 140 illustrations; G. Durrant, *William Wordsworth* (London, 1969), Cambridge British Authors paperback; C. Woodring, *Wordsworth* (Cambridge, Mass., 1968); J. Wordsworth, *The Music of Humanity: A Critical Study of Wordsworth's "Ruined Cottage" Incorporating Texts from a Manuscript of 1799-1800* (London, 1969); J. A. W. Heffernan, *Wordsworth's Theory of Poetry: The Transforming Imagination* (Ithaca, N. Y., 1969); J. Wordsworth, *William Wordsworth: 1770-1969* (London, 1969), British Academy Chatterton Lecture.

D. Wesling, *Wordsworth and the Adequacy of Landscape* (London, 1970); G. Durrant, *Wordsworth and the Great System* (London, 1970); J. R. Watson, *Picturesque Landscape and English Romantic Poetry* (London, 1970); A. S. Byatt, *Wordsworth and Coleridge in Their Time* (London, 1970); W. Heath, *Wordsworth and Coleridge* (Oxford, 1970); S. Prickett, *Coleridge and Wordsworth: The Poetry of Growth* (Cambridge, 1970); J. Wordsworth, ed., *Bicentenary Wordsworth Studies in Memory of John Alban Finch* (Ithaca, N. Y., 1971); F. Garber, *Wordsworth and the Poetry of Encounter* (Urbana, Ill., 1971); G. K. Thomas, *Wordsworth's Dirge and Promise* (Lincoln, Nebr., 1971); J. R. Curtis, *Wordsworth's Experiments with Tradition* (Ithaca, N. Y., 1971); R. Noyes, *William Wordsworth* (New York, 1971); R. J. Onorato, *The Character of the Poet* (Princeton, N. J., 1971); G. McMaster, ed., *William Wordsworth* (Harmondsworth, 1972), Penguin Critical Anthology; A. R. Jones and W. Tydeman, eds., *Wordsworth, Lyrical Ballads* (London, 1972), a casebook; W. J. Harvey and R. Gravil, eds., *Wordsworth, The Prelude* (London, 1972), a casebook; R. Sharrock, *The Figure in a Landscape: Wordsworth's Early Poetry* (London, 1972), British Academy Warton Lecture; S. M. Parrish, *The Art of the Lyrical Ballads* (Cambridge, Mass., 1973); P. D. Sheats, *The Making of Wordsworth's Poetry* (Cambridge, Mass., 1973); A. Grob, *The Philosophic Mind* (Columbus, Ohio, 1973); A. O. Wlecke, *Wordsworth and the Sublime* (Berkeley, 1973); M. H. Abrams, ed., *Wordsworth, a Collection of Critical Essays* (Englewood Cliffs, N. J., 1973); L. M. Johnson, *Wordsworth and the Sonnet* (Copenhagen, 1973); F. D. McConnell, *The Confessional Imagination* (Baltimore, 1974); M. L. Reed, *Wordsworth: The Chronology of the Middle Years, 1800-1815* (Cambridge, Mass., 1975); R. E. Brantley, *Wordsworth's "Natural Methodism"* (New Haven, Conn., 1975); E. L. Stelzig, *All Shades of Consciousness: Wordsworth's Poetry and the Self in Time* (The Hague, 1975); S. Prickett, *Wordsworth and Coleridge: The Lyrical Ballads* (London, 1975); M. Jacobus, *Tradition and Experiment in Wordsworth's Lyrical Ballads (1798)* (Oxford, 1976); J. E. Jordan, *Why the Lyrical Ballads?* (Berkeley, 1976); F. Ferguson, *Wordsworth: Language as Counter-Spirit* (New Haven, Conn., 1977); J. Beer, *Wordsworth and the Human Heart* (London, 1977).

SIR WALTER SCOTT

(1771-1832)

Ian Jack

I

ALMOST fifty years ago Edmund Wilson remarked on the anomalous place occupied by Charles Dickens among the great English writers. He pointed out that although Dickens had come to be taken for granted as an institution, his true stature as a writer was not appreciated. Today the position of Dickens is very different, and there are signs that it is Scott who has fallen heir to this prominent but neglected niche in the Temple of Fame. He too enjoys—if that is the word—the sort of household familiarity that has nothing much to do with being read. It is almost as true of Scott today as it was of Dickens a few decades ago that "the literary men from Oxford and Cambridge . . . rather snubbingly leave him alone." There have been a number of critical studies, but none of them is outstanding; while the most stimulating writers on the novel still tend to ignore Scott or to refer to him with an unbecoming condescension. The scholars have been more industrious, but they have not done enough. On the credit side we have Edgar Johnson's biography, a work of considerable merit, and (more importantly) James C. Corson's *Notes and Index to Sir Herbert Grierson's Edition of the Letters.* On the debit side, however, there is still no scholarly edition of the novels, no complete edition of the letters, and no edition of Lockhart's *Memoirs* corresponding to the Hill-Powell edition of Boswell's *Life of Johnson.*

It is not difficult to account for this state of affairs. The unevenness of Scott's work is notorious, and no service is done to his memory by enthusiasts who find *Woodstock* as rewarding as *The Heart of Mid-Lothian* and persist in prescribing *Ivanhoe* as a "set book" (prescribed text). The casualness with which Scott approached his literary undertakings, whether we regard it as a splendid magnanimity or a culpable indifference to his art, is calculated to make scholars feel small and ridiculous. He was not greatly concerned with the theory of fiction, and his books con-tain less to interest critics writing on the evolution of the modern novel than the work of many much less gifted men. And then there is Lockhart. His biography, admirable as it is, is not of a sort to give us much sense of kinship with its subject. Precisely because Scott was so fine a person—so much the man as well as the gentleman—we need a biography that should acknowledge such faults as he had. What his biographer gives us is a carefully edited Scott. We know now that the story of Scott on his deathbed telling Lockhart to be a good man may well be a fabrication, and we are on our guard. Remembering Lockhart's disingenuous career as a reviewer, we do not trust him. It is not so much that details here and there are faked; the scholars who know most about Scott assure us that there are not many of these. It is, rather, that the whole thing is too deliberately posed, too much of a Royal Academy portrait.

Scott was one of Sir Henry Raeburn's favorite subjects, as Samuel Johnson was of Sir Joshua Reynolds, and the difference between Boswell's biography and Lockhart's is precisely that between the portraits of these two painters. Boswell presents Johnson as Reynolds painted him: massive, impressive, uncouth, unmistakably true; Lockhart's Scott is Raeburn's Scott: nobly conceived, yet painted with a sentimentality that softens the outlines and detracts somehow from the reality of the sitter. The result is a figure curiously remote from the lives of most of us. It is hardly surprising that a critic as gifted as Edwin Muir was driven, as if in sheer desperation, to formulate a psychological theory to explain some of the surprising features of Scott as a man and as a writer—an unconvincing theory that may be regarded less as an attempt to pull Scott down from his pedestal than as an endeavor to confer on him a common humanity with ourselves.

There is something to be said for bypassing Lockhart, and fortunately we can go straight to Scott himself. Although he was one of the least introspective of authors, hardly any prose writer before

27

Henry James wrote so much about his own life and the composition of his books. In his late thirties, before he had published a single novel, he wrote a chapter of autobiography about twice the length of this essay in which he tells us precisely the things about his early life that we are most anxious to know. Throughout his life he was as voluminous a letter writer as any of the Victorians. In his later years he kept a journal in which we are admitted—or as nearly admitted as he was willing or able to admit anyone—to his private thoughts; and the prefaces he wrote for the collected edition of his writings form a series of chapters of literary autobiography that take up the story at about the point at which his autobiography proper had left it, and bring us within sight of the end.

II

SCOTT points out in his autobiography that every Scotsman has a pedigree, and he took great pleasure in tracing his descent through his great-grandfather, a Jacobite "well-known in Teviotdale by the name of Beardie," back to Auld Watt of Harden and beyond, liking to think of his remoter ancestors as "merry-men all, of the persuasion and calling of Robin Hood and Little John." His immediate origins were very different, his father being an Edinburgh solicitor, a writer to the signet; he was an unworldly man, a strict Calvinist, and an enthusiastic student of theology and of "the abstruse feudal doctrines connected with conveyancing." Scott's mother, Anne Rutherford, a woman of pronounced literary tastes, was the eldest daughter of a highly gifted professor of medicine at the University of Edinburgh. The contrast between the uneventful respectability of his early surroundings and what he conceived of as the romance of his remoter ancestry, which was to be the mainspring of so much of his writing, seems to have struck Scott at an early age. Crippled by paralysis in his infancy, he was as a child a great listener to the tales of his elders. He loved to listen to his uncle Thomas Scott, for example, and comments that "It was a fine thing to hear him talk over the change in the country which he had witnessed." There was also his grandmother, "in whose youth the old Border depredations were matters of recent tradition, [and who] used to tell me many a tale of Watt of Harden, Wight Willie of Aikwood, Jamie Telfer of the fair Dodhead, and other heroes." And there was George

Constable, on whom the Antiquary is partly modeled, who remembered the rebellion of 1745 and liked to talk about "subjects of history or auldlangsyne." Edinburgh is a highly antiquarian city, and few men are so apt to be antiquarians as elderly writers to the signet. It was Scott's good fortune as a boy to be surrounded by a sort of Greek chorus of Scots antiquaries, with the retentive memory and the love of moralizing characteristic of their classical counterparts, but with a satirical sense of humor superadded.

It is clear that the stories and traditions that he heard from his elders were the material of Scott's earliest daydreams. Like Waverley, he "would steal away to indulge the fancies they excited. In the corner of a large and sombre library . . . he would exercise for hours that internal sorcery, by which past or imaginary events are presented in action, as it were, to the eye of the muser." What he heard was soon supplemented by what he read. Classical literature made little appeal to him, but he read widely in the English poets, particularly those who "exercised themselves on romantic fiction." He was fond of historical works, and read "many picturesque and interesting passages from our old historical chronicles." Later he began to explore Italian and French literature in a random way. He was particularly struck by "the heart-stirring and eye-dazzling descriptions of war and of tournaments" in Jean Froissart, as well as by the historical works of Pierre de Brantôme and François de La Noue, from whom he "learned to compare the wild and loose and yet superstitious character of the nobles of the League, with the stern, rigid, and sometimes turbulent disposition of the Huguenot party"—a comparison that he must have remembered when he came to contrast Jacobite and Hanoverian, Highlander and Lowlander, Royalist and Roundhead, in his own books.

But that is to anticipate. From his earliest boyhood Scott loved to hear traditional songs, particularly those associated with Border raids or the adventures of the Jacobites. He had a remarkable facility in learning them by heart, and would interrupt visitors anxious to talk with his elders by shouting dozens of stanzas of the ballad of Hardicanute at the top of his voice: "One may as well speak in the mouth of a cannon as where that child is," as one of them complained. When, therefore, he came on Allan Ramsay's *Tea-Table Miscellany* and, a little later, Thomas Percy's *Reliques of Ancient English Poetry*, he was enchanted. "As I had been from infancy devoted to legendary lore of this nature," he comments, "it may be imagined . . . with what delight I saw pieces of the same kind which had amused my childhood, and still continued in secret the Delilahs of my imagination, considered as the subjects of sober research."

Though Scott never lost his limp, his health became in every other respect extremely robust, and he tells us that as a young man he would often walk thirty miles in a day, or ride a hundred. On these expeditions he was in the habit of persuading the old men and women who knew traditional songs and ballads to recite them for him (though how often he wrote these down, as distinct from begging written copies from his fellow enthusiasts, remains obscure). At first he was discouraged from publishing his collection "by the multitude of similar publications," but finally he decided to try his fortune. The result was the *Minstrelsy of the Scottish Border*, of which the first two volumes were published in 1802, and the third the following year. He regarded the "Raiding Ballads (as they are called) relating to the forays and predatory incursions made upon the Borders" as a special feature of his collection, but he also included ballads of other types as well as modern imitations. Like Percy he wanted to reach as wide an audience as possible, and did not hesitate to complete unfinished ballads or improve passages he regarded as unsatisfactory. He did the same with *Sir Tristrem*, a poem commonly attributed to Thomas the Rhymer, which he published in 1804 with a brief final "fytte" of his own composition.

The transition from this sort of editing to original composition was a very easy one, and although Scott was for a while fascinated by some modish German poetry—his first publication was entitled *The Chase, and William and Helen: Two Ballads from the German of Bürger*—his most important inspiration as a poet came to him from the traditional poetry of Scotland. When he determined to attempt a longer poem, his first desire was to write something in the ballad stanza, and for a subject he wanted a story "which might admit of being treated with the simplicity and wildness of an ancient ballad." Chance provided him with the story of the dwarf Gilpin Horner; and though he realized that a long poem in the ballad stanza would not be popular, he was able to evolve a metrical form that owed as much to traditional poetry as to the experiments of his contemporaries. Impressed by the metrical experiments of Southey and by Coleridge's "Christabel," he used a medley of meters that provided him with splendid opportunities for the effects of contrast of which he was so fond, yet in which the tetrameter couplet "so popular with our old minstrels" remained in the background as a sort of norm. His poetry has something in common with that of the Italian *improvisatori*: it is swift-moving verse in which eloquent passages alternate with others that are culpably careless, and yet it carries us on and on as if we were caught up by some powerful and irresistible current.

The historical and antiquarian interests so evident in the *Minstrelsy* are no less characteristic of Scott's original poems. *The Lay of the Last Minstrel* is "intended to illustrate the customs and manners which anciently prevailed on the Borders of England and Scotland." Scott recognized that the Borderers of the sixteenth century, "living in a state partly pastoral, and partly warlike, and combining habits of constant depredation with the influence of a rude spirit of chivalry, provided a subject peculiarly adapted to poetry." *Marmion* is "an attempt to paint the manners of the feudal times upon a broader scale," while *The Lady of the Lake* is introduced by the remark that "The ancient manners . . . of the aboriginal race by whom the Highlands of Scotland were inhabited, had always appeared to me peculiarly adapted to poetry."

Like the poetry of Samuel Rogers and Thomas Campbell, and the first two cantos of Byron's *Childe Harold*, Scott's long poems enjoyed a popularity in their own day that they will never recover. Written to suit the taste of the age, to provide the common reader with a first-rate pastime, they lack the seriousness of major poetry. Although the modern reader is still struck by the vigor of the verse and the boyish zest with which Scott describes his feuds and battles and pursuits, he may be impressed more deeply by a certain underlying sadness, as he reads:

> Of ancient deeds, so long forgot;
> Of feuds, whose memory was not;
> Of forests, now laid waste and bare;
> Of towers, which harbour now the hare;
> Of manners, long since changed and gone.[1]
> (*The Lay of the Last Minstrel*, interlude
> between cantos IV and V)

[1]All quotations from the poems are from J. L. Robertson, ed., *The Poetical Works* (London, 1904).

It is when Scott touches on the oldest of all poetic themes, the transitoriness of human life, that he comes nearest to memorable eloquence:

> Now is the stately column broke,
> The beacon-light is quenched in smoke,
> The trumpet's silver sound is still,
> The warder silent on the hill.
>   (*Marmion*, introduction to canto I)

There are two or three lyrics in *Waverley* and its successors that haunt the memory when *Marmion* has been forgotten: "Proud Maisie" in *The Heart of Mid-Lothian*, for example, or these lines from *The Bride of Lammermoor*:

> Look not thou on beauty's charming,
> Sit thou still when kings are arming,
> Taste not when the wine-cup glistens,
> Speak not when the people listens,
> Stop thine ear against the singer,
> From the red gold keep thy finger;
> Vacant heart and hand and eye,
> Easy live and quiet die.
>   (song in ch. 2)

III

WHEN we turn from the poems to *Waverley* and its successors, we turn from romances in verse to romances in prose. Scott tells us that he called his poems "romances" "because the description of scenery and manners was more the object of the Author than a combined and regular narrative." Although his practice was not consistent, he more often used the word "romance" than "novel" to describe his works of prose fiction, and the introductory epistle to *The Fortunes of Nigel* makes it clear that he recoiled from the labor of writing a novel with a regular plot "where every step brings us a point nearer to the final catastrophe" precisely as he recoiled from the task of writing a "regular" poem.

As many critics have noticed, in most of Scott's books elements of the romance may be found combined with elements of the novel. But what precisely is meant by the two terms? A romance is written simply to entertain. It is not a serious criticism of life, and it is not tied to the rules of probability. Its characterization is likely to be superficial—particularly the characterization of the hero and heroine—and it will probably describe exciting events, "moving accidents by flood and field." The setting may be romantic and unfamiliar, giving the author opportunities for picturesque description. There is often an element of wish fulfillment, the reader being encouraged to identify himself with the hero or heroine.

The novel, on the other hand, does aim at a criticism of life: its function is to entertain, but to do so by telling the truth about human existence. For this reason it is tied more or less strictly to the laws of probability, and satire may be prominent. The setting may well be that of the author's own daily life; the incidents, such as might happen to anyone. The characterization of one or two central figures will tend to be all-important; dialogue will matter more than description.

In the work of most of the English novelists there is something of both elements, though sometimes the romance is more prominent and sometimes the novel. In *Emma*, for example, there is a great deal of the novel, very little of the romance. In *Wuthering Heights* the element of the romance is much more prominent. It is interesting to remember that the work of Ann Radcliffe and her followers, satirized by Jane Austen, must have helped to nourish the strange creative genius of the Brontës. Scott resembled the Brontës (who were to be eager readers of his books) in being attracted by the remote, the mysterious, the picturesque.

From his boyhood onward Scott was a storyteller. When he was at school, he had a close friend named John Irving, and he tells us that they had an agreement by which each in turn would "compose a romance for the other's amusement." He was in no doubt about the importance of this early habit:

These legends, in which the martial and the miraculous always predominated, we rehearsed to each other during our walks. . . . Whole holidays were spent in this singular pastime, which continued for two or three years, and had, I believe, no small effect in directing the turn of my imagination to the chivalrous and romantic in poetry and prose.[2]

The first story in prose that we know Scott to have begun with the intention of publication was the offspring of these early romances. It was to be "a tale of chivalry . . . in the style of *The Castle of Otranto*, with plenty of Border characters and supernatural incident," and the part that was written was included

---

[2]From Scott's "Memoir" in J. G. Lockhart, *Memoirs of the Life of Sir Walter Scott, Bart.*, vol. I (Edinburgh, 1837), pp. 45–46.

as an appendix to the later editions of *Waverley.* Two other fragments written before the publication of *Waverley*—of which the first third was composed in 1805 and then thrown aside—are given in other appendixes, and each anticipates a direction that Scott was later to pursue more fully. One was set in Scotland in the seventeenth and eighteenth centuries, and was to be called "The Lord of Ennerdale." The other was a brief conclusion for a romance written by the antiquary Joseph Strutt; its scene was laid in the reign of Henry VI, and the intention was "to illustrate the manners, customs, and language of the people of England during that period." The failure of Strutt's book, *Queenhoo-Hall,* drove Scott to the conclusion that "The manners of the middle ages did not possess the interest which [he] had conceived."

Although the modern reader is more likely to recognize the element of the romance in Scott's later books, it is important to realize that he himself also thought of *Waverley* as falling into this category; he called it "a romance, founded on a Highland story, and more modern events" than *Queenhoo-Hall,* and considered that such a book "would have a better chance of popularity than a tale of chivalry." After his famous journey to the Highlands and Islands in 1773, Samuel Johnson had half rejoiced and half complained that "such is the effect of the late regulations, that a longer journey than to the Highlands must be taken by him whose curiosity pants for savage virtues and barbarous grandeur." By traveling backward in time, Scott was able to make this "longer journey." When Rose Bradwardine gave Waverley an account of a Highland feud, we are told, he

could not help starting at a story which bore so much resemblance to one of his own day-dreams. Here was a girl . . . who had witnessed with her own eyes such a scene as he had used to conjure up in his imagination, as only occurring in ancient times. . . . He might have said with Malvolio, "'I do not now fool myself, to let imagination jade me,' I am actually in the land of military and romantic adventures."[3]

(*Waverley,* ch. 15)

Scott had found, in Scotland's past, people and events as romantic as anything that he had discovered in imaginative literature. His aim in the Scotch novels (as they were originally called) was to communicate his imaginative excitement to his readers.

This intention explains the structure of *Waverley:*

or, *'Tis Sixty Years Since.* As Francis Jeffrey pointed out, all that really happens in the first half of the book is that the hero travels into Scotland and learns about "the manners and state of society that prevailed . . . in the earlier part of the last century." Such chapter headings as "A Horse-Quarter in Scotland," "A Scottish Manor-House Sixty Years Since," and "A Creagh[4] and Its Consequences" tell their own story. Since Waverley travels on behalf of the reader, everything is made easy for him; we are hardly surprised when the famous robber Evan Dhu invites him to study the methods of the cattle thieves at first hand. The people whom Waverley meets are as carefully chosen as those selected to be introduced to a royal personage: they are the best possible examples of characteristic types. Baron Bradwardine, for example, is "the very model of the old Scottish cavalier . . . a character . . . which is fast disappearing." When Waverley returns to the Lowlands, later in the book, he is just as privileged a spectator: he blunders into the rebellion of 1745, attends the Jacobite ball at Holyrood, meets the Chevalier, and witnesses the battle of Prestonpans.

Waverley's journey into Scotland and into a past more romantic than the present was to be taken by tens of thousands of readers in the years that followed. The six books that succeeded *Waverley* describe Scotland in the eighteenth century or at the end of the seventeenth, and this was Scott's true area of inspiration. When in *Ivanhoe* and many of the later romances he turned to other settings, he ceased to be a major writer. But what matters is a man's best work, and Scott's genius must be estimated by the series of books that ended with *The Heart of Mid-Lothian,* supplemented by those of the later volumes—such as *Redgauntlet*—in which he returned to the life he fully understood.

IV

Scott was delighted with the reception given to *Waverley,* and it is clear that he determined to follow it with a book exploiting the same rich vein, yet free from the glaring deficiencies of his first attempt. The central purpose of *Guy Mannering* is again to illustrate Scottish life at a certain period—in the last quarter of the eighteenth century—and its hero is again an Englishman coming to Scotland for the first

---

[3]Quotations from the *Waverley* novels are from the Oxford Scott edition of the *Waverley Novels,* 25 vols. (London, 1910).

[4]Raid.

time, but it improves on its model in at least three ways. Although it is not a masterpiece of construction, its plot is much superior to that of the first book. Second, while men and women characteristic of the period are the main actors, historical personages and events are avoided, so that it is a "historical romance" in a different sense. But what is most important is that *Guy Mannering* contains a number of the remarkable characters whose speeches form the element of greatness in all Scott's best work.

Dandie Dinmont, who is based on a type that Scott knew well, is a notable achievement. His speech on the education of dogs—"Beast or body, education should aye be minded"—is in itself better than anything in *Waverley*. Meg Merrilees is of particular significance. Scott had always been attracted by gypsies, as he was by any class of people who lived according to an older and freer code than that of his contemporaries; he refers to them as "the *Parias* of Scotland, living like wild Indians among European settlers, and, like them, judged of rather by their own customs, habits, and opinions, than as if they had been members of the civilized part of the community." Meg is not only the linchpin of the whole action; she also acts as a remarkably impressive chorus. Here is the curse that she pronounces when her tribe is turned away from the land where they had long been suffered to remain:

Ride your ways, ride your ways, Laird of Ellangowan—ride your ways, Godfrey Bertram!—This day have ye quenched seven smoking hearths—see if the fire in your ain parlour burn the blyther for that. Ye have riven the thack of seven cottar houses—look if your ain roof-tree stand the faster. —Ye may stable your stirks in the shealings at Derncleugh—see that the hare does not couch on the hearthstone at Ellangowan.—Ride your ways, Godfrey Bertram—what do you glower after our folk for? There's thirty hearts there, that wad hae wanted bread ere ye had wanted sunkets, and spent their lifeblood ere ye had scratched your finger. Yes, there's thirty yonder, from the auld wife of an hundred to the babe that was born last week, that ye have turned out o' their bits o' bields, to sleep with the tod and the blackcock in the muirs!—Ride your ways, Ellangowan.—Our bairns are hinging at our weary backs—look that your braw cradle at hame be the fairer spread up.[5]

(*Guy Mannering*, ch. 8)

This speech emphasized the theme that runs through the whole book. *Guy Mannering* is a study

in loyalties, a study in the changes that had come over Scotland. Harlot and thief though she is, Meg Merrilees recognizes ancient ties to which the "new men," and even the younger gypsies, are strangers. She is a sort of picturesque reincarnation of the Last Minstrel, lamenting the changes that have befallen Scotland as the feudal order has been hurried toward its end.

Edie Ochiltree's role in *The Antiquary* is in many ways analogous, but the spirit of comedy is prominent in this third of the *Waverley*s (set during the years when Scott was a young man), and his first appearance is one of the great comic moments in fiction. The Antiquary is explaining to the hero how he has discovered the remains of a Roman camp that will at last settle the question of the site of the battle of Mons Graupius:

"Yes, my dear friend, from this stance it is probably—nay, it is nearly certain, that Julius Agricola beheld what our Beaumont has so admirably described!—From this very Praetorium—"

A voice from behind interrupted this ecstatic description—"Praetorian here, Praetorian there, I mind the bigging o't."[6]

(ch. 4)

Edie Ochiltree, the wandering beggar "who kept his rounds within a particular space, and was the newscarrier, the minstrel, and sometimes the historian of the district, [a] rascal [who] knows more old ballads and traditions than any other man in this, and the next four parishes," is another example of the type of character that made the deepest appeal to Scott, and inspired his greatest speeches:

I have had many a thought, that when I faund mysell auld and forfairn, and no able to enjoy God's blessed air ony langer, I wad drag mysell here wi' a pickle aitmeal . . . and I wad e'en streek mysell out here, and abide my removal, like an auld dog that trails his useless ugsome carcase into some bush or bracken, no to gie living things a scunner wi' the sight o't when it's dead—Ay, and then, when the dogs barked at the lone farmstead, the gudewife wad cry, "Whisht, sirra, that'll be auld Edie," and the bits o' weans wad up, puir things, and toddle to the door, to pu' in the auld Blue Gown that mends a' their bonny-dies—but there wad be nae mair word o' Edie, I trow.[7]

(ch. 2)

---

[6]I remember its being built.

[7]forfairn, worn out; pickle, small supply of; streek mysell, lay myself out (like a corpse); ugsome, disgusting; scunner, disgust; bits o' weans, little children; bonny-dies, toys.

---

[5]thack, thatch; shealings, sheds, cottages; sunkets, delicacies; bits o' bields, poor shelters; tod, fox.

Edie's speeches are not the only examples of Scott's triumphant use of the Lowland vernacular in this book. One of the most Wordsworthian things in it occurs during the description of the funeral near the end:

"I'm fain to see ye looking sae weel, cummer; the mair, that the black ox has tramped on ye since I was aneath your roof-tree."

"Ay," said Elspeth; but rather from a general idea of misfortune, than any exact recollection of what had happened—"there has been distress amang us of late—I wonder how younger folk bide it—I bide it ill—I canna hear the wind whistle, and the sea roar, but I think I see the coble whombled keel up, and some o' them struggling in the waves—Eh, sirs, sic weary dreams as folk hae between sleeping and waking, before they win to the lang sleep and the sound."[8]

(ch. 40)

By the time he wrote *The Antiquary*, Scott was perfectly aware that the great strength of his writing lay in his creation of Scots character through his use of the Scots tongue. He points out in the preface that he has sought his principal characters

in the class of society who are the last to feel the influence of that general polish which assimilates to each other the manners of different nations . . . both because the lower orders are less restrained by the habit of suppressing their feelings, and because I agree with my friend Wordsworth that they seldom fail to express them in the strongest and most powerful language. This is, I think, peculiarly the case with the peasantry of my own country, a class with whom I have long been familiar. The antique force and simplicity of their language, often tinctured with the Oriental eloquence of Scripture . . . give pathos to their grief and dignity to their resentment.

We again find speeches of this sort in *Old Mortality*, the first book in which Scott wrote of a period about which his information was derived wholly from written sources; and we find them, most notably of all, in *The Heart of Mid-Lothian*, a remarkable work that must be regarded as the one great masterpiece of the *Waverley* series. In this book, for the first time, there is no upper-class hero or heroine. The central character, Jeanie Deans, speaks Scots. In *Rob Roy*, Scott was to show his boredom with the usual heroine of romance by creating the tomboy Di Ver-

non; but Jeanie Deans differs from convention much more profoundly.

The book was written to demonstrate "the possibility of rendering a fictitious personage interesting by mere dignity of mind and rectitude of principle, assisted by unpretending good sense and temper, without any of the beauty, grace, talent, accomplishment, and wit, to which a heroine of romance is supposed to have a prescriptive right." Jeanie Deans is in fact no more "born to be an heroine" than Catherine Morland in *Northanger Abbey*. It is characteristic that when the duke of Argyle carries her off and "a romantic heroine might have suspected and dreaded the power of her own charms," no such "silly thought" presents itself to her mind. Jeanie Deans has graver issues to deal with than those confronting the heroines of romance. What is at stake is her integrity of conscience. Time and again the great temptation is pressed on her: if only she will affirm that her sister had told her that she was pregnant, she will save her life; and she knows that her sister is innocent of the child murder of which she is suspected. In this dilemma her determination is simple and unshakable; for her sister she will sacrifice "all but truth and conscience."

In analyzing her response to a potentially tragic situation, Scott shows his understanding of the Lowland Scots character, as the product of environment and history, at a level far transcending the merely curious or picturesque. Jeanie Deans's journey southward to plead for her sister's life contrasts markedly with the journey northward made by so many of his heroes. This is a serious journey, undertaken as a quest for justice and mercy, an expedition closer to John Bunyan than to the guidebook. In the story as it came to Scott—in an anonymous letter written by a Mrs. Helen Goldie—it was the duke of Argyle who procured the pardon. Scott enhances the drama by introducing the Porteous riots as the background of the story—and so emphasizing the theme of confusion and uncertainty about human justice—and by making Jeanie herself plead for her sister's life before the queen. The words in which she does so have the resonance of the greatest human utterances:

O, madam, if ever ye kend what it was to sorrow for and with a sinning and a suffering creature, whose mind is sae tossed that she can be neither ca'd fit to live or die, have some compassion on our misery! Save an honest house from dishonour, and an unhappy girl, not eighteen years of age, from an early and dreadful death! Alas! it is not when we sleep soft and wake merrily ourselves that we think on

---

[8]fain, glad; cummer, gossip, neighbor; the black ox, death; bide, stand; coble, cobble, small boat; whombled, overturned.

other people's sufferings. Our hearts are waxed light within us then, and we are for righting our ain wrangs and fighting our ain battles. But when the hour of trouble comes to the mind or to the body—and seldom may it visit your Leddyship—and when the hour of death comes, that comes to high and low—lang, and late may it be yours—O, my Leddy, then it isna what we hae dune for oursells, but what we hae dune for others, that we think on most pleasantly. And the thoughts that ye hae intervened to spare the puir thing's life will be sweeter in that hour, come when it may, than if a word of your mouth could hang the haill Porteous mob at the tail of ae tow.[9]

(*The Heart of Mid-Lothian*, ch. 35)

The man who wrote that speech might have done anything. And yet Scott did not hesitate to add several hundred pages to his masterpiece to bring it to a length that suited his publisher, adding a novelettish postscript to his greatest imaginative achievement. "A rogue writes to tell me," he wrote in his journal, "rather of the latest, if the matter was of consequence—that he approves of the first three volumes of the *H. of Midlothian*, but totally condemns the fourth. However, an author should be reasonably well pleased when three fourths of his works are acceptable to the reader." It is surely the oddest remark ever made by a great writer.

V

YET it is typical of Scott. He shared Samuel Johnson's view that "no man but a blockhead ever wrote, except for money." Although he took a natural pleasure in exercising his gift of storytelling, from the first his principal object in writing was to make money, and in the end he had no other. Literary fame did not mean much to him, nor was literary immortality often in his thoughts. In his heart he despised literary people, if they were not also something more; as he listened to their talk, he must have felt the easy amusement of a millionaire who overhears a small shopkeeper boasting of his savings. This might suggest that Scott was an exceptionally well-balanced man; and in most ways he was. Yet perhaps no one is wholly sane, and he had his own obsession. He was obsessed by the idea of founding a family. There are no more illuminating pages in Lockhart—and none in which he speaks more frankly—than those in which he analyzes the motives that impelled Scott on his way:

[9]kend, have known; tail of ae tow, end of one rope.

His original pride was to be an acknowledged member of one of the "honourable families" whose progenitors had been celebrated . . . for following . . . in blind obedience . . . the patriarchal leader; his first and last worldly ambition was to be himself the founder of a distinct branch; he desired to plant a lasting root, and dreamt not of personal fame, but of long distant generations rejoicing in the name of "Scott of Abbotsford." By this idea all his reveries—all his aspirations—all his plans and efforts, were overshadowed and controlled.

Abbotsford, the house he purchased in 1811, and extended and elaborated almost until the end, mattered to Scott more than anything that he had ever written. This "romance in stone" was the symbol of what he was trying to do, the mistress for whom he labored longer than any knight of medieval legend and for whom he was to sacrifice life itself. This is not the place to trace his bewildering relations with his publishers, or to attempt any distribution of the blame. If you are not interested in money, it is wiser not to aim at becoming rich. The trouble with Scott was that he had a mind above money, yet he wanted a great deal of it. So he wrote and wrote, and in the end money brought him down.

In the preface to *Ivanhoe*, Scott acknowledges the dilemma that had faced him after the publication of *Rob Roy*. "Scottish manners, Scottish dialect, and Scottish characters of note, being those with which the author was most intimately and familiarly acquainted, were the ground upon which he had hitherto relied. It was, however, obvious that this kind of interest must in the end occasion a degree of sameness and repetition." The remarkable thing is that change of setting was the chief means of variety that occurred to Scott.

When Dickens sensed that the first impulse of his imaginative invention was flagging, he took stock of the position and made a sustained and remarkable effort to write on a new plan. With *Dombey and Son*, as Kathleen Tillotson has argued, he began the attempt to write novels "founded on a theme, embodied in a relation between characters." Scott's main resource was to move from country to country and from century to century. In the imaginary dialogue between the author and a critic prefaced to one of his last books, *The Surgeon's Daughter*, he admits that he would be delighted "to light upon any topic to supply the place of the Highlands," a theme that is "becoming a little exhausted." His friend replies: "Do with your Muse of Fiction . . . as many an honest man does with his sons in flesh and blood. . . . Send her to India." And so, twenty years before *Martin Chuzzlewit* was sent to America, Adam Hartley was dispatched to India, and this was only one of the last of the destinations in space and time to which Scott's heroes had been sent packing. It is no surprise that the part of *The Surgeon's Daughter* that is set in Scotland—the greater part—is much more successful than the Indian episode.

A writer can deal satisfactorily only with the life that he knows. In his "Life of Mrs. Radcliffe," Scott had pointed out the inferiority of her first book, *The Castles of Athlin and Dunbayne*, to its successors, commenting that "The scene is laid in Scotland during the Dark Ages, but without any attempt to trace either the peculiar manners or scenery of the country." Even if Mrs. Radcliffe had made the attempt, it may be doubted whether her book would have been much improved; she had never been in Scotland, and she had never lived in the Middle Ages. However conscientiously she had studied the background, therefore, it would have remained book knowledge. And book knowledge, for a creative writer, remains half knowledge.

Scott seems not to have realized how profoundly *The Heart of Mid-Lothian* differed even from his other books set in eighteenth-century Scotland. The reason must have been that he was not greatly interested in theory and technique. He did not give much thought (for example) to the possibility of varying the storyteller's point of view. The fictitious autobiographies of his contemporary John Galt—above all *The Provost*, that masterpiece of sustained dramatic irony—have a technical maturity to which he did not aspire. "I took up one of Scott's novels—*Redgauntlet*," Henry James was later to write, "it was years since I had read one. They have always a charm for me—but I was amazed at the badness of *R: l'enfance de l'art*." Among writers of prose fiction these two men may well stand as the extremes; and whereas Scott's heedlessness shocked the author of *The Portrait of a Lady*, James's concern with his art would have seemed to Scott a madman's obsession.

One reason for Scott's lack of interest in technique was simply the nature of his temperament, and another his pressing need for money; a third may possibly be found in what he believed to have been the practice of Shakespeare. Many English writers are influenced by Shakespeare, and the Shakespeare by whom each is influenced is the Shakespeare presented by the criticism of his day. Whereas modern critics emphasize such matters as Shakespeare's stagecraft and the persistence in his plays of elements originating in the medieval drama, the critics of the late eighteenth and early nineteenth centuries emphasized his spontaneity, contrasting it with the deliberateness of Ben Jonson in terms that sometimes seem to suggest that Jonson's method was that of the noncreative mind, Shakespeare's that of the creator par excellence. It is worth remembering this, and the complementary belief that Shakespeare was more concerned with writing fine speeches and creating great characters than with constructing dramatic wholes, when we read Scott's characteristic pronouncements on his own methods of working:

I have repeatedly laid down my future work to scale, divided it into volumes and chapters, and endeavoured to construct a story. . . . But I think there is a demon who seats himself on the feather of my pen when I begin to write, and leads it astray from my purpose. Characters expand under my hand; incidents are multiplied; the story lingers, while the materials increase; my regular mansion turns out a Gothic anomaly. . . . When I light on such a character as Bailie Jarvie, or Dalgetty, my imagination brightens, and my conception becomes clearer at every step which I take in his company. . . . If I resist the temptation . . . my thoughts become prosy, flat and dull . . . I am no more the same author . . . than the dog in a wheel, condemned to go round and round for hours, is like the same dog merrily chasing his own tail.

(introductory epistle to *The Fortunes of Nigel*)

The magnanimity of this is characteristic of Scott, and thoroughly disarming; he is so frank about his own shortcomings that a critic feels embarrassed when driven to acknowledge their existence and their importance. Yet there is a hint of complacency underlying the magnanimity. Captain Dalgetty is in a sense the most successful character in *A Legend of Montrose*, but he is quite out of keeping with the general tone of the book and goes far toward turning into farce what had been designed as tragedy. The whole account that Scott gives of his creative processes leads us to expect precisely what we find in the great majority of his tales—ramshackle wholes with magnificent parts.

VI

ONE of the most remarkable passages in the autobiography is that in which Scott tells us that as a young man he had been passionately anxious to paint landscapes. In spite of a great deal of effort, however, he had found himself quite unable

with the eye of a painter to dissect the various parts of a scene . . . [or] to assess the effect which various features of the view had in producing its leading and general effect. . . . Even the humble ambition which I had long cherished of making sketches of those places which interested me . . . was totally ineffectual. . . . I was obliged to relinquish in despair an art which I was most anxious to practise.[10]

The disabilities of men of genius are always of interest, and Scott's failure as an artist is no less revealing than the lack of capacity for philosophical discussion that he discovered as a member of the Speculative Society, or the defective ear for music that handicapped him as a collector of ballads. The result seems to have been that while he remained throughout his life a lover of beautiful scenery, he early began to specialize (as it were) in scenery with definite historical associations. He tells us that "the love of natural beauty" was one of his fundamental passions, "more especially when combined with ancient ruins, or remains of our fathers' piety or splendour." Earlier in the same passage he says:

To me, the wandering over the field of Bannockburn was the source of more exquisite pleasure than gazing upon the celebrated landscape from the battlements of Stirling Castle. . . . Show me an old castle or a field of battle, and I was at home at once, [and] filled it with its combatants in their proper costume. . . . I mention this to show the distinction between a sense of the picturesque in action and in scenery.

Although "the picturesque in action" is in a sense the clue to all Scott's books, he did not neglect "the picturesque . . . in scenery." One has only to glance into the various works of William Gilpin, particularly his *Observations Relative . . . to Picturesque Beauty . . . [in] the High-Lands of Scotland*, to see how closely many of the scenes that Scott describes conform to the canons of the picturesque; and when one finds him praising Mrs. Radcliffe for being "the first to introduce into her prose fictions a beautiful and fanciful tone of natural description . . . which had hitherto been exclusively applied to poetry," it becomes evident that he regarded picturesque description as one of the resources of the writer of romance. His favorite territory, the Highlands and the Borders, provided him with a rich storehouse of picturesque scenery, and when he moved further afield—to Zetland (Shetland) and Orkney in *The Pirate*, to the Isle of Man in *Peveril of the Peak*—his choice was always partly dictated by the picturesque potentialities of the country. "The site was singularly picturesque," he remarks at the beginning of *St. Ronan's Well*, and it is an observation that might stand at the beginning of the majority of his tales.

Scott's imagination was highly visual, and it seems likely that he sometimes conceived of individual episodes, or even whole stories, primarily in visual terms. It is tempting to assign such an origin to *The Bride of Lammermoor*. Near the end of the opening chapter, an imaginary painter shows Scott a sketch that contains the germ of the whole book:

The sketch . . . represented an ancient hall, fitted up and furnished in what we now call the taste of Queen Elizabeth's age. The light, admitted from the upper part of a high casement, fell upon a female figure of exquisite beauty, who, in an attitude of speechless horror, appeared to watch the issue of a debate betwixt two other persons. The one was a young man, in the Vandyke dress common to the time of Charles I, who with an air of indignant pride, testified by the manner in which he raised his head and extended his arm, seemed to be urging a claim of right.

The fact that Scott is composing in consciously pictorial terms is often emphasized by his mentioning the name of a particular painter, as he does in this passage. When Ellangowan looks back and sees the gypsies he has expelled from their home, we are told that "The group would have been an excellent subject for the pencil of Calotte." Scott was particularly fond of effects of chiaroscuro, and when he uses this device, Rembrandt is the painter he most often remembers. A fine example is the description of David Deans grieving over the sin of his daughter:

The sun sent its rays through a small window at the old man's back and . . . illumined [his] grey hairs . . . and the sacred page which he studied. His features, far from handsome, and rather harsh and severe, had yet from their expression of habitual gravity and contempt for earthly things an expression of stoical dignity amidst their sternness. . . . The whole formed a picture, of which the lights might have been given by Rembrandt but the outline would have required the force and vigour of Michael Angelo.

(*The Heart of Mid-Lothian*, ch. 12)

---

[10]From Scott's "Memoir" in J. G. Lockhart, *Memoirs of the Life of Sir Walter Scott, Bart.*, vol. I (Edinburgh, 1837), p. 51.

Most frequently it is his friend David Wilkie whom Scott mentions, as when he says that the scene before the funeral in *The Antiquary* was one "which our Wilkie alone could have painted, with that exquisite feeling of nature which characterizes his enchanting productions." The affinity between Fielding and Hogarth has often been pointed out: the affinity between Scott and Wilkie is no less striking, and no less revealing.

Unlike those of Jane Austen, Scott's finest characters are usually men and women we can readily visualize. Edie Ochiltree is a good example, with his "slouched hat of huge dimensions," his "long white beard, which mingled with his grizzled hair; an aged but strongly marked and expressive countenance hardened by exposure to a right brick-dust complexion; a long blue gown, with a pewter badge on the right arm; [and] two or three wallets or bags slung across his shoulder." One notices particularly the explicit contrast between Edie and the earl:

The contrast . . . was very striking. The hale cheek, firm step, erect stature and undaunted presence and bearing of the old mendicant, indicated patience and content in the extremity of age, and in the lowest condition to which humanity can sink; while the sunken eye, pallid cheek, and tottering form of the nobleman . . . showed how little wealth, power, and even the advantages of youth, have to do with that which gives repose to the mind, and firmness to the frame.

(*The Antiquary*, ch. 28)

This is only one example of a device to which Scott attached great importance, both in his poems and in his prose romances. Gilpin insists that contrast is an essential element of the picturesque, and one has only to glance through Scott's prefaces to see how often he refers to contrasts of different kinds. The opening chapter of *Quentin Durward* is headed "The Contrast," and there are many other chapters which could bear the same heading. He tells us that he chose a watering place as the scene of *St. Ronan's Well* because it is a setting "where the strongest contrast of humorous characters and manners may be brought to bear on and illustrate each other," while in the prefatory letter to *Peveril of the Peak* he explicitly mentions that once he has found a suitable subject, he "invests it with such shades of character, as will best contrast with each other." This desire for contrast lay very near the heart of Scott's imagination, and explains part of the appeal that such a character as Rob Roy had for him. Like Waverley's as he listened to Rose Bradwardine, Scott's imagination caught fire at the thought that "a character like his, blending the wild virtues, the subtle policy, and unrestrained license of an American Indian, was flourishing in Scotland during the Augustan age of Queen Anne and George I"; and he points out in so many words that it is "this strong contrast between the civilized and cultivated mode of life on the one side of the Highland line, and the wild and lawless adventures . . . [of] one who dwelt on the opposite side . . . which creates the interest attached to his name."

It is not surprising that Scotland in the eighteenth century was for Scott the ideal imaginative territory. Just as "the most romantic region of every country is that where the mountains unite themselves with the plains or lowlands," so

the most picturesque period of history is that when the ancient rough and wild manners of a barbarous age are just becoming innovated upon, and contrasted, by the illumination of increased or revived learning, and the instructions of renewed or reformed religion. The strong contrast produced by the opposition of ancient manners to those which are gradually subduing them, affords the lights and shadows necessary to give effect to a fictitious narrative; and while such a period entitles the author to introduce accidents of a marvellous and improbable character, as arising out of the turbulent independence and ferocity belonging to old habits of violence, . . . yet . . . the characters and sentiments of many of the actors may . . . be described with great variety of shading and delineation, which belongs to the newer and more improved period.

(introduction to *The Fortunes of Nigel*)

Scott was never quite certain whether it was a contrast between the enlightened present and the barbarous past or between the prosaic present and the romantic past, and from the heart of this uncertainty he wrote his books.

VII

ALTHOUGH there are few writers whose achievement is more difficult to assess, it is clear that Scott's importance is very great. The popularity of his books was prodigious; their circulation exceeded that of the work of any earlier novelist and revolutionized the status of the novel as a vendible commodity. That it has now been the dominant literary form for more than a century is in a considerable measure due to him. Richardson and Fielding had established the novel; Scott made it irresistible. He also confirmed its respectability, which had remained in some doubt throughout the previous century.

Few major writers have been so unadventurous in their moral judgments. Once Scott had written, it became increasingly difficult for even the strictest of fathers to forbid his daughters to read prose fiction. In this, as in so many other respects, he prepared the way for Dickens. What Dickens did only partially and under restraint, out of deference to the requirements of "dainty Delicacy," Scott did willingly and from conviction.

It is also evident that Scott extended the range of subject matter accessible to the novelist. Many writers followed his example in choosing Scottish subjects, while others explored the possibility of dealing with other regions of the British Isles. But his most obvious influence was in popularizing the historical romance. As he himself makes clear in the "Lives of the Novelists," this type of book was already familiar in the eighteenth century; yet since what matters in literature is not so much being the first to do a thing as being the first to do it outstandingly well and at the critical time, Scott was the important figure. He gave the historical romance a new popularity and a new prestige.

Scott also did something more important. If the nineteenth century was to prove (among other things) the Age of History, the period in which mankind became more conscious of historical perspectives than it had ever been before, it was due to no one more than to Scott. There is abundant evidence of his influence, and the witnesses are the historians themselves. Carlyle is particularly explicit, in an essay that does not err on the side of indulgence:

These Historical Novels have taught all men this truth, which looks like a truism, and yet was as good as unknown to writers of history and others, till so taught; that the bygone ages of the world were actually filled by living men, not by protocols, state-papers, controversies and abstractions of men.

("Sir Walter Scott")

Scott was not a man of ideas, and he shrank from innovation with an instinctive distrust. As William Hazlitt put it, "If you take the universe, and divide it into two parts, he knows all that *has been*; all that *is to be* is nothing to him. . . . The old world is to him a crowded map; the new one a dull, hateful blank." The paradox is that this man of genius with his gaze fixed on the past did more than most writers have done to change the way in which men and women think, and so to create the climate of ideas in which we are still living today.

SELECTED BIBLIOGRAPHY

The bibliography was compiled by the British Council.

I. BIBLIOGRAPHY. G. Worthington, *A Bibliography of the Waverley Novels* (London, 1931); W. A. Ruff, "A Bibliography of the Poetical Works," in *Edinburgh Bibliographical Society Transactions*, 1, nos. 2 and 3 (1937–1938); J. C. Corson, *A Bibliography of Sir Walter Scott: A Classified and Annotated List of Books and Articles Relating to His Life and Works, 1797–1940* (Edinburgh, 1943).

II. PRINCIPAL COLLECTIONS. *Poetical Works*, 12 vols. (Edinburgh, 1820); *Waverley Novels*, 48 vols. (Edinburgh, 1830–1834), with prefaces and notes by Scott; other eds. include Centenary ed., text rev., with notes by D. Laing, 25 vols. (London, 1870–1871); the Dryburgh ed., 25 vols. (London, 1892–1894); the Border ed., with notes by A. Lang, 48 vols. (London, 1892–1894); the Edinburgh ed., 48 vols. (Edinburgh, 1901–1903); the Oxford Scott ed., 25 vols. (London, 1910); a number of the novels published in Everyman's Library have been reedited by W. M. Parker, with biographical and bibliographical intros.; J. G. Lockhart, ed., *Poetical Works*, 12 vols. (Edinburgh, 1833–1834); *Miscellaneous Prose Works*, 30 vols. (Edinburgh, 1834–1840, 1871 [vols. XXIX and XXX]), including *The Life of Dryden, Memoirs of Jonathan Swift*, "Lives of the Novelists," *Paul's Letters to His Kinsfolk, Border Antiquities*, the essays on chivalry and romance, *The Life of Napoleon* (9 vols.), numerous reviews (some incorrectly ascribed), and the three series of *Tales of a Grandfather* (7 vols.), all of which had been printed previously; J. L. Robertson, ed., *Poetical Works* (London, 1904), in the Oxford Standard Authors series; D. Cecil, ed., *Short Stories* (London, 1934), in the World's Classics series; L. M. Watt, ed., *Poetical Works* (London, 1942).

III. SEPARATE WORKS. *Note*: Scott did not acknowledge the authorship of the *Waverley* novels until 1827. *Waverley* was unsigned and most of its successors were "By the author of *Waverley*." *The Chase, and William and Helen: Two Ballads from the German of Burger* (Edinburgh, 1796); *The Eve of Saint John: A Border Ballad* (Kelso, 1800); *The Lay of the Last Minstrel: A Poem* (London, 1805); *Ballads and Lyrical Pieces* (Edinburgh, 1806); *Marmion: A Tale of Flodden Field* (Edinburgh, 1806), verse; *The Lady of the Lake: A Poem* (Edinburgh, 1810); *The Vision of Don Roderick: A Poem* (Edinburgh, 1811); *The Bridal of Triermain: or, The Vale of St. John* (Edinburgh, 1813), verse; *Rokeby: A Poem* (Edinburgh, 1813); *Waverley: or, 'Tis Sixty Years Since*, 3 vols. (Edinburgh, 1814), novel; *The Field of Waterloo: A Poem* (Edinburgh, 1815); *Guy Mannering: or, The Astrologer*, 3 vols. (Edinburgh, 1815), novel; *The Lord of the Isles: A Poem* (Edinburgh, 1815); *The Antiquary*, 3 vols. (Edinburgh, 1816), novel; *Tales of My Landlord*, 4 vols. (Edinburgh, 1816), novel, contains *The Black Dwarf* and *Old Mortality*, published under the pseudonym Jedediah Cleishbotham; *Harold the Dauntless: A Poem* (Edinburgh, 1817); *Rob Roy*, 3 vols. (Edinburgh, 1818), novel; *Tales of My Landlord*, 2nd ser., 4 vols. (Edinburgh, 1818), novel, contains *The Heart of Mid-Lothian*; *Tales of My Landlord*, 3rd ser., 4 vols. (Edinburgh, 1819), novel, contains *The Bride of Lammermoor* and *A Legend of Montrose*.

The Abbot, 3 vols. (Edinburgh, 1820), novel; *Ivanhoe: A Romance*, 3 vols. (Edinburgh, 1820), novel; *The Monastery: A Romance*, 3 vols. (Edinburgh, 1820), novel; *Kenilworth: A Romance*, 3 vols. (Edinburgh, 1821), novel; *The Fortunes of Nigel*, 3 vols. (Edinburgh, 1822), novel; *Halidon Hill: A Dramatic Sketch from Scottish History* (Edinburgh, 1822), verse; *Peveril of the Peak*, 4 vols. (Edinburgh, 1822), novel; *The Pirate*, 3 vols. (Edinburgh, 1822), novel; *Quentin Durward*, 3 vols. (Edinburgh, 1823), novel; *Redgauntlet: A Tale of the Eighteenth Century*, 3 vols. (Edinburgh, 1824), novel; *St. Ronan's Well*, 3 vols. (Edinburgh, 1824), novel; *Tales of the Crusaders*, 4 vols. (Edinburgh, 1825), novel, contains *The Betrothed* and *The Talisman*; *Woodstock: or, The Cavalier. A Tale of the Year Sixteen Hundred and Fifty-One*, 3 vols. (Edinburgh, 1826), novel; *Chronicles of the Canongate*, 2 vols. (Edinburgh, 1827), novel, contains *The Highland Widow*, *The Two Drovers*, and *The Surgeon's Daughter*, with an intro. in which Scott acknowledges his authorship of the *Waverley* novels; *Chronicles of the Canongate*, 2nd ser., 3 vols. (Edinburgh, 1828), novel, contains *St. Valentine's Day: or, The Fair Maid of Perth*; *Anne of Geierstein: or, The Maiden of the Mist*, 3 vols. (Edinburgh, 1829), novel; *Tales of My Landlord*, 4th ser., 4 vols. (Edinburgh, 1832), novel, contains *Count Robert of Paris* and *Castle Dangerous*; D. Douglas, ed., *The Journal, 1825–32*, 2 vols. (Edinburgh, 1890), also in J. G. Tait, ed., 3 vols. (Edinburgh, 1939–1946), and W. E. K. Anderson, ed. (London, 1972); D. Cook, ed., *New Love-Poems* (Oxford, 1932).

IV. LETTERS. W. Partington, ed., *The Private Letter-Books of Sir Walter Scott* (London, 1930), contains letters to Scott now in the National Library of Scotland; W. Partington, ed., *Sir Walter's Post-Bag: More Stories and Sidelights from His Unpublished Letter-Books* (London, 1932), contains letters to Scott now in the National Library of Scotland; H. J. C. Grierson et al., eds., *The Letters*, 12 vols. (London, 1932–1937), W. M. Parker's index on cards is at the National Library of Scotland; F. E. Ratchford and W. H. McCarthy, eds., *Correspondence of Scott and C. R. Maturin* (Austin, Tex., 1937); J. C. Corson, *Notes and Index to Sir Herbert Grierson's Edition of the Letters of Sir Walter Scott* (Oxford, 1979).

V. MISCELLANEOUS WORKS. In addition to a great amount of literary journalism and miscellaneous writing (such as essays and prefaces), Scott edited *Minstrelsy of the Scottish Border*, 2 vols. (Kelso, 1802), 3 vols. (Edinburgh,

1803), also in T. F. Henderson, ed. (London, 1902; reiss., 1932); *The Works of Dryden*, 18 vols. (London, 1808); *Secret History of the Court of James the First*, 2 vols. (London, 1811); *The Works of Swift*, 19 vols. (London, 1814); and much more. His "Lives of the Novelists" were prefixed to Ballantyne's Novelist's Library, 10 vols. (London, 1821–1824).

VI. BIOGRAPHICAL AND CRITICAL STUDIES. A great deal of criticism is in the reviews of Scott's books that appeared in the *Edinburgh Review*, the *Quarterly*, and other periodicals of the time. Most of the points that have been made by modern critics are anticipated by someone writing in Scott's day. Some of the best of these reviews—those by Hazlitt and W. F. Jeffrey, for example—were repr.

J. L. Adolphus, *Letters to Richard Heber, Esq. Containing Critical Remarks on the Series of Novels Beginning with "Waverley," and an Attempt to Ascertain Their Author* (London, 1821), an admirable piece of criticism, in which Adolphus shows that *Waverley* and its successors were written by the author of *Marmion* and the other poems; J. Hogg, *The Domestic Manners and Private Life of Sir Walter Scott* (Glasgow, 1834), by the "Ettrick Shepherd" who knew Scott very well—Lockhart disliked Hogg and treats him unfairly; R. Chambers, *Life of Sir Walter Scott* (London, 1834; rev. and enl., 1871); G. Allan, *Life of Sir Walter Scott, Baronet: With Critical Notices of His Writings* (Edinburgh, 1834)—J. C. Corson points out that this appeared in 5 parts between 1832 and 1834 and that the marked difference in tone between the part dealing with Scott's early life and that dealing with his maturity is due to the fact that the first part was written by William Weir, not by Allan; W. Hazlitt, *The Spirit of the Age; or, Contemporary Portraits* (London, 1835), the "character" of Scott is one of the most brilliant and incisive criticisms of him ever written—much else on Scott is in Hazlitt's collected writings; J. G. Lockhart, *Memoirs of the Life of Sir Walter Scott, Bart.*, 7 vols. (Edinburgh, 1837–1838), most later biographies simply plunder Lockhart, who included Scott's account of his early life, written in 1808; T. Carlyle, *Critical and Miscellaneous Essays*, 4 vols. (London, 1839).

J. Ruskin, *Modern Painters*, 5 vols. (London, 1843; 1846–1860), here and elsewhere (notably in *Fors Clavigera*, *Praeterita*, and *Fiction, Fair and Foul*) Ruskin wrote a good deal on Scott and his influence—some of the most important passages are in A. H. R. Ball, *Ruskin as Literary Critic* (London, 1928); F. Jeffrey, *Contributions to the Edinburgh Review*, 4 vols. (London, 1844), this and subsequent collections of Jeffrey's criticism contain some of his reviews of *Waverley* and the later books; W. Bagehot, "The *Waverley* Novels," in *National Review* (April 1858), repr. in his *Works* and in collections of essays entitled *Literary Studies* and *Estimations in Criticism*; L. Stephen, *Hours in a Library*, 3rd ser. (London, 1874–1879), 1st ser. contains an excellent essay on the *Waverley* novels; R. H. Hutton, *Sir Walter Scott* (London, 1878), in the English Men of Letters series; M. Oliphant, *The Literary History of England in the End of the Eighteenth and Beginning of the Nineteenth*

Century, 3 vols. (London, 1882), contains a long ch. on Scott that is still of interest.

W. H. Hudson, *Sir Walter Scott* (London, 1901); A. Lang, *Sir Walter Scott* (London, 1906); A. Lang, *Sir Walter Scott and the Border Minstrelsy* (London, 1910); W. S. Crockett, *The Scott Originals* (London, 1912), an account of the originals of many characters in Scott's work; C. Whibley, ed., *Collected Essays of W. P. Ker*, 2 vols. (London, 1925), vol. I contains three essays on Scott; C. N. Johnston (Lord Sands), *Sir Walter Scott's Congé* (London, 1929), deals with Scott's unsuccessful love for Williamina Belsches—it is essential to consult the 3rd ed. of this book (1931), as it was only then that Lord Sands finally settled some very difficult problems of chronology; D. Carswell, *Sir Walter: A Four-Part Study in Biography* (London, 1930); J. Buchan, *Sir Walter Scott* (London, 1932), biographically unoriginal, yet containing perceptive comments on Scott as a man and an author by another Scottish writer of romances who understood him very well; M. C. Boatwright, "Scott's . . . Use of the Supernatural . . . in Relation to the Chronology of the *Waverley* Novels," in *PMLA*, 50 (March 1935); J. T. Hillhouse, *The Waverley Novels and Their Critics* (Minneapolis, 1936).

E. Muir, *Scott and Scotland: The Predicament of the Scottish Writer* (London, 1936), a stimulating book in which the author points to the "very curious emptiness . . . behind the wealth of his imagination" and tries to account for it—Muir also wrote about Scott in D. Verschoyle, ed., *The English Novelists: A Survey of the Novel by Twenty Contemporary Novelists* (London, 1936), and in *Sir Walter Scott Lectures* (below); H. J. C. Grierson, *Sir Walter Scott, Bart. A New Life Supplementary to, and Corrective of, Lockhart's Biography* (London, 1938); H. J. C. Grierson, *Essays and Addresses* (London, 1940), contains "Scott and Carlyle" and the important essay "Lang, Lockhart and Biography"; *Essays on the Eighteenth Century Presented to David Nichol Smith* (Oxford, 1945), contains an outstanding essay by F. A. Pottle, "The Power of Memory in Boswell and Scott"; R. D. Mayo, "The Chronology of the *Waverley* Novels: The Evidence of the Manuscripts," in *PMLA*, 63 (September 1948), argues convincingly against the theory of U. Pope-Hennessey and others—Mayo's view is that the novels were written in the order they were published; U. Pope-Hennessey, *Sir Walter Scott* (London, 1948), in two parts, "The Man" and "The Work"—this brief study makes some interesting critical suggestions, but the theory that some of Scott's novels were written before *Waverley* is irritatingly ubiquitous.

Sir Walter Scott Lectures, 1940–1948 (Edinburgh, 1950), with an intro. by W. L. Renwick, contains the first four series of Scott lectures by H. J. C. Grierson, E. Muir, G. M. Young, and S. C. Roberts, repr. from *University of Edinburgh Journal*, which also contains the subsequent lectures (1950–1956) by D. N. Smith, J. R. Sutherland, J. C. Corson, M. Lascelles, and J. A. Smith; M. Praz, *La crisi dell'eroe nel romanzo vittoriano* (Florence, 1952), in A.

Davidson, trans., *The Hero in Eclipse in Victorian Fiction* (London, 1956), argues that "The novels of Sir Walter Scott made a notable contribution to the process by which Romanticism turned bourgeois"; H. Pearson, *Walter Scott: His Life and Personality* (London, 1954); J. Kinsley, ed., *Scottish Poetry: A Critical Survey* (London, 1955), contains J. W. Oliver, "Scottish Poetry in the Earlier Nineteenth Century"; D. Daiches, *Literary Essays* (Edinburgh, 1956), contains the admirable appreciation "Scott's Achievement as a Novelist"; W. Gell, *Reminiscences of Sir Walter Scott's Residence in Italy, 1832*, J. C. Corson, ed. (London, 1957), Lockhart made a rather cavalier use of Gell's reminiscences, and it is interesting to compare the full text with what appears in his *Life*—Gell's *Reminiscences* also in G. H. Needler, ed. (Toronto, 1953).

D. Davie, *The Heyday of Sir Walter Scott* (London, 1961); C. S. Lewis, *They Asked for a Paper* (London, 1962), contains an essay on Scott; G. Lukács, *The Historical Novel*, trans. H. Mitchell and S. Mitchell (London, 1962), a penetrating study, written from a Marxist point of view; P. F. Wilson and B. Dobrée, eds., *The Oxford History of English Literature* (Oxford, 1945–   ): W. L. Renwick, ed., vol. IX, *English Literature, 1789–1815* (1963), contains a brief discussion of Scott's poetry; I. Jack, ed., vol. X, *English Literature, 1815–1832* (1963), contains the ch. "The *Waverley* Romances"; A. Welsh, *The Hero of the Waverley Novels* (New Haven, 1963), Yale Studies in English no. 154; F. R. Hart, *Scott's Novels: The Plotting of Historic Survival* (Charlottesville, Va., 1966); M. Mack and I. Gregor, eds., *Imagined Worlds: Essays . . . in Honour of John Butt* (London, 1968), contains M. Lascelles, "Scott and the Art of Revision"; E. Quayle, *The Ruin of Sir Walter Scott* (London, 1968), using the Ballantyne papers, argues that Scott was responsible for his own financial downfall; J. H. Raleigh, *Time, Place, and Idea: Essays on the Novel* (Carbondale, Ill., 1968), includes the ch. "What Scott Meant to the Victorians"; I. Williams, ed., *Sir Walter Scott on Novelists and Fiction* (London, 1968), a very useful compilation; A. Melville Clark, *Sir Walter Scott: The Formative Years* (Edinburgh, 1969); A. O. J. Cockshut, *The Achievement of Walter Scott* (London, 1969); A. Norman Jeffares, ed., *Scott's Mind and Art* (Edinburgh, 1969), ten essays on various aspects of Scott.

J. O. Hayden, ed., *Scott: The Critical Heritage* (London, 1970), a valuable collection of nineteenth-century criticism of Scott; E. Johnson, *Sir Walter Scott: The Great Unknown*, 2 vols. (London, 1970), the most comprehensive biography since Lockhart's, and an important study; D. D. Devlin, *The Author of Waverley: A Critical Study of Walter Scott* (London, 1971); F. R. Hart, *Lockhart as Romantic Biographer* (Edinburgh, 1971), contains the fullest discussion of Lockhart's biography; A. Bell, ed., *Sir Walter Scott Bi-centenary Essays* (London, 1974); J. Rubenstein, ed., *Sir Walter Scott: A Reference Guide* (London, 1974); D. Brown, *Sir Walter Scott and the Historical Imagination* (London, 1979).

SAMUEL TAYLOR COLERIDGE
(1772-1834)

R. L. Brett

"So Coleridge passed, leaving a handful of golden poems, an emptiness in the hearts of a few friends, and a will-o-the wisp light for bemused thinkers." With these words E. K. Chambers, ended his *Samuel Taylor Coleridge: A Biographical Study* (1938), and this, perhaps, is the way the general public still regards Coleridge: as the author of "The Ancient Mariner," "Kubla Khan," and "Christabel," a poet *manqué* whose gifts were dissipated in abstruse speculation and whose will was undermined by drug addiction. On this view, Coleridge was a brilliant failure, who after a few years of virtuosity burned himself out.

One charge that has been decisively dismissed since Chambers' biography is that of Coleridge's indolence. The picture of Coleridge as a broken man, sponging on his friends, and accomplishing nothing but "a handful of golden poems," has been demolished by modern editions of his writings. The *Collected Works* (not yet completed) will run to some twenty-two volumes; the *Collected Letters* (many of them more like essays), completed in 1971, totals six large volumes, and the *Notebooks* another five large volumes of text and five more of commentary. The sheer bulk of this work challenges the idea of Coleridge as ineffectual and lazy and presents a picture of sustained industry, but sustained often against great odds and threatened by personal misfortunes. But what of the contents of this work? No one would challenge Coleridge's claim to be one of England's greatest poets, not only for "The Ancient Mariner," "Kubla Khan," and "Christabel" but also for his conversational poems such as "This Lime Tree Bower My Prison," "Frost at Midnight," and "Dejection," which were novel combinations of meditative reflection and a sensitive appreciation of landscape. But now we recognize in Coleridge England's greatest philosophical critic, who analyzed in *Biographia Literaria* the workings of the poetic imagination and used this analysis as an instrument of fine critical discrimination in his lectures on Shakespeare and the other English poets. More than this, his *Confessions of an Inquiring Spirit* and *On the Constitution of the Church and State* add to these roles those of religious philosopher and political theorist. Such works are now seen as classics of English literature and have caused us to revise the estimates of his contemporaries.

Coleridge's own generation never doubted that he was a man of prodigious gifts. Even William Hazlitt, who first gave currency to the notion of Coleridge as the "lost leader," as one who had betrayed his ideals and dissipated those gifts, was ready to acknowledge the genius of Coleridge as a young man. In his *Lectures on the English Poets* (1818) he could write,

I may say of him here, that he is the only person I ever knew who answered to the idea of a man of genius. . . . He was the first poet I ever knew. His genius at that time had angelic wings, and fed on manna. He talked on for ever; and you wished him to talk on for ever. . . . His voice rolled on the ear like the pealing organ, and its sound alone was the music of thought. His mind was clothed with wings; and raised on them, he lifted philosophy to heaven.

(lecture VIII, "On the Living Poets")

But as Hazlitt looks back over the years, he qualifies his admiration. "And shall I, who heard him then, listen to him now?" he asks. "Not I! . . . That spell is broke; that time is gone for ever!" William Wordsworth, Thomas De Quincey, Charles Lamb (who had been at Christ's Hospital with Coleridge and who was his friend for fifty years), and many others were all united in their conviction that in Coleridge they had known a man of genius. But others began to echo the reservations Hazlitt had expressed, and in time it was the reservations alone that were heard. The most influential of these critics was Carlyle, who, though he owed him so much, wrote the most maliciously damaging account of Coleridge's last years in his *Life of Sterling*:

Coleridge sat on the brow of Highgate hill, . . . looking down on London and its smoke-tumult, like a sage escaped from the inanity of life's battle. . . . His express contributions to poetry, philosophy, or any specific province of human literature or enlightenment, had been small and sadly intermittent.   (ch. 8, p. 63)

Carlyle describes Coleridge's physical appearance:

. . . the face was flabby and irresolute. . . . The whole figure and air, good and amiable otherwise, might be called flabby and irresolute.   (ibid., p. 65)

And then he dismisses him in a sentence that was to become the judgment of the majority:

To the man himself Nature had given, in high measure, the seeds of a noble endowment; and to unfold it had been forbidden him.   (ibid., p. 72)

No doubt a superficial account of Coleridge's career can be used to project this image of a broken and irresolute figure whose early promise was never fulfilled, but it is one that does not stand up to scrutiny.

Coleridge was the youngest child of the Reverend John Coleridge, vicar of Ottery St. Mary in Devon. He was born on 21 October 1772, the tenth child of a second marriage and the youngest of thirteen children. As the youngest, he was petted and made much of; and his father, especially, fostered his precocious talents. His imagination was stimulated at an early age by tales from the *Arabian Nights* and other stories of the supernatural—overstimulated, in fact, for he developed a morbid fascination for stories that frightened him, until his father realized what was happening and threw the books on the fire. His precocity did not always endear him to his elder brothers. In a letter written on 16 October 1797, one of a series of autobiographical letters to his friend Thomas Poole, he recalls a childhood incident with such graphic detail that one feels it must have left its mark on an already sensitive personality. He relates how in the course of a fight he seized a knife and ran at his brother Frank, but was stopped by their mother, who had just entered the room. He dashed from the house in panic and stayed out all night. Filled with fear and remorse, he wandered in the meadows by the river Otter until, overcome by fatigue, he sank down in the wet grass to sleep. When he woke he was crippled with rheumatism and lay there helpless, listening to the distant search party, which could not hear his cries. He was found, of

course, and restored to his anxious parents, but one can discern in this incident the origins of much that went to the making of Coleridge the man. He himself traced to this experience the beginnings of the so-called rheumatic attacks he suffered in later life and which drove him to seek relief in opium. It is likely that some of these attacks were partly psychosomatic and connected with the deep sense of guilt that pervaded his personality, and, if so, we can see why the story of Cain had such a hold on his imagination and why he made it the subject of a poem he abandoned, but of which he said "the Ancient Mariner was written instead."

Certainly Coleridge had a personality plagued by self-doubt, was unassertive, dependent, and at times self-indulgent. Nevertheless, he combined these traits with an acute power of self-analysis, which helped him to combat his shortcomings, but which in turn could also lead to an obsessional and paralyzing habit of introspection. His adult personality owed something not only to his early childhood but also to his removal at the age of nine from the security of home to the harsh life of Christ's Hospital. Coleridge left Devon on his father's death and spent the next nine years at school in London. He recorded in his notebooks in later life the nightmares he suffered and described how many of them took him back to Christ's Hospital. We also get a vivid account of Coleridge's feelings at the time from Lamb's essay "Christ's Hospital Five-and-Thirty Years Ago," written in the assumed person of Coleridge:

I was a poor friendless boy. My parents, and those who should care for me were far away. . . . O the cruelty of separating a poor lad from his early homestead! The yearnings which I used to have towards it in those unfledged years! How, in my dreams, would my native town (far in the west) come back, with its church, and trees, and faces!

From Christ's Hospital Coleridge went to Jesus College, Cambridge, where he became a Unitarian and a "democrat"; that is, a member of the student Left of his day. However intellectually sophisticated Coleridge's views may have been, he was innocent in the ways of the world, and in his third year he fell in debt to the tradesmen of the town. This, coupled with the rejection of his love for Mary Evans, the sister of a school friend, perhaps caused him to leave the university and enlist in the Light Dragoons. He joined the colors in December 1793 under the assumed name of Silas Tomkyn Comberbacke, and it was some time before he was tracked down and bought out by his brothers. Coleridge made a poor soldier, and no doubt it was with some relief that he found himself back in Cambridge the following April. But he remained unsettled and at odds with the university and left at the end of the year without taking his degree. Wordsworth had left Cambridge as Coleridge arrived and the two men did not meet until 1795, when they were both in Bristol. Coleridge had gone there to join forces with Robert Southey in launching pantisocracy, a utopian scheme to found a community of a few families on the banks of the Susquehanna; Wordsworth was staying in the city with his friends the Pinneys. It was not until 1797, however, when Coleridge visited Wordsworth and his sister Dorothy at Racedown in Dorset, that they became close friends. Wordsworth recalled the visit over forty years later and how Coleridge " . . . did not keep to the high road, but leaped over a gate and bounded down a pathless field by which he cut off an angle."[1] Coleridge stayed for three weeks and was soon back again with a chaise to transport the Wordsworths to Nether Stowey, in the Quantock Hills in Somerset, where his friend Thomas Poole had found him and his wife a cottage. A fortnight later Wordsworth and his sister moved to nearby Alfoxden, and the two men became neighbors and collaborators.

It was a critical period in the lives of both men. Wordsworth had been in France during the Revolution and had been caught up in the intoxication of great political events. He had fallen in love with a French girl, Annette Vallon, and was the father of her child. At the time it had seemed the beginning of a new life, and he later described his feelings in *The Prelude* in the famous lines:

> Bliss was it in that dawn to be alive,
> But to be young was very heaven.

But family disapproval had brought him home just as England declared war against France. His political hopes had turned to a deep sense of betrayal when the Revolution turned into the Terror and the collapse of his personal plans and public aspirations had left him in a state of emotional turmoil on his return. Five years passed before Wordsworth recovered his

mental equilibrium in the quiet countryside of the Quantocks, with the companionship of his sister Dorothy and the encouragement of Coleridge.

Wordsworth had tried to cure his breakdown by rational control, a doctrine he had met in the pages of William Godwin's *Political Justice*, but Coleridge taught him "to keep alive the heart in the head," for to repress the emotions was to deny an important part of oneself. Coleridge himself was passing through a difficult time. He had married, rather reluctantly, Southey's sister-in-law, Sarah Fricker, but only because pantisocracy would not accept bachelors. The scheme itself had never materialized, but now he was faced with the responsibility of earning a living not only for himself but for his wife and baby. The only weapons he had to fight what he called the two giants, "Bread and Cheese," were his journalism and his poetry. Little wonder, perhaps, that he was suffering from depression and anxiety.

When he met Wordsworth, Coleridge was a disciple of David Hartley, whose psychological theory saw human personality as the product of environment rather than innate forces. Hartley confirmed what Coleridge had come to believe from his own experience: that emotional health was not a matter of rational control but of allowing the mind to develop in natural surroundings away from the corruptions of city life. This conviction, which he shared and explored with Wordsworth, inspired the memorable poetry they produced together in that *annus mirabilis* of 1797.

When Coleridge moved to Nether Stowey he was already developing a new and simpler style of poetry. After leaving Cambridge he had continued his interest in radical politics and combined with it the ambition to be a poet. While in Bristol he had delivered lectures in 1795 attacking the government and its policy of war against France, and in the following year had started his own radical journal, the *Watchman*. Also in 1796 he had published a collection entitled *Poems on Various Subjects*, which contained sonnets first published in the *Morning Chronicle*, such as "To William Godwin" and "To Lord Stanhope." These, together with "Religious Musings," express his strong political and religious beliefs (and the two are not really separate). Others such as "Lines Composed While Climbing the Left Ascent of Brockley Combe" show an interest in landscape. Much of his early poetry had been in the manner of the eighteenth-century imitators of Milton, written in an inflated and artificial diction owing

---

[1]From E. de Selincourt, ed., *The Letters of William and Dorothy Wordsworth, the Later Years* (Oxford, 1935–1939), vol. III, p. 1584.

more to books than nature; but his interest in landscape now led him toward writers such as Shenstone, Goldsmith, Gray, and Cowper, whose verse used the description of nature as an occasion for reflection. We see how Coleridge began to experiment with this form in his poem on Brockley Combe and how he took it further in his "Reflections on Leaving a Place of Retirement," as he prepared to leave Clevedon, where he and his wife had started their married life, to return to Bristol in 1795. The poem begins with a description of their cottage on the shores of the Bristol Channel:

> Low was our pretty Cot: our tallest Rose
> Peep'd at the chamber-window. We could hear
> At silent noon, and eve, and early morn,
> The Sea's faint murmur.
>
> (1–4)

Coleridge sees Clevedon as a "Valley of Seclusion" that he and his bride must leave so that he can take up the fight for justice and freedom. He then surveys the scene from the hill above their home; in front of him the sea, behind the countryside stretching in the far distance to the spires of Bristol. The end of the poem returns to the cottage and expresses his belief that the memory of the scene will sustain him in the days to come:

> Yet oft when after honourable toil
> Rests the tir'd mind, and waking loves to dream,
> My spirit shall revisit thee, dear Cot!
> Thy Jasmin and thy window-peeping Rose,
> And Myrtles fearless of the mild sea-air.
> And I shall sigh fond wishes—sweet Abode!
>
> (63–68)

The poem provides a procedure that he was to develop into a new and successful poetic form in "This Lime Tree Bower My Prison" and "Frost at Midnight," written after his move to Nether Stowey in 1796. It starts with natural description, embraces the realization of a reciprocity between the mind and what it perceives, and expresses the conviction that the experience it recounts will be stored in the memory to enliven the mind in times of depression or adversity. This poetic procedure served as a model for Wordsworth's "Lines Composed . . . above Tintern Abbey," which was indebted to Coleridge not only for its poetic form but for its content. Especially, one can hear Coleridge's confident assertion in "This Lime Tree Bower My Prison":

> Henceforth I shall know
> That Nature ne'er deserts the wise and pure

echoed in Wordsworth's affirmation

> that Nature never did betray
> The heart that loved her.

The best of Coleridge's poems in this kind is "Frost at Midnight," written in 1798; in the same year and perhaps under its influence, Wordsworth wrote his Tintern poem traveling from the Wye Valley to Bristol, where he was just in time to include it in their joint venture *Lyrical Ballads*, about to be published by Joseph Cottle, the Bristol bookseller. In the poem Coleridge speaks to his infant son (named Hartley after the philosopher) of his own childhood at Christ's Hospital, "In the great city, pent 'mid cloisters dim," and promises him an upbringing close to nature:

> . . . so shalt thou see and hear
> The lovely shapes and sounds intelligible
> Of that eternal language, which thy God
> Utters, who from eternity doth teach
> Himself in all, and all things in himself.
>
> (58–62)

In much the same language Wordsworth addressed his sister on the banks of the Wye.

The other kind of poetry Coleridge made especially his own, but which he did not share with Wordsworth, was the poetry of the supernatural. His most famous poems, "The Ancient Mariner," "Kubla Khan," and "Christabel," all belong to this kind and, although the last of them was added to later, they were all composed at this time. Writing many years later in chapter 14 of *Biographia Literaria* about his collaboration with Wordsworth in *Lyrical Ballads*, Coleridge describes the difference between their contributions to the collection:

The thought suggested itself that a series of poems might be composed of two sorts. In the one, the incidents and agents were to be, in part at least, supernatural; and the excellence aimed at was to consist in the interesting of the affections by the dramatic truth of such emotions as would naturally accompany such situations, supposing them real . . . for the second class, subjects were to be chosen from ordinary life; the characters and incidents were to be such as will be found in every village and its vicinity where there is a meditative and feeling mind to seek after them, or to notice them when they present themselves.

"With this view I wrote the 'Ancient Mariner,'" he continues, but although "The Ancient Mariner" was the only one of the three poems mentioned above to appear in *Lyrical Ballads*, the passage applies to all three.

In *Biographia Literaria* Coleridge recounts the story of his early allegiance to the philosophy of associationism and his growing dissatisfaction with it. It was only later, after he had moved to Keswick, that he began to construct a system of thought more congenial to his mind than the empiricist tradition of the eighteenth century. But much earlier than this, he tells us, when he was only twenty-three, that is, in 1795–1796, he heard Wordsworth read the manuscript of his poem "Guilt and Sorrow" and was impressed by

. . . the union of deep feeling with profound thought; the fine balance of truth in observing with the imaginative faculty in modifying the objects observed; and above all the original gift of spreading the tone, the *atmosphere* and with it the depth and height of the ideal world, around forms, incidents and situations of which, for the common view, custom had bedimmed all the lustre, had dried up the sparkle and the dewdrops.

(ch. 4)

In December 1794 he had written to Southey,

I am a compleat Necessitarian—and understand the subject as well almost as Hartley himself—but I go farther than Hartley and believe the corporeality of thought, —namely, that it is motion.

But prolonged reflection about the experience of listening to Wordsworth, he tells us, had led to a new development in his thought. Wordsworth's poetry showed an awareness that marked it off from the devitalized writings of the eighteenth century; it had a quality of poetic genius that caused Coleridge to give an important place to the imagination when he came to construct his own philosophy. His discipleship of Hartley had brought him into a state of paralysis, religious doubt, and a darkness of mind from which he had been partly delivered by a reading of the early Neoplatonic writers Plotinus, Proclus, and Gemistus Pletho, from whom he had progressed to the seventeenth-century mystics George Fox, Jacob Boehme, and Boehme's English disciple William Law. "They contributed," he wrote in chapter 9 of *Biographia Literaria*,

to keep alive the heart in the head; gave me an indistinct, yet stirring and working presentiment, that all the products of the mere reflective faculty partook of death, and were as the rattling twigs and sprays in winter into which a sap was yet to be propelled. . . . If they were too often a moving cloud of smoke to me by day, yet they were always a pillar of fire throughout the night, during my wanderings through the wilderness of doubt, and enabled me to skirt, without crossing, the sandy deserts of utter unbelief.

His meeting with Wordsworth brought him the friendship of a man whose vision of life confirmed the "working presentiment" of these mystics and whose poetry brought the heart and the head together in "the union of deep feeling with profound thought" that so attracted Coleridge.

The story Coleridge recounts in *Biographia Literaria* strikes the reader by its religious overtones and images; it tells us how he was lost in the wilderness of doubt but eventually reached the promised land of renewed faith and how he passed through darkness into light. After meeting Wordsworth he became convinced that this salvation could be identified with an imaginative awareness that saw the world of nature as more than matter in motion but as possessing a spiritual significance. Later he was to make this conviction part of his philosophy of religion, but the poetry that was inspired by it sits rather loosely to dogmatic Christianity. "The Ancient Mariner" uses biblical and even medieval Catholic imagery, but naturalizes it in a narrative that becomes an internalized and psychological version of redemption; nevertheless, few can doubt that it deals with a profound spiritual experience that haunts the mind with a compulsive power.

The creation of the old seaman was a great triumph in Coleridge's construction of the poem, for he gives the poem dramatic force and credibility. Because we accept him, we accept his story and grant it that "willing suspension of disbelief for the moment" the poem demands. Criticism of the poem has been endless. At the start it was seen as a narrative in the Gothic and romantic style of Gottfried August Bürger, the German poet whose poems in the translations by Sir Walter Scott and others enjoyed such a vogue in the 1790's. Southey, when he reviewed *Lyrical Ballads* soon after its appearance, thought it a poor specimen even of this kind and called it "a Dutch attempt at German sublimity," adding, "Genius has here been employed in producing a poem of little merit." Even Wordsworth, in a letter to Joseph Cottle on 24 June 1799, maintained that it had been "upon the whole . . . an injury to the volume, . . . the old words and the strangeness of it have deterred readers from going on." Since then, and especially in the last few decades, interpretations of the poem have increased in number and in ingenuity. The albatross, for instance, has been seen as a representation of Coleridge himself, of his imagination, of Mrs. Coleridge, and of God's creation. Many have ignored Coleridge's distinction between allegory, which he defined as a one-to-one relation, and "the Symbolical," which, he said in lecture VIII of his 1818 lectures,

cannot, perhaps, be better defined in distinction from the Allegorical, than that it is always itself a part of that, of the whole of which it is the representation.[2]

This is important when we come to consider the shooting of the albatross, for it implies that this central act, the pivot on which the action turns, is not an arbitrary token of something else, nor something whose significance has been obscured or repressed by the censorship of the poet's superego. It is a representative example of a whole class of actions. This suggests that those critics are correct who see it as a violation of the principle of the "one-life" that Coleridge proclaimed in lines he later added to "The Eolian Harp," and which begins:

> O! the one Life within us and abroad,
> Which meets all motion and becomes its soul.
>
> (26–27)

An essential element of the crime is its motivelessness. The poem goes out of its way to isolate it and show it as an act of gratuitous cruelty without any advantage to the Mariner or his shipmates; only after the killing do they hold the albatross responsible for the bad weather. In this respect the crime is like man's original disobedience. Some readers think the Mariner's crime too petty to have had such tremendous consequences, but again the eating of the apple in Eden, insignificant in itself, had catastrophic results. By relating it to the Fall we are made aware of the mystery surrounding the action of the poem. Why should men act wantonly and cruelly, why should they violate the principle of the "one-life," when there is no advantage to themselves? The mystery of evil puzzled Coleridge for most of his life

and some would say he had a pathological sense of guilt. Certainly "The Ancient Mariner" cannot be interpreted in clear conceptual terms. Its story is close to the story of mankind as told in the biblical narrative, and this itself parallels the religious experience of the individual believer. The hero of the poem is a kind of Adam, unreflective, proud in the assumption that he is master of nature rather than part of it. His disobedience is followed by a journey through the wilderness until he is rescued by God's grace. The grace of God is given and not won, and this seems to be so in the poem when the Mariner is moved by the beauty of the water snakes and "blessed them unawares." The Christian echoes and references throughout the poem are undeniable. It is difficult, but certainly not impossible, to accommodate the figures of Death and Life-in-Death to a Christian framework, just as Milton in *Paradise Lost* brought the figures of pagan mythology within a biblical dispensation. To those who say that the Mariner's redemption is incomplete we can point to the doctrine of purgatory, a state, like heaven and hell, that one can inhabit here and now.

Coleridge's preoccupation with the Fall of man can also be seen in "Kubla Khan," probably written in 1798 just after "The Ancient Mariner," or in the autumn of 1797, although it was not published until 1816, when it was printed with a note informing the reader that it appeared at Lord Byron's request. The note also described it as "a psychological curiosity" and explained that it had been written at a farmhouse between Porlock and Linton where Coleridge had retired in ill health and fallen asleep after taking "an anodyne." He had been reading the account in *Purchas's Pilgrimage* of how the Khan Kubla had ordered the building of a palace within a walled garden. After three hours he woke and started to write the "two to three hundred lines" he had composed during his profound sleep, but as he wrote he was disturbed by "a person on business from Porlock." This interruption lasted "above an hour" and when the interview was over he found that the rest of the poem had vanished from his mind. A manuscript version of the poem was acquired by the British Museum in 1962, and attached to this was a short note of Coleridge's that added a few more details. In this he specifically mentions that the anodyne was "two grains of Opium taken to check a dysentry," and he describes his sleep as "a sort of Reverie." For many years the poem was regarded as a meaningless fragment, a congeries of images and

[2] From T. M. Raysor, ed., *Coleridge's Miscellaneous Criticism* (London, 1936), p. 99.

memories from Coleridge's unconscious mind, the product of automatic writing. A moment's reflection reminds us, however, that not all drug-takers are poets and that even if opium had a necessary part in the genesis of the poem, it is not sufficient to explain its marvelous character. Coleridge not only took opium, he was also a poet of genius, and the poem bears all the marks of his artistry.

Modern scholarship and criticism from J. L. Lowes's *Road to Xanadu* onward have laid bare the influence of Coleridge's wide reading upon the poem; less attention has been paid to the influence of landscape and the part played by the memory images of places Coleridge had visited. Coleridge was not only "a library cormorant" (to use his own description of himself), but also a keen observer and recorder of natural scenery. It is likely, then, that the language and imagery of the poem would show a conflation not only of literary sources but also of remembered scenes. One cannot be certain of these, but the combe in which the farmhouse stands where Coleridge fell asleep would probably have been in his mind, and not far away was the rocky gorge through which the river Lyn dashes down to the sea. Even closer to the descriptive language of the poem is Wookey Hole in the Mendip Hills, which Coleridge must have visited when he walked from Cheddar to Bridgwater. Here the river Axe plunges underground from the Ebbor gorge and runs through a great cavern in which the stalagmites and stalactites have the appearance of a fairy palace made of ice. Closest of all to the poem was the fabulous estate at Hafod, near Aberystwyth, which Coleridge visited during his walking tour of North Wales in 1794. Geoffrey Grigson, in an article in the *Cornhill* magazine for 1947, first drew attention to the similarity between the landscapes of "Kubla Khan" and Hafod. Hafod, by the Devil's Bridge in Cardiganshire, was laid out by its owner, Thomas Johnes, in the 1780's to be a recreation of the Happy Valley described in Samuel Johnson's *The History of Rasselas Prince of Abyssinia* (1759), an earthly paradise enfolded in the steep hills that descend to the river Ystwyth. Johnes had the advice of the two great landscape artists of the time, Richard Payne Knight and Uvedale Price, but the idea of creating a paradise was his own, as was the little Garden of Eden that lies within it, hidden in woods and overshadowed by a great cedar tree above the river and approached by a stone gateway bearing the figures of Adam and Eve. The house itself (later destroyed by fire) was finished in

1788, only a few years before Coleridge's visit, and was an exercise in romantic Gothic architecture. It stood at the head of the valley and the river flowed before the lawns in front of its windows. After its completion the owner added a large octagonal library, which was built on the roof and was surmounted by a beautiful dome in the style of a Mogul palace. Not only did Coleridge see this elaborate and fantastic representation of an earthly paradise but his memory of it was probably revived by *An Attempt to Describe Hafod*, published in 1796 and written by George Cumberland, who was a friend of Joseph Cottle, the publisher of *Lyrical Ballads*.

J. L. Lowes demonstrated that "The Ancient Mariner" in several places owed something to Coleridge's visit to Wales and it seems very likely that the same was true of "Kubla Khan," that here, too, the literary memories merge with the topographical ones. Coleridge's readings of Purchas, Bartram's *Travels*, Bruce's *Travels to Discover the Sources of the Nile*, Maurice's *History of Hindostan*, and of several classical writers, were brought together and given a focus by the passage in *Paradise Lost* where Milton describes the false paradise at Mount Amara near the source of the Nile in Abyssinia. Just as several remembered landscapes coalesce to form the scenery of "Kubla Khan" so the names *Ebbor*, *Aber*ystwyth, *Aby*ssinia, and *Amara* come together in Coleridge's invention of "Abora."

No genetic account can determine the meaning of a poem; and Lowes himself, although he laid bare so many of its literary sources, thought "Kubla Khan" lacked unity. Most critics now would argue that the elements that come together in the poem form a whole with a discernible meaning. The first two sections of the poem describe the creation of an earthly paradise. Like the Garden of Eden, it is built by the side of a river. "Alph," which is close to the first letter of the Greek alphabet, suggests the beginning of things, but also brings to mind the river Alpheus (another river supposed to run underground), which in ancient legend was often associated with the Nile. But unlike the Garden of Eden this paradise has been built by an earthly potentate. It is another of those follies that try to make a new heaven on earth, like Milton's false paradise, or the Happey Valley of Johnson's *Rasselas*, or Johnes's palace at Hafod. Its impermanence is foreshadowed by the "Ancestral voices prophesying war."

The third section moves toward Plato's doctrine of Ideas, which informs the rest of the poem. We know

Coleridge was reading intensively in Plato and the Platonists when he wrote the poem, and an entry in one of his notebooks at the end of 1796 (vol. 1, p. 204) copies a sentence from book VII of Plato's *Republic.* This comes from the beginning of the allegory of the cave, where Socrates tells Glaucon that ordinary men cannot perceive the absolute directly, that only after a gradual progression from the shadows into the light of day can they "look at the sun and observe its real nature, not its appearance in water." The fountain and the cave both symbolize time and eternity: the waters of the fountain are always changing while its shape remains the same, and the cave in Plato's allegory, where the prisoners discern only the shadows of the world outside, represents this earthly life where we see only the appearances of things. In this section of the poem we no longer perceive the dome itself; all we catch is its reflection on the surface of the river:

> The shadow of the dome of pleasure
> Floated midway on the waves.
> (31–32)

The sun, which in Coleridge's poetry generally symbolizes God's presence, casts its light upon the dome, but this too is only a reflection and the icy interior of the shadow palace is as cold as the water it floats on. And yet our vision of the dome is not an illusion since it gives us a glimpse of perfection, and as we contemplate it we can hear Plato's cosmic harmony:

> . . . the mingled measure
> From the fountain and the caves.
> (33–34)

The last section of the poem takes up the theme of music in the figure of the Abyssinian maid, whose song brings before us the paradise hidden in her native mountains. She inspires the poet to believe that he, too, through his poetry could build "That sunny dome! those caves of ice!" The picture of the poet with his "flashing eyes" and "floating hair" comes from Plato's *Ion,* in which Socrates presents a more ambiguous opinion of poets than in the *Republic,* and speaks of them as not in their right minds but as " . . . like Bacchic maidens who draw milk and honey from the rivers when they are under the influence of Dionysus." This Platonic echo also leaves an ambiguity at the end of "Kubla Khan," for we do not know whether the poet is claiming for himself an Orphic power or whether he regards poetry as a divine madness, whether he regards poetry as an ac-

cess to ultimate truth or whether, as Plato argued, it deals only with appearances. We do not even know whether Coleridge himself is speaking in the poem, but it was a question he was to return to when he came to assess the powers of the imagination.

The other great poem that was started at this time was "Christabel." The first part was written in Somerset in 1797–1798, the second at Keswick in 1800, but when it was published in 1816 it still remained uncompleted. Coleridge was persuaded by Byron and Scott, both of whom read the poem in manuscript, to publish it along with "Kubla Khan" and "The Pains of Sleep." Scott had adapted its meter for *The Lay of the Last Minstrel* (1805), and Coleridge felt that others were beginning to plagiarize his work. There is a marked difference between the two parts of "Christabel," and this goes further than the change of landscape that parallels the removal from Nether Stowey to Keswick. The first part is dramatic and, since drama can only live in the present, Coleridge employs the historic-present tense and the device of question-and-answer to give the action immediacy. In the second part the dramatic is replaced by narrative and the poem becomes less effective. The poem starts successfully with its evocation of unexplained horror, but as the story unfolds this sense of inexplicable dread is dispelled. In 'The Ancient Mariner" Coleridge takes the kind of supernatural story made fashionable by the translations of Bürger and gives it "the depth and height of the ideal world." "Christabel" starts out with this quality, but fails to sustain it, and it was the realization of this, perhaps, that prevented him from finishing it.

Like "The Ancient Mariner," "Christabel" is concerned with the theme of evil and guilt. The heroine, Christabel, whose innocence is symbolized by the image of a dove, meets at midnight in the woods that surround her father's castle the sorceress Geraldine, who is likened to a snake. Christabel is defenseless; her mother is dead and her father is bewitched by Geraldine's charms. The action of the poem suggests that Christabel will pass from unreflecting innocence to a knowledge of good and evil; but through grace and her own faith, in acquiring the wisdom of the serpent she will retain the innocence of the dove.

There were three contemporary accounts of how Coleridge planned to complete it, two of them by James Gillman, the physician with whom he lived from 1816 until his death, the other by his son Derwent. The shorter of the two accounts by James

Gillman and that by Derwent Coleridge suggest vicarious suffering as the central theme of the poem and that Christabel's trial would be revealed as a means of saving "her lover that's far away." The remaining account, without contradicting this, reads like the synopsis of a Gothic horror story, but this does not necessarily discredit it, for a prose sketch of "The Ancient Mariner" would be equally unconvincing; nevertheless, Coleridge's inability to finish the poem suggests that it was turning into a work of fancy rather than imagination.

In 1798 Coleridge and Wordsworth left *Lyrical Ballads* with Joseph Cottle and set off with Dorothy Wordsworth for Germany. The Wordsworths settled at Goslar, in the Hartz mountains; Coleridge spent the time at the University of Göttingen, where he was a considerable success and made much of by the professors. Following their return the next year, the two families settled in the Lake District. Coleridge moved his family to Keswick in July 1800, and less than two years later, in April 1802, he wrote the saddest of all his poems, "Dejection." It was published in a shortened version the following October, but in its original and more private form it was addressed to Wordsworth's sister-in-law, Sara Hutchinson. By this time Coleridge's fortunes were at a low ebb. His wife had resented the move to the north and was jealous of the intimate circle of friends at Grasmere, and more especially of Sara Hutchinson, with whom Coleridge had fallen in love. The recriminations and strife of his own home contrasted sadly with the happiness at Grasmere, and his misery was increased by rheumatic illnesses brought on by the damp climate. He now began to seek relief from pain, depression, and guilt in ever increasing doses of opium. He could look from his windows at Greta Hall on the splendor of the mountains, but in vain, for now he discovered that nature could betray the heart that loved her. He had lost all sense of joy and with it the capacity for creative work. It was no good turning to nature, for as he cried out in despair:

I may not hope from outward forms to win
The passion and the life, whose fountains are within.

Nature cannot act on a blank mind; it needs a ready and active cooperation for its healing power to work:

O Lady! we receive but what we give,
And in *our* life alone does Nature live
Our's is her Wedding Garment, our's her Shroud—

To the outside world and often to his friends, Coleridge's life from then on seemed to be a story of decline and even degradation, broken from time to time by achievements that fell below his real capacity. In 1804 he left for Malta, where he acted as private secretary to Sir Alexander Ball, the high commissioner, who thought so highly of him that he persuaded Coleridge to stay on some months beyond the departure date he had set himself. He returned home in 1806, but it was ten weeks before the Wordsworths saw him in October, almost three years since they had parted at Grasmere. His appearance shocked them, as Dorothy Wordsworth reported in a letter to Catherine Clarkson on 6 November 1806:

Never, never did I feel such a shock as at first sight of him. . . . He is utterly changed; and yet sometimes, when he was animated in conversation . . . I saw something of his former self. . . . He did not complain of his health, . . . but that he is ill I am well assured, and must sink if he does not grow more happy. His fatness has quite changed him—it is more like the flesh of a person in dropsy than one in health.

They failed to realize at first that Coleridge had not freed himself from opium and that he was beginning to drink brandy to overcome the depression that followed his use of the drug. Coleridge had decided to live apart from his wife, but it was not until the next year that the separation came about. He now turned once more to lecturing and journalism, the two activities he could always fall back on and that at his best he did superbly well. But he was not at his best in the lectures on poetry he delivered at the beginning of 1808 at the Royal Institution. De Quincey, who attended the lectures and knew something of opium addiction himself, described him in terms curiously like those Coleridge had used for his own Ancient Mariner:

His appearance was generally that of a person struggling with pain and overmastering illness. His lips were baked with feverish heat, and often black in colour; and, in spite of the water which he continued drinking . . . he often seemed to labour under an almost paralytic inability to raise the upper jaw from the lower.

Coleridge had worked for the *Morning Post* as early as 1797, when England was renewing its war against Napoleon. At that time he had been anti-Pitt and antiwar, but when he returned from Germany in 1799 he realized the dangers that could come about if Napoleon were to dominate Europe. It was this change of mind that caused William Hazlitt to charge him with apostasy, but Coleridge maintained that he had been consistent and that it was the revolutionaries who had forsaken their principles. It was at this time that he started to use the signature made up from the initials of his name to rebut the charge of apostasy. "Εστησε signifies—," he wrote to William Sotheby in September 1802, "*He hath stood*—which in these times of apostasy from the principles of Freedom, or of Religion in this country . . . is no unmeaning Signature." On returning from Malta, Coleridge moved to the *Courier*, an evening paper to which he contributed some 140 pieces spread over fourteen years. Reading these pieces one is struck by their liberalism rather than their reactionary opinions. Whether he is writing on the rights of women, the place of Jews in society, child labor in the factories, the cotton operatives of Lancashire, or Quakers and military service, he shows a deep humanitarianism; and on the tortuous questions of Irish independence and Catholic emancipation, he has a far better grasp of the issues than most of his contemporaries. Although these essays were occasional pieces, they were informed by the philosophical approach to politics that he worked out in the *Friend*, the periodical he decided to launch in 1808.

In September of that year Coleridge went to stay with the Wordsworths at Grasmere, and it was here that he drew up the plans for his new periodical. The first number did not appear until June 1809, but it ran until March 1810, when it closed after the publication of the twenty-seventh number. The financial and practical arrangements for the publication of the periodical were complicated and troublesome and would have created problems even if Coleridge had been in better health. As it was, they became too much for him and it was this, coupled with Sara Hutchinson's departure to join one of her brothers in Wales, that brought the venture to an end. Coleridge had dictated the contents to her and most of these were his own contributions. They were the product of an impressive and sustained program of work, much of it involving original thought. But with Sara Hutchinson gone, Coleridge rapidly deteriorated, and it was then that the notorious quarrel with Wordsworth occurred. It came as the culmination of a long worsening in their relationship. Coleridge was a difficult person to have living for so long in their house, but the Wordsworths put up with his apathy, depression, and unsocial habits with forbearance, until at last they could take no more. The break finally came in October 1810, and the effect on Coleridge was catastrophic. The breach was finally closed, but their relationship was not quite the same; and after 1812 Coleridge never again visited the Lakes. He moved to London, spent some time in Bristol and then with his friends the Morgans at Calne, where he dictated *Biographia Literaria* in 1815. He finally settled at the house of Dr. and Mrs. Gillman in Highgate, where he spent the last eighteen years of his life. It was only then that he gained some control of his opium addiction and achieved peace of mind. It was, and still is, easy enough to condemn Coleridge for his lack of will, but in his day laudanum could be bought across the counter of any apothecary's shop and was regarded much as we now regard alcohol, something to be condemned only when it has done its worst, and then with a varying mixture of censure and pity for its victim.

To Hazlitt, to Carlyle, and to many others Coleridge seemed a failure, but there were some, and these more far-sighted even in his own generation, who recognized his genius and the importance of what he was still able to achieve; not merely the brilliance of his youth, but his lasting importance. Chief among them was John Stuart Mill, who in the memorable essay "Coleridge" in the *Westminster Review* in 1840, called him one of the two great "seminal minds" of the century. The other, according to Mill, was Jeremy Bentham, who carried on the eighteenth-century tradition of thought Coleridge sought to overthrow. Mill's tribute is even more impressive because his own philosophy finally came down on the side of Bentham rather than Coleridge.

When Coleridge wrote "Dejection" he faced the ruin of his own personal fortunes, and could find no answer to his problems in the philosophy of Hartley and eighteenth-century empiricism. He had already been reading deeply Plato and the English Platonists of the seventeenth century, and while in Germany he had acquired a knowledge of German philosophy, in particular that of Kant, who, he declared in *Biographia Literaria*, took hold of him "as with a giant's hand." It was at this time of depression and blighted hopes that he opened the box of books he had brought back with him from Germany and began the work of constructing a system of thought that would provide an answer to his intellectual, spiritual, and moral problems. He never completed this task, but what strikes the modern reader who has the hindsight to appreciate his achievement is not the failure but the heroic struggle to wrest, out of personal unhappiness, a faith to meet not only his own needs but also the challenges to religious belief in the century to come.

Coleridge's starting point was his dawning conviction that empiricism was wrong in its view of the mind as a tabula rasa, or an empty receptacle fed by sense experience, in which knowledge is built up by the association of ideas. Writing to his friend Thomas Poole in 1801, he declared:

If the mind be not *passive*, if it be indeed made in God's Image, and that, too, in the sublimest sense—the Image of the *Creator*—there is ground for suspicion, that any system built on the passiveness of the mind must be false as a system.

Coleridge came to believe that the mind is active in perception, turning the raw material of sensation into objects by a power that he called the "primary imagination." Alongside this in Coleridge's thought ran a vitalistic conception of nature that matched his view of the mind as creative in knowledge. As God created the world out of chaos and gave it order and form, so the human mind imposes order and form upon the manifold data of sensory experience. The world was not created by God and left to run in accordance with the laws of Newtonian physics; it is sustained in being by God's spirit and is, to use a phrase of Coleridge's, *natura naturans* and not *natura naturata*. So by analogy, though in a real sense too, the human mind creates the world it perceives. Coleridge described the primary imagination in *Biographia Literaria* as "a repetition in the finite mind of the eternal act of creation in the infinite I AM."

This creative process applies to art as well as to perception. The eighteenth century accounted for the poetic imagination in terms of memory images associated in the mind under the influence of the emotions. Coleridge admitted that some poetry could be explained in this way, but described it as the poetry of fancy, and the poet who composed it, the poet of talent. The poet of genius, on the other hand, is endowed with a creative power that can form from the materials of sensation a new world; one like the everyday world, but reorganized and raised to a higher level of perception. This secondary or poetic imagination creates a world of "seeming objects," a world like the world of our ordinary experience, but one whose features carry a weight of meaning and significance. So the world of *Hamlet* or *King Lear* is not the world of the chronicler or historian and even the characters and events in Shakespeare's history plays are more universal than those we meet in Holinshed's *Chronicles*; they "may be termed ideal realities."

They are not the things themselves, so much as abstracts of the things, which a great mind takes into itself, and there naturalizes them to its own conception.[3]

Coleridge's work on Shakespeare marks the beginning of a new period in the history of Shakespearean criticism and, indeed, of literary studies generally in England. His admiration and understanding of Shakespeare informed the development of his critical theory, and this in turn led to a new and greater discrimination when he came to analyze and discuss the plays. His criticism of Shakespeare is both inductive and deductive. Although Coleridge is rightly called a philosophical critic and some of his Shakespearean criticism echoes the writings of the German critics, it was his own poetic sensibility that formed the threshold to this achievement. Just as his reading of Wordsworth's poems when a young man, he tells us in *Biographia Literaria*, led to his growing conviction that a distinction must be made between fancy and imagination, so his poetic insight into Shakespeare's mind gave him a new appreciation of the plays. It was this rare combination of the poet and philosopher that made Coleridge the great critic he was. It enabled him to recognize, before anyone else, the promise of genius in Wordsworth and to reassess the achievement of Shakespeare, free from neoclassical restrictions.

Unfortunately, much of Coleridge's Shakespearean criticism comes to us in incomplete or corrupt form, from lectures that were often given extemporaneously and for which no accurate or full record remains. When still a young man, Coleridge had lectured in Bristol on political and theological topics, but it was not until 1808, two years after his return from Malta, that he gave, at the invitation of Humphry Davy, the course of lectures on literature at the Royal Institution, which has already been mentioned. Apart from De Quincey's brief account of these we know little, but certainly Shakespeare was included in the syllabus. From November 1811 to January 1812, he gave a series of seventeen lectures

[3]From T. M. Raysor, ed., *Coleridge's Shakespearean Criticism*, vol. II (London, 1930; rev. ed., 1960), p. 125.

in London, which Byron attended. Southey arranged for a shorthand transcript to be made, so that they would not be lost, as those at the Royal Institution had been. Remains of two such reports survived: one by a Mr. Tomalin, who was probably employed by Southey; the other by John Payne Collier, whose literary dishonesty later became well known, but whose account agrees substantially with others, including that of Henry Crabb Robinson. *The Diary, Reminiscences and Correspondence of H. Crabb Robinson* (1869) furnishes us with the commentary of a cultivated man who was friendly to Coleridge, but who had a capacity for objective criticism. According to him the level of the lectures was uneven; at times brilliant and perceptive, but at others digressive and prolix. Later in the year, after some postponements, Coleridge gave a further course of five or six lectures, of which the last at least was devoted to Shakespeare and the contents of which were probably incorporated in the lectures he was to give in Bristol, of which Coleridge's own notes survived. Further lectures followed at the Surrey Institute in 1812–1813, and those at Bristol in 1813–1814. We learn from Robinson's diary that those at the Surrey Institute concentrated on Shakespeare and Milton and that Coleridge's performance was uneven, that he improvised and wandered into digressions. Those at Bristol, according to Joseph Cottle, were a great success and the report of the second lecture in the *Gazette* said that the lecture room was filled to overflowing. The six lectures on Shakespeare in this series were discovered in Bristol much later and published in 1883 in the Bohn edition of Coleridge's *Lectures on Shakespeare*. It was only when he needed money for the university expenses of his son Derwent that he returned to the lecture room and in 1818 gave another course of fourteen lectures on literature, three of which were on Shakespeare. Again, in 1818–1819 he gave some lectures on Shakespeare as a parallel series to a course he gave on the history of philosophy. The philosophy lectures were fully reported and have since been edited by Kathleen Coburn, but the only record of the literature lectures are the brief comments in the *Champion*, which have now been published along with the rest of this Shakespeare material in T. M. Raysor's edition.

In the prospectus to these last lectures Coleridge described Shakespeare as "the great Philosophic Poet." From Ben Jonson to Samuel Johnson all the critics had regarded Shakespeare as a writer whose fancy outran his judgment. Coleridge realized that what the eighteenth century called judgment and fancy were in Shakespeare, two sides of the same coin; that Shakespeare's genius, like Wordsworth's, combined deep feeling and profound thought. This was the focus of all his lectures on Shakespeare, in which, he said, his object was

to prove that in all points from the most important to the most minute, the judgement of Shakespeare is commensurate with his genius—nay, that his genius reveals itself in his judgement, as in its most exalted form.

(*Coleridge's Shakespearean Criticism*, vol. I, p. 114)

The genius and the judgment were united in a power of the imagination that revealed itself not in mechanically contrived plots but in works of art that had an organic life of their own, understood not by their correspondence to outside rules but by the recognition of an inner coherence.

Coleridge was, then, a philosophical critic. He believed that his distinction between the fancy and the imagination

would in its immediate effects furnish a torch of guidance to the philosophical critic; and ultimately to the poet himself. In energetic minds, truth soon changes by domestication into power; and from directing in the discrimination and appraisal of the product, becomes influencive in the production.

(*Biographia Literaria*, ch. 4)

In other words, Coleridge was not concerned with formal criticism, with the application of rules, or the attempt to assess how far a literary work conformed to a norm. Historically speaking, he hastened the end of neoclassicism and the notion that there are fixed literary kinds to which all works must belong. For him the task of the literary critic is to discover how a work of art realizes the laws implicit in its own nature. In every work there is an organic principle giving it shape and form. A work of art is not an assemblage of bits and pieces put together by mechanical rules; it is the embodiment of the creative force of the poet's imagination.

The poet "in ideal perfection," he tells us in chapter 14 of *Biographia Literaria*, "diffuses a tone and spirit of unity," which comes about by

the balance or reconciliation of opposite or discordant qualities; of sameness, with difference; of the general, with the concrete; the idea, with the image; the individual, with the representative; the sense of novelty and freshness, with old and familiar objects; a more than usual state of emotion, with more than usual order; judgement ever awake and steady self-possession, with enthusiasm and feeling profound or vehement.

This chimes in with his earlier argument in chapter 9 that "all symbols of necessity involve an apparent contradiction." They bring together especially the two qualities he admired so much in Wordsworth's poetry: "the fine balance of truth in observing" and "the imaginative faculty in modifying the objects observed."

The creations of the poetic imagination are symbols, and Coleridge maintains in chapter 9 of *Biographia Literaria* that "An IDEA in the *highest* sense of the word cannot be conveyed but by a symbol." To grasp the significance of this one needs to appreciate the distinction he draws between the understanding and the reason. The understanding is that power of the mind which frames concepts, that is concerned with abstract and discursive knowledge derived from the world of perception. The reason goes beyond this; it is the "source and substance of truths above sense" that have their evidence in themselves. The reason is concerned with principles that, although not empirically verifiable, have to be accepted if experience itself is to make sense. It is significant that Coleridge called the secondary imagination "the agent of the reason," for the constructions of the poet's imagination go beyond discursive and conceptual knowledge to explore a world that can be represented only in symbols.

Kant, too, believed that the reason could go beyond the understanding, but he discounted the notion that it could reach more than what he called "phenomenal knowledge" or that it could know the noumena or "things in themselves." Coleridge was reluctant to accept this and even refused to believe that this is what Kant had meant. Coleridge's earlier attraction to Neoplatonism might have led him at this point to elaborate a philosophy which claimed that art can penetrate the world of perception and apprehend the supersensuous. The difference between Kant and the Neoplatonists was that one saw art as the representation of an idea in the artist's mind whereas the others saw it as a representation of reality itself. In places Coleridge flirted with Schelling, who tried to bring these two viewpoints together; but as he carried forward his philosophical speculation he abandoned this line of inquiry, and

the imagination, though it retained its importance, ceased to hold the central place in his thinking.

Coleridge always looked to philosophy to meet the needs of his own personal life, and one of these needs was his longing for forgiveness and the lifting of his sense of guilt over missed opportunities—the waste of his own great gifts, his broken marriage, and his addiction to opium. This is given plangent expression in a brief entry in one of his notebooks:

But O! not what I understand, but what I *am*, must save or crush me!
(*Notebooks of Samuel Taylor Coleridge*, vol. III, item 3354)

And so from the time of *Biographia Literaria* onward he increasingly devoted his energies to the construction of a philosophy of religion in which the will rather than the imagination played the central part.

When Coleridge's *Aids to Reflection* was published in 1825 natural theology was at a low ebb. Of the traditional arguments for God's existence only the argument from design commanded any intellectual conviction, but this was tied to a deism that had been bled white from the wounds inflicted by skeptics like Hume. Revealed religion, which had rested upon the twin authorities of the church and the Bible, had also been weakened; the church was still suffering from the onslaughts of Gibbon, and the authority of the Bible had been undermined by the Higher Criticism from Germany. For Coleridge the truth of Christianity is a living thing, and he develops the existential approach to religious belief he had advanced in the final chapter of *Biographia Literaria*, where he wrote, " . . . we can only *know* by the act of *becoming. Do the will of my Father, and ye shall KNOW I am of God.*"

In *Confessions of an Inquiring Spirit*, published posthumously in 1840, he outflanked the attacks of the German critics on the Scriptures by claiming that the Bible carried the evidence of its own truth. "The Bible and Christianity," he declared, "are their own sufficient evidence." He rejected the crude literalism that thought the Bible had been "dictated" by God, and he distinguished between revelation and inspiration. Not everything the biblical authors wrote is revealed truth, for they were men of their own times with patterns of thought and even prejudices that influenced their narrative; but they were inspired. Every part of Scripture is inspired, but not every part is revealed truth. We can only leap what Lessing had called "the wide and ugly ditch" between the events of the Gospel narrative and the claims of the evangelists by an act of faith that starts with a recognition of our own need. Our realization of the weakness of our wills and inability to meet the demands of a moral imperative are met in the Bible with the promise of forgiveness and grace. The two come together as a key fits a lock.

Coleridge's vitalistic view of nature was matched by his conviction that society is best understood in organic rather than atomistic terms. He had started by supporting the French Revolution, but changed his mind, though not his principles, when it turned into a tyranny. He came to believe that it was wiser to change institutions than to overthrow them, for society is not a machine to be scrapped at will for a new model, but something with a life of its own. This was also Edmund Burke's reaction to eighteenth-century notions, but Coleridge goes beyond Burke in his Christian and Platonic theory of the state. The state should act not merely as a referee in the conflict of self-interests between individuals and groups, nor simply to formulate a contract between government and the governed. It has a more positive role; it should encourage and should provide opportunities for the self-fulfillment of all members of society. In *On the Constitution of the Church and State* (1830), he discerned two opposed principles in society, one of progression and the other of permanence, and he saw them embodied in his own day in the landed classes and the commercial interests. The balance of power today may be different, but the analysis itself remains valid. Coleridge also recognized a mediating and balancing force in society, embodied in what he called the "clerisy" and consisting of the educators, especially the clergy and teachers. This modern version of Plato's Guardians he termed a National Church, a body that embraced but was not identical with the Church of England. Its duty was

to preserve the stores, to guard the treasures of past civilization, and thus to bind the present with the past; to perfect and add to the same, and thus to connect the present with the future.

(ch. 5)

When Coleridge settled with the Gillmans at Highgate, the turbulence of his earlier years was over. He was never free of dependence upon opium, but his use was controlled and limited. He became the center of an admiring circle of disciples who, from 1822 on, visited Highgate for their "Thursday-evening class."

This was a group of five or six young men to whom Coleridge lectured on philosophy. But there were less formal gatherings that included the Gillmans and old friends such as Lamb, as well as younger friends like Joseph Henry Green, who was to become his literary executor, and John Sterling, who was to transmit Coleridge's thought to F. D. Maurice and J. C. Hare, the leaders of the Broad Church movement. Hazlitt's tribute to Coleridge's power as a talker has already been quoted, and he was still able to hold an audience spellbound by his eloquence. Even as a young man he was better as a monologuist than as a conversationalist, and Caroline Fox recounts in her *Journal* how (probably at one of the Highgate evenings) Coleridge appealed to Lamb with the question "You have heard me preach, I think?", to be met with the reply "I have never heard you do anything else." At the end this habit of soliloquizing became a little disconcerting to the visitors who made their way to Highgate. Ralph Waldo Emerson, who was one of several Americans to visit him, recalled in his *English Traits* (1856) how

. . . the visit was rather a spectacle than a conversation, of no use beyond the satisfaction of my curiosity. He was old and pre-occupied, and could not bend to a new companion and think with him.

But that was in 1833, at the end of Coleridge's life. Before that, in 1828, he and Wordsworth had managed a visit to the Continent that lasted a few weeks, though both men seemed very old for such an expedition. There were disappointments, some of them severe, as when his son Hartley failed to have his Oriel fellowship renewed. There was a sadness that flowed from his hopeless love for Sara Hutchinson, whom he saw only a few times after they parted in 1810, but who made several visits in 1834 when she knew his death was near. Highgate was a safe harbor after the stormy seas he had crossed. Like the wedding guest in his own "Ancient Mariner" he found himself "a sadder and a wiser man" at the end of his voyage. Although he had not thought of his great poem in autobiographical terms when he wrote it, he came increasingly to see it as a prophecy of his own life, and it was in his mind when he composed the epitaph that adorns his grave in Highgate Church. When he wrote the following lines, which form part of that epitaph, he was thinking not of his reputation but of his immortal destiny; and yet in one sense at least his prayer has been answered, for his reputation today is very much alive.

Beneath this sod
A poet lies, or that which once seem'd he.
O, lift one thought in prayer for S.T.C.;
That he who many a year with toil of breath
Found death in life, may here find life in death!

SELECTED BIBLIOGRAPHY

Detailed bibliographical information can also be found in the appropriate volumes of *The New Cambridge Bibliography of English Literature* and *The Oxford History of English Literature*.

I. BIBLIOGRAPHY. T. J. Wise, *A Bibliography of the Writings in Prose and Verse* (London, 1913; supp., 1919), also reiss. with Coleridgeana (London, 1970); T. J. Wise, *Two Lake Poets: A Catalogue of Printed Books, Manuscripts and Autograph Letters by W. Wordsworth and S. T. Coleridge* (London, 1927), a section of the Ashley Library in the British Museum; V. W. Kennedy and M. N. Barton, *Samuel Taylor Coleridge: A Selected Bibliography of the Best Available Editions of His Writings, of Biographies and Criticisms of Him, and of References Showing His Relations with Contemporaries* (Baltimore, 1935), contains a useful list of critical and biographical studies; R. Haven, J. Haven, and M. Adams, eds., *Samuel Taylor Coleridge: An Annotated Bibliography of Criticism and Scholarship*, vol. I, *1793–1899* (Boston, 1976), vol. II will bring this to 1975; J. D. Caskey and M. M. Stapper, eds., *Samuel Taylor Coleridge: A Selective Bibliography of Criticism, 1935–1977* (Westport, Conn., 1977).

II. COLLECTED WORKS. The first collected ed. of the works of Coleridge is in progress under the general editorship of K. H. Coburn (see below). Until this is finished the only complete ed. is W. Shedd, ed., *The Complete Works of Samuel Taylor Coleridge*, 7 vols. (New York, 1853).

The Poetical Works, 3 vols. (London, 1828; 2nd ed., 1829; rev. ed., 1834), published originally by W. Pickering in an ed. of 500 copies, includes the dramas *Wallenstein, Remorse*, and *Zapolya*—2nd ed. is the basis of J. D. Campbell's ed. and E. H. Coleridge used the rev. ed.; *The Poetical Works of Coleridge, Shelley and Keats* (Paris, 1829); D. Coleridge, ed., *The Dramatic Works* (London, 1852); D. and S. Coleridge, eds., *Poems* (London, 1852; 1870), the latter includes an intro. essay by D. Coleridge and repr. the 1798 text of "The Ancient Mariner"; W. M. Rossetti, ed., *The Poetical Works* (London, 1872), with a critical memoir by Rossetti; R. H. Shepherd, ed., *The Poetical and Dramatic Works*, 4 vols. (London, 1877); J. D. Campbell, ed., *The Poetical Works* (London, 1893), contains valuable explanatory notes and biography; J. D. Campbell and W. H. White, eds., *Coleridge's Poems. A Facsimile Reproduction of Proofs and MSS* (London, 1899).

E. H. Coleridge, ed., *The Complete Poetical Works*, 2 vols. (Oxford, 1912), the definitive ed. of the poems, the only complete text, with full textual and biographical notes, also repr. in 1 vol., with minor omissions; H. W. Garrod, ed., *Coleridge: Poetry and Prose. With Essays by Hazlitt, Jeffrey, De Quincey, Carlyle, and Others* (Oxford, 1925), a substantial selection; S. Potter, ed., *Coleridge: Select Poetry and Prose* (London, 1933); K. H. Coburn, *Inquiring Spirit: A New Presentation of Coleridge from His Published and Unpublished Prose Writings* (London, 1951); K. Raine, comp., *Poems and Prose* (London, 1957), with an intro. by Raine; J. Beer, ed., *Poems* (London, 1963; 1974), the latter has a new intro.; K. H. Coburn, gen. ed., *Collected Works* (London, 1969–   ), in progress, will include 16 titles in 22 vols. plus an index vol.; vol. I: L. Patton and P. Mann, eds., *Lectures, 1795*, on politics and religion; vol. II: L. Patton, ed., *The Watchman*; vol. III (in 3 pts.): D. V. Erdman, ed., *Essays on His Times*; vol. IV (in 2 pts.): B. E. Rooke, ed., *The Friend*; vol. VI: R. J. White, ed., *Lay Sermons*; vol. X: J. Colmer, ed., *On the Constitution of the Church and State*.

III. LETTERS. T. Allsop, ed., *Letters, Conversations and Recollections of S. T. Coleridge*, 2 vols. (London, 1836; 2nd ed., 1858; 3rd ed., 1864); *Unpublished Letters from Samuel Taylor Coleridge to the Rev. John Prior Estlin, Communicated by H. A. Bright* (London, 1884); W. Knight, ed., *Memorials of Coleorton*, 2 vols. (Edinburgh, 1887), letters to Sir George and Lady Beaumont; *Letters from the Lake Poets to Daniel Stuart* (London, 1889); A. H. Japp, ed., *De Quincey Memorials . . . with Communications from Coleridge* [and others], 2 vols. (London, 1891); E. H. Coleridge, ed., *Letters*, 2 vols. (London, 1895); R. B. Litchfield, *Tom Wedgwood: The First Photographer* (London, 1903), contains Coleridge's letters to the Wedgwoods; E. Betham, *A House of Letters* (London, 1905), contains Coleridge's letters to Matilda Betham; A. Turnbull, ed., *Biographia Epistolaris: Being the Biographical Supplement of Coleridge's Biographia Literaria with Additional Letters*, 2 vols. (London, 1911); E. L. Griggs, ed., *Unpublished Letters, Including Certain Letters Republished from Original Sources*, 2 vols. (London, 1932); S. Potter, ed., *A Minnow Among Tritons* (London, 1936), Mrs. Coleridge's letters to Thomas Poole, 1799–1834; M. K. Joseph, *Charles Aders . . . with Some Unpublished Letters by S. T. Coleridge* (Auckland, 1953); E. L. Griggs, ed., *Collected Letters, 1785–1834*, 6 vols. (Oxford, 1956–1971).

IV. SEPARATE WORKS IN VERSE. *The Fall of Robespierre: An Historic Drama* (Cambridge, 1794), Act I by Coleridge, Acts II and III by R. Southey; *Ode on the Departing Year* (Bristol, 1796); *Poems on Various Subjects* (Bristol, 1796), includes poems by C. Lamb and C. Lloyd; *Fears in Solitude . . . To Which Are Added "France, an Ode" and "Frost at Midnight"* (London, 1798); *Lyrical Ballads* (Bristol, 1798; 2 vols., London, 1800), written with Wordsworth, the 1800 ed. includes changes in Coleridge's contribution and a rev. of "The Ancient Mariner"; in R. L. Brett and A. R. Jones, eds. (London, 1963; rev. ed., 1965); *The Piccolomini, or,*

The First Part of Wallenstein: A Drama in Five Acts. The Death of Wallenstein: A Tragedy in Five Acts (London, 1800), a trans. of Schiller's *Die Piccolomini* and *Wallenstein's Tod; Remorse: A Tragedy in Five Acts* (London, 1813); *Christabel. Kubla Khan: A Vision. The Pains of Sleep* (London, 1816); *Sibylline Leaves: A Collection of Poems* (London, 1817); *Zapolya: A Christmas Tale, in Two Parts* (London, 1817); *The Devil's Walk: A Poem* (London, 1830), written with Southey, first published anonymously in the *Morning Post* in 1799, later enlarged by Southey.

V. Separate Works in Prose. *Conciones ad Populum, or, Addresses to the People* (Bristol, 1795); *A Moral and Political Lecture* (Bristol, 1795); *The Plot Discovered, or, An Address to the People Against Ministerial Treason* (Bristol, 1795); *The Watchman*, 10 numbers (1796); *The Friend: A Literary, Moral and Political Weekly Paper*, 28 numbers (1809–1810), also reiss. with supplementary matter (1812) and with new matter, 3 vols. (London, 1818); R. Southey, ed., *Omniana, or Horae Otiosiores*, 2 vols. (London, 1812), with many articles by Coleridge; *The Statesman's Manual, or, The Bible the Best Guide to Political Skill and Foresight: A Lay Sermon* (London, 1816); *Biographia Literaria, or, Biographical Sketches of My Literary Life and Opinions*, 2 vols. (London, 1817), the best ed. is J. Shawcross, ed., 2 vols. (Oxford, 1907), also recommended is G. Watson, ed. (London, 1956); *"Blessed Are Ye That Sow Beside All Waters": A Lay Sermon* (London, 1817); *Treatise on Method* (London, 1818), first published as *General Introduction [to the Encyclopaedia Metropolitana], or, Preliminary Treatise on Method*—definitive ed. is A. D. Snyder, ed. (London, 1934); *Aids to Reflection in the Formation of a Manly Character* (London, 1825); *On the Constitution of the Church and State* (London, 1830); H. N. Coleridge, ed., *Specimens of the Table Talk of the Late Samuel Taylor Coleridge*, 2 vols. (London, 1835); H. N. Coleridge, ed., *The Literary Remains*, 4 vols. (London, 1836–1839).

Confessions of an Inquiring Spirit (London, 1840; 2nd ed., 1849; 3rd ed., 1853; reiss., 1956, 1971); S. B. Watson, ed., *Hints Towards the Formation of a More Comprehensive Theory of Life* (London, 1848); S. Coleridge, ed., *Essays on His Own Times: Forming a Second Series of "The Friend,"* 3 vols. (London, 1850); *Notes on English Divines* (London, 1853); D. Coleridge, ed., *Notes Theological, Political and Miscellaneous* (London, 1853), partly repr. from *The Literary Remains*, the rest new; J. P. Collier, ed., *Seven Lectures on Shakespeare and Milton* (London, 1856), edited from Collier's shorthand notes; T. Ashe, ed., *Lectures and Notes on Shakespeare and Other English Poets* (London, 1883), from *The Literary Remains* with Collier's notes and reports of lectures; T. Ashe, ed., *Miscellanies, Aesthetic and Literary; to Which Is Added the Theory of Life* (London, 1885); W. F. Taylor, ed., *Critical Annotations: Being Marginal Notes Inscribed in Volumes Formerly in the Possession of Coleridge* (Harrow, 1889);

E. H. Coleridge, ed., *Anima Poetae: From the Unpublished Notebooks* (London, 1895); J. W. Mackail, ed., *Coleridge's Literary Criticism* (London, 1908); T. M. Raysor, ed., *Coleridge's Shakespearean Criticism*, 2 vols. (London, 1930; 2nd ed., 1960); R. R. Brinkley, ed., *Coleridge on the Seventeenth Century* (Durham, N. C. 1935), includes previously unpublished material; T. M. Raysor, ed., *Coleridge's Miscellaneous Criticism* (London, 1936); K. H. Coburn, ed., *The Philosophical Lectures of S. T. Coleridge, Hitherto Unpublished* (London, 1949); K. H. Coburn, ed., *The Notebooks* (London, 1957–   ), vol. I: *1794–1804* (1957); vol. II: *1804–1808* (1961); vol. III: *1808–1819* (1973); each vol. in 2 pts., 5 vols. in 10 pts. plus index vol. are projected.

VI. Biographical and Critical Studies. W. Hazlitt, *Lectures on the English Poets* (London, 1818; 2nd ed., 1819; 3rd ed., with additional material, 1841); C. Lamb, *Essays of Elia* (London, 1822); W. Hazlitt, *The Spirit of the Age, or, Contemporary Portraits* (London, 1825), in the 2nd ed. (1835) the material on Coleridge was amplified; T. Allsop, ed., *Letters, Conversations and Recollections of S. T. Coleridge*, 2 vols. (London, 1836); J. Cottle, *Early Recollections, Chiefly Relating to the Late Samuel Taylor Coleridge, During His Long Residence in Bristol*, 2 vols. (London, 1837), rev. in 1 vol. as *Reminiscences of S. T. Coleridge and R. Southey* (London, 1847; reiss. 1970); J. Gillman, *The Life of Samuel Taylor Coleridge* (London, 1838); J. S. Mill, "Coleridge," in *Westminster Review*, vol. XXXIII (March 1840), repr. in *Dissertations and Discussions* (London, 1857); *The Autobiography of Leigh Hunt, with Reminiscences of Friends*, 3 vols. (London, 1850), best ed. by J. Morpurgo (London, 1949); J. S. Mill, *Dissertations and Discussions: Political, Philosophical and Historical*, 4 vols. (London, 1859–1875); J. H. Green, *Spiritual Philosophy, Founded on the Teaching of S. T. Coleridge*, J. Simon, ed., 2 vols. (London, 1865); H. Crabb Robinson, *Diary, Reminiscences and Correspondence*, T. Sadler, ed., 3 vols. (London, 1869); *Memoir and Letters of Sara Coleridge, Edited by Her Daughter* [S. Coleridge], 2 vols. (London, 1873); A. C. Swinburne, *Essays and Studies* (London, 1875); H. D. Traill, *Coleridge* (London, 1884), in the English Men of Letters series; T. H. H. Caine, *Life of Samuel Taylor Coleridge* (London, 1887), with a bibliography by J. P. Anderson; Mrs. H. Sandford, *Thomas Poole and His Friends*, 2 vols. (London, 1888), a valuable biographical source book; W. Pater, *Appreciations* (London, 1889).

J. D. Campbell, *Samuel Taylor Coleridge: A Narrative of the Events of His Life* (London, 1894); A. W. Gillman, *The Gillmans of Highgate, with Letters from S. T. Coleridge etc.* (London, 1895); T. De Quincey, *Reminiscences of the English Lake Poets* (London, 1907), later selections include E. Sackville-West, ed. (London, 1948) and D. Wright, ed. (London, 1970); J. M. Murry, *Aspects of Criticism* (London, 1920); E. J. Morley, ed., *Blake, Coleridge, Wordsworth, Lamb, etc.: Selections from Crabb*

Robinson's Remains (London, 1922); H. W. Garrod, *The Profession of Poetry* (Oxford, 1924; repr. with other lectures, 1929, 1970); L. E. Watson, *Coleridge at Highgate* (London, 1925); J. L. Lowes, *The Road to Xanadu* (London, 1927; enl. ed., 1930), a study of the sources of Coleridge's poetic inspiration; E. J. Morley, ed., *Correspondence with the Wordsworth Circle*, 2 vols. (Oxford, 1927); J. H. Muirhead, *Coleridge as Philosopher* (London, 1930); M. H. Abrams, *The Milk of Paradise* (Cambridge, Mass., 1934), a study of opium dreams and their bearing on the poetry of Coleridge (among other subjects); E. Blunden and E. L. Griggs, eds., *Coleridge: Studies by Several Hands* (London, 1934), commemorating the centenary of Coleridge's death; I. A. Richards, *Coleridge on Imagination* (London, 1934; 2nd ed., 1955; 3rd ed., 1960); S. Potter, *Coleridge and S.T.C.* (London, 1935); E. K. Chambers, *S. T. Coleridge: A Biographical Study* (Oxford, 1938); L. Hanson, *The Life of S. T. Coleridge* (London, 1938); E. L. Griggs, ed., *Wordsworth and Coleridge: Studies in Honor of G. M. Harper* (Princeton, N. J., 1939); A. H. Nethercott, *The Road to Tryermaine* (Chicago, 1939; repr. New York, 1962); G. McKenzie, *Organic Unity in Coleridge* (Berkeley, 1939).

B. Willey, *Coleridge on Imagination and Fancy* (London, 1946), the Warton Lecture before the British Academy, 1946; W. L. Kennedy, *The English Heritage of Coleridge of Bristol* (New Haven, Conn., 1947); H. Read, *Coleridge as Critic* (London, 1949); T. M. Raysor, ed., *The English Romantic Poets: A Review of Research* (New York, 1950); H. House, *Coleridge* (London, 1953), the Clark Lectures at Cambridge, 1951–1952; H. M. Margoliouth, *Wordsworth and Coleridge, 1795–1834* (London, 1953); H. Read, *The True Voice of Feeling: Studies in English Romantic Poetry* (London, 1953); G. Whalley, *Coleridge and Sara Hutchinson and the Asra Poems* (London, 1955); J. V. Baker, ed., *The Sacred River: Coleridge's Theory of the Imagination* (Baton Rouge, La., 1957); W. F. Kennedy, *Humanist Versus Economist: The Economic Thought of Samuel Taylor Coleridge* (Berkeley–Los Angeles, 1958); J. B. Beer, *Coleridge the Visionary* (London, 1959); J. A. Colmer, *Coleridge: Critic of Society* (Oxford, 1959); I. A. Richards, *Coleridge's Minor Poems: A Lecture* (Missoula, Mont., 1960); M. Suther, *The Dark Night of Samuel Taylor Coleridge* (New York, 1960); J. D. Boulger, *Coleridge as Religious Thinker* (New Haven, Conn., 1961); C. R. Woodring, *Politics in the Poetry of Coleridge* (Madison, Wis., 1961); R. H. Fogle, *The Idea of Coleridge's Criticism* (Berkeley–Los Angeles, 1962); P. Deschamps, *La Formation de la pensée de Coleridge, 1772–1804* (Paris, 1963); M. F. Schultz, *The Poetic Voices of Coleridge* (Detroit, 1964).

J. A. Appleyard, *Coleridge's Philosophy of Literature* (Cambridge, Mass., 1965); M. Suther, *Visions of Xanadu* (New York–London, 1965); D. P. Calleo, *Coleridge and the Idea of the Modern State* (New Haven, Conn.–London, 1966); G. G. Watson, *Coleridge the Poet* (London, 1966); P. M. Adair, *The Waking Dream: A Study of Coleridge's Poetry* (London, 1967); M. H. Coburn, ed., *Coleridge: A Collection of Critical Essays* (Englewood Cliffs, N. J., 1967); G. Yarlott, *Coleridge and the Abyssinian Maid* (London, 1967); W. Walsh, *Coleridge: The Work and the Relevance* (London, 1967); A. C. Hayter, *Opium and the Romantic Imagination* (London, 1968); J. R. Barth, *Coleridge and Christian Doctrine* (Cambridge, Mass., 1969); W. J. Bate, *Coleridge* (London, 1969); R. L. Brett, *Fancy and Imagination* (London, 1969); G. N. Giordano-Orsini, *Coleridge and German Idealism: A Study in the History of Philosophy. With Unpublished Materials from Coleridge's Manuscripts* (Carbondale, Pa., 1969); J. R. de J. Jackson, *Method and Imagination in Coleridge's Criticism* (London, 1969); T. MacFarland, *Coleridge and the Pantheist Tradition* (Oxford, 1969); D. Sultana, *Samuel Taylor Coleridge in Malta and Italy* (Oxford, 1969); A. S. Byatt, *Wordsworth and Coleridge in Their Time* (London, 1970); J. R. de J. Jackson, ed., *Coleridge: The Critical Heritage* (London, 1970); B. Lawrence, *Coleridge and Wordsworth in Somerset* (Newton Abbot, 1970); A. T. S. Prickett, *Coleridge and Wordsworth: The Poetry of Growth* (Cambridge, 1970); W. Heath, *Wordsworth and Coleridge: A Study of Their Literary Relations in 1801–1802* (Oxford, 1970); R. L. Brett, ed., *S. T. Coleridge* (London, 1971), a collection of critical essays with a useful bibliography by G. Whalley; O. Barfield, *What Coleridge Thought* (London, 1972); N. Fruman, *Coleridge the Damaged Archangel* (London, 1972); G. H. Hartman, ed., *New Perspectives on Coleridge and Wordsworth* (London–New York, 1972); B. Willey, *Samuel Taylor Coleridge* (London, 1972); M. M. Badawi, *Coleridge: Critic of Shakespeare* (Cambridge, 1973); A. R. Jones and W. Tydeman, eds., *"The Ancient Mariner" and Other Poems; A Casebook* (London, 1973); J. B. Beer, ed., *Coleridge's Variety: Bicentenary Studies* (London, 1974); K. H. Coburn, *The Self-Conscious Imagination: A Study of the Coleridge Notebooks in Celebration of the Bicentenary of His Birth* (London, 1974); A. J. Harding, *Coleridge and the Idea of Love* (London, 1974); R. Parker, *Coleridge's Meditative Art* (Ithaca, N. Y.–London, 1975); S. Prickett, *Romanticism and Religion: The Tradition of Coleridge and Wordsworth in the Victorian Church* (Cambridge, 1976); J. R. Barth, *The Symbolic Imagination: Coleridge and the Romantic Tradition* (Princeton, N. J., 1977); J. B. Beer, *Coleridge's Poetic Intelligence* (London, 1977); K. H. Coburn, *In Pursuit of Coleridge* (London, 1977); L. S. Lockridge, *Coleridge the Moralist* (Ithaca, N. Y., 1977); G. Dekker, *Coleridge and the Literature of Sensibility* (London, 1978); J. S. Hill, ed., *Imagination in Coleridge* (London, 1978).

ROBERT SOUTHEY

(1774-1843)

Geoffrey Carnall

I

ROBERT SOUTHEY saw himself as a dominating figure in the England of his day. He was the author of several major poems, and an intrepid innovator in his subjects and his meters. His literary achievement had been publicly recognized when he was made poet laureate—the king's own poet. As a prominent contributor to the *Quarterly Review*, he exercised a powerful influence on public life. As a historian, he was a pioneer in recording the development of the vast new nation of Brazil. In his *History of the Peninsular War*, he celebrated what seemed to him the most inspiriting event of his time—the Spaniards' general and spontaneous insurrection against the mighty military power of Napoleon's France.

Southey shared to the full in that restless energy so characteristic of the Napoleonic era. It was a time of grandiose political and philosophical systems, and he was prolific in plans for treatises, histories, and epic poems. The results were often disappointing, and Southey would certainly have been disappointed at the relatively small part later assigned to him in English literary history. His most memorable work is seldom even thought of as his: few people associate "The Story of the Three Bears" with his name. His *Life of Nelson* is still being reprinted, but it is for the great admiral's sake, not Southey's. "The Battle of Blenheim" and "The Inchcape Rock" have almost acquired the anonymity of folklore.

If Southey is remembered as a man, it is as the ridiculous figure in Lord Byron's *Vision of Judgment*. He is still a stock example (partly because of his association with William Wordsworth and Samuel Taylor Coleridge) of the ardent young reformer who is corrupted and turns conservative. Social historians, though, sometimes honor him as an early critic of the evils that the new factory system brought to early nineteenth-century Britain. He made a notable protest against the commercial spirit,

regarding it as deeply injurious to the kindly and generous feelings of human nature. Yet his protests are no longer read, as those of Thomas Carlyle and Charles Dickens are.

Southey was endowed with a strong sensibility— too strong, in fact. His senses, he confessed, were perilously acute: "impressions sink into me too deeply. . . . I fly from one thing to another, each new train of thought neutralizing, as it were, the last." Such a method of writing would seem to guarantee a failure to achieve fully satisfactory expression. Yet his work constantly betrays the feelings that he found almost unendurable. This is particularly true of his copious and unguarded correspondence; but from nearly all his work the attentive reader will learn something of the stresses under which men lived in his time, a time of exceptionally rapid social change and insecurity.

II

SOUTHEY was born in Bristol on 12 August 1774. He came from a family of farmers and tradespeople; his father was a linen draper. Much of his childhood was spent under the capricious care of Miss Tyler, a maiden aunt with some pretensions to gentility. She utterly dominated his mother: "Never," Southey wrote later, "did I know one person so entirely subjected by another." This early experience of domestic despotism probably helped to create the rather bleak view of life that casts a shadow over nearly all his writings. He was a sensitive child, and his family enjoyed making him cry by forcing him to listen to sad songs and dismal stories. Southey reacted against this overmastering sensibility by developing military ambitions. At the age of nine, he read William Shakespeare's history plays, concluded that England was once again on the brink of civil war, and made up his mind to take a leading part in the conflict. In

58

order to enlist followers, he set up as an interpreter of dreams, referring his schoolfellows' dreams to the coming great civil wars and the appearance of a very great man—meaning himself.

The stratagem was ingenious, but apparently did not work. His literary ambitions developed later, and were much more successful. Being an enthusiastic admirer of Edmund Spenser's *Faerie Queene*, Southey decided to finish the poem. Before he was fifteen, he had sketched a plan based on every hint he could gather from the six books that Spenser himself had completed. Southey actually wrote three cantos of this projected continuation. Nothing, he said, ever gave him so much delight as the dream of what he intended to do in it.

The predominant impulse in this and other early projects seems to have been one of constructing a world of his own, in which the menacing forces outside him could be contended with on terms more advantageous than everyday life often allowed. The appeal of the remote and exotic is especially apparent in the plan he formed to illustrate various national mythologies, each with its own heroic poem. His later epics were in part a fulfillment of this scheme.

Southey was fifteen when the French Revolution began, and he soon became a passionate sympathizer with the revolutionary cause. He was expelled from Westminster School for writing an attack on flogging (he proved it to be an invention of the Devil). Later, at Balliol College, Oxford, he felt himself increasingly at odds with the course of life arranged for him. His uncle, the Reverend Herbert Hill, who was chaplain to the British trading station at Lisbon, wanted his nephew to become a clergyman. But Southey had little relish for this. Modern geology and Edward Gibbon's history had undermined his belief in the Bible. As a democrat he objected to a system that gave bishops incomes of £10,000 a year. As an enthusiastic reader of Johann Wolfgang von Goethe's *Werther*, he was inclined to question the ethical doctrines of Christianity. It is true that he learned to reject the sensibility of *Werther* for the fortitude and self-control of stoicism as interpreted by Epictetus, but this was not enough to overcome his distaste for the church. He could see only one way out; he must emigrate.

The idea of emigration took a firm shape in 1794, when he met Coleridge, then an undergraduate at Cambridge. Between them they evolved a plan for a settlement in America (first in Kentucky, and later in Pennsylvania), to be run on egalitarian, "pantisocratic" principles. Although the plan came to nothing, for a time it had an intoxicating effect on both men. They lived in Bristol, and took a prominent part in radical agitation there. They gave lectures and wrote propagandist pieces. The one that became most famous was Southey's poetic play about Wat Tyler. This leader of the Peasants' Revolt in the fourteenth century had become a type of the spirit of radical reform. Southey affected to regard him as an ancestor: Was not his genteel aunt a Miss Tyler? Inspired by this personal association, he denounced the aristocrats with uninhibited enjoyment:

> Be he villain, be he fool,
> Still to hold despotic rule,
> Trampling on his slaves with scorn!
> This is to be nobly born.[1]
> (vol. II, p. 34)

As the prospect of emigration receded, Southey's revolutionary ardor cooled. It no longer seemed so difficult to make a living in England. A school friend, Charles Wynn, gave him an annuity; and the Bristol bookseller Joseph Cottle, who later published the *Lyrical Ballads* of Wordsworth and Coleridge, issued a handsome edition of Southey's first epic poem, *Joan of Arc*. This soon gained him a considerable literary reputation. After some desultory efforts to study law, he gradually settled into the life of a professional man of letters, a vocation that was confirmed when, in 1803, he went to live at Greta Hall, Keswick, in the Lake District. Coleridge was already staying there. The scheme of pantisocracy had included matrimonial arrangements for those taking part, and Southey had persuaded Coleridge that Sarah Fricker, a sister of Southey's wife, Edith, would be a suitable mate for him. She proved to be as unsuitable as could well be imagined, but in spite of this the two families formed the nucleus of a remarkable household, of which Southey's letters give a pleasant picture.

Before this final settlement in Keswick, Southey spent two considerable periods with his uncle in Portugal, where he developed his interest in Portuguese and Spanish history and literature, subjects on which he became the leading English authority. His

[1] All quotations except those from *Joan of Arc* are from *The Poetical Works of Robert Southey, Collected by Himself*, 10 vols. (London, 1837–1838).

first impressions of Portugal were unfavorable. He found the squalid poverty repulsive, and had little good to say about the Roman Catholic church. Still, he preferred Catholicism to the Calvinistic forms of Protestantism he knew in England, because it did more to kindle and satisfy the feelings and the imagination:

Bad indeed must the sinner be who will not be burnt white at last! Every prayer at a crucifix helps him—and a Mass on purpose is a fine *shove* towards Paradise. It is a superstition of hope.

(MS letter to Charles Danvers, 13 September 1800)

The power lent by Catholic belief, in alliance with the strong national feelings of the people, enabled the Spaniards to resist the French after the invasion of 1808. Southey heard country people talk of their old heroes, and "witnessed the passionate transfiguration which a Spaniard underwent when recurring from the remembrance of those times to his own." In the chivalric literature of Spain, much of which Southey translated into English, it was possible to discover an antidote to the sense of weakness that he found so difficult to tolerate. As the Cid smote down his enemies, so Southey delighted to trample on his.

He never found any difficulty in provoking opposition. *Joan of Arc* is a calculatedly controversial poem: English readers were not used to seeing their heroic King Henry V consigned to hell. His shorter poems and ballads, like Wordsworth's, are particularly concerned with the common people and their sufferings. In his "Botany Bay Eclogues" Southey enters sympathetically into the condition of convicts who were transported to Australia. He exploits popular traditions, and deliberately avoids sophistication. As the Scots critic Francis Jeffrey remarked, the new sect of poets had a "perverted taste for simplicity" and a "splenetic and idle discontent with the institutions of society." Southey's most scoffed at poems were his experiments in meters borrowed from Greek and Latin poetry. The trouble was that he wrote about subjects his readers found ludicrously unclassical—beggars and screaming babies.

Thus, although Southey was no longer the young revolutionary of 1794, he was still seen by the public as an unorthodox poet, hostile to the established order of things. After 1810, though, he acquired a very different reputation. He became a warm partisan of public order, an outspoken Tory. His views

changed in the first instance because of political controversies over the Peninsular War. When the Spaniards rose against the French in 1808, the news was enthusiastically welcomed in Britain, eager for new allies in the long and exhausting war with France. Southey's joy was unbounded. All that the chivalry of Spain had meant to his imagination seemed now to be realized in political action. But as the Spanish campaign dragged on, and Napoleon continued to dominate Europe, a mood of war-weariness began to increase in Britain. The opposition parties took a gloomy view of the war in Spain, and Southey came to feel that only the conservative government of Spencer Perceval could be relied on to back the Spaniards. Hence Wat Tyler's apologist was converted to support for the unreformed British constitution, which may have kept power in the hands of a few rich men but at least ensured a strong administration. Any reform that gave more influence to the middle and lower classes would be intolerable.

It was not only the war that made Southey conservative. He was also alarmed at the increasingly turbulent state of British politics. The industrial system had shattered traditional social loyalties. It had created a society that was callous and irresponsible. He was appalled by the conditions of life in towns like Birmingham and Manchester, and especially by the employment of children in factories. "I thought," he wrote in his *Letters from England*, "that if Dante had peopled one of his hells with children, here was a scene worthy to have supplied him with new images of torment." Prosperity was founded on the brutalization of the great mass of the people. As he put it in the *Quarterly Review* (vol.51, March 1834, p.279), the modern industrial system

carries in itself the sure cause of its own terrible destruction. That physical force which it has brought together as an instrument of lucration—a part of its machinery—will one day explode under high pressure.

There would be a terrible war of the poor against the rich. With serious riots in London in 1810, the Luddite machine-breaking in some factory areas in 1812, and above all, in the same year, the assassination of Spencer Perceval, the prime minister, it looked as though violent revolution were an immediate danger. Southey's own radicalism had been violent, and he detected the same mood in the reform movement as a whole. Many well-disposed friends of order were not, he felt, sufficiently disturbed by the trend of events. From his retreat in Keswick, Southey sought to sound the alarm, and to point out the means of reforming society so that the pressures making for revolution could be contained and removed.

From its first number in 1809, Southey had been a leading contributor to the *Quarterly Review*, a journal closely associated with Perceval's administration. In it he expounded his views on the measures necessary to save the country. Strong government was the first need: troublemakers should be transported to Australia, where they would have less scope for mischief. But his articles were not mere pleas for repression. He recognized that social inequality like that found in England was utterly wrong. He sympathized with the pioneering socialist plans of Robert Owen, seeing in them a practical application of the ideals of pantisocracy, to which he still felt a strong attachment. He even commended the revolutionary society of "Spencean philanthropists," insofar as they aimed at building experimental socialist communities. His main interests, though, were in universal education (on sound and law-abiding principles) and in assisted emigration.

Southey's services to public order and social reform were not confined to journalism. In 1813 he agreed to accept the office of poet laureate. The duties of this office consisted mainly in supplying poems for royal weddings and other court occasions; and Southey's immediate predecessor, Henry James Pye, had been a poet of very modest talents. For a reputable man of letters it required much boldness to undertake the work at all. But Southey had conceived the idea of using his laureate poems to strengthen the spirit of order and true patriotism. The poet laureate was to give utterance to the soul of the nation. He wrote odes to keep up the people's will to win the war, to commend schemes of welfare, and to deplore insane faction, rabid treason, and erring zeal. When Princess Charlotte married, he wrote "Lay of the Laureate," in which her royal duties were clearly detailed, and her ultimate fate plainly set before her:

> Is this the Nuptial Song? with brow severe
> Perchance the votaries of the world will say:
> Are these fit strains for Royal ears to hear?
> What man is he who thus assorts his lay,
> And dares pronounce with inauspicious breath,
> In Hymeneal verse, the name of Death?
>
> (vol. X, p. 171)

A year later the princess did die. Unabashed, Southey wrote a decorous funeral song. His most ambitious, and most disastrous, laureate poem was inspired by the death (in 1820) of George III. *A Vision of Judgement* relates how the poet witnesses the king's triumphant entry into heaven—a ceremony that the powers of darkness would like to prevent, but cannot. George, rejuvenated and restored to sanity, is greeted by his royal ancestors and by great Englishmen of the past. Southey is particularly delighted to catch a glimpse of Spenser, whose poetry caught him up into a world of romance that made the real world "weary, and stale, and flat." Indeed, the poet laureate was so eager to join the departed worthies that he pressed forward to enter the gates of heaven—but in vain. The poem ends, as it began, with Southey listening to a church bell tolling for the king's death.

In a controversial preface Southey attacked what he called the "Satanic school" among modern poets. Their work, he said, was sometimes lascivious, sometimes loathsome, and was "more especially characterized by a Satanic spirit of pride and audacious impiety, which still betrays the wretched feeling of hopelessness wherewith it is allied." The poet Southey had chiefly in mind here was Byron, who retaliated with truly diabolical effectiveness. The "Satanic" poet's *Vision of Judgment* broadly accepts Southey's account of what happened before the gates of heaven, but gives it an interpretation much less flattering to George III and the laureate. Southey alleged that the Devil had put up two of the king's chief antagonists to testify against him—John Wilkes and the mysterious Junius; but they were ashamed of themselves, and held their tongues:

> Caitiffs, are ye dumb? cried the multifaced Demon in anger.
> Think ye then by shame to shorten the term of your penance?
> Back to your penal dens! . . . And with horrible grasp gigantic
> Seizing the guilty pair, he swung them aloft, and in vengeance
> Hurl'd them all abroad, far into the sulphurous darkness.
>
> (vol. X, p. 225)

Byron agrees that they refused to testify, but attributes Wilkes's refusal to his habitual good nature, and Junius' to disdain. He also agrees that Southey was snatched up to the gates of heaven on this occa-

sion—but the snatching was done by the devil As-
modeus, anxious to have Southey damned forthwith
for scribbling as though he were "head clerk to the
Fates."

There undoubtedly was something irresistibly
ludicrous about Southey's attempt to be the national
poet. He was not particularly deferential to those in
authority, and he had too much of a radical past to
live down, a fact neatly underlined in 1817, when his
youthful poetic drama *Wat Tyler* made its first appearance (in a pirated edition) before a delighted
public. After 1822, moreover, he stood for a point of
view that became steadily more remote from political realities. It was a time of accelerating reform.
Some of this was acceptable to him: Robert Peel, for
example, was drastically reducing the number of of-
fenses punishable by death. But Southey was whole-
heartedly against letting Roman Catholics enter the
British Parliament—an attitude that could not be
maintained in the face of mounting pressure from
Ireland. In 1829 "Catholic Emancipation" was accepted by Parliament, and the following year a new
government came into power, pledged to a general
reform of the House of Commons. It seemed to
Southey that the "state Omnibus" was rolling
smoothly "down an inclined plane, and towards a
precipice." When he was in London in the autumn of
1830, he met the duchess of Kent and her young
daughter, the future Queen Victoria, who was
brought in to tell him that she had read his *Life of
Nelson.* The family seemed to Southey to be "as unconcerned about the state of affairs, and passing
their days as pleasantly, as Marie Antoinette in her
time of coming troubles."[2]

He was not as disheartened by politics in his later
years as some of his gloomy predictions might suggest. He became a friend of Lord Ashley's (afterward
Lord Shaftesbury), and saw in him the type of man
who would come forward, after the revolution had
run its course, to reedify the constitution. Southey
encouraged him in his interest in factory reform, the
more so since most conservatives in Parliament neglected the issue. ("Verily, verily," said Southey, in a
moment of exasperation, "they seem to be demented.") He warned Ashley, though, against actually visiting the manufacturing districts, for fear
that his health might suffer from "the distressful
recollections which would be impressed upon you

and *burnt in.*"[3] Even then, Southey had evidently
not lost his overmastering sensibility.

He himself took no active part in politics. Nothing
could tempt him to quit his retreat in Keswick—certainly not the offer he received to join the *Times*
newspaper, nor the seat in Parliament that Lord Rad-
nor wanted him to take in 1826. Apart from his occasional journeys, he spent his life in quiet and constant literary work. He was a model father, a kindly
and diplomatic president of a small pantisocratic
republic in which no servant was allowed to address
the children as "Master" or "Miss." The atmosphere
of his home is suggested by a letter Southey wrote in
1812, when Keswick was alarmed by the presence of
"ugly fellows," unemployed laborers from neighboring industrial towns. He was asking a friend to send
two pistols and a watchman's rattle. The rattle was
to give the alarm when the ugly fellows arrived, but
Southey looked forward to "the glorious tunes, the
solos and bravuras, that I shall play upon that noble
musical instrument before any such fellow makes his
appearance." Southey's son Cuthbert commented
gravely that "these musical anticipations were fully
realized."[4]

Unfortunately, the ills of life were not always to be
warded off so cheerfully. Southey was tenderly attached to his eldest son, Herbert, and had great
hopes for him. But he died in 1816, when only nine
years old. Southey was so deeply distressed that his
spirits never fully recovered. His wife was even more
severely affected by the death ten years later of their
daughter Isabel, and eventually lost her reason.
After her death (in 1837) Southey married the poet
Caroline Bowles, but shortly afterward his mind
began to fail. He became incapable of recognizing his
friends or of reading. It can be said, though, that he
never lost his love of books. He was to be seen in his
magnificent library, patting his books affectionately, like a child. He died on 21 March 1843.

III

Is Southey's poetry still worth reading?

He himself put a high value on his long narrative
poems. They have had their admirers, it is true, in-

[2]See Henry Taylor, *Correspondence,* edited by E. Dowden (London, 1888), p. 29.

[3]MS letters to Lord Ashley, 6 April and 11 May 1833. See E. Hod-
der, *Life of the Seventh Earl of Shaftesbury* (London, 1886), vol. I,
p. 168.
[4]See C. C. Southey, *The Life and Correspondence of Robert
Southey* (London, 1849–1850), vol. III, pp. 326–327.

cluding Percy Shelley and John Henry Newman, but readers generally have agreed to ignore them. Richard Porson remarked, with a fine ambiguity, that " 'Madoc' will be read—when Homer and Virgil are forgotten"; and, as Byron was careful to explain, "not till then."

If Southey's epics fail to hold the attention, it is because he so often fails to involve himself deeply enough in the situations he describes. He lived in a time of appalling political earthquakes, and the subjects of his poems reflect this quite explicitly—too explicitly. In such an epoch, Southey believed, the indispensable virtue was courage, the willingness to act; and action sometimes depends on shutting out perceptions that might be disconcerting. More than once he remarked that "Composition, where any passion is called forth, excites me more than it is desirable to be excited." The writing of poetry could make his face burn and his heart throb. The real themes of his poetry haunted the threshold of his consciousness, but seem always to have been held back, except when disguised in comic forms. He recorded many of his dreams, and these are sometimes illuminating. In one dream he was haunted by evil spirits. He tried to reason himself into a belief in their unreality, but the horrors continued to increase:

At length an arm appeared through the half-opened door, or rather a long hand. Determined to convince myself that all was unsubstantial and visionary, though I saw it most distinctly, I ran up and caught it. It was a hand, and a lifeless one. I pulled at it with desperate effort, dragged in a sort of shapeless body into the room, trampled upon it, crying out aloud the while for horror.[5]

Southey's cries were real enough, and woke up his wife, who in turn woke him, thus delivering him from the most violent fear that ever possessed him. He felt, he said, like a medieval monk engaged in a contest with the Devil—though one imagines that a devil with horns and tail would have been less frightening than this shapeless horror. Only the annihilation of the feared object would give him a feeling of security, or so it seemed during the dream.

Southey rarely explored the sense of impotence that haunted him in this nightmare, though there is a fine example in his *History of the Peninsular War*. In 1808, Ferdinand VII of Spain went to Bayonne and thus entered a trap prepared for him by the French:

[5]From E. Dowden, ed., *The Correspondence of Robert Southey with Caroline Bowles* (Dublin, 1881), p. 367.

Confused and terrified as Ferdinand was, and feeling himself in the power of the French, the only ease he could find was by endeavouring implicitly to believe their protestations of friendship.

(vol.I, p.205)

Southey could hardly have endured this story if he had not known there was to be a happy ending. A power lay dormant in Spain of which the possessors had not suspected the existence until the insurrection broke out. "The holiest and deepest feelings of the Spanish heart were roused, and the impulse was felt throughout the Peninsula like some convulsion of the earth or elements."

"The sense of power," Southey said of one of his heroes, "revived his heart." Much of his poetry was written to reinforce that sense of power, and his epics glorify the man who never loses his nerve in unpredictable and frightful situations. They are, above all, poems of violence. The domestic pieties, and what he calls "the healing power of nature," are evident enough, but it is the battle scenes that really engage his poetic energies. This is already clear in his earliest major poem, *Joan of Arc*. It is best read in the first edition of 1796, where the author's revolutionary sentiments have not been toned down. Not that any revisions could ever do much to soften an English epic that presents the English as wolfish invaders. But later editions somewhat moderate the "fierce and terrible benevolence" of the original:

To England friendly as to all the world,
Foe only to the great blood-guilty ones,
The masters and the murderers of mankind.
(bk.8, p.295)

The poem is informed with a faith that the oppressed can be roused to

Dash down his Moloch-idols, Samson-like,
And burst his fetters—only strong whilst strong
Believed.
(bk.9, p.359)

The climax comes with Joan's address to the newly crowned king of France. She bids him rule justly, assuring him that

. . . hireling guards,
Tho' flesh'd in slaughter, would be weak to save
A tyrant on the blood-cemented Throne
That totters underneath him.
(bk.10, p.409)

The burning of Joan of Arc, although at one time Southey thought of writing a play on the subject, is not given any prominence. Passive suffering was too uncongenial to his imagination. If an innocent maiden were condemned to be burned alive, his natural impulse was to save her by miracle and blast the perpetrators of the wicked deed, as he contrived to do in one of his shorter poems, "The Rose." But with Joan history would not permit this.

In *Thalaba the Destroyer* (1801) the shackles of history are cast aside. The hero is an Arabian youth destined to destroy the evil magicians who live in the Domdaniel Caverns "underneath the roots of Ocean." The magicians try to destroy Thalaba, but are always cheated by the courage and piety inspired by his sense of mission, or by the direct intervention of Providence. Thus, Abdaldar seeks to stab Thalaba while the latter is prostrate in prayer. The hot blast of the Simoom passes just at the right moment, and Abdaldar is suffocated while the pious worshippers remain unharmed beneath the poisonous whirlwind. At one point Thalaba is taunted with trusting in the magic powers of a ring he took from Abdaldar's corpse. He replies:

> Blindly the wicked work
> The righteous will of Heaven!
> Sayest thou that diffident of God,
> In Magic spells I trust?
> Liar! let witness this!
> (vol. IV, p. 196)

He throws the ring into the abyss, where it is caught by a skinny hand. Thus to renounce the aid of magic is no great sacrifice, because high-wrought feeling

> Infused a force portentous, like the strength
> Of madness through his frame
> (vol. IV, p. 197)

and he is able to throw his antagonist after the ring.

The poem ends with Thalaba's mysteriously guided journey to the Domdaniel Caves. He travels in a dog sled, and then in a little boat—a part of the poem that delighted the young Shelley, whose *Alastor* is plainly indebted to it. Thalaba is parachuted down a deep cavern to the roots of ocean, and there stabs the giant idol of the magicians' god, Eblis. The ocean vault falls in, destroying the magicians along with Thalaba, whose soul is immediately translated to paradise.

The poem has an incantatory energy that is par-

ticularly striking in the spells. Giddily whirling round, the sorceress Khawla invokes Eblis

> Till her voice is a shapeless yell,
> And dizzily rolls her brain,
> And now she is full of the Fiend.
> She stops, she rocks, she reels!
> Look! look! she appears in the darkness!
> Her flamy hairs curl up
> All living, like the Meteor's locks of light!
> Her eyes are like the sickly Moon!
> (vol. IV, p. 311)

Cardinal Newman greatly admired the "irrepressible onward movement" of this poem, leading as it did to a "tremendous catastrophe in which the hero dying achieves his victory." What is surprising in this judgment is Newman's feeling that the catastrophe is "tremendous." The perils of Thalaba's adventures are so readily overcome that it is difficult to feel much concern about them. For Newman, perhaps, this was one of the poem's merits.

The perils in *Madoc* (1805) are felt much more intensely. It tells the story of a medieval Welsh prince who leaves his native land to settle in America. The first part, "Madoc in Wales," describes the hero's recruitment of a party of emigrants; the second part, "Madoc in Aztlan," describes the merciless struggle with the people of Aztlan—ancestors of the Mexicans the Spaniards discovered in the sixteenth century. The war includes a battle on a lake, in which the Welsh ships run down the light Aztec craft. Many Aztec warriors drown, and those who try to save themselves by clinging to the sides of boats either have their hands hacked off or drag the boats under the water. Even more striking is a contest with a huge snake, which could be destroyed only by crushing it beneath rocks rolled down a precipice, and then stabbing it in the mouth, the eye, and the neck. The climax of the poem is the night when Aztec priests and people wait for the sun to rise at the beginning of a new era—wait with a torturing fear that it may never rise again:

> . . . Oppressive, motionless,
> It was a labour and a pain to breathe
> The close, hot, heavy air. Hark! from the woods
> The howl of their wild tenants! and the birds,
> The day-birds, in blind darkness fluttering,
> Fearful to rest, uttering portentous cries!

What follows in fact is a devastating volcanic explosion:

Anon, the sound of distant thunders came:
They peal beneath their feet. Earth shakes and yawns,
And lo! upon the sacred mountain's top,
The light . . . the mighty flame! A cataract
Of fire bursts upward from the mountain head, . . .
High, . . . high, . . . it shoots! the liquid fire boils out;
It streams in torrents down!

(vol. V, p. 380)

Even though the Aztecs are presented as an exceedingly dangerous enemy, Southey allows his imagination to overwhelm them here with a violence understandable only when one remembers the shapeless horror of his nightmare.

The Curse of Kehama (1810) is closer to the manner of *Thalaba*. The exotic subject, suggested by Southey's reading of Hindu myth and legend, gives considerable scope to his predilection for images of power. Power in this poem is concentrated in the great and wicked figure of Kehama. By the performance of prescribed sacrifices, he has attained semidivine status, and is attempting to consolidate his conquest of the lower regions of the universe. His son Arvalan has tried to rape Kailyal, a peasant girl, but has been killed in the attempt by her father, Ladurlad. Ladurlad is condemned to the severest torture Kehama can devise: a total deprivation of all satisfactions of the senses. He can never sleep, and must endure an everlasting fire in his heart and brain.

To prolong the punishment, Ladurlad is protected by a charm from all possible causes of death. He is thus able to thwart Kehama's will, intervening to desecrate the great sacrifice that was to have made Kehama absolute master of hell and earth and the lower heavens. The setback is only temporary, for at the end of the poem Kehama appears to be achieving the final step to omnipotence by drinking the amreeta cup. In fact he is condemning himself to an eternity of torment. Three statues already support the throne of judgment in the underworld: one is the first man who heaped up superfluous wealth, another the first king and conqueror, and another the first deceiving priest. Kehama is transformed into the fourth statue. Ladurlad is then released from the curse, while his daughter joins a beautiful spirit, the Glendoveer, with whom she lives in heaven happily ever after.

Kehama was for Southey a type of the presumptuous will and intellect that threatened old pieties and released infernal energies to devastate the world. In his letters he compares Kehama with Napoleon,

and the poem itself makes clear the alliance between Kehama and demonic subversion. In Padalon, the Hindu hell, the rebel spirits lie in chains, but Kehama has filled them with hope. Gigantic demons are constantly having to rivet the rebels' chains to repress their rage:

Loud around,
In mingled sound, the echoing lash, the clash
Of chains, the ponderous hammer's iron stroke,
With execrations, groans, and shrieks and cries
Combined in one wild dissonance, arise;
And through the din there broke,
Like thunder heard through all the warring winds,
The dreadful name. Kehama, still they rave,
Hasten and save!
Now, now, Deliverer! now, Kehama, now!
Earthly Almighty, wherefore tarriest thou?

(vol. VIII, pp. 190–191)

The stoic resistance and domestic piety of Ladurlad and his daughter, the ethereal daring of the Glendoveer, can offer no decisive act of resistance to Kehama. But their firm conviction that "they who suffer bravely save mankind" enables them to cooperate with the ultimately beneficent purposes of Providence. Kehama is defeated only by the mightiest of the gods: "Seeva," the Destroyer.

The fifth of Southey's epic poems, *Roderick, the Last of the Goths*, has a wider range of feeling than any of its predecessors. He was more genuinely involved in this Spanish subject than he had been in the others. It tells the story of the Moorish invasion of Spain in the eighth century, and is obviously inspired by Southey's admiration for Spanish and Portuguese resistance to the French during the Peninsular War. It appeared in 1814, not long after the end of the fighting. The theme of resistance to disbelievers is combined with others that deeply interested him. Roderick, the last Gothic king of Spain, rapes Count Julian's daughter. Count Julian calls in the Moors to avenge the wrong, and thus leads to the subjection of his country. Roderick, repentant, travels about Spain in disguise as a priest, helping the forces that are consolidating behind Prince Pelayo, until the first victories against the Moors are achieved. In the battle at the end of the poem, Roderick reveals himself, thus adding to the confusion of the Moors, but afterward disappears again.

The poem is exceptional in the extent of the interest that Southey shows in the relationship between Roderick and Count Julian's daughter,

Florinda. He is not usually much attracted to love as a subject for poetry, and once remarked that he would like to see the tales that Jean-Pierre Camus, bishop of Belley, wrote to inspire horror and disgust for the passion. Although Southey does not go so far as the bishop, he certainly tends to relate the passionate forms of love to pain and destruction. If he puts Sappho into one of his early monodramas, she is about to commit suicide. If the beautiful Laila, in "The Lovers' Rock," runs away from her Moorish home with her lover Manuel, they are trapped on the way and throw themselves down a precipice rather than risk dying separately. In three major poems— *Wat Tyler*, *The Curse of Kehama*, and *Roderick*—rape or attempted rape forms a conspicuous part of the plot. In *Roderick*, though, the guilty man is a sympathetic character. We come to see that the rape is hardly a rape at all: Florinda is in love with Roderick, and she resists him on account of a rash vow she has made to live as a hermit.

As in all the other epics, it is the violence that impresses itself most memorably. The experience that Southey finds unendurable is the sense of "joyless, helpless, hopeless servitude," not only to the Moors but also to the very nature of things. In fighting the Moors, the Spaniards are comforted and reconciled to life, above all at such a moment as during the battle of Covadonga, when the Moorish army is lured into a deep valley, and then crushed by a landslide set in motion by Pelayo's force:

> The Asturians shouting in the name of God,
> Set the whole ruin loose! huge trunks and stones,
> And loosen'd crags, down, down they roll'd with rush
> And bound, and thundering force.
>
> (vol. IX, p. 220)

The poem reaches its climax in the battle, when Roderick throws off his disguise, rejoicing in his strength. He lays about him with his good sword,

> . . . and smote
> And overthrew, and scatter'd, and destroy'd,
> And trampled down.
>
> (vol. IX, p. 247)

Much as Southey might enjoy celebrating battles in poetry, he did not care for the real thing. In the late summer of 1815, he visited the field of the battle of Waterloo. He was much distressed by the condition of the soldiers who were recovering from their wounds, and remarked that he had never before seen the real face of war so closely. "God knows!" he added, "a deplorable sight it is." His laureate poem on the subject, "The Poet's Pilgrimage to Waterloo," is a resolute attempt to digest this melancholy experience. After an account of his visit, he dreamed that he met a tempter who argued that life was sickening and meaningless, undirected by any purpose:

> The winds which have in viewless heaven their birth,
>   The waves which in their fury meet the clouds,
> The central storms which shake the solid earth,
>   And from volcanoes burst in fiery floods,
> Are not more vague and purportless and blind,
> Than is the course of things among mankind!
>
> (vol. X, p. 74)

Southey recovers his optimism when the Heavenly Muse reassures him that human progress is real, and that the civilizing mission of Great Britain in the world will make a great contribution to it. The earlier doubts are suppressed by a firm effort of the will, though, rather than through any deeply felt assurance.

The most pleasing of Southey's longer poems is also the most unreservedly somber. This is *A Tale of Paraguay*, which was published in 1825. It tells of a small family who are the only survivors of a smallpox epidemic among a tribe of Guariní Indians. Mother, son, and daughter are eventually brought into one of the Jesuit settlements, where, although kindly treated, they soon die. The poem is Southey's most extensive and deliberate account of the insecurity to which human life is exposed. Disease, war, predatory animals—all help to make men's hold on life a frail one. Settlement in the Jesuit "reduction" appears to remove the most apparent causes of insecurity, but in fact the change in the way of life of "these poor children of the solitude" proves more deadly than anything else. Dobrizhoffer, the Austrian Jesuit who rules the reduction, is deeply grieved when first the mother, then the daughter, dies; but neither of them feels distress. The daughter sees him weep,

> . . . and she could understand
> The cause thus tremulously that made him speak.
> By his emotion mov'd she took his hand;
> A gleam of pleasure o'er her pallid cheek
> Pass'd, while she look'd at him with meaning meek,
> And for a little while, as loth to part,
> Detaining him, her fingers lank and weak,

Play'd with their hold; then letting him depart
She gave him a slow smile that touch'd him to the heart.
(vol. VII, p. 92)

Something is expressed here of Southey's own most painful experiences, the deaths of his children. It was made bearable for him by the remoteness of the subject, and by the feeling that it was better for these Indians to die under Dobrizhoffer's benevolent care than to survive his expulsion along with the other Jesuits in 1767, when "all of good that Paraguay enjoy'd" was overthrown "by blind and suicidal Power."

Impressive in its own way as *A Tale of Paraguay* is, though, it is not resilient enough to be fully characteristic of Southey. His buoyancy finds its most natural expression in many of his shorter poems, especially those in which the Devil plays a part. There is St. Romuald, for example, who used to fight with Satan "all through a winter's night" until

> . . . his face became
> All black and yellow with the brimstone flame,
> And then he smelt—O Lord! how he did smell!
> (vol. VI, p. 94)

Although Southey usually contrives to keep the Devil at bay, some of his most memorable ballads reenact the nightmare of being overpowered by an alien will. This experience could be made palatable by attributing great wickedness to the victim, as in "God's Judgement on a Wicked Bishop." It is mere poetic justice to be eaten by thousands of rats when you have just burned a barn crowded with women and children. "The Old Woman of Berkeley" is a little more disquieting. It tells how a witch is carried off by the Devil in spite of the devoted efforts of a large company of priests, choristers, and bellmen, and the protection of a stone coffin fastened by iron bars and tied down by three chains, blessed and sprinkled with holy water. The old woman may be a witch, but one cannot help feeling for her—or at least for her son the priest and her daughter the nun, who labor so diligently for their mother's salvation, but to no effect. This ballad was translated into Russian by Vasily Zhukovsky; but because the Devil was shown entering a church, the censors objected to its publication.

By contrast, the Russian authorities would have found "The Young Dragon," a poem that Southey wrote some thirty years later, positively edifying. It is founded on a Spanish legend about Antioch in ear-

ly Christian times. Satan is alarmed at the number of conversions to Christianity there, and hatches a dragon to punish the city. This dragon requires a Christian virgin every day; and when a certain Marana is chosen, her father (a pagan) takes active measures to save her life. He steals the thumb of John the Baptist, preserved as a relic in Antioch; and just as the dragon is about to devour his daughter, lobs it down the dragon's throat. The effect is remarkable:

> A rumbling and a tumbling
>   Was heard in his inside,
> He gasp'd, he panted, he lay down,
>   He roll'd from side to side:
> He moan'd, he groan'd, he snuff'd, he snor'd,
> He growl'd, he howl'd, he raved, he roar'd;
>   But loud as were his clamours,
> Far louder was the inward din,
> Like a hundred braziers working in
>   A caldron with their hammers.
> (vol. VI, p. 279)

His body swells up, rises slowly from the ground, and, when three miles up, explodes with a sound that can be heard a hundred leagues away. The debris is dispersed like the fallout from a nuclear explosion, and the holy thumb ascends to heaven.

Southey's best work is often his most playful, as is shown by "The Story of the Three Bears."[6] It is a beautifully poised treatment of the theme of the unamiable protagonist whose sins get her into trouble. (The amiable Goldilocks belongs to a decadent version.) The impudent old woman who eats the little bear's porridge, pushes the bottom out of his chair, and goes to sleep in his bed is surely well advised to jump out of the window when the bears discover her. But nothing worse happens than complaints from the Great Huge Bear in his great, rough, gruff voice—represented by great huge gothic type.

The story belongs to a world that Southey did not generally believe in: a golden world in which bears do nobody any harm, and never suspect that anybody will harm them. A more characteristic view of life is suggested in that famous early poem "The Battle of Blenheim." Here he is content to juxtapose the world of domestic decency with the dreadful world of power. It reflects both sides of his character: his inborn kindliness and sensitivity, and his unwilling

[6]First published in vol. IV of his desultory novel *The Doctor* (London, 1837).

conviction that the world is a savage place. Old Kaspar, talking to Peterkin and Wilhelmine about the many thousands of bodies that "lay rotting in the sun," makes Southey's point with a fine economy:

> "Great praise the Duke of Marlbro' won
>   And our good Prince Eugene."
> "Why 'twas a very wicked thing!"
>   Said little Wilhelmine.
> "Nay—nay—my little girl", quoth he,
> "It was a famous victory."
>
> (vol. VI, p. 153)

IV

SOUTHEY's prose is vigorous and direct, and covers much ground in little time. "My way," he said once, "is when I see my object, to dart at it like a greyhound." Unfortunately he often pays for this vigor by oversimplifying the issues. He is too anxious to reach an assured position to have time to unravel complexities. He does not suppress the contradictory feelings that influence his views, but they appear as fluctuations of opinion and feeling, not as constituents of a consistent attitude. When he was considering Roman Catholicism in the context of current British politics, he used language of unqualified hostility:

Whenever the Roman Catholic superstition predominates, it offers only these alternatives:—Unbelief, with scarce a decent covering of hypocrisy, and all the abominations of vice, as exhibited in Italy and France, among the higher ranks; or base, abject, degrading destructive bigotry in all, as in Spain, Portugal, and the Austrian States. These are the effects which always have been, and always must be, produced by a Catholic establishment.[7]

Southey wrote these words while he was working on *Roderick*, a poem that might have come from the pen of a Catholic apologist. *A Tale of Paraguay* and the *History of Brazil* show how warmly he felt toward the Jesuits of South America. It might be possible to reconcile the various opinions Southey expresses so vehemently, but Southey himself did not make any very adequate attempt.

The same is true of his attitude toward the Protes-

---

[7]From the *Edinburgh Annual Register for 1808*, vol. I, pt. 1 (Edinburgh, 1810), p. 131.

tant sect of the Quakers. He was united with them in steadfast opposition to slavery, in their warm but undogmatic religious feeling, in their stoic discipline and their practical goodwill. He once expressed a wish that he could bring up his son Herbert as a Quaker. In some moods he could feel that pacifism was a practical policy. He believed that the Quakers of Pennsylvania had shown that "a people whose principle it is never to resist evil, and always to bear testimony against it, cannot be crushed by any exertion of human power short of universal massacre." At one time he supported the abolition of all capital punishment, on the ground that this example would produce a more general reverence for life. He also proposed that the management of British prisons should be handed over entirely to the Quakers. But even at the time of his greatest sympathy with Quakerism, around 1807, he was apt to express warlike and un-Quakerly views. Quakerism, he told someone, is the true system of the Gospel, "but I want to have the invasion over before I allow it to be so."

His attitude toward John Wesley and the Methodist movement was more consistent, and his *Life of Wesley* is in many ways a valuable contribution to the religious history of Great Britain in the eighteenth century. Southey was well versed in Methodist literature, and reduces a mass of documentation to a clear and workmanlike narrative. But he is not fully in sympathy with his subject. His imagination could be stirred deeply by Catholicism; he could contemplate bringing up his best-loved son as a Quaker. He felt no such involvement with this predominantly working-class religious movement. Originally fiercely hostile to it, he gradually developed an attitude of measured respect. He recognized that Wesley had reclaimed many from a course of sin; supported many in poverty, sickness, and affliction; and imparted to many a triumphant joy in death. But one continually feels that Southey has a certain distaste for the Methodists, and the book leaves one with a sense of having surveyed Methodism from the outside, not with having gained much understanding of the inner dynamics of the movement.

In his *Letters from England*, though, this kind of detachment is turned to good account. It was published (in 1807) as the work of a Spanish traveler, Don Manuel Alvarez Espriella, and Southey enters spiritedly into the part of a Catholic and a foreigner. He speaks of fashions in dress, furniture, and religion, of quackery and dishonesty of many kinds. He is deeply impressed by "the ingenuity, the activity, and the indefatigable watchfulness of roguery in England." He visits the picturesque Lake District, and tells of the cheap boarding schools in Yorkshire —later to be pilloried by Dickens in *Nicholas Nickleby*. There is an eloquent account of the evils of life in industrial Manchester. He is interested in crowd behavior, and gives several striking examples of it. He goes into great detail about the religious underworld, seeing here evidence of a deep social current flowing he knows not where. Southey is obviously fascinated by incidents like Joanna Southcott's debate with the Devil: it is a subject he might have used in a ballad. The book lives because of its vivid presentation of the surface of life in early nineteenth-century England; but it is a surface that invites the reader to speculate, with Don Manuel, about what is going on below.

His critique of industrial society is more fully developed in a series of imaginary conversations between himself and the ghost of Sir Thomas More that he published in 1829: *Colloquies on the Progress and Prospects of Society*. In spite of More's Catholicism, Southey felt deeply in sympathy with him. Had he not conceived the original Utopia? And might not Southey have resisted the Protestant Reformation if he had been a contemporary of More's? "I resisted opinions," he makes More say, "which in their sure consequences led to anarchy in all things."[8] Southey's revulsion against anarchy led him to endorse the cooperative projects of Robert Owen, and to revive the idea of a Protestant order of Sisters of Charity. His book is a notable monument of the nineteenth-century rebellion against "the devouring principle of trade."

None of Southey's other prose works, though, has quite the vitality of *The Life of Nelson*. There was a real sympathy of spirit between the poet and the admiral. Southey saw in this man who could not bear tame or slow measures a superb example of the leadership needed in such portentous times as his. Vexed and disappointed as he might sometimes unavoidably be, Nelson had the resilient spirit that Southey valued in himself. Nelson, he said, had "that lively spring of hope within him, which partakes enough of the nature of faith to work miracles in war." Once he was engaged in action, "his conversation became joyous, animated, elevated, and delightful." Even in his death agonies during the battle of Trafalgar, the same spirit persisted. When the surgeon asked him whether his pain was very great, "he replied, 'So great, that he wished he was dead. Yet,' said he, in a lower voice, 'one would like to live a little longer too!'" The affinity to Thalaba and Roderick is evident, but Southey's Nelson is a finer creation than his other heroes. None of them combines the qualities of courage and kindliness so convincingly:

He governed men by their reason and their affections: they knew that he was incapable of caprice or tyranny; and they obeyed him with alacrity and joy, because he possessed their confidence as well as their love. "Our Nel," they used to say, "is as brave as a lion, and as gentle as a lamb." Severe discipline he detested, though he had been bred in a severe school. He never inflicted corporal punishment if it were possible to avoid it and when compelled to enforce it, he, who was familiar with wounds and death, suffered like a woman.[9]

On his own initiative Southey would not have made one of his heroes irritable through "fatigue, and anxiety, and vexation at the dilatory measures of the commander-in-chief." Not that such irritation was outside his experience. On the contrary, as a reviewer for the *Quarterly*, Southey was constantly complaining that his most effective blows were spoiled by the cowardly editor. Nelson among the Neapolitans plainly looked, in Southey's eyes, just like himself among the politicians who controlled the *Quarterly Review*. Nelson, he said, saw

. . . selfishness and knavery wherever he looked; and even the pleasure of seeing a cause prosper, in which he was so zealously engaged, was poisoned by his sense of the rascality of those with whom he was compelled to act.[10]

But Southey did not write poetry about such complexities.

Southey has been much criticized for his censorious comments on Nelson's attachment to Lady Emma Hamilton. It is true that irregular love affairs were as uncongenial to Southey as the finer points of tactics; but he admired Lady Hamilton in her role as encourager of heroism, and acknowledged her "uncommon intellectual endowments." Her worst sin, from Southey's point of view, was undue devotion

---

[8]See *Colloquies*, vol. II (London, 1829), p. 40.

[9]From G. Callender, ed., *Life of Nelson* (London, 1922), p. 267.
[10]*ibid.*, p. 179.

to the Neapolitan court. He thought it was about the worst government that had ever existed. If the revolutionary spirit of the 1790's had been allowed to sweep away such rotten regimes—if Britain had not interfered in their favor—Southey would have been well pleased. When Lady Hamilton appeared to him to act as the agent of such a government, no words of condemnation could be too strong. It must be admitted, though, that Southey's considered opinion of Lady Hamilton is as difficult to assess as his considered opinion of the Roman Catholic church.

V

SOUTHEY himself is not much easier to sum up. The virtuosity he displays as a poet is impressive, but the feeling behind it is too often harsh and cold. The sympathetic reader can still find much to excite him in Southey's work, but there is too little sense of sheer pleasure in life for the enchantment to be sustained. His friend Wordsworth was able, as one sees most vividly in his sonnet to Toussaint L'Ouverture, to find strength in human agonies and human exultation alike. It is precisely this deep-rooted strength that is absent from Southey's writings, and the deficiency perhaps accounts for some of the less agreeable features of his personal character. There can be no doubt of his kindness, his willingness to help, and the utter reliability that made such help really useful. But there is an unmistakable element of hardness in his character. He could be a severe judge of other people, especially if political issues were involved. Once outside the security of his domestic life, he felt himself to be in a world in which ruthlessness was necessary to survival. He was always at the mercy of his emotions. Even in his sixties he would still blush with pleasure like a girl, or turn slate-colored with anger. Thomas Carlyle, much impressed by the poet's "vehement brown eyes" and "huge white head of hair," wondered that he had "not been torn to pieces long since under such furious pulling this way and that." But he could be extraordinarily timid, too—at least in unfamiliar situations. In 1834, John Lingard summoned Wordsworth and Southey to give evidence on a literary point in a lawsuit. Wordsworth spoke boldly, looking the very figure of a robust mountaineer, "his shirt unbuttoned in the front, disclosing a tough and hairy breast." But there was nothing so robust about Southey. He could be

brought to say no more than that he agreed with Wordsworth's testimony.[11]

Southey often contemplated the idea of emigrating, thinking not only of North America but also, at various times, of Switzerland, Portugal, Brazil, and Australia. A similar impulse prompted his enthusiasm for projects of large-scale emigration for the working classes, as well as for the transportation of seditious journalists and politicians. Anything that relieved the menacing pressure of life in industrial England was welcome. The appeal of emigration was purely ideal, of course, so far as he himself was concerned. Keswick served well enough as a retreat, and his library of 14,000 volumes was a secure vantage point for viewing the problems of man and society —as he did in his *Colloquies* with the ghost of Sir Thomas More. Southey's poems and histories were inspired by current events and feelings, but the source materials (cited in notes that often crowd out the text) interpose a thick screen between the world and his sensibility:

> My days among the Dead are pass'd;
>   Around me I behold,
> Where'er these casual eyes are cast,
>   The mighty minds of old. . . .
>   (vol. II, p. 257)

The "casual" is significant. Here at least Southey could afford to take his ease. Downstairs young Herbert might be playing at Apollyon in *The Pilgrim's Progress*, roaring at his sisters like a lion seeking whom he might devour; but that was as near as the Devil, and the alarming energies that he symbolized, ever got to Greta Hall. Except in dreams.

SELECTED BIBLIOGRAPHY

I. BIBLIOGRAPHY. W. Haller, *The Early Life of Robert Southey* (New York, 1917), app. A is a detailed descriptive list of Southey's works but does not include contributions to periodicals; C. W. Houtchens and L. H. Houtchens, eds., *The English Romantic Poets and Essayists* (New York, 1957; rev. ed., 1966), ch. on Southey by K. Curry is an excellent bibliographical guide, but for most purposes it has been superseded by Curry's *Robert Southey: A Reference Guide* (Boston, Mass., 1977); J. Raimond,

[11]See T. Carlyle, *Reminiscences*, edited by C. E. Norton and I. Campbell (London, 1972), p. 349; and M. Haile and E. Bonney, eds., *Life and Letters of John Lingard* (London, 1911), p. 254.

Robert Southey: L'homme et son temps, l'oeuvre, le rôle (Paris, 1968), includes a very full bibliography.

II. COLLECTED WORKS. *The Poetical Works of Robert Southey* (Paris, 1829); *The Poetical Works of Robert Southey, Collected by Himself*, 10 vols. (London, 1837–1838), repr. several times in one vol.; M. H. Fitzgerald, ed., *Poems of Robert Southey* (London, 1909), contains bibliographical notes but omits *Joan of Arc, A Vision of Judgement*, and some minor poems.

III. SELECTED WORKS. S. R. Thompson, ed., *Selections from the Poems* (London, 1888); E. Dowden, ed., *Poems* (London, 1895); J. Zeitlin, ed., *Select Prose of Robert Southey* (New York, 1916); G. Grigson, ed., *A Choice of Robert Southey's Verse* (London, 1970).

IV. SEPARATE WORKS. *The Fall of Robespierre: An Historic Drama* (Cambridge, 1794), verse, Act I by Coleridge and Acts II and III by Southey; *Poems: . . . by Robert Lovell, and Robert Southey* (Bath, 1795); *Joan of Arc: An Epic Poem* (Bristol, 1796; rev. eds., 1798, 1806, 1812), further revs. were made in *The Poetical Works* (1837–1838); *Letters Written During a Short Residence in Spain and Portugal* (Bristol, 1797); *Poems* (Bristol, 1797; 2nd, rev. ed., 1797; vol. II, 1799); *Thalaba the Destroyer*, 2 vols. (London, 1801), verse; *Madoc* (London, 1805), verse; *Metrical Tales and Other Poems* (London, 1805); *Letters from England: By Don Manuel Alvarez Espriella*, 3 vols. (London, 1807), in J. Simmons, ed. (London, 1951); *The Curse of Kehama* (London, 1810), verse; *History of Brazil*, 3 vols. (London, 1810–1819); *Omniana, or, Horae otiosiores*, 2 vols. (London, 1812), written with Coleridge, in R. Gittings, ed. (Fontwell, 1969); *The Origin, Nature, and Object of the New System of Education* (London, 1812); *The Life of Nelson*, 2 vols. (London, 1813; rev. eds., 1814, 1830), best modern ed. by G. Callender (London, 1922), text of first ed. available in Everyman's Library and Nelson Classics; *Carmen Triumphale, for the Commencement of the Year 1814* (London, 1814); *Odes to His Royal Highness the Prince Regent, His Imperial Majesty the Emperor of Russia, and His Majesty the King of Prussia* (London, 1814); *Roderick, the Last of the Goths* (London, 1814), verse.

The Minor Poems of Robert Southey, 3 vols. (London, 1815), repr. *Poems* and *Metrical Tales*; *The Lay of the Laureate: Carmen Nuptiale* (London, 1816); *The Poet's Pilgrimage to Waterloo* (London, 1816), verse; *A Letter to William Smith, Esq., MP* (London, 1817); *Wat Tyler* (London, 1817), verse; *The Life of Wesley and the Rise and Progress of Methodism*, 2 vols. (London, 1820), in M. H. Fitzgerald, ed. (London, 1925); *The Expedition of Orsua and the Crimes of Aguirre* (London, 1821), repr. from the *Edinburgh Annual Register*, III, pt. ii; *A Vision of Judgement* (London, 1821), verse; *History of the Peninsular War*, 3 vols. (London, 1823–1832); *The Book of the Church* (London, 1824); *A Tale of Paraguay* (London, 1825), verse; *Vindiciae Ecclesiae Anglicanae: Letters to Charles Butler, Esq., Comprising Essays on the Romish*

Religion and Vindicating the Book of the Church (London, 1826); *All for Love; and, The Pilgrim to Compostella* (London, 1829), verse; *Sir Thomas More: or, Colloquies on the Progress and Prospects of Society*, 2 vols. (London, 1829); *Essays, Moral and Political*, 2 vols. (London, 1832); *Letter to John Murray, Esq., "Touching" Lord Nugent* (London, 1833); *Lives of the British Admirals*, 5 vols. (London, 1833–1840), vols. I–IV by Southey, vol. V by R. Bell, repr. without the introductory "Naval History of England" as *English Seamen*, D. Hannay, ed., 2 vols. (London, 1895–1904); *The Doctor*, 7 vols. (London, 1834–1847), also an abr. ed. by M. H. Fitzgerald (London, 1930).

The Life of the Rev. Andrew Bell, 3 vols. (London, 1844), vol. I by Southey, vols. II and III by his son C. C. Southey; *Oliver Newman: A New-England Tale (Unfinished): With Other Poetical Remains* (London, 1845); *Robin Hood: A Fragment, by the Late Robert Southey, and Caroline Southey* (London, 1847), verse; J. W. Warter, ed., *Southey's Common-place Book*, 4 vols. (London, 1849–1851); W. R. Nicoll, ed., *Journal of a Tour in the Netherlands in the Autumn of 1815* (London, 1903); C. H. Herford, ed., *Journal of a Tour in Scotland in 1819* (London, 1929); A. Cabral, ed., *Journals of a Residence in Portugal, 1800–1801, and a Visit to France, 1838* (Oxford, 1960). See the following section for Southey's biographies of Kirke White, John Bunyan, Isaac Watts, and William Cowper.

V. WORKS EDITED OR TRANSLATED BY SOUTHEY. J. Necker, *On the French Revolution*, 2 vols. (London, 1797), vol. II trans. from the French by Southey; V. de Lobeira, *Amadis of Gaul*, 4 vols. (London, 1803), trans. from the Spanish; *The Works of Thomas Chatterton*, 3 vols. (London, 1803), R. Southey and J. Cottle, eds.; Francisco de Moraes, *Palmerin of England*, 4 vols. (London, 1807), trans. from the Portuguese; *The Remains of Henry Kirke White*, 3 vols. (London, 1807–1822), includes a short biography by Southey; *Specimens of the Later English Poets*, 3 vols. (London, 1807); *Chronicle of the Cid* (London, 1808), trans. from the Spanish; *The Byrth, Lyf, and Actes of King Arthur*, 2 vols. (London, 1817); *The Pilgrim's Progress. With a Life of John Bunyan* (London, 1830); *Attempts in Verse, by John Jones, an Old Servant: With . . . an Introductory Essay on the Lives and Works of Our Uneducated Poets* (London, 1831), the *Essay* was repr. by J. S. Childers, ed. (London, 1925); *Select Works of the British Poets, from Chaucer to Jonson, with Biographical Sketches* (London, 1831); *Horae Lyricae. Poems . . . by Isaac Watts . . . with a Memoir of the Author* (London, 1834); *The Works of William Cowper. . . . With a Life of the Author*, 15 vols. (London, 1835–1837).

VI. CONTRIBUTIONS TO PERIODICALS. *Flagellant* (1792), No. 5, contains Southey's attack on flogging. Contributions from Southey appeared in *Monthly* magazine (1796–1800); *Morning Post* (1798–1799), poems; *Critical Review* (1798–1803); *Annual Anthology*, edited by Southey in Bristol (1799–1800); *Annual Review* (1802–1808); *Athe-*

naeum (1807–1809); *Edinburgh Annual Register* (1808–1811), to which he contributed "History of Europe"; and *Foreign Review* (1828–1830). For his contributions to *Quarterly Review* (1809–1839), see H. Shine and H. C. Shine, *The Quarterly Review Under Gifford* (Chapel Hill, N. C., 1949), and C. C. Southey, *The Life and Correspondence of Robert Southey*, VI (London, 1850), 400–402 (incomplete). Southey also contributed poems to such annuals as *Literary Souvenir* (1826–1828); *Amulet* (1829); *Anniversary* (1829); and *Keepsake* (1829).

VII. LETTERS. J. W. Robberds, *Memoir of the Life and Writings of the Late William Taylor*, 2 vols. (London, 1843), contains Taylor's correspondence with Southey; C. C. Southey, *The Life and Correspondence of Robert Southey*, 6 vols. (London, 1849–1850); J. W. Warter, ed., *Selections from the Letters of Robert Southey*, 4 vols. (London, 1856); J. Forster, *Walter Savage Landor: A Biography*, 2 vols. (London, 1869); E. Dowden, ed., *The Correspondence of Robert Southey with Caroline Bowles* (Dublin, 1881); O. Williams, *Lamb's Friend the Census-Taker: Life and Letters of John Rickman* (London, 1912); E. Braekman, ed., "Letters by Robert Southey to Sir John Taylor Coleridge," in *Studia Germanica Gandensia*, 6 (1964), 103–230; K. Curry, ed., *New Letters of Robert Southey*, 2 vols. (New York, 1965).

VIII. BIOGRAPHICAL AND CRITICAL STUDIES. F. Jeffrey, review of *Thalaba the Destroyer*, in *Edinburgh Review*, 1 (1802), 63–83, repr. in R. B. Johnson, ed., *Famous Reviews* (London, 1914); J. Foster, review of *The Curse of Kehama*, in *Eclectic Review*, 7 (1811), 185–205, 334–350, repr. in Foster's *Contributions to the Eclectic Review*, vol. II (London, 1844), an evangelical-Christian critique; W. Hazlitt, *The Spirit of the Age* (London, 1825); T. B. Macaulay, review of *Colloquies of Society*, in *Edinburgh Review*, 50 (1830), 528–565, repr. in Macaulay's *Critical and Historical Essays*, vol. I (London, 1843); J. Cottle, *Early Recollections*, 2 vols. (London, 1837), rev. as *Reminiscences of Samuel Taylor Coleridge and Robert Southey* (London, 1847); T. De Quincey, "Lake Reminiscences, from 1807 to 1830. No. IV—William Wordsworth and Robert Southey," in *Tait's Edinburgh Magazine*, 6 (1839), 453–464, repr. in De Quincey's *Works*, edited by D. Masson, vol. II (Edinburgh, 1889), and in J. E. Jordan, ed., *Reminiscences of the English Lake Poets* (London, 1961); E. Dowden, *Southey* (London, 1879), in the English Men of Letters series; T. Carlyle, *Reminiscences*, vol. II (London, 1881), contains material on Southey; G. Saintsbury, *Essays in English Literature, 1780–1860*, 2nd ser. (London, 1895), the essay on Southey is repr. in Saintsbury's *Collected Essays and Papers*, vol. I (London, 1923); L. Stephen, *Studies of a Biographer*, vol. IV (London, 1902), contains material on Southey.

A. V. Dicey, *Lectures on the Relation Between Law & Public Opinion in England During the Nineteenth Century* (London, 1905), lecture 7 briefly relates Southey to "Tory philanthropy"; A. Symons, *The Romantic Movement in English Poetry* (London, 1909), states that "Southey had a small but genuine talent of a homely and grotesque order"; L. Pfandl, "Robert Southey und Spanien," in *Revue hispanique*, 28 (1913), 1–315, an exhaustive study; W. Haller, *The Early Life of Robert Southey, 1774–1803* (New York, 1917), an outstanding study of Southey as poet; M. Beer, *A History of British Socialism*, vol. I (London, 1919), discusses Southey as critic of capitalism; E. K. Broadus, *The Laureateship: A Study of the Office of Poet Laureate in England* (Oxford, 1921); C. C. Brinton, *The Political Ideas of the English Romanticists* (London, 1926), ch. II; F. Walter, *La Littérature portugaise en Angleterre à l'époque romantique* (Paris, 1927), ch. III; H. N. Fairchild, *The Noble Savage* (New York, 1928), ch. VI; A. Cobban, *Edmund Burke and the Revolt Against the Eighteenth Century* (London, 1929), Southey's political and social thinking related to that of Burke, Wordsworth, and Coleridge; E. Bernbaum, *Anthology of Romanticism*, 5 vols. (New York, 1930), vol. I in *Guide Through the Romantic Movement* (2nd ed., rev. and enl., New York, 1949), an excellent brief study and bibliography; H. G. Wright, "Southey's Relations with Finland and Scandinavia," in *Modern Language Review*, 27 (1932), 149–167; T. P. Peardon, *The Transition in English Historical Writing, 1760–1830* (New York, 1933), Southey's place in the development of historiography.

J. de Sousa Leao, "Southey and Brazil," in *Modern Language Review*, 38 (1943), 181–191; J. Simmons, *Southey* (London, 1945), the standard biography; B. N. Schilling, *Human Dignity and the Great Victorians* (New York, 1946), ch. IV, Southey as opponent of orthodox political economy; M. Elwin, *The First Romantics* (London, 1947), biographical account of Wordsworth, Coleridge, and Southey; K. Hopkins, *The Poets Laureate* (London, 1954); A. M. Allchin, *The Silent Rebellion: Anglican Religious Communities, 1845–1900* (London, 1958), emphasizes Southey's contribution to the revival of the idea of Sisters of Charity; R. Williams, *Culture and Society, 1780–1950* (London, 1958), brief discussion of Southey's critique of modern industrial society; A. Cabral, *Southey e Portugal, 1774–1801* (Lisbon, 1959); G. Carnall, *Robert Southey and His Age: The Development of a Conservative Mind* (Oxford, 1960); W. W. Beyer, *The Enchanted Forest* (Oxford, 1963), app. V, "Southey, Orientalism, and *Thalaba*"; J. Raimond, *Robert Southey: L'homme et son temps, l'oeuvre, le rôle* (Paris, 1968), an exceptionally detailed study; M. Jacobus, "Southey's Debt to *Lyrical Ballads, 1798*," in *Review of English Studies*, 22 (February 1971), 20–36; L. Madden, ed., *Robert Southey: The Critical Heritage* (London, 1972), a useful collection of critical assessments from Southey's own time and the years immediately after his death; K. Curry, *Southey* (London, 1975), a compact and comprehensive survey of every aspect of his work; E. Bernhardt-Kabisch, *Robert Southey* (Boston, Mass., 1977), in the Twayne English Authors series.

CHARLES LAMB

(1775-1834)

Edmund Blunden

INTRODUCTION

IN November 1835, William Wordsworth, a man who can hardly be described as effusive, wrote a poem that was printed as "Extempore Effusion on the Death of the Ettrick Shepherd"—that is, the then well-known author James Hogg. The poem was of a wider scope than the title suggests, for Hogg was one of several poets over whom the grave had lately closed, leaving Wordsworth in old age and in a mood of isolation. His stanzas accordingly formed a lament for all these, whom he had known. Among them two had been friends from childhood until death. One was Samuel Taylor Coleridge; the other was mentioned thus, next to him:

> And Lamb, the frolic and the gentle,
> Has vanished from his lonely hearth.
> (19–20)

It was also desired of Wordsworth, as the master poet and surviving friend, that he should compose an epitaph for Lamb's gravestone. He missed that aim, but he hit another mark by completing in 1835 a lengthy meditation on Lamb's history and personality, from which the following passage is taken:

> So genius triumphed over seeming wrong,
> And poured out truth in works by thoughtful love
> Inspired—works potent over smiles and tears.
> And as round mountain tops the lightning plays,
> Thus innocently sported, breaking forth
> As from a cloud of some grave sympathy,
> Humour and wild instinctive wit, and all
> The vivid flashes of his spoken words.
> ("Written after the Death of
> Charles Lamb," 15–22)

These tributes were not the first of Wordsworth's public expressions of his attitude toward Charles Lamb. Another, in courteous prose, had accompanied the narrative poem called "The Waggoner" in 1819; it was, indeed, the dedication of that long-withheld work, and Wordsworth gave as his main reason for dedicating it to Lamb the "acknowledgement of the pleasure I have derived from your Writings and of the high esteem with which I am Very truly yours, William Wordsworth."

It is easy to understand that as time goes on, critical commentary on Lamb is often based virtually upon the celebrated essays that he put forth over the signature "Elia." Wordsworth probably had those writings chiefly in mind when he wrote the passage on Lamb's genius defeating hard circumstance quoted above. But the "Essays of Elia" did not begin to appear in the *London* magazine before 1820, and we have seen that Wordsworth had already done honor to Lamb as a writer. The compliment in "The Waggoner" (1819) was almost certainly called forth by Lamb's *Works* in two volumes, edited by some of his friends the year before. These volumes did not sell in large numbers, but they were prized by good judges of literature, of whom Wordsworth was one. That fact alone requires that Lamb's literary life and experiments should be looked at by those who desire to estimate him, to enjoy his pages, or to do both on a plan extending beyond the limits of the two series of *Essays of Elia*. The present study is intended as a help toward such an ampler appreciation.

Lamb never made authorship his profession, yet during forty years largely spent in accountancy and other business of the East India Company, he wrote and printed an abundance of varied literary pieces. Sometimes, to increase his chances of an occasional holiday excursion, if for no deeper reason, he played the journalist; and his friends who edited newspapers or magazines were glad to have his articles. He lost sight of many of these fugitive pieces, but other readers remembered a number of them long after their first purpose was served. He wrote for the theater. With his sister or alone he wrote prose and verse for children; sometimes he ventured into the field of critical disquisition, and examined the principles of greatness in art and in literature. His serious poetry began when he was a schoolboy, and was never afterward far from his desire. Thus, without methodical intention Lamb left enough writings to make him appear almost voluminous in the collected editions. While the *Essays of Elia* cannot be denied the central and highest part in his achievement, Lamb's readers can make many discoveries elsewhere in the collections. Had the disguise or dramatization of Elia never occurred to him, Lamb would still have his place in the annals of English authorship by virtue of different contributions: by his remarks on Shakespeare and the dramatists of Shakespeare's age, whose excellences he especially revealed; his delineations of the stage and its performers in his own age; a number of inimitable poems in contrasting moods; and (to abridge the list) his often flowing, imaginative, and warmhearted letters.

EARLY INFLUENCES

In those instances where the heredity and the early life of an author are well recorded, it is not always easy to connect them with the author's literary turn or bent. We know something of John Lamb, Charles' father, and can at least note that he wrote and published verses in the middle of the eighteenth century; his three children, John, Mary, and Charles, all had the trick of verse (and all wrote prose with feeling). The *Poetical Pieces* of John Lamb the elder were written, mostly in humorous style, for a small "Friendly Society" of which he was "laureate." Beyond its members few people can have distinguished the clever rhymer in the man whose daily work was that of a clerk and steward. Mr. Lamb was officially a "scrivener," worked in the Inner Temple (which was and is one of the law colleges of London), and lived there in the house and the service of the generous Samuel Salt, Esq.

John Lamb and his wife Elizabeth had seven children, three of whom survived to adulthood. John the younger was born in 1763, Mary Anne in 1764, and the last of the seven, Charles, on 10 February 1775. At that date John was a scholar at Christ's Hospital, the ancient school for fatherless or needy London children that stood no great way from St.

Paul's Cathedral; he was therefore usually away from home. When he came, he was a self-centered and citified youth, and it was to Mary that the child Charles looked for companionship, which was given with the greatest joy. The understanding endured as long as Lamb lived, and made its impression through the written word on his own and later generations, at home and beyond the seas. It endured inescapable trials which in the lifetime of Charles and Mary were kept as secret as possible but which, now that they are mentioned in every biography, may suggest that the artist does not always devote himself to pleasing the world, but sometimes to defying the outer darkness.

To pass through the Inner Temple even now, if the weather is sweet, is to experience something of that retirement from the mill of life that Lamb, as Elia, beautifully illustrated. "Its church, its halls, its gardens, its fountain, its river!" Even in the essay "The Old Benchers of the Inner Temple," he had to complain of alterations, of fountains choked, sundials removed, and (almost worse) dignities and sacrednesses overwhelmed. His essay explains in its measure the kind of garden beauty that was his solace and something more through life, and the singular observance of the beloved setting and moment that he maintained in other places. "My first hint of allegory" was here. Nobody excels Lamb in the power of perceiving the symbol or the outward sign of the inward or the visionary grace. But the title "The Old Benchers of the Inner Temple" appears to imply that in his childhood there he became prepared for another interest of his maturity, the enjoyment and the portrayal of human character. If we conjecture that when he came to describing those wonderful magnificoes who formerly paraded the terrace in the Inner Temple, he worked partly in the reminiscences of his sister, we do not fall into any gross improbability.

Among the benchers Lamb presents "the pensive gentility of Samuel Salt," and well he might; for he was born in Salt's house, and that house was as much the child's as the Temple was. Salt, as E. V. Lucas pointed out, "gave to Charles and Mary the freedom of his library, . . . a privilege which, to ourselves, is the most important of all." Lamb, in general, had a theory that children should not be shepherded into reading only pretty little books designed for their presumed limitations or appetites, but should be let loose among "good old English reading, without much selection or prohibition"; and Salt the barrister seems to have come to the same conclusion in his day. Yet it was not on Salt's shelves but in his father's "book-closet" that the small boy encountered an immense work, bound up after being bought in installments, called Stackhouse's *History of the Bible*. This monster consists in part of illustrations; and one of them, showing the Witch of Endor raising up the phantasm of Samuel, tormented Charles Lamb's nightly fancy from his fourth year to his seventh. At last he poked his finger by mishap through the ridiculous picture of Noah's Ark in Stackhouse, and was forbidden to unclose that book again.

In his seventh year Lamb was being considered for a privilege both valuable and formidable. He was to leave his first simple school for Christ's Hospital, which had equipped his elder brother for a safe job in the South Sea House. Mr. Salt was one of those good-natured men who have had a passion for enriching Christ's Hospital and, as governors, securing education there for promising but needy children. The school had been founded by King Edward VI (and the City of London) during the Reformation; a monastery had been converted into a school; and the school had become a source of strength for the church, the universities, the teaching world, and above all the commercial City. Lamb might even become a captain in the Royal Navy or enter trade if he was admitted. He was admitted, and "clothed" —in the blue coat and yellow stockings still worn by Christ's Hospital boys—on 9 October 1782. His attainments were such that he was at once included in the senior school, a mile or less from home; at the same time one Samuel Taylor Coleridge, from distant Devonshire, was sent there.

Some of the distresses that children like Coleridge might feel in the strange and gigantic school, before they found their way in it, were narrated by Lamb in one of his Elia essays, but this was mainly an instance of his imaginative sympathy. He had long before summed up his own school days as "joyful." If the daily routine of Christ's Hospital had been bitter to him, as it apparently was to others, he could count on being in the Temple and among his consolations at least twice a week. But he found Christ's Hospital as romantic as the Temple, though less spacious and flower-grown. Its cloisters alone were a noble antiquity. The hall was noble, and its walls were hung with great pictures of royal and other benefactors, still seeming to watch over the destinies of their Bluecoat boys. If the diet prescribed was not such as boys could call good, Lamb was not much con-

cerned, for his Aunt Hetty would soon be plodding into the quadrangles with her basket of interesting food from the Temple. It is not known that Lamb ever met with the sharp violence that others aroused by misdeeds or misfortune; he observed the tyranny of the upper grammar master, Dr. James Boyer, and the toughness of the mathematical head, William Wales, F.R.S. (Fellow of the Royal Society), almost as an envoy from another country. Here too, we may say, Lamb fed on character.

Coleridge was speedily selected by Dr. Boyer as a boy to be trained for the university, and at that period Christ's Hospital could foster only a few of them at a time. However often Coleridge was thundered at and flogged, he remained to become head boy of the school, and to be sent to Cambridge with an extraordinary reputation. Boyer did not overlook Lamb, who was three years younger, yet perceived the genius of his friend Coleridge. Lamb was not of the same versatility, but he was a good classical scholar as far as his years allowed, and his English compositions were precise and sensible. It was a mystery to later generations of studious Blues that Lamb had not been made a Grecian, or sixth-form boy, and many declared that he had been one; but at the point when he might have been promoted, and so set on the road to a university career, some impediment appeared. An impediment in his speech, some say; others believe that the comparative poverty of his parents obliged him to turn away from "the sweet food of academic institution" and follow his brother John out of Christ's Hospital and into City life. Nothing was easier then for a Blue of good report. Yet all through his City life something of the collegian persisted in Lamb's outlook and spoke in his writings, even if in a humorist's accents; if he had a perpetual sadness, this disappointment after his exemplary studies at Christ's Hospital was part of it.

Lamb was at the school from 1782 to 1789. It was at one of its highest points, if the energetic lives and achievements of many of its alumni are acceptable as evidence. They did well in all sorts of professions and enterprises, and nowhere more than in literature, both classical and original. Most of those writers are forgotten now in the mass of ingenious productions that their period called for, but in some one may catch certain likenesses to Lamb. And this may be connected with what he himself interpreted, the character of the boys in their cloistered school, their Tudor costume, their dependence and independence, their responsibility to a generous nursing mother, their ceremonies and courtesies, their unity in variety, their dream of returning to their old school as good men who would spur on the latest comers in it. Lamb tells us that the Christ's Hospital boy's friends were commonly his friends through life; and Coleridge was not his only reason for saying so, nor was he thinking of his own circle only.

The contrast between the two chief classical masters who taught in the old grammar school at Christ's Hospital amused Lamb and his contemporaries, and thanks to Lamb will amuse readers still to come; he is laughing at Coleridge as he writes, for Coleridge was at the unlucky end of the stick.

The Upper and Lower Grammar Schools were held in the same room; and an imaginary line only divided their bounds. Their character was as different as that of the inhabitants on the two sides of the Pyrenees. The Rev. James Boyer was the Upper Master: but the Rev. Matthew Field presided over that portion of the apartment, of which I had the good fortune to be a member. We lived a life as careless as birds. We talked and did just what we pleased, and nobody molested us. We carried an accidence, or a grammar, for form; but, for any trouble it gave us, we might take two years in getting through the verbs deponent, and another two in forgetting all that we had learned about them. There was now and then the formality of saying a lesson, but if you had not learned it, a brush across the shoulders (just enough to disturb a fly) was the sole remonstrance. Field never used the rod; and in truth he wielded the cane with no great good will—holding it "like a dancer." It looked in his hands rather like an emblem than an instrument of authority; and an emblem, too, he was ashamed of. He was a good, easy man, that did not care to ruffle his own peace, nor perhaps set any great consideration upon the value of juvenile time. He came among us, now and then, but often stayed away whole days from us; and when he came, it made no difference to us—he had his private room to retire to, the short time he stayed, to be out of the sound of our noise.

But then:

Though sufficiently removed from the jurisdiction of Boyer, we were near enough (as I have said) to understand a little of his system. We occasionally heard sounds of the *Ululantes*, and caught glances of Tartarus. B. was a rabid pedant. His English style was cramped to barbarism. His Easter anthems (for his duty obliged him to those periodical flights) were grating as scrannel pipes—He would laugh, ay, and heartily, but then it must be at Flaccus's quibble about *Rex*—or at the *tristis severitas in vultu*, or *inspicere in patinas*, of Terence—thin jests, which at their first broaching could hardly have had *vis* enough to move a

Roman muscle.—He had two wigs, both pedantic, but of different omen. The one serene, smiling, fresh powdered, betokening a mild day. The other, an old, discoloured, unkempt, angry caxon, denoting frequent and bloody execution. Woe to the school, when he made his morning appearance in his *passy*, or *passionate wig*. No comet expounded surer. [1]

(''Christ's Hospital Five and Thirty Years Ago,''
Essays of Elia, vol. II, pp. 12–21)

So far we have looked only at the child Lamb in London, and some would have it (he was apt to take this line himself) that he was absolutely a Londoner. But his mother is the refutation of this. Elizabeth Field was a village girl. In Hertfordshire even now there may be rural relatives of Lamb, and country corners where he once paused as not quite a townee. His grandmother, who was housekeeper at Blakesware House, a residence of almost too great a charm to think of now, did not forget the Lamb children. Hence, before and during his Christ's Hospital days, Charles was transferred northward by coach, away from the din of London and even the pomps of the Temple, and into the country, into the sleepy great house and its museum of relics and treasures of art, and whatever its lawns, copses, ponds, and running waters comprehended. If he could, Lamb would take with him a schoolfellow whose means were insufficient for his longer journey home. At ''Blakesmoor'' (as he called it in the *Essays of Elia*), an estate since broken up, Lamb was a country child, and so he was elsewhere on occasion; nevertheless, it was a place that very curiously continued the chain of his first experiences. ''From cloister to cloister'' he passed from the Inner Temple to Christ's Hospital; and when he sought out the essence of his holidays in the country mansion that his grandmother had as if it were hers, things were much the same. His reflections after many years are undeniably Lamb's own, even if they were offered as Elia's:

The solitude of childhood is not so much the mother of thought, as it is the feeder of love, and silence, and admiration. So strange a passion for the place possessed me in those years, that, though there lay—I shame to say how few roods distant from the mansion—half hid by trees, what I judged some romantic lake, such was the spell which bound me to the house, and such my carefulness not to pass its strict and proper precincts, that the idle waters lay unex-

[1] All quotations are from E. V. Lucas, ed., *The Works*, 7 vols. (London, 1903–1905).

plored for me . . . . So far from a wish to roam, I would have drawn, methought, still closer the fences of my chosen prison; and have been hemmed in by a yet securer cincture of those excluding garden walls.

("Blakesmoor in H———shire," *Last Essays of Elia*, vol. II, pp. 405–409)

Lamb did not need to go very far in order to betray himself, in another aspect, to anybody with eyes to see. Not long after the death of Mrs. Plumer, the lady to whom "Blakesmoor" belonged, he must have written one of his first letters to his grandmother, inviting himself and friend to stay with her. The friend was a Bluecoat boy of no little ability, at school the rival of Coleridge and afterward a man of wealth who delighted in his famous friends. Charles Valentine Le Grice (to name him) remembered how Lamb had persuaded him to "Blakesmoor," and how, when the two were there, his junior had shown him around until they came to the stables. There on the wall was hanging the harness that had been used for Mrs. Plumer's carriage. Le Grice (then growing old) recorded how Lamb had drawn his attention to it and to the fact that it was never to be used again, and added how much he had felt the seriousness of this communication from so young a boy.

A YOUNG POET

WHEN Lamb was about to leave Christ's Hospital, the headmaster gave him the chief distinction—as Lamb and his schoolfellows would think—that he could. There was an almost sacred book in Dr. Boyer's keeping, into which he would sometimes request his senior students to transcribe their English essays or poems, and very occasionally one from the class below. Lamb was asked to add a poem to this remarkable anthology. The meter is good, the style correct, on eighteenth-century lines; but it is a piece in which an odd humor plays across a "vision" of mortality. Thus, in 1789 Lamb showed the wit-melancholy that became subtle in years burdened with experience.

To what degree is it sound to build on the fact that Lamb's first known writing is a poem? We see him for the next ten years or so continuing, with a natural hesitancy, to live inwardly and to try his genius in expression as a young poet. That period, from 1789 to 1798, was a curious time for English poetry; while it was difficult to name any mighty contemporary

masters, there was plenty of new writing in the form of psychologically sensitive verse being composed both by men and by women. In its profound development, as time unfolded, this preoccupation became obvious and conspicuous as the romantic movement in England; and one small volume, *Lyrical Ballads*, published by Coleridge and Wordsworth in 1798, was to take rank as its most definitive and influential pronouncement. One or two forms of verse, which had been gaining ground in Samuel Johnson's days—he must have seen Charles Lamb as a child among the children in the Temple—and which he had deplored as a mere mode, were beloved by the young poets of sensibility in that period. They were blank verse and the sonnet, the meditation in fourteen lines of rhyme. Lamb was content with both.

Here we may interpose a few details of his career. Not being allowed to follow Coleridge to Cambridge, Lamb was first shown countinghouse duties in the office of Joseph Paice, a merchant of unsurpassed gentleness; thence he was sent in 1791 to the South Sea House, where his forceful brother John was prospering; and next to the East India House, through the influence, it is believed, of Samuel Salt. In India House, Charles Lamb remained, and his portrait remains. His clerkship there began in 1792, and the presumptions that he idled and anticked through that official world are wrong. From the first he had to consider, and did consider, a great deal of work and a great complexity of personalities and conventions. In his published allusions to his office work Lamb surrounds it with a profusion of fancy and jest, but in reality he so studied it as to become a sort of hero to his successors.

Samuel Salt died in 1792, and the Lamb family, living mainly on bequests, had to leave their home in the Temple. It was a household such as, perhaps, some French novelist might best have represented. It was most hospitable, most intelligent; but John Lamb the elder was losing his mind. His sister, "Aunt Hetty," was loving, simple, unnecessary. His wife, Elizabeth, was socially remote from her sister-in-law, but her strong character came out most in rebuffs for her daughter Mary. Charles had his own claims on Mary's uncommon unselfishness; he confided in her while he was in love with a "fair-hair'd maid" in Hertfordshire, and when that dream was fading. But, it may be judged, Mary herself had a love, and had nobody to tell it to—and she was overworked as a "mantua-maker" and even as a teacher of dressmaking. All this and much else came to a head "in a day of horrors" in September 1796. That day Charles Lamb, on his way to the office, had tried to catch the family physician so that he might call on Mary, who had been suspiciously quiet. When he returned home, he found Mary brandishing a carving knife over her mother, whom she had just stabbed to death after failing to slay her screaming apprentice.

The madness of which this was the tragic discovery was never cured, but was not incessant. Charles, who did what his elder brother probably ought to have done, accepted the guardianship of his sister; and that was in the end a security for all that was great in himself. Their father died in 1799, and thenceforward it was Charles and Mary Lamb.

At this point we resume the theme of Lamb as a young poet—a character that, in the winter of 1796, he declared he had cast away forever with other vanities, but soon found to be a necessity. Probably he destroyed some notebooks, and we have no great quantity of his early work. He published some of it in Coleridge's *Poems on Various Subjects* (1796); some more in Charles Lloyd's *Poems on the Death of Priscilla Farmer* (1796) and *Blank Verse* (1798), where his name appeared with Lloyd's on the title page; and for some time he contributed to a new and agreeable periodical, the *Monthly* magazine. These appearances and his association with two young poets of a slightly revolutionary outlook in politics called some attention to Lamb's name. The delicacy and the religious quality of his poetry made their appeal to a few readers. Coleridge both encouraged and disheartened him, by being his senior and by his restless power and ideas, now praising, now rewriting, and at last burlesquing Lamb's verses. It was not so much the implied literary criticism that distressed Lamb as the obscuring of his honestly uttered feelings.

These sonnets of lost or fancied love, these soliloquies on altered fortune, on family history, on friendship, on loneliness, on the mystery of things and the eternal foundations of man in the divine, form quite an individual "progress" of poetry. Lamb had not then the art of original, bold observation or peculiar novelty of phrase, but was happy in a general and melodious simplicity; and sometimes his simple lines excelled for the emotion they conveyed: "I passed the little cottage which she loved"; "Beloved, who shall tell me where thou art?"; "How shall we tell them in a stranger's ear?"

Such unforced speech, in its right order, may go deep. In January 1798, Lamb seemed to sum up what he had known of life, with its vicissitudes, in the impromptu that became a classic, "The Old Familiar Faces." He had amused himself with light verses in the Latin meter then being adapted to English poetry by his friend Robert Southey and others, and suddenly, when a new disappointment in friendship was on his mind, the thought of the past fitted the tune exactly: "All, all are gone, the old familiar faces." It was not literally true, but it was for him the adieu to youth. It was composed in the Inner Temple.

One of the characteristics of Lamb's literary company was that most were devoted to English authors of a remoter time than their own century, then closing; from J. M. Gutch, with whom he sometimes lodged, a Blue and an editor, to William Godwin, the political philosopher and novelist, all of them had their idolatries of the ages of Shakespeare and Milton. Lamb had many, and among his "antiques" the dramatic poets of the early seventeenth century stood out. It was a consequence easily to be understood that in 1798 this young enthusiast began work on a play in an old manner, entitled *Pride's Cure* but subsequently and on publication *John Woodvil*. It hardly asks to be judged as drama now, but as a work of art—a form in which the poet conveyed the sense of the qualities he loved in the old plays, and something of himself besides. It was the brook-clear style, not the robustious profusion, that he still liked most, and followed delightfully; here is one of Margaret's speeches (or was it Lamb's Anna in Hertfordshire, whom he imagined speaking to himself?):

Dost yet remember the green arbour, John,
In the south gardens of my father's house,
Where we have seen the summer sun go down.
Exchanging true love's vows without restraint?
And that old wood, you call'd your wilderness,
And vow'd in sport to build a chapel in it,
There dwell
                 "Like hermit poor
                   In pensive place obscure",
And tell your Ave Maries by the curls
(Dropping like golden beads) of Margaret's hair;
And make confession seven times a day
Of every thought that stray'd from love and Margaret;
And I your saint the penance should appoint—
Believe me, sir, I will not now be laid
Aside, like an old fashion.

                       (V. i)

When *John Woodvil* was published in 1802, the reviewers missed the point and ridiculed it; but they had their own ideas of Elizabethan tragedy, and

Lamb called it "a tragedy." It was, rather, a study in a style, which demanded an aesthetic fineness more likely to be found in musical criticism than in the book-reviewing organizations of Lamb's day. A host of neo-Elizabethan dramas was being composed, and many were suited for the stage, but Lamb's "variation" was not paralleled.

PROSE

As in verse, so in prose: Lamb's first surviving attempts were marked by his responsiveness to style, and he had—from the hours in Samuel Salt's library and through his book-hunting vacations—a discoverer's instinct that way. His own work might spring from this kind of stimulus usually not as imitation but as variation. We cannot say with certainty what Lamb's share was in a book published in 1796, *Original Letters &c. of Sir John Falstaff*, which was principally the work of James White, his schoolfellow and friend until death. It was topical (a hit at the Shakespeare forgeries then flourishing) and it lives still. Lamb openly presented as an appendix to *John Woodvil* his *Curious Fragments* as they might have been found in the writer Robert Burton, whose *Anatomy of Melancholy* always captures some tastes at any period.

Of greater importance and personal significance was *A Tale of Rosamund Gray and Old Blind Margaret*, written in 1797 and 1798, and published in the latter year. It is a kind of novel, though it would not occupy many more pages than this essay; and it was, however anxiously conceived as a story of innocence and calamity in the light of sensibility, an experiment in method and style. Something of Laurence Sterne's way of breaking off and beginning as if in another direction is in it, and more of Henry Mackenzie's "fragmentary" narrative in brief; for Lamb had been reading, as so many had, *The Man of Feeling* and other works by Mackenzie. Lamb included much in this tale beyond the evident needs of telling it, and contrived to digress even within those narrow limits chosen for the whole; much in it was concise and homely, the humor was everyday, and yet there are interludes of romance and of speculation. It is seen that already his notion of prose was that it can be elaborate in design where the theme suggests a specially imaginative movement. The third chapter is a sort of song for Rosamund Gray, and then an invocation to the moon shining upon the writer's window is harmonized with that song. But Lamb ends his book with a paragraph of four words only: "Matravis died that night."

Lamb picked up the name of the villain Matravis from one of his Elizabethan authors. To these—to the dramatists at least—he gave much of his leisure from the India House; and after an immense range of intense reading, he put forth in 1808 the most striking anthology perhaps ever made from English literature. It was called *Specimens of English Dramatic Poets*, and in later life Lamb read and chose supplementary passages—for he could not pretend that his book was other than a masterpiece of inquiry into a magnificent and neglected subject. But it is mentioned here with particular allusion to the prose notes that accompany the poetic selections. Whether they are invariably to be endorsed as canons of criticism is not my interest; indeed, not much criticism is as likely to be accepted by all as the tide tables; the prose itself, sounding like the voice of a full intellectual and spiritual devotion, is noteworthy. "Their dignity," Frank Morley writes of those notes on Christopher Marlowe, John Webster, George Chapman, and the rest, "cannot be disregarded. They could not have been written except by a man of grave and energetic spirit; a spirit of larger motions than some have credited to Lamb."

One of the most congenial criticisms delivered by Lamb was prompted by Thomas Middleton's play *The Witch* and some prevailing talk about Shakespeare's indebtedness to Middleton. Lamb clears that away.

The Witch.—Though some resemblance may be traced between the charms in Macbeth, and the incantations in this play, which is supposed to have preceded it, this coincidence will not detract much from the originality of Shakespeare. His witches are distinguished from the witches of Middleton by essential differences. These are creatures to whom man or woman, plotting some dire mischief, might resort for occasional consultation. Those originate deeds of blood, and begin bad impulses to men. From the moment that their eyes first meet with Macbeth's, he is spell-bound. That meeting sways his destiny. He can never break the fascination. These witches can hurt the body, those have power over the soul. Hecate in Middleton has a son, a low buffoon: the hags of Shakespeare have neither child of their own, nor seem to be descended from any parent. They are foul anomalies, of whom we know not whence they are sprung, nor whether they have beginning or ending. As they are without human passions, so they seem to be without human relations. They come with thunder and lightning, and vanish to airy music. This is all we know of them. Except Hecate, they have no *names*;

which heightens their mysteriousness. The names, and some of the properties, which the other author has given to his hags, excite smiles. The Weird Sisters are serious things. Their presence cannot co-exist with mirth. But, in a lesser degree, the witches of Middleton are fine creations. Their power too is, in some measure, over the mind. They raise jars, jealousies, strifes, "like a thick scurf" over life.

("Characters of Dramatic Writers Contemporary with Shakespeare," *Miscellaneous Prose*, vol. I, p. 47)

It is the same with two long critical essays contributed by Lamb in 1810–1811 to *Reflector*, a quarterly edited by Leigh Hunt, "On the Genius and Character of Hogarth" and "On the Tragedies of Shakespeare, Considered with Reference to Their Fitness for Stage-Representation." Both pieces were paradoxical or aggressively unorthodox. Lamb set out to demonstrate that the common view of Hogarth "as a mere comic painter, as one whose chief ambition was to *raise a laugh*," was wrong, and that instead Hogarth's works were a grand school of life. In the other essay he maintained that Shakespeare was reduced by the details of the material stage from that infinite scale on which he addresses the imagination of his reader. In both instances, whether we concede his argument or not, the vitality of the critic's mind and the abundance of his armory brought into action with rapid freshness—and, be it added, the noble construction of the whole—are beyond the ordinary. The two essays served at once as classics often quoted by Lamb's contemporaries.

Lamb expresses the difference between seeing Shakespeare acted and reading him in terms that must move us strongly, even if we do not accept the conclusion:

The state of sublime emotion into which we are elevated by those images of night and horror which Macbeth is made to utter, the solemn prelude with which he entertains the time till the bell shall strike which is to call him to murder Duncan,—when we no longer read it in a book, when we have given up that vantage-ground of abstraction which reading possesses over seeing, and come to see a man in his bodily shape before our eyes actually preparing to commit a murder, if the acting be true and impressive, as I have witnessed it in Mr. K.'s performance of that part, the painful anxiety about the act, the natural longing to prevent it while it yet seems unperpetrated, the too close pressing semblance of reality, give a pain and an uneasiness which totally destroy all the delight which the words in the book convey, where the deed doing never presses upon us with the painful sense of presence: it rather seems to belong to history—to something past and inevitable, if it has any-

thing to do with time at all. The sublime images, the poetry alone, is that which is present to our minds in the reading.

("On the Tragedies of Shakespeare, Considered with Reference to Their Fitness for Stage-Representation," *Miscellaneous Prose*, vol. I, p. 106)

Tales from Shakespeare, Mrs. Leicester's School, and the like, written before 1811, have carried the names of Charles and Mary Lamb into reading circles where his theories about Hogarth and Shakespeare do not arise. The *Tales*, undertaken for some desirable guineas, were completed with many groans, for Lamb saw that the task was really impossible; but, as his sister commented, "he has made something of it," and of her share people say the same.

WORKS, *1818*

THE first decade of the nineteenth century was spent by the Lambs mainly in their old home, the Inner Temple, though for a time Lamb tried going off to a room or two away from it so that he might write with less interruption. His sister was sometimes absent for the more melancholy reason that her mind was occasionally darkened again; she well knew when she must place herself under restraint for a period. Her case is a strange one, indeed, since ordinarily she was recognized by their increasing circle of friends as a woman of conspicuous wisdom and poise. She superintended while she enjoyed the great hospitality of the household; she was the counselor of Coleridge, of William Hazlitt, and foremost of her brother. When she wrote, as in *Mrs. Leicester's School*, the calm beauty of her nature achieved completeness of style and story. Her few poems also were simple and wise.

The Lambs were theatergoers and made friends with many men and women connected with the stage; it is not surprising that Lamb tried to write for it. A success there would have golden effects on the spirit of their days and on the question of paying their bills, for although Lamb was gradually rising in the ranks of the East India House clerks, the money came in slowly. In 1806 his farce *Mr. H——* was accepted at Drury Lane, and on 10 December it was acted. It contains plenty of amusing dialogue and light satire, but depends on the delayed revelation of Mr. H——'s name in full; and when it comes, it is insufficient to justify all the expectation. Consequently the audience at Drury Lane first applauded briskly; but when H—— was found to be only Hogflesh, they hissed, and so did the author, seated near the orchestra. *Mr. H——* was withdrawn. Its failure was very near indeed to a lasting popularity.

From Mitre Court Buildings the Lambs moved— but still within their accustomed range—to 4 Inner Temple Lane, where they remained until 1817. The plan of their life was unaltered. It allowed a number of journeys and visits outside London. Lamb's only sojourn among Wordsworth's lakes and mountains had satisfied Wordsworth that he could take delight in such scenes in spite of his usual protestations, but probably his contentment was fullest in less romantic regions, such as the Thames Valley or near the southern coast of England. Lamb meanwhile produced articles for newspapers and miscellanies, and was valued by most of those who knew him not only for these but also for his conversation on writers and books. Much of it, though not in all its original brilliance, is sketched in the vast diary of his watchful friend Henry Crabb Robinson, who tried to make him read Goethe.

The sign of Lamb's recognition as a "great contemporary" was the publication, arranged by others, of his two-volume *Works* in 1818. Here were some poems to prove that he had enlarged his scope and released his imagination since 1798. The new sonnets were of a new energy. But the longest and the best of the poems, "A Farewell to Tobacco," won many admirers. In meter it was a revival of seventeenth-century verse, and like that too in the play of the mind, moving swiftly from the homely and colloquial to the far allusion and powerful fancy. The "Great Plant" in that poem, as Lamb said, made a bold attempt to overcome the imagery of the god of the vine and grape.

One of the prose pieces was a typical appreciation of a forgotten writer who, thanks largely to Lamb, has been since a favorite. It was George Wither, the seventeenth-century poet, whom Lamb's schoolfellow Gutch collected and privately reprinted about 1810. The reader of this beautiful criticism will notice that Lamb was not merely a hunter of rare poetry in distant places, for he makes a comparison between the spirit of liberty in Wither and that in "every page of our late glorious Burns." Before long he was to read John Keats and announce his excellences in a quite poetical review.

The biography of Lamb cannot be condensed here, but the reappearance of his sonnet to the actress Fanny Kelly in his *Works* requires the mention of one of its principal episodes. In 1819, having been secretly haunted by Miss Kelly's kind nature and unassuming genius for years, Lamb sent her his proposal of marriage: "In many a sweet assumed character I have learned to love you, but simply as F. M. Kelly I love you better than them all. Can you quit these shadows of existence, and come and be a reality to us?" Much moved—for she was Lamb's friend—but seeing that such a marriage would involve her in the "sad mental uncertainty which surrounded his domestic life," Miss Kelly declined the proposal. Out of this disappointment, like others, Lamb appears even to have gained in fortitude, but perhaps toward his death the accumulation of "failures" told on him.

ELIA *DEVELOPED*

At the age of forty-five, Lamb did not give his friends any impression that he was growing old, but he might well think with Ralph Waldo Emerson (in his poem "Terminus"), "It is time to be old," and

> A little while
> Still plan and smile,
> And, fault of novel germs,
> Mature the unfallen fruit.

His personal life promised to go on with little change of design to the end, governed by the deep mutual dependence of Mary and himself, and by his genuine allegiance to the office at the India House, which was to him as a company of soldiers is to a good company commander. In literature, what more? One thing was certain: he could look back on thirty, even on thiry-five, years of love of human life, its changing scenes, its enigmatic presences, its men and women. From childhood he had been a collector of characters, even of places.

When he was invited to contribute to the *London* magazine, edited by John Scott, in 1820, Lamb was certainly pleased; it was no casual offer. He was to have a regular place. Reminiscence would furnish him with materials enough for most of the monthly papers desired. The first of these appeared in August 1820, "The South-Sea House"—and Lamb, who does not oblige us with many peeps behind the screen concerning his literary methods, explains its signature "Elia": "A person of that name, an Italian, was a fellow clerk of mine at the South Sea House." He says that he used the name as a protection, in case his brother John, still in that house, were offended by "certain descriptions" in the text. Yet Elia was, or became, more than a pseudonym. Elia also was a personality, for the purpose of these writings. The argument whether he was equivalent to Lamb's conception of himself will long continue.

So far as Elia is indicated as "a phantom," a recluse living in the past and speaking in a language antique and remote, he may be described as an invention. He is to that extent a kinsman of such figures as the Spectator or the Gentleman in Black who had been devised by eighteenth-century essayists, and of the "I" who is put forward to tell the tale of many a novel. But Lamb could not be so formal in his compositions as Joseph Addison and Richard Steele, or his predecessor in the Temple, Oliver Goldsmith; and he neither imposed distinctness upon his "poor gentleman" nor employed him or remembered his function with regularity in the essays signed Elia. In January 1823, Lamb tried to convince his friends and readers at large, by a farewell essay declaring that Elia was dead and gone, that he had carried on his fantasy as far as he wished or ought. It was not accepted; the name had become an attraction, and the humor and sadness that Elia's style had presented were regarded as Lamb's undoubted self-expression. He agreed that he had on occasion communicated his own story through the disguise, and noted that sometimes he had done the opposite.

The *London* magazine passed from John Scott's hands to John Taylor's, and drifted thence again. Lamb contributed to it from 1820 to 1825, but some papers from other, and especially later, magazines are gathered into *The Essays of Elia*. It consists of two volumes arranged by Lamb himself, *Elia* (1823) and *The Last Essays of Elia* (1833), and the standard reached in the paper on the South Sea House was kept up surprisingly well to the last. It is true that *The Last Essays* ends with a set of comments on "Popular Fallacies" that do not attempt to be more than table talk, but among them Lamb also shows his varied power, now describing the uniqueness of an outwardly ugly countenance, now movingly insisting that poverty is no blessing to childhood, presently arguing against early rising in a mood of approaching death. Apart from this series *Elia* closes with no less an essay than "Old China," wherein he uses to the fullest advantage his method of seeming, but only seeming, to desert his stated subject.

Lamb did not think that his critics were all wrong in objecting to the "affected array of antique modes and phrases" of *Elia*; he hints that the trouble was not the choice of style but want of control of it. To dwell on Elianism for a moment, I reflect that it is sometimes elaborate and fanciful to a fault, but that it can be perfect in point and sound. Here are two paragraphs on two kinds of borrowers:

> When I think of this man; his fiery glow of heart; his swell of feeling; how magnificent, how *ideal* he was; how great at the midnight hour; and when I compare with him the companions with whom I have associated since, I grudge the saving of a few idle ducats, and think that I am fallen into the society of *lenders*, and *little men*.
>
> To one like Elia, whose treasures are rather cased in leather covers than closed in iron coffers, there is a class of alienators more formidable than that which I have touched upon; I mean your *borrowers of books*—those mutilators of collections, spoilers of the symmetry of shelves, and creators of odd volumes. There is Comberbatch, matchless in his depredations!
>
> ("The Two Races of Men," *Essays of Elia*, vol. II, p. 25)

How could this mock-serious charge against the mighty Coleridge (who denied it) have been delivered better?

The manner and tune of the essays are as changeful as their occasions and topics, for Lamb saw English prose as an instrument with stops enough for every use and grace. If he is moved to speak direct thoughts, he lets Elia go and is as laconic as can be. "When I am not walking, I am reading; I cannot sit and think. Books think for me." "I called upon you this morning, and found that you were gone to visit a dying friend. I had been upon a like errand." But the comic spirit in Lamb may come in upon his realities of feeling with instant change of note. "There is no home for me here. There is no sense of home at Hastings. It is a place of fugitive resort, an heterogeneous assemblage of sea-mews and stock-brokers, Amphitrites of the town, and misses that coquet with the Ocean." Such allusions as occur there, of course, make Elia difficult to catch in all his meaning and picturing at first glance.

"To the Shade of Elliston," written in 1831 as an in memoriam for an illustrious actor who had (once) played Mr. H———, might be misconsidered as a piece of artificial word spinning, if it were not seen as an address to a man remarkable for his classical training and his being an actor all the time. It is a caprice, judged exactly for the occasion. It begins with an echo of, and with scholarly references to, elegies of antiquity, and inwoven touches upon Robert Elliston's merriest stage characters. Even classical hexameter and pentameter verse is heard.

Joyousest of once embodied spirits, whither at length hast thou flown? to what genial region are we permitted to conjecture that thou hast flitted?

Art thou sowing thy *Wild Oats* yet (the harvest time was still to come with thee) upon casual sands of Avernus? or art thou enacting ROVER (as we would gladlier think) by wandering Elysian streams?

(*Last Essays of Elia,* vol. II, p. 106)

In a second paper Lamb describes Elliston as he had known him for the general reader, in a different, an explanatory, rhythm and thought.

The essays in the *London* magazine were appreciated, reprinted in other journals, toilingly imitated; and on the strength of them, Lamb found himself invited by the lord mayor of London to a banquet at the Mansion House. His artistry in them might be properly perceived by the few; the many were moved by the characters he depicted, not least "Bridget Elia"—but the full history of Mary Lamb would never be guessed from Elia's page.

No inescapable death-in-life molests her there, presented as Elia's cousin; she is a spirit of security and life for all who come.

It has been the lot of my cousin, oftener perhaps than I could have wished, to have had for her associates and mine, free-thinkers—leaders, and disciples, of novel philosophies and systems; but she neither wrangles with, nor accepts, their opinions. That which was good and venerable to her, when a child, retains its authority over her mind still. She never juggles or plays tricks with her understanding.

We are both of us inclined to be a little too positive; and I have observed the result of our disputes to be almost uniformly this—that in matters of fact, dates, and circumstances, it turns out, that I was in the right, and my cousin in the wrong. But where we have differed upon moral points; upon something proper to be done, or let alone; whatever heat of opposition, or steadiness of conviction, I set out with, I am sure always, in the long-run, to be brought over to her way of thinking.

("Mackery End, in Hertfordshire," *Essays of Elia,* vol. II, p. 76)

POSTSCRIPTS

WHERE the Lambs could live was a question depending on Mary's mental health and on the provision of a nurse in an emergency. In the hope of a normal home life, as well as from pure benevolence, they adopted a little girl named Emma Isola, whose grandfather had taught Wordsworth Italian. She lived with them in a house they had at Islington for some years after 1823, a cottage beside Lamb's well-known stream, the New River. Their devotion to Emma was faultless, and Lamb took the greatest pains to make his knowledge of literature and his gifts as a writer serve her education and her young friendships. For Emma he compiled manuscript anthologies and wrote all sorts of verses. In 1833 she married Edward Moxon, one of the young men who gathered around Lamb in those years and whose lifework (Moxon became a publisher) owed some of its quality to Lamb. Perhaps Emma never saw clearly what she had owed to Lamb; but once married, she had small opportunity for brightening his solitariness.

Did Lamb fall in love with Emma? It has been supposed. If he did, he told nobody, especially her. Charles Lamb could endure anything. He came home from the East India House "for ever," a pensioner, on 29 March 1825, and celebrated his freedom in one of his most resourceful essays, "The Superannuated Man." But its joy is not as peaceful as might seem; now that he had time to himself, Lamb wondered what allotment of time it would be. He did not like to think of his old office team still at it. And what had time in store for Mary? At all events, while she was well, they could see something more of the country, and he could speed into town by coach, stay with friends, read at the British Museum, call on editors.

A new house was taken at Enfield Chase in 1827, but in 1829 they became boarders next door; Mary was growing weaker, and her attacks lasted longer. It was necessary at length to move nearer London and to board at Edmonton with Mr. and Mrs. Walden, who had previously taken care of Mary in her illnesses. Those "encroached on her yearly"; and yet there were great calms, and revivals of old bright pleasures, long walks, days with friends, new books. (Mary tackled the novels. Will someone recapture her comments on Jane Austen?)

Since his retirement Lamb had not neglected to seek some sustained plan of writing, and in occasional prose and verse he produced an equivalent to what he might have done had he been a more regular and prolific writer. His willingness to please was in part responsible for the *Album Verses* that he gave Moxon to publish in 1830. Not many poems have been penned in this occasional manner to surpass "In My Own Album," but the volume contains a few others of a noble nature, some sonnets among them: "Work," "Leisure," and one more to Fanny Kelly. In 1833, Lamb wrote an allegorical lyric on the vanished world of Grecian beauty, which his young friend Keats should have been living to enjoy. His longest effort of those closing years was *Satan in Search of a Wife* (1831), a comedy of the devil's private life, a diversion for the writer that should at least be read for minor brilliances of wit and versification. It is probable that Lamb's last piece of poetry was in the gentler vein of his *Album Verses*, a pretty compliment and wish to Margaret W. on 8 October 1834.

One of Lamb's last prose pieces went into the album of Keymer, a bookseller, on 21 November 1834. "When I heard of the death of Coleridge, it was without grief. It seemed to me that he long had been on the confines of the next world—that he had a hunger for eternity. I grieved then that I could not grieve. But, since, I feel how great a part he was of me. . . ." Five weeks later, after a fall on a graveled road, at a time when Mary was amid the darkness of one more mad period, Lamb died; he had told Mary where he would like his grave in Edmonton churchyard to be, and she managed to point out the place to his friends. Of the numerous public tributes to him that followed, none would have pleased him better (even if he had made his jokes on the circumstances) than a passage of eulogy in the annual Latin oration at Christ's Hospital, spoken by the senior Grecian, Joseph Christian, before the lord mayor and the usual parade of rank and talent in September 1835.

Mary lived on harmlessly, no longer the equal of herself in her brother's time but still able to astonish people now and then by her memory, insight, and imagination, until 1847. She lies buried in the same grave as Charles. John Lamb had died in 1821, and no reason remained why the history of Charles and Mary, so much like an Elizabethan tragedy in its principal theme, should be kept from their readers any longer. Sometime after 1860 the stack of volumes in which Lamb had declared that his true works consisted—"more MSS. in folio than ever Aquinas left, and full as useful"—the ledgers at the India House—were destroyed in a general abolition of such gear. There is grief among the research students of today that this was done, and nobody has felt able to invent in Lamb's way what he may have written in verse or prose in the margins of those monumental account books.

One group of writings by him, little noticed in this account so far, was not meant for publication any more than the India House ledgers, but has become a classic of its kind. The letters of Lamb now in print—the edition by E. V. Lucas dated 1935 is the best—number about a thousand, and some of the long ones are singly comparable with his full-scale essays. There are readers who are more pleased with them than with the essays in general, since they are more direct and unmoderated in expression, and some of the ideas repeated in the essays come out in them with a cheerful vehemence. If it is the full story of Lamb's life and friendships that is looked for, this great series of records surpasses in its original intensity the skill of the biographer. It must lack some passages known from other sources to the modern biographer, for many letters are lost or mislaid, but that is a minor deficiency. Above all, the capability of Lamb as the friend of a multitude of people, old or young, and his equal range and fineness of mental sympathies, lie open in the letters and even in the short notes, which mostly have his original touch in dealing with things quite ordinary.

Lamb the letter writer spoke to each recipient as to an individual, and that sympathetic gift distinguishes the last letter he is known to have sent. It was to the wife of his schoolfellow George Dyer, and the date is five days before his death. The book in question was found with the leaf turned down at the description of the death of Sir Philip Sidney. Mr. Cary wrote a poem to Lamb in eternity on regaining his book.

Dec. 22nd, 1834

Dear Mrs. Dyer—I am very uneasy about a *Book* which I either have lost or left at your house on Thursday. It was the book I went out to fetch from Miss Buffam's, while the tripe was frying. It is called Phillip's Theatrum Poetarum; but it is an English book. I think I left it in the parlour. It is Mr. Cary's book, and I would not lose it for the world. Pray, if you find it, book it at the Swan, Snow Hill, by an Edmonton stage immediately, directed to Mr. Lamb, Church Street, Edmonton, or write to say you cannot find it. I am quite anxious about it. If it is lost, I shall never feel like tripe again.

With kindest love to Mr. Dyer and all.

Yours truly,

C. Lamb.

Notwithstanding his beginnings in literature on the poetical side and his belief through life that he was a poet and might write something next, by heaven's blessing, like a great poem, it was not for Lamb to come near his friends of the Lake School as a reformer of English poetry. But we may attribute the name that he won in prose in his own time and afterward to a cause that can easily be overlooked. It was Lamb who more than anyone else brought about an imaginative treatment of English prose in exchange for the formality and solidity of much eighteenth-century writing. He was not a hard theorist, and he valued the Johnsonian and the Gibbonian traditions, but both from his disposition and from his reading he rejoiced in a far larger spectrum of prose style than he had first found in use. If it had been true that he had no ear for music (but this claim is soon disproved), it would still be his distinction to have heard newly the many musical possibilities of language and to have created new examples of them answering in melody or in harmony to earth's many voices.

EPILOGUE

Charles Lamb, to those who know thee justly dear
For rarest genius, and for sterling worth,
Unchanging friendship, warmth of heart sincere,
And wit that never gave an ill thought birth,
Nor ever in its sport infixed a sting;
To us, who have admired and loved thee long,
It is a proud as well as pleasant thing
To hear thy good report, now borne along
Upon the honest breath of public praise:
We know that with the elder sons of song,
In honouring whom thou hast delighted still,
Thy name shall keep its course to after days. . . .
     Robert Southey, Poet Laureate
     The Times, 6 August 1830

SELECTED BIBLIOGRAPHY

I. Bibliography. L. S. Livingston, *A Bibliography of the First Editions . . . of Charles and Mary Lamb, Published Prior to . . . 1834* (New York, 1903); J. C. Thomson, *Bibliography of the Writings of Charles and Mary Lamb* (Hull, 1908); "Bibliographical List (1794–1834)," in T. Hutchinson, ed., *The Works*, vol. I (London, 1908); T. J. Wise, *The Ashley Library Catalogue*, vol. III (London, 1923).

II. Collected Works. *The Works of Charles Lamb*, 2 vols. (London, 1818); *The Poetical Works of Rogers, Lamb . . .* (Paris, 1829); *The Prose Works*, 3 vols. (London, 1835); *The Poetical Works* (London, 1836; 2nd ed., 1848); T. N. Talfourd, ed., *The Works*, 5 pts. (London, 1840; 4 vols., 1850); J. E. Babson, ed., *Eliana . . . Hitherto Uncollected Writings* (Boston, 1866–1867); T. Purnell, ed.,

The Complete Correspondence and Works, 4 vols. (London, 1870); R. H. Shepherd, ed., *The Works* (London, 1874); P. Fitzgerald, ed., *Life, Letters and Writings*, 6 vols. (London, 1875); C. Kent, ed., *The Works* (London, 1875); A. Ainger, ed., *Life and Works*, 12 vols. (London, 1899–1900); W. Macdonald, ed., *The Works*, 12 vols. (London, 1903); E. V. Lucas, ed., *The Works*, 7 vols. (London, 1903–1905; 6 vols., including rev. ed. of *Letters*, 1912); T. Hutchinson, ed., *The Works*, 2 vols. (Oxford, 1908); *Collected Essays*, 2 vols. (London, 1929), illus., the Gregynog Press ed.

III. Selected Works. E. M. W. Tillyard, ed., *Lamb's Criticism. A Selection* (Cambridge, 1923); A. C. Ward, ed., *Everybody's Lamb* (London, 1933); J. L. May, ed., *Selected Essays, Letters, Poems* (London, 1953); J. M. Brown, ed., *The Portable Charles Lamb* (New York, 1964); F. B. Pinion, ed., *A Lamb Selection: Letters and Essays* (London–New York, 1965), with intro. and notes.

IV. Works Written with Mary Lamb. *Mrs. Leicester's School* (London, 1807); *Tales from Shakespeare*, 2 vols. (London, 1807); *Poetry for Children* (London, 1809).

V. Works Containing Contributions by Lamb. *Original Letters &c. of Sir John Falstaff* (London, 1796), also in I. Gollancz, ed. (London, 1907), written by Lamb and White; *Poems on Various Subjects by S. T. Coleridge* (London, 1796), contains four sonnets signed C. L.; *Poems on the Death of Priscilla Farmer* (London, 1796); *Poems by S. T. Coleridge, Second Edition. To Which Are Now Added Poems by Charles Lamb and Charles Lloyd* (Bristol, 1797); *Blank Verse, by Charles Lloyd and Charles Lamb* (London, 1798), written with Lloyd; J. Thelwall, ed., *The Poetical Recreations of the Champion* (London, 1822), contains many contributions by Lamb.

VI. Separate Works. *A Tale of Rosamund Gray and Old Blind Margaret* (Birmingham, 1798); *John Woodvil, a Tragedy* (London, 1802); *The Adventures of Ulysses* (London, 1808), also in E. A. Gardner, ed. (Cambridge, 1921); *Specimens of English Dramatic Poets* (London, 1808); *Mr. H———, or Beware a Bad Name* (Philadelphia, 1813); *Elia. Essays Which Have Appeared Under That Signature in the London Magazine* (London, 1823); *Album Verses, with a Few Others* (London, 1830); *Satan in Search of a Wife* (London, 1831), published anonymously; *The Last Essays of Elia* (London, 1833); *Elia. Both Series*, 2 vols. (London, 1835); *Recollections of Christ's Hospital* (London, 1835); A. Ainger, ed., *Essays of Elia*, 2nd ser. (London, 1883), also in L. N. Hallward and S. C. Hill, eds., 2 vols. (London, 1895–1900); O. C. Williams, ed., *Essays of Elia* (Oxford, 1911), also in A. H. Thompson, ed., 2 vols. (Cambridge, 1913); E. Blunden, ed., *The Last Essays of Elia* (Oxford, 1929), notes by F. Page; M. Elwin, ed., *The Essays of Elia. Including Elia and The Last Essays of Elia* (London, 1952); F. W. Robinson, ed., *The Essays of Elia* (London, 1959).

Note: Lamb's early journalism (about 1800) in newspapers has not been fully documented. Later he contributed to many periodicals, chiefly Hunt's *Reflector* (1810–

1812), *Examiner* (1812–1821), and *Indicator* (1819–1821); the *London* magazine (1820–1825); *New Monthly* magazine (1825–1827); Hone's *Every-Day Book* (1825–1826); *Table Book* (1827); *Year Book* (1831); *Blackwood's Edinburgh* magazine (1828–1830); *Athenaeum* (1832–1834).

VII. LETTERS. T. N. Talfourd, ed., *Letters, with a Sketch of His Life*, 2 vols. (London, 1837); T. N. Talfourd, ed., *Final Memorials; Consisting Chiefly of His Letters, Not Before Published*, 2 vols. (London, 1848); W. Hazlitt, ed., *Letters*, 2 vols. (London, 1886); A. Ainger, ed., *Letters*, 2 vols. (London, 1888); H. H. Harper, ed., *Letters*, 5 vols. (Boston, 1905), the most splendid of all the eds., with many facs.; E. V. Lucas, ed., *Letters*, 2 vols. (London, 1905); E. V. Lucas, ed., *The Letters of Charles Lamb, to Which Are Added Those of His Sister, Mary Lamb. The First Complete Edition*, 3 vols. (London, 1935; abridged ed., 2 vols., 1945); G. Woodcock, ed., *Letters. A Selection* (London, 1950); E. W. Marrs, ed., *The Letters*, vol. I (Ithaca, N. Y., 1976); vol. II (Ithaca, N. Y., 1976); vol. III (Ithaca, N. Y., 1978).

VIII. BIOGRAPHICAL AND CRITICAL STUDIES. W. Hazlitt, *Table Talk*, 2 vols. (London, 1821–1822); W. Hazlitt, *The Spirit of the Age* (London, 1825); L. Hunt, *Lord Byron and Some of His Contemporaries* (London, 1828), developed into his *Autobiography*, 3 vols. (London, 1850; rev. ed., 1860); A. Cunningham, *Biographical and Critical History of the Last Fifty Years* (Paris, 1834); E. Moxon, *Charles Lamb* (London, 1835); W. Wordsworth, *To the Memory of Charles Lamb* (London, 1835), privately printed; J. Cottle, *Early Recollections*, 2 vols. (London, 1837); S. C. Hall, *The Book of Gems. Modern Poets* (London, 1838); T. Hood, *Hood's Own (Literary Reminiscences)* (London, 1839); C. Mathew, *Memoirs*, 4 vols. (London, 1839); T. B. Macaulay, *Critical and Miscellaneous Essays*, 5 vols. (Philadelphia, 1841–1844); P. G. Patmore, *My Friends and Acquaintances*, 4 vols. (London, 1853); T. Taylor, ed., *The Life of Benjamin Robert Haydon, from His Autobiography and Journals*, 3 vols. (London, 1853–1854); T. De Quincey, *Leaders in Literature* (London, 1862); P. Fitzgerald, *Charles Lamb. His Friends, His Haunts and His Books* (London, 1866); B. W. Procter (Barry Cornwall), *Charles Lamb. A Memoir* (London, 1866); H. Crabb Robinson, *Diary*, 3 vols. (London, 1869), also in E. J. Morley, ed. (Oxford, 1927), with additional material.

W. C. Hazlitt, *Mary and Charles Lamb* (London, 1874); C. C. Clarke and M. C. Clarke, *Recollections of Writers* (London, 1878); T. Carlyle, *Reminiscences*, 2 vols. (London, 1881); A. Ainger, *Charles Lamb* (London, 1882); Mrs. Gilchrist, *Mary Lamb* (London, 1883); A. C. Swinburne, *Miscellanies* (London, 1886); A. Birrell, *Obiter Dicta*, 2nd ser. (London, 1887); W. Pater, *Appreciations* (London, 1889), contains an essay on Lamb; B. E. Martin, *In the Footprints of Charles Lamb* (London, 1891); R. B. Johnson, *Christ's Hospital. Recollections of Lamb, Coleridge and Leigh Hunt* (London, 1896); W. C. Hazlitt, *The Lambs: Their Lives, Their Friends and Their Correspondence* (London, 1897); E. V. Lucas, *Charles Lamb and the Lloyds* (London, 1898); B. Dobell, *Sidelights on Charles Lamb* (London, 1903); J. R. Rees, *With Elia and His Friends* (London, 1903); A. Derocquigny, *Charles Lamb; sa vie et ses oeuvres* (Lille, 1904); A. Ainger, *Lectures and Essays*, 2 vols. (London, 1905); W. Jerrold, *Charles Lamb* (London, 1905); E. V. Lucas, *Life of Charles Lamb* (London, 1905); S. L. Bensusan, *Charles Lamb* (London, 1910), illus.; O. Elton, *A Survey of English Literature 1780–1830*, 2 vols. (London, 1912); F. Masson, *Charles Lamb* (London, 1913); E. Blunden, *Christ's Hospital, a Retrospect* (London, 1923); G. A. Anderson, ed., *The Letters of Thomas Manning to Charles Lamb* (London, 1925); E. Blunden, *Votive Tablets* (London, 1931); S. M. Rich, *The Elian Miscellany* (London, 1931); F. V. Morley, *Lamb Before Elia* (London, 1932); E. Blunden, *Charles Lamb and His Contemporaries* (Cambridge, 1933); E. Blunden, *Charles Lamb, Recorded by His Contemporaries* (London, 1934).

M. H. Law, *The English Familiar Essay in the Early Nineteenth Century* (Philadelphia, 1934); A. C. Ward, *The Frolic and the Gentle* (London, 1934); E. C. Johnson, *Lamb Always Elia* (London, 1935); E. Morley, *Henry Crabb Robinson on Books and Their Writers*, 3 vols. (London, 1938); E. C. Ross, *The Ordeal of Bridget Elia* (London, 1940); R. C. Bald, "Charles Lamb and the Elizabethans," in *Studies in Honor of A. H. R. Fairchild* (New York, 1946); G. Gordon, *The Discipline of Letters* (London, 1946); K. S. Anthony, *The Lambs: A Study of Pre-Victorian England* (London, 1948); J. E. Morpurgo, ed., *Charles Lamb and Elia* (London, 1948); R. L. Hine, *Charles Lamb and His Hertfordshire* (London, 1949); E. C. Ross, *Charles Lamb and Emma Isola* (London, 1950); C. W. Houtchens and L. H. Houtchens, *The English Romantic Poets and Essayists: A Review of Research and Criticism* (Oxford, 1958).

Note: The Charles Lamb Society has issued a *Monthly Bulletin* since May 1935.

WALTER SAVAGE LANDOR

(1775-1864)

G. Rostrevor Hamilton

THE MAN

IT is one thing to read a biography of Landor. But if you had met him face to face and heard him talk, I wonder how impressed you would have been. With luck it might have been when he was in his early fifties, say in 1827 at the Villa Castiglione, two miles outside of Florence. I am supposing that you were then, as nearly as possible, like your present-day self. Yet living in the 1820's would have given a different tone to your personal qualities. Take your emotions: though more formal in expression than now, they would have had freer rein. You would have been more sentimental. Even if, as with Landor and his friend Robert Southey, your natural leaning had been to the objective and classical, you would have felt a pull toward the romantic, the Oriental, the flamboyant. You would have taken easily to such "barbaric" names as Gebir or Kehama.

You were, I will imagine, lately down from Cambridge, and the name Walter Savage Landor meant something to you; for in 1824 the first volumes of *Imaginary Conversations* had created a stir in the university. So distinguished in style, so adventurous in scope, often so questionable in their opinions, they were much debated in the common rooms.[1] I will not assume that you had any but a casual acquaintance with the author's verse, even with *Gebir.* You had a vague awareness of the course of his past life. He was born at Rugeley, Staffordshire, on 30 January 1775. It is possible you found out his reputation for being quarrelsome and arrogant: that he was called a "mad Jacobin" at Oxford; that he was sent down for shooting at the windows—they seem in fact to have been shuttered—of an undergraduate he despised, who was holding a party rivaling his own. That was in 1794, when Landor was nineteen. There

was talk of his having tried, some fourteen years later, to set up as a great landed personage at Llanthony, near the border of Wales. He had quarreled violently with the Welsh, and had been forced to leave the country, with debts unpaid, after squandering a fortune in half a dozen years. It was told also how, at the beginning of that period, he had contrived to join the rebels in Spain who were fighting for freedom against Joseph Bonaparte and the French. This magnanimous adventure had petered out; but Landor was thanked in the *Madrid Gazette* for gallant personal service and gifts of money, and he was even granted the honorary rank of colonel.

Altogether, in 1827 you must have approached Landor with high expectation and curiosity. He was a formidable figure: a big, bluff man with a resonant voice and with much of the grand manner, even in his exclamations and in the pealing laughter that ran up to a surprisingly high note. Beneath the broad sweep of his forehead, where the hair was already whitening, were candid eyes that suggested a challenge. You might have thought they held the hint of fanaticism; or you might, like his biographer John Forster, when he met him for the first time in 1836, have been persuaded that you saw "a depth of composed expression that even startled by its contrast to the eager restlessness looking out from the surface." He loved to throw out his opinions, and to listen to those of others when he deemed them worthy of respect. He was intolerant all through his life of contradiction, and averse to sustained reasoning.[2] This apart, he had cast off the roughness of earlier days, when he had been unsure of himself, and, now that he felt his high worth was recognized, would often exercise a winning charm. Landor was markedly courteous toward women. You would have guessed he was attractive to them, making them feel worthy of homage. It was in 1836 that Lady Blessington first

[1]See also J. Forster, *Walter Savage Landor, A Biography* (London, 1869), vol. II, p. 86.

[2]*ibid.,* vol. I, p. 113.

met him; she became his fervent admirer, and a lasting friend.

On a good day you would have learned to admire Landor's astonishing range, his familiarity with Greek and Latin classics, his enthusiasm for Alexander Pope and John Milton, or his erratic generosity to younger writers of the time. Or he might have led the way over wide fields of political history, with wit, with ardor, with an undercurrent of nobility, waving the banners of liberty and truth, "as if" (to quote Southey) "he spoke in thunder and lightning." It would have been unlike him if he had not mingled public events with personal narrative. It would have been unlike him if he had not said things that were outrageous and extravagant. The French, or it might be the Florentines, were the most treacherous rascals on earth; there was little good to be said of the English, from whom he had suffered many insults; and as for the Welsh—by heavens!—they were mean, ungrateful tricksters, the most barbarous race. All the time there would be the changing play of expression, now and then the disarming smile, and, when he trod near to offense, that crescendo of laughter. As a performance it was overwhelming. You would, I think, have been swept away by it.

It is well to submit oneself in imagination to the spell of Landor. One carries away something of value, not afterward to be lost when one considers the man more soberly. For it will not do to picture him always on tap or always amenable; nor must one be too much influenced by the eccentric if lovable image of Boythorn, the caricature that Charles Dickens drew in *Bleak House* when Landor was much older. Often, in fact, he preferred to dine alone or with a few personal friends. Only two years before the not impossible gathering I have pictured, Landor had written to his mother, "Here in Florence I have two or three friends, a manageable number, and some dozens who call on me, but whom I cannot receive." He was not very sociable. Society might mean competition, the idea of which, with the possibility of being defeated or laughed at, he could not abide. As for riding or dancing, in which he lamented his lack of skill, the remedy was simple: he gave up both. He could not do that with study or writing, whether in English or Latin, for his devotion to letters was too genuine. Pluming himself on his own superiority, yet afraid of failure, he had, both at Rugby and at Oxford, avoided competing for prizes. When sent down from the university in 1794, Landor took books, and his own brilliant but fallible instinct, for masters. It may be that in those early days

his rough independence was encouraged by the formidable Samuel Parr, who was held to be a successor to some extent to Samuel Johnson.[3] Parr, twenty-seven years older than Landor, took a strong liking to him, admiring his spirit and treating him like an equal in argument.

Landor's character held many apparent contradictions, but it changed little through his eighty-nine years, except that in later life he grew less domineering. He was impulsive and exuberant, yet often self-contained, an egoist who was capable of warm admiration. In politics he was a partisan, shrewd if reckless in judgment. He was a fine scholar, not exact but with great facility and a strong feeling for classical form. Essentially he was a proud man, stubborn in prejudice, liable to flare up—sometimes from personal touchiness, but often in defense of a generous ideal. Landor was violent in expression, but in repose betrayed a deep tenderness. It has become a commonplace to remark on the contrast between the turbulence of his character and the serenity of his art. There was indeed a strange opposition; but it did not, as usually supposed, mark off the man from the writer—it existed, rather, within the day-to-day life of the man. For the mood of contemplation, usually weak in exuberant people, was remarkably strong in him, and would absorb him for hours. It was not solely incidental to his writing, but belonged, by nature as well as self-discipline, to his regular habit of mind. The turmoil of action and adversity could not long suppress it.

After leaving Oxford in 1794, Landor spent much time in south Wales, where he wooed his first love, Nancy Jones, the "Ione" of his verse. But he was also working hard, and following up the ancient classics with *Paradise Lost*—"even the great hexameter sounded to me tinkling when I had recited aloud in my solitary walks on the sea-shore the haughty appeal of Satan and the deep penitence of Eve."[4] It was here that he formed an idealized attachment to Rose Aylmer, who died young and whose memory inspired the famous lines beginning "Ah, what avails the sceptred race." His pen was already busy with verse, and it was from a book lent to him by Rose that he took the story of *Gebir*, published in 1798. Then, perhaps early in 1803, Landor fell passionately in love with Jane Swift, the "Ianthe" on whom so

[3]James Boswell reports Johnson as meeting Parr in 1780 and being much pleased with his conversation: "Parr is a fair man. I do not know when I have had an occasion of such free controversy."
[4]From "The Abbé Delille and Walter Landor," in *Imaginary Conversations*.

many of his finest short poems were to center. Sometime in 1803 she was married to a Swift cousin, who died in 1814. Early in her marriage she came to return Landor's passion, but was not prepared to abandon her husband, to whom she bore seven children. After the husband's death Landor did not see her again until 1829, when she had been widowed a second time. From then on, the romance never faded, but friend rather than lover is the final and inclusive word. "It was to see Landor at his very best," wrote Forster, "to see him in the presence of this lady. In language, manner, look, voice, even in the minutest points of gesture and bearing, it was all that one could possibly imagine of the perfection of chivalrous respect."

In 1808 began the dramatic episode of Llanthony. Landor lavished money on the large estate he had purchased; he planted woodlands, made roads, built houses, bred sheep. It was a great enterprise but inevitably doomed, for he was countered on all sides by enmity and suspicion. Tenants refused to pay rent and, aided by the ingenuity of local attorneys, disputed his title over their land. Agents mismanaged his affairs and let him in for extravagant charges, and his own headstrong temper could not long be restrained. We have his vivid account of tracking down a tenant who was poaching. "He broke down the fence of my wood, and was in no foot-path. He stood before me with his arms folded and told me I had better not touch him. I instantly took him by the arm and swung him through the hedge . . . I trust I can punish the rascal for having a net." On another occasion he went about the streets of Monmouth, distributing a libelous handbill against a youth whom he had charged with uprooting newly planted trees. These and other incidents gave rise to law cases and, along with the general breakdown of his finances, led to his leaving the country in 1814.

For the first three of these disastrous years, Landor did not make Llanthony his headquarters. It was from Bath that he wrote to Southey in April 1811, announcing in a lighthearted manner that, while beginning to transcribe his tragedy *Count Julian*, he had fallen in love. His bride-to-be was Julia Thuillier, a pretty girl of seventeen. They married in May, and in June settled at Llanthony, although no house was ready for them. Through a lonely and harassing time Julia behaved remarkably well, supporting her husband and even helping to distribute his handbills at Monmouth. But the prospect of leaving England permanently was too much for her; and

in Jersey, en route to France, a quarrel blazed up that led to their parting. Landor was "resolved to see her no more," but relented on hearing that she was ill. A reconciliation took place, and for twenty years they managed to live together in Italy. But they were an ill-suited couple; and even their four children, of whom Landor was too possessively fond, were the cause of jealousy and unhappiness. The twenty years were not outwardly eventful, being much occupied with domestic affairs, the occasional visit of friends from England, and the withdrawn activities of a writer; *Imaginary Conversations* began to appear in 1824, bringing a new breath of fame. But it was still the same turbulent Landor, often threatening to run into trouble. On one occasion he took offense at his landlord, an Italian marquis, who strutted into the drawing room before Julia and some visitors without removing his hat. Landor strode up to him, knocked his hat off, rushed him out, and then broke into such peals of laughter at his own anger that no one in the party could resist.

In 1829, Ianthe visited Florence. Landor paid her a great deal of attention; and in a book of poems published two years later, thirty-one pieces were addressed to her. All this contributed, no doubt, to the worsening domestic atmosphere. Julia's tongue was increasingly waspish, and the "gentlemanly demeanor"[5] of her husband was unlikely to conciliate her. The break came, as it was bound to do; and in 1835 Landor returned alone to England, where he remained—mostly at Bath—until 1858.

Some of his best work was done in the earlier part of this phase, including further *Imaginary Conversations* and two long compositions on an equally high level, *Pericles and Aspasia* (1836) and *The Pentameron and Pentalogia* (1837). Little further need be said here. Old friendships took firmer root and new ones began, including those with Forster and Dickens. There were many deaths that he felt keenly, especially those of Southey in 1843 and of Ianthe in 1851. All through these years, in contrast with his political letters and the slashing attacks on Lord Brougham in the *Examiner*, runs a delightful thread of correspondence[6] with Rose Paynter, afterward Lady Graves-Sawle, a niece of Rose Aylmer. The interchange continued after his retreat to Italy in 1858.

The occasion for this last flight was a foolish and wretched case in which Landor was provoked to a

---

[5]The phrase of Landor's friend Armitage Brown.
[6]S. Wheeler, ed., *Letters of Walter Savage Landor, Private and Public* (London, 1899).

flagrant libel by a Mrs. Yescombe. He was vilified by the press for his part in what remains a somewhat obscure affair; at the time his friends were, for the most part, dismayed but loyal. He was now eighty-three, and there were six years of exile ahead. It was a sad close to his career, but pride did not desert him nor—despite a failing memory—did an occasional power of forceful expression. And he was not cut off from friendship. After an unhappy interval the Robert Brownings welcomed him most kindly; and in the year of his death (1864), he received a visit of enthusiastic homage from a young man of twenty-six, Algernon Swinburne. Landor died in Florence on 17 September 1864, too soon to read the dedication to him of *Atalanta in Calydon* (1865).

THE PROSE

"POETRY was always my amusement," Landor declared, "prose my study and business"; and it was to *Imaginary Conversations* that he looked for fame, as he went on to prophesy "I shall dine late; but the dining-room will be well lighted, the guests few and select." It may be proper, then, to take the prose before the verse, considering not only the *Conversations* but *Pericles and Aspasia* and *The Pentameron* as well.

It is altogether in keeping with Landor's character —his pride, his courtesy, his feeling for classical form—that, although his prose runs easily, ceremony should be a constant feature of his writing, seldom absent for long. The ceremonious style came naturally to him; and to see how easily it can rise from a humble context, we may look at the opening sentences of "Marchese Pallavicini and Walter Landor":

At Albaro near Genoa I rented the palace of Marchese Pallavicini. While he was presenting the compliments on my arrival, the wife of his bailiff brought me fish and fowl from the city and poured upon the table a basketful of fruit.

Landor. The walk has tired you, my good woman. The hill indeed is rather steep, but it is short; and you appear, like the generality of Genoese countrywomen, strongly built.[7]

(III.171)

[7]Quotations of prose and poetry except where noted are from T. E. Welby and S. Wheeler, eds., *The Complete Works*, 16 vols. (London, 1927-1936). References for prose are to volume and page numbers; for poetry, lines are also cited.

Landor's address to the bailiff's wife bears his hallmark. The emphatic monosyllables "steep" and "short" prepare for a leisurely floating rhythm, "the generality of Genoese countrywomen," brought to a firm finish in "strongly built." They are small strokes, but we recognize the fine brushwork. And the tone to which they contribute is formal, kindly, and a little patronizing.

Landor was well aware of the virtue of flexibility; and early in *The Pentameron*, in the first of the five days' talk between Giovanni Boccaccio and Petrarch, there are signs that he was then (1837) consciously aiming at a simpler manner. Boccaccio has thought, in a sickbed repentance, of burning his *Decameron*. Petrarch has urged him, greatly to his comfort, to do no such thing, but to cast out a few stories that were too indecorous and to put others in their place. He goes on to give some purely literary advice—"In what you may substitute hereafter, I would say to you as I have said to myself, do not be on all occasions too ceremonious in the structure of your sentences." As for Landor, it is amusing to notice how ceremonious he can be a page or two later, when commending the quality of plainness:

In the loftiest rooms and richest entablatures are suspended the most spider-webs; and the quarry out of which palaces are erected is the nursery of nettle and bramble.

(IX.163)

Ceremony was too deeply rooted in him to be easily corrected; it was not only in the structure of his sentences but also in the whole cast of his mind.

Nevertheless Landor has a remarkable range. For ceremony, while it most often has dignity for companion, as in the fine "Conversation" between the brothers Cicero, can also subsist with tenderness or with lively satire. And in *The Pentameron* are long passages where it goes with a kind of transparent peacefulness. The third day in particular opens with a deliciously fresh narrative. Petrarch rises early and, when the maid Assunta has given much-needed help—for he is no horseman—in saddling and equipping his steed, he sets out somewhat perilously to the parish church of Certaldo to hear mass:

And now the sound of village bells, in many hamlets and convents and churches out of sight, was indistinctly heard, and lost again; and at last the five of Certaldo seemed to crow over the faintness of them all. The freshness of the morning was enough of itself to excite the spirits of youth; a portion of which never fails to descend on years that are far removed from it, if the mind has partaken in innocent mirth while it was its season and its duty to enjoy it.

(IX.206)

Petrarch continues on his way through increasing sights and sounds of country people's happiness, and reaches Certaldo with time to spare, surprised to find laurels put up over the gates and a concourse to greet him:

A young poet, the most celebrated in the town, approached the canonico with a long scroll of verses, which fell below the knee, beginning
How shall we welcome our illustrious guest?
To which Ser Francesco immediately replied, "Take your favourite maiden, lead the dance with her, and bid all your friends follow; you have a good half-hour for it".

(IX.207)

The "Conversation" between Cicero and his brother is a sustained piece that was a favorite of William Wordsworth's. The whole of it should be read, even if the grave and bookish talk on Roman history has its turns of dullness. Landor was deeply in sympathy with the noble Romans and Greeks, whom today we take too much pleasure in debunking. Yet we must feel the nobility of thought and expression in such a saying as "We cannot conquer fate and necessity, yet we can yield to them in such a manner as to be greater than if we could." The talk is supposed to take place not long before the brothers were put to death, and it is fitting that the atmosphere should be burdened. Relief comes with an exquisite passage evoking the seashore at night, and then Cicero pursues his philosophy of life and death:

Everything has its use: life to teach us the contempt of death and death the contempt of life. Glory, which among all things between stands eminently the principal, although it has been considered by some philosophers as mere vanity and deception, moves those great intellects which nothing else could have stirred, and places them where they can best and most advantageously serve the Commonwealth. Glory can be safely despised by those only who have fairly won it: a low, ignorant, or vicious man should dispute on other topics.

(II.143)

The themes taken by Landor extend from Greece and Rome down through the centuries: kings and statesmen, poets and scholars, famous men and renowned women; war and peace; the manners of people in this country or that, with sometimes the intimate and homely setting; religion; law; government; and the turmoil of the contemporary scene. Ceremony, I said, may sometimes go with satire. A seventeenth-century "Conversation," "Bishop Burnet and Humphrey Hardcastle," is used to stage an attack on Lord Byron ("Mr. George"). It is the voice of Landor with a difference, for he seeks to reproduce the racy idiom of the bishop; but here his own manner breaks out unmistakably:

Mr. George began with satirizing his father's friends, and confounding the better part of them with all the hirelings and nuisances of the age; with all the scavengers of lust, and all the link-boys of literature; with Newgate solicitors, the patrons of adulterers and forgers, who, in the long vacation, turn a penny by puffing a ballad, and are promised a shilling in silver for their own benefit, on crying down a religious tract. He soon became reconciled to them, and they raised him upon their shoulders above the heads of the wittiest and the wisest. This served a whole winter. Afterwards, whenever he wrote a bad poem, he supported his sinking fame by some signal act of profligacy: an elegy by a seduction, a heroic by an adultery, a tragedy by a divorce.

(IV.262)

Virulent though the passage is, it is built up in a formal, ceremonious manner: a long, mounting rhythm carries it over phrases that stand in rhetorical apposition; then the movement slows down, and steadies itself for the final thrust—once again in parallel phrases, but now carefully measured and short.

Among other lively "Conversations" I would point especially to "Alfieri and Salomon the Florentine Jew," with the superb Landor-like arrogance of Alfieri's final remark, "As a writer and as a man I know my station: if I found in the world five equal to myself, I would walk out of it, not to be jostled"; "Diogenes and Plato," a most unfair attack by Diogenes, but mischievous and entertaining, with quick turns of fancy and no little wisdom; and "La Fontaine and La Rochefoucault," a well-balanced argument, light and brilliant, in which the former speaks up for a kindly view of human nature—"I consider your *Maxims* as a broken ridge of hills, on the shady side of which you are fondest of taking your exercise; but the same ridge hath also a sunny one."

We must expect, unless we are specialists, to find some of the dialogues overly difficult. Without having the peculiar background, we cannot be intelligent readers of, say, "The Emperor Alexander and Capo d'Istria" or "King James I and Isaac Casaubon," though in the latter we feel the speakers to be alive and credible. We are likely to be daunted by long discussions of verbal usage and spelling, especially in "Samuel Johnson and John Horne (Tooke)." Even when Landor is dealing with ideas in a more general and familiar field, we have to read with alert attention, able to relish the rich flow and aptness of expression, able also to enjoy differing as well as agreeing. Many of his sayings have the steady light of wisdom. Yet he is inclined to be wayward, quick to leap to conclusions, slow to check them. Despite enthusiasm for justice, he is liable to break out in small prejudices and is obsessed by a few big ones, strangely assorted—his biases, for example, against the Roman Catholic Church, against Plato and his philosophy, against George Canning and his statecraft. All this can be tiresome and irritating. "Never," said Southey (going, I think, too far), "never did man represent himself in his writings so much less generous, less just, less compassionate, less noble in all respects than he really is."

As to the "compassionate" and "noble," we need to penetrate to the central tone of Landor's writing. Often we are reminded of the qualities he displayed in life; there is much of compassion and nobility or—to use terms that seem both wider and more appropriate—of tenderness and pride. Poetic contemplation, moreover, allows free interplay between diverse passions, imparting to them an ideal tinge. Thus the tenderness and pride of Landor sometimes grow toward each other in a rare exaltation. The best examples occur in the epigrammatic poems addressed to Ianthe. But there is a fine moment in "Kosciusko and Poniatowski," when the union of the two passions is felt in love of country. Kosciusko is living in Switzerland; he will not be persuaded to return to his home and take command, but he dwells there continually in vision:

> Were I in Poland, how many things are there which would disturb and perhaps exasperate me! Here I can think of her as of some departed soul; not yet indeed clothed in light nor exempted from sorrowfulness, but divested of passion, removed from tumult, and inviting to contemplation.

(VIII.71-72)

Yet Landor's tenderness and pride are each insecure. Tenderness is liable to lapse into a sentiment where the relationship with life is untrue, and the reader must discriminate. What drew tears of approval in the early nineteenth century may well be embarrassing in the late twentieth. At all times, too, it is a personal matter. Speaking for myself, I cannot endure the sentimentality, in "Blucher and Sandt," of Sandt's effusion over a flower in his cell[8] ("Thou hast been out upon the dew, my little one! . . ."). There are a few other cases that trouble me. On the other hand, I feel that the sentiment in "Roger Ascham and Lady Jane Grey," while it trembles on the verge of prettiness, is kept pure and fresh. This piece is one of several sketches from English history—others include "Henry VIII and Ann Boleyn" and "Oliver Cromwell and Walter Noble" —that were founded on a keen study of records, not so much of event as of character and turn of speech. While a new scene took shape, from whatever country or age, Landor would meditate on his personae until they assumed a life of their own with, inevitably, an infusion of his. He would not only direct their growth but also watch them grow, not only search within himself, "with care, difficulty and moroseness,"[9] for the right words but also listen to them speaking. They were creatures of his imagination, and he was not too much hampered by stern historical requirement. Thus he confesses of *Pericles and Aspasia*, the long series of letters with classical Athens as their center and inspiration, that "The characters, thoughts and actions are all fictions. Pericles was somewhat less amiable, Aspasia somewhat less virtuous, Alcibiades somewhat less sensitive."

As I have suggested, Landor's pride, no less than his tenderness, is dangerously poised. When not merely self-regarding, it can be a noble quality, going out in scorn of what is base or in contemplation of an ideal, seeking glory in the Ciceronian sense. Yet Landor, although drawn by human greatness, remains an egoist; and the great men he imagines reflect his own proud spirit, sometimes magnanimous but sometimes overly solemn and portentous. The most obvious cause of offense is the overbearing tone in which he asserts his views, as when, in "The Abbé Delille and Walter Landor," he treats the abbé to a long attack on Nicolas Boileau, setting himself to pull to pieces one line or phrase after another. This

[8]Sandt was a student who had assassinated August von Kotzebue as an enemy of Germany and liberty.
[9]For this phrase see note to second edition of the Burnet and Hardcastle "Conversation."

"Conversation" is full of rewarding digressions. Among its riches is a glorious sentence that pictures Edward Gibbon (whom he admired) "pacing up and down the unventilated school of rhetoric with a measured and heavy step."

In all his most serious writing, whether as critic, essayist, or poet, Landor devoted meticulous attention to detail, the shape and sound of a sentence or a line. Love of the small perfection both sharpened and limited his powers. It helped him to condense a finely rhythmical prose into moments of unique grace and solidity, and made it possible for him to become a supreme epigrammatist in verse. On the other hand, in long compositions it caused—or at least was accompanied by—an insufficient sense of the whole, a weakness in architecture. And so, too, with criticism. A line-by-line method was applied not only to Boileau, whom he disliked, but also to poets for whom he professed a deep admiration, and he set himself mainly to attack. He had, indeed, a scorn for vague generalities, and a sense of the harm that can be done to a poet's fame by excessive praise. But he went too far in the opposite direction.

The extreme case is that of Dante, the relentless harrying of whom overcasts the otherwise serene sky of *The Pentameron*. *The Divine Comedy* must surely be approached as a whole. Landor takes it part by part, one scene at a time, one passage at a time, and actually makes Petrarch say that "at least sixteen parts in twenty of the *Inferno* and *Purgatorio* are detestable, both in poetry and principle." Again, while no one can doubt his ardent enthusiasm for Milton, one feels in "Southey and Landor," as he lops off lines from *Paradise Lost* by tens and hundreds, that here also something is lacking in his comprehension. He has an acute eye for small points but, even when just, these are not always worth making; and sometimes, as when he amusingly objects that Atlantean shoulders could no more support "the weight of monarchies" than the shoulders of a grasshopper, he is overly literal.

After a long scrutiny of *Paradise Lost*, Southey remarks to Landor, "We shall lose our dinner, our supper, and our sleep, if we expatiate on the innumerable beauties of the volume: we have scarcely time to note the blemishes." The reader will be grateful for the minutes of praise among the hours of correction; grateful, too, for the occasional access of fervor that is more true to Landor's generosity:

After I have been reading the *Paradise Lost*, I can take up no other poet with satisfaction . . . I recur to it incessantly

as the noblest specimen in the world of eloquence, harmony and genius.

(V.279–280)

But now, in order to suggest something of the variety of Landor's criticism at its best, I will turn to remarks in "Southey and Porson," first on John Dryden, and then on Edmund Spenser. On Dryden, whom he is comparing with William Cowper, he is plain and judicious:

Dryden possesses a much richer store of thoughts, expatiates upon more topics, has more vigour, vivacity and animation. He is always shrewd and penetrating, explicit and perspicuous, concise where conciseness is desirable, and copious where copiousness can yield delight.

(V.202)

Now for Spenser, and an incrustation of warm images:

Spenser's is a spacious but somewhat low chamber, hung with rich tapestry on which the figures are mostly disproportioned, but some of the faces are lively and beautiful; the furniture is part creaking and worm-eaten, part fragrant with cedar and sandalwood and aromatic gums and balsams; every table and mantelpiece and cabinet is covered with gorgeous vases, and birds and dragons, and houses in the air.

(V.204)

The similitude is much more elaborate than usual. Suffice it that Landor's ready command of images, whether simple or ornate, adds very much to his persuasiveness, not least when he seeks to lay down bare principles for the writer's art. "Do not fear," Isaac Barrow advises Isaac Newton, "to be less rich in the productions of your mind at one season than at another":

Marshes are always marshes, and pools are pools; but the sea, in those places where we admire it most, is sometimes sea and sometimes dry land; sometimes it brings ships into port, and sometimes it leaves them where they can be refitted and equipped. The capacious mind neither rises nor sinks, neither labours nor rests, in vain.

(IV.153)

Conversation, distinguished by Landor from the dialogue in which we "adhere to one point," gave him the freedom he desired to pass from one subject or mood to another. However refreshing this may be, it entails a looseness of structure, and the freedom can be carried too far. In "Scipio, Polybius, and Panaetius," the talk opens in the stateliest manner just after Carthage has fallen. Scipio, the Roman commander, is shaken by reflections on the mortality of man and his empires. He receives in his tent two Greek friends of much learning, one of whom, Polybius, narrates a terrifying episode within the ruined city. Soon the speeches turn to the right and wrong employment of elephants in war. Then, in the hope of bringing a smile to Scipio's face, Polybius diverges into a story of lovemaking, an idyllic scene enchantingly laid, in which Euthymedes, a philosopher, is led on to pay his address to the lovely Thelymnia. After the moralizing, and the elephants, and still within the perimeter of the tragic city, the scene is strangely inappropriate. Yet Landor's prose here is at its most melodious: not a consonant is out of place to trip up the music.

The love episode has a parallel in "Epicurus, Leontion and Ternissa." It may be said that Epicurus on the brink of passion should not be so cool and fastidious a teacher as he shows himself, even though he is the apostle of restraint. But the piece does not fall apart as the previous example does. The prose, while beautifully modulated, is firmer and less ornate; and Epicurus, in his composed manner, is a fountain of wisdom. Here are only two of the many sayings that invite us to join in debate:

Paradox is dear to most people: it bears the appearance of originality, but is usually the talent of the superficial, the perverse and the obstinate.... (I.220)

Certainly there is a middle state between love and friendship, more delightful than either, but more difficult to remain in.... (I.222)

These two "Conversations" impress us with the easy continuity of their rhythm; it has few knots or thickenings. But sometimes, in the even course of his prose, Landor's feeling for words assumes a special concentration in the superb molding of a short passage. The most famous example occurs in "Aesop and Rhodopè":

There are no fields of amaranth on this side of the grave: there are no voices, O Rhodopè, that are not soon mute, however tuneful: there is no name, with whatever emphasis of passionate love repeated, of which the echo is not faint at last.

We cannot help speaking of the sensuous appeal of the language. The effect, though, is not due to language in abstraction from meaning. An abstract poem (or prose poem), if it could exist, would be a disembodied and dispirited thing. The passage is saved from such vacuity by the simple thought of mortality, and the simple but universal feeling it arouses. Taken as a mere expression of the thought, it would be emptily artificial. Rather, it is an issue of thought, feeling, and the artifice of language, so united as to be past final analysis. It does not challenge the beauty that may spring from deep thought or complex experience, neither of which is here. It is more limited than such a beauty, but within the narrower limit we are brought near to perfection.

Not so familiar is this word picture from *Pericles and Aspasia:*

There is a gloom in deep love, as in deep water: there is a silence in it which suspends the foot, and the folded arms and the dejected head are the images it reflects. No voice shakes its surface: the Muses themselves approach it with a tardy and a timid step, and with a low and tremulous and melancholy song.

(letter 47, X.33)

No one but Landor has drawn from the English language an effect of this kind, suggesting in its serenity and amplitude an Elysian repose. It requires the utmost delicacy to harmonize a quality so static and remote with the stir of human emotion. The beauty must not be flaunted; the elaboration must not be carried too far. Occasionally we are made aware of the risk. Time and again there are approaches to this highly wrought manner that owe their safety, and their force, to a properly classical restraint.

In *Pericles and Aspasia*, Landor seems to have been divided between two aims, that of giving ease and naturalness to the correspondents, and that of developing his own ideas with a considered and balanced art that was better suited to the work. When we find, as we quite often do, an easy and intimate tone, we shall be grateful for the refreshment; but we shall also accept formal discourses. These are much in the manner of the *Conversations*. On the whole, though, the letters are gentler. Most of them pass between women, Aspasia and her friend Cleone; and Cleone, we may note, suggests that all reflections that are "quiet, compassionate and consistent" are peculiarly womanish. Pericles feels the burden of his position, but can on occasion forget his need to be great; when he makes a stinging reply to a charge of embezzling public money, there is no stiffness in his self-vindication. The speech occurs at the end of a particularly lively sequence of letters (142–145). Through them pass the figures of Polynices—a fishmonger, who is the occasion of trouble with the comic writers—of Thucydides at work on his history, and of Sophocles exercising his personal charm. It is a fascinating panorama of Athens, created by the very personal vision of Landor. And here is one of many charming sidelights. Weary at last of war and public affairs, Aspasia writes to Pericles, yearning for a holiday:

When the war is over, as surely it must be in another year, let us sail among the islands of the Aegean, and be young as ever. O that it were permitted us to pass together the remainder of our lives in privacy and retirement! This is never to be hoped for in Athens.
I inherit from my mother a small yet beautiful house in Tenos: I remember it well. Water, clear and cold, ran before the vestibule: a sycamore shaded the whole building. . . .

(letter 173, X.170)

For Pericles there could be no retirement but death. There is a noble pride, worthy of Landor himself, in his farewell to Aspasia:

It is right and orderly, that he who has partaken so largely in the prosperity of the Athenians, should close the procession of their calamities. The fever that has depopulated our city, returned upon me last night, and Hippocrates and Acron tell me that my end is near.

(letter 235, X.244)

He reviews the course of his life and his friendship with great men:

And now, at the close of my day, when every light is dim and every guest departed, let me own that these wane before me, remembering, as I do in the pride and fullness of my heart, that Athens confided her glory, and Aspasia her happiness, to me.

(letter 235, X.245)

THE VERSE

IN order finally to reach Landor's epigrams, we must pass through the colonnade of *Gebir*, a poem that extends to seven books, or a little under two thousand lines. The main part of it was written when Landor was only twenty-two. At that age there could not be the control of mature years, but he never in fact became a master of big design. *Gebir* is a confused poem, the syntax and meaning often congested and obscure, while the quick changes of the narrative are joined by perfunctory links. Even line by line it is unsure, wavering between such felicities as

And the long moon-beam on the hard wet sand
Lay like a jasper column half-uprear'd . . .

(bk. I, 227–228)

or

Fears, like the needle verging to the pole,
Tremble and tremble into certainty . . .

and so insensitive a handling of alliteration as

Crown'd were tame crocodiles, and boys white-robed
Guided their creaking crests across the stream.

(bk. IV, 157–158)

The poem has an interesting place in the English tradition. It was published in 1798, a few weeks before the *Lyrical Ballads* of Wordsworth and Samuel Taylor Coleridge. Landor had not cast off the influence of Pope, but he had newly fallen under the spell of *Paradise Lost*. At the same time he drew direct sustenance from the ancient classics and had been rereading Pindar: "What I admired," he wrote to Forster in 1850, "was what nobody else had ever noticed—his proud complacency and scornful strength. If I could resemble him in nothing else, I was resolved to be as compendious and exclusive." The verse rises at best to an impressively sonorous quality, new and not imitative, though partly descending from the pomps of Milton. At least half a dozen times it carries us forward twenty years to the more assured Miltonics of John Keats's *Hyperion*: lines, to quote a single example, like these:

The wonted buzz and bustle of the court
From far through sculptured galleries met her ear.

(bk. I, 54–55)

Another passage, besides pointing forward in a general way to the romantics, was to have a parallel in Wordsworth's *Excursion* (1814)—Landor thought it a case of theft. Wordsworth does not at any point equal the climax reached in the last two of the lines quoted below. Yet by an irony these lines seem to be, par excellence, Wordsworthian in the grand manner:

> But I have sinuous shells, of pearly hue
> Within, and they that lustre have imbibed
> In the sun's palace porch, where, when unyoked,
> His chariot wheel stands midway in the wave.
> Shake one, and it awakens; then apply
> Its polisht lips to your attentive ear,
> And it remembers its august abodes,
> And murmurs as the ocean murmurs there.
>
> ("The Shepherd and the Nymph")

That, along with parts of *Chrysaor*, will retain our admiration, even though we find the poems difficult to read at length.

As with *Gebir*, which stands at the front of the narrative pieces, so with *Count Julian*, the leading tragedy, finished on the eve of Landor's marriage in 1811. It is a bewildering play. The reader, without the help of notes or stage directions, is puzzled by numerous cross-purposes and fluctuations of attitude. Yet there are enough fine passages to make it surprising that Landor did not develop as a dramatist. He even shows, for a spell of twenty lines near the end, that he could at times write remarkably "simple and lucid" English, in spite of Coleridge's assertion[10] that he had never learned to do so. The Moorish prince is being addressed by his son, who intercedes for Julian:

> Pity, release him, pardon him, my father!
> Forget how much thou hatest perfidy.
> Think of him, once so potent, still so brave,
> So calm, so self-dependent in distress,
> I marvel at him: hardly dare I blame
> When I behold him fallen from so high,
> And so exalted after such a fall.
> Mighty must that man be, who can forgive
> A man so mighty; seize the hour to rise,
> Another never comes: O say, my father!
> Say, "Julian, be my enemy no more".
> He fills me with a greater awe than e'er
> The field of battle, with himself the first,
> When every flag that waved along our host
> Droopt down the staff, as if the very winds
> Hung in suspense before him. Bid him go
> And peace be with him, or let me depart.
> Lo! like a god, sole and inscrutable,
> He stands above our pity.
>
> (V.iv.315-333)

---

[10] *Table Talk* (January 1834).

Landor was very disappointed with the reception to his work. As time passed, he persuaded himself that poetry was his "amusement." Indeed it very often was. I am not thinking so much of the trifles—a hundredweight of feathers—that he ought never to have published, such as the middle-length poems of *The Hellenics*. These are starred with felicities; and two, "The Hamadryad" and "Enallos and Cymodameia," are altogether charming. Some (though neither of these two) were originally composed in Latin. All are the work, and pastime, of a talented scholar, illuminated here and there by a genius for phrase; the latter poem, for example, tells how the lovers had arisen from the sea floor:

> . . . From the ground,
> Ere she had claspt his neck, her feet were borne.
> He caught her robe; and its white radiance rose
> Rapidly, all day long, through the green sea.
> Enallos loost not from that robe his grasp,
> But spann'd one ancle too. The swift ascent
> Had stunn'd them into slumber, sweet, serene,
> Invigorating her, nor letting loose
> The lover's arm below; albeit at last
> It closed those eyes intensely fixt thereon,
> And still as fixt in dreaming.
>
> (149-159)

In the best pieces there is no more than a pleasant appeal to our emotions, and death comes with a gentle elegiac sadness; here the verse is rightly deliberate and cool, sometimes with a notable purity of sound. Yet it is liable to fall into stiff folds. Again, the ingenuous stories depend so much on a meticulous shaping that small blemishes are not unimportant. Tongue and ear are not seldom troubled by a run of syllables like "unlovely things she shuns."[11] It is surprising that Landor, who could be a fine—and in epigram a supreme—craftsman, was yet so fallible.

To compose an epigram is largely, and sometimes from beginning to end, a matter of craft, depending on skill and practice. But among serious pieces, going back to the Greek anthology, the best are surprised into poetry. The unseen transformation takes place, a gift to the conscious mind—sometimes sudden, sometimes rising slowly out of the depths of contemplation. Let me take as a first example the quatrain "Dirce." I think Landor must have been brooding over a passage in his favorite "Conversation," "Epicurus, Leontion and Ternissa":

---

[11] From "Pan and Pitys," in *The Hellenics*.

Ternissa. I cannot bear to think of passing the Styx, lest Charon should touch me; he is so old and wilful, so cross and ugly.

Epicurus. Ternissa! Ternissa! I would accompany you thither, and stand between. Would not you too, Leontion?

(I.205)

In "Dirce" it is the same scene, even if those who are to shield the lovely passenger from Charon have become a "Stygian set." But now the whole image shines with magic, and in few syllables has become a consummate poem:

> Stand close around, ye Stygian set,
>   With Dirce in one boat conveyed!
> Or Charon, seeing, may forget
>   That he is old and she a shade.
>
>   (XVI.72)

Landor's great mastery was in such miniatures. But I must refer also to the many poems that, though often only a little longer, unfold beyond the confines of epigram. As a representative of these I would like to set down a tender twelve-line address to Ternissa:

> Ternissa! you are fled!
> I say not to the dead,
> But to the happy ones who rest below:
>   For, surely, surely, where
>   Your voice and graces are,
> Nothing of death can any feel or know.
>   Girls who delight to dwell
>   Where grows most asphodel,
> Gather to their calm breasts each word you speak:
>   The mild Persephone
>   Places you on her knee,
> And your cool palm smooths down stern Pluto's cheek.
>
>   (XVI.356–357)

It is unlike an epigrammatic movement, too leisurely and slow, ending almost deathly slow in the artful succession of full-sounding closed monosyllables.

The craft of epigram is somewhat narrowly traditional, for the form suitable to the English language is simple and definite in meter and regular in rhyme. Yet, where feeling and imagination are deeply engaged, the slightest inflection of cadence may work a miracle and the author's individual mark may be felt. This cannot happen, to anything like the same extent, with pieces that depend on a turn of satirical humor or wit. Landor wrote comparatively few of these that deserve special note, though some are excellent, such as the lines on Melville:

> God's laws declare
> Thou shalt not swear
> By aught in heaven above or earth below.
>   *Upon my honour!* Melville cries;
>   He swears, and lies,
> Does Melville then break God's commandment? No.
>
>   (XV.31)

It seems that Landor himself did not set a very high value on the epigrammatic art. In the "Conversation" between Southey and Porson, he makes the latter say that "certainly the dignity of a great poet is thought to be lowered by the writing of epigrams"; Southey replies that "the great poet could accomplish better things; the others could not." The best way I can defend the epigram is by developing the distinction I have already suggested between one kind and another, between those that stop at being delightful specimens of craft and those that go on to be poems in a full sense. In the first kind I include not only sallies of wit but also every miniature that, though assuming shape in the poet's mind, is yet in a sense external, like a piece of jade under the hand of a studious carver. The poet's work bears some resemblance to an exercise in a set subject, with a delicate but limited instrument. In this kind of epigram the distance between the writer of genius and the artificer of talent is much lessened. They are both, so to speak, in the same art class, trying their skill of execution. And so it happens on occasion that the little-known man is able to hold his own with the great. It may be difficult to tell them apart.

In the other kind of epigram there is still good craftsmanship, but there is also a going beyond the nice calculation of craft. Whether this is an inspiration from outside, Heaven or the Muses or a memory that transcends the individual, there is a release that brings into active harmony the inner powers of the poet—in Coleridge's ideal, the poet's "whole soul." And suffusing these powers there is a tinge or strain, intimately the poet's own, that deepens in the comtemplative mood.

It may seem that a distinction in the above terms is more suited to the dignity of a long poem, the "better thing" that a great poet can accomplish. Yet it can be applied also to the epigram, so long as we remember its minuteness of scale. And there is one other condition. For the sake of clarity we make a sharp division between talent and genius, craftsman and poet; but between one and the other there are in fact infinite gradations. As in so many things it is a case not of this or that, but of more or less. If we recognize the nature of the transition, it need not worry us that no one can say exactly where the dividing line falls. A bridge, after all, is a man-made or critic-made convenience.

Let me now attempt some application of what I have said, and let me begin with the tinge personal to the poet. It will not become fully apparent until his work develops. Yet I suggest that an essence of Landor can be felt in this simple quatrain, dated 1793:

> "Tell me what means that sigh", Ione said,
> When on her shoulder I reclined my head;
> And I could only tell her that it meant
> The sigh that swells the bosom with content.
> (XV.335)

The essence is faint, but will be perceptible to anyone sufficiently steeped in his work. But some of his more impressive pieces are not so unmistakably his: this, for example, which he wrote on seeing a single hair from the locks of Lucretia Borgia:

> Borgia, thou once wert almost too august
> And high for adoration; now thou'rt dust.
> All that remains of thee these plaits unfold,
> Calm hair, meandering in pellucid gold.
> (XV.30)

It is in its way a model, especially in the workmanship of its last line. Yet it may find a challenge in lines in Bowyer Nicholls' "On the Toilet Table of Queen Marie-Antoinette"[12]:

> This was her table, these her trim outspread
> Brushes and trays and porcelain cups for red;
> Here sate she, while her women tired and curled
> The most unhappy head in all the world.

Both these beautiful pieces are impersonal. They deserve a high place, but the signature is immaterial.

A good number of Landor epigrams can stand among the best in the language. These best include an inner ring of such perfection—two or three of Hilaire Belloc's are there—that, viewing them separately, I would hardly dare to call one better than another. But Landor has a more brilliant constellation than anyone else. I would not single out as its chief luminary either the famous epigram-lyric to Rose Aylmer or the equally well-known "I strove

with none; for none was worth my strife." The former, for all its exquisite grace, does not move me deeply, perhaps because one "night of memories and sighs" hardly seems an adequate offering. (Indeed, more than thirty years later Landor chanced to say in a letter to her niece, Rose Paynter, that "there are things in the world fairly worth even *two* sleepless nights."[13]) Again, I find the exalted note of "I strove with none" a little inhuman. The proud old man appeals to me more surely in a less well-known quatrain, where the sublime—and it is sublime—is lightly touched with the ridiculous:

> "Call me not forth", said one who sate retired,
> Whom Love had once, but Envy never, fired.
> "I scorn the crowd: no clap of hands he seeks
> Who walks among the stateliest of the Greeks".
> ("On Some Obscure Poetry," XVI.209)

The constant themes are age and death and love, sometimes interwoven. The wisdom is rarely so detached as here:

> How soon, alas, the hours are over,
> Counted us out to play the lover!
> And how much narrower is the stage,
> Allotted us to play the sage!
> But when we play the fool, how wide
> The theatre expands; beside,
> How long the audience sits before us!
> How many prompters! what a chorus!
> ("Plays," XVI.84)

Although words are not wasted, room is found for reflection. In other pieces there is a stringent brevity—in "Death stands above me, whispering low," and still more in

> Various the roads of life; in one
> All terminate, one lonely way.
> We go; and "Is he gone?"
> Is all our best friends say.
> ("From the Greek," XVI.193)

Age and death are faced with the old classical pride, and in the pieces that celebrate love this quality is found, along with the deep tenderness that is Landor's other great characteristic. It is the partnership of these two—not quite as equals, for tenderness

---

[12]Reprinted from *Love in Idleness* (London, 1885) in *Poems* (Oxford, 1943).

[13]*Letters of Walter Savage Landor, Private and Public*, p. 64; italics added.

as a rule dominates—that issues in the most moving and perfect of the poems. But first consider this, the last of three stanzas in which a minor piece is all at once pierced with tender feeling:

> Only two months since you stood here!
>   Two shortest months! then tell me why
> Voices are harsher than they were,
>   And tears are longer ere they dry.
>
> (XV.392)

And then, in these other lines, recognize, when pride comes in, a new power like the swell of an organ note:

> Remain, ah not in youth alone,
>   Tho' youth, where you are, long will stay,
> But when my summer days are gone,
>   And my autumnal haste away.
> *"Can I be always by your side?"*
>   No; but the hours you can, you must,
> Nor rise at Death's approaching stride,
>   Nor go when dust is gone to dust.
>
> (XV.391)

Here we are on the heights. There is little to do but quote, and I must resist the temptation to go on too far. The enchanting poem addressed to Ianthe beginning "Past ruin'd Ilion Helen lives" is well known from anthologies, and no one must miss it. But I cannot forbear from setting down two others, less widely familiar, that are unsurpassed; each is self-sufficient, as an epigram must be, yet each increases the light of the other:

> Proud word you never spoke, but you will speak
>   Four not exempt from pride some future day.
> Resting on one white hand a warm wet cheek
>   Over my open volume you will say,
> "This man loved *me!*" then rise and trip away.
>
> "Do you remember me? or are you proud?"
> Lightly advancing thro' her star-trimm'd crowd,
>   Ianthe said, and lookt into my eyes.
> "A *yes*, a *yes*, to both: for Memory
> Where you but once have been must ever be,
>   And at your voice Pride from his throne must rise".
>
> (XV.393, 395)

What is perfect may be wrongly praised, but never overpraised. The long life of Landor and the great expanse of his work show us sometimes a spectacle of high powers running to waste or marred by folly.

Here, in such handfuls of verse, all dross is refined away. A classical poet, he rises to an ecstasy that no romantic could outdistance. The pride is still there—the very word rings in the last two pieces—but, as it does homage, it is a noble pride. Landor was always the rebel, but at this moment we see him exempt from weakness and above strife.

SELECTED BIBLIOGRAPHY

I. BIBLIOGRAPHIES. T. J. Wise and S. Wheeler, *A Bibliography of the Writings in Prose and Verse* (London, 1919), additional contributions to periodicals are recorded in *Notes and Queries* (November 1952); T. J. Wise, *A Landor Library. A Catalogue of Printed Books, MSS and Autograph Letters* (London, 1928), privately printed catalog of the extensive collection in the Ashley Library, now in the British Museum; R. H. Super, *The Publication of Landor's Works* (London, 1952), an important study.

II. COLLECTED WORKS. *The Works*, 2 vols. (London, 1846): vol. I, *Imaginary Conversations*, and vol. II, *Poems; The Works*, 8 vols. (London, 1876), with a Life by J. Forster, based on his biography (1869); G. C. Crump, ed., *Imaginary Conversations*, 6 vols., *Poems, Dialogues in Verse, and Epigrams*, 2 vols., and *The Longer Prose Works*, 2 vols. (London, 1891–1893); T. E. Welby and S. Wheeler, eds., *The Complete Works*, 16 vols. (London, 1927–1936), the standard ed., with full bibliographical and textual apparatus; S. Wheeler, ed., *The Poems*, 3 vols. (Oxford, 1937), from *The Complete Works*.

III. SELECTIONS. S. Colvin, ed., *Selections from the Writings* (London, 1882), in the Golden Treasury series; E. de Selincourt, ed., *Imaginary Conversations, a Selection* (London, 1915), in the World's Classics; H. Ellis, ed., *Imaginary Conversations and Poems* (London, 1933), in Everyman's Library; T. E. Welby, comp., and F. A. Cavanagh and A. C. Ward, eds., *Imaginary Conversations* (Oxford, 1934); E. K. Chambers, ed., *Poetry and Prose* (Oxford, 1946), includes Swinburne's poem on Landor and essays by E. de Selincourt, W. Raleigh, and O. Elton; J. B. Sidgwick, ed., *The Shorter Poems* (Cambridge, 1946); R. Buxton, ed., *The Sculptured Garland: A Selection from the Lyrical Poems* (London, 1948); G. Grigson, ed., *Poems* (London, 1964); *Poetry and Prose* (London, 1978).

IV. SEPARATE WORKS. *Moral Epistle, Respectfully Dedicated to Earl Stanhope* (London, 1795); *The Poems* (London, 1795), suppressed by Landor; *Gebir, a Poem in Seven Books* (London, 1798), also in A. Symons, ed. (London, 1907); *Poems from the Arabic and Persian: With Notes by the Author of Gebir* (Warwick, 1800; type facs., London, 1927); *Poetry by the Author of Gebir* (London, 1802); *Gebirus, poema* (Oxford, 1803), Landor's Latin version of *Gebir*; *Simonidea* (Bath, 1806); *The Dun Cow; an Hyper-Satirical Dialogue in Verse. With Explanatory Notes* (London, 1808), published anonymously; *Three Letters, Written in Spain, to D. Francisco Riguelme* (London, 1809); *Ode ad Gustavum regem. Ode ad Gustavum exulem* (London, 1810); *Commentary on "Memoirs of Mr. Fox"* (London, 1812), published anonymously and suppressed, also in S. Wheeler, ed. (London, 1907); *Count Julian: A Tragedy* (London, 1812); *Letters Addressed to Lord Liverpool, and the Parliament, on the Preliminaries of Peace. By Calvus* (London, 1814), suppressed; *Idyllia nova quinque heroum atque heroidum &c* (Oxford, 1815); *Idyllia heroica decem* (Pisa, 1820); *Imaginary Conversations of Literary Men and Statesmen*, 3 vols. (London, 1824–1828; 2nd ser., 2 vols., 1829); *Gebir, Count Julian and Other Poems* (London, 1831); *Citation and Examination of William Shakespeare Touching Deer-Stealing to Which Is Added a Conference of Edmund Spenser with the Earl of Essex* (London, 1834); *The Letters of a Conservative: In Which Are Shown the Only Means of Saving What Is Left of the English Church* (London, 1836); *Pericles and Aspasia* (London, 1836); *A Satire on Satirists, and Admonition to Detractors* (London, 1836); *Terry Hogan, an Eclogue. Edited by Phelim Octavius Quarle* (London, 1836), published anonymously.

The Pentameron and Pentalogia (London, 1837); *Andrea of Hungary, and Giovanna of Naples* (London, 1839); *Fra Rupert: The Last Part of a Trilogy. The First Being Andrea of Hungary, the Second Being Giovanna of Naples* (London, 1840); A. Symons, ed., *The Hellenics of Walter Savage Landor. Enlarged and Completed* (London, 1847), with *Gebir* (London, 1907); *Poemata et inscriptiones* (London, 1847); *Imaginary Conversation of King Carlo Alberto and the Duchess Belgioioso* (London, 1848); *The Italics of Walter Savage Landor* (London, 1848); *Popery: British and Foreign* (London, 1851); *Imaginary Conversations of Greeks and Romans* (London, 1853); *The Last Fruit off the Old Tree* (London, 1853); *Letters of an American, Mainly on Russia and Revolution* (London, 1854); *Antony and Octavius. Scenes for the Study* (London, 1856); *Letters from W. S. Landor to R. W. Emerson* (Bath, 1856); *Dry Sticks, Fagoted* (London, 1858); *Savonarola e il priore di San Marco* (Florence, 1860), Landor's English version is in *Letters and Other Unpublished Writings* (1897); *Heroic Idylls, with Additional Poems* (London, 1863), first appearance of most of the Latin poems; S. Wheeler, ed., *Letters and Other Unpublished Writings* (London, 1897); S. Wheeler, ed., *Letters of Walter Savage Landor, Private and Public* (London, 1899); H. C. Minchin, ed., *Last Days, Letters and Conversations* (London, 1934); R. H. Super, ed., *To the Burgesses of Warwick* (London, 1949).

V. BIOGRAPHICAL AND CRITICAL STUDIES. R. W. Emerson, *English Traits* (London, 1856); K. Field, "Landor's Last Years in Italy," in *Atlantic Monthly* (April–June 1856); J. Forster, *Walter Savage Landor, A Biography*, 2 vols. (London, 1869); E. L. Lynton, "Reminiscences of Walter Savage Landor," in *Fraser's* magazine (July 1870); R. M. Milnes, *Monographs, Personal and Social* (London, 1873); L. Stephen, *Hours in a Library*, 3rd ser. (London, 1879), contains an essay on Landor's *Imaginary Conversations*; S. Colvin, *Landor* (London, 1881), in the English Men of Letters series; A. C. Swinburne, *Miscellanies* (London, 1886), contains Swinburne's essay on Landor in *Encyclopaedia Britannica*; E. W. Evans, *Walter Savage Landor. A Critical Study* (New York, 1892); F. Thompson, "Landor," in *The Academy* (27 February 1897); W. Bradley, *The Early Poems of Walter Savage Landor* (London, 1914); W. B. D. Henderson, *Swinburne and Landor* (London, 1918); A. H. Mason, *Walter Savage Landor, poète lyrique* (Paris, 1924); G. Fornelli, *Landor e l'Italia* (Forli, 1930); F. Elkin, *Walter Savage Landor's Studies of Italian Life and Literature* (Philadelphia, 1934); M. Elwin, *Savage Landor* (London, 1941); R. H. Super, *Landor: A Biography* (New York, 1954); M. Elwin, *Landor: A Replevin* (London, 1958); R. Pinsky, *Landor's Poetry* (Chicago, 1968); R. H. Super, *Walter Savage Landor: A Biography* (London, 1977); C. L. Proudfit, ed., *Landor as Critic* (London, 1979).

JANE AUSTEN

(1775-1817)

Brian Southam

It seems a contradiction in terms to talk in the same breath about literary greatness and popularity. Almost by definition a literary classic implies a minority audience, the professional attention of scholars and critics, and the enforced attention of students. In this light the case of Jane Austen is remarkable. This is a writer whose novels are among the acknowledged classics of English literature, studied in schools and universities throughout the world (at the latest count in thirty-five languages, including Chinese, Japanese, Persian, and Bengali), with an enormous bibliography of scholarship and criticism. Yet the six novels also attract an audience quite unconcerned about Jane Austen's critical reputation and status, who turn to the novels simply for enjoyment. This is the only instance in English literature where Samuel Johnson's image of "the common reader" really comes alive: the idea that the ultimate test of literary greatness is not in the formal recognition of the academics but rests with "the common sense of readers, uncorrupted by literary prejudices," and that this individual judgment should prevail over "the refinements of subtlety and the dogmatism of learning."

To stress Jane Austen's popularity is not to disparage the interest of critics and scholars. Literary historians delight in her ramified allusiveness. She is a critics' novelist par excellence, a writer whose subtlety and sophistication have always attracted subtle and sophisticated minds. The novels have proved to be wonderfully rewarding for interpretative critics who light on such a richness of meaning in their structure of language and the vibrations of irony. Rhetoricians of fiction have developed some of their finest discussions upon the study of her narrative methods. She is recognized as a supreme artist of the novel, a judgment that comes with special authority from other novelists as well as critics. The dramatic power of her characters led some nineteenth-century writers, including Macaulay and George Lewes, to regard her as no less than a "prose Shakespeare"; and in our own day Brigid Brophy has described Jane Austen as "the greatest novelist of all time."

In these terms Jane Austen's achievement sounds forbidding. But this is precisely what the novels are not. Whatever their dignity as works of literature, as books for reading their stance is completely unpretentious. They seem to offer themselves as no more than entertainment. Even after more than a century and a half, they continue to provide what is for most people the prime satisfaction of reading— the chance to escape from the pressures of ordinary life into the security of a created world, where another order of reality takes over for a while. As Clerihew Bentley put it, "The novels of Jane Austen / Are the ones to get lost in." His doggerel captures a popular truth. Her picture of Regency England still exerts a containing and hypnotic realism. For all its selectivity and exclusions, its remoteness from us in time and culture, it is a fictional world into which the reader can move easily and within which there is a powerful illusion of completeness and truth. The distance in time is bridged by the momentum of the writing, its brilliance, stylishness, and drive, by the fascination of the characters, by the skill of the storytelling, and by the appeal of the author's sane and sympathetic humanity. The novels offer us the excitement of sharing the vision of a creative mind and of responding to its energies of wit and understanding. Many critics have devoted many books to the analysis of these effects. But in the end, we are left with the plain fact of Jane Austen's readability, and within this her capacity to engage us imaginatively, emotionally, and intellectually.

The publication of the six novels between 1811 and 1817 marked a turning point in the development of English fiction. To Jane Austen's contemporary audience they revealed that the novel was capable of unsuspected power, that it was not to be dismissed as a mere pastime but was to be taken seriously as a form of literature, on a level with poetry and drama; and the early reviews by Sir Walter Scott and Richard Whately proved that criticism of the novel could itself rank as a serious intellectual activity. In the words of George Moore, Jane Austen turned the washtub into the vase. In effect, she transformed the eighteenth-century novel—which could be a clumsy and primitive performance, uncertain in its technique—into a work of art. She gave elegance and form to its shaping, style to its writing, and narrative skill to the presentation of the story. She invented her own special mode of fiction, the domestic comedy of middle-class manners, a dramatic, realistic account of the quiet backwaters of everyday life for the country families of Regency England from the late 1790's until 1815. Her account of this world is limited and highly selective. Its focus is upon the experiences of young women on the path to marriage; and there is no attempt to present a social panorama (as earlier novelists, such as Fielding and Smollett, had done), nor to describe the condition of industrial England and its appalling scenes of poverty and social unrest (a task which many Victorian novelists, from Dickens onward, were to set themselves). The modesty of Jane Austen's fictional world is caught in her remark to a novel-writing niece that "3 or 4 Families in a Country Village is the very thing to work upon," and her famous comment to a novel-writing nephew about "the little bit (two inches wide) of Ivory on which I work with so fine a Brush," which "produces little effect after much labour."

However, the claim to be a miniaturist is not to be taken at face value. There is certainly a miniaturism in the artistry of Jane Austen's language and the refinements of verbal style, and another kind of miniaturism in the tight social and geographical boundaries of the stories. But the novels themselves give an impression of size and strength; their fictional world is lucidly defined; they have dimensions of space and time and a firm logic of structure and organization. And within the limits of the "Country Village" scene and its neighborhood of respectable families, the novels communicate a profound sense of this moment in English history—when the old Georgian world of the eighteenth century was being carried uneasily and reluctantly into the new world of Regency England, the Augustan world into the romantic. The detailed account of its manners and fashionable pursuits is the descriptive groundwork for a highly analytical portrait of the age, which in turn conveys an implication of the deeper processes of change in early nineteenth-century society and in the individual's understanding of himself and the world around him.

II

HISTORICALLY, the novels are a challenge to the idea of society as a civilizing force and to the image of man's fulfillment as an enlightened social being. They question the driving optimism of the period—that this, in the development of English society, was triumphantly the Age of Improvement. Improvement was the leading spirit of Regency England, its self-awarded palm. Certainly it was unequaled as a period of economic improvement, in the wake of the industrial revolution. The wartime economy accelerated this new prosperity. Alongside this material improvement there was an air of self-conscious, self-congratulatory improvement in manners, in religious zeal, in morality, in the popularization of science, philosophy, and the arts. It was the age of encyclopedias, displaying the scope and categories of human knowledge in a digestible form. Books and essays paraded "Improvement" in their titles. In an essay "On the means of improving the people" (meaning the working people), Southey struck a common chord of complacent Englanderism, rejoicing to belong "to the middle rank of life . . . which in this country and at this time [1818] is beyond doubt the most favourable situation wherein man has ever been placed for the cultivation of his moral and intellectual nature."

But many of the achievements of Regency improvement were more apparent than real. This is nicely symbolized in its most conspicuous manifestation across the countryside itself. Landscape improvement was celebrated as the latest of the fine arts, much theorized about by contemporary aestheticians and brandished as a distinctively English contribution to the sum of civilization. Country houses and their grounds were expensively and elaborately improved, as General Tilney's "improving hand" has transformed the pre-Reformation convent of Northanger Abbey into a modern home of extravagant and faintly ludicrous luxury, and as in *Mansfield Park*, Repton, the fashionable improver of the day, is to transform Sotherton Court, a fine old Elizabethan country house, destined to be adorned in "a modern dress."

Throughout the novels Jane Austen plays deftly with the terminology of improvement, carrying its negative overtones of novelty, showiness, and superficiality into the realm of manners, behavior, and morality. Improvement can be a facade, a veneer. Jane Austen's skeptical, testing irony is the acid solution to peel it off, exposing the ramshackle foundations of social and personal morality which improvement could flashily conceal. For Mr. Rushworth, Sotherton is "a prison—quite a dismal old prison," crying out for the hand of Repton, whose specialty was making old houses look "cheerful." But the improving hand that first gets to work is Henry Crawford's. The cheerfulness and freedom he brings to Sotherton's "prison" is a sexual escapade with the owner's wife!

Socially and politically, improvement had a very bitter ring. Essentially it was a middle-class conceit. Outside the gentry's world of property and privilege was a wholly different scene. Throughout this period a third of the country, its laboring population, lived permanently on the verge of starvation, while the rich became even richer, their prosperity more blatant. In this fertile ground revolutionary ideas took root; and the period from the beginning of the 1790's until the Peterloo Massacre of 1819 was the most violent and repressive time in English history since the Civil War. Habeas corpus was suspended. Freedom of speech and freedom of assembly were curtailed. Bread riots were met with force, and with that blunt instrument the masses were kept down. Jane Austen gives no more than a fleeting glimpse of England's violence. In *Northanger Abbey* the London mobs come in as a joke. We never see the grinding misery of the poor; they are simply objects of charity, to be visited with a bowl of soup. It was not that Jane Austen was unaware. Hampshire and Kent, where she spent most of her adult life, were as badly hit by agricultural poverty as any other part of England. She must have seen it for herself and read about it in the essays and pamphlets of crusading reformers; and met it poignantly in her favorite poet, Crabbe, who delivered a starkly unpastoralizing report of what he observed, "the Village Life a Life of Pain."

There is no answer to the charge that Jane Austen should have devoted her genius to portraying the condition of England in all its misery and horror.

That would have been the great heroic task for a Tolstoy, a Dickens, a Zola, a Steinbeck, or a Lawrence; and she would never have succeeded. Writing out of the experiences that she knew intimately, and with the particular artistic gifts of ironic commentary and observation, she was able to do something else. The restricted social vision of the novels is a satire in itself. It presents a faithful image of the gentry's state of mind. Its limitations and exclusions are those of the prosperous, leisured, middle-class consciousness—self-regarding and self-centered, with its trivial, time-filling preoccupations. Its gaze was steadily averted from the unpleasant social realities of an economic system which enabled the gentry to enjoy this way of life. Their turning away from the visible truth was culpable. John Cartwright protested in 1812, "English gentlemen are perpetually travelling. Some go to see lakes and mountains" (as Elizabeth Bennet travels north with the Gardiners on a tour of the Peak district); "Were it not as allowable to travel for seeing the actual conditions of a starving people?"

One of Jane Austen's major achievements in the novels is to have captured the total illusion of the gentry's vision, the experience of living in privileged isolation, of being party to a privileged outlook, of belonging to a privileged community, whose distresses, such as they are, are private, mild, and genteel. Each of the homes and neighborhoods is its own "little social commonwealth," a microcosm, the center of a minute universe. The irony is implicit. The miniature issues of these little worlds, so realistic, so much the center of the stage, vivid and magnified to the point of surrealism, imply another, larger world beyond: "the flourishing grandeur of a Country, is but another term for the depression and misery of the people . . . to speak of the expensive luxury and refinements of the age, is but, with cruel irony, to remind us how many myriads are destitute." John Thelwall, in *The Peripatetic* (1793), was presenting a line of argument which was familiar to Jane Austen's audience and which the novels artfully exploit. "The depression and misery" of the common people was a theme she could never handle directly; her way was to treat it by silent implication.

But the silence is not total. Just once or twice there is an oblique glimpse of the macabre reality that lies outside the image of the gentry's mind. This happens, for example, when Jane Austen describes Lady Catherine de Bourgh's activities in the parish of Hunsford: "Whenever any of the cottagers were disposed to be quarrelsome, discontented or too poor, she sallied forth into the village to settle their differences, silence their complaints, and scold them into harmony and plenty." The scolding is a black joke. Hunsford's "poor" were people starving. Several chapters earlier in *Pride and Prejudice*, Catherine and Lydia Bennet bring home the latest military gossip: "Much had been done, and much had been said in the regiment since the preceding Wednesday; several of the officers had dined lately with their uncle, a private had been flogged, and it had actually been hinted that Colonel Forster was going to be married."

The device here is incongruity (compare Pope's "Puffs, powders, patches, bibles, billets-doux"). The wit is literary but the joke is not. The "private . . . flogged" was the recipient of lashes to the number of 750 or 1,000. Such punishments were widely reported. When the book appeared in 1813, these facts were in the public mind. The British army was then distinguished as the only European army outside Russia to retain flogging as a punishment. Its abolition was debated in Parliament in 1811 and 1812. In 1810, Cobbett had been charged with seditious libel and sentenced to two years' imprisonment for an anti-flogging article in the *Political Register*; Leigh Hunt got eighteen months for printing a similar article in the *Examiner*. Writing from prison, Cobbett continued his attack upon its hideous inhumanity and the nauseating hypocrisy of its official circumlocution, "corporal infliction": "Why not name the thing? *Flog is flog.*" Simply and laconically, Jane Austen did just that.

Flogging was one aspect of national repression. It was a punishment handed out to the militia, to wartime conscripts on duty in England, rather than to the regular troops serving in Europe. A similar reality of English life comes into chapter 14 of *Northanger Abbey*, where Henry Tilney makes fun of his sister for supposing that Catherine's mysterious hinting about "something very shocking indeed" in London—"uncommonly dreadful. I shall expect murder and every thing of the kind"—refers to a calamity that has actually happened. Catherine is merely talking about the latest Gothic novel; and Tilney enjoys himself, elaborating on his sister's fearful imaginings: ". . . she immediately pictured to herself a mob of three thousand men assembling in St. George's Fields; the Bank attacked, the Tower threatened, the streets of London flowing with blood. . . ." His tone is mocking and lighthearted. How could anyone be so silly?

But historically his sister's train of thought is completely credible. The novel is set at the turn of the century, and in July 1795 there was a meeting of the radical London Correspondence Society, 100,000 strong, at St. George's Fields. The speeches were inflammatory, with talk of "the holy blood of Patriotism, streaming from the severing axe. . . ." In October, George III was jeered on his way to the state opening of Parliament, his carriage was pelted, and a window cracked by a stone. The next day horse guards and troops had to clear the mobs out of his way to the theater. So Eleanor's misunderstanding and Tilney's joke touch upon circumstances bizarrely close to the truth. In this passage Jane Austen raises the specter of revolutionary uprising, a fear that haunted the establishment and the middle classes throughout this period and found a terrible nemesis in the deaths of Peterloo.

Jane Austen uses Tilney again in this historical function in chapter 24, when he reproves Catherine for her Gothic imaginings about his father and his dead mother, the half-formed idea that General Tilney might have murdered her:

Dear Miss Morland, consider the dreadful nature of the suspicions you have entertained. What have you been judging from? Remember the country and the age in which we live. Remember that we are English, that we are Christians. Consult your own understanding, your own sense of the probable, your own observation of what is passing around you—Does our education prepare us for such atrocities? Do our laws connive at them? Could they be perpetrated without being known, in a country like this, where social and literary intercourse is on such a footing; where every man is surrounded by a neighbourhood of voluntary spies, and where roads and newspapers lay every thing open? Dearest Miss Morland, what ideas have you been admitting?[1]

After this lecture Catherine runs off "with tears of shame." Tilney is laying Gothic ghosts. But for the readers of *Northanger Abbey* in 1818, the joke is hollow; the passage rings with a disquieting truth, and his reference to "a neighbourhood of voluntary spies" is a figure of speech unpleasantly literal. "Spies" were paid informers. At this time there was an extensive "spy system" (as it was then known), maintained by the government to infiltrate workingmen's organizations. Informing was promoted as a citizen's patriotic duty. In parliamentary debates in

[1] All quotations from the novels are from R. W. Chapman, ed., *Novels: . . .*, 5 vols. (Oxford, 1923; repr. 1926, 1933; 2 vols., 1934).

the summer of 1817, the foreign secretary, Robert Castlereagh, maintained that "morality, religion, and social order, are best defended at home by spies and informers." But the spy system was vigorously challenged then, as it had been years before, in the early 1790's, when it was employed to counter the earliest radical groups. While there was deep fear that the horrors of the French Revolution would be enacted in England, nonetheless the incursions of state repression were strongly opposed. In 1812 one critic went so far as to describe the police as "a system of tyranny; an organized army of spies and informers, for the destruction of all public liberty, and the disturbance of all private happiness." This was a Gothicism of Regency life, all too real, that Tilney's well-bred and enlightened reasonableness could never rob of its terrors.

It is with such momentary and glancing allusions that Jane Austen reminds the reader of the England unseen, which lies beyond the blinkered social focus of the gentry's vision. But these are pinpoints of light. There was another "depression and misery" that she knew intimately, and could command fully and creatively. This was the private, personal history of women like herself, trapped and stifled within the confines of a hothouse society, recognizing its brittleness and artificiality, but with no other world to exist in. These historical issues bear most immediately upon Jane Austen as a _woman_ novelist, presenting an account of society from the woman's point of view—the woman's experience of men, of other women, of their families, the social circles to which they were confined, and, ultimately, their experience of themselves and of life. For the first time in English literature, outside Shakespeare, we meet heroines who are credible, with minds, with the capacity to think for themselves, with ambition and wit, with an interior life independent of men and the will to challenge them emotionally and intellectually, with the energy to shape their relationships.

The intense inner drama of the novels arises from the conflict between the individuality of the heroines, their private needs and aspirations, and the leveling, restrictive pressures of a tight social morality. Their predicament is to be born into a world which values them for their marriageability, where the culmination of womanhood is to be a wife and mother, where their lives are regulated by the artificial ideals of polite femininity. The six novels are repeated dramatizations of this theme. Each of the heroines has to learn to understand herself and her relationships with other people. She has to practice the morality of compromise and discover her own way of accepting the demands of society while preserving the integrity of her own values and beliefs. Each of the heroines travels the path of self-discovery and growth; they struggle toward self-determination and fulfillment; and Jane Austen leaves it an open question, open to us as readers to decide, how far they win through, how far they fail.

The recognition of this theme shows us how inadequate it is to label Jane Austen as a "woman" writer or as "the novelist of Regency England." These labels are accurate, and they draw attention to important aspects of her work. But her theme has as much to do with men as with women, and it relates to any society which imposes a strict code of manners and tightly defined roles upon the people who exist within it. Jane Austen's attitude may seem unheroic. She has no stirring message, no doctrine of personal liberation. Her view is coldly realistic. She presents the sad truth that however much people may dream of personal freedom, of escaping from the constrictions of their family or of society at large, we are nonetheless tied by blood and time and circumstance, with bonds of need and dependence, to people we hate or despise or are bored by, yet cannot do without. Man's inhumanity to man can be polite, intimate, and domestic. The novels confirm that life is a comedy to those who think. A thinking novelist, she casts her heroines in a thinking mold. But this single truth is not exclusive: life is also a tragedy to those who feel. And the deepest and most powerful tension arises from Jane Austen's struggle to maintain a hold over experiences that threaten the comic surface of the novels with the "feeling" tones of tragedy.

III

SOME books leave us totally incurious about their authors. In the novels of Jane Austen, however, the writer's presence is strongly marked, not just in an official role, as narrator or commentator, but as an active, pervasive "artistic" presence—controlling, arranging, manipulating—reminding us continually that the realism of the novels is wholly artificial, wholly an effect of technique; not "realism" created out of the vast, detailed sprawl of "naturalism," but an economic, succinct realism formed out of the selection of detail and the synergy of its relationships. The realism is moral as well as aesthetic; it offers an interpretation and criticism of life, as well as a picture of it; and unless the reader deliberately switches off, its assertion of values leaves no room for indifference, and a great deal of room for reservation and disagreement.

Many readers respond to the novels at an extremely personal level, finding a "Gentle Jane," a presence that is intimate and lovable. Katherine Mansfield declared that "Every true admirer of the novels cherishes the happy thought that he alone—reading between the lines—has become the secret friend of their author." These are sentimental delusions but proudly confessed to. A. C. Bradley, the great Shakespearean critic, spoke of Elizabeth Bennet as a girl we are meant to fall in love with, as he did. Kipling wrote two poems in Jane Austen's honor, one of which ends with the stirring cry, "Glory, love, and honour unto England's Jane." The other, entitled "Jane's Marriage," has her transported to Paradise. When she asks for "Love," Captain Wentworth is called up from "a private limbo," where he has been reading a copy of *Persuasion*, which "told the plain / Story of love between / Him and Jane." These two poems frame a story called "The Janeites." This is narrated by a soldier in the trenches in World War I. In full, fruity Cockneyese, he holds forth on his discovery that the ladies and gentlemen of the novels "was only just like people you run across any day," and connects them incongruously with figures in his own life. He has learned about Jane Austen from his officers, the Janeites of the title, who form their own little secret society, with its code of knowing catchwords and allusions to the novels. The fiction is answered in fact, for the Janeites still exist, enthusiasts who know the novels through and through, read and reread them, see her characters in the world around them, and talk and write about Jane Austen with an amazing intimacy and affection. Some critics dismiss the Janeite following as cultish and sentimental. This may or may not be so. What is indisputable is the depth of the Janeite response to a quality of the author's personality that comes across with a living force.

But other readers find this personality unsympathetic, even repellent. Charlotte Brontë discovered a writer altogether out of touch with the "Passions," "a complete and most sensible lady, but a very incomplete, and rather insensible (*not senseless*) woman." Mark Twain boasted that she awakened in him nothing less than an "animal repugnance." D. H. Lawrence admired the vivid presentation of her characters, but he abhorred the writer, "a narrow-

gutted spinster." He enlarged upon this remark in "A Propos of *Lady Chatterley's Lover*," where he mourned the loss of what he calls the "blood-connexion" that linked the classes in the England of Defoe and Fielding: "And then, in the mean Jane Austen, it is gone. Already this old maid typifies 'personality' instead of character, the sharp knowing of apartness instead of knowing in togetherness, and she is, to my feeling, thoroughly unpleasant, English in the bad, snobbish sense of the word, just as Fielding is English in the good, generous sense."

These comments have a historical force as well as a personal validity. Charlotte Brontë is voicing a mid-nineteenth-century romantic position, objecting to Jane Austen's morality of self-discipline, good sense, and rational feeling, and classifying her as a "society" novelist, not a novelist of humanity. Lawrence invokes a twentieth-century psychological romanticism, arbitrary but illuminating. During the later eighteenth century, English society lost the last vestiges of social unity, its paternalistic "blood-connexion," the better side of feudalism. By Jane Austen's day this had given way to a divisive class system with its elaborate snobberies of money and rank. To this extent the "knowing of apartness" that Lawrence identified in the novels is an authentic social experience, not solely a projection of some psychological apartness in Jane Austen's own makeup.

Jane Austen's spinsterdom is also taken up in W. H. Auden's verse epistle "Letter to Lord Byron," in which he asks the poet to tell her "How much her novels are beloved down here," and continues with a confession of his own discomfort at finding such a streak of cold realism in her nature:

> You could not shock her more than she shocks me:
> Beside her Joyce seems innocent as grass.
> It makes me most uncomfortable to see
> An English spinster of the middle class
> Describe the amorous effects of "brass",
> Reveal so frankly and with such sobriety
> The economic basis of society.

Auden's point is that Jane Austen behaves out of character—fancy an English lady, a spinster at that, betraying the secrets of her class! Auden's "shock" is a silent allusion to the popular myth of "Gentle Jane"—an eternal maiden aunt, an inspired amateur in the best English tradition, the homely spinster who put down her stitching to pick up her pen, who wrote in odd moments snatched from her domestic round, a kind of Sunday writer who scribbled just to please herself and entertain the family, who sat quietly in the corner, silently observing the world go by, catching a turn of phrase, the flow of conversation, sketching the characters and mannerisms of her neighbors and friends, describing their comings and goings, their contretemps, their joys and sadnesses, their follies, stupidities, and mentionable vices. This notion of Jane Austen's unpretentious amateurism is a touching picture with some fragments of truth. The novels were indeed based upon direct observation; and we can see from her letters that the world of the fiction is a faithful account of the small social world in which she passed her days—with its local balls, its gossip, chatter, and scandalizing, its marriageable young ladies and eligible young men.

But there the myth dissolves. The facts of Jane Austen's life tell a different story, one which confirms everything that the novels convey of their author's professionalism, her capacity for critical, creative detachment, and her total artistic command over the daily experiences by which her writing was fed. The sheer readability of the novels seems so natural and effortless that we take it for granted, just as we accept the feat of realism and the vitality of the characters. As Virginia Woolf recognized, "Of all great writers she is the most difficult to catch in the act of greatness." How difficult, and deceptive, we can see in the remarks of Henry James, who identified the "little touches of human truth, little glimpses of steady vision, little master-strokes of imagination," but put them down to "the extraordinary grace of her facility . . . of her unconsciousness." He was deceived by the art that conceals art. Seeing no evidence of effort, he supposed there was none, unaware that the achievement of the novels was the fruit of twenty years' apprenticeship, of a style and technique evolved through constant experiment, and that the story of her life is not just that of a writer, but of a writer determined to be published, determined to find an audience beyond the admiring circle of her family and friends, and determined to formulate a mode of social satire that would enable her to practice as a critic from within, delighting her audience with a portrait of themselves, flattering and entertaining in its mimetic accuracy but scathing in its judgment and in the implication of its silent exclusions. G. K. Chesterton observed that "Jane Austen may have been protected from truth: but it was precious little of truth that was protected from her." The novels wear a deceptive charm—as Richard

Simpson explained it, "a magnetic attractiveness which charms while it compels"—and their air of modesty is the modesty of Swift's *A Modest Proposal*, insidious and explosive.

IV

JANE AUSTEN's life was private and uneventful, and by modern standards extraordinarily narrow and restricted. Her forty-two years, from 1775 to 1817, were passed entirely among her family and friends. She visited London from time to time, but never mixed in fashionable society and avoided literary circles like the plague: "If I am a wild beast, I cannot help it." She never married; she never traveled abroad; she was unknown to the public. The novels were published anonymously and her authorship was revealed only after her death, through a biographical notice that came out with *Northanger Abbey* and *Persuasion* at the end of 1817. The pattern of her life was set by her dedication to writing; and this in turn may help us to understand her obsessive need for privacy, her choice of spinsterdom, and her role in the family as a dutiful daughter, an affectionate sister, and a favorite aunt to hordes of nephews and nieces. The circumstances of her life also help us to understand certain qualities in her writing: its highly personal tone; its allusiveness; its dramatic aspect, in the prominence of dialogue and in the scenelike staging of the characters and action; and its concentration on personal and family relationships.

Her childhood was spent in the small Hampshire village of Steventon, where her father, George Austen, was the parish clergyman. It was a large and literary household. Her father was a classical scholar with a taste for fiction, including the Gothic thrillers that Jane Austen was to make fun of in *Northanger Abbey*. Her mother was well known for her impromptu poems and stories. While at Oxford her brothers Henry and James edited a literary periodical, the *Loiterer*, in 1789–1790. There was a tradition of reading aloud; and with two daughters and five sons in the household, the family was able to put on plays. Friends and relatives were recruited and the rectory barn was converted into a small theater for summer performances, while during the winter they played in the rectory itself. Among the productions were farces whose humor could be very broad and unrectorylike.

From the outset Jane Austen enjoyed the encouragement of a close and appreciative audience. Her early writing, dating from about 1787, the so-called juvenilia, has come down to us in three manuscript notebooks, which contain pieces going up to about 1793. Soon after that she wrote her first important work, a novel in letters, entitled *Lady Susan*. About 1795 she began another epistolary novel, "Elinor and Marianne," which was eventually turned into *Sense and Sensibility*. In 1796–1797 she completed the earliest version of *Pride and Prejudice*, then called "First Impressions," which her father tried unsuccessfully to get published. In the next year *Northanger Abbey* was written.

Until this time Steventon had provided an ideal context for her work. The family was a keen audience. There was a wide neighborhood of visitable families, of clergymen and local gentry; and further afield, throughout southern England, the West Country, and the Midlands, there was an extensive network of Austens and Leighs (her mother's family) to be visited. But this pattern of life changed in 1801, when Mr. Austen gave up his parish and retired to Bath with his wife, Jane, and Cassandra. He died in 1805, and until 1809, they had to put up with a succession of temporary lodgings or long visits to their relatives in Bath, London, Clifton, Stoneleigh Abbey, Warwickshire (the family seat of the Leighs), and Southampton. During this period Jane Austen wrote little. The moves upset her, and there were other disappointments. In 1803 the manuscript of *Northanger Abbey* had been sold to a publisher, but was never printed. In December 1804 she lost her closest friend, Anne Lefroy, and a month later her father died. These events seem to have stopped her work on *The Watsons*, a manuscript she abandoned altogether. Its social picture is one of unrelieved bleakness, its heroine distressed, and its satire sharp to the point of cruelty. It signals a failing of generosity, a loss of creative power, which may stem from the sadness of these years.

In 1809, Jane Austen came to her last home, Chawton Cottage, two miles south of Alton on the Winchester road, and not far from Steventon. Here she spent the remaining years of her life. The return to a settled domestic existence seems to have revived her energies. She took up the manuscripts of *Sense and Sensibility* and *Pride and Prejudice* to get them ready for publication; and in 1811 a publisher agreed to produce the first of these novels with her guarantee against loss. In 1811 she also began *Mansfield Park*, which was completed in the summer of 1813

and published in 1814. Between January 1814 and March 1815 she wrote *Emma*, which appeared at the end of 1815. *Persuasion* was written between August 1815 and August 1816; and in 1816 she also revised *Northanger Abbey*.

In January 1817 she began *Sanditon*, her seventh novel, writing and revising more than 24,000 words in eight weeks. But by then she was far into her last illness, and the manuscript was put aside. It is an amazing document, a fierce and energetic satire on invalidism and hypochondria, Jane Austen's wry protest at her own condition. In May she was taken to Winchester to be under the care of a surgeon. Her illness was then unidentified; we now know it to have been Addison's disease. On the morning of 18 July, at 4:30, she died. Asked for her last wishes, she replied, with characteristic dignity, economy, and wit, "I want nothing but death." Six days later she was buried in Winchester Cathedral.

The course of Jane Austen's emotional life is obscure. The earliest of her surviving letters date from 1796, when she was twenty-one. They tell us of the parties and dances she went to locally, about visits to London, Bath, and to the coast. But there is virtually nothing about her relationships with men. The few comments are ironic and evasive. All we have are some tantalizing stories in the family recollections and memoirs: that there was a mild flirtation with a young Irishman in 1796; that two or three years later she may have turned down a fellow of Emmanuel College, Cambridge, staying in the locality; that in November 1802 she agreed to marry a Hampshire man, but that she changed her mind the very next morning. There are a number of other stories connecting her with someone—a naval officer, an army officer, or a clergyman—with whom she is said to have fallen in love but who died before their friendship could develop. There is no way of enlarging upon these vague and contradictory reports, for Cassandra destroyed her sister's most intimate letters. What remains, in the novels themselves, in *Sense and Sensibility* and *Persuasion* most of all, is the unquestionable proof that their author profoundly understood the experience of love, of love broken and disappointed, and the pains of loss and loneliness. As the Victorian novelist Julia Kavanagh observed, "If we look under the shrewdness and quiet satire of her stories, we shall find a much keener sense of disappointment than of joy fulfilled. Sometimes we find more than disappointment."

It seems unlikely that we shall ever know why Jane

Austen remained unmarried. There may be a faint clue in *Lady Susan*. The heroine is a woman with a dominant, aggressive personality, talents which lead her to the brink of social self-destruction. It is a study in frustration, of a woman's fate when society has no use for her stronger, more "masculine" talents. How far are we entitled to read this as a self-admonitory fable? Certainly Jane Austen at seventeen was already in command of a powerful intellect which was to be turned more and more searchingly upon the people around her. Later in life she was described as "a poker of whom everyone is afraid." The remark is malicious. But it conveys an element of truth. Jane Austen must have been a formidable woman to meet, even as a young woman. In Kipling's sympathetic fantasy-poem Jane Austen is a sadly resigned Anne Elliot who missed her Wentworth. This image of the older woman needs to be balanced with an image of Jane Austen when young—an Elizabeth Bennet, brilliant, vivacious, and witty, yet critical, challenging, and demanding, a woman who asked something of life and who never met a Darcy who could match her.

V

THE six novels fall into two distinct groups. The early novels—*Sense and Sensibility, Pride and Prejudice,* and *Northanger Abbey*—were begun in the 1790's and were rewritten and revised before their eventual publication; whereas the three later novels —*Mansfield Park, Emma,* and *Persuasion*—belong entirely to Jane Austen's years of maturity. This order helps us to trace her technical development in the art of narration and to follow the changes in her view of life. Qualities in the early novels seem to mark them as the work of a younger woman, while the imaginative temper of the second group is different. There is also the question of historical change. Jane Austen was thinking of this when she revised *Northanger Abbey* in 1816. She provided an "Advertisement" warning readers that the book had originally been intended for publication in 1803, "that thirteen years have passed since it was finished, many more since it was begun, and that during that period, places, manners, books, and opinions have undergone considerable changes."

This warning was more necessary than Jane Austen could have guessed, for the publication of *Northanger Abbey* was delayed until the end of 1817,

when it came out as part of a four-volume set alongside *Persuasion*. Both novels have a Bath setting. But a great deal had happened to society during these years. While the story of *Northanger Abbey* is undated, its fashions and literary jokes belong firmly to the turn of the century. In *Persuasion* the story is precisely dated and the sequence of contemporary events is used to work the plot: its beginning in "the summer of 1814" is a prelude to Wentworth's return from duty at sea; in April 1814, Napoleon abdicated; and in the autumn, released from active service, Wentworth comes back on leave to Somerset. Eight years before, as a penniless lieutenant, with a chancy life at sea, he was not considered a fit match for a baronet's daughter. But now the situation has changed. He is a captain, with a modest fortune in prize money. Although the Wentworths are nobodies alongside the ancient lineage of the Elliots, he has been made socially respectable by the new heroic dignity of his profession. The nation was indebted to its navy, both for the victories at sea and the safeguarding of its trading routes.

The historical distance between *Northanger Abbey* and *Persuasion* brings out another major feature of Jane Austen's development, the gradual shift of emphasis from literary to social satire. Her earliest creative impulse, as we can see it in the juvenilia, was distinctively *critical.* The childhood pieces parody virtually every style of fiction around her in the 1790's, and the three early novels develop directly out of that tradition. Although none of the manuscripts survive, we can reconstruct the process by which they were transformed from straight parody into realistic comedy of manners. *Northanger Abbey* looks as if it was put together from two separate pieces: a skit on the Fanny Burney style of social novel, telling of a young woman's first experience of polite society, added to a satire on Gothic fiction. *Sense and Sensibility* began as a novel in letters, mocking Marianne Dashwood as a heroine of sensibility from sentimental fiction, and exposing her correspondence to the comments of her sensible sister Elinor, who would give her sound advice on controlling her feelings, in the style of conduct fiction. "First Impressions," the original version of *Pride and Prejudice,* takes its title directly from the terminology of sentimental fiction, where it meant trust in one's immediate feelings, usually love at first sight.

In rewriting these early versions, it was not Jane Austen's purpose to remove the literary satire altogether, but to adjust it to a more realistic social setting. The final *Northanger Abbey* remains a Gothic satire; Marianne Dashwood still carries traces of her literary origin, and occasionally shifts back into her former role as a joke heroine; and the "First Impressions" theme is carried strongly into *Pride and Prejudice*. Neither did Jane Austen's interest in literary satire peter out. It was an experience that she shared with her readers and it continued, at a more subdued level, throughout the later novels until *Sanditon*, where, strangely, literary satire comes to the fore again. Today this may seem to be a rather specialized matter. But for Jane Austen and her contemporaries, literature carried an important social and cultural significance and the novel in particular played a vital part in creating an image of middle-class identity; indeed, the novel was a product of middle-class society, catering to its interests and tastes.

Its rise in England came in the eighteenth century with the growth of an increasingly prosperous and leisured reading public. With the new wealth of the industrial revolution, this audience grew rapidly. By the 1770's novel writing had become a largely commercial activity, and literary hacks produced a flood of popular reading, the "mere trash of the circulating library," as Jane Austen described it. The character of this fiction was determined largely by the character of its public, an audience of women with time and money on their hands and an appetite for easy reading. There was still an audience for the picaresque stories of Defoe, Fielding, and Smollett, with their coarse vitality and the knock-about humor of low life. But the fashionable female audience ("our fair readers" to the writers and reviewers) wanted a literature flattering to them, that celebrated the arrival in English life of an improved level of society, and in which women were seen to have the good taste to cultivate their finer feelings and to develop an elaborate code of manners.

There developed a bewildering variety of fictional types and subtypes. But one principle runs throughout the "society" literature of this period: the cult of feeling. This is one aspect of the eighteenth-century shift from the Age of Reason to romanticism; and its significance as a symptom of deeper cultural change should not be ignored. But in fiction it had a very degraded "social" manifestation for readers who practiced a snobbery of feeling to differentiate themselves from previous generations. Sensibility became the class badge of polite society, and the central figure of its literature was the so-called sentimental heroine of feeling. Her heroism is measured by the strength of her passions and the delicacy with which her sensibility trembles. Heroines prove their ladylikeness in displays of feeling, in blushes, tears, hysterics, swoonings, and madness. Lovers fall in love at sight; they are wracked by passion and the pangs of separation, and are elevated by the portrayable ecstasies of union. The plots were designed to throw them into a succession of dangers, both moral and physical, from which they could be rescued by heroes of exemplary courage and virtue. In Gothic versions they would be swept away, in distant times, to the remote medieval gloom of crumbling fortresses ruled over by Germanic or Italianate barons.

The cult of sensibility runs throughout the fiction of this period, in historical romances (where there was often a quieter responsiveness to the charms of the past or to an evocative, melancholic landscape), even in the novels of Fanny Burney, the only writer at this time to make a genuine attempt to portray the realities of life for a young woman entering polite society. Jane Austen was not the only one to react critically. Moralists attacked the cult as a dangerous, deceptive poisoner of impressionable young minds, while satirists made fun of it.

Northanger Abbey itself stands in a flourishing tradition of the mock Gothic. However, Jane Austen was alone in understanding the potentialities of fiction as a form of literature, a belief that she doesn't force upon her readers, but which she tried to realize in her own writing, and to which she alluded jokingly in chapter 5, where she reports a typical 1790's conversation:

"I am no novel reader—I seldom look into novels—Do not imagine that I often read novels—It is really very well for a novel."—Such is the common cant.—"And what are you reading, Miss—?" "Oh! it is only a novel!" replies the young lady; while she lays down her book with affected indifference, or momentary shame.—"It is only Cecilia, or Camilla, or Belinda;" or, in short, only some work in which the greatest powers of the mind are displayed, in which the most thorough knowledge of human nature, the happiest delineation of its varieties, the liveliest effusions of wit and humour are conveyed to the world in the best chosen language.

The rhetorical claim of the last five lines is an irony in itself. This is exactly what the contemporary novel was *not*, not even the works of Fanny Burney named here; and Jane Austen is able to say this because she knew so clearly what had once been achieved half a century before in the hands of Fielding and Richardson, and what could be achieved again, through her own work.

In Catherine Morland, Jane Austen presents a stock figure of current satire, the young woman so captivated by the exotic thrills of the Gothic that she is ready to see the world through the lens of her latest reading, in this case the most popular of all such novels, *The Mysteries of Udolpho* (1794) by Anne Radcliffe. Employing this common satirical device, Jane Austen's special twist was to show that the heroine doesn't have to look for excitement in books since there is a Gothicism of ordinary life, which can be experienced in the clear light of day.

This is the literary beginning to an issue raised again and again for the heroines of the six novels: the need to distinguish between illusion and reality, to be aware that the imagination has the power to enforce its own slanted vision upon the world. It is part of the struggle that the heroines have with the forces of pride and prejudice and with sense and sensibility, and which Emma Woodhouse faces in romantically casting Harriet Smith in the role of a distressed heroine and herself as a confidante-savior. The educative process of the novels is to take the heroines along the path of disillusionment toward a clearer, unimpeded knowledge of themselves and their relationships; and the literary delusion is one of the blocks that they have to overcome.

Jane Austen's anti-romanticism was identified by Sir Walter Scott in 1816 in his review of *Emma*. He remarked that the story has "cross purposes enough (were the novel of a more romantic cast) for cutting half the men's throats and breaking half the women's hearts." No throats are cut; no hearts are broken. The novel plays with the devices and situations of romantic fiction, adjusting them to a story whose dramas and distresses are personal and domestic. Scott was looking at *Sense and Sensibility* and *Pride and Prejudice* as well; and he used this review as an occasion for placing Jane Austen's achievement in a new realist tradition of contemporary life. Whereas the sentimental romance purported to be an imitation of *la belle nature*, a higher and a nobler reality to be aspired to, Jane Austen provided its antithesis, an imitation of the tempo and character of ordinary existence, to be faced as Elizabeth Elliot in *Persuasion* faces "the sameness and the elegance, the prosperity and the nothingness of her scene of life . . . a long uneventful residence in one country circle." In the

works of Jane Austen, Scott declares, we have the accuracy and realism of "the modern novel."

We can extend this historical placing by a glance sideways to the situation in poetry at this time. Jane Austen's critical response to fiction is almost exactly matched in Wordsworth's critical reaction to the state of verse. Like her, he found himself surrounded by a tired, imitative school of writing, highly conventionalized and remote from the language and lives of ordinary people. His creative counterstatement was the poetry of the *Lyrical Ballads* (1798); and his formal protest was the "Advertisement" to that volume and the preface to the second edition (1800), where he complained, in words that Jane Austen could very well have used herself, of the public appetite for melodrama and extravagance, "this degrading thirst after outrageous stimulation" and the "frantic novels" which were currently so popular. He drew attention to his choice of "incidents and situations from common life," presented, as far as possible, in "a selection of language really used by men," a formula which applies, with only a modification upward into middle-class life, to Jane Austen's procedure in the novels. Just as the *Lyrical Ballads* set a standard in poetry, so her writing provided an implicit commentary on the state of English fiction as she found it in the 1790's. Her work was in effect a liberation of the novel from its servile function as a class entertainment and as an instrument of cultural self-flattery. She showed instead that fiction could present an artistic image, delightful for its accuracy and realism, yet disturbing, too, for within this accuracy and realism lay the incisive, anatomizing, analytical truth of its commentary upon middle-class life and manners.

VI

JANE AUSTEN's contemporary readers paid her the highest possible tribute to an artist in the realist tradition—they confused her fiction with reality. She was plagued by people who went round finding originals for the characters. In June 1814, a month after the publication of *Mansfield Park*, she met a fantasticating Miss Dusautoy, who had "a great idea of being Fanny Price—she and her youngest sister together, who is named Fanny." Then there was the deluded Miss Isabella Herries, who, having read *Emma*, was "convinced that I had meant Mrs. & Miss

Bates for some acquaintance of theirs—People whom I never heard of before." We can smile at their naiveté and share Jane Austen's annoyance that strangers should foist such silly identifications upon her (including the suggestion that the Dashwood sisters in *Sense and Sensibility* were portraits of herself and her sister Cassandra). But, in all their simplicity, these comments testify to the convincing dramatic life of her characters. This quality was more deeply experienced by a Mrs. Cage, who came away from *Emma*, her imagination bemused: "I am at Highbury all day," she reported, "and I can't help feeling I have just got into a new set of acquaintances." A cooler, more analytical note is struck by Lady Harriet Gordon, who read *Mansfield Park* when it first appeared and whose comments Jane Austen considered important enough to place in a collection of "Opinions":

In most novels you are amused for the time with a set of Ideal People whom you never think of afterwards or whom you the least expect to meet in common life, whereas in Miss Austen's works, and especially in Mansfield Park you actually *live* with them, you fancy yourself one of the family; and the scenes are so exactly descriptive, so perfectly natural, that there is scarcely an incident or conversation, or a person that you are not inclined to imagine you have at one time or other in your Life been a witness to, born a part in, and been acquainted with.[2]

The same point was developed more systematically by contemporary reviewers. An anonymous contributor to the *British Critic* for March 1818 remarked that "we instantly recognize among some of our acquaintances, the sort of persons she intends to signify, as accurately as if we had heard their voices"; "she seems to be describing such people as meet together every night in every respectable house in London; and to relate such incidents as have probably happened one time or other, to half the families in the United Kingdom." One of the characters picked out is Isabella Thorpe from *Northanger Abbey*, "a fine handsome girl, thinking of nothing but finery and flirting, and an exact representation of that large class of young women in the form they assume among the gayer part of the middling ranks of society." Like other reviewers, he was struck by the accuracy as well as the lifelikeness of Jane Austen's social portraiture; her characters are seen to be representative types, and in these comments we

[2]From *Plan of a Novel. . . . With Opinions . . .* (Oxford, 1926).

can gauge the immediate success of the novels in the comedy of manners tradition.

In English fiction we are familiar with the comedy of manners through the works of Thackeray, Trollope, George Eliot, E. M. Forster, and more recent novelists including Evelyn Waugh and Anthony Powell. But in Jane Austen's day it was essentially a dramatic tradition, beginning in the Restoration theater and revived in the later eighteenth century by Garrick and Sheridan. It was a tradition in which Jane Austen was well grounded. The Steventon productions had included plays by Sheridan and Garrick, as well as by a number of minor dramatists of the time; and as a girl she had experimented with scenes of burlesque drama. This theatrical tradition was a potent force in shaping Jane Austen's method in the novels, where so much of the action is realized dramatically in dialogue and where the positions, movements, and relationships of the characters— whether they are alone or in a room with other people or out walking or traveling—are so graphically drawn and convey such a full awareness of other people, their gestures, their expressions and moods. In many scenes we are led to visualize the figures; they stand before us like actors on a plain and shallow stage, in a clear, defining light.

But this is not theater manqué, as anyone will know who has tried to dramatize the novels. Dialogue which seems perfect to the eye and sounds perfectly on the internal ear, loses something in the speaking; and professional scriptwriters have foundered on this problem. What we have in Jane Austen is the true *fictional* comedy of manners, which creates the effect of mental theater, of an imaginative visualization. It is the reader himself who contributes the backdrop of reality to the furniture of Jane Austen's spare, essential detail. The scenes are enriched, as no performance can be, by the author's frame of commentary and the angle of vision, as, for example, the wholly dramatic dialogue between Mr. and Mrs. Bennet in the first chapter of *Pride and Prejudice* is sharply framed by the opening lines, the aphoristic pearl of worldly wisdom, "It is a truth universally acknowledged, that a single man in possession of a good fortune must be in want of a wife." Then follows an immediate shift, descending from the realms of universal bathos to the banality of a grubby neighborhood view:

However little known the feelings or views of such a man may be on first entering a neighbourhood, this truth is so well fixed in the minds of the surrounding families, that he is considered as the rightful property of some one or other of their daughters.

The effect is of a camera panning in from outer space, to fasten on a single spot, telescopically enlarged, as chapter 1 places "this truth" so solidly and comically before us in the person of Mrs. Bennet, fired by the arrival of Mr. Bingley, "a single man of large fortune," within calling distance of her household of marriageable daughters. Her husband is tired, has heard it all before, plays dumb, draws her on, mocks her. The comedy of repartee is hard and precise. It turns on the twin forces of money and marriage, upon the weary, sardonic, baiting sarcasm of Mr. Bennet and the stupid single-mindedness of his wife, "a woman of mean understanding" whose "business" in life "was to get her daughters married."

The comedy of manners thrives best in a climate of social uneasiness and change, when people are preoccupied with the cultivation of manners, the pursuit of fashion, and the show of respectability. Regency England provided just that situation, with its small and compact layer of middle-class gentry (estimated at about 25,000 families). Although the country was at war almost continuously from 1793 until 1814, middle-class life went on, virtually unaffected. But structurally it was not a static society. The crucial distinction of gentlemanly birth was disappearing. The lower middle classes were becoming prosperous. Successful farmers, merchants, manufacturers, tradesmen, and lawyers were ambitious to share the social standing of the gentry, as far as that could be achieved—by money, by mixing with them, by imitating their manners and their ways of speech. They could be "gentlemanlike"; could behave with "civility"; could start to drink tea in their summerhouses and have parlors, as the Martins dare to do in *Emma*; can dare, like Mrs. Elton, the daughter of a Bristol merchant, to act "the Lady Patroness" of the neighborhood, usurping the place of Emma Woodhouse, the daughter of the neighborhood's first gentleman.

For young women fashionable respectability meant being able to play the piano, to sing snatches of French and Italian, to know the gems of English verse, to be knowledgeable about the picturesque, to reel off the titles of the latest novels. These are the fashionable "accomplishments" that Jane Austen exposes and itemizes. Music, literature, and art were reduced to being the trappings of a culture specifically social, components in a shallow display put on for the sake of polite gentility and ornamental wifeliness.

The snobberies of rank became even sharper during the time that Jane Austen was writing, one of the things she may have had in mind when she added the "Advertisement" to *Northanger Abbey*. Bath of the 1790's had been a social mixing pot. Everyone jostled together in the public rooms of the spa. This is how such a nonentity as a Catherine Morland, the unremarkable daughter of an obscure country clergyman, could meet a Henry Tilney, the son of a great landowner—and how both of them could meet the Thorpes, the children of a rising lawyer. In the postwar Bath of *Persuasion*, their paths would never have crossed. By that time the gentry had left the public rooms, and entertained in private. A Tilney would have passed his time with one social set, a Morland in another.

Writing for a contemporary audience, Jane Austen's social notation is swift and economical. Money and rank place people on the social map as precisely as a grid reference. It is enough for Jane Austen to tell the reader that Mr. Bingley's fortune is £100,000, his sisters' dowries £20,000 each, and that this money is inherited from a father in "trade" in the North. This signals a family on the way up. The sisters have very superior airs. They patronize the Bennets, disapprove of Elizabeth's "most country town indifference to decorum" in walking three miles through the mud to visit her sick sister, to arrive with her cheeks a "blowsy" and unladylike red from the wind. Their "darling wish" is to see their brother further make the family respectable by the purchase of a landed estate, which he does.

Jane Austen pairs Bingley with Darcy. He too comes from the North. But there the resemblance ends. His name alone announces an aristocratic Anglo-Norman lineage, a far cry from the plebeian Yorkshire thud of "Bingley." He belongs to one of the ancient families of England. His income of £10,000 a year from family estates establishes him as one of a select group of only four hundred such landowners in the whole country. Although he has no title and is technically not a member of the aristocracy, his blood and wealth would make him persona grata at the highest levels. So Jane Austen's readers would savor the full comedy of his presence in the dingy small-town atmosphere of Meryton, with its petite bourgeoisie of tradesmen, merchants, and working lawyers.

Jane Austen had no illusions about the society she lived in. She could see its shallownesses and superficialities and she let them speak for themselves. That Bingley was a northerner with a northern name, a nouveau riche of lowly origin, meant nothing to her. She records the data. He is part of the social scene, and this is the way in which society would assess him. He has a function in the story and in the pattern of relationships. His extrovert warmth and friendliness, his ease in company, and his other social virtues provide a foil to Darcy's introvert coldness and unsociability. But Jane Austen passes judgment on Bingley's human worth, not on his social pleasantry—on the fact, for example, that his "manners" have "something better than politeness; there was good humour and kindness."

The novels provide us with a historically accurate picture of a society under stress, its values and its groups in a state of change. The picture is dynamic, analytical, and evaluative, as well as descriptive. The pejorative meaning of "vulgar" and "vulgarity" is a gentlemanly coinage, to identify and put down the lowness of the lower middle classes and their manners. Jane Austen takes these words and breaks them open. Technically Mrs. Jennings is vulgar. She is a Cockney, the widow of a man who traded in an unfashionable part of London. She tramples on every protocol, transgresses every rule of polite behavior. She is emotionally vulgar, coarsely insensitive, a burden to the Dashwood sisters with her sly hints and loud whispers of suitors, lovers, and marriage. She is comically vulgar in her imbecilic fancy that as a glass of Constantia wine cured her husband's "old cholicky gout," so will it mend Marianne's broken heart. But her "blunt sincerity" and warmhearted, innocent kindliness toward Marianne redeem everything. Jane Austen does not ask us to forget her vulgarity—it happened and it hurt people—nor does she ask us to discount this vulgarity against Mrs. Jennings' motherliness. What she does do is to present us with a woman in whom these qualities and defects stand together in a critical relationship. "Vulgarity" takes on a new meaning once we have read *Sense and Sensibility*. And a further meaning still when we encounter the brand of vulgarity displayed by Isabella Thorpe, an energetic social climber, who behaves to Catherine Morland as a treacherous and spiteful bitch.

There is also the vulgarity of the gentry. Isabella's transparent deceit is trivial alongside the hollowness of General Tilney's urbane and charming courtesies; and nothing that she does to Catherine Morland can match his callousness in sending the girl home in disgrace from Northanger Abbey. Lady Catherine de Bourgh is aristocratic in name and nature but, an arch snob, she is supremely vulgar toward her social inferiors. Emma Woodhouse suffers from snobbish, vulgarizing fantasies. Without knowing Robert Martin, she caricatures him as a straw-chewing yokel, "clownish," "gross," uncouth, and ill mannered. This is her notion of yeoman farmers. But when she meets him, she discovers a man who is quiet, neat, sensible, and well mannered. He writes a good letter. He even reads the same books as she does!

Darcy's "prejudice" produces the same vulgarizing slant. Until he gets to know them, Elizabeth's uncle and aunt, the Gardiners, belong to the unvisitable, unknowable world of her "lowly connexions." In trade, they live within sight of their warehouse in a part of London that a Darcy wouldn't be seen in. But in the flesh he finds them pleasant and likable; and although the Gardiners are unimportant as characters, Jane Austen bothers to underline his discovery in the last sentences of *Pride and Prejudice*: "With the Gardiners they were always on the most intimate terms. Darcy, as well as Elizabeth, really loved them. . . ."

VII

JANE AUSTEN's comedy of manners is a comedy of meanings. Language is behavior; and the conventional, clichéd language of Regency society is an expression of the people themselves. Jane Austen identified both the slang of fashionable social culture and what she called the "novel-slang" of its literature. In chapter 14 of *Northanger Abbey*, Henry Tilney takes Catherine to task for her use of "nice" and complains about its loss of meaning.

"Oh! it is a very nice word indeed!—it does for everything. Originally perhaps it was applied only to express neatness, propriety, delicacy, or refinement;—people were nice in their dress, in their sentiments, or their choice. But now every commendation on every subject is comprised in that one word."

Jane Austen could have repeated this lecture many times over. The strength and discrimination of language that Johnson inherited from Swift and Pope, and before them, from Dryden, Milton, and the metaphysical poets, had by this time been dissipated in the rhetoric of sentimental and moralizing fiction. Words passed from writer to writer like worn coins, a currency with an accepted face value, but its meanings blurred and thin.

The semantic drama of *Sense and Sensibility*, *Pride and Prejudice*, and *Persuasion* is signaled in their titles; and within the novels we can follow the scheme of characterization that brings the meaning of these words to life in the complexities and contradictions of human nature. Jane Austen denies the black-and-white morality of conduct fiction. "Sense" can be as tiresome or as dangerous as "sensibility." "Pride" and "prejudice" can be strengths as well as weaknesses. "Persuasion" can be interference. Other words are tested and searched—"principle," "judgement," "improvement," "propriety." There is a prominent cluster of social words— "civil," "civility," "civilities," "civilly," "uncivil," "incivility"—relating to the principles of etiquette, of meeting the social obligations of politeness, an issue upon which Jane Austen builds a wide-ranging conflict between compromise and integrity. These terms are not fixed and passive counters. *Pride and Prejudice* gives "civility" a very personal meaning. It is the quality that Elizabeth and Darcy have to acquire to temper their superiority and aggressiveness. Her brilliance of mind and sharpness of tongue, his arrogant patricianism, threaten to isolate them from other people. So for them "civility" means adjustment, tolerance, sympathy, and understanding.

"Duty" is a key word in *Mansfield Park* and *Persuasion*. In the later eighteenth century it had come to carry the most solemn overtones of moral obligation and religious observance. Jane Austen takes nothing on trust; the word is flooded with a dispassionate irony. Its force as a moral absolute of Christianity is slyly questioned in the sententious invocations of Sir Thomas and Edmund Bertram. In *Persuasion* an overdeveloped sense of filial duty brings Anne Elliot years of needless suffering. Duty is what you make it, what you want it to be. At the age of twenty-one, Maria Bertram "was beginning to think matrimony a duty"; and as there is a young man conveniently at hand, with a grand country house and a princely income of £12,000 a year, "it became, by the same rule of moral obligation, her evident duty to marry Mr. Rushworth if she could."

The semantic energies of Jane Austen's language are as powerful as the characters and human situations to which they are attached. They are mobilized within a total structure of meaning, a field of force capable of exerting the most delicate vibrations of feeling and tone, and of adumbrating the entire range of social and cultural usage that the language brings from outside. The novels can be regarded as semantic organisms, analytical works of art that test and display the very language they are composed of; and the novelist herself belongs to that small group of writers for whom language is not only the medium of literature but a part of its subject.

VIII

THE underlying theme of Jane Austen's social comedy is the predicament of being a woman in a man's world—a world ruled by men and run for their advantage, in which marriage looms as the central and decisive act of the woman's life, and where the prevailing view is (to quote Coleridge) that "Marriage has . . . no *natural* relation to love. Marriage belongs to society; it is a social contract." Other than marriage, no career or occupation was open to her. Her education was a grooming for polite society, providing her with fashionable "accomplishments" to catch the eye of a future husband. The alternatives were unthinkable. To be a governess was to sell yourself into the slavery of superior servanthood. Jane Austen put it neatly in a letter: "Single women have a dreadful propensity for being poor—which is one very strong argument in favour of matrimony." The force of this idea is conjured up in Emma Woodhouse's fearful image of the elderly spinster ridiculed by the children of the village. At worst, then, marriage could be the solution to an economic and human problem, as Jane Austen presents it in *Pride and Prejudice*: "the only honourable provision for well-educated young women of small fortune, and however uncertain of giving happiness, must be their pleasantest preservative from want." This sardonic generalization is attached to Charlotte Lucas in her choice of Mr. Collins. Elizabeth Bennet is saddened that her friend should humiliate herself with such a man, should "have sacrificed every better feeling to worldly advantage." But Charlotte makes this choice with her eyes open. She is twenty-seven, on the verge of becoming "an old maid." "I am not romantic," she tells Elizabeth, "I never was. I ask only a comfortable home."

There were other pressures toward marriage, the

right marriage, a marriage acceptable to the family, whose status and respectability were defined by the networks of relationship and association established through marriage. For the traditional landowning gentry these values were vital to the framework of society and their own survival. The crushing force of this system is expounded succinctly in the opening pages of *Sense and Sensibility*, with a history of the Dashwood estate, its preservation from generation to generation through the elaborate legalities of inheritance and succession. The measured rhetoric of the exposition asserts the weight and solidity of the system and the need to maintain the respectability of a family name. It is a system that calls for individual sacrifice. One of the recent Dashwoods was unable to provide for "those who were most dear to him" by selling any part of the estate, so tight was the knot of its legal bondage. Within this large social-historical image is embodied the ideology of property, its power and mystique, set at the opening of the novel to guide our understanding of the relationship between the individual and society dramatized in the story of Marianne Dashwood. An individualist, a rebel against convention, she has her own romantic "systems," "systems" which "have all the unfortunate tendency of setting propriety at nought," declares Elinor, the censorious voice of social "sense." Marianne is eventually tamed and disciplined into behaving politely and dutifully, as a young lady should, turning her back on visions of romantic love and yoked in marriage to the respectable middle-aged suitor promoted by her family and friends—Coleridge's "social contract" to the letter.

In *Sense and Sensibility*, Jane Austen shows a woman broken by these pressures; in *Pride and Prejudice* she shows how a woman can triumph over them. In this case, it is not the force of the heroine's own family but the weight of "family" snobbery, pride of caste from the man's side, from Darcy himself and his aunt. This comes to a head in chapter 56, in one of the great comic scenes of English literature, where Lady Catherine confronts Elizabeth in an attempt to warn her off, facing her with the weighty dynastic claims of the Darcys against the vulgar upstartism of the Bennets.

"Hear me in silence. My daughter and my nephew are formed for each other. They are descended on the maternal side, from the same noble line; and, on the father's, from respectable, honourable, and ancient, though untitled families. Their fortune on both sides is splendid. They are destined for each other by the voice of every member of their respective houses; and what is to divide them? The upstart pretensions of a young woman without family, connexions, or fortune. Is this to be endured? But it must not, shall not be! If you were sensible of your own good, you would not wish to quit the sphere in which you have been brought up."

This is comic melodrama, part of a wonderfully contrived scene. Lady Catherine's swelling indignation is pricked by Elizabeth's quiet contempt. Pope would have envied the artistry of Jane Austen's mock heroics—Lady Catherine thundering with biblical eloquence, "Heaven and earth!—of what are you thinking? Are the shades of Pemberley to be thus polluted?"—and the skill of their deflation. But Lady Catherine's bombast is not all hot air. Its hard core is an argument whose authority comes from centuries of social theory and practice. She calls upon ancient sanctities: the dogma of order and hierarchy, whereby the harmony of the whole depends upon the human atoms keeping to their divinely ordained and fixed positions, the great to remain great in the company of their peers, the "young woman without family, connexions, or fortune" to stay put in the "sphere" in which she has "been brought up."

Elizabeth's social offense is to have her eyes on Darcy. Her offense, as a woman, is to dare to stand up and assert herself as a person, to think for herself, to hold opinions, and to expose herself as an individual with a will of her own. The woman's accepted role was to be passive and submissive. Her function was to be decorative in society, comforting at home, an appendage to the man. Henry Tilney puts the idea playfully to Catherine Morland: "man has the advantage of choice, woman only the power of refusal . . . he is to purvey, and she is to smile." In chapter 11, the idea takes a more serious turn in the words of Anne Elliot to Captain Harville on the woman's experience of love:

"We certainly do not forget you, so soon as you forget us. It is perhaps, our fate rather than our merit. We cannot help ourselves. We live at home, quiet, confined, and our feelings prey upon us. You are forced upon exertion. You have always a profession, pursuits, business of some sort or other, to take you back into the world immediately, and continual occupation and change soon weaken impressions."

In Anne's reference to "our fate" there is no hint of rhetoric, no false note. Her own life has given her the right to use these words. The bitter truth of separation, loss, and remembrance she knows only too well, and she touches on them here with dignity and restraint. Again there is no hint of rhetoric when Emma Woodhouse reflects on "the difference of woman's destiny," comparing the social eminence of the great Mrs. Churchill and the nonentity of Jane Fairfax, soon to enter the "governess-trade," "the sale—not quite of human flesh—but of human intellect." Jane Austen is expressing the woman's cause but in a way which is totally unpolemical, totally undoctrinaire. The urgent tones of Mary Wollstonecraft and the other crusading feminists of the time only get into the novels as a parody-echo, in the pert aggressiveness of Mrs. Elton's warning to Mr. Weston:

"I always take the part of my own sex. I do indeed. I give you notice—You will find me a formidable antagonist on that point. I always stand up for women—"

Jane Austen's standing up for women is not argumentative, but dramatic. It is implicit in the creation of heroines whose claim to existence is human, whose reality comes from their self-awareness, their possession of minds and feelings, and not as a result of their conformity to some stereotype in either fashionable life or fashionable literature.

When Captain Wentworth asserts that naval vessels are no place for ladies, Mrs. Croft corrects him sharply: "But I hate to hear you talking so, like a fine gentleman, and as if we were all fine ladies, instead of rational creatures." When Mr. Collins refuses to credit Elizabeth's rejection, she has to reprimand him in the same terms: "Do not consider me now as an elegant female intending to plague you, but as a rational creature speaking the truth from her heart." Their rationality is something that these women have to argue for in the face of male attitudes, which are not so much a consequence of prejudice or stupidity but of habit, a block much more difficult to shift. When the Dashwood sisters are locked in argument, the contest is real; they are not the author's ventriloquial dummies. Marianne is a romantic, passionate woman, but she is far from mindless. Jane Austen underlines Anne Elliot's "strong mind," her "maturity of mind," phrases we might think superfluous, since these qualities are so evident in all she does. In this emphatic labeling we can glimpse Jane Austen's anxiety to press home to her Regency public the message that a woman could have qualities traditionally a man's and that a woman could surpass him in maturity and understanding, as Anne surpasses Wentworth and everyone else in *Persuasion.*

There was indeed a battle to be fought. In *Mansfield Park,* Sir Thomas Bertram comes down heavily on Fanny Price for refusing to accept Henry Crawford. Given the young man's interest and eligibility, the woman's consent is taken for granted. So her refusal is momentous, unnatural, arouses him to an angry diatribe against the new, unfeminine "independence of spirit, which prevails so much in modern days, even in young women, and which in young women is offensive and disgusting beyond all common offence." Lady Catherine sees this new spirit in Elizabeth Bennet. In her, it is something deliberate and self-conscious, a part of her attraction for Darcy, which she is eager to discuss with him. In Jane Austen's new brand of intellectual romance, the lady can even invite her beloved to analyze the bonds of affection. At the end of the story, she wants him "to account for his having ever fallen in love with her"; and she is just as keen to present her view of the affair: "The fact is, that you were sick of civility, of deference, of officious attention. You were disgusted with the women who were always speaking and looking, and thinking for *your* approbation alone. I roused and interested you, because I was so unlike *them.*" Lady Catherine interpreted her nephew's interest as a sexual infatuation, the sordid outcome of Elizabeth's "arts and allurements." Her suspicions are correct; but only half correct. What attracted Darcy was the challenge of a woman whose vitality and presence are intellectual as well as physical.

Each of the heroines presents a different face to the world and is attractive to men for different reasons. None of them can match Elizabeth's high spirits, her aggressive outspokenness and sheer argumentative brilliance. But they are all alike in their possession of an interior life, a dimension of psychological reality, which forms an area of action as important as the action outside and which is drawn with equal care and precision. Jane Austen's method is not stream of consciousness nor an elaborate psychoanalytical psychologizing. Her technique is essentially realistic in connecting the ebb and flow of experience to the circumstances of the story and to the heroine's immediate situation. Its credibility comes partly from the thoughtful, reflective nature of the heroines, partly from the train of events, and partly from the fact that the patterns of thought and feeling are so patently normal and recognizable.

While visiting the newlywed Collinses, Elizabeth Bennet has plenty of time to digest the contents of Darcy's second letter as she goes on solitary walks to escape the company of Mr. Collins and Lady Catherine:

After wandering along the lane for two hours, giving way to every variety of thought; re-considering events, determining probabilities, and reconciling herself as well as she could, to a change so sudden and so important, fatigue, and a recollection of her long absence, made her at length return home; and she entered the house with the wish of appearing cheerful as usual, and the resolution of repressing such reflections as must make her unfit for conversation.

(ch. 36)

Elizabeth's mental and emotional existence is here traced as an active and conscious state of mind. Its progression is geared to the sequence of her movements; and through this technique Jane Austen is able to convey the processes of thought and feeling as well as their quality and content.

There is often a precise enumeration of the levels of experience, the ways in which the same impression can be registered differently, sometimes contradictorily. When Marianne Dashwood hears the news of Lucy Steele's marriage, "To her own heart it was a delightful affair, to her imagination it was even a ridiculous one, but to her reason, her judgement, it was completely a puzzle." The impact of feeling can be registered in moral terms. At Portsmouth, Fanny Price was "quite shocked" by a squabble in the family: "Every feeling of duty, honour, and tenderness was wounded by her sister's speech and her mother's reply." Jane Austen's drive is continually discriminative, toward a clarity of mind which is moral as well as rational, toward judgment based upon clear thinking and right feeling. Fanny receives a "stab" when she concludes that Edmund Bertram's marriage to Mary Crawford is inevitable. She grieves to see someone she loves like a brother caught in the toils of a seductress whom she detests. She is heartbroken, dejected, but rallies herself and determines to "endeavour to be rational, and to deserve the right of judging Miss Crawford's character and the privilege of true solicitude for him by a sound intellect and an honest heart."

Jane Austen sets a high value on self-knowledge and each of the novels can be analyzed in terms of the heroine's progress along this path. But self-knowledge on its own is not enough and Jane Austen joins to it the idea of a second kind of knowledge, knowledge of our duty in life. This concept appears in *Mansfield Park*, where Edmund Bertram sends Mary Crawford off with an admonitory reference to "the most valuable knowledge we could any of us acquire—the knowledge of ourselves and of our duty." And his father, Sir Thomas, comes to the conclusion that the sexual misbehavior of his daughters must be put down to the fact that in their upbringing "active principle had been wanting, that they had never been properly taught to govern their inclinations and tempers, by that sense of duty which can alone suffice." At the end of *Persuasion*, Anne Elliot is able to congratulate herself on having done the right thing, eight years before, in following Lady Russell's advice by giving up any idea of marrying Wentworth. Lady Russell stood in the place of a mother and, dutifully, as a child, she obeyed. So her conscience remained clear, even if her heart was broken, and she is in a position to reflect: "If I mistake not, a strong sense of duty is no bad part of a woman's portion."

These concepts of duty are not presented to us uncritically. Sir Thomas and Edmund both deliver judgment; they enjoy putting other people right and fault-finding in themselves; and there is a glib and defensive rationalization in Anne Elliot's conclusion. But these qualifications are local. The idea of duty was important to Jane Austen—not just the formal duties of religion and family, but the internal duty of individual women toward themselves. To thyself be true. It is this concern which ultimately connects us with Jane Austen, which enables us to understand the heroines in their struggle for individuality and fulfillment, a theme at the heart of nineteenth- and twentieth-century literature, from the romantic poets onward; and at the heart, too, of the slow social revolution in England that followed the political revolutions in America and France. In *A Vindication of the Rights of Women*, published in 1792, Mary Wollstonecraft had argued radically that women should not seek "power over men; but over themselves"; that they should fight free from the degradation of being regarded as mere sexual and social objects, not by overturning society but by valuing themselves as individuals with a right to fulfill themselves in their own way. This message sounds again at the end of *A Doll's House* in Nora's challenge to Torvald. Above the responsibilities of marriage and motherhood, she sees other duties:

Nora: My duties toward myself.
Torvald: Before all else you are a wife and a mother.
Nora: That I no longer believe. I think that before all

else I am a human being, just as much as you are—or, at least, I should try to become one. I know that most people agree with you, Torvald, and that they say so in books. But henceforth I can't be satisfied with what most people say, and what is in books. I must think things out for myself and try to get clear about them.

"Let other pens dwell on guilt and misery," Jane Austen begins the final chapter of *Mansfield Park*. She declares herself "impatient to restore every body, not greatly in fault themselves, to tolerable comfort, and to have done with all the rest." Without exception the novels close on a note of dismissive irony, with a rapid tying up of loose ends. Jane Austen never follows her heroines into the reality of marriage; nor does she carry them to the bitter and tragic point that Nora reaches, where life falls apart and has to be put together again, slowly, painfully, and alone. Nevertheless, the comic mask is only a mask. Her heroines' experiences and the meaning of their lives, as much as we are shown of them, are touched with an irony beyond laughter.

In the foreword to *Women in Love*, D. H. Lawrence declared the importance of man's "struggle for verbal consciousness." It is Nora's struggle, her fight to escape from the doll's house in which Torvald has locked her; before her it is the struggle of Jane Austen's heroines; and today many men and women would accept it as their struggle too. Lawrence's enunciation of this process touches the very center of Jane Austen's art, and it helps us to understand the depth of engagement with the compelling force of these "verbal" heroines and the "verbal" structures in which they have their life:

Any man of real individuality tries to know and to understand what is happening, even in himself, as he goes along. This struggle for verbal consciousness should not be left out in art. It is a very great part of life. It is not superimposition of a theory. It is the passionate struggle into conscious being.

IX

JANE AUSTEN's verbalism is most crucially exposed in the treatment of love. In this area the logic is relentless. Coleridge's axiom—"Marriage has . . . no *natural* relation to love"—defines the premise of Jane Austen's husband-and-wife comedy. The married couples duly exhibit the gamut of comic symptoms

—from lovelessness and boredom to irritation aged into resentment. But the novels also deliver a stern counteraxiom: that marriage does have a *moral* relation to love; and by that test the quality of marriage is to be judged, with the equally decisive qualification that love is not necessarily related to passion or to the feelings conventionally regarded as romantic. For the heroines a part of love is the recognition of their own needs—Fanny Price for an elder brother, Emma Woodhouse for a kindly, admonitory uncle, the broken Marianne Dashwood for a father-protector. The discovery of mutual affinities, sympathies, and understandings is the justification for marriage on human and moral grounds, as distinct from the worldly contracts made for profit or convenience, or the "social contract" marriages made for the sake of the family. Love is an awareness of the other person, sharpened by judgment into a learning experience. At the close of *Pride and Prejudice*, *Emma*, and *Persuasion*, the heroes and heroines are brought even closer together as they talk about the ways in which they have affected one another morally and intellectually as well as emotionally. This is the final stage in their process of mutual education. These scenes present a remarkable combination of analysis and personal contact in which the sense of emotional intimacy is deepened in the act of discussion.

But what of love as passion? When the couples come together in the full recognition of their feelings, Jane Austen is discretion itself—we are not to intrude upon such tender scenes, not to overhear lovers' talk. Edward Ferrar's declaration is made "very prettily." George Knightley delivers himself "in plain, unaffected, gentlemanlike English." The "happiness" Fanny Price inspires in Edmund Bertram is conjectured to "have been great enough to warrant any strength of language in which he could cloathe it to her or to himself." Darcy "expressed himself on the occasion as sensibly and as warmly as a man violently in love can be supposed to do." Only in *Persuasion* is Jane Austen more forthcoming. The reconciliation of Anne and Wentworth, which leads on without interruption to their declaration of love, is drawn with unequaled richness and intensity of feeling. Yet even here the emphasis remains verbal, the reporting oblique. Their deepest contact is through "words enough . . . the power of conversation . . . those retrospections and acknowledgements, and especially in those explanations of what had directly preceded the present moment, which were so poignant and so ceaseless of interest."

Here, as so often in the novels, Jane Austen renders the experience of people discovering and exploring their love for one another, simply through being together, through awarenesses and understandings, spoken and unspoken. This is their making love. If we accept the playful irony of style, the narrator's pose of mock discretion, Darcy's warmth and the violence of his love are not in question. They are proposed to us verbally, as qualities to take on trust, part of a mild joke against lovers in general. But in the flesh there is no warmth or violence of love whatsoever in Darcy. He admires a good figure, but no more than that. This absence from *Pride and Prejudice* and from the relationships in all the later novels is something we have to question if our reading of Jane Austen has begun with *Sense and Sensibility*. For Marianne Dashwood is a woman passionately in love, a woman whose attractiveness and vitality have a genuinely sensuous vibration, and in Willoughby she is matched by a man who has the power to disturb women. Elinor finds her judgment endangered by his presence, and the physical aspects of his hold over her are spelled out.

Elinor's problem was also Jane Austen's. She too was disturbed by the power of sexuality, its threat to the security of reason and self-control, its melting attack upon the certainties of selfhood and identity (a point that Lawrence hints at). The tension is evident in *Sense and Sensibility*. The writer's engagement in Marianne and Willoughby is unmistakable. Their destruction—Willoughby blackened with a murky past, the thin and distant melodrama of having seduced a seventeen-year-old schoolgirl. Marianne devitalized through illness and cast off as a "reward" to the patient Colonel Brandon—is gratuitous and forced, a betrayal of the novel's dramatic commitment, however neatly and maliciously their punishment completes the scheme in which the sickness of "sensibility" is purged with a stiff dose of "sense."

After this exercise in suppression, Jane Austen tried to turn her back on the problem. Her heroes are a dull and unvirile crew; her heroines are untroubled by passion. Sexuality is outlawed, reserved for the villains and villainesses and the silly little girls and the married women who should know better: for Wickham and Lydia, who were "only brought together because their passions were stronger than their virtue"; for the Crawfords, whose dangerous, seductive charm has to be smeared with the taint of corruption (again, some readers have felt, gratuitously). Whatever the solid virtues of George

Knightley, whatever the truth to life in his marriage to Emma Woodhouse, there is some shadowy objection to his avuncular and tutelary union with a girl of such brilliance, beauty, and the "bloom of full health." *Persuasion* is *Sense and Sensibility* safely rewritten, with the rational "romance" of maturity and quieter, more tender, poetic charms substituted for the impulsive infatuation of youth.

Charlotte Brontë wondered where in Jane Austen is "that stormy Sisterhood . . . the Passions." It is a question that has been raised by many of Jane Austen's critics; it lurks within Lawrence's "narrow-gutted spinster." One answer is in *Sense and Sensibility*, which Charlotte Brontë had not read. Marianne Dashwood is a heroine whose courage and love she would have applauded and whose suffering she would have wept for; and surely Lawrence would have cheered her too, if ever he had read the book with an open mind. The other answer is that Jane Austen tried to undercut the passions with irony, to detach herself from them, and to subject them to the pressure of her own compelling need for order and control, the driving necessity of her imagination and her whole being, the force which stands behind the achievement of the novels both in their scope and their limitations.

X

As far as her fellow countrymen are concerned, Jane Austen can properly be described as the most beloved of English novelists. Like Shakespeare, she has transcended literary greatness to become part of the national heritage and something of a cult. Her anniversaries are commemorated, her homes are visited, and Chawton Cottage is preserved by the Jane Austen Society as a place of pilgrimage. Strictly speaking, these circumstances have more to do with social anthropology than literary criticism. But the fact remains that of all the great English novelists, Jane Austen is the only one to survive into the late twentieth century with such a devoted following. Her works are known with more intimacy than those of Shakespeare himself. If he is revered as the English national poet, Jane Austen is loved as the national novelist, the most widely enjoyed and in many ways the most English of all English writers.

Generations of readers have treasured the novels nostalgically. They seem to immortalize a golden age in English society ("the last voice of a happier age," commented V. S. Pritchett). There are still people who can identify themselves and their acquaintances, charitably and uncharitably, with Jane Austen's characters and their way of life. For them the novels can be potently authenticating, as they were for their Regency audience. There is a special pleasure, the joy of recognition, in discovering oneself drawn so accurately and artistically. Like family portraits and domestic interiors of a Dutch fidelity, they flatter by the very perfection of the rendering. The basis of Jane Austen's social comedy has not dated, with its attention to manners and the refinements of social behavior, its play upon vulgarity and the distinctions of class. The forms have changed, but the system remains; and for those who live within it, the novels can be read as a celebration of traits that are cherished as typically and endearingly English—a proud insularity; a bluff and determined philistinism; an anti-intellectualism; a wariness of Mediterranean passion and French gallantry; a sense of order, decorum, and self-control; anxieties about social background and breeding; a respect for duty, propriety, and tradition; and, the ultimate saving grace of the English, a thick-skinned capacity to laugh at themselves and so draw the sting of any joke.

Nostalgic, wishful, chauvinistic and unliterary, jealous, possessive, and snobbish—this view of the novels is partial, blind to their irony and to the force of their social judgment. Nonetheless, it is a view which has been held firmly and continuously in England from Jane Austen's time until the present day. Its voice can still be heard, and occasionally breaks into print. In the summer of 1974, when a current domestic worry was the rising price of bread, this short letter appeared in the correspondence columns of an English national paper:

Sir,
We hear a lot about the cost of bread and even the shortage of this essential commodity. There is a perfectly simple answer which is to bake one's own bread; we have done this for years and my cook produces much finer bread than you can obtain in the ordinary way. It is also much cheaper and requires no expensive equipment.

Jane Austen would have greeted the unconscious irony of this letter with a smile of recognition. Bread was expensive in her day too; and there was no shortage of advice from the gentry, just as well-meaning, suggesting how the poor could feed themselves economically.

According to Hobbes, "laughter is a bad infirmity of human nature which every thinking man will attempt to overcome." The novels of Jane Austen offer a different moral: that laughter comes to our rescue, is a necessary strength, a realistic response, an understanding, which enables "thinking" people to hold out in the face of life's irrational and chaotic ironies. Jane Austen's vision would place her far along Nietzsche's scale of laughing philosophers, by which they are ordered "according to the rank of their laughter—rising to those capable of *golden* laughter." In the passage in *Beyond Good and Evil* where he presents this idea, Nietzsche goes on to speculate upon "the Olympian vice," divine laughter:

And if gods too philosophize, as many an inference has driven me to suppose—I do not doubt that while doing so they know how to laugh in a new and superhuman way— and at the expense of all serious things! Gods are fond of mockery; it seems they cannot refrain from laughter even when sacraments are in progress.

Jane Austen's laughter is directed at the secular sacraments and sacred cows of the Regency world —at its fashionable modes of feeling and thinking; at its idols of class and culture; at its categoricalisms; at its rage for order, inherited from the Age of Reason; at its sentimental romanticism; at its litany of "improvement," "duty," "sense," "civility." Her laughter is amused, intellectual, and sardonic. But there the superhumanism, the Godlike mockery ends. For behind the laughter is sadness and compassion. And behind that is anger and frustration, the tensions of a satirist who uncovers the shams, shabbinesses, and inhumanities of her world, its oppressions and claustrophobias, yet who nevertheless belongs to it, needs it, and cannot exist outside it. Its profoundest critic and historian, she is its victim herself.

SELECTED BIBLIOGRAPHY

I. Bibliography. Detailed bibliographical information will also be found in *The New Cambridge Bibliography of English Literature*, vol. III. G. L. Keynes, *Jane Austen: A Bibliography* (London, 1929), the standard methodical bibliography, published in a lim. ed. by the Nonesuch Press, includes a list of secondary material up to 1928;

R. W. Chapman, *Jane Austen: A Critical Bibliography* (Oxford, 1953; 2nd ed., 1955), a selective list, covering historical and biographical material.

II. COLLECTED WORKS. *Novels*, 5 vols. (London, 1833; repr. 1866, 1869), the first collected ed., published by R. Bentley—a vol. titled *Lady Susan &c* was added to the ed. of 1878–1879, which also contained "A Memoir of Jane Austen" by her nephew J. E. Austen-Leigh, first published separately in 1870; *Works*, 6 vols. (London, 1882), the Steventon ed., vol. VI contains the "Memoir" by her nephew, *Lady Susan*, and other fragments; R. B. Johnson, ed., *Novels*, 10 vols. (London, 1892), illus. by W. C. Cooke and ornaments by F. C. Tilney; R. B. Johnson, ed., *Novels*, 10 vols. (London, 1898), illus. by C. E. and H. M. Brock; *Novels*, 10 vols. (London, 1898), the Winchester ed.; *Works*, 10 vols. (London, 1899), the Temple ed.; *Novels*, 6 vols. (London, 1902), the Hampshire ed., decorated by B. MacManus; *Works*, 6 vols. (London, 1907–1931), with intro. by Lord D. Cecil, R. W. Chapman, M. Lascelles, M. Sadleir, and F. Reid, in the World's Classics series; R. B. Johnson, ed., *Works*, 10 vols. (London, 1908–1909), illus. by A. W. Mills, in the St. Martin's Illustrated Library of Standard Authors.

Novels, 6 vols. (London, 1922), intro. by R. B. Johnson, illus. by C. E. Brock; *Novels: The Text Based on Collation of the Early Editions by R. W. Chapman. With Notes, Indexes, and Illustrations from Contemporary Sources*, 5 vols. (Oxford, 1923; repr. without colored plates, 1926; repr. with corrs., 1933; repr. in 2 vols., 1934), vol. VI, *Minor Works* (Oxford, 1954; rev. ed., 1969)—the definitive ed., outstanding for its careful scholarship; *Works*, 7 vols. (London, 1923), the Adelphi ed., vol. VII contains *Lady Susan* and *The Watsons*; *Works*, 5 vols. (London, 1927), the Georgian ed., with an intro. to each vol. by J. C. Bailey—the intros. were repr. in a separate vol. (London, 1931); *The Complete Novels* (London, 1928), an omnibus ed. in one vol., with an intro. by J. C. Squire; *Works*, 7 vols. (London, 1933–1934), with an intro. by R. B. Johnson and illus. by M. Vox, vol. VII contains *Sanditon, The Watsons, Lady Susan*, and other miscellanea; *Novels*, 6 vols. (London, 1948), the Chawton ed.; M. M. Lascelles, ed., *Novels*, 5 vols. (London, 1961–1964), in the Everyman Library; *Novels*, 6 vols. (London, 1969–1972), in the Penguin English Library; J. Kinsley, ed., *Novels*, 6 vols. (London, 1971), in the Oxford English Novels series.

III. LETTERS. E. Brabourne, ed., *Letters*, 2 vols. (London, 1884), with intro. and critical remarks by Brabourne; J. H. and E. C. Hubback, *Jane Austen's Sailor Brothers* (London, 1906), contains unpublished letters to her brother Francis; W. Austen-Leigh and R. A. Austen-Leigh, *Jane Austen: Her Life and Letters* (London, 1913), contains numerous extracts from her letters; R. W. Chapman, ed., *Five Letters from Jane Austen to Her Niece Fanny Knight* (Oxford, 1924), facs.; R. B. Johnson, comp., *Letters* (London, 1925), with an intro. by Johnson; *Jane Austen's Letters to Her Sister Cassandra and Others. Collected and Edited by R. W. Chapman*, 2 vols. (Oxford, 1932; repr. in 1

vol., with adds., 1952), the only complete ed. and a definitive text, with notes and indexes—a selection of letters appeared in the World's Classics series (London, 1955).

IV. SEPARATE WORKS. *Sense and Sensibility: A Novel by a Lady*, 3 vols. (London, 1811; 2nd ed., corr., 1813); *Pride and Prejudice*, 3 vols. (London, 1813); *Mansfield Park*, 3 vols. (London, 1814; 2nd ed., corr., 1816); *Emma*, 3 vols. (London, 1816); *Northanger Abbey* and *Persuasion*, 4 vols. (London, 1817), contains a biographical notice of the author by her brother Henry (included in Bentley's ed. of 1833); *Lady Susan* and *The Watsons* (London, 1871), unfinished novels first printed in J. E. Austen-Leigh, *A Memoir of Jane Austen* (2nd ed., London, 1871), and repr. together in 1939 with an intro. by J. Bailey—*The Watsons* was repr. separately in 1923 with an intro. by A. B. Walkley, in 1927 from the MS (by R. W. Chapman), and in 1928, completed by E. and F. Brown in accordance with Austen's intentions; *Love and Freindship [sic] and Other Early Works. Now First Printed from the Original MSS* (London, 1922), with a preface by G. K. Chesterton, comprises the MS juvenilia in the Bodleian Library, Oxford; R. W. Chapman, ed., *Sanditon. Fragment of a Novel Written January–March 1817. Now First Printed from the Manuscript* (Oxford, 1925), repr. 1934 with *The Watsons, Lady Susan*, and "Other Miscellanea," by R. B. Johnson, ed.; *Plan of a Novel, According to Hints from Various Quarters. With Opinions on Mansfield Park and Emma, Collected and Transcribed, and Other Documents (with Facsimiles)* (Oxford, 1926); R. W. Chapman, ed., *Two Chapters of "Persuasion"* (Oxford, 1926), the first draft of chs. 10 and 11 in vol. II; R. W. Chapman, ed., *Volume the First. Now Printed from the Manuscripts in the Bodleian Library* (Oxford, 1933), with a preface by Chapman, contains the first of three MS notebooks in which Jane Austen collected (*ca.* 1793) her juvenilia; R. W. Chapman, ed., *Volume the Third. Now First Printed from the MS (in the Possession of Mr. R. A. Austen-Leigh)* (Oxford, 1951), with a preface by Chapman, the third of Austen's MS notebooks; B. C. Southam, ed., *Volume the Second [Love and Freindship] [sic]* (Oxford, 1963).

V. BIOGRAPHICAL AND CRITICAL STUDIES. Articles marked (L) are repr. in D. Lodge, *Jane Austen: Emma: A Casebook*; those marked (S), in B. C. Southam, *Jane Austen: The Critical Heritage*; those marked (W), in I. Watt, *Jane Austen: A Collection of Critical Essays*.

W. Scott, review of *Emma*, in *Quarterly Review*, 14 (1815), the most important contemporary statement (S); R. Whately, review of *Northanger Abbey* and *Persuasion*, in *Quarterly Review*, 24 (1821), a classic essay (S); T. B. Macaulay, "The Diary and Letters of Madame D'Arblay," in *Edinburgh Review*, 76 (1843); G. H. Lewes, "The Novels of Jane Austen," in *Blackwood's* magazine (July 1859); J. Kavanagh, *English Women of Letters* (London, 1862), ch. 18, "Miss Austen's Six Novels" (S); J. E. Austen-Leigh, *A Memoir of Jane Austen* (London, 1870; 2nd ed., 1871), the latter contains *Lady Susan, The Watsons, Sanditon, Plan of a Novel*, and other items; R. Simpson, review of *Memoir* of *Jane Austen*, in *North British Review*, 52 (1870) (S); "S. Tytler" [H. Keddie], *Jane Austen and Her Works* (London, 1880); W. G. Pellew, *Jane Austen's Novels* (Boston, 1883); S. F. Malden, *Jane Austen* (London, 1889), in the Eminent Women series; G. Smith, *Life of Jane Austen* (London, 1890), contains a bibliography by J. P. Anderson; O. F. Adams, *The Story of Jane Austen's Life* (Chicago, 1891; rev. ed., Boston, 1897); A. Jack, *Essays on the Novel as Illustrated by Scott and Miss Austen* (London, 1897); W. H. Pollock, *Jane Austen, Her Contemporaries and Herself: An Essay in Criticism* (London, 1899).

W. D. Howells, *Heroines of Fiction* (New York, 1901); C. Hill, *Jane Austen: Her Homes and Her Friends* (London, 1901); H. H. Bonnell, *Charlotte Brontë, George Eliot, Jane Austen: Studies in Their Works* (New York, 1902); G. E. Mitton, *Jane Austen and Her Times* (London, 1905); J. H. and E. C. Hubback, *Jane Austen's Sailor Brothers* (London, 1906); W. L. Phelps, *Introduction to Jane Austen's Novels* (London, 1906); W. H. Helm, *Jane Austen and Her Country-House Comedy* (London, 1909); A. C. Bradley, "Jane Austen: A Lecture," in the English Association's *Essays and Studies*, vol. II (Oxford, 1911), essay repr. in Bradley's *A Miscellany* (London, 1929); P. H. Fitzgerald, *Jane Austen: A Criticism and an Appreciation* (London, 1912); M. Sackville, *Jane Austen* (London, 1912); W. and R. A. Austen-Leigh, *Jane Austen: Her Life and Letters, a Family Record* (London, 1913), the authoritative biography and an indispensable record, based on family papers; F. W. Cornish, *Jane Austen* (London, 1913), in the English Men of Letters series; K. and P. Rague, *Jane Austen* (Paris, 1914), in the Les Grands Écrivains Étrangers series; L. Villard, *Jane Austen, sa vie et son oeuvre, 1775–1817* (Lyons, 1915), trans. in part by V. Lucas as *Jane Austen: A French Appreciation*, with a new study of Jane Austen by R. B. Johnson interpreted through *Love and Freindship* [sic] (London, 1924); R. Farrer, "Jane Austen," in *Quarterly Review*, 228 (1917) (extracts in L); F. Pollock, *Jane Austen Centenary Memorial: A Record of the Ceremony of Its Unveiling at Chawton, Hampshire* (London, 1917).

M. A. Austen-Leigh, *Personal Aspects of Jane Austen* (London, 1920); O. W. Firkins, *Jane Austen* (New York, 1920); R. B. Johnson, *Jane Austen* (London, 1925); V. Woolf, *The Common Reader* (London, 1925), contains an appreciation of Austen (W); M. Sadleir, *The Northanger Novels: A Footnote to Jane Austen* (Oxford, 1927), English Association Pamphlet no. 68; S. Alexander, *The Art of Jane Austen* (Manchester, 1928); H. W. Garrod, "Jane Austen: A Depreciation," in *Transactions of the Royal Society of Literature*, n.s. 8 (1928); C. L. Thomson, *Jane Austen: A Survey* (London, 1929); R. B. Johnson, *Jane Austen: Her Life, Her Work, Her Family and Her Critics* (London, 1930); J. C. Bailey, *Introductions to Jane Austen* (London, 1931); G. L. Apperson, *A Jane Austen Dictionary* (London, 1932); D. Rhydderch, *Jane Austen: Her Life and Art* (London, 1932); G. Rawlence, *Jane Austen* (London, 1934); D. Cecil, *Jane Austen* (Cambridge, 1935), the Leslie Stephen lecture, 1935; E. Bowen, *Jane Austen*

(London, 1936), in the English Novelists series; E. Austen-Leigh, *Jane Austen and Steventon* (London, 1937); B. K. Seymour, *Jane Austen: Study for a Portrait* (London, 1937); E. Jenkins, *Jane Austen: A Biography* (London, 1938); M. Ragg, *Jane Austen in Bath* (London, 1938); M. Wilson, *Jane Austen and Some Contemporaries* (London, 1938); E. Austen-Leigh, *Jane Austen and Bath* (London, 1939); M. M. Lascelles, *Jane Austen and Her Art* (London, 1939), the first systematic study of Jane Austen's achievement, an indispensable intro. essay.

E. Austen-Leigh, *Jane Austen and Lyme Regis* (London, 1940); D. W. Harding, "Regulated Hatred: An Aspect of the Work of Jane Austen," in *Scrutiny*, 8 (1940) (W); S. Kaye-Smith and G. B. Stern, *Talking of Jane Austen* (London, 1943); R. Brower, "The Controlling Hand: Jane Austen and *Pride and Prejudice*," in *Scrutiny*, 13 (1945), an outstanding essay, repr. in Brower's *Fields of Light* (New York, 1951) (W); R. A. Austen-Leigh, *Jane Austen and Lyme Regis* (London, 1946); S. Kliger, "Jane Austen's *Pride and Prejudice* in the Eighteenth-Century Mode," in *University of Toronto Quarterly*, 16 (1947); R. W. Chapman, *Jane Austen: Facts and Problems* (Oxford, 1948), the Clark lectures, Trinity College, Cambridge, 1948; D. Daiches, "Jane Austen, Karl Marx and the Aristocratic Dance," in *American Scholar*, 17 (1948); M. Schorer, "Technique as Discovery," in *Hudson Review*, 1 (1948); H. Ashton, *Parson Austen's Daughter* (London, 1949); R. A. Austen-Leigh, *Jane Austen and Southampton* (London, 1949); *Jane Austen and Jane Austen's House* (Winchester, 1949); M. Schorer, "Fiction and the 'Matrix of Analogy,'" in *Kenyon Review*, 11 (1949); E. N. Hayes, "*Emma*: A Dissenting Opinion," in *Nineteenth-Century Fiction*, 4 (1950) (L); S. Kaye-Smith and G. B. Stern, *More Talk of Jane Austen* (London, 1950); M. Kennedy, *Jane Austen* (London, 1950); S. T. Warner, *Jane Austen* (London, 1951; rev. eds., 1957, 1964), a British Council pamphlet; Caroline Austen, *My Aunt Jane Austen: A Memoir*, R. W. Chapman, ed. (Alton, Hants., 1952), from a MS dated March 1867; M. Mudrick, *Jane Austen: Irony as Defense and Discovery* (Princeton, N. J., 1952); M. L. Becker, *Presenting Miss Jane Austen* (London, 1953); A. Kettle, *An Introduction to the English Novel* (London, 1953), vol. I includes the essay "Jane Austen: *Emma*" (W,L); D. Van Ghent, *The English Novel: Form and Function* (New York, 1953), includes a ch. on *Pride and Prejudice*; A. H. Wright, *Jane Austen's Novels: A Study in Structure* (London, 1953; 2nd ed., 1972).

C. S. Lewis, "A Note on Jane Austen," in *Essays in Criticism*, 4 (1954) (W); M. Schorer, "Pride Unprejudiced," in *Kenyon Review*, 18 (1956); E. F. Shannon, "*Emma*: Character and Construction," in *PMLA*, 71 (1956) (L); D. Cecil, *Literary Studies* (London, 1957), contains notes on *Sense and Sensibility* and Austen's scenery; *The Pelican Guide to English Literature* (Harmondsworth, 1957), vol. V, *From Blake to Byron*, pt. 2, includes D. W. Harding, "Jane Austen and Moral Judgement"; I. Watt, *The Rise of the Novel: Studies in Defoe, Richardson and Fielding* (London, 1957), the best account of Austen's relationship to the eighteenth-century novel; L. Trilling, intro. to Austen's *Emma* (New York, 1957), the Riverside ed., repr. as *"Emma* and the Legend of Jane Austen" in Trilling's *Beyond Culture* (New York, 1965) (L); J. Coates, *The Watsons: Jane Austen's Fragment Continued and Completed* (London, 1958); A. D. McKillop, "The Context of *Sense and Sensibility*," in *Rice Institute Pamphlets*, 44 (1958); R. C. Rathburn and M. Steinmann, eds., *From Jane Austen to Joseph Conrad* (Minneapolis, 1958), includes A. D. McKillop, "Critical Realism in *Northanger Abbey*," and C. Murrah, "The Background of *Mansfield Park*"; C. Gillie, "*Sense and Sensibility*: An Assessment," in *Essays in Criticism*, 9 (1959); M. Schorer, "The Humiliation of Emma Woodhouse," in *Literary Review*, 2 (1959).

J. Hubback, *The Parents in Jane Austen's Novels* (London, 1960); W. Watson, *Jane Austen in London* (London, 1960); W. C. Booth, *The Rhetoric of Fiction* (London, 1961), includes the essay "Control of Distance in Jane Austen's *Emma*" (L); F. W. Bradbrook, *Jane Austen: Emma* (London, 1961); W. W. Heath, *Discussions of Jane Austen* (Boston, 1961); H. S. Babb, *Jane Austen's Novels: The Fabric of Dialogue* (Columbus, Ohio, 1962); M. Bradbury, "Jane Austen's *Emma*," in *Critical Quarterly*, 4 (1962) (L); S. Ebiike, *Jane Austen* (Tokyo, 1962); R. E. Hughes, "The Education of Emma Woodhouse," in *Nineteenth-Century Fiction*, 16 (1962) (L); R. Liddell, *The Novels of Jane Austen* (London, 1963); I. Watt, *Jane Austen: A Collection of Critical Essays* (Englewood Cliffs, N. J., 1963); G. Hough, *The Dream and the Task* (London, 1964), includes the essay "*Emma* and 'Moral' Criticism" (L); B. C. Southam, *Jane Austen's Literary Manuscripts: A Study of the Novelist's Development Through the Surviving Papers* (London, 1964); H. Ten Harmsel, *Jane Austen: A Study in Fictional Conventions* (The Hague, 1964); W. A. Craik, *Jane Austen: The Six Novels* (London, 1965); W. A. Litz, *Jane Austen: A Study of Her Artistic Development* (London, 1965); F. Bradbrook, *Jane Austen and Her Predecessors* (London, 1966); I. Brown, *Jane Austen and Her World* (London, 1966); G. Ryle, "Jane Austen and the Moralists," in *Oxford Review*, 1 (1966); N. Sherry, *Jane Austen* (London, 1966); R. A. Colby, *Fiction with a Purpose* (London, 1967), ch. 3, "*Mansfield Park*: Fanny Price and the Christian Heroine"; A. Fleishman, *A Reading of "Mansfield Park": An Essay in Critical Synthesis* (Baltimore, 1967), the most detailed historical study; W. J. Harvey, "The Plot of Emma," in *Essays in Criticism*, 17 (1967) (L); L. Lerner, *The Truthtellers: Jane Austen, George Eliot, D. H. Lawrence* (London, 1967); J. Wiesenfarth, *The Errand of Form: An Assay of Jane Austen's Art* (London, 1967).

D. Lodge, ed., *Jane Austen: Emma: A Casebook* (London, 1968); K. L. Moler, *Jane Austen's Art of Allusion* (Lincoln, Neb., 1968); B. C. Southam, ed., *Critical Essays on Jane Austen* (London, 1968); B. C. Southam, ed., *Jane Austen: The Critical Heritage* (London, 1968); W. A. Craik, *Jane Austen in Her Time* (London, 1969); T. Tanner, intro. to *Sense and Sensibility* and *Mansfield Park* (London, 1969, 1970), in the Penguin English Library eds.; Y. Gooneratne, *Jane Austen* (Cambridge, 1970); G. Hough, "Narrative and Dialogue in Jane Austen," in *Critical Quarterly* (Autumn 1970); J. O'Neill, ed., *Critics on Jane Austen* (London, 1970); K. C. Phillipps, *Jane Austen's English* (London, 1970); R. Williams, *The English Novel from Dickens to Lawrence* (London, 1970), the intro. discusses Austen; A. M. Duckworth, *The Improvement of the Estate: A Study of Jane Austen's Novels* (Baltimore, 1971); K. Kroeber, *Styles in Fictional Structure: The Art of Jane Austen, Charlotte Brontë, George Eliot* (Princeton, N. J., 1971); B. C. Southam, "General Tilney's Hot-houses: Some Recent Jane Austen Studies and Texts," in *Ariel* (October 1971); J. A. Hodge, *The Double Life of Jane Austen* (London, 1972); N. Page, *The Language of Jane Austen* (Oxford, 1972); J. M. D. Hardwick, *The Osprey Guide to Jane Austen* (Reading, 1973); D. Mansell, *The Novels of Jane Austen: An Interpretation* (London, 1973); F. B. Pinion, *A Jane Austen Companion: A Critical Survey and Reference Book* (London, 1973); S. M. Tave, *Some Words of Jane Austen* (Chicago, 1973); C. Gillie, *A Preface to Jane Austen* (London, 1974); G. Leeming, *Who's Who in Jane Austen and the Brontës* (London, 1974); D. Bush, *Jane Austen* (London, 1975); M. Butler, *Jane Austen and the War of Ideas* (Oxford, 1975); D. D. Devlin, *Jane Austen and Education* (London, 1975); J. Halperin, ed., *Jane Austen: Bicentenary Essays* (Cambridge, 1975); B. Hardy, *A Reading of Jane Austen* (London, 1975); J. Rees, *Jane Austen: Woman and Writer* (London, 1976); B. C. Southam, ed., *Sense and Sensibility, Pride and Prejudice and Northanger Abbey: A Casebook* (London, 1976); J. McMaster, ed., *Jane Austen's Achievement* (London, 1976); J. Halperin and J. Kunert, *Characters in the Fiction of Jane Austen, the Brontës and George Eliot* (London, 1977); K. L. Moler, *Jane Austen's Art of Allusion* (Lincoln, Nebr., 1977); D. Cecil, *A Portrait of Jane Austen* (London, 1978); J. P. Brown, *Jane Austen's Novels: Social Change and Literary Form* (Cambridge, Mass., 1979); D. Cleverdon, *Innocent Diversion: Music in the Life and Writings of Jane Austen* (London, 1979); B. J. Paris, *Character and Conflict in Jane Austen's Novels* (London, 1979); W. Roberts, *Jane Austen and the French Revolution* (London, 1979); B. C. Southam, ed., *Sir Charles Grandison* (Oxford, 1981).

WILLIAM HAZLITT

(1778-1830)

R. L. Brett

I

THOSE who dislike biographical criticism and maintain that an author's life is irrelevant to his writings will find it difficult to come to terms with Hazlitt. For Hazlitt was a biographical critic who believed that ideas are best seen as an expression of personality. For him character was always more important than abstract notions. Even when dealing with fictional writing his preoccupation with people manifests itself. His criticism of William Shakespeare concentrates on character, and in *Lectures Chiefly on the Dramatic Literature of the Age of Elizabeth* he expresses a dislike of the "German" type of tragedy as compared with Shakespeare's, because its characters are merely "mouthpieces," the symbolization of "speculative opinions," and not flesh-and-blood people with lives of their own. Not only was Hazlitt a great exponent of biographical criticism but nearly all his writing is autobiographical and personal, recording his opinions, airing his prejudices, expressing his likes and dislikes, and defending his views. Above all, he advances with passionate conviction what he believes to be true and demolishes what he thinks is false. He is a master of rhetoric whose task, as he sees it, is not only to please his readers but also to persuade them, to convince them, and to rouse them. Ideas are not so much a matter of intellectual assent as of how one lives.

This means that Hazlitt's writing was often argumentative, a quality strengthened by the realization that most of his contemporaries disliked him and by a determination to command their attention and respect, even if he could not win their affection. There is often in his writing the feeling that he is an outsider, a sense at times of injured merit, though to do Hazlitt justice, later generations have acknowledged his merit and recognized that he was treated unfairly in his own day. One can discern the seeds of this sense of alienation in Hazlitt's upbringing. His father was a Unitarian minister and he was educated at a Unitarian academy. To be a Unitarian at this time was more than a matter of religious opinion; it meant that one was a radical in politics, probably with republican sympathies, an enemy of the aristocracy and of the established church with its state patronage and traditional privileges. Those who held these views naturally supported the French Revolution, and it was Hazlitt's unswerving allegiance to this cause that increasingly isolated him from popular opinion in England. He once told Samuel Taylor Coleridge that he had not changed any of his opinions since the age of sixteen. Coleridge, who had been an ardent supporter of the French Revolution as a young man, retorted, "Why then, you are no wiser now than you were then!" and his reply indicates how public sentiment had shifted during their lifetime. To understand this more clearly, we must turn to the details of Hazlitt's birth and education.

William Hazlitt was born on 10 April 1778 at Maidstone, Kent. His father was a dreamer rather than a man of action, taken up with theological speculation and disputes concerning religious and civic liberty, but Hazlitt always loved him for his piety and unworldliness. After moving to Ireland in 1780, the family left in 1783 for America: there Hazlitt's father thought he might find a more congenial atmosphere than at home, where his sympathy for the American colonists was looked at askance and where he felt a lack of freedom. But experience dashed these hopes. After four years of disappointment and illness, the family returned to England and settled in the little town of Wem in Shropshire, where the elder Hazlitt became minister of the Unitarian congregation. The quiet simplicity of his home at Wem, with its emotional security and firm radical principles, remained with Hazlitt as a memory to sustain and console him throughout a turbulent life. His first departure from home came in his fifteenth year, when he was sent to New College, Hackney, an academy that trained candidates for the ministry.

Hazlitt entered New College in 1793, the year in which the British government declared war against France. The declaration came as a profound shock to him. He had grown up in circles that welcomed the French Revolution; his father's distinguished friends Richard Price and Joseph Priestley, the intellectual and spiritual luminaries of the Unitarians, had both defended the revolution, not only on philosophical and political grounds but also as the expression of God's purposes in history. The tradition in which he had been nurtured saw the history of the previous hundred years as a great movement of ideas and events that had started with the Glorious Revolution of 1688, had led to the demand for American independence, and had given birth to the French Revolution. Dr. Price, in his *Discourse on the Love of Our Country*, delivered on 4 November 1789 at the Meeting House in the Old Jewry in London, had welcomed the events in France with an apocalyptic fervor and discerned in them the realization of his millennarian hopes:

After sharing in the benefits of one Revolution, I have been spared to be a witness of two other Revolutions, both glorious. And now methinks, I see the ardour for liberty catching and spreading; a general amendment beginning in human affairs; the dominion of kings changed for the dominion of laws, and the dominion of priests giving way to the dominion of reason and conscience.

Those of Hazlitt's generation, at least those of spirit and generous impulses, could say with William Wordsworth, "Bliss was it in that dawn to be alive,/But to be young was very Heaven." Looking back at this period in "On the Feeling of Immortality in Youth," Hazlitt wrote:

For my part, I set out in life with the French Revolution, and that event had considerable influence on my early feelings, as on those of others. Youth was then doubly such. It was the dawn of a new era, a new impulse had been given to men's minds, and the sun of Liberty rose upon the sun of Life in the same day, and both were proud to run their race together. Little did I dream, while my first hopes and wishes went hand in hand with those of the human race,

that long before my eyes should close, that dawn would be overcast, and set once more in the night of despotism.[1]

(essay 18)

Hazlitt's disillusionment was profound and in some ways permanent, but its first consequence was its unsettling effect on his career at the Hackney academy. Even without the pressure of great events, Hazlitt would probably have been unsettled, for the college was renowned for its freethinking, and the prescribed courses of study did not come easily to him. It is no wonder, perhaps, that a boy of his years and in such circumstances should find it difficult to retain his Christian faith. After three years in Hackney, Hazlitt left, minus his faith and determined not to enter the ministry. There followed a period at Wem spent in desultory reading with no definite career in mind. This was brought to an end in 1798, when Hazlitt first met Coleridge and realized that he had reached a turning point in his life.

The account of their meeting is given in "My First Acquaintance with Poets," the eloquence of which witnesses to the effect Coleridge had on Hazlitt as a young man of nineteen. Coleridge at this time was a neighbor of William and Dorothy Wordsworth in the Quantock Hills in Somerset, and the two poets were engaged in writing and compiling the poems that were to appear in September 1798 as *Lyrical Ballads*. Coleridge, without any prospect of a secure income, was considering entering the Unitarian ministry and had traveled to Shrewsbury to preach a trial sermon before the congregation there. Hazlitt graphically describes Coleridge's appearance in the pulpit and his announcement of the text, "And he went up into the mountain to pray, HIMSELF, ALONE." He was, of course, listening to the greatest talker of the age, and Coleridge's mastery of language seemed to him "like an eagle dallying with the wind." "Poetry and Philosophy had met together. Truth and Genius had embraced, under the eye and with the sanction of Religion." As he walked back to Wem, he viewed the landscape with a new enthusiasm, "for there was a spirit of hope and youth in all nature, that turned every thing into good."

The next day Coleridge visited the elder Hazlitt,

[1]From "Uncollected Essays" in P. P. Howe, ed., *The Complete Works* (London, 1930–1934), vol. XVII. All quotations from the works are, unless otherwise indicated, from the Howe edition, which is the standard.

and the young man was entranced by his conversation. He learned with disappointment that Coleridge, while at Shrewsbury, had received the offer of an annuity from the Wedgwoods and that this genius was not to become their neighbor after all. But he recovered when Coleridge invited him to visit Nether Stowey. The invitation was given in January 1798, and the visit did not take place until May, but the delay did nothing to diminish the excitement and pleasure Hazlitt gained from his month in the Quantocks. He was fascinated by Coleridge's wide-ranging mind and eloquence, and impressed with Wordsworth's personality and poetic power. Both men treated him as an equal and gave him a new self-confidence. He had entered a world in which poetry, politics, philosophy, and psychology were the topics of everyday conversation, and found the experience exhilarating. Indeed, although he did not realize it at the time, never again were Hazlitt's relations with the two poets to be so cordial.

The grounds of future discord lay partly in Hazlitt's awkward and touchy personality, but there were larger issues that were to divide them. These had their origins in the great shift of political opinion that was beginning to take place in England. While some saw in the French Revolution the realization of their dearest hopes, the majority looked across the Channel with mounting alarm. Already in 1790, Edmund Burke had published his *Reflections on the French Revolution* and he followed this in 1796 with his *Letter to a Noble Lord.* These works had a great influence in encouraging resistance to the revolution, and were all the more impressive because their author had sided with the cause of American independence. Burke argued that political institutions were not simply mechanical contrivances erected to serve the will of the people, to be scrapped and replaced according to some new blueprint of society, but that society develops by a principle of organic growth, and that to tear down institutions is to risk anarchy. The swing of public opinion made even radical reform unpopular, and this was increased by the appearance in 1798 of Thomas Malthus' *Essay on the Principle of Population.*

Malthus' book argued with what seemed to be scientific irrefutability that reform was not only irrelevant but also positively dangerous, since "a strong . . . check on population from the difficulty of subsistence," manifested in such forms as famine and disease, was always inevitable. To upset the natural processes of self-preservation and to put benevolence in their place would be to meddle with the design of Providence and to court disaster. Hazlitt's unstinted admiration of Burke as a prose stylist did little to modify his dislike of Burke's doctrines, and for Malthus he had nothing but contempt. Hazlitt's *Reply* to Malthus had to wait until 1807, when a new edition of the *Essay on Population* and Malthus' *Letter to Samuel Whitbread* both appeared, and then his attack on their author was savage in its abuse. Whitbread had brought a poor-law bill before Parliament, and the spectacle of Malthus lobbying members of Parliament in an attempt to abolish poor-law relief roused Hazlitt's fiercest anger. He preferred to believe with those, like William Godwin, who argued that if existing social institutions could be modified or new ones brought into being, human nature would respond and a just society could realize the dreams of the reformers. For him, society was made for man, not man for society.

Hazlitt spent the years from 1798 to 1803 trying to follow in the footsteps of his elder brother, John, who was a painter. He studied first in London and then in Paris. When he arrived in Paris in 1802, England and France were at peace; when he left it in 1803, England was about to declare war again. The great majority of the English people supported the war, and again Hazlitt found himself in a dwindling minority. He saw the war as an attack on democracy, and during his time abroad he developed an affection for the French people and an admiration for their first consul, Napoleon. These were grounds enough for the rift that was to open up between Hazlitt and Wordsworth and Coleridge, for the two poets now regarded the French Revolution as a god who had failed; but it was the personal element that was to make their quarrel especially acrimonious.

When Hazlitt returned from France in 1803, Wordsworth and Coleridge were living with their families in the Lake District, and he joined them there the following summer. He now saw himself as a portrait painter, and this was how Coleridge wrote of him in a letter to Tom Wedgwood in September of that year: "William Hazlitt is a thinking, observant, original man, of great power as a Painter of Character Portraits, and far more in the manner of the Old Painters, than any living Artist." He was more experienced than the youth who had visited the Quantocks, but even so the picture Coleridge gives is that of an odd and immature character.

His manners are to 99 in 100 singularly repulsive: brow-hanging, shoe-contemplative, *strange* . . . he is, I verily believe, kindly-natured—is very fond of, attentive to, and patient with, children, but he is jealous, gloomy, and of an irritable Pride—and addicted to women, as objects of sexual Indulgence. With all this, there is much good in him . . . he is strangely confused and dark in his conversation and delivers himself of almost all his conceptions with a Forceps, yet he says more than any man I ever knew. . . . He sends well-headed and well-feathered Thoughts straight forwards to the mark with a Twang of the Bow-string.

II

THE two poets and their circle welcomed Hazlitt in their midst, but perhaps he felt they did not take him seriously enough. Though his talents as a painter were undeniable, the portraits he painted did not meet with unqualified praise. Dorothy Wordsworth, who always had a sharp tongue, told Lady Beaumont that the portrait of Coleridge made her think of the poet as "not merely dying, but dying of sorrow and raised up upon his bed to take a last farewell of his Friends." Robert Southey, who had recently moved to Keswick, said of Wordsworth's portrait that it represented him "At the gallows—deeply affected by his deserved fate—yet determined to die like a man." But it was what Coleridge referred to in his letter as "sexual Indulgence" that brought an ignominious end to Hazlitt's visit. The letters of both Wordsworth and Coleridge give details of the incident that caused Hazlitt to leave, and while they were written later and after Hazlitt had attacked their reputations, there is no reason to doubt their essential truth. Apparently Hazlitt attempted sexual assaults on some of the local girls, and one attack in particular so incensed the community that the men chased him out of the village, from which he escaped over the hills in clothes and with money provided by either Coleridge or Wordsworth. In view of the revelations Hazlitt was to make later in *Liber Amoris*, one can believe the substance of these accounts, for his personality reveals a man of great sexual passion, at once attracted to women and inhibited in their presence.

Following this debacle, Hazlitt's fortunes were at a low ebb, and remained so for eight years. After a retreat to Wem, he ventured again on the literary scene in London, and found true friends in Charles and Mary Lamb. The Lambs were the center of a talented circle, and at their Wednesday evening parties at Mitre Court, Hazlitt was variously tolerated, encouraged, and approved of. For the Lambs themselves he retained an enduring affection. Many of his essays look back on the warmth of their friendship, and his portrait of Charles Lamb in the National Portrait Gallery remains his best-known painting and a token of gratitude to one whose loyalty remained constant. Through the Lambs Hazlitt met his first wife, Sarah Stoddart, in 1807. She was the daughter of a retired naval officer who lived at Winterslow, near Salisbury, and upon his death she had inherited a house of her own and a modest income of £80 a year. She was three years older than Hazlitt, and had already been involved in a number of unfortunate love affairs. What induced Hazlitt to marry her remains a mystery. She had many virtues, including common sense and practicality, but she lacked any grace of manner or appearance and, above all, the romantic sensibility that would have inspired Hazlitt and aroused him from his constitutional melancholy. She brought him a measure of financial security and provided him with a home he could call his own; but though he was used to living in the country and loved the Wiltshire landscape, he felt that his future lay in London.

Even at the beginning he entered on married life with no enthusiasm, and as the years passed, he viewed his choice of a wife as another misfortune of life. He embarked on marriage with the grim realization that he had failed as a painter and as a man of letters. In 1805 he had published *An Essay on the Principles of Human Action*, but it had been virtually ignored; he had some political essays to his credit and a few commissioned works, and more recently had written his *Reply* to Malthus; but none of them gave him much of a reputation. In 1809 he started to edit the memoirs of the social reformer Thomas Holcroft, who died in March of that year; but the work had a checkered history and did not appear until 1816. In 1812 he turned, as so many other indigent authors were doing, to the delivery of a series of lectures. These lectures on philosophy commanded little attention, but helped Hazlitt to clarify his own ideas and were useful to the tasks that lay ahead. In the same year he became parliamentary and dramatic reporter for the *Morning Chronicle*, and at long last found an occupation that matched his genius and that was to establish his career.

At first Hazlitt was restricted to reporting parliamentary debates from the press gallery, but he soon began contributing short essays and occasional pieces that so pleased his editor that he became dramatic critic and literary reviewer. After eighteen months of apprenticeship, brought to an end by political differences, he moved to the *Champion*, then to the radical *Examiner*, run by John and Leigh Hunt, and finally to the *Times*. As a young man he had wrestled with words and found every piece of writing an agonizing process of making his ideas articulate; but now the pressure of working to a deadline and having to deal with current events seemed to have a liberating effect, and the six years he spent with these journals saw a tremendous output of writing on politics, philosophy, the theater, art, literature, and belles lettres. His contributions to "The Round Table," a feature of the *Examiner*, gave him freedom to develop the essay form in his own characteristic manner, especially to compound literature, politics, and personalities. His new-found confidence charged these pieces with great energy and gave them what he believed was the hallmark of great art, the quality he called "gusto." He also adopted a procedure that he was to use with increasing success: to cream off the best of his journalism and to publish it later in book form. From his essays in the *Examiner* and elsewhere, he gathered the works that appeared as *The Round Table* and some of the material that went into the making of his *Characters of Shakespeare's Plays*, and, when he left the *Times*, produced *A View of the English Stage* and *Political Essays*.

Hazlitt's attacks on Wordsworth, Coleridge, and Southey, whom he now regarded as renegades, and on the Tory politicians were venomous in tone and, as was to be expected, were answered in kind. The *Quarterly Review* and *Blackwood's* magazine were quick in their condemnation, and the latter in particular mounted a sustained campaign against him; but Hazlitt thrived on opposition and his style became stronger with debate. The passion that informed his language sprang from a deeply held conviction that after 1815 the cause of political reform was lost, that the government consisted of no more than a parcel of hypocrites and knaves who had little sense of justice and lacked even compassion for the poor and oppressed. His style may often have been vituperative and his arguments prejudiced, but the same could be said of his opponents; and *Blackwood's* in particular descended to the level of abusing not only his character but also his personal appearance. Public contention spurred Hazlitt to new

levels of achievement and improved his prospects by bringing him into a closer association with the *Edinburgh Review*, which, under the editorship of Francis Jeffrey, had become the scourge of the Tories and the romantic poets.

Jeffrey had invited Hazlitt to become a reviewer for the *Edinburgh Review* in 1814, the year in which he himself had reviewed Wordsworth's *Excursion* with the notorious and laconic comment, "This will never do." Although it became known for the forthright expression of its political opinions, the *Edinburgh Review* soon established a reputation for its literary reviews as well. It welcomed change in politics, but its literary values were traditional; Jeffrey disliked all modern poetry and looked back to the Elizabethan period as the high-water mark of literary achievement, and next best the Augustanism of the eighteenth century. He preferred George Crabbe to Coleridge, Samuel Rogers to Wordsworth, and Thomas Campbell to Southey. His criticism of Lord Byron brought about that splendid retaliatory poem, *English Bards and Scotch Reviewers*, and his review of *Marmion* made Sir Walter Scott swear he would never write for the *Edinburgh* again. Where other men, even other contributors to the *Edinburgh*, judged Jeffrey to be cantankerous and malicious, Hazlitt found in him a patron and benefactor. He paid Hazlitt liberally, and even went so far as to write a laudatory review of *Characters of Shakespeare's Plays* in his own periodical. Their good relations were checked for a time by the *Edinburgh's* cool review of *The Spirit of the Age* in 1825, almost certainly written by Jeffrey himself, in which Hazlitt was advised "to say sensible things in a plain way" rather than to write for effect, and to eschew "the eternal desire to strike and surprise." Hazlitt withdrew his services in dudgeon, and resumed them only when there was a change of editors; but their friendship was later repaired, and it was to Jeffrey that Hazlitt appealed on his deathbed for a loan of £10 to clear his debts. Jeffrey, generous with money as always, promptly sent £50 and allowed Hazlitt to die in peace and dignity.

In 1818–1819, Hazlitt gave three courses of lectures, the first of which was attended by John Keats, who had become a firm friend and admirer. These were subsequently published as *Lectures on the English Poets, On the English Comic Writers*, and *On the Dramatic Literature of the Age of Elizabeth*. Though written to earn money, they were the product of reflection and the wide reading he was able to do when freed from the demands of journalism. Together they form an extended survey of English literature with a concentration on those periods and authors that gave him special pleasure. The lectures provided him with an escape from contemporary disputes, into a world of disinterested pleasure.

To most of his contemporaries, Hazlitt must have appeared a man of bustle and contention, angry and disputatious, concerned only with the rancorous issues of the time. But there was another side to his character; behind this angry polemicist lay a contemplative man who sought relief in an ideal world of artistic delight. Not that he had much time for the "pure" pleasures of literature, for literature to him was a reflection of life, and its values were the values of life as we know it. Nevertheless, the world of books was a kingdom of the mind to which he could escape from the distractions of the present. In his lecture "On Poetry in General," which introduced his *Lectures on the English Poets*, he wrote: "If poetry is a dream, the business of life is much the same. If it is a fiction, made up of what we wish things to be, and fancy that they are, because we wish them so, there is no other nor better reading."

Hazlitt was not a scholarly critic, for he was impatient of dates and chronology, nor was he a prescriptive critic who judged literature by principles and rules; he was above all a critic who tried to communicate his personal enthusiasm for what he admired. This gave his criticism greater generosity and less rancor than his political writings, but it did not prevent the expression of prejudice, for prejudice is often a kind of personal preference.

Hazlitt had already demonstrated his critical generosity in his comments on Burke in *The Eloquence of the British Senate* in 1807. He admired Burke as a thinker and even more as a writer, though he disagreed profoundly with him on the French Revolution. One of Burke's principles was what Hazlitt described as a natural prejudice.

He was therefore right in saying that it is no objection to an institution, that it is founded on *prejudice*, but the contrary, if that prejudice is natural and right; that is, if it arises from those circumstances which are properly subjects of feeling and association, not from any defect or perversion of the understanding in those things which fall properly under its jurisdiction. On this profound maxim he took his stand.

In this sense it is natural and right for a man to be prejudiced in favor of his own wife and children, even if they are not superior to those of other men.

Hazlitt shows the same kind of prejudice in his treatment of those authors for whom he has some sympathy. When he is out of sympathy with their opinions, he can still write, at least in the *Lectures on the English Poets*, more in sorrow than in anger. Even his remarks on Wordsworth and Coleridge lose some of the acerbity of his earlier comments. So he can say of the one that "Mr. Wordsworth is the most original poet now living . . . and the less Mr. Wordsworth's general merits have been understood, the more necessary is it to insist upon them," and to pay to the other what amounts to a tribute, even if a sharply qualified one. Writing of Coleridge in "On the Living Poets," he remembers the glory that surrounded him at Shrewsbury.

He was the first poet I ever knew. His genius at that time had angelic wings, and fed on manna. He talked on for ever; and you wished him to talk on for ever. His thoughts did not seem to come with labour and effort; but as if borne on the gusts of genius, and as if the wings of his imagination lifted him from off his feet. His voice rolled on the ear like the pealing organ, and its sound alone was the music of thought. His mind was clothed with wings; and raised on them he lifted philosophy to heaven. In his descriptions, you then saw the progress of human happiness and liberty in bright and never-ending succession, like the steps of Jacob's ladder, with airy shapes ascending and descending, and with the voice of God at the top of the ladder.

(lecture 8)

But the earlier glory is used to point the contrast with Coleridge's present state. "And shall I, who heard him then, listen to him now? Not I! . . . that spell is broke; that time is gone for ever; that voice is heard no more: but still the recollection comes rushing by with thoughts of long-past years, and rings in my ears with never-dying sound."

III

FROM 1808 to 1812, the Hazlitts continued to live at Winterslow, though Hazlitt made lengthy stays in London. But from then on, Hazlitt, his wife, and their small son moved to a house in York Street, Westminster, which had once been the home of John Milton and more recently had been occupied by James Mill. His landlord was the philosopher Jeremy Bentham, with whom his relations were often strained because of failure to pay the rent. Many years later, when he had left York Street, Hazlitt gave an astringent account in *The Spirit of the Age* of Bentham's utilitarian cast of mind; this had connived at a scheme for desecrating the house and garden, which had been "the cradle of *Paradise Lost*," and permitting a road to be built so that "the idle rabble of Westminster" could pass across this hallowed ground. He sometimes returned to Winterslow and stayed at The Hut, a small inn where he could read and write, undistracted by the cares of business and the demands of journalism.

In the Wiltshire countryside Hazlitt could lie, as he wrote in one of his essays, "whole mornings on a sunny bank on Salisbury Plain, without any object before me, neither knowing nor caring how time passes, and thus 'with light-winged toys of feathered Idleness' to melt down hours to moments." It was here that he prepared his lectures on the English comic writers and wrote the essays for John Scott's *London* magazine that afterward were published in two of his best books, *Table Talk* (1821–1822) and *The Plain Speaker* (1826). Hazlitt needed a retreat from both professional and domestic troubles, for his marriage went from bad to worse. By 1819 his relations with his wife had reached the breaking point. No woman could have tolerated for long the strains he imposed upon Sarah Hazlitt. A few might have borne the financial straits to which he reduced her, and others, his ill temper and adultery, but no one could have borne these and accepted as well his flagrant promiscuity and his habit of taking their young son on his visits to the various women of easy virtue with whom he associated. At the end of the year, he and his wife separated, and in 1820 Hazlitt took lodgings in Southampton Buildings.

Here he became infatuated with his landlord's daughter, Sarah Walker. The strange story is chronicled in *Liber Amoris*, in which Hazlitt laid bare his heart with astonishing candor. He was now forty-two and Sarah Walker a girl half his age. She was anything but a paragon of beauty or virtue, though probably out of her depth in such an affair; and the tantalizing manner in which she trifled with him inflamed his passion until it assumed the character of an obsession. Hazlitt invested this unremarkable and flirtatious girl with a romantic aura that reflected his own emotional needs and had little objective reality. The rhapsodical flights of *Liber Amoris* read like the yearnings of a young man whose first experience of love expresses itself in a vision of idealized and unattainable perfection. We discern in them the dammed-up feelings that had never found satisfaction in his unhappy marriage.

Is my love then in the power of fortune, or of her caprice? No, I will have it lasting as it is pure; and I will make a Goddess of her, and build a temple to her in my heart, and worship her on indestructible altars, and raise statues to her: and my homage shall be unblemished as her unrivalled symmetry of form; and when that fails, the memory of it shall survive; and my bosom shall be proof to scorn, as hers has been to pity; and I will pursue her with an unrelenting love, and sue to be her slave, and tend her steps without notice and without reward; and serve her living, and mourn for her when dead.

(part II, letter 12)

Alongside these flights of fancy in *Liber Amoris* are passages that reveal a far more earthly and sensual love. This erotic passion was far removed from the purity of his visionary joy, but in Hazlitt's feverish state the two worked together in a gathering frenzy.

By the end of 1821, Hazlitt decided to seek a divorce and, because this was easier to secure under Scottish law, he devised a plan that took him and his wife to Edinburgh. In February 1822 he stayed for a month at Renton in Berwickshire, where he wrote a series of essays for the *New Monthly* magazine, later to appear as the second volume of *Table Talk*, and then journeyed to the Scottish capital, where his wife joined him in April. While the divorce proceedings were in train, Hazlitt paid a brief visit to London to see Sarah Walker, full of foreboding that she would reject him and that his love had been betrayed. In July the divorce was completed; and he and his wife parted on terms that, if not cordial, were at least civilized. She was practical and sensible, as always, and here perhaps was the core of what had always separated them.

Hazlitt returned to London at once, and found that his worst fears had been realized. The effect on him was catastrophic. He could end *Liber Amoris* in a state of sad resignation: "Her image seems fast 'going into the wastes of time,' like a weed that the wave bears farther and farther from me . . . no flower will ever bloom on earth to glad my heart again!" But before he reached that state, he had to pass through a period during which his unrequited love alternated with hatred and bitterness. Contemporary accounts all speak of him as insane or demented at this time, sending his associates to spy on Sarah, compulsively recounting his misfortune to any who would listen to him, and unable to work or pay his bills. This was a period when, in a lifetime of adversities, his spirits and his fortunes were at their lowest. The only relief he found was in art, and the first writings he managed to accomplish after his rejection were essays on the galleries he visited. He contributed these essays on the Dulwich Gallery, the pictures at Windsor Castle, the pictures at Hampton Court, and others to *London*; they appeared later as *Sketches of the Principal Picture-Galleries in England*.

We should not blame Sarah Walker unduly for the misery she caused Hazlitt, for she had been caught up in events that she did not understand and by a personality more complex than she could comprehend. Nor, perhaps, should we censure Hazlitt, for he was swept away by emotions that should have been liberated much earlier in life. Even *Liber Amoris*, which appeared in 1823 and so excited his enemies and fed their malicious prurience, should be seen as a kind of abreaction; and though its authorship was known at once, we should remember that it was published anonymously.

Hazlitt spent a good deal of this period at The Hut in Winterslow. His recovery was slow, but as the emotional forces that had been released in his personality became integrated, his work achieved a new power. At the end of 1821, he was asked to write for the *Liberal*, a new periodical launched by Byron, Shelley, and Leigh Hunt. The invitation was surprising, for in spite of their shared political opinions, Hazlitt did not admire Shelley as a poet, and his relations with Byron were less than cordial following his adverse reviews of Byron's poetry. But his association with them was short-lived. The *Liberal* was dogged with misfortune from the beginning. Shelley was drowned in July 1822; John Hunt was charged with libeling George III by printing Byron's "The Vision of Judgment," which appeared in the first number; and Leigh Hunt quarreled with Byron. The fourth number was its last; but during its brief lifetime, which provoked a storm of abuse, Hazlitt wrote some of his best essays for it. In its third number appeared "My First Acquaintance with Poets"; and to the second he contributed "On the Scotch Character" and "On the Spirit of Monarchy." All of these are written with a wonderful command of language and "My First Acquaintance with Poets" is one of his masterpieces.

To 1822 also belongs his *Characteristics: In the Manner of Rochefoucault's Maxims*, published anonymously in 1823 and made up of material he had intended for the *Liberal*. These worldly-wise observations on man and society reflect the cynicism and weariness that still clouded Hazlitt's mind. From the smartness of "Vice is man's nature: virtue is a habit—or a mask" or "There is often a good deal of spleen at the bottom of benevolence," it is a short step to the bruised sensibility that shows in "We grow tired of ourselves, much more of other people" and "An accomplished coquet excites the passions of others, in proportion as she feels none herself."

For evidence of a full recovery of spirits we have to turn to *The Spirit of the Age*, though Hazlitt told Walter Savage Landor that he had written it in a "depression of body and mind." His greatest book, it shows a renewed and, indeed, a greater mental energy than anything he had written before. A few of the essays he included in it came from his earlier periodical publications, but the great bulk of it was new. The work began at Winterslow late in 1823, when he wrote a short biographical study of his former landlord, Jeremy Bentham, that appeared in the *New Monthly* the next spring. This was followed by four sketches of eminent contemporaries for the same periodical, which together with one on George Canning written for the *Examiner*, he gathered with seventeen new essays to form his book.

The Spirit of the Age is more than a collection of separate biographies; it has a structure and coherence that give the work a cumulative effect and provide a synoptic view of the period. It can be seen as his *Biographia Literaria*, though it deals only with his contemporaries and not with earlier figures who had influenced him, and as his considered judgment on his own generation. He discusses, of course, not only those who have influenced him positively but also those with whom he disagrees, and most frequently those who manage to fall into both categories. He sees his own age animated by a great debate carried on by those who are traditionalists—some of them, indeed, reactionaries—and those who believe in reform and experiment. From his vantage point in middle life, he observes these opposing forces and considers that great opportunities have been lost, that his own period has been one of unfulfilled hopes and broken promises. He does not lack sympathy with tradition, but regards it as something that must be vitalized and carried forward by the talents of individuals in every generation. The tragedy of his own age is that though there have been men of great talents—some of them, indeed, geniuses—they have failed to do this. There is thus a certain sadness in his view of men and events, but never despair. He lives in hope that the failures of today may become the achievements of tomorrow.

The temper of Hazlitt's writing in *The Spirit of the Age* is more balanced and less strident than in much of his previous work. He can still express vehement dislike on occasion and his sarcasm can be biting, as when he says of William Gifford that he is admirably qualified to be editor of the *Quarterly Review*, since he is fitted to this situation "by a happy combination of defects, natural and acquired."

It would be asking too much of Hazlitt to write dispassionately of one who had attacked him personally throughout the years, but generally his tone is generous in its understanding of human motives and behavior, and ready to balance virtues against faults. In *Liber Amoris* he had preached what he called the religion of love, a strange compound of "eros" and "agape" but here he is moved by a religion of humanity. He realizes that any improvement in the condition of man must reconcile the claims of both the heart and the head, that plans for social reform must be made not only by the light of the intellect but also with regard for the emotions. Many schemes for improvement are too narrow in their view of human nature. So he criticized Bentham for basing everything on the principle of utility:

He has a great contempt for out-of-door prospects, for green fields and trees, and is referring every thing to Utility. There is a little narrowness in this; for if all the sources of satisfaction are taken away, what is to become of utility itself? It is, indeed, the great fault of this able and extraordinary man, that he has concentrated his faculties and feelings too entirely on one subject and pursuit and has not "looked enough abroad into universality."

Similarly, he attacks Malthus not for the strict theoretical side of the argument concerning population, but for his failure to acknowledge that men are free to arrange things for the good of all. The growth of population should be checked not by vice and misery, but by moral restraint; and the poor should not be treated as the victims of natural forces. His denunciation of William Wilberforce rests upon the charge that Wilberforce concentrated on the abolition of slavery abroad, but failed to expose evil at home. This myopic view was a fault not only of the intellect but also of moral sensibility, and led Wilberforce into hypocrisy.

His patriotism, his philanthropy are not so ill-bred, as to quarrel with his loyalty or to banish him from the first circles. He preaches vital Christianity to untutored savages, and tolerates its worst abuses in civilized states. . . . There is in all this an appearance of a good deal of cant and tricking. His patriotism may be accused of being servile, his

humanity ostentatious, his loyalty conditional, his religion a mixture of fashion and fanaticism.

One of the best portraits in *The Spirit of the Age* for understanding Hazlitt's analysis of the contemporary situation is that of Sir Walter Scott, for Scott's interpretation of history was very different from his own. Hazlitt had every reason for disliking Scott, whom he regarded as a reactionary Tory and timeserver, and his admiration for Scott's novels came to him late. This was the paradox he had to face: how a man whose political views were so antipathetic to him could write novels "whose worst is better than any other person's best." What he admired so much was Scott's ability to take the reader into a story that captured the imagination, that ranged over the whole of life from the highest to the lowest, and that showed sympathy and understanding for the human condition. "What a power is that of genius!" he exclaims. "What a world of thought and feeling is thus rescued from oblivion! How many hours of heartfelt satisfaction has our author given to the gay and thoughtless! How many sad hearts has he soothed in pain and solitude!" Scott's great gift is to be able to give concrete expression to the universal; it is the gift of the imagination and especially of the historical imagination, which can represent life as it really was. But Scott has fatal limitations and defects: his mind is timid; it "does not project itself beyond this into the world unknown, but mechanically shrinks back as from the edge of a precipice." Scott seeks refuge from the present in history: "Sir Walter would make a bad hand of a description of the Millennium, unless he could lay the scene in Scotland five hundred years ago." He is a writer "who, from the height of his genius looking abroad into nature, and scanning the recesses of the human heart, 'winked and shut his apprehension up' to every thought or purpose that tended to the future good of mankind."

It is a measure of Hazlitt's sympathetic understanding that his most eloquent tributes are paid to those with whom he disagreed most profoundly: Scott, Burke (who lies outside the purview of *The Spirit of the Age*), Wordsworth, and Coleridge. He comes once again in these portraits to a considered judgment of the last two, whose influence, through friendship and alienation, remained with him always. He regards Wordsworth as the archetypal figure of the period: "Mr. Wordsworth's genius is a pure emanation of the Spirit of the Age." His earlier poetry reflects the stirring of revolutionary change with which the age began: "It is one of the innovations of the time. It partakes of, and is carried along with, the revolutionary movement of our age: the political changes of the day were the model on which he formed and conducted his political experiments." Since then Wordsworth has withdrawn to a life of contemplation. Hazlitt gives him credit for resisting the beguilement of material ambitions and worldly fame, but regrets that he has retreated from the challenges of the times and has "passed his life in solitary musing or in daily converse with the face of nature." Wordsworth's later poetry now reflects this concern with the self, and is no more than an association of images in the poet's own mind: "He has dwelt among pastoral scenes, till each object has become connected with a thousand feelings, a link in the chain of thought, a fibre of his own heart." Hazlitt sees him rescued by a growing popular esteem from the sad fate that might otherwise have awaited him—"that of becoming the God of his own idolatry."

There, then, are two tendencies of the age: to retreat into history and to withdraw into the recesses of one's own mind. The third is to engage in endless talk as an escape from action: "The present is an age of talkers, and not of doers; and the reason is that the world is growing old." Nothing exemplifies this more clearly for Hazlitt than what he considers the wasted genius of Coleridge, whose voice, as he recalls it, "is like the echo of the congregated roar of the 'dark rearward and abyss' of thought." Hazlitt gives a brilliant sketch of Coleridge's intellectual and spiritual pilgrimage, tracing his progress from the time when he had been a revolutionary and a democrat, when he "had kindled his affections at the blaze of the French Revolution, and sang for joy, when the towers of the Bastille and the proud places of the insolent and the oppressor fell," through a discipleship of Godwin and David Hartley, and allegiance to the Platonists, mystics, and "Bishop Berkeley's fairyworld," until he "lost himself in the labyrinths . . . of the Kantean philosophy, and amongst the cabalistic names of Fichte and Schelling, and God knows who." It is a sorry story of dissipated powers, says Hazlitt. "Alas! 'Frailty, thy name is *Genius!*' . . . such and so little is the mind of man." Coleridge had given excuses by his "casuistry and a musical voice" for those who dared not risk unpopularity or who sought state favors; but while they entered the citadels of privilege and public acclaim, he remained outside, "pitching his tent upon the barren waste without, and having no abiding place nor city of refuge!" He had achieved neither position nor place, nor would he win lasting fame. It is a sad valedictory to one whom Hazlitt had once worshiped.

It would be an error, of course, to mistake Hazlitt's mellowness for objectivity, and his pronouncements often derive from a pattern of preconceived ideas that he imposes on his age. His insistence that Scott seeks to escape from the present into the refuge of the past does scant justice to Scott's belief that we see an image of ourselves in the mirror of history, and that history is the best discipline we can have for tackling present problems. He fails to see this, of course, because he has no sympathy with Scott's Tory philosophy. Equally he ignores Wordsworth's concern for "Joy in widest commonalty spread," which accompanied his "bliss in solitude." Worst of all is what amounts to his patronage of Coleridge, who merited his pity even less than his anger. Though he admires Coleridge's erudition, he fails to see the significance of his philosophical speculation, and does not recognize, as John Stuart Mill did a few years later, that Coleridge was one of the great seminal minds of the period. These are all limitations that spring from his deeply held convictions; they may be mistaken, and must detract from any claim he had to be a profound thinker, but at least they are free of malice.

While Hazlitt was completing *The Spirit of the Age*, he embarked upon marriage for the second time. We do not know the date of the marriage, though it was probably in April 1824 in Edinburgh, and very little about his new wife. Some said that Isabella Bridgewater was the widow of an army colonel; others, the widow of a barrister; but all agreed that she was a woman of character and that Hazlitt was lucky to have married her. By August of that year the couple left on a continental tour, staying in Paris for three months, when Hazlitt visited the Louvre once again, and proceeding in January 1825 to Italy. Hazlitt recounted their journey in *Notes of a Journey Through France and Italy*, published in that year. After a few weeks in Switzerland, they returned to England in the autumn.

In 1826, Hazlitt gathered together the essays that were published as *The Plain Speaker* and began writing as articles his "conversations" with the painter James Northcote, a friend of thirty years. In the summer he went to France, where he stayed for fourteen months, working on what he considered his magnum opus, *The Life of Napoleon Bonaparte*, and contributing articles to the periodicals at home. He returned in October 1825, but his wife did not accompany him and, as far as we know, they never met again. Some said that Hazlitt's son was unhappy with his stepmother and that this brought about a split, but Hazlitt has left no account of their separation.

Hazlitt's main concern on returning to England was the publication of his *Life of Napoleon Bonaparte*. The first two volumes appeared in January 1828, but his high hopes for what he regarded as the crowning achievement of his career were speedily dashed, for the reception they were given was decidedly cool. Undeterred by the bankruptcy of his publishers, which brought his arrest for debt, he set about preparing the third and fourth volumes for publication. These appeared in the year of his death, and he probably did not see them in print. This was just as well, for his attempt to defend the beliefs of a lifetime—the cause of the French Revolution and Napoleon as the embodiment of the aspirations that were then given birth, his attack on the Tories for refusing to see the need for reform, and his lamentation for Napoleon's final defeat—met with a stony silence. If one were able to share his exaggerated and partisan views, one would still have to confess that Hazlitt's work is prolix and tedious. Even Lamb, generous to the last in trying to see something to admire in the writings of his friend, had to admit that he skipped parts of it.

On returning from France, Hazlitt retired again to Winterslow. The failure of his publishers obliged him to continue his journalism, although in 1828 he had written one of his finest pieces, "A Farewell to Essay-Writing," which first appeared in the *London Weekly Review*. Though embroiled to the end in dispute and dissension, he seemed now to be more withdrawn into his own memories. His emotions are recollected and expressed in tranquillity: "Food, warmth, sleep, and a book; these are all I at present ask," he writes at the beginning of his "Farewell." ". . . give me the robin redbreast, pecking the crumbs at the door, or warbling on the leafless spray, the same glancing form that has followed me wherever I have been, . . . or the rich notes of the thrush that startle the ear of winter. . . . To these I adhere, and am faithful, for they are true to me. . . ." Though few now share his most cherished political convictions, and though events seem to have conspired against him, he remains true to his youthful vision:

One great ground of confidence and support has, indeed, been struck from under my feet; but I have made it up to myself by proportionable pertinacity of opinion. The success of the great cause, to which I had vowed myself, was to me more than all the world. . . . But my conviction of the right was only established by the triumph of the wrong; and my earliest hopes will be my last regrets.

He recalls earlier and happier years at Winterslow, when Charles and Mary Lamb had visited him:

I used to walk out at this time with Mr. and Miss Lamb of an evening, to look at the Claude Lorraine skies over our heads melting from azure into purple and gold, and to gather mushrooms, that sprung up at our feet, to throw into our hashed mutton at supper.

This association of ideas leads him to the pleasures afforded by art, and reminds him of his visits to picture galleries. It is these memories that give him strength to face what lies ahead:

It is in looking back to such scenes that I draw my best consolation for the future. Later impressions come and go, and serve to fill up the intervals; but these are my standing resource, my true classics. If I have had few real pleasures or advantages, my ideas, from their sinewy texture, have been to me in the nature of realities; and if I should not be able to add to the stock, I can live by husbanding the interest.

Not that Hazlitt had much future to look forward to. Back in London he worked as drama critic of the *Examiner* and found pleasure again in his old love of the theater. But his health began to deteriorate; worn out by constant industry, personal and professional disappointment, poverty, and calumny, he seemed prematurely old. Finally he suffered from cancer of the stomach. He died, aged fifty-two, on 18 September 1830, and was buried in St. Anne's Churchyard in Soho. His life had been marked by hardship and misery; and yet his last words, according to his son, were, "Well, I have had a happy life." He was sustained at the last, as he had always been in adversity, by memories of his childhood and youth, when the world lay bright before him. Always in times of misery he had found consolation in memories of the innocence of childhood (something that links him to William Blake and Wordsworth), and new hope in a vision of what life might be. In his essay "The Dulwich Gallery" he had written of himself as a boy:

See him there, the urchin, seated in the sun, with a book in his hand, and the wall at his back. He has a thicker wall before him—the wall that parts him from the future . . . he thinks that he will one day write a book, and have his name repeated by thousands of readers. . . . Come hither, thou poor little fellow, and let us change places with thee if thou wilt.

The urchin's wish had been granted; he had had to ". . . feed poor, and lie hard, and be contented and happy, and think what a fine thing it is to be an author, and dream of immortality." Nor would Hazlitt on his deathbed have had it otherwise.

Hazlitt's achievement as a man of letters lies in his essays and his literary criticism. As an essayist he belongs to that English tradition of writing that runs through Bacon, Addison, Steele, Johnson, and Hume, but he also owes something to the French writers Montaigne and Rousseau, whose work was more confessional and personal. Writing for him was not concerned with lifeless abstractions, but was the embodiment of a man's attitude to life, his values and passions as well as his intellect. That is why he could say in the "Character of Mr. Burke": "The only specimen of Burke is, *all that he wrote.*"

Nevertheless, while there is this personal reference in nearly all he wrote, Hazlitt was a keen observer and critic of human affairs and of his fellow men. The essay was for him the form above all others most suited to bringing together the mind of the author and the pageant of human experience. The essayist's art consists, he writes in "On the Periodical Essayists,"

. . . in applying the talents and resources of the mind to all that mixed mass of human affairs, which, though not included under the head of any regular art, science, or profession, falls under the cognizance of the writer, and "comes home to the business and bosoms of men" . . . it makes familiar with the world of men and women, records their actions, assigns their motives, exhibits their whims, characterises their pursuits in all their singular and endless variety, ridicules their absurdities, exposes their inconsistencies.[2]

He goes on to elaborate the notion that the essay is ideally fitted to approach life with a method that is concrete and particular rather than a priori and theoretical:

It is in morals and manners what the experimental is in natural philosophy, as opposed to the dogmatical method.

[2]Essay 5 in *Lectures on the English Comic Writers* (London, 1819).

It does not deal in sweeping clauses of proscription and anathema, but in nice distinctions and liberal constructions. It makes up its general accounts from details, its few theories from many facts.

One might find it difficult at first glance to apply this to his own practice as an essayist, for Hazlitt always seems prone to view things through the spectacles of his own preconceptions, to confuse politics and poetry, to see men as actors in a great historical drama that he has largely written himself. Few of his essays do not include at least a passing reference to his revolutionary convictions, and in many his radical opinions throw a shadow across the page. At times, indeed, this tendency becomes tedious, but what redeems him is that his polemicism is mitigated by common sense and honesty. In his essay "On Personal Character," for instance, Hazlitt observes that human character is much more intransigent than reformers would like to admit, that to change men's circumstances does not always lead to an improvement of behavior, that different nations have their own national characteristics that remain pretty constant, that genetic inheritance is more powerful than the habits we acquire by education and social convention:

We may refine, we may disguise, we may equivocate, we may compound for our vices, without getting rid of them; as we change our liquors, but do not leave off drinking. We may, in this respect, look forward to a decent and moderate, rather than a thorough and radical reform . . . we may improve the mechanism, if not the texture of society; that is, we may improve the physical circumstances of individuals and their general relations to the State, though the internal character, like the grain in wood, or the sap in trees, that still rises, bend them how you will, may remain nearly the same.[3]

Hazlitt was least doctrinaire when it came to human nature.

This understanding of, and sympathy for, human nature in all its complexity can be seen in his essays that deal with the novel and the theater. Scott's works, he wrote, "are almost like a new edition of human nature. This is indeed to be an author!" In his lecture "On the English Novelists" he says that fiction is a representation of life; what we learn from it is what we learn from life itself, not theoretical knowledge but knowledge given us by direct acquaintance. "We find there a close imitation of men

[3]Essay 21 in *The Plain Speaker: Opinions on Books, Men, and Things,* 2 vols. (London, 1826).

and manners; we see the very web and texture of society as it really exists, and as we meet with it when we come into the world." Similarly the theater teaches us not by precept but by extending and enriching our sensibilities; it holds up a mirror in which we see our faults, and brings before us a vision of what we might be. The players, he writes in "On Actors and Acting":

... show us all that we are, all that we wish to be, and all that we dread to be. The stage is an epitome, a bettered likeness of the world, with the dull part left out. . . . What brings the resemblance nearer is, that, as *they* imitate us, we, in our turn, imitate them. . . . They teach us when to laugh and when to weep, when to love and when to hate, upon principle and with a good grace! Wherever there is a playhouse the world will go on not amiss. The stage not only refines the manners, but it is the best teacher of morals, for it is the truest and most intelligent picture of life.[4]

Even further removed from polemics was Hazlitt's love of painting. Here was an activity that had no other end than itself. "You sit down to your task, and are happy," he wrote in "On the Pleasure of Painting":

No angry passions rise to disturb the silent progress of the work, to shake the hand, or dim the brow: no irritable humours are set afloat: you have no absurd opinions to combat, no point to strain, no adversary to crush, no fool to annoy—you are actuated by fear or favour to no man. There is "no juggling here", no sophistry, no intrigue, no tampering with the evidence, . . . but you resign yourself into the hands of a greater power, that of Nature, with the simplicity of a child, and the devotion of an enthusiast. . . .[5]

Painting not only provided an escape but also sharpened Hazlitt's powers of observation, so that he could hit off a man's appearance or manner by the use of significant detail. Some of his essays demonstrate this ability of the portrait painter to depict character in visual description, as when he writes, perhaps unfairly, of Coleridge's habit of "shifting from one side of the foot-path to the other," and uses it as evidence of the poet's instability of purpose, or describes Wordsworth in *The Spirit of the Age* as

... grave, saturnine, with a slight indication of sly humour, kept under by the manners of the age or by the

pretensions of the person. He has a peculiar sweetness in his smile, and great depth and manliness and a rugged harmony in the tones of his voice. His manner of reading his own poetry is particularly imposing.

At bottom Hazlitt was a solitary, shy in company, ill at ease unless with a few intimate friends, and even then often gauche and silent. He found refreshment of spirit most at Winterslow, where alone with nature he could walk in the winter or lie upon a sunny bank in summer, where he could survey the landscape, delight in animal life, and feel himself part of the progress of the seasons. It was at Winterslow that he wrote his essay "On Living to One's-Self," in which he explains:

What I mean by living to one's-self is living in the world, as in it, not of it: it is as if no one knew there was such a person, and you wished no one to know it: it is to be a silent spectator of the mighty scene of things, not an object of attention or curiosity in it; to take a thoughtful, anxious interest in what is passing in the world, but not to feel the slightest inclination to make or meddle with it . . . this sort of dreaming existence is the best.

Those who see Hazlitt only as a partisan fail to take account of this more important side of him. Without this dreaming, contemplative, solitary nature, drawing upon a store of memories and associations, reflecting upon his own life and the experience of others, he would not have been the great writer he was.

Great writing depends also, of course, upon style, upon the ability to use language to express one's thoughts and feelings exactly and movingly. One of the best-known criticisms of Hazlitt's style is Thomas De Quincey's, though it relates to Hazlitt as a lecturer and not as a writer. In an essay on Charles Lamb that he contributed to the *North British Review* for November 1848, De Quincey declared:

No man can be eloquent whose thoughts are abrupt, insulated, capricious, and (to borrow an impressive word from Coleridge) non-sequacious. Eloquence resides not in separate or fractional ideas, but in the relations of manifold ideas, and in the mode of their evolution from each other. . . . Now Hazlitt's brilliancy is seen chiefly in separate splinterings of phrase or image. . . . A flash, a solitary flash, and all is gone.

It is a damaging charge, but Hazlitt had said as much as this himself when he described his essay writing in "On the Pleasure of Painting":

[4] From *The Round Table: A Collection of Essays on Literature, Men and Manners*, 2 vols. (Edinburgh, 1817).
[5] Essay 1 in *Table Talk*, 2 vols. (London, 1821–1822).

. . . I seldom see my way a page or even a sentence beforehand; and when I have as by a miracle escaped, I trouble myself little more about them. I sometimes have to write them twice over. . . . For a person to read his own works over with any great delight, he ought first to forget that he ever wrote them. . . . I have more satisfaction in my own thoughts than in dictating them to others. . . .

This is a strength as well as a weakness in Hazlitt's composition, for his style has spontaneity and freshness; it gives the pleasure of good conversation, and we feel, as we read his work, that we are getting to know an interesting acquaintance and entering his mind and personality. This is very much Hazlitt's intention, for in his essay "On Familiar Style" he tells us that "To write a genuine familiar or truly English style, is to write as any one would speak in common conversation, who had a thorough command and choice of words, or who could discourse with ease, force, and perspicuity, setting aside all pedantic and oratorical flourishes."

Though spontaneous, Hazlitt's style draws upon a wide range of reading, ever ready at his call, either by direct and apt quotation or by allusion. His cadences often echo Shakespeare, whose plays he knew intimately, and the Authorized Version of the Bible, which he must have heard Sunday by Sunday at his father's chapel in Wem; but there are also an elegance, an exactness, and a pithiness of expression that come from his reading of the great prose stylists of the eighteenth century: Burke, whom he admired above all as a writer, the essayists such as Addison and Steele (though not Johnson, whose orotundity seemed to him oppressive), and the philosophers, especially Hume, whom he thought Coleridge had dismissed too lightly.

We should not forget that Hazlitt regarded himself as a philosopher and that he had roots in the empiricist tradition of the eighteenth century. His first book, written after years of study, was an essay on the principles of human action; it was followed not very long after by his lectures on philosophy. Hazlitt is generally considered an impressionistic and not a philosophical critic; but behind his critical judgments are certain assumptions and principles, including an implicit theory of the mind, and these derive in the main from empiricism. This philosophy is often confused with rationalism, but empiricism believed that our knowledge is derived from experience; and while it tried to bring as great an area of human experience as possible within the bounds of rational explanation, it was often profoundly

skeptical of the powers of reason. At its most skeptical it could declare with Thomas Hobbes that "The thoughts are to the desires, as scouts, and spies, to range abroad, and find the way to the things desired" (*Leviathan*, I, viii), or with Hume that "Reason is, and ought only to be, the slave of the passions" (*A Treatise of Human Nature*, II, iii). This kind of skepticism accords well with Hazlitt's distrust of any attempt to explain man entirely in terms of reason and throws a clear light on his approach to literature.

Literature for Hazlitt is a matter of the emotions. He is impatient with neoclassical rules and categories; "Poetry," he writes in "On Poetry in General," "is the language of the imagination and the passions." It is not always easy to decide what he meant by "imagination." Though he was scornful of the new German philosophy that encouraged Coleridge to elaborate his famous distinction between the fancy and the imagination, in many places he adopts language reminiscent of Coleridge's. There is little to show, however, that he grasped the complexity of Coleridge's theory. He quotes with approval (though inaccurately) Bacon's famous dictum that poetry "has something divine in it, because it raises the mind and hurries it into sublimity, by conforming the shows of things to the desires of the soul, instead of subjecting the soul to external things, as reason and history do"; but what give it this character, according to Hazlitt, are the force of passion and the desire to gratify our own wishes. He does not regard the imagination as, in Coleridge's phrase, "the agent of the reason"; and the knowledge it gives comes not from an interplay between symbol and concept, but from our direct perception of the created world the poet presents, a world like the one we know, but shaped and given life by the poet's "gusto," a term much favored by Hazlitt. The romantic notion that poetry seeks to embody an idea in the poet's mind has to find a place in his thought alongside the Aristotelian view that poetry is a representation of life as it is or ought to be. When he turns from poetry to the novel—and he was the first critic to take the novel seriously—the Aristotelian view predominates.

Hazlitt's psychology is the eighteenth-century associationist one; but because he does not care for a mechanical interpretation of this doctrine, he shares Wordsworth's belief that our ideas are associated under the influence of emotion rather than simply by contiguity of space and time, and that poetry, to use the phraseology of the preface to *Lyrical Ballads*, is concerned with "the manner in which we associate ideas in a state of excitement" and is "the spontaneous overflow of powerful feelings." Equally our critical judgments are made not by reason, or the application of rules, but by what we would call emotional sensibility and what the eighteenth century called passion, which for Hazlitt included an imaginative sympathy.

This quality of sympathetic understanding has a central place amid the various critical ideas Hazlitt holds in suspension, and enriches his appreciation of literature. Indeed, it characterizes all he wrote. Although he was, above all, a personal writer, he could by an exercise of the imagination enter into the lives of men very different from himself. It is true that he was a good hater, but as he remarked in his essay on the subject, hatred is common to us all. "I have quarrelled with almost all my old friends (they might say this is owing to my bad temper), but they have also quarrelled with one another." Hatred, then, is not something that separates him from his fellows, but something that unites him to them. "Life," he says, "would turn to a stagnant pool, were it not ruffled by the jarring interests, the unruly passions, of men." The "passions of men," whether unruly or not, his own as well as those of others, are what concern him. This is why he will always have readers to admire and find pleasure in his work.

SELECTED BIBLIOGRAPHY

I. BIBLIOGRAPHIES. G. L. Keynes, *Bibliography of William Hazlitt* (London, 1931); C. W. Houtchens and L. H. Houtchens, eds., *English Romantic Poets and Essayists: A Review of Research and Criticism* (New York, 1957), contains ch. on Hazlitt by E. W. Schneider.

II. COLLECTED WORKS. A. R. Waller and A. Glover, eds., *The Collected Works*, 12 vols. (Cambridge, 1902–1906), with intro. by W. E. Henley; P. P. Howe, ed., *The Complete Works*, 21 vols. (London, 1930–1934), rev. of the Waller and Glover ed., with additional notes, *The Life of Napoleon Bonaparte*, and other uncollected material.

III. SELECTIONS. A. Ireland, ed., *Hazlitt: Essayist and Critic* (London, 1889); D. N. Smith, ed., *Essays on Poetry* (London, 1901); C. Whibley, ed., *Essays* (London, 1906); W. D. Howe, ed., *Selections* (Boston, 1913); J. Zeitlin, ed., *Hazlitt on English Literature* (New York, 1913); G. Sampson, ed., *Selected Essays* (Cambridge, 1917); P. P. Howe, ed., *The Best of Hazlitt* (London, 1923); G. L. Keynes, ed., *Selected Essays* (London, 1930), in the Nonesuch Library, the best comprehensive ed.; R. W. Jepson, ed., *Selections*

from Lamb and Hazlitt (London, 1940); R. Wilson, ed., *Selected Essays* (London, 1942); C. M. Maclean, ed., *Hazlitt Painted by Himself* (London, 1948); C. Morgan, ed., *Liber Amoris and Dramatic Criticisms* (London, 1948); C. M. Maclean, ed., *The Essays: A Selection* (London, 1949); R. Vallance and J. Hampden, eds., *Essays* (London, 1964).

IV. SEPARATE WORKS. *An Essay on the Principles of Human Action* (London, 1805), published anonymously; *Free Thoughts on Public Affairs: Or Advice to a Patriot* (London, 1806), published anonymously; *An Abridgement of the Light of Nature Pursued* (London, 1807), published under the pseudonym Abraham Tucker; *The Eloquence of the British Senate*, 2 vols. (London, 1807), published anonymously; *A Reply to the Essay on Population, by the Rev. T. R. Malthus. In a Series of Letters* (London, 1807; repr. New York, 1967), published anonymously; *A New and Improved Grammar of the English Tongue* (London, 1810); *Memoirs of the Late Thomas Holcroft, Written by Himself* [by Hazlitt] *and Continued to the Time of His Death*, 3 vols. (London, 1816), in E. Colby, ed., 2 vols. (London, 1925), and repr. in World's Classics (Oxford, 1926); *Characters of Shakespeare's Plays* (London, 1817), repr. in Everyman's Library (London, 1906) and World's Classics (Oxford, 1917); *The Round Table: A Collection of Essays on Literature, Men and Manners*, 2 vols. (Edinburgh, 1817); *Lectures on the English Poets* (London, 1818), repr. in Everyman's Library (London, 1910) and World's Classics (Oxford, 1924), also in F. W. Baxter, ed., (Oxford, 1929); *A View of the English Stage: Or, a Series of Dramatic Criticisms* (London, 1818), also in W. Hazlitt, Jr., ed. (London, 1851), and W. S. Jackson, ed. (London, 1906); *Lectures on the English Comic Writers* (London, 1819), also in W. C. Hazlitt, ed. (London, 1869), repr. in World's Classics (Oxford, 1907), and A. Johnson, ed., (London, 1965), in Everyman's Library; *A Letter to William Gifford, Esq.* (London, 1819); *Political Essays, with Sketches of Public Characters* (London, 1819).

Lectures Chiefly on the Dramatic Literature of the Age of Elizabeth (London, 1820); *Table Talk*, 2 vols. (London, 1821–1822), repr. in World's Classics (Oxford, 1901) and in Everyman's Library (London, 1908); *Characteristics: In the Manner of Rochefoucault's Maxims* (London, 1823), published anonymously, also in R. H. Horne, ed. (London, 1837; repr. 1927); *Liber Amoris: Or, the New Pygmalion* (London, 1823), published anonymously, also in R. Le Gallienne and W. C. Hazlitt, eds. (London, 1894), printed privately, with additional material, and C. Morgan, ed. (London, 1948); *Select British Poets, or New Elegant Extracts from Chaucer to the Present Time, with Critical Remarks* (London, 1824), withdrawn owing to infringement of copyright in the contemporary section, published without copyright material as *Select Poets of Great Britain* (London, 1825); *Sketches of the Principal Picture-Galleries in England* (London, 1824); *The Spirit of the Age: Or Contemporary Portraits* (London, 1825), repr. in World's

Classics (Oxford, 1904), also in E. D. Mackerness, ed. (London, 1969); *Notes of a Journey Through France and Italy* (London, 1826); *The Plain Speaker: Opinions on Books, Men, and Things*, 2 vols. (London, 1826), repr. in Everyman's Library (London, 1928); *The Life of Napoleon Bonaparte*, 4 vols. (London, 1828–1830).

Conversations of James Northcote, Esq., R. A. (London, 1830), also in E. Gosse, ed. (London, 1894), and F. Swinnerton, ed. (London, 1949); W. Hazlitt, Jr., ed., *Criticism on Art: And Sketches of the Picture Galleries of England*, 2nd ser. (London, 1834–1844), also in W. C. Hazlitt, ed., *Essays on the Fine Arts* (London, 1873); *Literary Remains of the Late William Hazlitt, with a Notice of His Life, by His Son* (London, 1836), 22 essays, mainly repr. from periodicals; *Painting* [by R. B. Haydon] *and the Fine Arts* [by Hazlitt] (Edinburgh, 1838); *Sketches and Essays, Now First Collected by His Son* (London, 1839), 18 essays repr. from periodicals, repr. in World's Classics (Oxford, 1902); W. C. Hazlitt, ed., *Winterslow: Essays and Characters Written There* (London, 1850), repr. in World's Classics (Oxford, 1902); W. C. Hazlitt, ed., *Memoirs of William Hazlitt, with Portions of His Correspondence*, 2 vols. (London, 1867); W. C. Hazlitt, ed., *Lamb and Hazlitt. Further Letters and Records* (London, 1900); P. P. Howe, ed., *New Writings of William Hazlitt*, 2nd ser. (London, 1925–1927), articles repr. from periodicals and Oxberry's *New English Drama* (1818–1819); S. C. Wilcox, ed., *Hazlitt in the Workshop: The MS of "The Fight"* (Baltimore, 1943).

V. Biographical and Critical Studies. L. Stephen, *Hours in a Library*, 2nd ser. (London, 1876), contains a discussion of Hazlitt and his work; W. C. Hazlitt, *Four Generations of a Literary Family*, 2 vols. (London, 1897); A. Birrell, *William Hazlitt* (London, 1902); R. H. Stoddard, *Personal Recollections of Lamb, Hazlitt and Others* (London, 1903); P. E. More, *Shelburne Essays*, 2nd ser. (London, 1905); P. P. Howe, *The Life of William Hazlitt* (London, 1922; rev. 1928, 1947), published in paperback by Penguin (Harmondsworth, 1949),·now superseded by H. Baker's study; W. P. Ker, *Collected Essays*, vol. I (London, 1925), includes an essay on Hazlitt; H. W. Garrod, *The Profession of Poetry* (Oxford, 1929), repr. the essay "The Place of Hazlitt in English Criticism"; V. Woolf, *The Common Reader* (London, 1932), contains an appreciation of Hazlitt; H. Pearson, *The Fool of Love* (London, 1934); C. M. Maclean, *Born Under Saturn: A Biography* (London, 1943); W. P. Albrecht, *Hazlitt and the Malthusian Controversy* (Albuquerque, N.M., 1950); W. J. Bate, *Criticism: The Major Texts* (New York, 1952); H. Baker, *William Hazlitt* (Cambridge, Mass., 1962), a major and excellent study of Hazlitt's life, ideas, and background; H. Bates, *William Hazlitt* (London, 1962); I. Jack, *English Literature 1815-32* (Oxford, 1963), ch. 9, "Hazlitt," contains a very useful bibliography; W. P. Albrecht, *Hazlitt and the Creative Imagination* (Lawrence, Kans., 1965); R. Park, *Hazlitt and the Spirit of the Age: Abstraction and Critical Theory* (Oxford, 1971); R. M. Wardle, *William Hazlitt* (Lincoln, Nebr., 1971).

THOMAS DE QUINCEY
(1785-1859)

Hugh Sykes Davies

I

THOMAS DE QUINCEY's best-known work, *Confessions of an English Opium-Eater*, was first published in *London* magazine in 1821, and it is characteristic of certain oddities in the pattern of his life and writings that both the year and the title give misleading impressions of his place in English literature. The year suggests that he was a romantic of the second generation, to be placed with Lord Byron, Percy Shelley, and John Keats; but in fact he was thirty-six when he wrote the *Confessions,* and for the past twenty years had been an admirer and friend of William Wordsworth and Samuel Taylor Coleridge. In literary taste and outlook, he belonged to the first generation of the English romantics, not to the second. The title is no less misleading, with its suggestion of Byron and Keats, the sensational and the exotic; for the book itself is of a sobriety in subject and treatment that owed nothing to Byron or Keats, and much to Wordsworth.

The year 1821 divides De Quincey's life into two parts almost equal in length, but in every other respect utterly different. Before it he had written nothing; after it he wrote the fourteen closely printed volumes that make up his collected works.[1] In the first part of his life, he moved in society, was the friend of literary men—the intimate friend of the greatest writers of his time. In the second part he dropped out of society, was cut off from all his friends, living almost as an exile from his past. He wrote of his later life:

the years came—for I have lived too long, reader, in relation to many things! and the report of me would have been

---

[1]The standard edition is D. Masson, ed., *The Collected Writings,* 14 vols. (Edinburgh, 1889–1890). Page references are to this edition. They are often needed, because De Quincey rarely divided his long essays into sections or chapters, which might be used to identify references.

better, or more uniform at least, had I died some twenty years ago—the years came in which circumstances made me an Opium-Eater; years through which a shadow as of sad eclipse sate and rested upon my faculties; years through which I was careless of all but those who lived within *my* inner circle, within "my heart of hearts."

(vol. II, p. 339)

In this second, eclipsed part of his life, De Quincey was almost entirely cut off from external experience, save that of writing for a living under a crushing weight of debt; and he came to depend, for mental and emotional sustenance, on his memories of the first and happier part. It was in this exploration of his earlier life, in his study of the role of memory in the human personality, that he most closely resembled Wordsworth. And as the reader of Wordsworth's poetry is inevitably involved in the events of his life, so the student of De Quincey's prose must become to some extent his biographer.

He was born on 15 August 1785, the second son of a Manchester merchant who died in 1793 after many years of ill health, leaving a modest fortune to his widow and family. These were at once the happiest years of De Quincey's life and also those, he came to believe, in which he had been marked out for ultimate misery. He was a small, gentle child, preferring the company of his sisters to that of his turbulent elder brother, and winning from them, rather than from his sternly dutiful mother, the warmth of affection that he so much needed. Their manner of life was peaceful, but rich in imagination. Like the Brontës a generation later, all the children of the family were writing long novels about elaborately conceived private worlds of their own. But this early happiness was destroyed, first by the death of his most dearly loved sister, and then by the removal of the whole family, after the father's death, from their large house outside Manchester. Mrs. De Quincey went to Bath, and it was there that she first sent Thomas to school. He at once showed a remarkable aptitude for Latin and Greek, and tasted the dangerous pleasure of being obviously the cleverest boy in a small school.

After a short experience of a private school conducted by a clergyman, where he learned nothing but fortunately forgot nothing either, he was sent to Manchester Grammar School. From the point of view of his mother, and of the guardians appointed by his father's will, the choice was a good one. The school was then, as it is now, outstanding among the older grammar schools; and it had the further advantage that three years' study there would gain him an exhibition to Oxford. But De Quincey disliked it from the first, for reasons that never emerge quite clearly, either from his long letters to his mother written at the time, or from the later accounts of his school life. There was hard work, but no question of ill treatment, and in many ways he enjoyed special privileges. Perhaps the most persistent source of irritation was that his favorite exercise, walking, could be indulged in only through the streets of a city that showed, perhaps more clearly than any other place in Britain, the immense brutalization of the physical conditions of life, and of intellectual and emotional standards, then being effected by the industrial revolution. In one of his letters to his mother, he wrote:

I am living in a town where the sole and universal object of pursuit is precisely that which I hold most in abhorrence. In this place trade is the religion, and money is the god. Every object I see reminds me of those occupations which run counter to the bent of my nature, every sentiment I hear sounds a discord to my own. I cannot stir out of doors but I am nosed by a factory, a cotton-bag, a cotton-dealer, or something else allied to that most detestable commerce. Such an object dissipates the whole train of romantic visions I had conjured up, and frequently gives the colouring to all my associations of ideas during the remainder of the day.[2]

It is easy to imagine with what force Wordsworth's *Lyrical Ballads* must have struck such a temperament, so situated. De Quincey seems to have read them in 1802, and at once became one of Wordsworth's earliest and most devoted disciples. They suggested to him the kind of life he really wished to lead and, by contrast, brought his dislike of Man-

[2]Bairdsmith MSS, quoted in H. A. Eaton, *Thomas De Quincey: A Biography* (Oxford, 1936), p. 68, the most fully documented biography of De Quincey yet written.

chester to a crisis. He fled from the school in the middle of the night, resolved never to return. It was the first of those flights from the stress of unpleasant realities that were to become a repeating pattern in his life, and its effect was to plunge him into difficulties in some ways greater than those he sought to escape.

His mother, deeply shocked by De Quincey's rebellion, and fearing his influence upon her other children, agreed that he should set off on a walking tour. His first intention was to go to Wordsworth, with whom he was already in correspondence; but shyness overcame him, and instead of going to the Lake Country, he went to north Wales. The allowance made to him was so small that he had to lodge in the humblest inns and farmhouses; and often he slept in the open, with no better shelter than a primitive tent, for which his walking stick served as a pole. As winter came on, this mode of life became impossible; but he was afraid to return home, lest he be sent back to Manchester. De Quincey fled again, breaking off all communication with his mother and guardians, resolved to lose himself in the anonymous vastness of London and to live by borrowing money on the security of his expectations under his father's will. His negotiations with the moneylenders were tortuous, and ultimately unsuccessful; but they kept him in London for five months, in destitution and near-starvation. Nevertheless he gained what was to prove more valuable than money—some of the most vivid and profound experiences of his early life.

Early in 1803, De Quincey seems to have received an assurance that he would not be sent back to Manchester, and he returned to his mother's home. Later in the year he went up to Worcester College, Oxford, the poorer by the exhibition that he might have had from Manchester Grammar School, and on an allowance that proved to be much too small. For the next five years he kept his terms there, reading avidly within the official syllabus, especially in Latin and in Greek, but even more widely outside it, in German philosophy and above all in English literature. In 1808, De Quincey sat for his final examination, wrote a few papers that are said to have been brilliant, and then fled, as abruptly and more inexplicably than he had fled from school. But now there was no question of returning home in disgrace. He was in possession of the small fortune left to him by his father, and he believed that it would be enough to enable him to lead the kind of life he had chosen for himself: that of a scholar and a gentleman, living in some remote and picturesque place, with a large library, and even larger but leisurely literary ambitions.

At Oxford, De Quincey seems to have had few friends, if any; perhaps there were few worth his making, for it was one of the less distinguished periods in the history of the university. But he had made friends elsewhere, and distinguished ones. While still at Oxford he had come to know Coleridge well; and soon after leaving it, he visited Wordsworth for the first time, though they had been in correspondence for some years. For several months he lived at Dove Cottage with the Wordsworths as an intimate friend, almost as a member of the family, and remained as tenant of the cottage when they moved to a larger house nearby. For a few years it seemed that he had succeeded in living the kind of life he had chosen, amid splendid scenery, in close friendship with the writer he admired above all others.

But it was not to last. In 1813, De Quincey suffered an access of grief and illness, from which he sought relief in massive doses of laudanum. He had first become acquainted with the drug in London, during one of his vacations from Oxford, and had continued to use it—so he assures us—in moderation. But now it took hold of him with the ineluctable strength of an addiction, and the Grasmere idyll was over. His relations with Wordsworth and his family grew more distant—they had already seen what laudanum could do to a man, in the case of Coleridge. De Quincey grew irritable and touchy, resentful of their disapproval and of what he took—perhaps rightly —to be a certain loftiness in Wordsworth's attitude to him. Matters were made worse when he courted the daughter of a small farmer, and married her after the birth of an illegitimate child. Dorothy Wordsworth, until now his intimate friend, thought the marriage unsuitable; though hardly a snob, she was sensitive to the special social hierarchy of the Lake and its peculiar local structure of peasants and small farmers. In a sense De Quincey had let the gentry down by his marriage.

Worst of all, by ill management and extravagance, above all in the purchase of books and in a generous but injudicious gift to Coleridge of several hundred pounds, the inheritance upon which De Quincey depended had been wasted away to almost nothing. Debts, bills, and creditors crowded in on him, and the leisurely literary ambitions of his youth were transformed into an urgent need to write for ready money. In 1819 he went to Edinburgh, in a desperate and unsuccessful attempt to write for *Blackwood's* magazine. In the following year he was in London, and by a great effort finished his first and perhaps his greatest work, the *Confessions*. Back at Grasmere he and his family lived as if besieged—"shut up as usual," Dorothy Wordsworth wrote, "the house always blinded—or left with but one eye to peep out of—he probably in bed—We hear nothing of him."[3]

The first, and happier, part of De Quincey's life was at an end. From that time on, his old friends "heard nothing of him." In 1825 his growing financial troubles drove him finally from Grasmere, from the last semblance of his life as a leisured scholar. He moved to Edinburgh and at last became a contributor to *Blackwood's* magazine, frequent but not regular—regularity was, and always remained, beyond him. The next twenty years were spent there or in Glasgow, hunted from one lodging to another by furious Scottish creditors, sometimes living with his family but often alone, in hiding, without books, with little food, sometimes without clothes. The lives of literary men have all too often been burdened by financial worries and follies, but it is impossible to read a detailed account of this second part of De Quincey's life without feeling that there was never one more harassed, more pitilessly overwhelmed by adversity and confusion.

In the last few years of his life, he was more at peace. His daughters took over the management of his affairs, his position as a writer was assured, and he was largely freed from the struggle to write day by day for his living. In 1850 he began to bring together his scattered papers into a collected edition, rewriting and adding much. He died on 8 December 1859, seventy-four years of age. Whatever opium had done for him, it had not much shortened his life.

II

In a diary kept in 1803, De Quincey had reviewed the literary projects of his boyhood. "I have always intended of course," he wrote, "that *poems* should form the corner-stone of my fame"; and he listed the poems, plays, and tales that he had, "at some time or other, seriously intended to execute." So far as is

[3]Letter to Edward Quillinan; 19 November 1822, in E. de Selincourt, *Dorothy Wordsworth* (London, 1933).

known, none of them was written. It was no great loss, for their titles suggest a dismal array of the most stilted and artificial "romantic" themes, most of them treated "pathetically." At the very time when he made this list, he was growing out of these juvenile aspirations, toward the very different ambition of his idyllic years at Grasmere. The aim of his studies there, of his large library, his long leisure, was to be a great work of philosophy that would transform education and reestablish mathematics in England. But this, too, failed to be written; and when at last he set pen to paper, it was not for the sake of fame or great ambition, but for money. The fate that befell him was one that he both feared and despised. In 1818 he wrote to his mother: "Like all persons who believe themselves in possession of *original* knowledge not derived from books, I was indisposed to sell my knowledge for money, and to commence trading author."[4] But that was to be his trade for the rest of his life.

In some ways De Quincey was unfitted for it, both by temperament and training. He lacked the self-discipline needed for the regular and punctual performance of routine tasks, and he had much of that ingenious indolence that knows how to avoid doing something arduous by elaborating the preparations for doing it. Rather than write the article expected of him, he would often compose a letter explaining his delay nearly as long as the article would have been, and quite as elaborate. Coleridge once described his turn of mind, rather unkindly but not inaccurately, as "anxious yet dilatory, confused from over accuracy, and at once systematic and labyrinthine."[5] When laudanum was added to these deficiencies of temperament, it is hard to imagine a man less fitted to the trade of writer for periodicals.

Yet for thirty years De Quincey drove this trade with outstanding success. The editors put up with his unpunctuality and his dreadfully elaborate excuses for it—or, at least, when one editor could bear it no longer, there was always another to take him on. For though his manner of driving his trade was outrageously unbusinesslike, he was extremely good at it. To get an article out of him might cost ten times the trouble; but when it came, it might be ten times as good as another's. The qualities of his mind and style were far above those usually found in writers for periodicals, and it was only because of the defects in his temperament that he was brought down to their level. The dilettantism that had kept him reading through the ambitious years of his youth, always preparing to write but never writing, now became an asset. He had a vast store of material of all kinds, and a memory so tenacious that even when the need to hide from his creditors severed him from his library—as it often did—he could draw on it freely and effectively. His writing, in fact, was entirely of a piece with the odd pattern of his life. The same underlying coherence is clearly illustrated in his first—and last—conversation with his tutor at Oxford:

On a fine morning, he met me in the Quadrangle, and, having then no guess of the nature of my pretensions, he determined (I suppose) to probe them. Accordingly, he asked me, "What I had been lately reading?" Now, the fact was that I, at that time immersed in metaphysics, had really been reading and studying very closely the *Parmenides*. . . . Yet, so profound was the benignity of my nature that, in those days, I could not bear to witness, far less to cause, the least pain or mortification to any human being. I recoiled, indeed, from the society of most men, but not with any feelings of dislike. On the contrary, in order that I *might* like all men, I wished to associate with none. Now, then, to have mentioned the *Parmenides* to one who, fifty thousand to one, was a perfect stranger to its whole drift and purpose, looked too *méchant*, too like a trick of malice, in an age when such reading was so very unusual. I felt that it would be taken for an express stratagem for stopping my tutor's mouth. All this passing rapidly through my mind, I replied, without hesitation, that I had been reading Paley. My tutor's rejoinder I have never forgotten: "Ah! an excellent author; excellent for his matter; only you must be on your guard as to his style; he is very vicious *there*." Such was the colloquy; we bowed, parted, and never more (I apprehend) exchanged one word.

(vol. II, pp. 61–62)

This sunlit encounter throws several kinds of light on De Quincey and his time. It shows, for example, how far the only two universities in England, Oxford and Cambridge, had narrowed their curricula to suit the needs of the Church of England and the training of its clergy. Indeed William Paley's *Evidences of Christianity* was still compulsory reading for some entrants early in this century. It reveals too something of the laxity with which even this limited education was pursued. Adam Smith had been at Oxford half a

[4]A. H. Japp, *De Quincey Memorials* (London, 1891), vol. II, p. 114.
[5]E. H. Coleridge, ed., *Letters from the Lake Poets to D. Stuart* (London, 1889), p. 155.

century earlier than De Quincey and had recorded, in *The Wealth of Nations*, that the professors had long ago given up all pretense to lecture. It seems that the tutors had similarly given up tuition.

Much of education in both English universities lay outside the official syllabus, which included some Latin, a little Greek, and a dash of Euclid for the few who fancied either themselves or mathematics. Many were there only for the sake of social life and making acquaintances who might be useful later. Many read their Paley and got their livings in the church. But a few, like De Quincey, read widely and deeply, and perhaps with more zest because their official studies were so undemanding and it was pleasant to be better read than the tutors. It was doubly rewarding to have read the *Parmenides* of Plato and to keep quiet about it, as if it was a possession to be treasured in privacy, like "the tremendous hold taken of my entire sensibilities at this time by our own literature" (vol. II, p. 72).

But De Quincey was also one of that still more select minority who had heard of another modern revolution: "In Kant, I had been taught to believe, were the keys of a new and a creative philosophy" (vol. II, p. 86). Only six weeks later his hopes had faded, but this intense encounter with a notoriously "difficult" thinker had developed some of the tougher powers hitherto latent in De Quincey, above all skill in handling nice distinctions and exact definitions. He displayed them especially in the essay published in 1836 that rounds off his intellectual autobiography with an intellectually rigorous, tough account of what he had grasped in Kant and its relation to Hume's crucial discussion of cause and effect. When, a decade later, he was suddenly roused from the torpor of laudanum by the chance gift of a treatise on economics by David Ricardo, it was with these same powers that he attacked the complexities of economics.

That brief encounter between De Quincey and his tutor was also, in a broader sense, symbolic of wider differences between them. The narrow limitations of the English universities had left something of a vacuum, which the Scottish universities, notably Edinburgh and Glasgow, were ready to fill. Their courses had a range and variety lacking in England, were more concerned with modern life and literature, with speculations touching on practical life. Their influence was widely extended by the publication from Edinburgh of periodical magazines, such as the *Edinburgh Review* and *Blackwood's*

magazine. It was largely for the sake of these periodicals that De Quincey moved to Scotland for the last two decades of his life, providing essays in abundance for a new and intelligent public, provincial rather than metropolitan, modern instead of ancient. He was, without quite knowing it, a leading contributor to the first wave of what we now call "adult education" (or "the open university"), while his tutor aptly symbolizes the kind of education that De Quincey helped to displace.

It was also lucky, though perhaps it never occurred to De Quincey to think so, that he lived at a time when there was a vigorous demand for periodical writing of high quality. The great periodical magazines that had begun in the eighteenth century were then at the height of their development, and enjoyed the support of a fairly large body of intelligent readers. A generation later they were already in their decline, in the process of being supplanted by cheaper competitors with wider circulations and lower standards. In that last age of great periodicals, De Quincey, with Charles Lamb and William Hazlitt, enjoyed the opportunity of continuing the tradition of essay writing that had come down to them from Joseph Addison, Samuel Johnson, and Oliver Goldsmith. Among them they made fine and varied use of it.

To read De Quincey's collected essays, even today, would be a liberal education of remarkable comprehensiveness. For it would include Greek literature and philosophy, much Roman history, German literature and philosophy, modern history and literature, politics and economics; even mathematics would not be wholly absent, for in his writings on economics he made some use of mathematical arguments and illustrations, along with others—such as the factors determining the price of a rhinoceros in the seventeenth century, or of a musical snuffbox on a steamboat on Lake Erie, entirely typical of his taste for oddities. This education, though, would be in many respects a little out-of-date. More than a century of scholarship, of philosophy, and of economic speculation has turned many of his essays into period pieces, of no more than historic interest. What has survived is a smaller body of writing, some literary criticism and biography, records of people and events he had known at first hand, and, above all, autobiography. Today, in fact, he is most readable in those writings that most involved his own experience. And it is in these that his literary achievement was the greatest.

III

DE QUINCEY's literary criticism differs from that of Lamb and Hazlitt in that it was only fitfully directed. He wrote nothing like Lamb's essays on the Elizabethans, or Hazlitt's lectures on William Shakespeare and his studies of contemporary writers in *The Spirit of the Age*. There is but one Shakespearean study, "On the Knocking at the Gate in Macbeth," remarkable in its way, but brief and restricted in scope. There is one long essay "On Milton," two on Alexander Pope—"The Poetry of Pope" and "Lord Carlisle on Pope"—and nothing else substantial on any older writers. There are striking and illuminating observations in all these essays, but in all of them also a tendency to slide into digressions; De Quincey often attempts, rather in the manner of Coleridge, large philosophic generalizations about the principles of literature and criticism.

In his writings on contemporaries, De Quincey's tendency was to move away from their actual work and into the details of their personalities and lives. Of this the outstanding example is his long series of essays on Wordsworth, Coleridge, and the other writers of the Lake School.[6] Only one of them, "On Wordsworth's Poetry," even tries to deal with the poetry as such; and on the whole it fails to make clear why he had been so swiftly carried away by it as a boy. All the rest are mainly studies in personalities and biographies—even "William Wordsworth," in which he draws upon his preview of *The Prelude* in manuscript only for information about the life, never for criticism of the poetry. One is left with a sense of opportunity missed, a revelation never made concerning the kind of impact made by the poetry on one of its earliest admirers. On the other hand, the impulse that carried De Quincey toward biography is valuable to us, and was entirely natural to him. Not only had he lived in intimate friendship with his subjects, but he was also a gifted observer of human beings, of their appearances, manners, conduct, and—a rarer gift—of those traits that are revealed in their bodily postures and gestures. For example, he records that

the total effect of Wordsworth's person was always worst in a state of motion. . . . This was not always perceptible,

[6]The dozen or so essays in this group are often collected under the title *Recollections of the Lake Poets*, as in the edition by E. Sackville-West (London, 1948).

and in part depended (I believe) upon the position of the arms; when either of these happened (as was very customary) to be inserted into the unbuttoned waistcoat, his walk had a wry or twisted appearance; and not appearance only—for I have known it, by slow degrees, to edge his companion from the middle to the side of the highroad. Meantime, his face—that was one which would have made amends for greater defects of figure.

(*Tait's* magazine, January 1839, p. 7)

Of Dorothy Wordsworth he wrote, with the same unflattering but revealing perception:

Her manner was warm and even ardent; her sensibility seemed constitutionally deep; and some subtle fire of impassioned intellect apparently burned within her, which, being alternately pushed forward into a conspicuous expression by the irrepressible instincts of her temperament, and then immediately checked, in obedience to the decorum of her sex and age, . . . gave to her whole demeanour, and to her conversation, an air of embarrassment, and even of self-conflict, that was almost distressing to witness.

(vol. II, p. 238)

It is not surprising that observations of such penetration and candor, published while their subjects were still living, should have given some offense. But there is little doubt that they are true in themselves, and they were not made entirely for their own sake; they are aspects of the larger picture that De Quincey built up of the remarkable relationship between Wordsworth and his sister, and of the special influence she had exercised on his work. This opportunity of observing the Wordsworth circle from within was certainly not missed, but recorded with perception and often with astringent objectivity.

There are similar compensations in De Quincey's digressions into the philosophy of literary art. True, they divert him from the actual writings of Shakespeare, John Milton, Pope, and the rest; but they have their own interest, being rarely less than ingenious, and sometimes illuminating. A few, moreover, serve to throw light on his own experience of writing. Perhaps the best-known of them is a distinction between "the literature of knowledge" and "the literature of power." It had been suggested to De Quincey in conversation by Wordsworth, but he made it his own by elaborating it over a long period. It appears first in "Letters to a Young Man" (1828), and again as an extensive digression in "The Poetry of Pope" (1848). The essential difference is that the function of "the literature of knowledge" is to teach, to convey information, while that of "the literature of power" is to move, to expand, and to exercise the reader's "latent capacity of sympathy with the infinite." From this follows a characteristic difference between the two kinds of writing in their capacity for survival:

> . . . hence the pre-eminence over all authors that merely *teach* of the meanest that *moves*, or that teaches, if at all, indirectly *by* moving. The very highest work that has ever existed in the Literature of Knowledge is but a *provisional* work: . . . Let its teaching be even partially revised, let it be but expanded,—nay, even let its teaching be but placed in a better order,—and instantly it is superseded. Whereas the feeblest works in the Literature of Power, surviving at all, survive as finished and unalterable amongst men.
>
> (vol. XI, p. 57)

The fate of De Quincey's own writings is enough to illustrate this principle and to confirm its general accuracy. Whenever he wrote to instruct, whenever his subject lay mainly in the field of erudition, he has been superseded; but whenever his material was taken from his own experience, from what he had seen and lived through, his writing has retained a life and power of its own.

Another of De Quincey's theories about the nature of literature was concerned with "rhetoric," of which the conception, set out in a treatise entitled "Rhetoric" (1828), was so eccentrically personal that it can only have been an expression of his own experience of literary creation. He rejected several accepted notions of rhetoric: it was not, for example, the mere addition of ornament to plain matter, nor was it the art of persuasion by sophistry, nor again identical with highly emotive utterance. His own definition was based upon a distinction between two opposing conditions in which any subject might exist. Much might be known about it, and with certainty; and in this condition it would leave no scope for rhetoric. On the other hand, fixed and certain knowledge about it might be lacking, so that consideration of it must necessarily move among mere guesses and the weighing of probabilities; in this case the art of rhetoric might legitimately be used in swaying belief to one side or the other. De Quincey himself never suggested, perhaps never consciously realized, how nearly this view of the function of rhetoric coincided with his definition of "the literature of power." The consistency of his thinking depended much more upon the unconscious similari-

ties of his insights and intuitions than upon his perception of logical relations between them. But it is clear that for him, rhetoric, like "power," was conceived as the antithesis of fixed and certain knowledge; its sphere of operation was the same as that of literary "power," and its function was to exercise and expand latent capacities of the mind.

Two descriptions of rhetoric given in the essay show more concretely how De Quincey conceived its mode of operation. In one he says that it is "to hang upon one's own thoughts as an object of conscious interest, to play with them, to watch and pursue them through a maze of inversions, evolutions, and harlequin changes." In the second he points to the absence of true rhetoric in French prose writers, for "there is no eddying about their own thoughts; no motion of fancy self-sustained from its own activities; no flux and reflux of thought, half meditative, half capricious." Of however slender use these definitions and descriptions of rhetoric may be in general, they could hardly be bettered as characterizations of one outstanding quality in De Quincey's own writing. Those parts of it that remain the most readable, that have the "power" to survive, are precisely those in which his mind gave itself up to this free imaginative play. Some aspect of his subject, or often some digression that it suggested to him, was picked up and carried on in the "flux and reflux of thought, half meditative, half capricious"; and what he had begun as forced labor came to life under his hand.

The third of De Quincey's more notable contributions to literary theory was at once the most original and the one most nearly related to his own writing. It was a close concern with the special qualities of prose and the technique of writing it. This is a subject not very fully treated by most theorists of literature, partly, no doubt, because they have usually ranked prose so far below verse as to make it beneath the dignity of their notice, but also, perhaps, because the structural aspects of prose are more fluid and complex than those of verse, and so more difficult to discuss. De Quincey forcefully corrects both errors in "Philosophy of Herodotus":

> . . . if prose were simply the negation of verse, were it the fact that prose had no separate laws of its own, but that to be a composer in prose meant only his privilege of being inartificial, his dispensation from the restraints of metre, then, indeed, it would be a slight nominal honour to have been the Father of Prose. But this is ignorance, though a

pretty common ignorance. To walk well, it is not enough that a man abstain from dancing. Walking has rules of its own the more difficult to perceive or to practise as they are less broadly *prononcés*. To forbear singing is not, therefore, to speak well or to read well: each of which offices rests upon a separate art of its own. Numerous laws of transition, connexion, preparation, are different for a writer in verse and a writer in prose. Each mode of composition is a great art; well executed, is the highest and most difficult of arts.

(vol. VI, p. 100)

Scattered liberally through his essays are reflections on these "laws" of prose, not only in English but also in Latin, Greek, French, and German. De Quincey wrote on diction and the "choice of words"; and his comments on the functions of Romance and Teutonic words in English, especially in the third "Oxford" paper and "The Poetry of Wordsworth," have hardly been bettered. But it was above all with what might be called the prosody of prose that he concerned himself, and some of his most perceptive and original observations are on the inner harmonies of sentence structure, such as this in the third "Oxford" paper:

The two capital secrets in the art of prose composition are these: 1st, The philosophy of transition and connection, or the art by which one step in an evolution of thought is made to arise out of another: all fluent and effective composition depends on the *connections*;—2dly, The way in which sentences are made to modify each other; for the most powerful effects in written eloquence arise out of this reverberation, as it were, from each other in a rapid succession of sentences. . . .

(vol. II, p. 65)

It is worth remarking again the consistency of De Quincey's intuitions: this notion of "reverberation" between sentences looks very like a structural aspect of that "flux and reflux of thought" which was at the heart of his special definition of rhetoric. And in his comments on the style of his contemporaries, his more abstract doctrines on prose are applied with the same kind of consistency to concrete cases. Thus, in "Charles Lamb" he says:

Hazlitt was not eloquent, because he was discontinuous. No man can be eloquent whose thoughts are abrupt, insulated, capricious, and (to borrow an impressive word from Coleridge) non-sequacious. Eloquence resides not in separate or fractional ideas, but in the relations of manifold ideas, and in the mode of their evolution from each other.

It is not indeed enough that the ideas should be many, and their relations coherent; the main condition lies in the *key* of the evolution, in the *law* of the succession.

(vol. V, p. 231)

In Lamb's prose he found some great merits, but also this characteristic defect:

. . . Lamb had no sense of the rhythmical in prose compositions. Rhythmus, or pomp of cadence, or sonorous ascent of clauses, in the structure of sentences, were effects of art as much thrown away upon *him* as the voice of the charmer upon the deaf adder. We ourselves, occupying the very station of polar opposition to that of Lamb,—being as morbidly, perhaps, in the one excess as he in the other,—naturally detected this omission in Lamb's nature at an early stage of our acquaintance.

(vol. V, p. 235)

The cause of this deficiency in Lamb, De Quincey insisted, was his lack of any response to music; whereas he himself was deeply interested in it throughout his life, and to this interest certainly owed much of his feeling for phrasing and structure in prose. The terms that naturally occur to him in speaking of it are often of musical origin: "key of the evolution," "rhythmus, or pomp of cadence, or sonorous ascent of clauses"; and in some of his descriptions of music he almost exactly reproduces his doctrines on the prosody of prose, as in the following passage from "On Style":

A song, an air, a tune,—that is, a short succession of notes revolving rapidly upon itself,—how could that, by possibility, offer a field of compass sufficient for the development of great musical effects? The preparation pregnant with the future; the remote correspondence; the questions, as it were, which to a deep musical sense are asked in one passage and answered in another; the iteration and ingemination of a given effect, moving through subtle variations that sometimes disguise the theme, sometimes fitfully reveal it, sometimes throw it out tumultuously to the blaze of daylight: these and ten thousand forms of self-conflicting musical passion,—what room could they find, what opening, what utterance, in so limited a field as an air or song?

(vol. X, p. 136)

The kind of prose that emerged from this sense of musical structure and almost symphonic complexity was specially fitted to be the instrument of De Quincey's most powerful autobiographical writings, the *Confessions* and "Suspiria de Profundis." Indeed, no other kind would have served his purposes there, in a genre for which, in his general introduction to the collected edition of his works (1853–1860), he modestly claimed originality for himself, under the title of "impassioned prose." But the same virtues were capable of more supple and rapid effects when they were needed. His narrative prose also is admirably swift and effective, when employed on a suitable subject. It is seen at its worst in his fiction, for there he was haunted by a crazy admiration for the most outrageous kind of German romantic writing, the results of which can be seen by the curious in his *Klosterheim.* But it is at its best in parts of the *Confessions* and in "The English Mail-Coach," which re-creates the romance of that mode of travel in its heyday, just before it was displaced by the railways. It contains one of the best descriptions in English of a fast ride by night on a crack mail coach, and of a hairbreadth escape from a mortal accident.

There are also at least two pieces of historical writing in which De Quincey's narrative power is seen to the full: "The Spanish Military Nun" and "Revolt of the Tartars." The first describes, at headlong pace, the adventures of a nun dressed as a soldier during a journey through South America; the second recounts the almost epic exodus of the Kalmuck Tartars from the Volga to China in 1771. In both he had sources for the facts, in French and in German, but he used them with a free imagination and to splendid effect. The second, especially, is a piece of his writing that has not received its due. It ends with an appalling but magnificent description of the final massacre of the fleeing Tartars by their Bashkir pursuers in the bloodstained waters of Lake Tengis, under the eyes of the Chinese emperor.

It is one of the paradoxical traits in De Quincey's character that though gentle to a degree, diminutive in person, and elaborately courteous in manner, he was curiously fascinated by scenes of violence. In 1818 he was for a short time editor of the *Westmorland Gazette*; instead of printing news of the day and political articles, as the proprietors wished, he filled his columns with long reports of lurid crimes collected from all over the country. Four years later he published his most famous piece of literary criticism, the short essay "On the Knocking at the Gate in Macbeth." It is as different from any other piece of Shakespearean criticism in English as it is typical of De Quincey, for it contains a digression, written with almost more care and interest than the main theme, a digression about a specially bloodthirsty

murder. The dramatic problem, as De Quincey posed it, was his strong feeling that the knocking "reflected back upon the murder a peculiar awfulness." For years he had been unable to find a rational cause for this feeling, until, in 1812, the same knocking on a door in the silence of the night had followed a multiple murder in London.

"The same incident," De Quincey observes, "did actually occur, which the genius of Shakespeare had invented; and all good judges, and the most eminent dilettanti, acknowledged the felicity of Shakespeare's suggestion as soon as it was actually realized." Its dramatic and imaginative function in the play, he thought, was to emphasize the enormity and inhumanity of Duncan's murder: "the re-establishment of the goings-on of the world in which we live first makes us profoundly sensible of the awful parenthesis that had suspended them." In Shakespearean criticism this was an isolated lucky hit, so far as De Quincey was concerned. And it remained isolated because what had really caught his imagination was not Shakespeare and Shakespearean interpretation, but the notion that there might, after all, be an imaginative, even an artistic, side to the most brutal murders—a side that would serve to explain to him his interest in them. The digression on the London murder tumbles suddenly, accidentally (though by a significant accident), on this idea:

. . . in 1812, Mr. Williams made his *début* on the stage of Ratcliffe Highway, and executed those unparalleled murders which have procured for him such a brilliant and undying reputation. On which murders, by the way, I must observe that in one respect they have had an ill effect, by making the connoisseur in murder very fastidious in his taste, and dissatisfied with anything that has been since done in that line.

(vol. X, p. 390)

It was this half-fanciful, but also half-serious, notion of connoisseurship, dilettantism in murder, that De Quincey picked up and made the basis of a series of three papers titled "Murder Considered as One of the Fine Arts," the first in 1827, the second in 1839, and the third specially written in 1854 for the collected edition of his works. It was a series of accounts of actual murders notable for their ferocity (including those committed by the immortal artist John Williams), and it shows De Quincey's narrative power at its gloomy best.

In some ways these strange productions anticipate the literature of crime and violence that has become so large a part of popular fiction since Edgar Allan Poe. But De Quincey's attitude toward his own interest in such themes was far more complex. He recognized its force, but at the same time saw that it was at odds with his fastidious sense of gentleness and culture. This deep-seated duality of feeling appears in his treatment of the subject as a continual coloring of irony, almost of mock morality, in which the moral issues are ingeniously reversed, as in the passage from the second paper on "Murder Considered as One of the Fine Arts":

> . . . if once a man indulges himself in murder, very soon he comes to think little of robbing, and from robbing he comes next to drinking and Sabbath-breaking, and from that to incivility and procrastination. Once begin upon this downward path, you never know where you are to stop. Many a man dated his ruin from some murder or other that perhaps he thought little of at the time.
>
> (vol. XIII, p. 56)

The same half-serious, half-jesting mock morality was elaborated into a formal defense of this new field of artistic criticism. In the first of his papers, De Quincey compared murders with large fires in respect of their artistic merits, and described an occasion when he had been taking tea with Coleridge, who was discussing Plato; news had been brought that a large building was on fire nearby, and the whole party had rushed out to see it, "as it promised to be a conflagration of merit." He had been compelled to leave before the climax; but, meeting Coleridge afterward, he had asked "how that very promising exhibition had terminated." "Oh, sir," said he, "it turned out so ill that we damned it unanimously." This did not mean, De Quincey points out, that Coleridge was incendiary-minded or lacking in moral feeling. "Virtue was in no request. On the arrival of the fire-engines, morality had devolved wholly on the insurance office. This being the case, he had a right to gratify his taste. He had left his tea. Was he to have nothing in return?" From examples such as these, De Quincey elicited a novel general principle:

> Everything in this world has two handles. Murder, for instance, may be laid hold of by its moral handle (as it generally is in the pulpit and at the Old Bailey), and *that*, I confess, is its weak side; or it may also be treated *aesthetically*, as the Germans call it—that is, in relation to good taste.
>
> (vol. XIII, p. 13)

This seems to be the first use of the word "aesthetic" in this sense in English—it is seven years earlier than the first examples given in the Oxford English Dictionary. De Quincey must certainly be credited, among his contributions to literary criticism, with having been the first to advance a theory that was to acquire great influence later in the nineteenth century, and not only in England: the theory that developed into the richer formulations of Walter Pater and Charles Baudelaire, and then into the vulgarized formula of "art for art's sake."

But this tentative and ironic aestheticism is not merely a curious fact in literary history. It is also striking evidence of the strength of the tensions within De Quincey's personality, of the strange contrast between the humdrum domesticity of his outward life and the exotic violence of his inner world. Of this tension the curious papers on "Murder Considered as One of the Fine Arts" are but a minor product. Its major expression is in the *Confessions* and its continuations, for there, without the disguise of ironic humor, he tries to explore and explain, above all to himself, the destiny that had placed such a gulf between his outward and inward lives.

IV

FOR the more lurid implications of the term "Opium-Eater," De Quincey himself was responsible. And he was exaggerating, no doubt for the sake of emphasis. Solid opium was at times in his possession, and on occasions he ate it. But his regular sustenance was the less sensational tincture of laudanum, on sale in every apothecary's shop and kept in the medicine cupboard of every well-run household, much as aspirin is today, as the normal remedy for all kinds of aches and pains. It was recommended for such purposes to the prudent housewife in William Buchan's *Domestic Medicine*, a widely used handbook of the time, but with the solemn warning that it might be abused as well as used. Its disadvantage was notoriously that some of those who took it first as a medicine might become addicted to it as a drug, and come to depend upon it not as a palliative for a cough or toothache, but as a means of blunting their reactions to the stresses and tensions of their lives. This is what had happened to Coleridge when De Quincey met him—on the first day of their acquaintance, the older man solemnly warned the younger against the drug. Later the same addiction overtook other writers, Keats and Wilkie Collins among them, and many who were not writers. But De Quincey was the only one who wrote about his addiction openly, studying it with an almost clinical detachment. Indeed, this air of scientific frankness, of a man laying his private secrets bare for the public good, was one of the ways in which he seems to have quieted his conscience and kept up his self-respect —and hoped to retain the respect of others.

De Quincey's verdict on opium as a drug, and on himself as an addict, was that his personality had not been changed, morally or mentally; that his faculties and his general health had been impaired temporarily, but not irrecoverably; and that the inevitable final pains of opium were much greater than its early pleasures. There was, though, one really important discovery, one really revealing aspect of his "case": the drug had greatly intensified the workings of some faculties, especially those of memory and of dreaming, and had enabled him to discover some laws of their operation that, without this intensification, he would never have been able to observe. In giving a careful account of them, he believed that he was saying something both true and useful not only about himself, but also about the growth and structure of the human personality in general. It is in this sense that the *Confessions* deserve to be looked on as something like a prose equivalent of Wordsworth's *Prelude*. Both are intensely personal, yet objective in their mode of observation and presentation; both are attempts to reveal, by the exploration of autobiographical material, common and fundamental aspects of the human spirit; and both are perhaps easier to understand in the light of modern psychology than they were in their own day. De Quincey's is, of course, by many degrees the lesser work: more limited in its scope, less sustained, less penetrating even at its best. But it deserves to be read and judged in the light of this comparison rather than that of the more lurid expectations aroused by its title.

Compared with *The Prelude*, the *Confessions* are not merely prose: they are prosaic, at any rate in their account of the outward events of De Quincey's early life. They rehearse that first crisis: the flight from Manchester Grammar School, the wanderings in Wales, and those months in London, cold and hungry, lying at night in a bleak room lent by the agent of a moneylender, by day walking miserably through streets and parks. And here, at least, the tone rises above the prosaic, as he tells of his friend-ship with Ann, a sixteen-year-old girl of the streets —he was seventeen. As two waifs in the vast friendlessness of London, they walked up and down Oxford Street, sometimes sitting on steps and under porticoes, always afraid of being moved on by the watchmen. One night he was ill from want of food, and she fetched him a stimulant that, he firmly believed, saved his life—and paid for it herself. A few days later he left London for a short time; and when he parted from her, agreed where they should meet on his return. But she was not at their meeting place, that night or any other:

To this hour I have never heard a syllable about her. This, amongst such troubles as most men meet with in this life, has been my heaviest affliction. If she lived, doubtless we must have been sometimes in search of each other, at the very same moment, through the mighty labyrinths of London; perhaps even within a few feet of each other—a barrier no wider, in a London street, often amounting in the end to a separation for eternity! During some years I hoped that she *did* live; and I suppose that, in the literal and unrhetorical use of the word *myriad*, I must, on my different visits to London, have looked into many myriads of female faces, in the hope of meeting Ann.

(vol. III, p. 375)

After this story of his first visit to London, the tone of the narrative sinks again to the entirely prosaic, until it comes to his first experience of opium, while he was still at Oxford but often spending vacations in London. At this stage he found it not only a refuge against physical pain but also a mental and physical stimulant. He would take it regularly on Saturday nights; and it would send him to the opera, or wandering among people and streets and faces, with curiously heightened sensibilities. There is a brief glimpse of his earlier days at Grasmere with the Wordsworths, and then the statement that in 1813 he had become "a regular and confirmed (no longer intermitting) opium-eater." The immediate cause was illness, which in turn had been brought about by his paroxysm of grief at the death of Kate Wordsworth, at the age of three. From this first period of deep addiction, when he was taking a daily dose of laudanum enough to have killed a hundred people not habituated to it, he was roused by the awful reaction of the drug itself, by "the pains of opium."

The worst of its symptoms was an uncontrollable stream of fearful dreams, which tyrannized over him not only in sleep but also in the whole of his waking life. And it is in the description of these dreams that

De Quincey rises decisively above the prosaic, into his own unique kind of "impassioned prose." The style reflects his long and careful study of prose as an artistic medium, above all his sense of its analogies with music. Many years later, in the general preface written for his collected works, he pleaded "the perilous difficulty besieging all attempts to clothe in words the visionary scenes derived from the world of dreams, where a single false note, a single word in the wrong key, ruins the whole music." And the substance of the dreams was woven from his earlier life, from the formative experiences of his childhood and youth:

In the early stage of the malady, the splendours of my dreams were indeed chiefly architectural; and I beheld such pomp of cities and palaces as never yet was beheld by waking eye, unless in the clouds . . . . To my architecture succeeded dreams of lakes and silvery expanses of water: . . . The waters gradually changed their character—from translucent lakes, shining like mirrors, they became seas and oceans. And now came a tremendous change, which, unfolding itself slowly like a scroll, through many months, promised an abiding torment; and, in fact, it never left me, though recurring more or less intermittingly. Hitherto the human face had often mixed in my dreams, but not despotically, nor with any special power of tormenting. But now that affection which I have called the tyranny of the human face began to unfold itself. Perhaps some part of my London life (the searching for Ann amongst fluctuating crowds) might be answerable for this. Be that as it may, now it was that upon the rocking waters of the ocean the human face began to reveal itself; the sea appeared paved with innumerable faces, upturned to the heavens; faces, imploring, wrathful, despairing; faces that surged upwards by thousands, by myriads, by generations: infinite was my agitation; my mind tossed, as it seemed, upon the billowy ocean, and weltered upon the weltering waves.

. . .

The scene was an oriental one; and there also it was Easter Sunday, and very early in the morning. And at a vast distance were visible, as a stain upon the horizon, the domes and cupolas of a great city— . . . And not a bowshot from me, upon a stone, shaded by Judean palms, there sat a woman; and I looked, and it was—Ann! She fixed her eyes upon me earnestly, and I said to her at length, "So, then, I have found you at last." I waited; but she answered me not a word . . . . Seventeen years ago, when the lamplight of mighty London fell upon her face, as for the last time I kissed her lips . . . her eyes were streaming with tears. The tears were now no longer seen. Sometimes she seemed altered; yet again sometimes *not* altered; and hardly older. Her looks were tranquil, but with unusual solemnity of expression, and I now gazed upon her with some awe. Suddenly her countenance grew dim; and, turning to the mountains, I perceived vapours rolling between us; in a moment all had vanished; thick darkness came on; and in the twinkling of an eye I was far away from mountains, and by lamp-light in London, walking again with Ann—just as we had walked, when both children, eighteen years before, along the endless terraces of Oxford Street.

(vol. III, pp. 439–441; 445–446)

The *Confessions* end with this procession of dreams, and with the equivocal assertion that the habit of opium had been nearly conquered. In a sense they were unfinished, since the addiction was not conquered either. De Quincey was to go further and deeper among the pains of opium, and into the history of his own spirit. But twenty-five years passed before the ability not only to dream but also to describe his dreams visited him again, probably in what modern physicians call the period of withdrawal, when, after heavy addiction to a narcotic, the doses are suddenly reduced. In 1845 he resumed his *Confessions*, and thought that what he had written was "the *ne plus ultra*, as regards the feeling and the power to express it, which I can ever hope to attain."[7] Like so many of his projects, this continuation was not achieved completely. All that is left, and probably all that he wrote, is a series of fragments, linked by no coherent plan but in some very significant ways deepening the self-analysis of the earlier work, and carrying the splendor of "impassioned prose" still further.

It would be a service to De Quincey's reputation, even now, to link these fragments with the original *Confessions* in such a way as to bring out the fundamental coherence of the whole sequence—a coherence not of logical structure but of emotion and of recollection. Certainly the beginning of such a rearrangement would be a paper written in the Indian summer of 1845, "The Affliction of Childhood."[8] In it he describes, for the first time fully, the death of his specially beloved sister Elizabeth, when he was seven years old—the sister who, more than any other human being, had given him the full security of real affection. With appalling clarity he writes of his clandestine visit to the room where her body lay in a blaze of sunlight, and of his last kiss on her dead lips. And he goes on, in some of his most perceptive ex-

[7]"Letter to Professor Lushington," 1845, in H. A. Page, *Thomas De Quincey: His Life and Writings* (London, 1877), vol. I, p. 338.
[8]Masson, vol. I, pp. 28–54.

plorations of his own memories, to explain to himself why death, and above all the death of young girls, should have become inextricably woven in his mind with the images of summer, sunlight, Palestine, Jerusalem, and Easter Day.

It is in this entangled mass of associations that he found the reason why he should have encountered Ann in his dreams beneath Judean palms, within sight of Jerusalem. And he became aware that her figure was, for him, only another incarnation of the sister who had died when he was a child. A third incarnation of the same image of death and the maiden was Kate Wordsworth, who had died at the age of three in 1813, and whose death had precipitated his first deep addiction to opium. In the earlier *Confessions* there is an Easter Day dream of the sun-drenched churchyard among the mountains where she was buried, but it needs to be rounded out by his account of his extraordinary affection for her and his grief at her death, published in 1840.[9]

These three girls—his sister Elizabeth, the street girl Ann, and Kate Wordsworth—were woven interchangeably into his recurring dream of death and summer—"having been once roused, it never left me, and split into a thousand fantastic variations, which often suddenly re-combined, locked back into startling unity, and restored the original dream."[10] Some of the most singular and lovely of these variations are in the new fragments, to which he gave the title "Suspiria de Profundis." Perhaps the best-known of all his pieces of "impassioned prose" is the triptych of three ambiguously allegorical female figures, shadowily representing the modes of grief in despair and madness. Here is one of them:

The second Sister is called *Mater Suspiriorum*, Our Lady of Sighs. She never scales the clouds, nor walks abroad upon the winds. She wears no diadem. And her eyes, if they were ever seen, would be neither sweet nor subtle; no man could read their story; they would be found filled with perishing dreams, and with wrecks of forgotten delirium. But she raises not her eyes; . . . She weeps not. She groans not. But she sighs inaudibly at intervals. Her sister, Madonna, is oftentimes stormy and frantic, raging in the highest against heaven, and demanding back her darlings. But Our Lady of Sighs never clamours, never defies, dreams not of rebellious aspirations. She is humble to abjectness. Hers is the meekness that belongs to the hopeless. Murmur she may, but it is in her sleep. Whisper she may, but it is to herself in

the twilight. Mutter she does at times, but it is in solitary places that are desolate as she is desolate, in ruined cities, and when the sun has gone down to his rest.

(vol. XIII, p. 366)

It would be hard to find a better example of what De Quincey described as "the capital secrets" of prose, for here it is by the connections between the sentences, and the "reverberations" between them, that the effect is attained. It is, indeed, a compressed demonstration of the devices by which the implied intonation of the speaking voice may be controlled. There is inversion of the usual order—"murmur she may"; a subtle use of parallelism and antitheses; and above all, in the last three sentences, a repetition of the same basic pattern, but with a lengthening of the variations so that they lead with musical inevitability to the final cadence. The whole effect is one rare in English prose—and perhaps not entirely to the taste of most readers and writers of English prose. In French it can be savored more frankly; and in Baudelaire's magnificent version of it, the strict harmony of its sentence structure emerges even more firmly than in the original.[11]

A few more dream fragments in De Quincey's highest strain are to be found in "The English Mail-Coach," another product of the second period of his creative dreams. Here is one from the "Dream-Fugue," which represents his last attempt to lift prose to the level of music, and gives another variation of his endless dream of dying girls, more purely, less rhetorically, than in the "Suspiria":

Sweet funeral bells from some incalculable distance, wailing over the dead that die before the dawn, awakened me as I slept in a boat moored to some familiar shore. The morning twilight even then was breaking; and, by the dusky revelations which it spread, I saw a girl, adorned with a garland of white roses about her head for some great festival, running along the solitary strand in extremity of haste. Her running was the running of panic; and often she looked back as to some dreadful enemy in the rear. But, when I leaped ashore, and followed on her steps to warn her of a peril in front, alas! from me she fled as from another peril, and vainly I shouted to her of quicksands that lay ahead. Faster and faster she ran; round a promontory of rocks she wheeled out of sight; in an instant I also wheeled round it, but only to see the treacherous sands

[9]Masson, vol. II, pp. 440–445.
[10]Masson, vol. III, p. 444.

[11]De Quincey's influence upon French literature was considerably greater than upon English. Alfred de Musset translated the *Confessions* in 1828, and Honoré de Balzac, Théophile Gautier, and Baudelaire made more or less extensive use of the images in them.

gathering above her head. Already her person was buried; only the fair young head and the diadem of white roses around it were still visible to the pitying heavens; and, last of all, was visible one white marble arm.

(vol. XIII, p. 321)

For writing in this mode, De Quincey is often enjoyed, sometimes praised—and rightly, for there is nothing quite like it in English. But he is also criticized for it, on the ground that it is overly elaborate, "Mandarin" prose. So far as this may be a matter of taste, there is no point in disputing it; but to whatever extent it may rest on preconceptions of the nature of language and of literature, it is open to argument. First, it should be remembered that modern linguistics lays stress upon the many "registers" of a single language, and happens to describe them by a musical metaphor from one of De Quincey's favorite instruments, the organ, in which a register is a set of stops producing the same quality of sound, in the same way. There are on the organ registers that need to be used with discretion; but so used, they are no less effective, no less essential than others. And in prose there are kinds of registration that are needed, that are artistically justified, for only a few special purposes; but for those purposes they are irreplaceable. De Quincey's own plea, of the rarity and difficulty of transcribing dreams, carries real weight. The dream rarely offers determinate shapes, hard outlines, and clear-cut detail; what overwhelms in it is the atmosphere, the immense suggestion of emotion. And for the rendering of this shadowy essence, De Quincey's prose was an admirable, an indispensable medium.

Secondly, it must not be forgotten that De Quincey was not concerned with dream writing for its own sake. It was no more, and no less, than the special material on which he founded his study of the growth of the human spirit. And just as it is possible—and very common—for Wordsworth to be read for the sake of the descriptions, while their purpose is nearly overlooked, so De Quincey is too often read for the sake of his purpler passages, without regard for the explorations of which they are merely a part. No doubt the reason is that his passages of reflection and analysis, like Wordsworth's occasional philosophic comments, are more soberly written, less superficially attractive and striking than the material on which they rest. But for him they were the justification of his enterprise, and not in any narrowly artistic sense. In the *Confessions*

there are some fine passages on memory, above all the memory of childhood, and its formative effect on the human personality; in its continuation, the "Suspiria," there are finer still, for they gain by his deeper understanding of himself, his more sensitive evocation of the experiences that had shaped his dreams and himself. In "The Affliction of Childhood," for example, there is this profound perception:

. . . far more of our deepest thoughts and feelings pass to us through perplexed combinations of *concrete* objects, pass to us as *involutes* (if I may coin that word) in compound experiences incapable of being disentangled, than ever reach us *directly*, and in their own abstract shapes.

(vol. I, p. 39)

Wordsworth continually exemplified this vital aspect of human experience, but never defined it quite so clearly. And in this passage on his own chosen ground, the theory of dreams, De Quincey shows not only that he has something of importance to report, but also that his prose, even at its most elaborate, is no less capable of precise exposition than of visionary description. And this was so because his "fine writing" depended not on a curious choice of words but upon the firm and supple structure of sentences musically molded, unfolding a theme and its development to the final cadence with that special sureness of phrasing that links each moment of melody with the whole magnificent composition:

. . . countless are the mysterious handwritings of grief or joy which have inscribed themselves successively upon the palimpsest of your brain; and, like the annual leaves of aboriginal forests, or the undissolving snows on the Himalaya, or light falling upon light, the endless strata have covered up each other in forgetfulness. But by the hour of death, but by fever, but by the searchings of opium, all these can revive in strength. They are not dead, but sleeping. In the illustration imagined by myself from the case of some individual palimpsest, the Grecian tragedy had seemed to be displaced, but was *not* displaced, by the monkish legend; and the monkish legend had seemed to be displaced, but was *not* displaced, by the knightly romance. In some potent convulsion of the system, all wheels back into its earliest elementary stage. The bewildering romance, light tarnished with darkness, the semi-fabulous legend, truth celestial mixed with human falsehoods, these fade even of themselves as life advances. The romance has perished that the young man adored; the legend has gone that deluded the boy; but the deep, deep tragedies of infan-

154

cy, as when the child's hands were unlinked for ever from his mother's neck, or his lips for ever from his sister's kisses, these remain lurking below all, and these lurk to the last. Alchemy there is none of passion or disease that can scorch away these immortal impresses. . . .

(vol. XIII, pp. 348–349)

His daughter described the moment of De Quincey's death thus:

Suddenly we saw him throw up his arms, which to the last retained their strength, and say distinctly, and as if in great surprise, "Sister! sister! sister!" The loud breathing became slower and slower, and as the world of Edinburgh awoke to busy work and life, all that was mortal of my father fell asleep for ever.[12]

He was a man, then, who had come to know himself and, without rhetoric, what for him would indeed lurk to the last.

SELECTED BIBLIOGRAPHY

I. Bibliography. J. A. Green, *Thomas De Quincey: A Bibliography Based upon the De Quincey Collection in the Moss Side Library* (Manchester, 1908); W. E. A. Axon, "The Canon of De Quincey's Writings, with References to Some of His Unidentified Articles," in *Transactions of the Royal Society of Literature*, 32 (1912), 1–46.

II. Collected Works. J. T. Fields, ed., *De Quincey's Writings*, 22 vols. (Boston, 1851–1859), unrev. text, repr. in Author's Library ed. (Boston, 1878); *Selections Grave and Gay from Writings, Published and Unpublished, of Thomas De Quincey, Revised and Arranged by Himself*, 14 vols. (Edinburgh, 1853–1860), author's collected ed. of his previously published writings, enl., recast, and rev.; D. Masson, ed., *The Collected Writings*, 14 vols. (Edinburgh, 1889–1890), with intro. and notes by Masson, the standard ed., several times repr.; A. H. Japp, ed., *The Posthumous Works*, 2 vols. (London, 1891–1893), edited from the original MSS, with intro. and notes by Japp.

III. Selected Works. D. Masson, ed., *Select Essays*, 2 vols. (Edinburgh, 1888); *Essays* (London, 1903), with intro. by C. Whibley; H. Darbishire, ed., *De Quincey's Literary Criticism* (London, 1909), with intro. by Darbishire; *The English Mail-Coach and Other Essays* (London, 1912), the Everyman's Library ed.; T. Burke, comp., *The Ecstasies of Thomas De Quincey* (London, 1928); A. H. R. Ball, ed., *Selections from De Quincey* (London,

1932); P. Van D. Stern, ed., *Selected Writings of Thomas De Quincey* (New York, 1937); E. Sackville-West, ed., *Recollections of the Lake Poets* (London, 1948), with intro. by Sackville-West; E. Sackville-West, ed., *Confessions of an English Opium-Eater, Together with Selections from the Autobiography of Thomas De Quincey* (London, 1950), with intro. by Sackville-West; B. Dobrée, ed., *Thomas De Quincey* (London, 1965).

IV. Separate Works. *Confessions of an English Opium-Eater* (London, 1822; rev. ed., 1823; enl. ed., 1856), published anonymously, also in Everyman's Library ed. (London, 1907), and in G. Saintsbury, ed. (London, 1927) —French trans. by A. de Musset (Paris, 1828), and by C. Baudelaire (Paris, 1860); *Klosterheim; or, The Masque* (Edinburgh, 1832); *The Logic of Political Economy* (Edinburgh, 1844); *China. A Revised Reprint of Articles from Titan, with Prefaces and Additions* (Edinburgh, 1857); *The Wilder Hope: Essays on Future Punishment, with a Paper on the Supposed Scriptural Expression for Eternity* (London, 1890); S. M. Tave, ed., *New Essays by De Quincey: His Contributions to the Edinburgh Saturday Post and the Edinburgh Evening Post, 1827–8* (Princeton, N. J., 1966), articles attributed with varying degrees of certainty to De Quincey.

Among the many periodicals to which De Quincey contributed were the *Westmorland Gazette* (1818–1819); *London* (1821–1825); *Blackwood's* (1826–1828; 1830–1834; 1837–1845; 1849); *Tait's* (1833–1841; 1845–1848; 1851); *Hogg's Instructor* (1850–1853); and *Titan* (1856–1857).

V. Letters and Diaries. A. H. Japp, ed., *De Quincey Memorials*, 2 vols. (London, 1891), includes "Letters and Other Records, with Communications from Coleridge, the Wordsworths . . . "; H. A. Eaton, ed., *A Diary of Thomas De Quincey, 1803* (London, 1928); W. H. Bonner, ed., *De Quincey at Work: As Seen in One Hundred and Thirty New and Newly Edited Letters* (Buffalo, N. Y., 1936); S. Musgrove, ed., *Unpublished Letters of Thomas De Quincey and Elizabeth Barrett Browning* (Auckland, 1954), from the originals in the Grey Collection, Auckland Public Library.

VI. Biographical and Critical Studies. H. A. Page (pseudonym of A. H. Japp), *Thomas De Quincey: His Life and Writings*, 2 vols. (London, 1877; rev. and enl. ed., 1890); T. Carlyle, *Reminiscences*, J. A. Froude, ed., 2 vols. (London, 1881); D. Masson, *De Quincey* (London, 1881), in the English Men of Letters series; J. R. Findlay, *Personal Recollections of Thomas De Quincey* (Edinburgh, 1886); J. Hogg, *De Quincey and His Friends: Personal Recollections, Souvenirs and Anecdotes* (London, 1895); G. T. Clapton, *Baudelaire et De Quincey* (Paris, 1931); V. Woolf, *The Common Reader*, 2nd ser. (London, 1932), contains "De Quincey's Autobiography"; M. H. Abrams, *The Milk of Paradise: The Effect of Opium Visions on the Works of De Quincey, Crabbe, Francis Thompson and Coleridge* (Cambridge, Mass., 1934); M. Elwin, *De*

---

[12]H. A. Page, *Thomas De Quincey: His Life and Writings*, vol. II, p. 305.

Quincey (London, 1935); H. A. Eaton, *Thomas De Quincey: A Biography* (Oxford, 1936); E. Sackville-West, *A Flame in Sunlight: The Life and Work of Thomas De Quincey* (London, 1936); G.-A. Astre, *Thomas De Quincey, mystique et symboliste* (Paris, 1937).

J. C. Metcalf, *De Quincey: A Portrait* (Cambridge, Mass., 1940); S. K. Proctor, *Thomas De Quincey's Theory of Literature* (Ann Arbor, Mich., 1943); J. E. Jordan, *Thomas De Quincey, Literary Critic: His Method and Achievement* (Berkeley–Los Angeles, 1952); C. Leech, "De Quincey as Literary Critic," in *Review of English Literature*, 2, no. 1 (January 1961), 38–48; G. Carnall, "De Quincey on 'The Knocking at the Gate,'" in *Review of English Literature*, 2, no. 1 (January 1961), 49–57; J. E. Jordan, *De Quincey to Wordsworth: A Biography of a Relationship* (Berkeley–Los Angeles, 1962); F. Moreux, *Thomas De Quincey: La vie—l'homme—l'oeuvre* (Paris, 1964); A. Goldman, *The Mine and the Mint: Sources for the Writings of Thomas De Quincey* (Carbondale–Edwardsville, Ill., 1965).

THOMAS LOVE PEACOCK
(1785-1866)

J. I. M. Stewart

I

THOMAS LOVE PEACOCK was born at Weymouth, Dorset, on 18 October 1785, the only child of a prosperous London glass merchant, Samuel Peacock, who so far disobliged the infant as to have him baptized in the Scotch Kirk, London Wall, thereby lending some color to the damaging conjecture that the future satirist's ancestry lay north of the Tweed. Three years later Samuel Peacock died. But this time he behaved handsomely enough, since he left his widow and child in a pleasant financial independence. They retired to Chertsey—an agreeable Thames-side village some twenty miles upriver from London—and to the society of Mrs. Peacock's father, a retired naval officer who had served under Lord Rodney. Mrs. Peacock was a cultivated woman who composed verse and read Edward Gibbon. Captain Love had lost a leg in the West Indies, but it may be presumed that he moved easily in polite society nevertheless. The boy had thus the good fortune to shed his mercantile background at a tender age, while retaining its material fruits into maturity.

Mrs. Peacock seems to have followed her favorite historian in setting no great store upon formal education. Peacock attended a private school only into his thirteenth year, thereafter making what appears to have been a more or less formal gesture in the direction of commercial pursuits. But this quickly faded; he had acquired at least the rudiments of Latin and Greek, and on the strength of this armory he proceeded to educate himself upon his own whim, whether agreeably in his mother's house or equally agreeably in the reading room of the British Museum. Had he shown any disposition to enter either Cambridge or Oxford, the matter would presumably have been arranged for him. He suggests himself as a youth with some skill in getting just what he wanted —and all he wanted for some years was books, rural surroundings, small expeditions within England and

Scotland, a few friendships or acquaintanceships of not too demanding a sort, and the affection and support of his mother. He was twenty-two before he wanted something that he failed to get. This was a young woman named Fanny Falkner, who, having been snatched from his advances and hastily married to another, died within the year.

> Frail as thy love, the flowers were dead
> Ere yet the evening sun was set;
> But years shall see the cypress spread,
> Immutable as my regret.[1]

When Peacock wrote these verses shortly after Miss Falkner's death, "regret" was a rather stronger word than it has since become. It could consume like fire—and for Alfred Tennyson, still, the days that are no more could be wild with it. And Peacock's regret was in a sense immutable, for this girl returned to his dreams in the last weeks of his life. Yet he was a mother's son. He may have lost Fanny Falkner, as his lifelong butt Samuel Taylor Coleridge lost Mary Evans, because his nature offered no unimpeded road to passionate love. At least he seems to have felt that distraction was required, since in the winter of 1808–1809 he took the only positive step in the direction of discomfort ever recorded of him—he had himself appointed secretary to Sir Home Riggs Popham, aboard H.M.S. *Venerable*. Finding himself, as a result, on board a "floating inferno"—and thus amid conditions little conducive to the composition of a comedy he had been meditating—he withdrew precipitately and, instead of being carried off by Sir Home to the Amazon or the Limpopo, spent the summer of 1809 in the more judicious pursuit of the source of the Thames. In the following year he published a poem celebrating the genius of this

[1]Quotations are taken from H. F. B. Brett-Smith and C. E. Jones, eds., *The Works*, 10 vols. (London, 1924–1934).

157

homely river. He had already published two metrical exercises: *The Monks of St. Mark* and *Palmyra*. He believed himself to be at least a minor poet. But he was a youth of the strongest good sense, and even this modest persuasion was scarcely to survive his meeting a major one. This major poet was Percy Shelley. And Shelley's was the major influence upon Peacock's career.

Peacock before meeting Shelley is a little like Coleridge before meeting William Wordsworth; there is the same spectacle of an immature talent groping uncertainly amid irreconcilable attitudes. He had just published *The Philosophy of Melancholy* (1812), which is not unlike the worst of Coleridge's early verse: degenerately Augustan in form, inchoately romantic in substance. Yet the effect of the meeting was not like that attending Wordsworth and Coleridge's alliance. For it is clear that Shelley quickly became established in Peacock's mind as a fascinating antitype of himself. In Shelley was enthusiasm, and in Shelley's circle was absurdity. And Peacock reacted to these things not as the simple romantic whom he had hitherto been inclined to personate, but as one whose complex affinities lay as much with Joseph Addison and Oliver Goldsmith as with the leaders of the romantic movement. He looked at Shelley—the twenty-year-old Shelley of the Bracknell period—and loved him. He looked at him again, looked at his companions, like Matthew Arnold murmured, "What a set!"—and upon that murmur the satirist Peacock was born. Yet the love survived, and the romantic in him survived as well. That is why Peacock is as good a satirist as he is.

Consider his account of the Bracknell coterie:

At Bracknell, Shelley was surrounded by a numerous society, all in a great measure of his own opinions in relation to religion and politics, and the larger proportion of them in relation to vegetable diet. But they wore their rue with a difference. Every one of them adopting some of the articles of the faith of their general church, had each nevertheless some predominant crotchet of his or her own, which left a number of open questions for earnest and not always temperate discussion. I was sometimes irreverent enough to laugh at the fervour with which opinions utterly unconducive to any practical result were battled for as matters of the highest importance to the well-being of mankind.

(vol. VIII, p. 19: "Memoirs of Percy Bysshe Shelley")

The novelist lurks in this distinguishably enough. So does another Peacock who was in the making.

"Opinions utterly unconducive to any practical result" were delectable to him as a writer, but the voice that censures them here is also the voice of the man who was to rise high in the service of the East India Company. Shelley's circle, and Shelley's difficulties, had their share in creating both these mature Peacocks.

The circle provided some irresistible figures of fun. For example, there was J. F. Newton, whose vegetarian principles were implicated with his great discovery that there were four compartments, as well as two hemispheres, in the ancient zodiac of Dendera. Peacock, interestingly enough, was not quite impervious to this sort of thing; it appears that he planned, and in part carried out, a poem based on Isaac Newton's cosmology. Nursing a fantastic bent of his own, he was capable of a sympathetic as well as a skeptical response to the fantastic in others. Had the balance been a little different—had it approached, for example, that which was to obtain in W. B. Yeats—something significantly imaginative might have emerged from Peacock's frequentation of a lunatic fringe. What was in fact to emerge was the Mr. Toobad of *Nightmare Abbey*. Not that poetry was abandoned at this time. On the contrary, he wrote a good deal of it, including *Rhododaphne*, the most successful of his longer works in verse.

But Peacock was not a poet—and what was growing in him in these years was, in the broadest sense, critical power. The mingling in Shelley of genius and absurdity was a perpetual challenge to analysis. Yet we misrepresent Peacock if we exhibit his part in the relationship as that of a merely detached and amused spectator. Sympathy was again important. His association with Shelley's studies was very close; the two evolved ideas and generated enthusiasms together. Peacock was older by seven years; it was his natural role to supply a more mature judgment, a moderating influence, as the emotional crises and practical perplexities constituting Shelley's daily life came along. Peacock's was not a powerful mind; but it was a mind existing in admirable balance, and one capable of forming and rendering persuasive, equitable views. Shelley's matrimonial vagaries constituted a worthy testing ground. Peacock saw and asserted the merits, as well as the limitations, of Harriet Shelley; despite much provocation he maintained an equally fair view of Harriet's more intellectual, if less attractive, supplanter, Mary Godwin. He entered the Shelley period as something of a dilettante poetaster. He emerged from it as a man of integrity and judgment, and also as a man of affairs. After Shelley left for Italy in 1818, Peacock—who was never to see him again—transacted his London business. When Shelley was drowned in 1822, Peacock and Lord Byron became his joint executors.

In 1818, Peacock was still living with his mother in rural seclusion. It may be that the departure of Shelley persuaded him to take stock of himself. He was writing a little verse; he was composing an essay on fashionable literature; he was reading and rambling as usual. The total picture may have come to him as not that of any sort of genius, as not even that of a dedicated and professional man of letters. Whether for this reason or on financial grounds, he now looked for a berth—but on dry land this time. He found it in the service of the East India Company. Interest was doubtless exerted on his behalf, but he appears to have been subjected to a fairly stiff probation, and even to something the hearty detestation of which was to become one of his ineradicable crotchets: competitive examination. Nor was his employment any kind of sinecure. He worked with colleagues of the first ability, including James Mill and John Stuart Mill; and in the wake of James Mill, he rose eventually to a position of major responsibility. The satirist of the Steam Intellect Society became, ironically, the chief expert of the company upon steam navigation; and in numerous ways this convinced opponent of rapid locomotion effectively speeded up physical communications with India. Shelley, before he died, was to laugh at Peacock as a powerful bureaucrat, and at the same time to suggest hopefully that his friend might secure him interesting employment as a political officer at the court of some rajah. It is amusing to speculate on what might have been the literary consequences of so strange a proposal, had it been carried out.

Bureaucrat or not, Peacock was not quite done with being a romantic—and in the first decades of the nineteenth century it was scarcely possible to support that character on the strength of a familiarity merely with the Cotswolds and the Chilterns. Mountains were essential to any full afflatus, and a mountain was better still if inhabited or frequented by a mountain maid. In 1811, Peacock had had the boldness to make an expedition to Wales. There had been mountains galore, and it had been a great success. Now, in 1819, casting a retrospective glance upon the occasion, he recollected that there had been a mountain maid as well—a certain Jane Gryffydh, a parson's daughter. He had neither seen the lady, nor

corresponded with her, since then. Now, though—being more comfortably provided for than hitherto—he sat down and wrote her a letter, the topic sentence of which is the following:

The same circumstances which have given me prosperity confine me to London, and to the duties of the department with which the East India Company has entrusted me: yet I can absent myself for a few days once in every year: if you sanction my wishes, with what delight should I employ them in bringing you to my home!

Shelley remarked that here was something very like the denouement of one of Peacock's novels. And we may feel it to be an oddly low-temperature technique in the establishing of a love relationship. Yet—as with a Sylvan Forester and an Anthelia Melincourt—there is no evidence that the marriage that followed it was unsatisfactory to either party.

Very little that is remarkable attended the long course of Peacock's middle and later life. His family having increased—children being born, his mother continuing to live—he established himself at Lower Halliford, on the Thames, where he remained for the rest of his days. A lover of Athens and Rome, and a wanderer amid all the literatures to which the Mediterranean basin has given birth, Peacock remained an untraveled Hyperborean to the end—an index of the extent to which he recognized that the larger world of his literary and historical imagination was an ideal world only. And we must notice that his convivial world was in some degree ideal too. He loved actual good talk. He loved actual good food and good wine—taking a hand, without doubt, in his elder daughter Mary's learned yet practical *Essay on Gastronomy and Civilization*, and giving careful thought to the ordering of his own dinner and the ritual of his own dinner table. Yet he moved comparatively little in literary and intellectual, as in any other, society. His family, his garden, and his river were enough for him, so that we have little record of him in the memoirs of his younger contemporaries. For a description of him in old age we have to turn to a granddaughter. After speaking of his wit and epicureanism, she goes on:

In public business my grandfather was upright and honourable; but as he advanced in years his detestation of anything disagreeable made him simply avoid whatever fretted him, laughing off all sorts of ordinary calls upon his leisure time. His love of ease and kindness of heart made it impossible that he could be actively unkind to any one, but he would not be worried, and just got away from anything that annoyed him. . . . He could not bear any one to be unhappy or uncomfortable about him.[2]

Peacock at least knew very well that care is not to be excluded even from a library or a riverbank or a garden, and in his domestic life he had perhaps more than an average share of worry. His wife's health failed, a favorite daughter died in early childhood, a son was unstable. In 1849, his eldest daughter, Mary Ellen, widowed as a young woman, married George Meredith, who was nine years her junior, and the couple lived with—and indeed on—Peacock for a number of years. Meredith was a good many things that Peacock disliked: Germanophile for one thing, and not quite confidently a gentleman for another. He had, moreover, the disgusting modern habit (as Peacock saw it) of smoking tobacco. In these things there was merely irritation, but the end of the story was tragedy. Mary Ellen ran away with a painter, Henry Wallis, in 1858, and returned a year later, alone and dying. Meredith was unforgiving and always remained so, declining further dealings with his father-in-law—from whom he had learned something about food and wine and a great deal about the possibilities of intellectual comedy.

In 1865, when Peacock was eighty, a fire broke out in the roof of his bedroom. He withdrew to his study, from which he refused to be moved. The fire was extinguished, but the shock had done its work; Peacock died a few weeks later, on 23 January 1866. Curiously, during his last years he developed a morbid fear of fire; it seemed the first symptom of an approaching senile dementia. The burned child fears fire. But so does the man who has declined it, or who has seen it decline him. In 1820 the mortal remains of Shelley had been consumed by fire—and, in a fitting symbolism, on an Italian beach. Peacock, who had taught Shelley so much good sense, lived on for another forty-six years, incombustible.

II

Headlong Hall was published anonymously in 1816, six months after the battle of Waterloo. *Mansfield Park* had appeared in the year preceding, and *Emma* was to appear in the year following. The Hun-

dred Days seem as remote from Peacock's world as from Jane Austen's. Yet *Headlong Hall* is, if in a restricted sense, a topical novel; it satirizes contemporary persons and their notions in the spheres of literature, science, and philosophy.

> All philosophers, who find
> Some favourite system to their mind,
> In every point to make it fit,
> Will force all nature to submit.

The epigraph, which is from Jonathan Swift, may be taken as announcing the governing idea of all Peacock's conversation novels. And all adopt, broadly, the same method: the drawing together in some generously and heterogeneously hospitable place, typically a country house, of a congeries of characters severally subscribing to every intellectual quirk, oddity, and crotchet under the sun. Perhaps because stage comedy affords him a primary model, Peacock starts off by aiming in this mode at a good deal of somewhat unambitious amusement. He throws in characters whose bonnets harbor some small and monotonously buzzing bee and who are entertainingly bizarre for a short appearance or two, but are of very limited utility thereafter. Squire Headlong falls into this category; we are told that he has been "seized with a violent passion to be thought a philosopher and a man of taste"; but his part in a speculative discussion is commonly a command to buzz the bottle, eschew heeltaps, and take due note that "as to skylight, liberty hall." The incompatibility of the squire and his guests is funny in a limited way, but on the whole he has to be left behind. In inventing him Peacock may have been remembering Samuel Johnson's Dick Minim. Or he may simply have hit upon him because he wanted a Welsh setting. He had spied a piquant incongruity in setting some of his very urban philosophers tramping among the mountains.

From the start Peacock reveals himself as so literary a writer that criticism is tempted to dwell on his sources. Yet from the start his virtues are so idiosyncratic that one feels the tracing of derivations to be of only minor interest. Besides the tradition of stage comedy there is, of course, that of the eighteenth-century English novel, from which he derives both an intermittent rough-and-tumble and the habit of using courtship as a light scaffolding around which to erect anything of greater interest and liveliness that comes along. From French *contes* of the same period he draws the notion of incorporating specula-

[2]J. B. Priestley, *Thomas Love Peacock* (London, 1927), p. 93.

tive debate, rendered in finished prose, in fiction. The embodying of opinion—the giving to this or that contention not merely a voice but also limbs, clothes, a wig, a valet or comic servant, even a mistress and a rudimentary disposition to action—is sufficiently widespread in literature; and in English literature it is percurrent from William Langland to Bernard Shaw. It is a device that can very easily go thin or dry, and it can take several fatal turns. For example, it can drift into the dialogue with unnecessary trimmings, as it does in the third act of Shaw's *Man and Superman*. Or the characters can come to look forbiddingly like personifications. *Headlong Hall* seems at first reading to be not at all a subtle performance; and when we find that its principal characters are a perfectibilist, a deteriorationist, and a "statu-quo-ite," we may feel that we are going to get very little flesh and blood. But this is not so. The doings of the people as people may be farcical or otherwise absurd, but the people do go through a sort of bustling course of things more or less congruous with their speculative persuasions. We are just able to maintain a sense of them as enjoying and suffering human beings; as a result, the book has life as fiction. Peacock's thread of connection with the novel proper here announces itself, once and for all, as slender enough. But he has the art never to sever it.

Take Mr. Escot, the deteriorationist, who does the lion's share of the talking in *Headlong Hall*. He is from the start a satisfactory monomaniac largely because he is able to summon so accomplished a rhetoric to the support of his *idée fixe*:

. . . these improvements, as you call them, appear to me only so many links in the great chain of corruption, which will soon fetter the whole human race in irreparable slavery and incurable wretchedness: your improvements proceed in a simple ratio, while the factitious wants and unnatural appetites they engender proceed in a compound one; and thus one generation acquires fifty wants, and fifty means of supplying them are invented, which each in its turn engenders two new ones; so that the next generation has a hundred, the next two hundred, the next four hundred, till every human being becomes such a helpless compound of perverted inclinations that he is altogether at the mercy of external circumstances, loses all independence and singleness of character, and degenerates so rapidly from the primitive dignity of his sylvan origin, that it is scarcely possible to indulge in any other expectation, than that the whole species must at length be exterminated by its own infinite imbecility and vileness.

(ch. 1)

This has the fullness and dignity, almost even the *gravitas*, of eighteenth-century moral prose. There is Johnson behind it. But in front of it, so to speak, is delicious absurdity—for in "the primitive dignity of his sylvan origin" there already peep out (when we know the books as a whole) the endearing features of Sir Oran Haut-ton from the next novel. Mr. Escot is typical of the chief personages in Peacock in being both cogent and extravagant. He illustrates, as they all do, something that, a little later in the book, Mr. Cranium expects us to take for granted: that "his own system is of all things the dearest to every man of liberal thinking and a philosophical tendency." In this irony lies the essence of Peacock's comic world. Liberal thinking and a philosophical tendency ought to make us tentative and openminded, but in fact they go along with the furious riding of one particular hobbyhorse. These people show an obsessive tenacity that renders them admirable material for the operations of the comic spirit. When, at the end of the story, Mr. Escot has gained the hand of the lovely Cephalis Cranium by bartering for it the skull of Cadwallader, he rashly declares himself to be the happiest man alive. But he quickly recovers, and adds that "a slight oscillation of good in the instance of a solitary individual" by no means affects the solidity of his opinions concerning the general deterioration of the civilized world. His marriage had no effect in weaning him from his faith in the Wild Man of the Woods, "the original, unthinking, unscientific, unlogical savage." At the same time he celebrates that marriage with an eminently thoughtful, scientific, and logical speech against the relations of the sexes as civilization orders them. His bride presumably is standing beside him as he orates. Regularly in Peacock there is at least the effective ghost of a dramatic setting. It is not so very far from this to the admirable finale of *Man and Superman*, with Jack Tanner caught, but speechifying still, and Ann Whitefield telling him encouragingly to go on talking.

Commentators, looking forward to the manner in which Peacock later developed his art, sometimes assert that Mr. Foster, believing in perfectibility, represents Shelley, and that Mr. Escot, being *laudator temporis acti*, must be Peacock himself. There is not very much in this. Among the characters who carry on a general philosophical debate in *Headlong Hall*, as distinct from those who chatter on minor topics, only one, Mr. Panscope, seems definitely related to a living person, Coleridge. Panscope is the first of a number of Coleridges in Peacock's books: a kind of sighting shot, and a poor one. One inadequacy appears at once. Coleridge, if we have studied him at all, comes to us, as does Henry James, preeminently as a voice—and here is not the voice we know as Coleridge's. But the presentation is in consonance with Peacock's presentation of all his characters. All speak with the same voice—at least in the sense that Walter Savage Landor's persons do in his *Imaginary Conversations*, or Ivy Compton-Burnett's in her novels. Peacock does later find means of rendering, within its embodiment in his own highly characteristic prose, the movement of mind of some actual persons. But that is a different matter.

There is one other point to be noted about Panscope—small, but of important implication. He has a good tailor and £10,000 a year. It is impossible to tell whether Peacock has simply thrown this in to give Panscope some eligibility as a suitor, or whether he is deliberately making the point that Panscope is not, in his personal character, Samuel Taylor Coleridge. In *Nightmare Abbey*, on the other hand, the Coleridge figure, Mr. Flosky, tells us why he has named his eldest son Emanuel Kant Flosky; and we know that Coleridge had called *his* eldest son Ernest Hartley Coleridge on the same principle of admiration for a philosopher. It is commonly said that Peacock does not bring real people into his books in the way of total caricature or travesty; rather, that he takes the publicly professed opinions of real people and infers appropriate imaginary characters from them. This holds only a limited truth. All his novels are, to some extent, romans à clef, and we can say only that Peacock exercises a good deal of civilized tact in exploiting only lightly the private character of his victims. We cannot say that he didn't "do" Coleridge again and again so as to make Coleridge appear very absurd, or that he didn't "do" Robert Southey more than once so as to make Southey appear very despicable.

The satire in *Headlong Hall* is blended with something like impartial debate on serious topics. When Escot sees in the fable of Prometheus a "symbolical portraiture of that disastrous epoch, when man first applied fire to culinary purposes," and when—helping himself to a slice of beef—he goes on to declare that both the Lotophagi and the Hindu "depose very strongly in favour of a vegetable regimen," he is delightfully absurd. But when, contemplating what we should think of as the first ad- vances of industrialism, he declares, "By enlarging and complicating your machines, you degrade, not exalt, the human animals you employ to direct them," or when he asserts that the manufacturing system tends "to multiply factitious desires, to stimulate depraved appetites, to invent unnatural wants, to heap up incense on the shrine of luxury, and accumulate expedients of selfish and ruinous profusion," he is of course the mouthpiece of Peacock and of most thoughtful men since Peacock's day. And although it is usually said that in *Headlong Hall*, as not in its successor *Melincourt*, Peacock preserves a sense of open debate and refrains from taking sides, it is surely undeniable that Escot on the whole is allowed to get the better of Foster. Foster, indeed, has an equal power of weighty disquisition; he will call upon us to mark "the slow, but immense, succession of concatenated intelligence" by which, for example, naval architecture has gradually attained its present state of perfection, or he will effectively oppose to Escot's "mere animal life of a wild man" the achievement of a civilization that produces an Isaac Newton, an Antoine Lavoisier, or a John Locke. But the last words tend to be with his adversary:

"You will allow", said Mr. Foster, as soon as they were again in motion, "that the wild man of the woods could not transport himself over two hundred miles of forest, with as much facility as one of these vehicles transports you and me through the heart of this cultivated country."

"I am certain", said Mr. Escot, "that a wild man can travel an immense distance without fatigue; but what is the advantage of locomotion? The wild man is happy in one spot, and there he remains: the civilised man is wretched in every place he happens to be in, and then congratulates himself on being accommodated with a machine that will whirl him to another, where he will be just as miserable as ever."

(ch. 2)

This looks back to Johnson's *Rasselas*, and forward to Matthew Arnold.

Nothing less than human destiny is the theme of the main sequence of debates in *Headlong Hall*. But there are subsidiary topics, two of which stand out. One centers on Mr. Cranium and his science of craniology or phrenology. The other centers on Mr. Milestone and his art of landscape gardening. Mr. Cranium's proposal for the institution of what would now be called vocational guidance on the basis of his discoveries is amusing, but we have quickly had enough of him. It is rather different with Mr. Milestone. We can no longer inspect extensive collections of skulls arranged to enforce the truths of phrenology, but we can still visit Blenheim and Stowe, Fountains and Stourhead. The vogue of the picturesque in its various phases has left its actual impress on the face of England; and its history, moreover, interdigitates with that both of imaginative literature and of the fine arts from the age of Alexander Pope to that of Wordsworth. Milestone's main scene, in which he produces his portfolio and shows what he has done for Lord Littlebrain, is made more effective for us if we have a look at some of the books put out by the improvers, in which an ingenious system of slides, to be drawn back from part of an illustration, gives a "before and after" view of their activities.

A further point may be made by way of Mr. Milestone. When "pickaxes and gunpowder, a hanging stove and a poker" are so combined as almost to emancipate the spirit of Mr. Cranium from its terrestrial bondage—the resulting explosion hurled him into the water, and being utterly destitute of natatorial skill, he was in imminent danger of final submersion—we come upon an element of straight slapstick that is to run through all the books. Ludicrous physical mishap has always been a resource of the English novelist. But in defending his use of it, Peacock would probably have appealed to a wider tradition: one including Samuel Butler's *Hudibras*, Miguel de Cervantes, and Aristophanes. In a much fuller context Aristophanes is the greatest of his masters, even if at a large remove. One has only to read *The Frogs* to realize this.

III

Aʙᴏᴜᴛ a year after the publication of *Headlong Hall*, Shelley wrote to Leigh Hunt:

Peacock is the author of *Headlong Hall*. . . . He is now writing *Melincourt* in the same style, but, as I judge, far superior to *Headlong Hall*. He is an amiable man of great learning, considerable taste, an enemy to every shape of tyranny and superstitious imposture.

There is certainly more of Shelley's influence in the second novel than in the first—and if Shelley had not been a genius, he would have been a prig. *Melincourt* (1817) is the work of a natural humorist and satirist who has become touched by this priggishness, very much to the detriment of his art. Thus the central figure of the story, Sylvan Forester, oscillates between being a fantastic creation (which is what he ought to be) and a heavily normative or exemplary one. He is a bore given large scope to be boring in a book that is a good deal longer than is judicious. Yet this last fact is one that we tend to rediscover with surprise upon a fresh reading. Looking back, we have a foreshortened view, recollecting the work as being dominated (as it is not) by the superb figure of Sir Oran Haut-ton. The greatest of Peacock's creations is, without doubt, the Seithenyn of *The Misfortunes of Elphin*. But Sir Oran surely comes next. And whereas Seithenyn has a great deal to say for himself, Sir Oran has nothing at all. The Wild Man of the Woods has not got around to articulate speech. He has an air of high fashion, bows gracefully, takes wine with due ceremony, and plays the flute. He even becomes a member of Parliament. But he doesn't speak. The grand characteristic of Peacock's people is, of course, their unquenchable loquacity. And here in the middle of them is Sir Oran, unmistakably the greatest gentleman of the lot. True civilization, we are almost persuaded, would consist in holding our tongue.

The skeleton of *Melincourt* is provided by the commonplace formula of the novel of courtship. Anthelia Melincourt is at once an independent heiress, a child of the mountains, and an authority on the five great poets of Italy. All this has given her, as a woman to be loved and won, "a visionary model of excellence which it was very little likely the modern world could realise." The modern world tries, sending various suitors to Anthelia's castle, including a wicked nobleman who, upon being rejected, abducts and proposes to ravish her—being prevented in the very act by one of Sir Oran's exercises in supersimian agility. Anthelia then pledges herself to Mr. Forester, who has been making cautious advances to her throughout the book.

This courtship must strike us as very stilted and insipid, but it is certainly not meant to appear in a satirical light. Peacock is taking it straight from a variety of the polite fiction of the age to which he cannot have attributed any very significant literary merit, but which he clearly regarded as wholesome and agreeable rather than absurd. What he did judge unwholesome and ridiculous—and pillory again and again—were those (as he conceived them) Germanic romances in which there is a morbid and unnatural confounding of virtue and vice, an exhibiting (as Mr. Flosky has it in *Nightmare Abbey*) of all the "blackest passions of our nature, tricked out in a masquerade dress of heroism and disappointed benevolence; the whole secret of which lies in forming combinations that contradict all our experience." So when Mr. Forester congratulates Anthelia on her library—

> You have an admirable library, Miss Melincourt: and I judge from the great number of Italian books, you are justly partial to the poets of that exquisite language. The apartment itself seems singularly adapted to the genius of their poetry, which combines the magnificent simplicity of ancient Greece with the mysterious grandeur of the feudal ages—
>
> (ch. 15)

we are decidedly not being asked to laugh at him. He is speaking out of real literary conviction—Peacock's literary conviction.

Nothing more need be said about the amatory or romantic part of *Melincourt*. We may turn to Sylvan Forester in his other character. He is first encountered as a young gentleman living in affluent retirement (he is the owner of Red Nose Abbey, which he has renamed Redrose Abbey) with a view, he says, "of carrying on in peace and seclusion some peculiar experiments on the nature and progress of man." These experiments concern Sir Oran, who "was caught very young in the woods of Angola." And what Mr. Forester is really proposing is an enormous joke at the expense of the English parliamentary system at its farthest stage of corruption. He explains this to his friend Sir Telegraph Paxarett:

> With a view of ensuring him the respect of society, which always attends on rank and fortune, I have purchased him a baronetcy, and made over to him an estate. I have also purchased of the Duke of Rottenburgh one half of the elective franchise vested in the body of Mr. Christopher Corporate, the free, fat, and dependent burgess of the ancient and honourable borough of Onevote, who returns two members to Parliament, one of whom will shortly be Sir Oran.
>
> (ch. 6)

This wonderful idea affords Peacock scope for a number of brilliant attacks upon the existing political system, including some admirable travesties of George Canning's speeches against parliamentary reform, in which "corruption" is pleasantly softened into "persuasion in a tangible shape," and in which the blessings of "virtual representation," and the arguments gravely adduced to the effect that the member for a rotten borough is far more gloriously independent and incorruptible than the member for a real one, are pilloried with a very sufficient sparkle of wit. At the actual election Mr. Corporate appears and is properly deferred to as "a respectable body of constituents." The occasion ends in a riot, and all that in fact exists of the honorable borough of Onevote (to wit, the hustings and a marquee, for Onevote has been for centuries a desolate stretch of heath) is reduced to ashes in a few minutes. All this is amusing today; it must have been more so in 1817, when Onevotes, Christopher Corporates, and the blessings of virtual representation for towns such as Novote actually existed and were defended by some of the most astute intelligences in the land.

If the high-mindedness of Shelley is responsible for some of the duller stretches of *Melincourt*, his potentialities as a figure of fun are the sole prompting occasion of the next, and much shorter, book, *Nightmare Abbey* (1818). The hard-worked term "tour de force" is perhaps the aptest that criticism can find for this performance. Out of Shelley's personality and intellectual persuasions, and even out of that matrimonial dilemma the resolution of which had been succeeded by tragedy, Peacock distills an essence that is at once farce and high comedy—and that was to prove entirely acceptable to a victim seldom showing much sense of humor, and very prone to imagine himself the object of malign attack.

Peacock cannot have been unaware of the hazards he ran, yet the book has the appearance of being casually entered upon. Once more there is the country house and the gathering of guests. The house—complete with its towers, moat, owls, and dismal fenland setting—is essential; Scythrop Glowry and his father could scarcely exist except against the background it provides. But the collecting within its moldering walls of a miscellaneous group of cranks is a carry-over from *Headlong Hall* not very well adapted to the higher organization at which the new book aims. Mr. Asterias, the ichthyologist, has small function in the story, and his son Aquarius has less; nor is Mr. Listless, the fashionable youth who is always listless, an impressive or useful invention. These old elements do not combine well with what is new.

On the other hand, certain others do. *Nightmare Abbey* is still a conversation piece; the passion of all its creatures is to talk, but now there is a situation as well as a dinner table. The incongruity of the talk and the situation, the absurdity of the characters' continued loquacity in the predicaments in which they find themselves, make the fine irony of the book. Thus, when Scythrop retires one evening to his tower, he is astonished to find a muffled figure that presently reveals itself as that of a young woman of dazzling grace and beauty. He is much taken aback, and the following exchange ensues:

"You are surprised", said the lady; "yet why should you be surprised? If you had met me in a drawing-room, and I had been introduced to you by an old woman, it would have been a matter of course; can the division of two or three walls, and the absence of an unimportant personage, make the same object essentially different in the perception of a philosopher?"

"Certainly not", said Scythrop; "but when any class of objects has habitually presented itself to our perceptions in invariable conjunction with particular relations, then, on the sudden appearance of one object of the class divested of those accompaniments, the essential difference of the relation is, by an involuntary process, transferred to the object itself, which thus offers itself to our perceptions with all the strangeness of novelty."

(ch. 10)

This is pleasing in itself; it would be so even if we did not recognize the raillery at the expense of David Hartley's sensationalist philosophy. Even better are the kindred passages at the climax, where Scythrop's loquacity is at one and the same time an endeavor to lead his father off the scent of the hidden lady and a genuine reflection of his inexpugnably theoretical mind.

IV

PEACOCK possessed little resource in drawing out and diversifying his fable. In *Headlong Hall* the house party assembles, dines, talks, breakfasts, dines, and so on. Its members perambulate (or, as Peacock likes to say, perlustrate) the squire's park; a few of them take slightly longer walks through the countryside; then they nearly all get married and—presumably —disperse. In *Nightmare Abbey* the scene is even more contracted: anybody proceeding beyond hooting distance of the owls disappears from our ken until he turns up again. The book is based on a single and simple comic situation and a variety of conver-

sations, with everything more or less focused upon the absurdities, and morbidities, as Peacock saw them, of the romantic sensibility. *Melincourt*, a much longer book, shows its author in real difficulty. He adopts a familiar resource of the novelist concerned with keeping going, and sends his characters traveling. But he is no Henry Fielding or Tobias Smollett, and the wanderers—who are supposed to be in urgent quest of a ravished maiden—simply go on talking, as if they were still around a dinner table.

In *Crotchet Castle* (1831)—the chief work of his full maturity—Peacock again tries traveling, this time in a peculiar manner and with more success. The house party members take to houseboats and are drawn up the Thames. They inspect Oxford and its "undisturbed libraries." Leaving Lechlade,

. . . they entered the canal that connects the Thames with the Severn; ascended by many locks; passed, by a tunnel three miles long, through the bowels of Sapperton Hill . . . ; descended by many locks again, through the valley of Stroud into the Severn; continued their navigation into the Ellesmere canal; moored their pinnaces in the Vale of Llangollen by the aqueduct of Pontycysyllty . . . .

(ch. 10)

This peregrination (which it is still possible to undertake, although soon after Lechlade the canal has become a dry bottom) transports the people of *Crotchet Castle* from one to the other of the only two localities that Peacock much cared for or knew about. The sense of familiar ground provides one of the pleasures of the novel.

But there is more that is familiar about it than that. For the formula is still the same: a host who collects indifferently crackpots and intellectuals, a hero with a stable full of hobbyhorses, a heroine who is devoted to books and mountain solitude. But it is all done better than ever before; and the cast members, although well-known to us, are almost without exception brilliant in their roles. Even so, one is preeminent. This is the clergyman Dr. Folliott, whose first entry has something of the splendor of the authentic Shakespearean Pericles in the third act of that imperfectly canonical tragedy:

"God bless my soul, sir!" exclaimed the Reverend Doctor Folliott, bursting, one fine May morning, into the breakfast-room at Crotchet Castle, "I am out of all patience with this march of mind. Here has my house been nearly burned down, by my cook taking it into her head to study hydrostatics, in a sixpenny tract, published by the Steam

Intellect Society, and written by a learned friend who is for doing all the world's business as well as his own, and is equally well qualified to handle every branch of human knowledge."

(ch. 2)

It is perhaps because in a state of irritation occasioned by this tiresome alarm—conjoined, as it was, with the dubious propinquity to Dr. Folliott's cook of Dr. Folliott's footman—that the doctor at once falls upon Mr. MacQuedy, a philosopher who has been so rash as to refer to his native Edinburgh as the modern Athens: "Modern Athens, sir! the assumption is a personal affront to every man who has a Sophocles in his library. I will thank you for an anchovy" (ch. 2).

The doctor is a Johnsonian bully, perhaps—but there are few instances in which there is not wit in his warfare. A propos of the ruling phobia of a certain Mr. Firedamp, he remarks that he himself judges the proximity of wine a matter of much more importance than the longinquity of water. And he finds in praise of education the single circumstance that it gives a fixed direction to stupidity. The eighth chapter of the novel, headed "Science and Charity," in which he first fustigates a couple of footpads whom he chooses to regard as swearing by "the learned friend" (who is Lord Brougham), and in which he is later interviewed by charity commissioners who solemnly admonish him upon the misappropriation of a shrunken and minute charitable endowment he has never heard of—this at great public expense and without even requiring or suggesting that the £1 a year involved should be charitably applied again—is one of the most amusing in the book. It is perhaps worth notice, as instancing the perfecting of Peacock's art, that it is only among his intimates that Dr. Folliott explodes about all this. To the itinerant commissioners he behaves with polite restraint. He is, in fact, a rounded character, and his foibles never take him beyond the bounds of good breeding or away from the gravity proper to his ministry. Even his attitude to the pleasures of the table is in every sense weighty. "The current of opinion," he says "sets in favour of Hock: but I am for Madeira; I do not fancy Hock till I have laid a substratum of Madeira." And there hovers in his mind the Platonic idea of a fish sauce that, could he but give it actuality, he would christen with the name of his college—thus handing down that college to posterity as a seat of learning indeed.

Peacock's final book, *Gryll Grange* (1861), is a work of old age. It has its novel facets, yet we shall be impatient with it if we are impatient at being rather lavishly offered the mixture as before. In Dr. Opimian there is a milder Dr. Folliott—but one still capable of saying much that is pertinent to us today. "Science is one thing and wisdom is another," he early remarks. "Science is an edged tool, with which men play like children, and cut their own fingers. . . . See how much belongs to the word Explosion alone. . . . I almost think it is the ultimate destiny of science to exterminate the human race."

Yet Dr. Opimian's philosophy is not exacting. "Whatever happens in this world," he advises a lovelorn young farmer, "never let it spoil your dinner"—and this advice he presently sharpens to "live in hope, but live on beef and ale." Generous in denunciation and reactionary in sentiment ("I have no wish," he says, "to expedite communication with the Americans"), he has yet concluded that there is more good than evil in the world. We are inclined to infer that this is Peacock's conclusion too—and it is scarcely one consonant with much fullness or sharpness of satire. The earlier novels are by a satirist who hangs his satire upon the peg of a love story for want of a better one; here the writer is an old man who likes to think that the young people about him are happy, and who is prompted to present prosperous courtship in rather more detail than hitherto. A good deal of it is tedious, but a little is fresh. Here, at the end of his life, very curiously, there is the ghost of a different sort of novelist haunting Peacock.

Miss Gryll, the squire's niece, has turned down many suitors, and seems hard to please. When the narrative opens, it is upon a new candidate, Lord Curryfin, who is an adherent of the Broughamian Pantopragmatic Society—and who, we are told, "valued what he learned less for the pleasure which he derived from the acquisition, than from the effect which it enabled him to produce on others." Lord Curryfin's grand subject is fish, and he has been going around watering places giving lectures designed alike to please the visiting gentry and to instruct the local fishermen in their business. This is scarcely promising—indeed, it is clear that at the start Lord Curryfin is designed as a merely comic character. But Peacock seems to feel that he should at least be given a fair run for Miss Gryll's hand, and to effect this the young man must be granted a greater degree of eligibility than is represented simply by his being a lord. So he is promptly endowed with a considerable amount of good sense, and a disposition to laugh at pantopragmatics as a youthful folly put behind him. He remains a pantopragmatist in the eagerness with which he takes up whatever project comes along; and he becomes, among other things, the mainstay of the amateur theatrical activity running through the book.

Lord Curryfin's rival, Mr. Falconer, is the most freakish of all Peacock's heroes. Like the poet Yeats after him—but on a much larger scale—he has reedified a ruined tower. In this he lives with a household of seven young women—not gentlewomen, but having the accomplishments of gentlewomen—who minister to him in the solitary, meditative, and medievalizing life he has designed for himself. He has always placed the summum bonum of life in tranquillity, not in excitement, so it is unfortunate that Miss Gryll is one day stunned by lightning more or less at his front door, and has to remain for a considerable period in his house, nursed by the seven handmaidens. But it is only when Dr. Opimian marshals seven young farmers prepared to marry Mr. Falconer's entourage that the match becomes feasible. Even so, we cannot feel that Mr. Falconer's views on courtship are of a kind likely to please a nice girl. He soliloquizes:

"It would be more fitting, that whatever I may do should be done calmly, deliberately, philosophically, than suddenly, passionately, impulsively."

. . .

He dined at his usual hour, and his two Hebes alternately filled his own glass with Madeira.

(ch. 20)

Clearly we are meant to find this amusing. But, equally clearly, we are not meant to dismiss Mr. Falconer from our regard as a young man displeasingly deficient in radical masculinity. And we may conclude that Peacock has not made up his mind whether the kind of wooing here described is exemplary. Perhaps we may further conclude that here is a particular instance of something pervasive in Peacock. George Saintsbury speaks of his "noble disregard of apparent consistency" and of his "inveterate habit of pillar-to-post joking." If he is, in the last analysis, supreme as a creator of fun rather than of satire, it is because he is content or constrained to bear a divided mind before a good many important topics. Perhaps all his superficial dogmatism compensates for, as all his quick laughter masks, a fundamental uncertainty of response to life. Or perhaps this is to take too seriously the dissection of one of the most amusing of writers.

V

So much for the conversation novels that have made Peacock famous. *Maid Marian* (1822) and *The Misfortunes of Elphin* (1829) may be styled romantic tales, but they derive their flavor from that ambiguity in Peacock that we have just been considering. His life's work, as Humphry House pointed out, can be viewed as the critique of romanticism—yet in regard to the romantic idea he never quite finally knew where his heart lay. Thus, like any romantic from Thomas Gray onward he was enchanted by mountain scenery, and celebrated it in verse as being likely to conduce to elevated feeling. At the same time there was a detached Peacock (as there was a detached Coleridge) who perceived that this is moonshine; that human beings in the highlands are as indifferently honest as human beings in the lowlands; and that what makes for moderate decency is not the contemplation of falls and cataracts but the reading of "ancient books." (Coleridge says the same thing, but names the Bible.) Again, Peacock had nourished his historical imagination not only on the classics but also on Welsh legend and Italian poetry. He could read Walter Scott in the spirit of one accepting Edmund Spenser's image of antique times; equally he could attack Scott—as he makes Dr. Folliott attack him—as a mere master of pantomime and fancy dress. He thus had ready to hand either of the moralist's ways of exploiting the past. A "goodly image" can be held up as a touchstone in Spenser's fashion, and it can be maintained that the march of mind has simply resulted in dragging us far beneath it. On the other hand, by showing people of a remote age and superficial strangeness behaving with just the rascality of the present age, one can bring that rascality freshly home. *Maid Marian*, which is little more than an episodic rehandling of the Robin Hood stories, with much interspersed verse, owes most of what interest it possesses to a mingling of these methods. At the same time it has more popular appeal than anything else that Peacock wrote, and it had a long and successful history as an operetta.

The Misfortunes of Elphin, based upon Welsh legendary material, is a similar romantic narrative refracted through the medium now of a simply comic, and now of an ironic, temper. As in *Maid Marian*, there is much laughing satire at the expense of common and perennial human nature as these peep through ancient habiliments—the humor being sufficiently dry to sustain itself vis-à-vis events sometimes violent and brutal rather than funny in themselves. But there is also—at least in one early stretch of the book—a more specific satirical intent in which the quarry is one we have already seen hunted in *Melincourt*, when Sir Oran is elected for Onevote. The felicitousness of the attack on the decay of parliamentary institutions in *The Misfortunes of Elphin* lies partly in the way it takes us by surprise. We may be reminded of Milestone in *Headlong Hall* who distinguished the quality of unexpectedness as important in the laying out of grounds.

At the beginning of the sixth century, the kingdom of King Gwythno existed in a state of easy prosperity. Much of it, though, was protected from inundation only by a massy stone wall, the maintenance of which was vested in Prince Seithenyn as Lord High Commissioner of Royal Embankment. He executed his charge "as a personage so denominated might be expected to do: he drank the profits, and left the embankment to his deputies, who left it to their assistants, who left it to itself."

A conscientious official, Teithrin, draws the attention of the king's son Elphin to the danger. Together they visit Seithenyn and find him in the middle of a carouse; he is first introduced to us as roaring aloud: "You are welcome all four"; and in the ensuing interview he develops a defense of his neglect in terms of a fuddled logic that represents the acme of Peacock's achievement as a humorist:

"Decay", said Seithenyn, "is one thing, and danger is another. Everything that is old must decay. That the embankment is old, I am free to confess; that it is somewhat rotten in parts, I will not altogether deny: that it is any the worse for that, I do most sturdily gainsay. It does its business well: it works well: it keeps out the water from the land, and it lets in the wine upon the High Commission of Embankment. Cupbearer, fill. Our ancestors were wiser than we: they built it in their wisdom; and, if we should be so rash as to try to mend it, we should only mar it."

"The stonework", said Teithrin, "is sapped and mined: the piles are rotten, broken, and dislocated: the flood-gates and sluices are leaky and creaky."

"That is the beauty of it", said Seithenyn. "Some parts of it are rotten, and some parts of it are sound."

"It is well", said Elphin, "that some parts are sound: it were better that all were so."

"So I have heard some people say before", said Seithenyn; "perverse people, blind to venerable antiquity: that very unamiable sort of people who are in the habit of indulging their reason. But I say, the parts that are rotten give elasticity to those that are sound. . . . It is well: it works well: let well alone. Cup-bearer, fill. It was half rotten when I was born, and that is a conclusive reason why it should be three parts rotten when I die."

(ch. 2)

This is very funny in itself. But the point of the satire is that statesmen were really talking much as Seithenyn talks, and Peacock is contriving to follow quite closely actual speeches made in opposition to current proposals for electoral reform.

VI

FINALLY, we may consider two of Peacock's nonfictional works. *The Four Ages of Poetry* (1820) is commonly said to owe its celebrity to its having provoked the writing of Shelley's famous *Defence of Poetry*; otherwise, it would remain in the obscurity attending the small body of Peacock's other minor and occasional writings. Clearly, it is not wholly serious. Indeed, like Maurice Morgann's essay on Falstaff, it is best regarded as a kind of poker-faced joke. But it differs from Morgann's essay in not being disinterested. Peacock has an axe to grind:

Mr. Scott digs up the poachers and cattle-stealers of the ancient border. Lord Byron cruises for thieves and pirates on the shores of the Morea and among the Greek Islands. Mr. Southey wades through ponderous volumes of travels and old chronicles, from which he carefully selects all that is false, useless, and absurd, as being essentially poetical; and when he has a common-place book full of monstrosities, strings them into an epic. Mr. Wordsworth picks up village legends from old women . . . .

(vol. VIII, p. 70: *The Four Ages of Poetry*)

Judged as a critical thesis, *The Four Ages of Poetry* is merely a concoction for the purpose of depreciating what it calls "that egregious confraternity of rhymesters, known by the name of the Lake Poets," and some others as well. Shelley cannot have been worried by all this. Nor can he have failed to see that the general trend of the piece is ironical, so that what

Peacock intends is a defense of true poetry. But Shelley was presumably sensitive to the ambiguity that we have remarked as fundamental to his friend's mind. The cyclic view of poetry propounded in the essay has very little substance. But there lurks in it—ready to take what weight we please—an argument drawing upon Locke and upon the empirical and utilitarian traditions that followed him: the argument that, in an age of advancing science, the poetic activity must be progressively circumscribed and finally wither away. It was this that roused Shelley and produced his finest venture into prose.

But Shelley might never have been aware of *The Four Ages of Poetry*—and *A Defence of Poetry*, in consequence, might never have been written—had Peacock not been his friend. To that friendship the principal memorial is the "Memoirs of Percy Bysshe Shelley," written forty years after the poet's death and made up of four separate contributions, variously occasioned, to *Fraser's* magazine between 1858 and 1862. The first begins with a certain amount of high-minded reluctance to write about the personal life of Shelley at all. There is no doubt that Peacock sincerely detested the sort of public tittle-tattle on the strength of private intimacy that he castigates in *Crotchet Castle* in the character of Mr. Eavesdrop. And his handling of the central point of scandal in Shelley's life is guarded as well as judicious. But when he comes to give his own reminiscences, he knows that a superb portrait is within his power, and the temptation is one that he is unable to resist. It would be quite wrong, though, to suggest that he sets the novelist in himself to work. The salient feature of his account is its avoidance of any exaggeration or heightening of effect. Much of it is extremely amusing, but this effect is achieved entirely without travesty. The Shelley of the "Memoirs" is much madder than Scythrop Glowry is ever depicted as being. But he is at the same time quite real. And one gets a fresh view of the extraordinary tact that went to the creating of Scythrop when one has had a close look at the Shelley whom Peacock knew.

Far more than with Thomas Jefferson Hogg, Thomas Medwin, Edward Trelawny, or anybody else until the egregiously dull Edward Dowden, we have a feeling that Peacock is a reliable chronicler. When he tells us of Shelley's living "chiefly on tea and bread and butter, drinking occasionally a sort of spurious lemonade, made of some powder in a box," we may be confident that the spuriousness of the lemonade hasn't been invented by way of good measure. When Shelley, accepting Peacock's prescription, changes his diet to "three mutton chops, well peppered" and Peacock declares "the success was obvious and immediate," we need have no hesitation in believing that it was so. And this holds, too, for his rather astonishing account of Shelley's delusions. This is the best part of the "Memoirs"—not so much because of its bizarre character as because of the perfection of tone with which the amusing, yet ominous, spectacle is presented. Reading the account of the mysterious incident of Williams in 1816, we may be disposed to doubt whether the maintenance of a cool and rational skepticism was as therapeutic as Peacock in his psychiatric innocence believed. But we cannot doubt that here, after a long interval of years, is one of the most consummate pieces of reporting in the language. Peacock is one of our greatest creators of the fantastic. And here was the fantastic created for him by God. It is wonderful that he felt no challenge, that he humbly and so perfectly re-created the thing in itself, forty years later.

SELECTED BIBLIOGRAPHY

I. Collected Editions. H. Cole, ed., *The Works*, 3 vols. (London, 1875); R. Garnett, ed., *Novels, Calidore, and Miscellanea*, 10 vols. (London, 1891); G. Saintsbury, ed., *Novels and Rhododaphne*, 5 vols. (London, 1895–1897); R. B. Johnson, ed., *Poems* (London, 1906), in the Muses' Library; A. B. Young, ed., *Plays* (London, 1910); H. F. B. Brett-Smith and C. E. Jones, eds., *The Works*, 10 vols. (London, 1924–1934), the definitive Halliford ed., with a biographical intro. superseding previous studies, and full bibliographical and textual notes; D. Garnett, ed., *The Novels* (London, 1948).

II. Selections. H. F. B. Brett-Smith, ed., *Selections* (London, 1928); B. R. Redman, ed., *The Pleasures of Peacock* (New York, 1948); H. L. B. Moody, ed., *A Peacock Selection* (London–New York, 1966).

III. Separate Works. *The Monks of St. Mark* (London, 1804), verse; *Palmyra, and Other Poems* (London, 1806); *The Genius of the Thames. A Lyrical Poem in Two Parts* (London, 1810), the 1812 ed. includes *Palmyra, and Other Poems* and two additional poems; *The Philosophy of Melancholy* (London, 1812), verse; *Sir Hornbook: or, Childe Launcelot's Expedition. A Grammatico-Allegorical Ballad* (London, 1814); *Sir Proteus, a Satirical Ballad* (London, 1814), written under the pseudonym P. M. Donovan; *Headlong Hall* (London, 1816), novel, with a new preface and with three other novels by Peacock in Bentley's Standard Novels series (London, 1837); *Melincourt*, 3 vols. (London, 1817), novel; *The Round Table, or, King Arthur's Feast* (London, [1817]), verse; *Nightmare Abbey* (London, 1818), novel; *Rhododaphne: Or the Thessalian Spell* (London, 1818), verse; *The Four Ages of Poetry* (London, 1820), criticism, also in H. F. B. Brett-Smith, ed. (Oxford, 1921), the Percy Reprints series; *Maid Marian* (London, 1822), novel; *The Misfortunes of Elphin* (London, 1829), novel; *Crotchet Castle* (London, 1831), novel; *Paper Money Lyrics, and Other Poems* (London, 1837), privately printed; "Memoirs of Percy Bysshe Shelley," in *Fraser's*, 4 pts. (July 1858, Jan. 1860, Mar. 1860, Mar. 1862), H. F. B. Brett-Smith, ed., with Shelley's letters to Peacock (London, 1909), see also Carl H. Pforzheimer Library, *Shelley and His Circle* (Cambridge, Mass., 1961); *Gryll Grange* (London, 1861), novel; *Ingannati: The Deceived. A Comedy Performed at Siena in 1531: and Aelia Laelia Crispis* (London, 1862), drama; *A Bill for the Better Promotion of Oppression on the Sabbath Day* (London, 1926), verse, privately printed; R. Wright, ed., *Nightmare Abbey* and *Crotchet Castle* (Harmondsworth, 1969), with an intro.

IV. Biographical and Critical Studies. A. M. Freeman, *Thomas Love Peacock. A Critical Study* (London, 1911); C. Van Doren, *The Life of Thomas Love Peacock* (London, 1911); J. B. Priestley, *Thomas Love Peacock* (London, 1927), in the English Men of Letters series; A. H. Able, *Meredith and Peacock. A Study in Literary Influence* (Philadelphia, 1933); O. W. Campbell, *Peacock* (London, 1953); H. Mills, *Peacock. His Circle and His Age* (Cambridge, 1968); C. Dawson, *Peacock: A Study of His Fine Wit* (London, 1970); L. Sage, ed., *Peacock—The Satirical Novels: A Casebook* (London, 1976); M. Butler, *Peacock Displayed: Satirist in His Context* (London, 1979).

GEORGE GORDON, LORD BYRON
(1788-1824)

Malcolm Kelsall

INTRODUCTION

GEORGE GORDON, LORD BYRON, was born on 22 January 1788, and died of fever on 19 April 1824, at Missolonghi, in Greece, where he had gone to fight for the patriot cause against Turkish imperialism. His life has exercised a magnetic attraction for generations of biographers. The personality is inextricably bound up with the poetry, and the confusion between the two was at times deliberately exploited by Byron, who posed as the real-life hero of his own romances. The sardonic misanthrope with a sublime imagination; or the guilty soul with a wellspring of scarcely concealed feeling: such characterizations in particular spoke to the nineteenth century of the essence of Byronism. The political and social rebel, the aristocratic outsider, the offspring of Satanism: these provide another nexus of Byronic ideas. More recently taste has responded rather to the comic than to the tragic aspects of the poet and his works. The wit, the good companion, the amiable, ill-used gentleman, "more sinned against than sinning," has emerged as a truer characterization both of the real man and of his personality as developed in his masterpiece *Don Juan* (1819–1824).

It is not a pertinent question to literary study to consider how far the poetry may be used as a key to the psychology of the man. But some knowledge of the man and the myth is required to understand the poetry because Byron utilized his experiences and reputation as the raw material for his creativity. He described his work at one time as the lava of the imagination, which implies that it was the uncontrolled outpouring of his mind. There are elements of symbolic suggestion and dark introspection in some of the poems that hint at inexplicable and uncoordinated self-revelation. But such elements are also common technical devices in much romantic art. They can be discussed in literary terms just as readily as narrative structure or verse form. Common sense indicates that no spontaneous eruption of the imagination ever found immediate utterance in verse. The following sketch of Byron's life, therefore, is an account of source material that the artist used.

Byron was not born the heir to a great title or a rich estate. The early years suggest more the origins of some picaro, the rogue hero of a novel by Henry Fielding, Tobias Smollett, or William Thackeray, rather than the English milord of European fame he was to become. His father, Captain John Byron, was a sexual adventurer, who, having run out of wives, money, and health, died in France in 1791 at the age of thirty-six. The infant Byron—lame from birth—was brought up in provincial obscurity in Aberdeen by a mother whom he found vulgar, and at the hands of servants and tutors who seem to have inducted him at early years to the gloom of Calvinistic Christianity and the dubious pleasures of premature sexuality.

At the age of ten he succeeded to the title of sixth Baron Byron of Rochdale and to an encumbered estate. Although he was to embark on the *cursus honorum* (career ladder) of the great—Harrow School; Trinity College, Cambridge; the House of Lords—there is at no time about him that complacent security of expectation not to be disappointed that characterizes many of the British ruling class. He was a parvenu, an upstart, "born for opposition." His first literary success was *English Bards and Scotch Reviewers* (1809), which is in the satiric tradition of Pope and the Latin poet Juvenal, poets who attacked society from without. The ultimate cantos of the uncompleted *Don Juan* castigate the British "establishment" from a personal position of exile, and in narrative terms, through the introduction of a hero who belongs to no social order: a Byronic alter ego, the wandering figure of "Donny Jonny."

Byron's grand tour of 1809–1811 took him through Portugal, Spain, Greece, and Turkey. It was a usual part of a gentleman's education, but it may also be seen as an act of symbolic liberation and exile rather than one fitting him for a patrician destiny in the classic way by the study of men, manners, and government. His meeting with the warlord Ali Pasha may have provided him with the inspiration for the heroes of his romances; the traditions and culture of the Mediterranean peoples fertilized his imagination for the rest of his life; his admiration for the ideal liberties of Greece found culminative expression in his death. His literary reputation was established by the works deriving from this tour: *Childe Harold's Pilgrimage* (cantos I and II, 1812) and the Turkish tales: *The Giaour* (1813); *The Bride of Abydos* (1813); *The Corsair* (1814); *Lara* (1814); and *The Siege of Corinth* (1816).

On his return to England, he found himself instantly famous. But fame as a writer was not the pathway to success associated with a lord. A great man of state might be an amateur of letters or a connoisseur of the arts, but he would not be a professional literary man like Pope, the son of a linen draper, or Johnson, a bookseller's son. For a time Byron affected to be in the Restoration tradition of "the mob of gentlemen who writ with ease"; he refused, initially, payment for his work, and looked, in vain, for a role in politics or in military adventure, which would be a more appropriate field of endeavor for a great man. He became acquainted with the leaders of the Whigs and spoke three times in the House of Lords in the service of that party, attacking the repressive measures of the Tories against industrial unrest and speaking in favor of Catholic emancipation and some degree of parliamentary reform. His later association with movements for national self-determination in Europe—the Carbonari in Italy and the insurrectionists in Greece—represents a practical extension of Whig politics into military action.

One result of this patrician tradition was to lead Byron sometimes to write carelessly and to devalue the craft of the "scribbler." He has none of the sustained sense of a dedicated spirit called to a high, prophetic mission we find in his contemporary Wordsworth or his friend Shelley. Yet his very hastiness and prolixity seem to have prepared the way for the emergence of his mature style from *Beppo* (1818) onward. The sequence of great comic poems, *The Vision of Judgment* (1822) and the sixteen cantos of *Don Juan*, remind one of *The Canterbury Tales*. The verse bears the impress of a speaking voice, a brilliant conversationalist and anecdotal narrator, a strong and experienced personality.

The reasons for Byron's permanent departure from England in 1816 are too complex psychologically to be guessed at. Simple practical reasons were debts and sexual scandal. England was too expensive for an impoverished lord, though later he set himself up financially by cheap living in Italy, parsimony, and payment, now accepted, for his writing. The sexual scandals have provided endless speculative fascination. On 2 January he had married Anne Isabella Milbanke, a prude, but loved his half sister Augusta Leigh. He may have had sexual intercourse with her. Buggery may have added variety to the marriage bed. The salacious gossip of his ex-mistress, Lady Caroline Lamb, who may not have been sane, poured oil on the flames. There are those who have read Byron's metaphysical tragedy *Manfred* (1817) as a confession to all Europe of incestuous passion.

He traveled through Germany and Switzerland to Italy, completing a third canto of *Childe Harold* (1816) and a fourth (1818). He had settled for a while at Lake Geneva with Shelley and Shelley's wife Mary (the daughter of William Godwin, the political philosopher), and a certain Claire Clairmont, Godwin's stepdaughter, who bore Byron a child, Allegra. Through Shelley he was exposed both to the metaphysical ideas of romanticism and a more radical political philosophy than would have been practical for the Whig party in London. Later, in Pisa, the conjunction of Leigh Hunt with Byron's entourage was to lead to an abortive venture into political journalism, the *Liberal* (1822–1823); but the death by drowning of Shelley, in 1822, removed an important catalyst. Byron, in any case, was shortly to turn his mind to Greece.

Byron's years in Italy are dull biographically. There was a period of sexual debauchery in Venice and a long period as *cavalier servente* (publicly accepted lover) to another man's wife, the prettily pedestrian Teresa Guiccioli. The Austrian police kept him under surveillance, but the nationalist secret society, the Carbonari, had neither the means nor the will to fight a war of liberation. Yet, in the period from 1818 onward, Byron produced what are now regarded as his comic masterworks: *Beppo, The Vision of Judgment,* and *Don Juan.* Enforced idleness, maturing years, a more assured social role in a tolerant society, a stable and undemanding sexual liaison with an agreeable woman, even "emotion recollected in tranquillity": these factors may have contributed to the development of his technique. In the later poems he frequently plays with the roles adopted in his earlier verses and his reputation or notoriety. Like the novels of Marcel Proust, these works go searching back into lost time, and in *Don Juan* he takes as one of his major motifs the waste and flight of years.

The embarkation for Greece in 1823, like the self-imposed exile of 1816, may be seen as a symbolic act. Eighteen-sixteen is the rejection of the insularity of English society; 1823 is the finding, at last, of a European role: as philhellene and champion of liberty. It is also recognized in the poetry that death would be welcome (though not by his shrewd and practical letters). To die for Greece would be to confirm a role that life denied. But the reality of the situation lacked all romance. The "patriots," Alexander Mavrokordatos, Odysseus Androutsos, and the rest, were divided against themselves. The Greek committee in London, on which Byron's friend John Cam Hobhouse served, at first dispatched a printing press to aid a cause that needed munitions. Byron himself never saw battle. He caught a fever, and died under the hands of his doctors in wretched circumstances. As a cynic he would have appreciated the irony of his fate. It is typical of the many situations in *Don Juan* that devalue human endeavor and pride. Yet the romantic side of his character longed for fame, and by dying he secured idealization as a hero and martyr. His reputation as a great man has been confirmed by posterity. Nothing is more typical of the man and artist than that the same act may be seen in terms of the grotesque and of the highest valor, an example of the vanity of human wishes, and of the power of the human imagination to strive, to seek, to find, and not to yield.

THE TURKISH TALES

BYRON's Turkish tales enjoyed a popular success. The versification is facile; the settings exotic; the staple fare the ever popular ingredients of sex and violence; the protagonists a stagy assortment of Byronic heroes, Gothic-satanical, sentimental-piratical. *Parisina* (1816), *Mazeppa* (1819), and *The Island* (1823) are later exercises more or less in the same mode but with different settings.

Beneath the racy sentimental melodrama there are suggestions of mythic ideas struggling for some form of representation. The poems have been seen as reiterative treatments of the theme of "the misery and lostness of man, the eternal death of love, and

the repetitive ruin of paradise" (R. F. Gleckner, *Byron and the Ruins of Paradise*). If this is so, then the subject finds a more appropriate treatment in the metaphysical and symbolic dramas *Manfred* (1817) and *Cain* (1821). The romances carry strong political overtones also, not only to the oppression of Greece but also to matters nearer home. The dedication of *The Corsair* expresses strong sentiments about the "wrongs" of Ireland, and it is easy to read into *Lara* echoes of the French Revolution. The impact of these slight poems upon European romanticism enhances the suggestion that important themes blend with naive matter. The imaginative ideas were reworked by Hector Berlioz and Eugène Delacroix. The Byronic hero was naturalized on the Yorkshire moors in the figure of Emily Brontë's Heathcliff. Byron himself plundered these early poems. *Don Juan* would not have its present form without the heroes of the Turkish romances to change and burlesque.

Sir Walter Scott wrote of the Byronic hero:

almost all, have minds which seem at variance with their fortunes, and exhibit high and poignant feelings of pain and pleasure; a keen sense of what is noble and honourable; and an equally keen susceptibility of injustice or injury, under the garb of stoicism or contempt of mankind. The strength of early passion, and the glow of youthful feeling, are uniformly painted as chilled or subdued by a train of early imprudences or of darker guilt, and the sense of enjoyment tarnished, by too intimate an acquaintance with the vanity of human wishes.

(cited in Byron's *Works* [1833], x.24)

The literary origins of this figure have been traced by P. L. Thorslev, Jr., in *The Byronic Hero: Types and Prototypes* and precisely analyzed in their various manifestations. The villain-hero of Elizabethan and Jacobean drama, John Milton's Satan, Friedrich von Schiller's *The Robbers* (*Die Räuber*) (1781), William Godwin's *Caleb Williams* (1794), Ann Radcliffe's *The Italian* (1797), the cult of sensibility—one may track the origins of the figure everywhere. But the effect in the earliest of the Turkish tales of the first appearance of Byron's Giaour (infidel) defies sober analysis. To respond to the verse is to yield to a wild intoxication:

Who thundering comes on blackest steed,
With slackened bit and hoof of speed?
Beneath the clattering iron's sound
The caverned Echoes wake around
In lash for lash, and bound for bound;
The foam that streaks the courser's side

Seems gathered from the Ocean-tide:
Though weary waves are sunk to rest,
There's none within his rider's breast;
And though to-morrow's tempest lower,
'Tis calmer than thy heart, young Giaour!
I know thee not, I loathe thy race,
But in thy lineaments I trace
What Time shall strengthen, not efface:
Though young and pale, that sallow front
Is scathed by fiery Passion's brunt;
Though bent on earth thine evil eye,
As meteor-like thou glidest by,
Right well I view and deem thee one
Whom Othman's sons should slay or shun.[1]

(180–199)

The speaker is a Turkish fisherman. The character is unimportant in himself, but the device enables Byron to enhance the mystery of the galloping figure by telling the tale in fragments of an onlooker's discourse: we have to guess at what has happened and what the characters feel. Equally important is the removal of the moral viewpoint outside Christendom. It is the European who is the infidel, and it is his romantic moral code of love that, in the Turkish setting, precipitates the tragedy. The passionate force of love is normally destructive in Byron, and the Byronic hero is already a prey to the canker of remorse, which neither revenge nor repentance will alleviate. The associative force of the trains of imagery enhance the significance of the figure. The image of the unbridled horse as symbolic of the danger of passion is one of the oldest European archetypes; the blackness of the steed suggests the powers of night, death, and the devil. The echoes that wake "beneath" the steed's "iron" hooves are "caverned," thus suggesting an affinity with the underworld, while "iron" is traditionally the metal associated with the worst of the seven ages of the world. The imagery then reaches out to embrace more elemental forces: ocean, tempest, meteor. Perhaps these are too easily conventional to be fully effective, but the words suggest that the infidel passions are eternally part both of the human psyche and the nature of things. Less commonplace in the portrayal may be the expression "What Time shall strengthen, not efface." Time cannot heal, repentance will not reform. Like Godwin's Falkland, Byron's Giaour corrodes inwardly with his crime. In

[1]All quotations from Byron's poems are from E. H. Coleridge, ed., *The Poetical Works* (London, 1905).

the monastery where ultimately he seeks refuge, he seems at times like Satan, at times like a vampire: one of those who, though dead, cannot die.

Although it would be absurd to seek to read too much into stories that never pretend to naturalism and are exotic and sensational in action and description, nonetheless the effectiveness of art does not always depend either on truth or craft. The mind feeds upon romance and delights in liberated images of other selves. Compare with the dark image of the Giaour the hero of *The Bride of Abydos* (1813), young Selim, about to die fighting for love against tyranny:

His robe of pride was thrown aside,
    His brow no high-crowned turban bore,
But in its stead a shawl of red,
    Wreathed lightly round, his temples wore:
That dagger, on whose hilt the gem
Were worthy of a diadem,
No longer glittered at his waist,
Where pistols unadorned were braced;
And from his belt a sabre swung,
And from his shoulder loosely hung
The cloak of white, the thin capote
That decks the wandering Candiote;
Beneath—his golden plated vest
Clung like a cuirass to his breast;
The greaves below his knee that wound
With silvery scales were sheathed and bound.
But were it not that high command
Spake in his eye, and tone, and hand,
All that a careless eye could see
In him was some young Galiongée.

(613–632)

Such an image suggests Lawrence of Arabia. The combination of youth, rebellion, simplicity, and exoticism is erotic. That erotic element I find ambivalent, combining the heterosexual and homosexual. Both qualities have been seen as present in Byron; his readers confused the man and his verse; many women were as ready to prostitute themselves to their image of the poet as the heroines of the poems adore with bovine submission their sexual masters. The image of Selim is potentially complex and disturbing.

The element of sexual politics implicit in this kind of character has been little examined. Yet the heroes of the romances are generally both lovers and rebels. Selim is the least corrupted of these figures because he is most justified. His father has been murdered.

He has come to carry away from an oppressor the woman he loves. The typical political situation of the poems is that the evils of despotism produce criminals or outlaws but that crime, though not condoned, is less wicked, less hypocritical, than the society which produces it. Such an argument is political dynamite, and if such were Byron's serious view, it was a subject that could be safely treated only in a remote setting and romantic form. Only *Lara* begins to come close to home when the serfs, rebelling against feudalism, take up the cry that they "dig no land for tyrants but their graves."

Yet Byron's robber chiefs are themselves as tyrannical as the forces they oppose. Young Selim's eye speaks "high command." So too does his hand. War is his medium. Force meets force destructively. The *Führerprinzip* (authoritarian principle) is most clearly obvious in *The Corsair*. "I form the plan, divide the spoil," he comments; "And all obey, and few enquire his will." His other self in *Lara* is always the "chieftain" of his serfs. When Selim's pirate band considers "equal rights, which man ne'er knew," he dismisses this talk as "prate," and cries, "I have a love for freedom too." For the Byronic hero freedom is the exercise of his will, and, in a sense, the existence of an opposing will is welcome, because it provides a force against which the hero may exercise himself. To the rebel leader men, militarily, and women, sexually, submit voluntarily. It is this voluntariness that distinguishes Selim or Conrad from tyrants. Their symbolic garb as common men appeals to democratic forces, but men know their masters even in the guise of a galiongee (Turkish sailor).

The outcome for the leader and his men is disastrous. At times Byron is moralistic about the evils of rebellion:

> And they that smote for freedom or for sway,
> Deemed few were slain, while more remained to slay.
> It was too late to check the wasting brand,
> And Desolation reaped the famished land;
> The torch was lighted, and the flame was spread,
> And Carnage smiled upon her daily dead.
>
> (*Lara*, 921–926)

Such Augustan sententiousness is not what the world recognized as Byronic. It is the fateful dash upon the reef of disaster—better to expire in a storm than rot in the torpor of stagnation—or the sentimental gesture at the critical instant, when blood and cunning were the only ways to success: these are the ways in which Byronic heroes are destroyed. Yet that destruction, paradoxically, is symbolic of the very freedom of the spirit to take what path it will. The pirate, free to wander over the tempestuous sea as his feelings direct, is the reiterated symbol. The beginning of *The Corsair*, though imaginatively far from the most exciting passage of the romances, provides a clear enunciation of the motif:

> O'er the glad waters of the dark blue sea,
> Our thoughts as boundless, and our souls as free,
> Far as the breeze can bear, the billows foam,
> Survey our empire, and behold our home!
> These are our realms, no limits to their sway—
> Our flag the sceptre all who meet obey.
> Ours the wild life in tumult still to range
> From toil to rest, and joy in every change.
> Oh, who can tell? not thou, luxurious slave!
> Whose soul would sicken o'er the heaving wave;
> Not thou, vain lord of Wantonness and Ease!
> Whom Slumber soothes not—Pleasure cannot please—
> Oh, who can tell, save he whose heart hath tried,
> And danced in triumph o'er the waters wide,
> The exulting sense—the pulse's maddening play,
> That thrills the wanderer of that trackless way?
> That for itself can woo the approaching fight,
> And turn what some deem danger to delight;
> That seeks what cravens shun with more than zeal,
> And where the feebler faint can only feel—
> Feel—to the rising bosom's inmost core,
> Its hope awaken and its spirit soar?
> No dread of Death—if with us die our foes—
> Save that it seems even duller than repose;
> Come when it will—we snatch the life of Life—
> When lost—what recks it by disease or strife?
>
> (1–26)

CHILDE HAROLD'S PILGRIMAGE III AND IV

BYRON initially describes Harold as "the wandering outlaw of his own dark mind." The image relates him, therefore, to the pirate or brigand heroes of the romances. As with *The Corsair* the sea is an important defining motif. The third canto of the pilgrimage opens with the poet upon the ocean, and a grammatical solecism confuses the speaker with the natural element: "Awaking with a start,/The waters heave around me." The fourth canto concludes with the invocation: "Roll on, thou deep and dark blue Ocean —roll!" For the corsairs, the sea was the place where they found freedom; the danger of their condition was the very stimulus of pleasure by which they "snatch the life of life"; "the wanderer of that trackless way" thrills to the exultation of his endless movement; energy is eternal delight. Harold, on the other hand, is the victim of that pessimistic weariness of life to which German romanticism has given the name *Weltschmerz*. He is upon the sea because society has exiled him, and he in turn has rejected the world to wrap himself in his own proud solitude, his sense of alienation, grief, and wrong. The waters are an emblem of trackless wandering—"I am as a weed, /Flung from the rock" (III.ii)—and he is hence the victim of circumstance rather than the master of his fate. At the end of the fourth canto the ocean is seen as "The image of Eternity" that subsumes all human endeavor and hence forever reminds the man of philosophical sensibility that all is vanity.

In these cantos the poet has chosen all the darker and more passive elements of the Byronic hero—his solitude, gloom, remorse, and excessive parade of feeling—and adopted them as his own. Hamlet brooding over a skull would be an appropriate emblem (and Byron's skull-cup is notorious). The dramatic being of Harold is of little importance. In the prentice work of the first two cantos the poet had attempted in vain to create a separate protagonist, but now the evocation "Long absent HAROLD reappears at last" is a mere ritual gesture. All pretense at distinguishing narrator from narrative persona soon dissolves. The cantos are Byron's journal of his physical and spiritual pilgrimage to the eternal city of Rome. This is, for him, *not* an emblem of a life and empire continuing to the end of time but a perpetual memento mori, a reminder of death and decay in which his blighted spirit may stand "a ruin among ruins."

There are obvious dangers in Byron's decision to adopt as his own, characteristics of romantic heroes who belong only in exotic fantasy. Fact and psychological fiction become strangely entwined. Much of the verse has a melodramatic and histrionic tone, and the ejaculations of feeling are often perilously close to rant. Yet this declamatory oratory has an extraordinary and insistent force that batters the sensibility:

There are some feelings Time can not benumb,
Nor Torture shake, or mine would now be cold and dumb.

But from their nature will the Tannen grow
   Loftiest on loftiest and least sheltered rocks,

Rooted in barrenness, where nought below
Of soil supports them 'gainst the Alpine shocks
Of eddying storms; yet springs the trunk, and mocks
The howling tempest, till its height and frame
Are worthy of the mountains from whose blocks
Of bleak, gray granite into life it came,
And grew a giant tree;—the Mind may grow the same.

Existence may be borne, and the deep root
   Of life and sufferance make its firm abode
In bare and desolated bosoms: mute
The camel labours with the heaviest load,
And the wolf dies in silence—not bestowed
In vain should such example be; if they,
Things of ignoble or of savage mood,
Endure and shrink not, we of nobler clay
May temper it to bear,—it is but for a day.

(IV.xix–xxi)

The sentiments are in the noblest tradition of European philosophy: the Stoic. The image of the wolf dying in silence was to inspire one of the finest of Alfred de Vigny's poems. Psychologically the fascination of the lines lies in the paradoxical struggle between feeling and "apathy" ($\dot{\alpha}\pi\dot{\alpha}\theta E\iota\alpha$); between the deep-seated human need to communicate and the ideal of that integrity which expresses itself in silence. Poetically the images suggest rich ambiguities. The invocation of the power of the mind to overcome "Time" and "Torture" suggests the sufferings of Prometheus and hence Titanic or Satanic rebellion or punishment, now seen, through the Alpine imagery, like a force in nature. This has rich mythic potential and may well have been inspirational for Shelley's *Prometheus Unbound* (1820). The use of the wolf as an emblem to raise the aspiration of the human mind is unusual, a beast of prey suggesting, in human terms, a figure like the Giaour or Conrad. Conversely, the comparison of social utility with the ignoble camel in some measure devalues the mundane with backhanded praise. The Stoic tradition in which Byron writes, therefore, is changed both under the pressures of acute personal sensibility and subtle poetic imagery.

The poet, throughout *Childe Harold*, is seeking to transform his own condition into some mythical representation of the eternal suffering of the human mind. At times, looking back into that Calvinistic tradition in which he was reared, he describes unhappiness as arising from the "uneradicable taint" of "sin"; or, in more modern and Freudian terms, he calls the mind "sick" and sees its disease arising from the alienation of man: "Our life is a false nature—'tis not in/ The harmony of things" (IV.cxxiv–cxxvi). These ideas are more centrally Byronic than the poet's occasional excursions into nature mysticism by way of consolation, especially in canto III, which are bastard Wordsworthianisms arising from Shelley's influence.

This pessimism is profoundly disturbing if true, yet its universal force is continually vitiated by the poet's posing like the protagonist of one of his own romances. He presents himself as immensely suffering from some dark secret—which *cannot* be told, he repeatedly *tells*—and he parades the scowl of nervous anguish as the badge of courage:

> But I have lived, and have not lived in vain:
> My mind may lose its force, my blood its fire,
> And my frame perish even in conquering pain;
> But there is that within me which shall tire
> Torture and Time, and breathe when I expire. . . .
> (IV.cxxxvii)

The "there is that within me" is no more specified than the "some feelings" of the earlier passage quoted. Again the ambiguous Titanic image is repeated, though now this figure, we shall be told, will move "In hearts all rocky now the late remorse of Love." This vague self-dramatizing utterance and self-pity have, in fact, a simple and mundane cause: Byron had quarreled with his wife. Should this be recalled, for instance as Thomas Peacock recalled it in *Nightmare Abbey*, it is difficult not to reject the grandiose pretensions of Byronism on the commonsense ground that the subject and the sentiments are ludicrously disproportionate. Shelley moved the matter into myth with Prometheus, and Byron was to explore something of the same line of development. In the metaphysical speculations of *Manfred* we find suggestions of the monstrous crime of incest, and in *Cain* there is overt Satanic speculation. Byron exploited these matters to add a heightened dramatic dimension to his tempest-riven mind. A domestic quarrel between a man and his wife is not large enough motivation for a poet to become the Titanic hero of his own poetry. There must be some great crime, the feelings must be intenser, the dark intellectual vision more daring. Byron will pile Pelion upon Ossa until suddenly the sublime topples into the ridiculous and he emerges with the domestic comedy of *Beppo*.

Granted these limitations in *Childe Harold*, cantos III and IV, nonetheless the oratorical vigor of utterance is united with an extraordinary synthesizing power of the imagination to interpret natural or artistic scene, present or historical character or event, in terms of the sensibility of the narrator, and yet always to find new variations upon the poem's themes. One of the usual "purple" passages may readily provide an example. The stanzas inspired by the statue of the dying gladiator follow shortly after the lines quoted above, which ended with a reference to "the late remorse of Love":

> I see before me the Gladiator lie:
>   He leans upon his hand—his manly brow
>   Consents to death, but conquers agony,
>   And his drooped head sinks gradually low—
>   And through his side the last drops, ebbing slow
> From the red gash, fall heavy, one by one,
>   Like the first of a thunder-shower; and now
>   The arena swims around him—he is gone,
> Ere ceased the inhuman shout which hailed the wretch
>   who won.
>
> He heard it, but he heeded not—his eyes
>   Were with his heart—and that was far away;
>   He recked not of the life he lost nor prize,
>   But where his rude hut by the Danube lay—
>   *There* were his young barbarians all at play,
>   *There* was their Dacian mother—he, their sire,
>   Butchered to make a Roman holiday—
>   All this rushed with his blood—Shall he expire
> And unavenged?—Arise! ye Goths, and glut your ire!
>   (IV.cxl–cxli)

The gladiator is another Byronic hero. The phrase "Consents to death, but conquers agony" goes straight to the heartland of Stoic tradition and is memorably terse. At the same time he is a man of feeling who recalls his children and his wife as he dies. So Byron in exile had recalled both his wife and daughter at the inception of the third canto. In a sense the poet has been butchered in reputation to make entertainment in England, just as the gladiator has been killed to amuse the Romans. Yet from these personal correlations a truth of more general importance arises, the more effective because of the poet's empathy with his subject. The gladiator is a type of all colonial peoples oppressed by imperialism. The scene arouses both pity and indignation as imagery and expectation are subtly modulated. After the lines on children and mother one might expect tears to "rush," but it is blood instead, and the expression "rushed with his blood" is used in two senses: to describe the literal death of the man but also with the usual metaphorical implication of the expression, a surge of angry emotion. That blood, earlier, had been described as falling like the first drops of a thundershower, proleptic thus of a storm to come: the storm of anger and of retribution on imperial Rome. Hence the cry to the barbarians: "Shall he expire/And unavenged?—Arise!" One need only compare Byron upon the gladiator's statue with Keats on the Grecian urn to appreciate the immeasurably greater kinetic energy of Byronism, despite whatever way one might judge the two poets' diverse verbal skills.

Yet the call to liberty is strangely placed within the structure of the poem. It follows on the passage ending with the expression of "the late remorse of Love" and leads into a meditation on the Coliseum that takes as its theme that all is vanity, and the ruins reecho with a sense of universal void (IV.cxlii–cxlv). The poem, therefore, is always modulating, tending to modify or even to contradict its own sentiments: love or hate, silence or impassioned utterance, universal vanity or passionate concern for human wrongs, selfhood or general typology. This complexity, or contradiction, is intrinsic in the poem's lack of structural principle. It flows in open-ended form on the stream of the poet's own life. Blake claimed that without contraries there is no progression, but he was a system builder, while we shall find that the essence of Byronism, as it comes to maturity, is to deny all system. One might rephrase Blake's aphorism for Byron: without contraries there is no life. Stasis is death.

It is difficult to illustrate without disproportionately long quotation. Consider another famous sequence, that on the battle of Waterloo, beginning III.xvii and ending perhaps around stanza xlv. The modulations here are continual from the confident eighteenth-century generalities of the lines "There was a sound of revelry by night" (xxi) to the personalized, even psychotic, introspection of the description of the broken heart like a mirror, "The same—and still the more, the more it breaks" (xxxiii); from the excitement of "And wild and high the 'Cameron's Gathering' rose!" (xxvi) to the bold gesture of the pathetic fallacy "Grieving, if aught inanimate e'er grieves,/Over the unreturning brave" (xxvii); the whole leading to the presentation of Napoleon as a real-life Byronic hero, a "Spirit antithetically mixed," greater, yet less than man, conqueror and captive, "sedate and all-enduring" whose "breath is agitation" and whose life a storm.

Byron condemned Wordsworth and his fellow "Lakers" for dabbling in a puddle while his own bark was driven over the ocean of eternity. It is a large claim, but the stanzas on Waterloo and Napoleon confront the major events of history in all their emotional complexity and endeavor to move from the local event to philosophical generality about the human condition. Local analysis is unjust because the part cannot be detached from the whole without interrupting the effect of the rhetorical flow; and verse that is conceived in terms of public oratory will not stand the rigorous scrutiny of petty detail.

> Their childrens' lips shall echo them, and say—
> "Here, where the sword united nations drew,
> Our countrymen were warring on that day!"
> (III.xxxv)

In lines like these, in a sequence such as this, Byron has broken free from the fictional stance of the Byronic hero to find, in history, an objective subject and a European voice and audience. It is a development that was to lead to the great passages of public commentary in the dedication of *Don Juan* and in *The Vision of Judgment*. That is a matter more readily seen in retrospect than apparent at the time. But the compulsive attraction for Byron of the Byronic hero as an alter ego was still strong, as the plays *Manfred* (1817) and *Cain* (1821) show.

THE PLAYS: MANFRED *AND* CAIN

Byron's interest in the drama was consistent. He had joined the management committee of the Drury Lane Theatre in 1815; he was the friend of Richard Brinsley Sheridan; his poems and letters are thickly sown with quotations from playwrights. His own dramas are of two main kinds: historical tragedies written on neoclassical principles such as *Marino Faliero* (1821), *Sardanapalus* (1821), and *The Two Foscari* (1821); and metaphysical fantasies such as *Manfred*, *Cain*, and *Heaven and Earth* (1823). None of the plays was written for performance, although in the historical dramas Byron wished to set an example to the times of the traditional virtues of seriousness and truth in subject, unity of time and place in structure. Certain Byronic themes reemerge in different form.

Sardanapalus attacks imperialistic tyranny through a hero usually condemned by history as a swinish sensualist and whose tragic fault, when he commits himself to necessary violence, is an excess of sentimental kindness for his enemies. *Marino Faliero* shows an aristocratic hero conspiring against a corrupt oligarchy. The treatment of the themes demonstrates little practical command of stagecraft in word or action, and the pieces inspired little theatrical interest.

The position of the two major metaphysical plays is different. *Cain* provoked the greatest intellectual scandal of Byron's career, and the amount of controversy that gathered around the piece has required major critical and editorial attention, notably Truman Guy Steffan's edition (1968) for the University of Texas. It has also attracted the interest of major practical craftsmen. The Moscow Art Theater and Jerzy Grotowski's Theatre Laboratory have both produced the play in this century because of the modernism of its theme and its symbolic form. *Manfred* achieved a respectable place in the nineteenth-century repertory because of its potentialities for "total theater," blending spectacle, music, and dance with the action. The boldness of its conception suggests analogies with Ibsen's *Peer Gynt*. By writing for a theater of the imagination, Byron helped, paradoxically, to enlarge the capabilities of the real stage.

Manfred has analogies with the first part of Goethe's *Faust*, which Byron knew through translation. The first scene in which the hero is discovered alone pondering in his study at midnight recalls, in general, the opening of Goethe's play. The hero is representative of human wisdom, which, having explored all earthly things, finds in them no solid joy or lasting treasure. "Sorrow is knowledge," Manfred concludes, a sentiment that the philosopher Nietzsche was to admire as immortal. There is no clear indication in the play of what spheres of learning Manfred has explored. He is a sage whose wisdom has given him direct contact with supernatural beings. He is also another typically Byronic hero, haunted by remorse for some dark crime (incest is suggested, and the "destruction" of his sister), alienated from human society, a rebel against the established order of things.

The treatment of the hero is different from that in the poems so far considered because Byron moves the story onto a metaphysical and allegorical level, suggesting the mode of later works like Shelley's *Prometheus Unbound* or the second part of Goethe's *Faust*. Lyric and dramatic elements are combined; dance and song are suggested by the text; the effects of light described would not only be scenically beautiful in performance but they are also interwoven with the allegory. The signification of these elements is not easily described and the ultimate meaning of the text is obscure. Like *Prometheus Unbound*, the play can be interpreted as a subjective and psychological work concerned with the powers and operations of the mind. What is represented as external is often internal. Allegory sometimes gives way to the kind of symbolism we find in dreams. We know that the images and words are important; they haunt us, but there are parts of the processes of our imaginations that we experience without ever fully understanding.

Not all the text is on this level. The chamois hunter, the witch of the Alps, and the abbot may all be easily interpreted allegorically in Manfred's quest for his lost sister, Astarte. The chamois hunter, who saves Manfred from suicide, is a romantic variant on the "happy husbandman": the simple man who finds contentment in his organic relationship with nature. The abbot, manifestly, represents the Christian religion. The witch of the Alps is less simply categorized but is described as the spirit of the place and of beauty and seems to represent something of the inspirational force of natural loveliness and of the power of pantheism.

The interpretative crux of the play is Astarte, Manfred's dead sister. To take her as merely being Augusta Leigh reduces the work at a stroke to absurdity. To read the play in terms of story—that is, as about incest—renders the metaphysical apparatus irrelevant. Astarte, therefore, must possess a symbolic signification, but what that is has proved mysterious. The original Astarte was a Phoenician fertility goddess and Byron may have chosen this form of the name rather than the biblical Ashtaroth because it suggests also *astra* (the Latin word for star). So Shelley was to combine the mythical Adonis and the Judaic word *Adonai* (a name for God) in *Adonais*. Seven stars appear to Manfred at the beginning of the play, the last of which seems to be an image of Astarte, for he faints with emotion on seeing her. She may represent something of the spirit of love and beauty with which the mind of man has so often been rapt, though it would be unwise to turn the play into a Platonic allegory. In earlier centuries the philosophy of Plato might have provided a framework for Byron, but for the romantic poet the thing sought is unknown and indefinable. To change to a Christian image: he is searching for the holy grail but does not know what it looks like.

The grail, according to the myth, was only for the pure in heart. The Byronic hero is impure, yet he still searches. After the vision of Astarte vanishes, an incantatory curse is spoken over the unconscious body of Manfred—possibly this indicates the workings of the unconscious mind:

> By thy cold breast and serpent smile,
> By thy unfathomed gulfs of guile,
> By that most seeming virtuous eye,
> By thy shut soul's hypocrisy;
> By the perfection of thine art
> Which passed for human thine own heart:
> By thy delight in others' pain,
> And by thy brotherhood of Cain,
> I call upon thee! and compel
> Thyself to be thy proper Hell!
>
> (I.i.242–251)

The paradox of the play is that the mind both creates the vision of love and beauty, and yet destroys it by its innate and inescapable mental corruption. The incest theme is a metaphor for this process. When Manfred eventually finds Astarte again she is a spirit in hell who cannot reply intelligibly to his passionate pleas. He cries:

> . . . I cannot rest.
> I know not what I ask, nor what I seek:
> I feel but what thou art, and what I am. . . .
>
> (II.iv.130–132)

One recognizes the desire, but the lines indicate that it is not possible to put a name to it. Possibly at this stage the vision of Astarte is contaminated. Since the scene is hell, if the Faust myth were still running in Byron's mind, the analogous figure here would be the visionary Helen of Troy, who destroys the hero by turning his mind to sensuality when he should think of God—so Marlowe: "Her lips suck forth my soul! See where it flies!"

Byron's hero also comes to die after this vision, though no logical reason is offered. But the play is not working within a theological system like Marlowe's *Dr. Faustus*. Instead it seems to be following a train of psychological causation: if Astarte is irredeemably in hell, then aspiration is in vain (such might be one interpretation). Yet Manfred dies defying the demons, just as he rejects the panacea of the Christian religion represented by the abbot. But, paradoxically, the ultimate demon declares that he is Manfred's "genius." Thus, the evil force which one believed was outside is revealed at the end as being within. The demonic agencies that the hero opposes even unto death may be his own creation. In support of this interpretation: precisely the same image dominates Werner Herzog's reworking of another fundamental romantic motif, the vampire myth in *Nosferatu*. Jonathan Harker creates Count Dracula by his own imagination and then becomes the vampire himself. His innocent wife (the Astarte figure) sacrifices herself in vain to the vampire's lust. This myth does not deny that innocence and beauty exist and that they are admired. But the darker and indestructible forces of the human mind always destroy them.

This is difficult and problematical ground. Byron complained of Coleridge's metaphysics: "I wish he would explain his explanation." Possibly *Manfred* is too obscure. But there is much in the working of the mind which is necessarily difficult to explain, and Byron observed that he was half-mad while writing the piece. At this time the props of Freudian imagery were not available as part of the subjective writer's stock in trade, and Byron was progressively exploring complex inner forces. The Byronic hero of a poem like *The Giaour* had become deliberately involved with the personality of the poet in the last cantos of *Childe Harold*. Now, in *Manfred*, the drama of the mind's *psychomachia* (spiritual war) shuts out more and more the objective scene. About this time Byron composed *The Prisoner of Chillon* (1816). The hero there is incarcerated so long in a dungeon below the level of the lake, scarcely able to glimpse anything of the outside world, that eventually he comes to love his own despair, and when liberty is eventually granted him, he is discontented with his freedom. The prisoner may be seen as a symbolic figure representing a mind entirely shut in upon itself.

Byron had returned to a more objective mood by 1821, when he came to write *Cain*. The extraordinary and famous change of direction in his writing after arriving in Italy seems, in retrospect, something like a self-willed therapeutic process to escape from the prison of his own subjectivity. But this is mere speculation. Although *Cain* has much in common with the earlier poetry thematically, the manner is markedly different. It is an intellectual and dialectical play built around formal arguments about theological ideas. Although these ideas are Byronic, there is little or no sense in the play that the poet himself is present in the characters. *Cain* argues about Manichaeism, or the "two principles" of good and evil, in the baldest of verse. The very directness of the iconoclasm was instrumental in causing contemporary outrage.

> *Lucifer.* Evil and Good are things in their own essence,
> And not made good or evil by the Giver;
> But if he gives you good—so call him; if
> Evil springs from *him*, do not name it *mine*,
> Till ye know better its true fount; and judge
> Not by words, though of Spirits, but the fruits
> Of your existence, such as it must be.
> *One good* gift has the fatal apple given,—
> Your *reason*:—let it not be oversway'd
> By tyrannous threats to force you into faith
> 'Gainst all external sense and inward feeling:
> Think and endure,—and form an inner world
> In your own bosom—...
>
> (II.ii.452–464)

The intellectual ideas of the play may be traced to the skepticism of Pierre Bayle and Voltaire. The cosmology of Cain's flight through space with Lucifer owes much to Fontenelle's *Entretiens sur la pluralité des mondes* (1686), and the vision back into the pre-Adamite world of long geological time derives from Cuvier's *Essay on the Theory of the Earth*. There have been other kinds of being in this world before man, and they have become disastrously extinct. There are other worlds in the infinity of space. What then of the special claims of the Christian revelation? If we must be skeptical about biblical truth, what will we conclude concerning the nature of God from the evidence of the creation? If God were good, all that we are and behold would be good. But since evil, death, and suffering are inextricably part of nature, then they are part of God's nature.

Lucifer's description of his relationship to God suggests a possible source in the philosopher William Godwin's account in *Enquiry Concerning Political Justice* (1793). Jehovah is a gloomy tyrant who demands submission from his sycophants:

> ... he is alone
> Indefinite, Indissoluble Tyrant;
> Could he but crush himself, 'twere the best boon
> He ever granted. ...
>
> (I.i.152–155)

To rebel against such a figure of political oppression is in itself an act of justice. This situation is similar to that of the rebel heroes of Byron's early romances; but now, not shrouded in the charms of exotic fiction, the idea is applied to the religious tenets of contemporary European society. Byron's pessimism makes the act of rebellion itself as evil as the system that provokes it. Lucifer is not like Shelley's Prometheus, who changes the world through sacrificial love. He is just as much a tyrant as God, and on this argument there would seem to be only one, not "two principles," in the universe. As in *Manfred*, knowledge of the nature of things brings sorrow. When Cain returns from his universal journey he brings with him death into the world by killing Abel in a fit of rage because Abel's blood sacrifice is acceptable to God, while his own innocent offering of fruits made without servility is rejected:

> ... If a shrine without victim,
> And altar without gore, may win thy favour,
> Look on it! and for him who dresseth it,
> He is—such as thou mad'st him; and seeks nothing
> Which must be won by kneeling. ...
>
> (III.i.266–270)

Byron, when attacked, claimed that the ideas of the piece were not his but appropriate only to the characters who uttered them: the evil figures Lucifer and Cain. This argument must be weighed. It may be granted that neither being seems to be an alter ego in the manner of Childe Harold, who merges with Byron, or of Manfred, who seems a projection of the poet's own deep mental disturbance. The characters in *Cain* are embodiments of ideas, for instance in the manner of the very similar modern morality plays of Edward Bond, and the great imaginative visions of the second act are objective in the sense that they represent what the universe is or was like. The myth also is traditionally given, whereas *Manfred* creates its own myth as an act of sublimated and darkly introspective self-revelation.

But the case for God is never put with the force of Lucifer's. Cain has already gone over to the other side intellectually before the devil appears and is distinguished from Lucifer only by his human sentiments, not by his principles. The "good" characters are loving to one another but totally submissive to a divinity who shows little sign of being anything but as Lucifer describes him, a gloomy tyrant who denies man knowledge and imposes submission by ignorance. That Cain is forced into murder by opposition to God merely shows that evil produces evil. Lucifer's interpretation of the universe appears to be the true one.

One may compare another parable for the modern world, Bertolt Brecht's *Galileo*. There the scientist (the Lucifer figure) disturbs the humble faith of the peasantry, which alone makes their poverty tolerable, by challenging the union of autocracy with ignorance that the Church (God) represents. In the process Galileo, by making himself unacceptable to authority, destroys the happiness of his daughter, who is prevented from marrying (Brecht's equivalent to the murder of Abel). But in Brecht's view such partial evil is justified by the greater good that will come from the advance of science in the service of humanity. He is in the tradition of philosophers such as Francis Bacon, Godwin, and Karl Marx, and believes in the essential union of science and reason with good. In Byron the disturbing thing about the vision of history that *Cain* represents is that "grief is knowledge" (I.354). Man's unconquerable mind burns to know truth and refuses to submit to evil, but the nature of things, and our own nature, always turns potential good to ill. Perhaps this is Byron's sense of original sin coming from Calvinism. A Brechtian answer (in the "enlightened" tradition of Lucretius) would be that Byron has simply not freed himself from superstitious guilt. But it can be seen from Byron's debates with Shelley, especially as presented in Shelley's *Julian and Maddalo*, that he has much more fundamental objections to optimism. They are based on observation of the processes of the mind and on the empirical data of history: plants, sick at germination, produce bad fruit. In *Cain* the Byronic hero has become an established literary type by which the poet can illustrate this intellectual proposition through myth and formal debate. The dramatic beings are no longer subsumed into his own personality like Harold or Manfred, but the iconoclastic ideas that they utter are centrally Byronic.

BEPPO

In *Beppo* (1818) Byron found the manner and form of the comic masterworks of his last years. The development is a surprise. His racy, vivid, and high-spirited letters are the only substantial evidence that there had long existed, in potential, a comic poet behind the mask of the satirist, sentimentalist, and misanthrope he had hitherto adopted. The new style was found almost by accident while he was still working in the vein of *Childe Harold* and *Manfred* and when, critically, his mind had seemed to be turning rather to Pope as an alternative poetical model. *Beppo* was no more than a hasty bagatelle offered to his publisher John Murray as a gift.

Two factors combined in the poem's inception. One is biographical. It had been a therapeutic experience for Byron to settle down to a life of comfortable promiscuity in Italy. His fraught nerves healed. His letters to Murray were so entertaining that the publisher asked him for some verse in the same manner. Murray wrote in January 1817: "Give me a poem,—a good Venetian tale describing manners formerly from the story itself, and now from your own observations, and call it 'Marianna.'" In the same year John Hookham Frere published two cantos of *Prospectus and Specimen of an Intended National Work, by William and Robert Whistlecraft, of Stow-market, in Suffolk, Harness and Collar-Makers*, a work familiarly known as *Whistlecraft* or, from its later title (1821), as *The Monks and the Giants*. This is an unfinished Arthurian burlesque written in the octave stanza (*ottava rima*) in the manner of the fifteenth-century Italian poet Luigi Pulci's tale of Charlemagne, the *Morgante Maggiore*. Byron's new style was given to him ready-made by Frere; witness the second stanza from Frere's first canto:

> Poets consume exciseable commodities,
>   They raise the nation's spirit when victorious,
> They drive an export trade in whims and oddities,
>   Making our commerce and revenue glorious;
> As an industrious and pains-taking body 'tis
>   That Poets should be reckon'd meritorious:
> And therefore I submissively propose
> To erect one Board for Verse and one for Prose.

The facetious whimsicality of the narrator, the outrageous rhymes and enjambment, and the easy conversational tone are exactly the new Byronic mode. Other literary sources may have contributed: Giovanni Battista Casti's *Novelle Galanti*, which Byron had acquired in 1816 (his *Animali Parlanti* and *Poema Tartaro* also show parallels with Byron's subsequent work); later Byron turned to Francesco Berni and the "parent" of this kind of writing, Pulci himself, whom he began to translate. But "*Whistlecraft* was *my* immediate *model*," he declared in a letter to Murray of 25 March 1818.

Frere's poem lacks both the deeper biographical resonances and the social immediacy of *Beppo*. Byron had all the literary expectations of the Byronic hero to exploit and his own notoriety. The tale he tells, although set a few years back, is about Venetian society vividly observed as he knew it now, and continually set in contrast with English society for satirical purposes. Frere, by going back to Arthur's days, usually loses connection with the actual and often writes what is little more than an amusing spoof of a chivalric poem.

Byron's new pose is of "a nameless sort of person, / (A broken Dandy lately on my travels)" (lii). He *was* a cynical man of fashion more concerned with the superficiality of society than with deep issues of emotion, morality, or philosophy, but he now is out of English society, perhaps even a little out-of-date (for fashions swiftly change). The word "nameless" contains a double meaning. It may refer to the difficulty of defining what sort of person an English gentleman "gone native" in Italy might be—"broken Dandy" is only one suggestion. It may also refer to Byron's abominable reputation in England. His is not the kind of name mentioned in polite society. This kind of persona was to be richly developed in *Don Juan*, but one should beware of defining the new role too precisely. The poet can change the mask through which he speaks, and the role played can vary from moment to moment from self-revelation to full dramatization of another being. The "broken Dandy" is a burlesque form of the Byronic hero, and like the tragic type it is not constant in its manifestations or its use.

The old form of Byronic hero appears momentarily as the dark Turk in the carnival, the alienated and mysterious figure of the husband whom we learn in his *Wanderjähre* (years of travel) has been slave, pirate, and renegade to his religion. But no tragic figure is likely to be called Beppo by a nagging wife. The poem works often by disappointing expectation:

> How quickly would I print (the world delighting)
>   A Grecian, Syrian, or *Assyrian* tale;
> And sell you, mixed with western Sentimentalism,
> Some samples of the *finest Orientalism.*
>
> (li)

The reader would expect a hot-blooded Mediterranean male to be jealous of his wife's lover, and Byron reminds his reader of the most famous of Venetian love tragedies, that "sooty devil" Othello, who "smothers women in a bed of feather." But this is the Venice of the carnival and of Carlo Goldoni, and when the husband returns after long years to find his wife unfaithful he merely strikes up a friendship with her lover, and she is merely curious about her husband's Turkish sexual and domestic life:

> "Are you *really, truly*, now a Turk?
>   With any other women did you wive?
> Is't true they use their fingers for a fork?
>   Well, that's the prettiest Shawl—as I'm alive!
> You'll give it me? They say you eat no pork.
>   And how so many years did you contrive
> To—Bless me! did I ever? No, I never
> Saw a man grown so yellow! How's your liver?"
>
> (xcii)

Insofar as the poem has a story, the tale is told with dramatic brilliance and a lively eye to social detail. But the anecdote is no more than a peg on which to hang the digressions. In this Byron resembles Laurence Sterne in *Tristram Shandy*. Anything that happens will set off a train of associated ideas, which beget fresh ideas, until by this process the most heterogeneous elements are yoked together. In *Don Juan* the method is used philosophically to satirize the pretensions of the human mind to build systems, especially systems of moral and metaphysical philosophy. In *Beppo* Byron is trying little more than to find a poetic speaking voice—as it were, a way of stretching his legs out before the fire and chatting a little facetiously upon anything that is likely to come into his head, especially what it is like to be an Englishman in Italy.

Yet the very act of comparison between the manners and climate of two societies begins to engender a far-reaching humorous skepticism:

> This feast is named the Carnival, which being
>   Interpreted, implies "farewell to flesh:"
> So called, because the name and thing agreeing,
>   Through Lent they live on fish both salt and fresh.
> But why they usher Lent with so much glee in,
>   Is more than I can tell, although I guess
> 'Tis as we take a glass with friends at parting,
> In the Stage-Coach or Packet, just at starting.
>
> (vi)

The poet has picked up the paradox of Venetian Catholicism represented by the feast of joy that is the prelude to the days of contrition and penance set aside by the church to mark Jesus's forty days fasting in the wilderness. He goes on to recommend that the English traveler should bring ample stock of sauces with him "if your religion's Roman/And you at Rome would do as Romans do" but concludes that no man

> If foreign, is obliged to fast; and you,
> If Protestant, or sickly, or a woman,
> Would rather dine in sin on a ragout—
> Dine and be d—d! I don't mean to be coarse,
> But that's the penalty, to say no worse.
>
> (ix)

Byron's satire is so tolerant of the human follies he mocks that he ends by reconciling the reader to his own folly. Human nature will have its way, and the flesh, if repressed in one fashion by the church, will have its Carnival another time. In any case, if the Lenten fish is so elaborately dressed with "ketchup, Soy, Chili-vinegar, and Harvey," what sort of contrition is this, and what is human nature that it can be so easily disturbed by the absence of ketchup? Perhaps even the church itself strives in every way to mitigate its own severities to the sick, to women (the weaker sex!), and as for Protestants, the word "d—d" has lost all its force in Byron's colloquialism (as well as all its middle letters). Do Christians really dispatch their fellow religionists to hell for not eating fish? Possibly. But the bantering tone of the lines never settles to anything of moral certainty. The broken Dandy's pose is that of a man who finds the reason for things "more than I can tell." Philosophically it is the pose of Socrates; in English verse it is closest to the technique of Chaucer. The Dandy merely reports on the surface of society as a naive Englishman abroad. It is for the reader to make what he will of the paradoxes and contradictions of the human situation the truth of which he is laughingly compelled to recognize.

The Dandy turns his mind back to the land he has left:

> "England! with all thy faults I love thee still,"
> I said at Calais, and have not forgot it;
> I like to speak and lucubrate my fill;
> I like the government (but that is not it);
> I like the freedom of the press and quill;
> I like the Habeas Corpus (when we've got it);
> I like a Parliamentary debate,
> Particularly when 'tis not too late. . . .
>
> (xlvii)

Like the ideals of Lent, the virtues of England slide away in this and subsequent stanzas, but are not totally devalued though never directly stated. On the contrary, the list of the good things is introduced by the phrase "with all thy faults," quoted from William Cowper's *The Task* (the sentiment is not Byron's), and "love" slides swiftly to "like," and the catalog ends in stanza xlix with Byron "forgiving" and "forgetting" unemployment, riots, bankruptcies, "Our cloudy climate, and our chilly women." Yet it was proper to recall in Italy, a land repressed by foreign domination, English freedom of speech and of the press, and parliamentary democracy. But when Byron writes "I like the government" one should recall that he was a strong opponent of the Tory regime, hence the caveat "but that is not it"; and that same Tory government, faced with substantial domestic disorder, was fast dismantling the very English freedom that Byron "likes"—hence the aside on habeas corpus. In parliamentary debate Byron had spoken with passion on some of these issues. Now he admits to no more than liking debate "when 'tis not too late." Is the Dandy a lazy man, or is he suggesting that such debates are a waste of time? Byron's indignation, coiled like a spring, was shortly to fly out in the dedicatory stanzas to *Don Juan*; witness the lines on Robert Stewart Castlereagh:

> Cold-blooded, smooth-faced, placid miscreant!
> Dabbling its sleek young hands in Erin's gore. . . .
>
> (xii)

But here, in *Beppo*, such a declamatory outburst would offend against comic decorum. The subversive possibilities of the comic mode were to prove a much more subtle and flexible tool than the devices of grand rhetoric, as *The Vision of Judgment* will show.

THE VISION OF JUDGMENT

BYRON was provoked by the Poet Laureate Robert Southey's *A Vision of Judgement* (1821). The quarrel between the poets had been festering for some time. Byron believed that Southey had accused him of living in Switzerland in "a league of incest," and in his preface to *A Vision* Southey had attacked the works of Byron and his "school" as being fit for a "brothel" and "Satanic" in their morality. The poet laureate had reneged on his earlier liberal sympathies expressed in poems like *Wat Tyler* (which he endeavored in vain to suppress) and had become the spokesman for high Toryism. In Southey's *Vision* the author is rapt into the skies from the Lake District and sees the recently dead king, George III, ascend to judgment. George is welcomed to heaven by the reactionary Prime Minister Spencer Perceval and is vainly accused by opposition speakers of the party of Satan like John Wilkes and the anonymous pamphleteer "Junius." Then he ascends to a blissful reunion with his family, helped on his way by figures like George Washington (who had fought against the king for the independence of America) and John Milton (who repents of his regicide opinions). The verse form is the Latin hexameter, which Byron called "spavined dactyls." The verse is as bad as the subject is silly; witness the account of the angel summoning the king's "absolvers":

Ho! he exclaim'd, King George of England standeth in
    judgment!
Hell hath been dumb in his presence. Ye who on earth
    arraign'd him,
Come ye before him now, and here accuse or absolve
    him!
For injustice hath here no place.

> From the Souls of the Blessed

Some were there then who advanced; and more from
    the skirts of the meeting—
Spirits who had not yet accomplish'd their
    purification,
Yet being cleansed from pride, from faction and error
    deliver'd,
Purged of the film wherewith the eye of the mind is
    clouded,
They, in their better state, saw all things clear; and
    discerning
Now, in the light of truth, what tortuous views had
    deceived them,
They acknowledged their fault, and own'd the wrong
    they had offer'd. . . .

(VI.1–12)

Southey, then, was more than a personal enemy. He stood as a type of the forces Byron opposed: a bad poet, a political apostate, a high Tory, above all an organ of what was for Byron one of the major ills of English society, cant: "in these days the grand '*primum mobile*' of England is *cant*; cant political, cant poetical, cant religious, cant moral."[2] Byron

[2]From R. E. Prothero, ed., *Letters and Journals* (London, 1898–1904), vol. V, p. 542.

had already attacked Southey and his circle of lakeland poets (Wordsworth and Coleridge) in "dedicating" *Don Juan* to him:

And now my Epic Renegade! what are ye at?
With all the Lakers, in and out of place. . .

but had chosen to let the lines remain unpublished. Now he had public as well as private cause for quarrel with the laureate. Byron's *The Vision of Judgment* was published in the first number of the opposition journal the *Liberal* with which Byron, Shelley, (now dead), and Leigh Hunt were editorially concerned.

The structure of Southey's poem is parodied. Satan, John Wilkes, and "Junius" reappear, and Wilkes even shows something of a Southeylike backsliding in forgiving a man he "beat. . . hollow" politically on earth—as the devil remarks, Wilkes "turned to half a courtier" before he died. But Junius remains fearless in his support of liberty and constant in his opposition to the king. The archangel Michael puts a Southeyian case to him:

"Repent'st thou not," said Michael, "of some past
    Exaggeration? something which may doom
Thyself if false, as him if true? Thou wast
    Too bitter—is it not so?—in thy gloom
Of passion?"—"Passion!" cried the phantom dim,
    "I loved my country, and I hated him.

"What I have written, I have written: let
    The rest be on his head or mine!"

(lxxxiii–lxxxiv)

The liberal reader's sympathy is meant to lie with "Junius." A passionate love for one's country in the teeth of an enemy of liberty is a real good, but it is typical of Byronism, and of the Byronic Satanism which Southey attacked, that "Junius" is a witness summoned by the devil; and his courageous declaration "What I have written, I have written" was also the expression of Pontius Pilate crucifying Christ as king of the Jews.

The major attack on the king is made by Satan himself in the guise of a disinherited nobleman called by his sense of duty to be an advocate. Compare Southey's Christian description of the devil accusing the king:

. . . a Demon came at the summons.
It was the Spirit by which his righteous reign had been
    troubled;

185

Likest in form uncouth to the hideous Idols whom
  India
(Long by guilty neglect to hellish delusions
  abandon'd)
Worships with horrible rites of self-immolation and
  torture.
Many-headed and monstrous the Fiend; with
  numberless faces,
Numberless bestial ears erect to all rumours, and
  restless,
And with numberless mouths which were fill'd with
  lies as with arrows.

(V.8–15)

with the Byronic:

But bringing up the rear of this bright host
  A Spirit of a different aspect waved
His wings, like thunder-clouds above some coast
  Whose barren beach with frequent wrecks is paved;
His brow was like the deep when tempest-tossed;
  Fierce and unfathomable thoughts engraved
Eternal wrath on his immortal face,
And *where* he gazed a gloom pervaded space.

(xxiv)

Byron's Satan is a figure of far greater power than Southey's. His original is the ruined archangel of Milton's *Paradise Lost*: the heroic and tragic antagonist of God. When he and Michael meet it is with "a high, immortal, proud regret" as if it were "less their will/Than destiny" for them to be engaged in eternal warfare (xxxii). The highest of the angelic powers recognizes another manifestation of himself in Satan, as it were, like Caesar shedding tears over the body of Pompey. This is a demonic entity as worthy of serious regard as Lucifer in *Cain* and another variation upon the Byronic hero: the man outcast because he will not submit to tyranny. The imagery associates him with thunder, traditionally seen as the instrument of the wrath of God. The Satanic, in this poem, comes close to being a voice that one might call, in another context, the justice of God.

The values that Satan expounds in his great piece of forensic oratory are such as he expects highest heaven to respond to with sympathy. Just as Southey expected heaven to be the home of the Tory party, so Byron turns the tables by expecting heaven to be liberal: to condemn tyranny, to oppose religious intolerance, and to reject wars waged to further those ends:

"He ever warred with freedom and the free:
  Nations as men, home subjects, foreign foes,

So that they uttered the word 'Liberty!'
  Found George the Third their first opponent. . . .

(xlv)

Selective quotation cannot do justice to the skill with which the attack spares the person of the "old, blind, mad, helpless, weak" octogenarian king rotting in his golden coffin—indeed, even acknowledges his personal virtues—and yet remorselessly reveals the public and political vice his reign occasioned. Such balance convinces that what is said is true more than mere polemic would do. Nor can short quotation reveal how dramatically in character is the devil's speech. It is appropriate that the first rebel should speak for liberty and claim as his own the shades of the tyrant-hater Junius Brutus and the insurrectionist George Washington. He also blatantly speaks to manipulate his audience. Although he addresses Michael as an equal, he cunningly works upon the prejudices of the silly Roman Catholic bigot St. Peter in revealing George as 'The foe to Catholic participation/In all the license of a Christian nation" (xlviii). Even in the most serious passages the derisive spirit of Byronic laughter mocks and subverts the cherished cant of society.

Byron himself appears in the poem as the sinning, tolerant, almost buffoonlike figure that is a development of the mask first adopted in *Beppo*. Even amid the condemnation of George III we find Byron, surprisingly, uttering the sentiment "God save the king!" but then subverting it with unusual reasons:

. . . It is a large economy
  In God to save the like; but if he will
Be saving, all the better; for not one am I
  Of those who think damnation better still:
I hardly know too if not quite alone am I
  In this small hope of bettering future ill
By circumscribing, with some slight restriction,
The eternity of Hell's hot jurisdiction.

. . .

God help us all! God help me too! I am,
God knows, as helpless as the Devil can wish. . . .

(xiii;xv)

From behind the comic mask one hears the voice of charity. We are asked to recognize the weakness of our common humanity. The lines are a mutation on the Calvinistic pessimism of the sense of original sin that is a constant quality of Byronism. "God save the king!" because the king is a sinner who needs to be saved; "God help us all!" because we are all sinners; "God help me too!" for we should not exclude ourselves when we condemn the wickedness of the world and delude ourselves with complacent pride—which is one of Southey's many failings. "God help me too!" has an additional resonance because it is Byron writing: notorious in his public capacity for "incest" and "Satanism" and a man who had deliberately involved his own poetic personality with that of his dark heroes.

The philosophical tradition that blends with Calvinism here I shall call "enlightened humanism" —there is no convenient critical shorthand for it. Eighteenth-century liberal philosophy had set itself constantly against Christian claims of exclusive revelation and of the universality of damnation for the infidel. Intellectual skepticism and comparative history had combined to undermine Christian doctrines, producing as their fruits deism, liberalism, and toleration. Byron always carried his learning lightly, but he had read in this enlightened school, and his charity is the product of the humane skepticism which that reading engendered.

Hence the salvation of George III in the poem. As in Southey's *Vision* the king gets into heaven, though merely through inadvertence on the part of the deity in Byron's story. To damn a man would be as wrong —and as arrogant in intellectual presumption—as Southey's claim that all good Tories go to God. In any case, since fellows like St. Peter are rather silly, and much of the best company seems to be in hell, Southey's Tory heaven is not so much of a reward after all. In Byron, George learns the 100th psalm because he must learn to enter heaven's gates with thanksgiving: "For the LORD *is* good; his mercy *is* everlasting." It is that quality of mercy that mankind most needs.

The real villain of the piece is Southey. Byron follows his original by having the "Laker" indeed rapt into the sky from Derwentwater, but the "truth" of the tale as *The Vision* recounts it is very different from what the lying renegade has reported in *A Vision*:

> . . . here's my 'Vision'!
> Now you shall judge, all people—yes—you shall
> Judge with my judgment! and by my decision
> Be guided who shall enter heaven or fall."
>
> (ci)

No case needs to be made against the poet laureate. He is condemned from his own mouth. Byron, though he invents speech for him, does not have to invent the grounds of his condemnation. The list of the man's own works speaks for itself:

> He had written praises of a Regicide;
> He had written praises of all kings whatever;
> He had written for republics far and wide,
> And then against them bitterer than ever;
> For pantisocracy he once had cried
> Aloud, a scheme less moral than 'twas clever;
> Then grew a hearty anti-jacobin—
> Had turned his coat—and would have turned his skin.
>
> (xcvii)

For great political crimes Byron had, at moments, allowed his style to rise to declamatory grandeur. Ridicule is enough for this sort of thing. He will never strike harder than he needs to achieve his end, but the ridicule is merciless in a way that the treatment of the king is not. Southey has nothing to redeem him. On the other hand, not even he is damned eternally. He is given the treatment Dante reserved for intellectual cowardice in the *Divine Comedy*: neither heaven nor hell will accept him. He is hurled back into the English lakes.

> He first sank to the bottom—like his works,
> But soon rose to the surface—like himself;
> For all corrupted things are buoyed like corks,
> By their own rottenness. . . .
>
> (cv)

A reader familiar with Pope will recognize that Byron is drawing upon the earlier poet's attacks on bad, hireling poetasters in *The Art of Sinking in Poetry* and *The Dunciad*. There was, Pope claimed, a profound depth in bad writing just as there is a sublime of the good. Poets diving in mud and excrement in the Fleet ditch were his imaginative illustration of this. Southey now joins another laureate, Pope's butt Colley Cibber, as a type of bad writer. He too "sinks" but like all rotten things "soon rose to the surface." George III is in heaven; his poet laureate, on top on earth. The satiric poet recognizes that no practical effect has been achieved by his protest. Byron the satirist, like the Byronic hero, is an outsider who fails in his war with corrupt society.

DON JUAN

BYRON began *Don Juan* in the summer of 1818 and continued work on it spasmodically until May 1823, when events in Greece made him lay it aside. His progress was checked by uncertainty about his purpose in the poem, the hostility with which the work was received by members of his circle—Teresa Guiccioli, Hobhouse, Moore—and the poor sales of the early cantos. For a time in 1821–1822 he abandoned the poem, which had progressed as far as canto V, but then, in the spring of 1822, he began work again in a sustained burst of creativity. Even then it is not certain in what way he intended to complete the poem, if at all.

While at work he issued several accounts of his purposes. Like the poem, they are self-contradictory. At one time he claimed, "Do you suppose that I could have any intention but to giggle and make giggle?" (letter to Murray, 12 August 1819), yet at other times he seriously defended the morality of his intention, calling the work "a *satire* on *abuses* of the present *states* of Society" (letter to Murray, 25 December 1822). Sometimes he claimed to have no plan or described the major part of the poem as merely prefatory to what he was about to write. But on another occasion he told Murray of his hero:

I meant to take him the tour of Europe—with a proper mixture of siege—battle—and adventure—and to make him finish as *Anacharsis Cloots*—in the French revolution. . . I meant to have made him a Cavalier Servente in Italy and a cause for a divorce in England—and a Sentimental "Werther-faced man" in Germany—so as to show the different ridicules of the society in each of those countries—and to have displayed him gradually *gaté* and *blasé* as he grew older—as is natural.—But I had not quite fixed whether to make him end in Hell—or in an unhappy marriage,—not knowing which would be the severest.

(16 February 1821)

This was about the time he laid the poem aside for a year, but it is not far removed in general from what he eventually accomplished. Juan travels widely; at the end a divorce seems likely; and an anarchic view of the French Revolution would provide a fitting climax to a work which so often mixes idealism and cynicism.

Although it is impossible to categorize this vast, sprawling, ragbag of a poem, some general indications may be offered. At the beginning of the fourth canto Byron wrote:

As boy, I thought myself a clever fellow,
    And wished that others held the same opinion;
They took it up when my days grew more mellow,
    And other minds acknowledged my dominion:
Now my sere Fancy "falls into the yellow
    Leaf," and Imagination droops her pinion,

And the sad truth which hovers o'er my desk
Turns what was once romantic to burlesque.

And if I laugh at any mortal thing,
    'T is that I may not weep; and if I weep,
'T is that our nature cannot always bring
    Itself to apathy. . . .

(IV.iii–iv)

The poem is a form of self-confession. As in *Beppo* the digressions frequently take over the story entirely, but the character of the narrator is now more fully developed and inextricably linked with Byron the man, poet, and public myth. The poem is about looking back. The "boy" he refers to is both his youthful self and the "Childe" of *Childe Harold's Pilgrimage*; the ideas are his early romantic conceptions, which experience now turns to burlesque. That growth of experience is not represented as intellectual progress. He has changed because "imagination" has declined, and what might be good for the philosopher may be deleterious for the poet. Nor has he rejected his pose as hero of his own romances. The quotation about the sere and yellow leaf is from *Macbeth*. Byron identifies himself with a regicide and a villain who, when he contemplates life, sees it as "a tale told by an idiot. . . signifying nothing." It is Macbeth as moral philosopher rather than man of action of whom he thinks. Beneath this is a more fundamental philosophic and satiric tradition. Byron refers to himself as sometimes laughing, sometimes weeping. It is an allusion to a famous commonplace in the Roman satirist Juvenal, who linked his work to the sages Democritus and Heraclitus: the former laughed at human follies, the other wept for them. The same tradition had inspired one of Byron's favorite poems: Johnson's imitation of Juvenal, *The Vanity of Human Wishes*. These stanzas, then, explain on biographical and moral grounds the tensions in the poem between the idealistic (romantic) and the comic (burlesque), between sorrow and mirth, that everywhere inform the writing.

A few lines later he acknowledges Pulci as the father of the burlesque, which is a clear connection between the inspiration of *Don Juan* and *Beppo*. More usually in the poem Byron refers to his genre as "epic." This has often been regarded as mockery. Obviously *Don Juan* is not in the least like the *Iliad* or *Aeneid*. Yet its story line is not dissimilar to that of the *Odyssey*: after many wanderings over land and sea the poet turns to his own land in his cantos on English society, and a divorce would be a burlesque reversal of the chastity of Homer's Penelope. In addition, the open-ended form and the emphasis in the story on love and war are reminiscent, in general, of the Italian chivalric epic of the school of Ludovico Ariosto. To descend later in a developing tradition: the sharp, satiric eye that the poet shows for social manners recalls the work of Henry Fielding, who argued that generically his new form of fiction, which we now call the novel, was a "comic epic poem in prose." If one comes closer to our own age and relates *Don Juan* to James Joyce's *Ulysses*, then it is easy to see that Byron's poem is part of a continuing process of evolution by which classical epic has remained alive for the modern world.

Renaissance tradition had emphasized the encyclopedic learning and educative function of the epic. *Don Juan* preserves both of these. The poem is about a modern-style hero's education in the chivalric topics of love and war. A common man like Juan is the proper representative of our age (so Joyce chooses an Irish Jew, Leopold Bloom, as his wandering Ulysses). His unheroic role is a comment by the poet on traditional themes: the uncertain nature of fame and the unworthy subjects of human renown. Cicero's *Somnium Scipionis* ("The Dream of Scipio") or the concluding stanzas of Chaucer's *Troilus and Criseyde* are *loci classici* (classic examples) that make the same general comment on the heroic life seen in the light of eternity. The difference between Byron and these earlier writers is that they view life from a serious religious viewpoint, whereas the Byronic universe is an absurd one in which even religion is belittled. This is the tragicomedy of the position of modern man.

The encyclopedic tradition provides the basis both for the action of the poem containing so much and for the poet's commentaries upon everything. It is an idea that Byron mocks even as he uses, just as he burlesques the heroic. Homer, it was claimed, was the master of all arts and sciences, which he incorporated into the structure of his epics, vatically inspired. Our modern poet is "A wanderer from the British world of Fashion,/Where I, like other dogs, have had my day" (II.clxvi), who has "picked up" bits of experience and knowledge of "no matter what" along the way. His usual pose is one of skepticism or ignorance, and his mind is in a state of constant mobility inspired as much by the state of his health or his bowels as by profound gazing into the heart of light; witness the modern Homer or Milton on how illness brought him to religion:

> The first attack at once proved the Divinity
> (But *that* I never doubted, nor the Devil);
> The next, the Virgin's mystical virginity,
> The third, the usual Origin of Evil;
> The fourth at once established the whole Trinity
> On so uncontrovertible a level,
> That I devoutly wished the three were four—
> On purpose to believe so much the more.
>
> (XI.vi)

The inspired poet of old was seen to have brought his worldwide knowledge into great structural order, uniting diversity in the heroic theme of his poem, uttering his vision in the loftiest style. Byron's poem, in contrast, is constructed on the principle of the "medley" where all kinds of his earlier poetry, including even lyric verse, are hung around the adventures of his hero with no pretense at any unity beyond that of the continuing authorial presence manipulating Juan. The style is that of the *improvvisatore*: "I rattle on exactly as I'd talk/With anybody in a ride or walk" (XV.xix), and it is this sense of easy spontaneity and flowing conversational invention that is the highest achievement of Byron's art. It is the very opposite of the great tradition of epic: "Hail, Muse! *et cetera* . . ." (III.i), and it is a deliberate attack on that now decadent tradition as a form of cant.

His burlesque mode is different from the mock-heroic intention of a writer like Pope, who also could not find a hero in the modern world. But Pope's heroes exist in the past in the great writers like Homer and Milton, and the captains, sages, and statesmen of antiquity with whom he liked to identify himself. It has frequently been said that Byron lacks these "positive" standards, and his verse wants the assurance of Pope's, which comes, partly, from these received traditions. But a poet's first moral duty is to truth; and if there is no firm assurance in anything past or present, then it is dishonest to take refuge behind an idealized antiquity or in the pretense that a true heroic style is still possible if only one chose to write it. There is nothing wanting in the confidence of craftsmanship in a stanza like this:

> What are the hopes of man? Old Egypt's King
> Cheops erected the first Pyramid
> And largest, thinking it was just the thing
> To keep his memory whole, and mummy hid;
> But somebody or other rummaging,
> Burglariously broke his coffin's lid:

Let not a monument give you or me hopes,
Since not a pinch of dust remains of Cheops.

(I.ccxix)

These lines still have about them suggestions of public rhetoric now subverted. The poet is a figure who orates as a wise man for us and our posterity. Equally typical of the Byronic mode of *Don Juan* is this stanza from the shipwreck canto on the sinking of the cutter:

Nine souls more went in her: the long-boat still
    Kept above water, with an oar for mast,
Two blankets stitched together, answering ill
    Instead of sail, were to the oar made fast;
Though every wave rolled menacing to fill,
    And present peril all before surpassed,
They grieved for those who perished with the cutter,
And also for the biscuit-casks and butter.

(II.lxi)

This is quite outside the range of a mock-heroic stylist like Pope. It is verse trying to be prose, a deliberate antistyle that is evolved because it is appropriate to the nature of the subject. At one extreme historically are the great shipwrecks in Homer and Vergil, at the other the ditched aircraft of Joseph Heller's *Catch-22*. In the modern world death by drowning has lost all religious or heroic significance; it matters to no one except those who are not quite drowned yet. The extraordinary thing about such acts is that the artist, because he cannot make them tragic, turns them to comedy. The last couplet is horrible, true, and funny. It is what is now called by the cliché "black comedy."

Lines like those were one of the principal causes of the outcry against the poem. Against the criticism of Francis Cohen, Byron defended himself in the well-known letter to John Murray of 12 August 1819 on the theme of "scorching and drenching" (mixing incompatible things):

did he [Cohen] never inject for a Gonorrhea?—or make water through an ulcerated Urethra?—was he ever in a Turkish bath—that marble paradise of sherbet and sodomy?

The stylistic twists in the poem from tragedy to comedy, from the sentimental to the vulgar, from high to low, are an assertion by the poet concerning the multiplicity of simultaneous human experience. A single stylistic decorum, such as the traditional lofty utterance of epic, falsifies. Something far more flexible is necessary to respond to the true, the experiential, nature of subjects like love and war. Once again Byron is part of a continuing process of literary evolution of old forms. One may compare Miguel de Cervantes' *Don Quixote*, which blended the sentimental and the comic, the idealistic and the vulgar, in a tale long, rambling, digressive, and irresistible. *Don Juan* is stylistically midway between a rejection of the Homeric epic and Cervantes' inception of the modern novel. When Byron wrote that his earlier cantos were merely prefatory to the story in England, he had, carelessly, hit on a central truth about his poem. His epic turns into a novel. The English cantos especially are far closer to Thackeray or Dickens than they are to eighteenth-century mock heroic, and they settle into an easy conversational style that is for long periods far more assured in tone and secure in attitude than the initial burlesque cantos:

Thrice happy he who, after a survey
    Of the good company, can win a corner,
A door that's *in* or boudoir *out* of the way,
    Where he may fix himself like small "Jack Horner,"
And let the Babel round run as it may,
    And look on as a mourner, or a scorner,
Or an approver, or a mere spectator,
Yawning a little as the night grows later.

(XI.lxix)

Unfortunately, in the years during which the poem evolved and Byron was finding this style, he was inclined to wobble like a would-be cyclist who cannot combine velocity with balance. At times he seems to be fighting a guerrilla war both with the epic and his own earlier romantic styles. He will be deliberately funny out of place. The story of the siege of Ismail, for example, is one of the most severe and graphic indictments of the true nature of war to be found in "epic" poetry, yet, notoriously, it collapses into mere vulgarity in the account of the rape that follows the capture. The idyll of Juan and Haidée shows flashes of the finest sentimental poetry conjoined with the sinister in the person of Lambro, who is a Byronic hero become real pirate. Yet for no intrinsic reason the poet will sidetrack into the jocular at the most inappropriate moments as though he does not trust his own ability to inspire pathos. These are severe faults. Yet, all the time, despite the wobbling, as the ramshackle poem evolves, unpredictably the diverse elements continually fuse creatively in new combinations. The poem is not a final-ized object "out there" that we are invited to admire, but something with which the reader is involved in its endless development:

> But Adeline was not indifferent: for
> (*Now* for a common-place!) beneath the snow,
> As a Volcano holds the lava more
> Within—*et cetera.* Shall I go on?—No!
> I hate to hunt down a tired metaphor,
> So let the often-used Volcano go.
> Poor thing! How frequently, by me and others,
> It hath been stirred up till its smoke quite smothers!
>
> I'll have another figure in a trice:—
> What say you to a bottle of champagne?
> Frozen into a very vinous ice,
> Which leaves few drops of that immortal rain,
> Yet in the very centre, past all price,
> About a liquid glassful will remain;
> And this is stronger than the strongest grape
> Could e'er express in its expanded shape. . . .
>
> (XIII.xxxvi–xxxvii)

The poem is like the process of life itself. There is no over-all plan except catholic inclusiveness. For these reasons any illustrative quotation of a part is not true of the whole. It interrupts the flow, and when we look again, everything is different. For instance, compare in the first canto the style of Julia's letter (where she so manifestly finds pleasure as well as pathos in her own sentimental tragedy) with the comic tirade with which she greets her husband hunting for Juan in the bedroom; or, in the English cantos, compare the tone of Byron the satirist of society with the fascinated regret of the exile record-ing his own graphic memories of the "Paradise of Pleasure and *Ennui.*"

The great life-force of the poem remains the poet himself, and it is his life experience as man and artist, and all the mobility and richness of his temperament, that continually renews the narrative. He claims even the freedom of an old friend to bore his ac-quaintances with anecdote, recollection, and essay. These elements cannot be systematized into a struc-ture of ideas. As William Parry observed in his ac-count of Byron's *Last Days*: "His opinions were the results of his feelings" and these continually fluc-tuate. But through all the multiplicity of the ex-perience of *Don Juan* three major themes might be picked out in the poet's pursuit of truth. One is the relativity of all systems and ideas and the inex-tricable confusion of the ideal with the physical in human behavior. The baseness of the flesh tests and devalues all abstract conceptions. Another is a burn-ing commitment to the ideals of personal and politi-cal liberty. Inevitably this cannot be expressed as a positive system. It is the negative pathway of the man "born for opposition" (XV.xxii). Then there is the sense of the hurry of the years that carry all men, societies, and systems away. The fullest formal ex-pression is in the famous *Ubi sunt* stanzas beginning XI.lxxvi: "'Where is the World' cries Young, at *eighty.* . . ." and ending in the traditional advice of Epicurean philosophy to enjoy each day, for each day flies:

> But "*carpe diem*," Juan, "*carpe, carpe!*"
> To-morrow sees another race as gay
> And transient, and devoured by the same harpy.
> "Life's a poor player,"—then "play out the play. . . ."
>
> (XI.lxxxvi)

The guarantee of the authenticity of these sen-timents in the poem is Byron the man. The truth of which he writes is known because he has himself ex-perienced it. He is no better or wiser than other men, but he has lived fully and he is honest about his own life. The extraordinary culmination of Byron's poetic career is that a writer who began by posing as the fictional hero of his own improbable romances now, by process of evolution, has found the way of revealing himself as a type of Everyman through his art:

> But now at thirty years my hair is grey—
> (I wonder what it will be like at forty?
> I thought of a peruke the other day—)
> My heart is not much greener; and, in short, I
> Have squandered my whole summer while 'twas May,
> And feel no more the spirit to retort; I
> Have spent my life, both interest and principal,
> And deem not, what I deemed—my soul invincible.
>
> . . .
>
> Ambition was my idol, which was broken
> Before the shrines of Sorrow, and of Pleasure;
> And the two last have left me many a token
> O'er which reflection may be made at leisure:
> Now, like Friar Bacon's Brazen Head, I've spoken,
> "Time is, Time was, Time's past:"—a chymic treasure
> Is glittering Youth, which I have spent betimes—
> My heart in passion, and my head on rhymes.
>
> (I.ccxiii;ccxvii)

191

GEORGE GORDON, LORD BYRON

SELECTED BIBLIOGRAPHY

I. BIBLIOGRAPHY. R. Noel, *The Life of Lord Byron* (London, 1890), includes a bibliography by U. P. Anderson, containing extensive lists of magazine articles about Byron and of musical settings; E. H. Coleridge, ed., *The Works of Lord Byron. Poetry*, vol. VII: *A Bibliography of Successive Editions and Translations* (London, 1904), the best general bibliography of the poems; S. C. Chew, *Byron in England* (London, 1924), contains an extensive list of Byroniana; R. H. Griffith and H. M. Jones, eds., *A Descriptive Catalogue of . . . Manuscripts and First Editions. . . at the University of Texas* (Austin, Tex., 1924); *Bibliographical Catalogue of the First Editions, Proof Copies and Manuscripts of Books by Lord Byron. Exhibited at the First Edition Club, January 1925* (London, 1925); *Byron and Byroniana. A Catalogue of Books* (1930), an important sale catalog, valuable for reference, issued by Elkin Mathews, the London booksellers; T. J. Wise, *A Bibliography of the Writings in Verse and Prose of George Gordon Noel, Baron Byron. With Letters Illustrating His Life and Work and Particularly His Attitude Towards Keats*, 2 vols. (London, 1932–1933), the standard technical bibliography, incorporates the material of the same author's *A Byron Library* (1928), the privately printed catalog of the Byron Collection in the Ashley Library, now in the British Museum; *The Roe-Byron Collection, Newstead Abbey* (Nottingham, 1937), the catalog of the collection at Byron's ancestral home.

II. COLLECTED WORKS. *The Poetical Works*, 2 vols. (Philadelphia, 1813), the first collected ed., followed throughout the nineteenth century by numerous other collected eds. in several vols., published in London, Paris, New York, and elsewhere; *The Works*, 4 vols. (London, 1815), new eds.: 8 vols. (1818–1820), 8 vols. (1825), 6 vols. (1831); J. Wright, ed., *The Works, with His Letters and Journals, and His Life, by Thomas Moore*, 17 vols. (London, 1832–1833); *The Poetical Works. New Edition, with the Text Carefully Revised*, 6 vols. (London, 1857); *The Poetical Works, Edited, with a Critical Memoir by W. M. Rossetti. Illustrated by Ford Madox Brown*, 8 vols. (London, 1870); *The Works. A New, Revised, and Enlarged Edition with Illustrations, Including Portraits*, 13 vols. (London, 1898–1904), comprising *Poetry*, E. H. Coleridge, ed., 7 vols., and *Letters and Journals*, R. H. Prothero, ed., 6 vols.; *The Poetical Works. The Only Complete and Copyright Text in One Volume. Edited with a Memoir*, by E. H. Coleridge (London, 1905), the standard ed., often repr.; *The Complete Poetical Works*, J. J. McGann, ed., vol. I (Oxford, 1980), full textual apparatus and notes, will include many previously unpublished poems and fragments.

III. SELECTIONS. *A Selection from the Work of Lord Byron*, edited and prefaced by A. C. Swinburne (London, 1866); *Poetry of Byron* (London, 1881), chosen and arranged by M. Arnold; H. J. C. Grierson, ed., *Poems* (London, 1923); E. Rhys, ed., *The Shorter Byron. . .* (London, 1927); R. A. Rice, ed., *The Best of Byron* (New York, 1933); L. I. Bredvold, ed., *Don Juan and Other Satiric Poems* (New York, 1935); S. C. Chew, ed., *Childe Harold's Pilgrimage and Other Romantic Poems* (London, 1936); J. Bennett, ed., *Satirical and Critical Poems* (Cambridge, 1937); *Byron, Poetry and Prose* (London, 1940), with essays by Scott, Hazlitt, Macaulay, intro. by A. Quiller-Couch, and notes by D. N. Smith; P. Quennell, ed., *Selections from Poetry, Letters and Journals* (London, 1949); J. Barzun, ed., *The Selected Letters of Lord Byron* (New York, 1953).

IV. SEPARATE WORKS. *Fugitive Pieces* [Newark, 1806], privately printed and anonymous; facs. repr., H. B. Forman, ed. (London, 1886); *Poems on Various Occasions* (Newark, 1807), privately printed and anonymous; *Hours of Idleness: A Series of Poems Original and Translated* (Newark, 1807), 2nd. ed.: *Poems Original and Translated* (Newark, 1808), contains five new pieces; *English Bards and Scotch Reviewers: A Satire* (London, 1809), the early eds. of this poem were frequently counterfeited; *Address Written by Lord Byron. The Genuine Rejected Addresses, Presented to the Committee of Management for Drury Lane Theatre: Preceded by That Written by Lord Byron and Adopted by the Committee* (London, 1812); *Childe Harold's Pilgrimage: A Romaunt*, 2 vols. (London, 1819), previously published cantos I and II (1812), III (1816), and IV (1818); *The Curse of Minerva: A Poem* (London, 1812); *Waltz: An Apostrophic Hymn by Horace Hornem, Esq.* (London, 1813); *The Giaour: A Fragment of a Turkish Tale* (London, 1813); *The Bride of Abydos: A Turkish Tale* (London, 1813); *The Corsair: A Tale* (London, 1814); *Ode to Napoleon Buonaparte* (London, 1814), published anonymously; *Lara: A Tale* (London, 1814).

Hebrew Melodies, Ancient and Modern with Appropriate Symphonies and Accompaniments (London, 1815), also in T. L. Ashton, ed. (Austin, Tex., 1972); *The Siege of Corinth: A Poem* and *Parisina: A Poem* (London, 1816), published anonymously; *Poems on His Domestic Circumstances* (London, 1816), these two poems, "Fare Thee Well" and "A Sketch from Private Life," had been privately printed and separately printed in the same year; various eds. of this collection with additional poems were published in 1816; *Poems* (London, 1816); *The Prisoner of Chillon and Other Poems* (London, 1816); *Monody on the Death of the Right Hon. R. B. Sheridan. Written at the Request of a Friend, to Be Spoken at Drury Lane* (London, 1816); *The Lament of Tasso* (London, 1817); *Manfred: A Dramatic Poem* (London, 1817); *Beppo: A Venetian Story* (London, 1818), published anonymously; 4th ed., with additional stanzas (London, 1818); *Mazeppa: A Poem* (London, 1819).

Don Juan, cantos I–II (1819), III–V (1821), VI–VIII (1823), IX–XI (1823), XII–XIV (1823), XV–XVI (1824) originally published anonymously; first collected ed., 2 vols. (Edinburgh, 1825), the fullest ed. is that of T. G. Steffan and W. W. Pratt, 4 vols. (Austin, Tex., 1957), and vol. I contains a detailed study of the composition of the poem; *Marino Faliero, Doge of Venice: An Historical Tragedy* and *The Prophecy of Dante: A Poem* (London, 1821); *Sardanapalus: A Tragedy, The Two Foscari: A Tragedy*, and *Cain: A Mystery* (London, 1821), also in T. G. Steffan, ed. (Austin, Tex., 1968); *The Vision of Judgment* (London, 1822), a product of Byron's feud with Southey, first printed in the *Liberal* (1822), an ephemeral paper promoted by Byron and Leigh Hunt, and published as *The Two Visions* with Southey's "Vision of Judgement" in the same year; *Heaven and Earth: A Mystery* (London, 1823), published anonymously, first printed in the *Liberal* (1823); *The Age of Bronze: Or, Carmen Seculare et Annus Haud Mirabilis* (London, 1823), published anonymously; *The Island: Or, Christian and His Comrades* (London, 1823); *Werner: A Tragedy* (London, 1823); *The Parliamentary Speeches of Lord Byron. Printed from the Copies Prepared by His Lordship for Publication* (London, 1824); *The Deformed Transformed: A Drama* (London, 1824).

V. DIARIES AND LETTERS. *Letter to [John Murray] on the Rev. W. L. Bowles' Strictures on the Life and Writings of Pope* (London, 1821); A. R. C. Dallas, ed., *Correspondence of Lord Byron with a Friend, Including His Letters to His Mother in 1809–11*, 3 vols. (Paris, 1825); *Letters and Journals of Lord Byron, with Notices of His Life*, by T. Moore, 2 vols. (London, 1830; rev. ed., 1875); R. E. Prothero, ed., *Letters and Journals*, 6 vols. (London, 1898–1904); W. N. C. Carlton, *Poems and Letters, Edited from the Original Manuscripts in the Possession of W. K. Bixby* (Chicago, 1912), privately printed; J. Murray, ed., *Lord Byron's Correspondence, Chiefly with Lady Melbourne, Mr. Hobhouse, the Hon. Douglas Kinnaird, and P. B. Shelley*, 2 vols. (London, 1922); *The Ravenna Journal, Mainly Compiled at Ravenna in 1821, with an Introduction by Lord Ernle [R. E. Prothero]* (London, 1928), printed for the members of the First Edition Club; P. Quennell, ed., *Byron Letters and Diaries: A Self Portrait*, 2 vols. (London, 1950); E. J. Lovell, ed., *Byron: His Very Self and Voice: Collected Conversations of Lord Byron* (London, 1954); L. A. Marchand, ed., *Byron's Letters and Journals* (London–Cambridge, Mass., 1973–   ), the definitive ed.

VI. BIOGRAPHICAL AND CRITICAL STUDIES. J. C. Hobhouse, *A Journey Through Albania and Other Provinces of Turkey* (London, 1813); P. B. Shelley, *History of a Six Weeks' Tour* (London, 1817); J. Watkins, *Memoirs of the Life and Writings of the Rt. Hon. Lord Byron, with Anecdotes of Some of His Contemporaries* (London, 1822); T. Medwin, *Journal of the Conversations of Lord Byron: Noted During a Residence with His Lordship at Pisa, in the Years 1821 and 1822* (London, 1824), also in E. J. Lovell, ed. (Princeton, N. J., 1966); J. Murray, *Notes on Captain Medwin's Conversations of Lord Byron* (London, 1824), privately printed, and repr. in *Works* (1898–1904); R. C. Dallas, *Recollections of the Life of Lord Byron, from the Year 1808 to the End of 1814* (London, 1824); W. Hazlitt,

The Spirit of the Age (London, 1825), contains an essay on Byron; P. Gamba, *A Narrative of Lord Byron's Last Journey to Greece* (London, 1825); A. Kilgour, *Anecdotes of Lord Byron from Authentic Sources* (London, 1825); W. Parry, *The Last Days of Lord Byron: With His Lordship's Opinions on Various Subjects, Particularly on the State and Prospects of Greece* (London, 1825); E. Blaquière, ed., *Narrative of a Second Visit to Greece, Including Facts Connected with the Last Days of Lord Byron, Extracts from Correspondence, Official Documents, etc.* (London, 1825); *The Life, Writings, Opinions and Times of the Rt. Hon. George Gordon Noel Byron, Lord Byron, by an English Gentleman in the Greek Military Service, and Comrade of His Lordship. Compiled from Authentic Documents and from Long Personal Acquaintance*, 3 vols. (London, 1825), ascribed to the publisher, Matthew Iley; L. Hunt, *Lord Byron and Some of His Contemporaries* (London, 1828).

J. Galt, *The Life of Lord Byron* (London, 1830); J. Kennedy, *Conversations on Religion with Lord Byron and Others* (London, 1830); J. Millingen, *Memoirs of the Affairs of Greece, with Various Anecdotes Relating to Lord Byron, and an Account of His Last Illness and Death* (London, 1831); M. Gardiner, *Conversations of Lord Byron with the Countess of Blessington* (London, 1834), also in E. J. Lovell, ed. (Princeton, N. J., 1969); T. B. Macaulay, *Critical and Historic Essays* (London, 1842), includes a review of *Letters and Journals of Lord Byron; with Notices of His Life* by T. Moore (1830); W. Hazlitt, *Lectures on the English Poets* (London, 1858); E. J. Trelawny, *Recollections of the Last Days of Shelley and Byron* (London, 1858; repr., E. Dowden, ed., 1906), see also the same author's *Records of Shelley, Byron, and the Author*, 2 vols. (London, 1878; new eds., 1887, 1905), and in D. Wright, ed. (Harmondsworth, 1973), the Penguin English Library; T. Guiccioli, *Lord Byron jugé par les témoins de sa vie*, 2 vols. (Paris, 1868), also in English trans. (London, 1869); E. M. Leigh, *Medora Leigh: A History and an Autobiography*, C. Mackay, ed. (London, 1869); J. C. Hobhouse, *A Contemporary Account of the Separation of Lord and Lady Byron: Also of the Destruction of Lord Byron's Memoirs* (London, 1870), privately printed, repr. in Hobhouse's *Recollections of a Long Life* (see below); J. Nichol, *Byron* (London, 1880), in the English Men of Letters series; J. C. Jeaffreson, *The Real Lord Byron: New Views of the Poet's Life*, 2 vols. (London, 1883); W. G. Smith, *Byron Re-Studied in His Dramas. An Essay* (London, 1886); M. Arnold, "Byron," in *Essays in Criticism*, 2nd ser. (London, 1888); R. Noel, *The Life of Lord Byron* (London, 1890); W. Graham, *Last Links with Byron, Shelley and Keats* (London, 1898).

Journal of Edward Ellerker Williams, Companion of Shelley and Byron in 1821 and 1822. With an Introduction by R. Garnett (London, 1902); R. Millbanke, *Astarte: A Fragment of Truth Concerning Lord Byron* (London, 1905), privately printed (enl. ed., London, 1921); J. Murray, *Lord Byron and His Detractors: Astarte. Lord Byron and Lord Lovelace* (London, 1906) and R. E. Prothero, *Lord Lovelace on the Separation of Lord and Lady Byron* (London, 1906), both privately printed for members of the Roxburghe Club; R. J. F. Edgcumbe, *Byron: The Last Phase* (London, 1909); J. C. Hobhouse, *Recollections of a Long Life*, 6 vols. (London, 1909–1911); W. M. Rossetti, *The Diary of Dr. John William Polidori, Relating to Byron . . .* (London, 1911); C. M. Fuess, *Lord Byron as a Satirist in Verse* (London, 1912); E. C. Mayne, *Byron*, 2 vols. (London, 1912; new ed., 1924), see also the same author's *The Life and Letters of Lady Noel Byron* (London, 1929); W. Fletcher, *Lord Byron's Illness and Death as Described in a Letter to the Hon. Augusta Leigh, Dated from Missolonghi April 20, 1824* (Nottingham, 1920), privately printed; E. J. Trelawny, *The Relations of Lord Byron and Augusta Leigh. With a Comparison of the Characters of Byron and Shelley* (London, 1920), privately printed; S. C. Chew, *Byron in England: His Fame and After Fame* (London, 1924); H. Nicholson, *Byron: The Last Journey, April 1823–April 1824* (London, 1924; new ed., 1948); J. D. Symon, *Byron in Perspective* (London, 1924); W. A. Briscoe, ed., *Byron, the Poet. A Centenary Volume* (London, 1924), contains essays by Haldane, Grierson, and others; H. J. C. Grierson, *The Background of English Literature* (London, 1925), contains "Byron and English Society"; M. Praz, *La fortuna di Byron in Inghilterra* (Florence, 1925), see also *The Romantic Agony*, A. Davidson, trans. (London, 1933); A. C. Gordon, *Allegra: The Story of Byron and Miss Clairmont* (New York, 1926); E. Railo, *The Haunted Castle* (London, 1927); C. Du Bos, *Byron et le besoin de la fatalité* (Paris, 1929), English trans. by E. Colburn Mayne (London, 1932); H. Richter, *Lord Byron: Persönlichkeit und Werk* (Halle, 1929).

A. Maurois, *Byron*, 2 vols. (Paris, 1930), English trans. by H. Miles (London, 1930); P. Quennell, *Byron: The Years of Fame* (London, 1935); I. Origo, *Allegra* (London, 1935); W. J. Calvert, *Byron: Romantic Paradox* (London, 1935); F. R. Leavis, *Revaluation* (London, 1936), contains his influential essay "Byron's Satire"; B. Dobrée, ed., *From Anne to Victoria* (London, 1937), contains "Byron" by T. S. Eliot, repr. in *On Poetry and Poets* (London, 1957); E. W. Marjarum, *Byron as Skeptic and Believer* (Princeton, 1938); G. Paston and P. Quennell, *To Lord Byron: Feminine Profiles, Based upon Unpublished Letters 1807–1824* (London, 1939); "Byron and the East: Literary Sources of the Turkish Tales," in H. Davies, W. C. de Vane, and R. C. Bald, eds., *Nineteenth Century Studies* (London, 1940); P. Quennell, *Byron in Italy* (London, 1941); E. F. Boyd, *Byron's Don Juan* (London, 1945); W. A. Borst, *Lord Byron's First Pilgrimage* (New Haven, Conn., 1948); E. J. Lovell, *Byron: The Record of a Quest* (Austin, Tex., 1949); I. Origo, *The Last Attachment. The Story of Byron and Teresa Guiccioli* (London, 1949); E. M. Butler, *Goethe and Byron* (London, 1951); H. Read, *The True Voice of Feeling* (London, 1951), contains an essay on Byron; G. W. Knight, *Lord Byron, Christian Virtues* (London, 1952); T. Spencer, *Fair Greece, Sad Relic: Literary Philhellenism from Shakespeare to Byron* (London, 1954); E. J. Lovell, ed., *His Very Self and Voice: Collected Conversations of Lord Byron* (New York, 1954); E. M. Butler, *Byron and Goethe* (London, 1956); R. Escarpit, *Lord Byron, un temperament littéraire*, 2 vols. (Paris, 1956–1957); B. Ford, ed., *The Pelican Guide to English Literature*, vol. V (London, 1957), contains "Lord Byron" by J. D. Jump; G. W. Knight, *Lord Byron's Marriage* (London, 1957); C. D. Thorpe, ed., *Major English Romantic Poets* (London, 1957), includes "Irony and Image in Byron's Don Juan"; L. A. Marchand, *Byron*, 3 vols. (London, 1957), the standard biography; L. Weinstein, *The Metamorphoses of Don Juan* (London, 1959); T. S. Eliot, *On Poetry and Poets* (London, 1957), contains an essay on Byron, first published in 1937.

P. West, *Byron and the Spoiler's Art* (London, 1960); G. M. Ridenour, *The Style of Don Juan*, Yale Studies in English vol. 144 (New Haven, Conn., 1960); D. L. Moore, *The Late Lord Byron* (London, 1961); A. Rutherford, *Byron* (London, 1961); B. Blackstone, *The Lost Travellers* (London, 1962), contains a ch. expanded from "Guilt and Retribution in Byron's Sea Poems," in *Review of English Literature*, 2 (January 1961); M. Elwin, *Lord Byron's Wife* (London, 1962); P. L. Thorslev, Jr., *The Byronic Hero: Types and Prototypes* (Minneapolis, 1962); W. H. Marshall, *The Structure of Byron's Major Poems* (Philadelphia, 1962); P. West, ed., *Byron: A Collection of Critical Essays* (Englewood Cliffs, N. J., 1963); M. K. Joseph, *Byron the Poet* (London, 1964); L. A. Marchand, *Byron's Poetry* (London, 1965); G. W. Knight, *Byron and Shakespeare* (London, 1966); W. W. Robson, "Byron as Poet," in his *Critical Essays* (London, 1966); J. J. McGann, *Fiery Dust: Byron's Poetic Development* (Chicago, 1968); M. K. Stocking, ed., *The Journals of Claire Clairmont* (Cambridge, Mass., 1969); R. F. Gleckner, *Byron and the Ruins of Paradise* (Baltimore, 1967); E. Bostetter, ed., *Twentieth Century Interpretations of Don Juan* (Englewood Cliffs, N. J., 1969); M. G. Cooke, *The Blind Man Traces the Circle* (Princeton, N. J., 1969); A. Rutherford, ed., *Byron. The Critical Heritage* (London, 1970); J. D. Jump, *Byron* (London, 1972); *The Byron Journal* (1973–   ); D. L. Moore, *Lord Byron Accounts Rendered* (London, 1974); B. Blackstone, *Byron. A Survey* (London, 1975); J. D. Jump, ed., *Byron. A Symposium* (London, 1975); J. J. McGann, *Don Juan in Context* (London, 1976); C. E. Robinson, *Shelley and Byron* (Baltimore, 1976).

PERCY BYSSHE SHELLEY

(1792-1822)

G. M. Matthews

I

It is no good making up one's mind too hastily about Shelley. Contemporary reviewers called various of his works a "dish of carrion," "drivelling prose run mad," "the production of a fiend, and calculated for the entertainment of devils in hell." The Victorians thought his lyrics "absolutely perfect"; he was "the Divine" poet. Early twentieth-century critics could see at a glance that there was "no brain work" in Shelley's poetry; it was "antipathetic to the play of the critical mind." Generalizations about him have always differed wildly. To Charles Kingsley, Shelley was "utterly womanish"; to D. H. Lawrence, he was "transcendently male"; and the man whose friends thought him "full of life and fun" while they knew him, T. S. Eliot in 1933 found humorless and pedantic.

Shelley was no perfectibilist. He saw human society in terms of unending struggle, and controversy delighted him, so his work is understandably controversial. But most judgments of it have been impressionistic: rationalizations of instant liking or distaste. The hostile criticism of the 1930's plainly took no trouble to understand the material it was dismissing: that "Alastor," for instance, was not a form of the name "Alastair" but Greek for an avenging fury; that "The Indian Serenade" was Indian, and a serenade; that when a snake renewed its "winter weeds outworn" (in Shelley or in William Shakespeare), it was changing its skin, not raising a fresh crop of nettles. Only in the last fifty years, and chiefly by Americans, has it been shown how complex this deceptively fluent verse often is, and how patiently its symbolic language needs learning.

Poor texts are still a handicap, and there is still room for disagreement. In this language, for example, electricity or "lightning" pervades the physical, as love pervades the moral, world; the fire of sun and stars is the counterpart of the One, the Unity or Spirit that shapes the beauty of the world; and the changing forms of cloud and vapor represent the mutations of matter that "veil" or refract this brightness and resist its influences. Some of the vocabulary is Platonic, perhaps Neoplatonic; but the language is Shelley's. His "Intellectual Beauty" (a phrase from William Godwin and James Burnett, Lord Monboddo, not from Plato) may express itself in revolutionary action (as in the "Ode to Naples," 149-176) and in sexual intercourse (as in *Laon and Cythna*, 2650-2665).

What fascinated Shelley was not *being* but *process*; not John Keats's timeless urn or William Wordsworth's "permanent forms of nature," but the sun-awakened avalanche, the destroying and preserving wind, the "unpastured sea hungering for calm." So it is true that as a poet he never looked steadily at an object for long, and this elusiveness can be irritating to his readers. By a principle of indeterminacy he passed on to what the object was becoming, or to what caused it. But accurate knowledge was generally taken for granted as the starting point of his invention. He was a country boy; most of his life was spent out-of-doors; and he read a good deal about the workings of nature. In many ways he was a very exact poet—more exact and knowledgeable than some of his critics.

Shelley was also a versatile craftsman. Unlike Geoffrey Chaucer, or George Gordon, Lord Byron, he was not interested in the full scope of human activity, but only in the great problem of humanity's place in the universe and of the achievement of happiness. Can man, through self-conquest, master his own future? Shelley's poetry was the changing comment of his own life experience on this unvarying question. But the angle of the comment, the stylistic range, was very wide. He wrote well in many different "kinds": epic, epigram, pastoral elegy, political ballad, familiar epistle, tragedy, lyric, burlesque. He is best known as the poet of fiery imaginings:

And the green lizard, and the golden snake,
Like unimprisoned flames, out of their trance awake[1]
(*Adonais*, 161–162)

The colors are heraldic, and oppressed creatures
break like volcanic fire out of the "trance" of winter;
yet as a physical picture every detail is vivid and apt.
He could also write with a sensuous verbal relish not
unlike Keats's:

Blue thistles bloomed in cities; foodless toads
Within voluptuous chambers panting crawled
(*Prometheus Unbound*, I. 170–171)

Again a symbolic description, with a strong undertone of social criticism; yet again it recalls eyewitness
accounts of Hiroshima a few months after atomic
bombardment. Or his imagery could be plain and
familiar: "like a flock of rooks at a farmer's gun"; "as
bats at the wired window of a dairy"; "like field
smells known in infancy."

One important quality in Shelley's later verse, expressing itself in both rhythm and tone, might be
defined as witty play:

Where light is, chameleons change:
Where love is not, Poets do:
("An Exhortation," 14–15)

This "power of entering thoroughly into the spirit of
his own humour," as Shelley's cousin Thomas Medwin remembered it, not only informs long poems like
"The Witch of Atlas" and the "Hymn to Mercury,"
but also can be recognized in the absorbed dramatic
roles of lyrics such as "The Cloud" and "The Two
Spirits." Until recently readers have been unwilling
to notice this quality. When Francis Palgrave and
Alfred, Lord Tennyson, put "The Invitation" into
The Golden Treasury in 1861, they left out the
playfully mocking middle passage, presumably because they thought it spoiled the serious idealism of
the poem.

Shelley was not a particularly self-centered poet.
Less than six percent of the poems in his *Collected
Works* begin with the first-person pronoun, compared with more than fifteen percent of those in
William Butler Yeats's; and only nineteen percent of
his first lines contain "I," "me," "my," "mine," compared with nearly twenty-three percent of John Dryden's. The test is a rough one, of course, since the
pronoun "I" does not necessarily mean the writer;
but that is as true in Shelley as in Yeats or Dryden.

[1]All quotations are from G. M. Matthews, ed., *Shelley: Selected
Poems and Prose* (Oxford, 1964).

II

PERCY BYSSHE SHELLEY was born on 4 August 1792 at
Field Place, near Horsham, Sussex. His father was
the heir of an American-born adventurer who had
twice married money, and who became a baronet in
1806. His family called him Bysshe, after his grandfather; his first wife called him Percy; and everyone
else has simply called him Shelley.

As the indulged eldest son of a country gentleman
and member of Parliament, Shelley became a fair
horseman, an excellent shot, and a memorable practical joker; and by his early teens he was already
romantically devoted to a pretty cousin, Harriet
Grove. But in adolescence he could not take his conventional, rather dim-witted father seriously as an
advocate of Whig ideals such as parliamentary reform, and sometimes mocked his shortcomings not
only to friends but even—less openly—in letters to
his father himself.

Shelley's uncompetitive home life had not fitted
him for survival at Eton, where he was savagely
ragged for his non-conformism. (He entered in
1804.) But though vulnerable, he was fearless; and it
was probably at Eton that the self-commitment recorded in his dedication to *Laon and Cythna* was
made:

I will be wise,
And just, and free, and mild, if in me lies
Such power, for I grow weary to behold
The selfish and the strong still tyrannize
Without reproach or check.
(31–35)

He would not learn what his "tyrants" taught, he
decided, but would "Heap knowledge from forbidden mines of lore"—from science, for example (then
outlawed at Eton), and the writings of Godwin and
the French skeptics. His tyrants did succeed in
teaching him Latin and Greek.

Just before Shelley entered University College,
Oxford, in October 1810, the parents concerned
broke off his friendship with Harriet Grove, alarmed
at its effects on her beliefs, and she dutifully married
the nephew of a clergyman. In the spring of 1811,
Shelley was sent down from Oxford for circulating
an unsigned leaflet, *The Necessity of Atheism*, written with his friend Thomas Jefferson Hogg, who
shared the same fate.

The shock of these arbitrary acts confirmed
Shelley's intellectual revulsion from Christianity.

196

His reaction, in August 1811, was to elope with a sixteen-year-old friend of his sister's, Harriet Westbrook. This marriage failed, but not before it had inspired his first important poem. Even at twenty-one Shelley was a well-published author, with two prose thrillers to his discredit and two volumes of mainly sensational, "gothic" verse.

Queen Mab, never regularly published, was, ironically, the one popular success of Shelley's career. From 1821 on, it was frequently reprinted—more to the author's amusement than dismay—and became one of the most respected texts in the Radical working-class movement, "the Chartists' Bible."

There is much in it to deserve respect. The fairy title was camouflage to cover "long notes against Jesus Christ, & God the Father and the King & the Bishops & marriage & the Devil knows what," as Shelley later remembered them, so that *Queen Mab*, like all his political verse, was solidly buttressed by prose argument. But the poem has a plain, simple structure—a perspective of the past, present, and future conditions of mankind—and the writing, though modeled on the irregular verse of Robert Southey's *Thalaba the Destroyer* (1801), is hard and clear. Many features of *Queen Mab* have a continuous development throughout Shelley's subsequent work. Human society is always seen in a cosmic setting, and human history as inseparable from the history of stars and insects. From the vantage point to which Mab has carried her, the soul of Ianthe (Harriet) is shown

> The flood of ages combating below,
> The depth of the unbounded universe
>   Above, and all around
> Nature's unchanging harmony.
>   (II. 254–257)

The order of nature is unchanging, a "wilderness of harmony," but its constituent parts are "combating below" in a continual storm of change. Thus the ruined civilizations that Mab exhibits are not—as in many eighteenth-century poems—mere illustrations of human pride humbled by time; they are part of a process in which man is endlessly implicated with nature. Necessity, "mother of the world" and moving in it everywhere like the West Wind, rules this "Imperishable change/That renovates the world." Only man does not yet cooperate. "Matter, with all its transitory shapes,/Lies subjected and plastic at his feet"; but he cannot master it, not by reason of his supposed

> evil nature, that apology
> Which kings who rule, and cowards who crouch, set up
> For their unnumbered crimes
>   (IV. 76–78)

but because his false institutions and superstitions offend the natural law. "Nature rejects the monarch, not the man."

Yet life goes on aspiring, "like hungry and unresting flame," and must triumph in the end. Then the playthings of man's social childhood—thrones, cathedrals, prisons—will be abandoned, and man will take his place among his fellow creatures in the natural order:

> . . . Man has lost
> His terrible prerogative, and stands
> An equal amidst equals . . .
>   (VIII. 225–227)

Men and women, too, will be equal, and thus truly free to love; the old quarrel between passion and reason will end once sexual relations are no longer distorted by commercial exploitation or venereal disease. And eventually the nightshade berries will outgrow their old habit of being poisonous, and the lions their customary fierceness.

Much of the egalitarianism of *Queen Mab*, its sun that shines as sweetly on cottage thatch as on the domes of palaces, was traditional. The style, too, was still eighteenth-century rather than romantic. Shelley did not find his way back to this sort of harsh clarity until the very different "Triumph of Life" a decade later.

For some three years after the writing of *Queen Mab*, Shelley's hectic life gave him little time for poetry; and the forms of direct action that he tried first—agitation in Ireland, land reclamation in Wales—resulted in prose tracts and manifestos rather than poems. Harriet's role as wife of a "committed" poet was hard to keep up, and the gap between their interests widened. In 1814, Shelley met Mary Godwin, daughter of Mary Wollstonecraft and the radical thinker William Godwin; and after a brief agony of indecision, they fled to Switzerland together, accompanied by Mary's stepsister Claire Clairmont.

The practical result of this second elopement was a year desperately spent in trying to raise credit on which to live and in dodging creditors. The strain made Shelley ill; he was told he was dying of consumption. Not until the summer of 1815, when his grandfather died, was there a reasonable subsistence for all concerned.

But in August, Shelley, now permanently addicted to boats, made a ten-day voyage up the Thames that mended his health and resulted in the first poem of his early maturity. *Alastor* is exploratory, a languidly beautiful product of convalescence. It is broadly in the eighteenth-century tradition of James Beattie's *The Minstrel*, that of moralizing on the way various experiences affect the sensibility of a young genius, but its landscapes are no longer diagrams thrown on a cosmic screen: they are symbolic, inseparable from the psychic and emotional states of the Poet passing through them.

The Greek title "Alastor," an avenging power, applies to the "self-centred seclusion" that tempts the Poet to waste his life in pursuing a dream lover of impossible perfection instead of making do with the love of his fellow beings. Was Shelley thinking mainly of himself? (He had given up direct political action, and a quiet country life certainly tempted him: a little later he was styling himself the "Hermit of Marlow.") Or Wordsworth? Or Coleridge? Short poems critical of both were included in the *Alastor* volume, but Shelley always took care that the minor poems in his collections matched the principal one. In any case, as the preface admits, his sympathies were on both sides; and the poem tends to romanticize what it was supposed to condemn.

Six weeks of the summer of 1816 were spent on the Lake of Geneva, near Lord Byron. The meeting was occasioned by Byron's liaison with Claire Clairmont; but the two poets liked each other, and their mutual literary admiration, at least, remained to the end. At this time Wordsworth's intuition in "Tintern Abbey" of

> A motion and a spirit, that impels
> All thinking things, all objects of all thought,
> And rolls through all things

was beginning to haunt Shelley's imagination. In "Mont Blanc," a poem the obscurity of which is partly due to technical clumsiness, the mountain embodies a secret Power, perhaps identical with Necessity, that, once acknowledged, could regenerate the world. In a companion "Hymn to Intellectual Beauty," reworked after his return home, Shelley celebrates "Intellectual Beauty" almost as the spiritual aspect of this immanent power, a radiance that invests Necessity with sympathy and loveliness, somewhat as Asia in *Prometheus Unbound* spiritualizes the inscrutable Demogorgon.

Back in England, the suicide of Fanny Imlay (Mary Shelley's half sister) on 9 October 1816 was swiftly followed by Harriet's suicide, in obscure circumstances; and early the following year the lord chancellor, John Scott, 1st earl of Eldon, ruled that Shelley was not fit to take care of Harriet's two children, although he had regularized his claim on them by marrying Mary. His friendships with Hogg, Thomas Love Peacock, and especially Leigh Hunt helped Shelley through these disastrous months. Hunt introduced him to John Keats, and the two young poets agreed each to complete a 4,000-line poem during the summer of 1817. Shelley's poem was *Laon and Cythna; or, The Revolution of the Golden City: A Vision of the Nineteenth Century*, a romance epic in Spenserian stanzas. Despite its Turkish setting, it was intended as a lesson to those supporters of the French Revolution who had been disillusioned by events since 1789. There is no easy optimism here (nor, indeed, anywhere else in Shelley's poems). Although the road to egalitarian objectives is always open, it leads through disappointment, bloody defeat, sacrifice, and death. To "break through the crust of those outworn opinions on which established institutions depend," Shelley made his revolutionary lovers brother and sister (the biological hazards not then being understood), and also stressed the bloodthirstiness of Christianity; but his publisher prevailed on him to modify these features, and to adopt a tactfully distancing title, *The Revolt of Islam*.

This poem has had very few to praise, and none to love it. Whereas the realism of its great prototype, *The Faerie Queene*, vitalizes the allegory, Shelley's symbolic treatment undermines the intended human interest. What stay in the mind are single images, as of the sunlit sea depths from which a diver "Passed like a spark sent up out of a burning oven," and single episodes, such as the opening duel between the eagle of darkness and the snake of light, the description of plague and famine in canto X, and Laone's hymn of hope during the "winter of the world" in canto IX, which anticipates the seasonal imagery of the "Ode to the West Wind."

Shelley was very depressed by the failure of *The Revolt of Islam*, still feeling, three years later, that its "date should have been longer than a day." This and the move to Italy in the spring of 1818—partly for the sunshine, partly to take Claire Clairmont's illegitimate daughter Allegra to her father, Byron— temporarily unsettled him. When he could "absolutely do nothing else," he translated Plato's *Sym-*

posium and the *Cyclops* of Euripides. But August brought the stimulus of a reunion with Byron in Venice. Claire wanted to see her little girl again, and Shelley had gone alone to negotiate a meeting. He succeeded—but when his family joined him at the villa near Este that Byron had lent them, the long, hot journey from Leghorn proved too much for his own year-old daughter Clara. She died of dysentery soon after arrival.

Out of this loss came the "Lines Written Among the Euganean Hills," a minor masterpiece. From the highest point of the Colli Euganei, on the lower slopes of which the Shelleys were living, could be seen Padua and Venice to the east, the Alps to the north, and the Apennines to the south. Islanded in space, making one October day an island in the flux of time, Shelley moves out of the storms of his own life to prophesy over the cities of the plain, enslaved and corrupted by foreign occupation, yet transfigured momentarily under the eternal sunlight. As usual he writes best when his private feelings dissolve into feeling for others; but even the "mariner" of the opening lines is not himself only, for the date is only a week from the anniversary of Fanny Imlay's suicide.

Just as individual lives are wrecked because love is willfully withheld until it is too late, so Venice and Padua face destruction because they lack the will to assert their ancient greatness. The line "Men must reap the things they sow" is bitterly ironical, for the harvests are being gathered—to supply the invader. The meter is that of John Milton's "L'Allegro," a favorite measure in the eighteenth century used, for instance, in John Dyer's Grongar Hill poems, and one with a flexibility that appealed to Shelley:

> And of living things each one,
> And my spirit which so long
> Darkened this swift stream of song,
> Interpenetrated lie
> By the glory of the sky:
> Be it love, light, harmony,
> Odour, or the soul of all
> Which from heaven like dew doth fall,
> Or the mind which feeds this verse
> Peopling the lone universe.
>
> (310–319)

There was reason for the new note of artistic assurance in this poem. Act I of *Prometheus Unbound* had just been finished.

Prometheus Unbound, Shelley's central poetic achievement, was composed over three widely spaced sessions that it will be necessary to treat as one. All but this first act was written during 1819: Acts II and III in the spring, at Rome, and Act IV in the autumn, at Leghorn and Florence. The "myth" of the poem is the great European humanist myth of the Titan who steals fire from the sun and teaches man all the arts and sciences, in defiance of an outraged deity. Shelley's version derives from that of Aeschylus' *Prometheus Bound* (and it is Aeschylus' Prometheus, not Shelley's, that is discussed in the preface); but he reminds readers of his great predecessor partly in order to underline the differences. *Prometheus Bound* was one play of a trilogy in which the hero eventually compromised with Jupiter; Shelley reorders the myth so that it will incorporate the knowledge gained in the struggle for human emancipation since the fifth century B.C.

Prometheus Unbound, as Shelley explained in the preface, was not a program of action, which could better be provided in prose tracts such as the "Essay on Christianity" and the "Philosophical View of Reform"; it was an "idealism"—an imaginative picture of "what ought to be, or may be"—meant to condition people's minds for the stupendous changes that society must undergo in becoming truly human. "Man must first dream the possible before he can do it." So even where the poem is closest to allegory, its characters cannot be translated exactly into moral or political terms, and different aspects of their significance are emphasized at different moments. Nor can the poem be summed up as a "drama in the mind"—or even in a universal Mind—although some of its actions are mental, such as Prometheus' renunciation of the curse, and his torture by the Furies, who represent his own temptations to despair.

At one level the poem mirrors the contemporary social order. Jupiter represents the ruling classes of Europe with their apparatus of repression and propaganda:

> Thrones, altars, judgement-seats, and prisons; wherein,
> And beside which, by wretched men were borne
> Sceptres, tiaras, swords, and chains, and tomes
> Of reasoned wrong, glozed on by ignorance . . . .
>
> (III. iv. 164–167)

Freedom can come only when this entrenched order is overthrown from below. But from another viewpoint all these repressive institutions, and the prestige that makes them effective, exist because mankind installed them and tolerated them: they "were, for his will made or suffered them," and man is able to undo his own mistakes. Jupiter is in this sense the creation of Prometheus. This is why he is described at his fall as "sunk, withdrawn, covered, drunk up/By thirsty nothing"—a mere hole in social and moral space that Love fills up.

At the beginning of the drama, the position is deadlocked. To defy power keeps hope alive, yet defiance alone cannot either dislodge the old regime or create a new one. Necessity, the natural law, cannot operate as one day it must, until the right conditions are met; and one essential condition is that Prometheus should give up his adversary's vindictive attitude of mind. Milton's God in *Paradise Lost* had allowed Satan freedom to act, "That with reiterated crimes he might/Heap on himself damnation." But Prometheus learns through centuries of suffering to forgo revenge; then Asia (Love, his wife and natural counterpart) can be inducted willingly into the realm of Demogorgon. Thus Love, the law that governs the moral world, interacts with Necessity, the law that governs all other worlds, and the Hour of liberation is released.

The imaginative implications of this unusual "plot" are many-sided. Appropriately in a drama about Prometheus, Shelley made part of the action into a geophysical metaphor. The scientist James Hutton had recently explained how the earth recreated itself by periodic cycles of volcanic activity, and it was believed that eruptions were triggered by the entry of water from the sea. So when Asia and her sea sisters penetrate the mountain of Demogorgon, who is described as if he were made of molten lava, they activate an eruption out of which the old earth is reborn. As Sir Humphry Davy had observed of volcanoes in 1811, "The evil produced is transient; the good is permanent. The ashes which buried Pompeii have rendered a great country continually productive. The destruction is small and partial—the benefit great and general." Shelley constantly used volcanic imagery in his poetry. Christianity placed God in Heaven and the Devil in the Pit; but for Shelley evil was rained from above, while the ultimate source of power and energy was located below, at the center. So the earth produced "fountains," or springs, and breathed up exhalations; these might be mischievous, corrupted as earth was under Jupiter, but in origin they were the "wine of life," sources of inspiration, prophecy, and action.

The dramatic center of Act I is the confrontation between Prometheus and the Furies, who are brought by Mercury to force him into despair. The contrast between the mealy-mouthed, self-indulgence of Mercury and the tight-lipped, dismissive irony of Prometheus is very effective:

> *Mercury.* Thou canst not count thy years to come
>   of pain?
>   *Prometheus.* They last while Jove must reign; nor
>   more, nor less
> Do I desire or fear.
>   *Mercury.* Yet pause, and plunge
> Into Eternity, where recorded time,
> Even all that we imagine, age on age,
> Seems but a point, and the reluctant mind
> Flags wearily in its unending flight,
> Till it sink, dizzy, blind, lost, shelterless;
> Perchance it has not numbered the slow years
> Which thou must spend in torture, unreprieved?
>   *Prometheus.* Perchance no thought can count them,
>   yet they pass.
>   *Mercury.* If thou might'st dwell among the Gods the
>   while
> Lapped in voluptuous joy?
>   *Prometheus.* I would not quit
> This bleak ravine, these unrepentant pains.
>   *Mercury.* Alas! I wonder at, yet pity thee.
>   *Prometheus.* Pity the self-despising slaves of
>   Heaven,
> Not me, within whose mind sits peace serene,
> As light in the sun, throned: how vain is talk!
> Call up the fiends.
>
>   (I. 414–432)

To the Furies, Prometheus is curt and laconic:

> Pain is my element, as hate is thine;
> Ye rend me now: I care not.
>   (I. 477–478)

And there is equal economy of language in a Fury's demoralizing summary of human impotence: even the greatest human figures

> . . . dare not devise good for man's estate,
> And yet they know not that they do not dare.
> The good want power, but to weep barren tears.
> The powerful goodness want: worse need for them.
> The wise want love, and those who love want wisdom;
> And all best things are thus confused to ill.
>   (I. 623–628)

The wintry poetic language of the alpine first act matches the dramatic situation; the language of the second act, borrowing its scenery from the luxuriant area around Naples, opens with a burst of colors to match the revitalizing forces set in motion by Prometheus' change of heart. In one dialogue—virtually a monologue—Asia is inspired to speculate, to the limit of her own insight (and Shelley's), on the authorship of evil; but some of the most original writing in this act is lyrical. In the "Semichorus of Spirits," a key passage with its remarkable reconcilement of free will and determinism in the final stanza, the clogged movement, the intricate syntax, the images of vegetation, gloom, and moisture aptly suggest the dense forest surrounding the causal source of material life:

> Nor sun, nor moon, nor wind, nor rain
> Can pierce its interwoven bowers,
> Nor aught, save where some cloud of dew,
> Drifted along the earth-creeping breeze
> Between the trunks of the hoar trees,
> Hangs each a pearl in the pale flowers
> Of the green laurel, blown anew;
>   . . .
> And the gloom divine is all around;
> And underneath is the mossy ground.
>   (II. ii. 5–11; 22–23)

The "Voice in the Air, Singing" in celebration of Asia is at another extreme, for here Asia is to Demogorgon as spiritual light is to physical heat:

> Child of Light! thy limbs are burning
> Through the vest which seems to hide them,
> As the radiant lines of morning
> Through the clouds ere they divide them;
> And this atmosphere divinest
> Shrouds thee wheresoe'er thou shinest.
>   (II. v. 54–59)

In Act III, after Jupiter has fallen, the gradual change to a new civilization is abridged for formal reasons; there seems to be little difference in things at first, but by the end the old idols are moldering ruins. And as in *Queen Mab*, not only is man reaching out into the deeps of space, but his morality is affecting the ecology of nature. The precision and quality of the lines in which the Spirit of the Earth rejoices over this development prove how seriously Shelley took it:

> All things had put their evil nature off:
> I cannot tell my joy, when o'er a lake

> Upon a drooping bough with nightshade twined,
> I saw two azure halcyons clinging downward
> And thinning one bright bunch of amber berries
> With quick long beaks, and in the deep there lay
> Those lovely forms imaged as in a sky . . . .
>   (III. iv. 77–83)

Act IV, the lyrical "cosmic dance" added to the poem when it was already half-copied for the printer, is patchy, but fascinating, as Mary Shelley said, for its "abstruse and imaginative theories with regard to the Creation." The extraordinary song of the Moon to the Earth, which turns gravitation into a metaphor of sexual love, is an example of the unique kind of analogical vitality that Shelley could derive from physical science:

> I, thy crystal paramour
> Borne beside thee by a power
> Like the polar Paradise,
> Magnet-like, of lovers' eyes;
>   . . .
> Sheltered by the warm embrace
> Of thy soul, from hungry space . . . .
>   (IV. 463–466; 479–480)

The end of the act is, in effect, a proclamation by Demogorgon to his reclaimed empire, summarizing the central experience of the poem:

> To defy Power, which seems omnipotent;
> To love, and bear; to hope, till Hope creates
> From its own wreck the thing it contemplates;
>   Neither to change, nor falter, nor repent;
> This, like thy glory, Titan! is to be
> Good, great and joyous, beautiful and free;
> This is alone Life, Joy, Empire and Victory.
>   (IV. 572–578)

From Este, with *Prometheus* one-quarter finished, the Shelleys traveled south to winter in Naples, an obscure and unhappy period in which only the "Stanzas Written in Dejection" were completed. But it is probable that "Julian and Maddalo," though planned at Este, was mostly written between Acts I and II of *Prometheus*; if so, Shelley was already experimenting consciously in a very different, familiar style, and a *"sermo pedestris* way of treating human nature,"* in the middle of his lyrical drama. The successful parts are in fact its vivid descriptions of Venice and its imitations of "the actual way in which people talk with each other"—in this case Julian

(Shelley) and Maddalo (Byron), on the shores and canals of Venice:

> Of all that earth has been or yet may be,
> All that vain men imagine or believe,
> Or hope can paint or suffering may achieve,
> We descanted, and I (for ever still
> Is it not wise to make the best of ill?)
> Argued against despondency, but pride
> Made my companion take the darker side.
>
> (43–49)

So Julian maintains, once more, that men are enslaved to evil because they make no effort to be otherwise; "it is our will/That thus enchains us to permitted ill." "You talk Utopia," Maddalo retorts; men are too weak ever to control their own destinies. And he supports his case by showing Julian someone whose reason has been destroyed by personal suffering. Perhaps the concept of this maniac derives from the madness of Torquato Tasso, and parts of his story from the private affairs of Shelley or Byron, but the episode as a whole is a "comment for the text of every heart." The poem ends with the argument still unsettled.

"Julian and Maddalo," subtitled "A Conversation," was a stylistic bridge between *Prometheus Unbound* and the "sad reality" of *The Cenci*, which Shelley wrote for the stage. All that he ironically called "mere poetry" was banished from the script, which was to be objective and lucid, "a delineation of passions which I had never participated in, in chaste language," and the principal part was angled toward a particular actress, Eliza O'Neill. But the true-life plot proved too unchaste for the theater management; Miss O'Neill could not be asked even to read it.

The heroine, Beatrice, is a mortal Prometheus who, because her oppressor is hateful, cannot help hating him, and answers rape with murder. Her conviction that a just God endorses her deed is so sustained and passionate that a puzzling dramatic tension is set up by "the restless and anatomizing casuistry with which men seek the justification of Beatrice, yet feel that she has done what needs justification." She is given other motives for her pose of innocence, including the fear of death. In the Old Vic production of 1959, Barbara Jefford spoke Beatrice's final words of the play, "Well, 'tis very well," with a stinging derision that epitomized the vitality and complexity of this remarkable heroine. *The Cenci* cannot properly be judged away from the theater, and in the theater it is powerful but defective. It is also memorably original. Except in the most trivial ways it is quite un-Shakespearean, in versification as in content.

Most of *The Cenci* was written near Leghorn. Mary Shelley had been grief-stricken by the death of their son William in June 1819; and the Shelleys had fled from Rome, now childless, to seek consolation from an old friend, Maria Gisborne, who had nursed Mary as a baby. Shelley did, of course, write private verses to express his feelings, but the two public poems composed during this unhappy summer were entirely objective. The second of these was "The Masque of Anarchy," a vigorous fusion of biblical prophecy, poetic vision, and street balladry:

> As I lay asleep in Italy
> There came a voice from over the Sea,
> And with great power it forth led me
> To walk in the Visions of Poesy.
>
> (1–4)

Asleep at his post of duty to others, Shelley meant. The news of the Peterloo massacre of 16 August, when a peaceful reform demonstration in Manchester was ridden down by drunken yeomanry, had reached him on 5 September; next day he told his publisher, "The torrent of my indignation has not yet done boiling in my veins"; and within three weeks a ballad of ninety-one stanzas was on its way to Leigh Hunt for publication. Again a poem was addressed to a popular audience, and again it was held back for fear of the consequences. Perhaps with reason, for although its appeal is to the advantages of passive resistance and (shrewdly) to "the old laws of England," the refrain "Ye are many—they are few" would hardly have tranquilized the frightened leaders of Lord Liverpool's government, nor would the opening stanzas, in which each leader is made to seem a mere "front" for the evil that inhabits him:

> I met Murder on the way—
> He had a mask like Castlereagh . . . .
>
> (5–6)

Murder wears the face of Lord Castlereagh (foreign secretary); Hypocrisy, that of Lord Sidmouth (home secretary and builder of churches for the starving poor); Fraud is a mock-up of Lord Eldon (a judge). Thus the title is a pun: "masque," pageant play, and "mask," disguise. Once more the constructive side of the poem takes the form of a prophetic vision, but the writing is forceful and concrete. "Freedom" is no abstract slogan: it means bread on a table, a home, and clothes.

Shelley's other political songs are less interesting than the long, incomplete prose essay "A Philosophical View of Reform," written soon after "The Masque of Anarchy." Its modest proposals to abolish the national debt, to disband the army, to make religious intolerance illegal, to extend the jury system and the franchise were not, of course, all that Shelley wanted, but only what he thought it possible to get. The long-range aspirations of his poetry always have somewhere behind them this sort of short-term prose practicality.

From this time on, with minor exceptions, Shelley gave up trying to reach a wide audience on subjects of topical concern, as he had earlier given up direct action. But one major poem, the "Ode to the West Wind," ends this period of passionate commitment. Shelley had just read an attack on *The Revolt of Islam* in the *Quarterly Review*, full of innuendo against the poet's private life and concluding, "Instead of relying on his own powers, he must feel and acknowledge his weakness, and pray for strength from above." Shelley takes this advice with ironic literalness: he acknowledges his weakness, and prays to the wind. The West Wind he invokes is the "breath of Autumn's being," the essence of seasonal change, one aspect of that universal Power operating at every level in all the elements, from the star-fretted sky to the weed on the seabed: the Power that destroys leaves and people of all colors but also resurrects them as children of another spring.

The reviewer (who had known Shelley at Eton) called him "unteachable in boyhood." If only he could be an unteachable boy again, or if the Wind would simply order him about, as it orders all inanimate things: wave, leaf, and cloud! So it does, for he too is subject to the universal Law; his own leaves are falling. But he is a man, not a leaf, and must use the Wind as well as serve it, just as Asia on her journey used as well as obeyed the "plume-uplifting wind" steaming from Demogorgon's mountain. He is a poet, and must give back music to the Wind; he is a prophet, and the Wind must trumpet his words abroad. Cause and effect interpenetrate to proclaim the same message of hope.

The ode is one of the great lyrics of the language, unique for its athletic swiftness within a tightly con-troling form. Its imagery and diction, which a few critics have thought suspiciously beautiful, have turned out on closer inspection to be equally exact and subtle.

The day "West Wind" was begun in Florence was probably the day after *Peter Bell the Third* was finished, this last a shrewd joke at Wordsworth's expense, with much hard-hitting contemporary satire:

> Hell is a city much like London —
> A populous and a smoky city;
> There are all sorts of people undone
> And there is little or no fun done;
> Small justice shown, and still less pity.
> (147–151)

There was also a literal "new birth" in November 1819. Percy Florence Shelley, who survived his father, owed his second name to the suggestion of a visiting friend, Sophia Stacey. Sophia flirted amicably with Shelley, sang to him, and was courted in a resourceful variety of poetic attitudes: with playful practicality in "Love's Philosophy," with oriental sensuality in "The Indian Serenade," and ethereally in "Thou art fair and few are fairer" (a lyric evidently once intended for Asia, but re-addressed from a "nymph of air" to a "nymph of earth"). Perhaps the unclaimed flowers of "The Question" would have been Sophia's too, if she had stayed to accept them.

In January 1820, Shelley took his family to Pisa, where a small group of friends later began to gather: Edward Williams and Jane Johnson early the following year, he a young officer on half-pay, she a refugee from her real husband; and in 1822, Edward Trelawny, a supposed former privateer who was as devoted as his credentials were unreliable.

The severe winter in Florence, and perhaps Miss Stacey's departure, influenced Shelley's first poem of 1820, "The Sensitive Plant" (*Mimosa pudica*), a parable of man's precarious situation within nature. This was followed by the grandiloquent "Ode to Liberty," inspired by news of the revolution in Spain against Ferdinand VII. Perhaps some of the shorter poems of this spring were more successful within their limits. Shelley obviously enjoyed the challenge to his craftsmanship of commissioned work, and it was probably after writing what is known as the "Hymn of Apollo," which the sun god sings in the first person, for a verse play of his wife's that Shelley went on to write, in the same manner but just for fun, his dazzling meteorological nursery rhyme "The Cloud."

The other long poems written in 1820 are all light in tone, especially the accomplished (and funny) translation of Homer's "Hymn to Mercury." "The Witch of Atlas" is more serious than it seems, but is still a holiday poem. And early in July, Shelley wrote the verse letter that Maria Gisborne called "that delightful and laughable and exquisite description in verse of our house and Henry's workroom"—the poem generally entitled "Letter to Maria Gisborne," although it was sent to the family. It was not that he was especially lighthearted. What the playful tone represents is a new artistic maturity in Shelley, a sort of Mozartian wryness, compounded of sadness and self-mockery, that is characteristic of some of his best work from 1820 on.

The Gisbornes had gone to London, and Shelley was writing from the workroom of Maria's son Henry, who was a nautical engineer. It is a true letter to close friends, not a public poem, and its deceptively careless form gives the illusion of spontaneous informality. The spider and silkworm of the opening introduce several themes—"threads of friendship," "machinery," and "habitation"—that permeate the poem. These verses are not to catch readers, Shelley says; they are just an expendable way of making my friends remember me. What really counts is not the apparatus of constraint, but the ties of affection, natural beauty, and domesticity. Later the spider's meretricious web becomes equivalent to London, and the silkworm's mulberry tree to the peaceful environment of Italy (silk was the chief industrial product of Italy). All this with playful courtesy— for instance, in the recollection of how Maria Gisborne, who had cared for Shelley's wife as a baby, had nursed him also through his infancy in the Spanish language. Topics of every degree of seriousness grow effortlessly out of one another: torture, toy boats, tea, life after death, prostitution, mince pies; and the appropriate modulations of tone are managed with a happy confidence:

> You will see Coleridge, he who sits obscure
> In the exceeding lustre and the pure
> Intense irradiation of a mind
> Which, with its own internal lightning blind,
> Flags wearily through darkness and despair—
>
> . . .
>
> But we will have books, Spanish, Italian, Greek,
> And ask one week to make another week

> As like his father as I'm unlike mine,
> Which is not his fault, as you may divine.
>
> (202–206; 298–301)

There is throughout a concrete particularity—a sense of locality and of things—which is not often credited to Shelley:

> . . . a shabby stand
> Of hackney coaches, a brick house or wall
> Fencing some lordly court, white with the scrawl
> Of our unhappy politics . . .
>
> (265–268)

The poem is a triumph of graceful craftsmanship and civilized feeling.

A more intense but much narrower poem resulted from Shelley's celebration of a young Italian girl, Emilia Viviani, as the final embodiment of the Ideal Beauty he had been seeking all his life. In a way *Epipsychidion* ("a little soul beside a soul") is the most "typical" of all Shelley's works, an extreme concentration of a single element in his genius. But Keats would have called it "too smokeable"—too easy to smile at. When, eventually, Shelley found Emilia "a cloud instead of a Juno," he reacted against the poem too, and sent word to stop its further publication.

He was still under the spell of this platonic friendship when he wrote his best-known prose work, "A Defence of Poetry," unpublished until 1840. It was part of an answer to Thomas Love Peacock's half-serious argument that poetry in a utilitarian age was obsolescent, and his treatment is therefore very general. But his metaphors are generally used, as in Francis Bacon, not for mere eloquence but in order to make complex meanings intelligible ("the mind in creation is as a fading coal, which some invisible influence, like an inconstant wind, awakens to transitory brightness"); and some of the incidental discussions are of much interest: for example, the question why a great poem such as *Paradise Lost* will go on revealing new significances long after its social context, and even the religion that inspired it, have disintegrated. "Veil after veil may be undrawn, and the inmost naked beauty of the meaning never exposed." This is an important commentary on Shelley's own adaptations of myth.

News came in April 1821 of Keats's death in Rome. Shelley had not known him well; but he had seen from *Hyperion* that Keats was a major poet, and the supposed primary cause of his death—the *Quarterly*

Review attack on *Endymion* in 1818—roused him to fury. Yet *Adonais* is "a highly wrought *piece of art*," for in this most complimentary of English elegies, Shelley purposely followed Keats's advice to "curb his magnanimity" (that is, his humanitarian zeal) and "be more of an artist." So it is statelier, more conscious of its own verbal substance, than many of Shelley's poems.

To counter the reviewers' dismissal of Keats as an illiterate Cockney, Shelley chose to honor him by adopting the graceful classical artifice of the pastoral elegy, as Edmund Spenser had mourned Sir Philip Sidney in *Astrophel*, and Milton his friend Edward King in "Lycidas." The classical pastoral transfers personal emotions and relationships to a more or less idealized country community; the shepherd with his pipe, living in close contact with nature, becomes a type of the poet, and the death of a shepherd-poet is lamented by his fellow shepherds and by nature itself. The convention derives from Theocritus and his Latin imitator Vergil; but Shelley's more immediate influences were Moschus' elegy on the Greek poet Bion, and Bion's own *Lament of Venus for Adonis*, lines from both of which he had translated. Thus *Adonais* belongs to a tradition extending from the Greek idyll to Matthew Arnold's "Thyrsis"—and even, in some respects, to T. S. Eliot's *The Waste Land*.

Keats had used the myth of Adonis, whose name suggested "Adonais," in his *Endymion*. He was a boy loved by the goddess Venus, but one day a boar killed him while he was hunting. He was permitted to return to life for half the year, spending the other half asleep in the underworld. This was a close fit: Keats was loved by immortal Poetry (Urania) and killed by a reviewer, yet in death he had rejoined the Spirit whose "plastic stress" shapes the beauty of the material world. Like Asia, Urania is composite. She is not Adonais' love but his mother, and she is imagined as being Milton's spiritual widow, with Adonais as their youngest offspring. This is because Shelley regarded the author of *Hyperion* as the poetic heir of Milton, who had adopted Urania as his single "heavenly born" Muse in *Paradise Lost*; so, after Milton's death, Keats was the "nursling of her widowhood." But at times she is also Venus Genetrix, goddess of love and organic life.

The almost unrelieved grief of the opening stanzas, expressed in imagery of cloud and vapor, is not to be dispelled by the return of spring, although

> The leprous corpse touched by this spirit tender
> Exhales itself in flowers of gentle breath;
> Like incarnations of the stars . . .
>
> (st. 20)

The flowers are earthly versions of the stars, radiating perfume instead of light. But for the dead man there is no renewal of life, as Moschus had said in his lament for Bion. Death is the price paid on earth for the colors of sky and field. Even Urania, undying mother of generation, cannot revive Adonais.

Adonais' own poetic imaginings lament him, and there are many references to Keats's poems: the "pale flower by some sad maiden cherished" is "Isabella"; Adonais is washed from a "lucid urn"; his spirit's sister is the nightingale; like his own Hyperion he could scale Heaven. His fellow poets lament him, too, mountain shepherds in honor of Endymion, who kept sheep on Mount Patmos; these include Byron, Thomas Moore, and Leigh Hunt. Shelley's own presence among them is often thought an embarrassment to the poem, and there is some evidence that he meant to omit these stanzas in a second edition. But the episode is not irrelevant; an obscure mourner, who identifies his fate with that of Adonais, asks: If the enemies of the imagination could not even discriminate between the extremes represented by Cain and Christ, what justice can be expected for any of us? Yet, in some sense at least, Adonais is with the "enduring" dead, like pure metal melted down and returned to the furnace, whereas the reviewer and his kind are ashes only:

> Thou canst not soar where he is sitting now—
> Dust to the dust! but the pure spirit shall flow
> Back to the burning fountain whence it came,
> A portion of the Eternal . . . .
>
> (st. 38)

So the poem reaches its final affirmation, expressed in imagery of light and fire. Adonais has "awakened from the dream of life"—this life the flowers, arts, and cultures of which can only partially embody the Power working through them—and has become identified with that Power:

> He is a portion of the loveliness
> Which once he made more lovely: he doth bear
> His part, while the one Spirit's plastic stress
> Sweeps through the dull dense world, compelling there
> All new successions to the forms they wear;

Torturing the unwilling dross that checks its flight
To its own likeness, as each mass may bear;
And bursting in its beauty and its might
From trees and beasts and men into the Heavens' light.

(st. 43)

In death the white sunlight of Unity is no longer refracted into colors by the "dome" of the mundane atmosphere. And that Unity, to attain which Shelley would almost accept a death like Keats's ("why shrink, my Heart?"), touches him in the act of writing his poem and authorizes its final daring paradoxes of grammar and metaphor:

That Light . . .

. . .

Which through the web of being blindly wove
By man and beast and earth and air and sea,
Burns bright or dim, as each are mirrors of
The fire for which all thirst, now beams on me,
Consuming the last clouds of cold mortality.

(st. 54)

In the autumn Shelley completed *Hellas* ("Greece") in honor of the Greeks' insurrection against their Turkish overlords. It was written, like W. H. Auden's *Spain*, for the cause; and though it has some fine lyrical choruses, the blank verse tends to be strained. Shelley called it "a mere improvise."

Byron had moved to Pisa late in 1821, to write for *The Liberal*, which Leigh Hunt was coming from England to edit; and in March and April 1822, Shelley translated some scenes from Pedro Calderón de la Barca and from *Faust* for publication in the new journal. But he was again in a very unsettled state. He had already abandoned work on a new play, *Charles I.* Some of his uncertainty related to Edward and Jane Williams—especially Jane, whom he found increasingly attractive. As the months of 1822 passed, the eight lyrics he gave her came to form the best—indeed, the only—group of unequivocally personal love poems he ever wrote. For all their tact and delicacy, these poems have a new undertone of skepticism, almost earthiness:

. . . the sweet warmth of day
Was scattered o'er the twinkling bay;
And the fisher with his lamp
And spear, about the low rocks damp
Crept, and struck the fish who came
To worship the delusive flame.

(43–48)

These "Lines Written in the Bay of Lerici" were composed when the Williams and Shelley families were in joint occupation of Casa Magni, the only house available to them on that beautiful coast. Claire's little Allegra had died of fever, and it had been imperative to get her mother well away from Byron, whom she was bound to blame for this tragedy. In May, Shelley's new boat, the *Don Juan*, arrived; and the outward things of life seemed very favorable to him, for once:

Williams is captain [he wrote], and we drive along this delightful bay in the evening wind, under the summer moon, until earth appears another world. Jane brings her guitar, and if the past and the future could be obliterated, the present would content me so well that I could say with Faust to the passing moment, "Remain, thou, thou art so beautiful".[2]

(letter to John Gisborne, 18 June 1822)

Inwardly it was otherwise. His poetry had failed, and the popular cause had been defeated over almost all of Europe. Four children he had loved were dead; his wife was ill and unhappy; and he was in love with someone unobtainable. In this complex of troubles he began "The Triumph of Life."

Shelley's last, unfinished, poem is difficult and enigmatic. Stylistically it is like a combination of "The Masque of Anarchy" and *Adonais*—that is, of directness and economy with a "highly wrought" verbal texture—but the literary influences behind it are no longer English or Greek, but Italian: Petrarch and Dante. Although most of the poem exists only in rough draft, the movement of the verse is so fluent that Shelley's technical mastery of the terza rima goes almost unnoticed. The homage of all creation to the sun, at the opening, is followed by a vision of the car of light, in front of which the young execute a frenzied erotic dance, until

One falls and then another in the path
    Senseless, nor is the desolation single,

Yet ere I can say *where*, the chariot hath
    Passed over them; nor other trace I find
·But as of foam after the ocean's wrath

    Is spent upon the desert shore.—Behind,
Old men and women foully disarrayed
    Shake their grey hair in the insulting wind,

[2]From F. L. Jones, ed., *The Letters of Percy Bysshe Shelley* (Oxford, 1964), vol. II, pp. 435–436.

Limp in the dance and strain with limbs decayed
 To reach the car of light which leaves them still
Far behind, and deeper in the shade.

 But not the less with impotence of will
They wheel, though ghastly shadows interpose,
 Round them and round each other, and fulfil

Their work, and to the dust whence they arose
 Sink, and corruption veils them as they lie,
And frost in these performs what fire in those.

(159–175)

One fallen worshipper, Jean Jacques Rousseau, describes how the car seduced him from what seemed an early ideal, a "fair Shape" brighter than the sun, and then destroyed him as it had destroyed these others.

What is being repudiated in this poem? The "suicidal selfishness" of *Queen Mab*, the "loathsome mask" of *Prometheus Unbound*, all the moral and social targets of Shelley's earlier attacks? These, certainly; but some feel that earthly life is now being rejected altogether, that Rousseau's "fair Shape" was a double agent, a delusive embodiment of the true Ideal. The poem breaks off, and no one knows whether there would have been another side to this somber vision, or whether it was already almost complete.

Leigh Hunt's arrival must have interrupted the answer to that final question, "What is Life?" After a busy but happy reunion with him in Leghorn, Shelley and Williams sailed for home on 8 July; but on the way the boat was wrecked in a squall. Because of the quarantine laws, the bodies of Shelley and his friend were burned on the foreshore under Trelawny's supervision; and Shelley's ashes were interred in the Protestant cemetery in Rome on 21 January 1823, that "flame transformed to marble" that had been celebrated in *Adonais*. At about the same age of twenty-nine, Wordsworth, who considered Shelley "one of the best *artists* of us all," was just thinking of writing a preface to his *Lyrical Ballads*.

SELECTED BIBLIOGRAPHY

I. Bibliography. H. B. Forman, *The Shelley Library* (London, 1886), pt. I: "Shelley's Own Books, Pamphlets and Broadsides; Posthumous Separate Issues; and Posthumous Books Wholly or Mainly by Him"; no pt. II was published; W. Sharp, *Life of Percy Bysshe Shelley* (London, 1887), includes bibliography by J. P. Anderson, still useful for critical articles 1822–1887; F. S. Ellis, comp., *A Lexical Concordance to the Poetical Works of Shelley* (London, 1892), repr. with app. by T. Saito (Tokyo, 1963), based on H. B. Forman's 1882 ed. of the poems; R. Granniss, *A Descriptive Catalogue of the First Editions in Book Form of the Writings of Shelley* (New York, 1923), with 30 plates; T. J. Wise, *A Shelley Library. A Catalogue of Printed Books, Manuscripts and Autograph Letters* (London, 1924), privately printed, essentially vol. V of *The Ashley Library* (London, 1924); S. de Ricci, *A Bibliography of Shelley's Letters, Published and Unpublished* (Paris, 1927), privately printed; *Keats-Shelley Journal* (1952–   ), contains an annual bibliography; L. Patton, *The Shelley-Godwin Collection of Lord Abinger, Duke University Library Notes*, 27 (1953), 11–17; C. H. Taylor, *The Early Collected Editions of Shelley's Poems: A Study in the History and Transmission of the Printed Text* (New Haven, Conn., 1958); K. N. Cameron, ed., *Shelley and His Circle 1773–1822* (Cambridge, Mass.–London, 1961–   ), vols. I–II (1961); D. H. Reiman, ed., vols. III–IV (1970); vols. V–VI (1973); to be completed in about 8 vols.; D. B. Green and D. E. G. Wilson, comps., *Keats, Shelley, Byron, Hunt and Their Circles: A Bibliography 1 July 1950–30 June 1962* (Lincoln, Nebr., 1964); I. Massey, *Posthumous Poems of Shelley: Mary Shelley's Fair Copy Book, Bodleian MS. Shelley Adds. d.9* (Montreal, 1969); C. Dunbar, *A Bibliography of Shelley Studies: 1823–1950* (Folkestone, 1976).

II. Principal Collected Editions. *The Poetical Works of Coleridge, Shelley, and Keats* (Paris, 1829), the Galignani ed., with a memoir by C. Redding; M. W. Shelley, ed., *The Poetical Works*, 4 vols. (London, 1839), *Queen Mab* printed with omissions; new rev. ed. in 1 vol., adding *Swellfoot, Peter Bell the Third*, and *Queen Mab* complete (London, 1839 [title page dated 1840]); W. M. Rossetti, ed., *The Poetical Works, Including Various Additional Pieces from MS and Other Sources, the Text Carefully Revised, with Notes and a Memoir*, 2 vols. (London, 1870; rev. ed., 3 vols., 1878); H. B. Forman, ed., *The Poetical Works*, 4 vols. (London, 1876–1877), new eds. in 2 vols. (London, 1882), with Mary Shelley's notes, and in 5 vols. (London, 1892), the Aldine ed.; H. B. Forman, ed., *The Works in Prose and Verse*, 8 vols. (London, 1880); G. E. Woodberry, ed., *Complete Poetical Works*, 4 vols. (Boston, 1892; London, 1893), also in 1 vol. (Boston, 1901), the Cambridge Poets ed.; T. Hutchinson, ed., *Complete Poetical Works* (London, 1904), with textual notes by Hutchinson, also published in Oxford Standard Authors ed. (London, 1905), with intro. by B. P. Kurtz (New York, 1933), and without intro. (London, 1934; 2nd ed., 1970), the latter rev. by G. M. Matthews; A. H. Koszul, ed., *The Poetical Works*, 2 vols. (London, 1907), with intro. by Koszul, also rev. ed. with new intro., 2 vols. (London,

1953), in Everyman's Library, poems published in chronological order; C. D. Locock, ed., *The Poems*, 2 vols. (London, 1911), with intro. by A. Clutton-Brock, the only complete ed. with explanatory notes; R. Ingpen and W. E. Peck, eds., *The Complete Works*, 10 vols. (London, 1926–1930; repr. New York, 1965), the Julian ed.; D. L. Clark, ed., *Shelley's Prose* (Albuquerque, N. M., 1954; repr. with corrs., 1967), a usefully full collection, but very unreliable textually and in dating; N. Rogers, ed., *The Complete Poetical Works*, vol. I: *1802–1813* (Oxford, 1972); vol. II: *1814–1817* (Oxford, 1975); to be completed in 4 vols.

III. SELECTIONS. R. Garnett, ed., *Select Letters* (London, 1882); E. Rhys, ed., *Essays and Letters* (London, 1886); J. Shawcross, ed., *Shelley's Literary and Philosophical Criticism* (London, 1909), with intro. by Shawcross; H. F. B. Brett-Smith, ed., *Peacock's Four Ages of Poetry; Shelley's Defence of Poetry; Browning's Essay on Shelley* (London, 1921; expurgated ed., 1923); A. M. D. Hughes, ed., *Poetry and Prose, with Essays by Browning, Bagehot, Swinburne, and Reminiscences by Others* (London, 1931); C. Baker, ed., *Selected Poetry and Prose* (New York, 1951), the Modern Library ed.; A. S. B. Glover, ed., *Selected Poetry, Prose and Letters* (London, 1951), the Nonesuch ed.; M. Spark and D. Stanford, eds., *My Best Mary: The Selected Letters of Mary W. Shelley* (London, 1953), with intro. by the eds.; E. Blunden, ed., *Selected Poems* (London, 1954), with a long intro. and notes; K. N. Cameron, ed., *Selected Poetry and Prose* (New York, 1956); J. Holloway, ed., *Selected Poems* (London, 1960), with intro. by Holloway; D. S. R. Welland, ed., *Selections from Shelley's Poetry and Prose* (London, 1961); G. M. Matthews, ed., *Shelley: Selected Poems and Prose* (Oxford, 1964), contains a new poem; H. Bloom, ed., *Selected Poetry and Prose* (New York, 1966); B. R. McElderry, ed., *Shelley's Critical Prose* (Lincoln, Nebr., 1966); P. Butter, ed., *Alastor and Other Poems: Prometheus Unbound with Other Poems: Adonais* (London, 1970); R. A. Duerksen, ed., *Political Writings Including "A Defence of Poetry"* (New York, 1970); N. Rogers, ed., *Selected Poetry* (London, 1970), an Oxford Paperback; D. H. Reiman and S. B. Powers, eds., *Shelley's Poetry and Prose* (New York, 1977), includes new texts and fifteen critical articles; T. Webb, ed., *Selected Poems* (London, 1977), with new texts.

IV. SEPARATE WORKS IN VERSE AND PROSE. *Original Poetry by Victor and Cazire* [Shelley and his sister Elizabeth] (Worthing, 1810), photofacs. in S. J. Hooker, *Shelley, Trelawny and Henley* (Worthing, 1950); John Fitzvictor [P. B. Shelley], ed., *Posthumous Fragments of Margaret Nicholson, Being Poems Found Amongst the Papers of That Noted Female Who Attempted the Life of the King in 1786* (Oxford, 1810), also privately printed by H. B. Forman (London, 1877); *Zastrozzi: A Romance* (London, 1810), repr. in E. Chesser, *Shelley and Zastrozzi: Self-Revelation of a Neurotic* (London, 1965); *The Necessity of Atheism* (Worthing, 1811), published anonymously by Shelley and T. J. Hogg, photofacs. in S. J. Hooker, *Shelley, Trelawny and Henley* (Worthing, 1950); *St Irvyne or the Rosicrucian: A Romance, by a Gentleman of the University of Oxford* (London, 1811; reiss., 1822); *An Address to the Irish People* (Dublin, 1812); *Declaration of Rights* (Dublin, 1812), an unsigned broadside, two copies are in the Public Record Office; *The Devils' Walk: A Ballad* (Barnstaple [?], 1812), unsigned broadside, one copy in the Public Record Office and one at the University of Texas, Austin; *A Letter to Lord Ellenborough* (London, 1812), privately printed, one copy in the Bodleian Library; *Proposals for an Association of . . . Philanthropists . . .* (Dublin, 1812); *Queen Mab: A Philosophical Poem, with Notes* (London, 1813), privately printed, many unauthorized eds. 1821–1857; *A Vindication of a Natural Diet, Being One in a Series of Notes to Queen Mab, a Philosophical Poem* (London, 1813); *A Refutation of Deism, in a Dialogue* (London, 1814), published anonymously; *Alastor: or The Spirit of Solitude, and Other Poems* (London, 1816).

History of a Six Weeks' Tour Through a Part of France, Switzerland, Germany and Holland (London, 1817), published anonymously by Percy and Mary Shelley; *A Proposal for Putting Reform to the Vote Throughout the Kingdom, by the Hermit of Marlow* [Shelley] (London, 1817), facs. of the MS published by H. B. Forman (London, 1887); *Laon and Cythna; or, The Revolution of the Golden City: A Vision of the Nineteenth Century in the Stanza of Spenser* (London, 1818), suppressed, rev. and reiss. as *The Revolt of Islam: A Poem in Twelve Cantos* (London, 1818), some copies dated 1817; *The Cenci: A Tragedy in Five Acts* (Leghorn, 1819; 2nd ed., London, 1821), repr. by G. E. Woodberry (Boston, 1909), with bibliography; *Rosalind and Helen: A Modern Eclogue; with Other Poems* (London, 1819); *Oedipus Tyrannus: or, Swellfoot the Tyrant: A Tragedy in Two Acts, Translated from the Original Doric* (London, 1820), this unsigned ed. was suppressed; *Prometheus Unbound: A Lyrical Drama in Four Acts, with Other Poems* (London, 1820), the principal separate modern eds. are V. Scudder, ed. (Boston, 1892), R. Ackermann, ed. (Heidelberg, 1908), A. M. D. Hughes, ed. (Oxford, 1910; repr. 1957), L. J. Zillman, ed. (Seattle, 1959; New Haven, Conn.–London, 1968); *Adonais: An Elegy on the Death of John Keats, Author of Endymion, Hyperion, etc.* (Pisa, 1821; 2nd ed., Cambridge, 1829), annotated ed. by W. M. Rossetti (Oxford, 1890) was rev. by Rossetti and A. O. Prickard (London, 1903), photofacs. in N. Douglas, ed. (London, 1927); *Epipsychidion: Verses Addressed to the Noble and Unfortunate Lady Emilia V— Now Imprisoned in the Convent of——* (London, 1821; facs. ed., Menston, 1970), this unsigned ed. was withdrawn; *Hellas: A Lyrical Drama* (London, 1822).

V. POSTHUMOUS WORKS. M. W. Shelley, ed., *Posthumous Poems* (London, 1824), this ed. was suppressed; *The Masque of Anarchy: A Poem Now First Published* (London, 1832), with preface by L. Hunt, photofacs. of the

"Wise" MS published by H. B. Forman (London, 1887); *The Shelley Papers: Memoir by T. Medwin and Original Poems and Papers by Shelley* (London, 1833), includes a spurious poem, "To the Queen of My Heart"; M. W. Shelley, ed., *Essays, Letters from Abroad, etc.,* 2 vols. (London, 1840), includes "A Defence of Poetry"; *An Address to the People on the Death of Princess Charlotte, by the Hermit of Marlow* (London, ca. 1843), probably from a MS written ca. 1817 and now lost; Lady J. Shelley and R. Garnett, eds. *Shelley Memorials* (London, 1859), includes "An Essay on Christianity"; R. Garnett, ed., *Relics of Shelley* (London, 1862); H. B. Forman, ed., *The Daemon of the World* (London, 1876), privately printed; H. B. Forman, ed., *Notes on Sculptures in Rome and Florence, Together with a Lucianic Fragment and a Criticism on Peacock's Poem "Rhododaphne"* (London, 1879), privately printed; B. Dobell, ed., *The Wandering Jew* (London, 1887); C. D. Locock, *An Examination of the Shelley Manuscripts in the Bodleian Library* (Oxford, 1903); A. H. Koszul, ed., *Shelley's Poetry in the Bodleian Manuscripts* (Oxford, 1910), "A Defence of Poetry," "Essay on Christianity," and fragments; *Note Books of Shelley, from the Originals in the Library of W. K. Bixby,* deciphered, transcribed, and edited by H. B. Forman, 3 vols. (Boston, 1911), privately printed; T. W. Rolleston, ed., *A Philosophical View of Reform* (Oxford, 1920); W. E. Peck, ed., "An Unpublished Ballad by Shelley" ("Young Parson Richards"), in *Philological Quarterly,* 5 (1926), 114–118; G. E. Woodberry, ed., *The Shelley Notebook in the Harvard Library* (Cambridge, Mass., 1929), a photofacs., autograph ascriptions were corrected by H. Darbishire in *Review of English Studies,* 31 (July 1932), 352–354.

J. C. E. Shelley-Rolls and R. Ingpen, eds., *Verse and Prose from the Manuscripts of Shelley* (London, 1934), privately printed; D. Cook, ed., " 'Sadak the Wanderer': An Unknown Shelley Poem," in *Times Literary Supplement* (16 May 1936), 424; E. H. Blakeney, ed., *A Shelley Letter* (Winchester, 1936), Shelley's verse epistle to Feargus Graham (1811); J. A. Notopoulos, *The Platonism of Shelley* (Durham, N. C., 1949), includes "Shelley's Translations from Plato: A Critical Edition," edited by the author, and unpublished material; G. M. Matthews, ed., "The Triumph of Life: A New Text," in *Studia Neophilologica,* 32 (1960), 271–309; K. N. Cameron, ed., *The Esdaile Notebook: A Volume of Early Poems* (New York, 1964; slightly rev., London, 1964); D. H. Reiman, *Shelley's "The Triumph of Life": A Critical Study Based on a Text Newly Edited from the Bodleian MS* (Urbana, Ill., 1965); N. Rogers, ed., *The Esdaile Poems* (Oxford, 1966); J. Chernaik, "Shelley's 'To Constantia,' " in *Times Literary Supplement* (6 February 1969), 140, a new text of "To Constantia Singing"; T. Webb, ed., "Shelley's 'Hymn to Venus': A New Text," in *Review of English Studies,* n.s. 21 (August 1970), 315–324; J. Chernaik and T. Burnett, eds., "The Byron and Shelley Notebooks in the Scrope Davies Find," in *Review of English Studies,* 29 (February 1978), 36–49.

VI. LETTERS AND JOURNALS. Lady J. Shelley and Sir P. F. Shelley, eds., *Shelley and Mary,* 3 (or 4) vols. (London, 1882), privately printed; R. Ingpen, comp. and ed., *The Letters,* 2 vols. (London, 1909), new ed., adding five letters (London, 1912; rev. ed., 1914); R. H. Hill, ed., *The Shelley Correspondence in the Bodleian Library* (Oxford, 1926), contains lists of MSS, letters, and relics; L. Hotson, ed., *Shelley's Lost Letters to Harriet* (London, 1930), with intro. by Hotson; S. Norman, ed., *After Shelley. The Letters of T. J. Hogg to Jane Williams* (Oxford, 1934); F. L. Jones, comp. and ed., *Letters of Mary W. Shelley,* 2 vols. (Norman, Okla., 1944); F. L. Jones, ed., *Mary Shelley's Journal* (Norman, Okla., 1947); W. S. Scott, ed., *New Shelley Letters* (London, 1948), letters by Shelley and members of his circle from the papers of T. J. Hogg; F. L. Jones, ed., *Maria Gisborne and Edward E. Williams, Shelley's Friends: Their Journals and Letters* (Norman, Okla., 1951); F. L. Jones, ed., *The Letters of Percy Bysshe Shelley,* 2 vols. (Oxford, 1964); M. K. Stocking, ed., *The Journals of Claire Clairmont* (Cambridge, Mass., 1968).

VII. BIOGRAPHICAL AND CRITICAL STUDIES. T. Medwin, *Journal of the Conversations of Lord Byron* (London, 1824), in E. J. Lovell, ed. (Princeton, N. J., 1966); L. Hunt, *Lord Byron and Some of His Contemporaries* (London, 1828), also in J. E. Morpurgo, ed. (London, 1949), see also Hunt's *Autobiography,* 3 vols. (London, 1850); W. Bagehot, *Estimates of Some Englishmen and Scotchmen* (London, 1858), repr. in his *Literary Studies,* vol. I, R. B. Hutton, ed. (London, 1879); T. J. Hogg, *Life of Shelley,* 2 vols. (London, 1858), the MS of two further vols. has been lost; T. L. Peacock, "Memoirs of Shelley," in *Fraser's* magazine (June 1858–March 1862), in H. F. B. Brett-Smith, ed. (Oxford, 1909); E. J. Trelawny, *Recollections of the Last Days of Shelley and Byron* (London, 1858; repr. 1906, 1952), rev. as *Records of Shelley, Byron and the Author,* 2 vols. (London, 1878; repr. London, 1905; New York, 1968); Lady J. Shelley and R. Garnett, eds., *Shelley Memorials* (London, 1859); T. Hunt, "Shelley, by One Who Knew Him," in *Atlantic Monthly,* 11 (February 1863), 184–204; D. F. MacCarthy, *Shelley's Early Life, from Original Sources* (London, 1872), Shelley's activities and publications in Ireland; E. Dowden, *Life of Shelley,* 2 vols. (London, 1886), the 1-vol. rev. and abr. version (1896) in H. Read, ed. (London, 1951); M. Arnold, *Essays in Criticism,* 2nd ser. (London, 1888), includes an essay on Shelley; H. S. Salt, *Shelley: Poet and Pioneer* (London, 1896).

W. B. Yeats, *Ideas of Good and Evil* (London, 1903), includes "The Philosophy of Shelley's Poetry," repr. in his *Essays and Introductions* (London, 1961); A. Droop, *Die Belesenheit Shelleys* (Weimar, 1906); E. S. Bates, *A Study of Shelley's Drama "The Cenci"* (New York, 1908; repr. 1969); A. C. Bradley, *Oxford Lectures on Poetry* (London, 1909), includes "Shelley's View of Poetry"; *Bulletin of the Keats-Shelley Memorial, Rome,* vol. I (1910), vol. II (1913), both repr. (1961), journal subsequently published yearly from vol. III (1950); A. Clutton-Brock, *Shelley: The Man and the Poet* (London, 1910; rev. ed., 1923); A. H. Koszul, *La jeunesse de Shelley* (Paris, 1910); H. R. Angeli, *Shelley and His Friends in Italy* (London, 1911); H. N. Brailsford, *Shelley, Godwin and Their Circle* (London, 1913; rev. ed., Oxford, 1951); R. Ingpen, *Shelley in England: New Facts and Letters from the Shelley-Whitton Papers* (London, 1917); S. de Madariaga, *Shelley and Calderón and Other Essays* (London, 1920); A. T. Strong, *Three Studies in Shelley* (Oxford, 1921); O. W. Campbell, *Shelley and the Unromantics* (London, 1924); E. Blunden, *Shelley and Keats as They Struck Their Contemporaries* (London, 1925); M. T. Solve, *Shelley: His Theory of Poetry* (Chicago, 1927; repr. New York, 1964).

C. H. Grabo, *A Newton Among Poets: Shelley's Use of Science in Prometheus Unbound* (Chapel Hill, N. C., 1930); *The Life of Percy Bysshe Shelley as Comprised in the "Life of Shelley" by T. J. Hogg, "The Recollections of Shelley and Byron" by E. J. Trelawny, "Memoirs of Shelley" by T. L. Peacock*, 2 vols. (London, 1933), with intro. by H. Wolfe; B. P. Kurtz, *The Pursuit of Death: A Study of Shelley's Poetry* (New York, 1933); C. H. Grabo, *Prometheus Unbound: An Interpretation* (Chapel Hill, N. C., 1935); C. H. Grabo, *The Magic Plant: The Growth of Shelley's Thought* (Chapel Hill, N. C., 1936); H. Read, *In Defence of Shelley and Other Essays* (London, 1936), rev. and repr. as *The True Voice of Feeling* (London, 1953); E. Barnard, *Shelley's Religion* (Minneapolis, 1937; repr. New York, 1964); R. G. Grylls, *Mary Shelley: A Biography* (Oxford, 1938); N. I. White, *The Unextinguished Hearth: Shelley and His Contemporary Critics* (Durham, N. C., 1938; repr. 1968), a full collection of the early reviews of Shelley.

N. I. White, *Shelley*, 2 vols. (New York, 1940; rev. ed., London, 1947), abr. to the 1-vol. *Portrait of Shelley* (New York, 1945), the standard biography; E. Blunden, *Shelley: A Life Story* (London, 1946); J. Barrell, *Shelley and the Thought of His Time* (New Haven, Conn., 1947); A. M. D. Hughes, *The Nascent Mind of Shelley* (Oxford, 1947); C. Baker, *Shelley's Major Poetry: The Fabric of a Vision* (Princeton, N. J., 1948); D. G. James, *The Romantic Comedy* (Oxford, 1948), has a section on *Prometheus Unbound*; R. H. Fogle, *The Imagery of Keats and Shelley* (Chapel Hill, N. C., 1949); J. A. Notopoulos, *The Platonism of Shelley* (Durham, N. C., 1949).

K. N. Cameron, *The Young Shelley: Genesis of a Radical* (New York, 1950; London, 1951), Shelley's life and work up to 1814; P. H. Butter, *Shelley's Idols of the Cave* (Edinburgh, 1954); S. Norman, *Flight of the Skylark: The Development of Shelley's Reputation* (Norman, Okla., 1954); C. E. Pulos, *The Deep Truth: A Study of Shelley's Scepticism* (Lincoln, Nebr., 1954); N. Rogers, *Shelley at Work: A Critical Inquiry* (Oxford, 1956; rev. ed., Oxford, 1968); H. Bloom, *Shelley's Mythmaking* (New Haven, Conn., 1959); D. Perkins, *The Quest for Permanence: The Symbolism of Wordsworth, Shelley and Keats* (Cambridge, Mass., 1959); E. R. Wasserman, *The Subtler Language* (Baltimore, 1959), essays on "Mont Blanc," "The Sensitive Plant," and *Adonais*; M. Wilson, *Shelley's Later Poetry: A Study of His Prophetic Imagination* (New York, 1959).

D. King-Hele, *Shelley: His Thought and Work* (London, 1960); L. S. Boas, *Harriet Shelley: Five Long Years* (Oxford, 1962); H. Lemaitre, *Shelley, poète des éléments* (Paris, 1962); G. M. Ridenour, ed., *Shelley: A Collection of Critical Essays* (Englewood Cliffs, N. J., 1965); E. R. Wasserman, *Shelley's Prometheus Unbound: A Critical Reading* (Baltimore, 1965); B. Wilkie, *Romantic Poets and Epic Tradition* (Madison, Wis., 1965), on *The Revolt of Islam* as epic; E. J. Schulze, *Shelley's Theory of Poetry: A Reappraisal* (The Hague, 1966); R. B. Woodings, ed., *Shelley* (London, 1968), 17 critical essays (1943–1968), in the Modern Judgments series; D. H. Reiman, *Percy Bysshe Shelley* (New York, 1969); J. P. Guinn, *Shelley's Political Thought* (The Hague, 1969); G. McNiece, *Shelley and the Revolutionary Idea* (Cambridge, Mass., 1969); S. Curran, *Shelley's "Cenci": Scorpions Ringed with Fire* (Princeton, N. J., 1970); E. R. Wasserman, *Shelley: A Critical Reading* (Baltimore, 1971); J. Chernaik, *The Lyrics of Shelley* (Cleveland, Ohio, 1972), new texts of 25 lyrics, with full commentary; K. N. Cameron, *Shelley: The Golden Years* (Cambridge, Mass., 1974); R. Holmes, *Shelley: The Pursuit* (London, 1974), a full biography; J. E. Barcus, ed., *Shelley: The Critical Heritage* (London, 1975); G. Carey, *Shelley* (London, 1975); S. Curran, *Shelley's Annus Mirabilis: The Maturing of an Epic Vision* (San Marino, Calif., 1975); C. E. Robinson, *Shelley and Byron: The Snake and Eagle Wreathed in Fight* (Baltimore, 1976); T. Webb, *The Violet in the Crucible: Shelley and Translation* (Oxford, 1976); T. Webb, *Shelley: A Voice Not Understood* (Manchester, 1977); N. Brown, *Sexuality and Feminism in Shelley* (Cambridge, Mass., 1979); E. Duffy, *Rousseau in England: The Context for Shelley's Critique of the Enlightenment* (Berkeley, 1979), a study of "The Triumph of Life"; J. V. Murphy, *The Dark Angel: Gothic Elements in Shelley's Works* (Lewisburg, Pa., 1979).

JOHN KEATS

(1795-1821)

Miriam Allott

INTRODUCTION

JOHN KEATS was born in London on 31 October 1795 and died of tuberculosis in Rome, where he had been sent for recovery, on 23 February 1821, having been unable to write any poetry during the last fourteen months of his life because of his illness. His brief poetic career falls roughly into four stages: 1816–1817, when he wrote most of the thirty-three poems in his first collection; 1817, when he was chiefly engaged in writing *Endymion*; 1818, a year bringing crucial personal experiences that deeply affected his imagination and that closed with his first attempts at *Hyperion*; and 1819, when he wrote his major poems. The precipitating events of 1818 included his parting with his brother George, who emigrated to America that June; the loss of his other brother, Tom, who died of tuberculosis in December, aged nineteen; his first sight, during his summer walking tour with his friend Charles Brown, of the dramatic mountain scenery in the Lake District and Scotland; and his introduction in the autumn to Fanny Brawne, the girl he loved and whom he was unable to marry, first because they lacked means and later because he was too ill.

Keats had little longer in which to discover his individual poetic voice and learn something of his craft than many students need to study for a first arts degree in a British university; but he lived to see published his two collections, *Poems* (1817) and *Lamia, Isabella, The Eve of St. Agnes, and Other Poems* (1820), and, in the interval between these, his lengthy *Endymion: A Poetic Romance* (1818). Much of the rest of his work, including a selection of his remarkable letters, appeared posthumously in two small volumes published in 1848 by Richard Monckton Milnes as *Life, Letters and Literary Remains of John Keats*. Milnes added to these in 1856 by printing for the first time *The Fall of Hyperion*, a reworking of the earlier, unfinished *Hyperion*.

The total output is not large and its quality is uneven; but it became a seminal influence for other poets in the nineteenth century, remains widely familiar today, even if only by hearsay, and receives from modern scholars the serious critical attention given to major writers. It is the product of a young talent wholly dedicated to its poetic calling and to poetry as a supreme expression of the beautiful, approaching perfection only with the writer's approach to maturity. This was a state reached, as Keats saw it, by growing away from unreflecting delight in external nature and into a wise understanding of the harsher realities of existence and the annihilation of self-regarding impulses through empathic identification with others. This he called "negative capability" and associated it above all with the Shakespearean creative imagination. He did not reach it in his own poetry, though the quick human intelligence and breadth of feeling in his letters make us think that with time he might have done so.

But Keats constantly sought to further the dual development of his poetic and his personal selves by working hard at his craft, experimenting with different genres and metrical structures, submitting himself to various literary influences, and searching for a balance between what he called "sensations"—responsiveness to the concrete particulars of life—and "thoughts"—the exercise of his powers of intellect and understanding, and the nourishing of them by wide reading and varied personal experience.

If we look in turn at Keats's first collection of verse, his narrative poems, his major odes, his final effort to forge a new kind of poetic statement by reworking his abortive "epic," *Hyperion*, into a highly personal "vision," and certain passages in his letters, we can distinguish, at least in outline, the movements of this self-discipline and something of the quality of the work it helped to produce. Critical judgments of Keats have sometimes been drawn out of true, partly because the human appeal of an existence haunted by poverty and fatal disease, which nonetheless finds compensation in the activity of a vivid creative intelligence, can distract attention from the work to the life (the tendency is still common in some modern studies of the Brontë sisters).

In the case of Keats it encouraged the legendary image of a chlorotic youth too sensitive to withstand hardship and done to death by hostile reviewers. Readers fastened on passages that suggested exclusively the poet of luxurious "sensations" and exquisite longing for death, a habit that encouraged a simplistic view of romanticism in general and of Keats's romanticism in particular. It became easy to isolate his confession in the "Ode to a Nightingale":

> . . . many a time
> I have been half in love with easeful Death,
> Called him soft names in many a musèd rhyme,
> To take into the air my quiet breath,
> Now more than ever seems it rich to die,
> To cease upon the midnight with no pain,[1]
>
> (st. 6, 1–6)

to overlook his recognition that death, after all, means insentience:

> Still wouldst thou sing, and I have ears in vain—
> To thy high requiem become a sod.
>
> (st. 6, 9–10)

and with this to ignore the entire movement of thought and feeling that at first carries the poet from "The weariness, the fever and the fret" into an ideal world of beauty and permanence, and finally returns him to what is actual and inescapable.

This curve of feeling shapes, in some degree, all Keats's major poetry. It is connected with that side of his creative temper where a flexible intelligence seeks to penetrate feeling with the vitality that certain Victorian readers anticipated modern criticism in recognizing. An arresting instance is William Howitt's remark, in a book published in 1847, that Keats's poetry was "a vivid orgasm of the intellect." David Masson, in his long article of November 1860 for *Macmillan's* magazine (he was then its editor), saw as outstanding in Keats "the universality of his sensuousness," but found the true sign of poetic greatness in the evidence, even in early poems, "of that power of reflective and constructive intellect by which alone so abundant a wealth of the sensual element could have been ruled and shaped into artistic literary forms."

This "potentiality" adds to our difficulties. In longer-lived and more prolific writers we can follow the individual imagination developing in accordance with its own laws of growth and movement. In Keats we catch little more than a glimpse of these laws and of how they might have come to order and direct his work. Had he lived, he would probably have suppressed or destroyed a great many early poems and, judging by certain comments in his letters, perhaps even some of those we most admire. As it is, we have to understand a talent that made many false starts; produced hundreds of journeyman lines; took time to shake off the insipidities of various unfortunate adoptive styles (especially the current neo-Elizabethanisms most damagingly influential in Leigh Hunt); and produced only a handful of fully achieved poems. Among these are "The Eve of St. Agnes" and the major odes of 1819; one or two unfinished works that, paradoxically, convey a sense of fine poetic accomplishment, notably the first *Hyperion* and (on a different scale) "The Eve of St. Mark"; and a few passages elsewhere—outstandingly the description of Moneta in *The Fall of Hyperion*—that hint at the approach of a new poetic maturity.

But we must remember that except for poets of the very first rank, and perhaps even here too, there is in the canon a relatively small area in which the shadow falling between conception and execution is dispelled by a high noon of creative intensity. Keats had his own feelings about the not fully achieved work of art as early as March 1817, when, at the age of twenty-one, he wrote a sonnet on first seeing the Elgin Marbles, the celebrated sculptures from the Parthenon brought to England by Thomas Bruce, seventh earl of Elgin, and bought for the nation in 1816, when they were housed in the British Museum. "I never cease to wonder at all that incarnate delight," he once said, when he was discovered gazing at them with his customary intentness.

> My spirit is too weak—mortality
> Weighs heavily upon me like unwilling sleep,
>
> (1–2)

he begins, expressing in the sonnet his baffled consciousness of his own artistic inadequacy, his long-

---

[1]Quotations from the poems are from M. Allott, ed., *The Poems of John Keats* (London, 1970).

ing to overcome it and the "dim-conceivèd glories of the brain," which "Bring round the heart an indescribable feud." "These wonders," broken but still withstanding the erosions of time, irradiate the imagination with gleams of something greater than either he or they, in their present form, can convey. They mysteriously mingle

> . . . Grecian grandeur with the rude
> Wasting of old Time, with a billowy main,
> A sun, a shadow of a magnitude.
>
> (12–14)

The architect Charles Robert Cockerell, contemplating Michelangelo's unfinished tondo of the Holy Family in 1823, found it "striking in its unfinished state . . . the subject seems growing from the marble and emerging into life . . . you trace and watch its birth from the sculptor's mind. . . ." A similar sense of emergent power distinguishes the "shadow of a magnitude" in Keats's unfinished *Hyperions* and the individual intelligence struggling to realize itself in the 1819 odes and the vivacious letters. We cannot scrutinize here what is "classical" and what "romantic," but Keats's writings remind us that incompleteness is a characteristic of one kind of romantic art. The aesthetic experience offered suggests "nature naturing," *natura naturans*, rather than "nature natured," *natura naturata*, which affords another kind of experience, one that we might be forgiven for identifying with what is "classical."

EARLY YEARS AND POEMS

THE prelude to Keats's poetic career runs from his birth in 1795—Thomas Carlyle was born that year, which should remind us that Keats would have been a man in his forties at the time of the Oxford movement, the last flare-up of Chartism, and Matthew Arnold's first volume of poems—to 1815, when he entered Guy's Hospital as a medical student; he had left the Clarke School at Enfield in 1811 to be apprenticed to Thomas Hammond, a surgeon and apothecary of Edmonton.

The events of a writer's life sometimes seem in retrospect to be designed exclusively for the needs of his creative imagination. Certainly Keats's early years suggest a necessary "set." On one side is the schoolboy, small in height—Keats was always rueful about his want of inches—and sensitive to hurt, who yet was robust, affectionate, and mettlesome; there are stories of his squaring up to boys who bullied his brothers and his routing of a butcher's boy who was cruel to a cat. On the other side are the experiences that constantly tested these qualities: fatal family illnesses, deaths, separations, material losses.

Keats's father, the head ostler at a local inn, died in an accident in 1804; his mother, for whom he felt deeply, remarried shortly after being widowed, and six years later died of tuberculosis, which also killed his brother Tom in 1818. His grandmother, who since 1804 had cared for the three brothers and their young sister, Fanny (the recipient of some of Keats's gayest and most tender letters), died in 1814. By this time Keats was away at Hammond's, and George—Tom accompanied him later—was taken on as a clerk by Richard Abbey, one of the two guardians appointed for the young family. Their latest loss brought more financial hardship because Abbey seemingly was slow to hand over money placed in trust for them. At this stage, though, he did keep on George and Tom, take Fanny into his home, and continue in the belief that he had secured a good professional opening for his eldest ward.

Keats's true calling announced itself in 1814, at the end of his eighteenth year, when, fired by *The Faerie Queene* and "enamoured of its stanza," he composed his first known poem, "Imitation of Spenser"; the calling was confirmed on 3 March 1817, when C. & J. Ollier published his *Poems* and set the seal on his abandonment of medicine for poetry. In intervals of walking the wards at Guy's Hospital, attending lectures, and passing, in July 1816, his qualifying examinations at Apothecary's Hall, he wrote most of the thirty-three poems in the collection. They reflect little of his student life except the loneliness and oppression he felt on leaving the Edmonton countryside to live in lodgings in the crowded capital.

> O Solitude, if I must with thee dwell,
> Let it not be among the jumbled heap
> Of murky buildings, . . .
>
> (1–3)

he writes in "To Solitude" (1815), picturing the wooded places

> . . . where the deer's swift leap
> Startles the wild bee from the foxglove bell.
>
> (7–8)

213

These two lines, with their Wordsworthian ring, are the best in this youthful piece, but it is momentous as his first published work. Its appearance in Leigh Hunt's *Examiner* for 5 May 1816 signaled his entry into the literary world.

Hunt, whom Keats admired not only for his verses but also for his liberal idealism and his admirable periodical (it served Keats as a kind of Open University), had been a hero since school days. The 1817 volume is suffused with his influence, and opens with a dedicatory sonnet rejoicing that though "Glory and loveliness have passed away," the author can feel

> . . . a free,
> A leafy luxury, seeing I could please
> With these poor offerings a man like thee.
>
> (12–14)

The first of the three sections of the *Poems* consists of eleven pieces, usually saluting in Hunt's sugary style the "Spenserian" delights of chivalric love and a natural world filled with "leafy luxury," white-handed nymphs, and "bowery" glades designed for poetic reverie. Two pieces, "Specimen of an Induction to a Poem" and "Calidore," inspired by Hunt's tripping style in *The Story of Rimini* (1816), are Keats's abortive first attempts at narrative poetry.

Of the three verse epistles in pentameter couplets in the second section, "To My Brother George" and "To Charles Cowden Clarke," composed in August and September 1816, show an advance on the earlier and more flowery "To George Felton Mathew," addressed to a poetaster associate of still more youthful days. (Clarke was the estimable schoolmaster and friend who fostered Keats's early enthusiasm for poetry and introduced his poems to the Hunt circle.) They emulate Hunt's informal verse letters recently published in the *Examiner* but, as elsewhere in the volume, are distinguished by the intermittent accents of an individual voice struggling for expression.

> With shattered boat, oar snapped, and canvas rent,
> I slowly sail, scarce knowing my intent,
>
> (17–18)

says Keats despondently in the epistle to Clarke, but his manner gathers buoyancy as he recalls the poetry that his friend taught him:

> The grand, the sweet, the terse, the free, the fine;
> What swelled with pathos, and what right divine;
> Spenserian vowels that elope with ease,
> And float along like birds o'er summer seas. . . .
>
> (54–57)

In the third section Keats grouped seventeen Petrarchan sonnets, mostly celebrating recent literary friendships and artistic enthusiasms. Among them are "On Seeing the Elgin Marbles," "Great Spirits Now on Earth Are Sojourning . . . ," which praises Hunt, William Wordsworth, and the painter Benjamin Haydon, and "On First Looking into Chapman's Homer," unquestionably the finest performance of this early period. He closed the volume with his reflective, confessional "Sleep and Poetry," running to some 400 lines in pentameter couplets and linked with "I Stood Tip-toe," written in the same meter and printed in the first section. Unequal in quality and awkward in meeting the simultaneous demands of sense, syntax, and rhyme, these nevertheless foreshadow later achievements. "I Stood Tip-toe" is a first gesture toward *Endymion*. Foremost among nature's "luxuries" that quicken poetic inspiration is the moon:

> O Maker of sweet poets, dear delight
> Of this fair world. . . .
>
> (116–117)

It was "a poet, sure a lover too" who, from his post on Mount Latmus,

> Wept that such beauty should be desolate.
> So in fine wrath some golden sounds he won
> And gave meek Cynthia her Endymion.
>
> (202–204)

Touched by Wordsworth's account of Diana, Apollo, and other rural deities in book IV of *The Excursion*, which was a profoundly influential work for the second generation of romantic poets, Keats too finds that myths originate in imaginative response to the beauties of nature, and "I Stood Tip-toe" singles out the haunting legends of Eros and Psyche (141–150), Pan and Syrinx (157–162), and Narcissus and Echo (163–180). The theme recurs in "Sleep and Poetry," which brings together for the first time central ideas concerning the interdependence of sleep, reverie, and poetic creativity; the vitalizing of the natural world through classical myth; and individual progress from what Keats later termed, in a letter of 3 May 1818 to John Hamilton Reynolds, the "Chamber of Maiden-Thought" to the darker world of "Misery and Heartbreak, Pain, Sickness and oppression." "Byron says, 'Knowledge is Sorrow,'" reflects Keats in the same letter, "and I go on to say that 'Sorrow is Wisdom.'"

The influence of Wordsworth's "Tintern Abbey," working on his own views about personal development, mitigates to some degree the debilitating prettinesses of Keats's poetic language.

> Oh, for ten years, that I may overwhelm
> Myself in poesy . . .
>
> (96–97)

he writes in "Sleep and Poetry," looking for the time when simple delight in "the realm . . . of Flora and old Pan" will yield to

> . . . a nobler life
> Where I may find the agonies, the strife
> Of human hearts—
>
> (123–125)

Keats conjures up an image of the creative imagination, partly inspired by the portrayal in certain of Nicolas Poussin's paintings of a chariot driven across the sky by Apollo, who was always an immensely potent figure for him. A charioteer descends to earth and communes with nature, but then focuses on the "shapes of delight, of mystery, and fear" embodied in the procession of men and women now passing before him. The conception is sufficiently striking, but ultimately eludes his poetic reach. At this stage of his career, the distance between Keats's available resources and his high sense of poetic vocation began to narrow when he freed his language from its fustian clutter by concentrating on "the object as in itself it is": in "To Charles Cowden Clarke" the moon seen among clouds,

> As though she were reclining in a bed
> Of bean blossoms, in heaven freshly shed,
> (95–96)

the uneven sound of Clarke's parting footsteps at night, sometimes resonant on the "gravelly" path, sometimes muffled as he stepped on the grass verge; or the attaching particularity found in his sonnet "To My Brothers,"

> Small, busy flames play through the fresh-laid coals,
> And their faint cracklings o'er our silence creep,
>
> (1–2)

and felt again in his description of setting out at night after the warm gathering at Hunt's Hampstead cottage:

> Keen, fitful gusts are whispering here and there,
>   Among the bushes, half leafless and dry;
>   The stars look very cold about the sky,
> And I have many miles on foot to fare.
>   ("Keen, Fitful Gusts," 1–4)

The clarity and immediacy usually peter out too soon; but the promise of poetic vigor is sustained in the Chapman sonnet, where the creative imagination as a "golden" realm filled with "wonders" generates the poem's unifying imagery of exploration and discovery and, for once (it was long before this happened again), the poem's structure and style are consistent with the movement of thought and feeling. Keats wrote it rapidly one October night in 1816, after he and Clarke had spent many hours poring excitedly for the first time over George Chapman's translation of Homer. (Homer had been familiar to them hitherto only in Alexander Pope's version, which never afforded Keats the keen delight he found, for instance, in his favorite line from Chapman on Odysseus shipwrecked: "The sea had soaked his heart through. . . .") In another sonnet of the period, "How Many Bards," Keats records the "thronging" in his mind of recollections from his favorite poets, which "make pleasing music" like the mingling of evening sounds—birdsong, "the whispering of the leaves," "the voice of waters"—as they lose their individual identity in the distance.

This sonnet vividly describes the working of Keats's densely associative literary memory, and the Chapman sonnet is a rare early illustration of his successful "alchemizing" of these recollections into his own idiom. It draws on wide literary memories, many of them probably half-conscious, some gathered from contemporary authors (Wordsworth included) and most of them echoed from his schoolroom reading: the most influential were accounts, in William Robertson's *History of . . . America*, of Balboa, Cortez, and the discovery of gold in the New World, and, in a schoolbook on astronomy, of the first sighting by William Herschel of the planet Uranus in 1781. The individual instances in the sestet of man's encounters with dazzling new experience and knowledge reinforce the fine opening breadth of the octave. Leigh Hunt celebrated the "prematurely masculine" vein in this "noble sonnet," which closed "with so energetic a calmness and which completely announced the new poet taking possession."

NARRATIVE POEMS

WITH his first volume of poems in print, Keats devoted the rest of 1817 to *Endymion*, the "Poetic Romance" that was to be "a test, a trial of my Powers of Imagination and chiefly of my invention by which I must make 4,000 lines out of one bare circumstance," the "circumstance" being the legend that the moon goddess—known variously in classical myth as Diana, Phoebe, and Cynthia—fell in love with the shepherd Endymion as he lay asleep on the mountain heights of Caria.

For his first major literary enterprise Keats obeyed the narrative impulse that prompted his fragmentary Huntian-Spenserian tales in 1816 and led him, in 1819 to compose "The Eve of St. Agnes," "La Belle Dame Sans Merci," and the more ambitious and uneven "Lamia." But, as A. C. Bradley saw in his *Oxford Lectures on Poetry* (1909), the "long poem" in the romantic period, adding its weight to a progressive breakdown of genres, contains lyrical, confessional, and reflective elements as well as a narrative interest. Keats usually relates a love story that expresses personal ideas and feelings rather more urgently than it arouses interest in "what happens next" to the lovelorn characters. *Endymion* uninhibitedly dramatizes his current aspirations for the supreme experience of an ideal passion. Later (as with William Butler Yeats, who met Maud Gonne after celebrating the legendary Niamh in *The Wanderings of Oisin*) his relationship with what he called in "Lamia" a "real woman" gave his work a new emotional charge.

"The Eve of St. Agnes" was written in January–February 1819, a few weeks after Keats's first "understanding" with Fanny Brawne on Christmas Day, and celebrates the warmth of a requited passion but, characteristically, cannot forget its attendant hazards or its vulnerability to time. His young brother had just died, and love and death are inextricably bound together in his imagination. In "La

Belle Dame Sans Merci" and "Lamia," written, respectively, on 21 April and between about 28 June and 5 September in the same year, where the destructiveness of passion is expressed as keenly as its delight, the emotion is still more ambivalent and the presence of death yet more haunting. The earlier "Isabella, or the Pot of Basil," on the other hand, written during March–April 1818, before the most overwhelming personal experiences of that year, is in spite of its authorial interpolations the least "personal" of these love stories. It led Keats a step or two along a road not taken elsewhere in his poetic life.

All these poems are consciously exploratory in their diverse techniques and source materials. *Endymion* continues in the pentameter couplets used for its precursor, "I Stood Tip-toe"; but Keats also handles ottava rima for his Italian "Isabella," Spenserians for "The Eve of St. Agnes," ballad-style quatrains for "La Belle Dame Sans Merci," octosyllabic couplets freely interspersed with seven-syllable lines for the fragmentary "The Eve of St. Mark," and Drydenesque couplets for "Lamia." The first and last draw on classical, the rest on medieval, sources. The latter suited Keats's liking for rich pictorial effects and, as it turned out, provided themes that allowed him to balance the inner and the outer, so that the work could be quickened by personal feeling without falling into disabling subjectivity.

Endymion, with more flats than elevations in its four long books, which here we can only glance at in passing, is for many readers a monument of misdirected effort. But its general style is an improvement on *Poems* (1817), reflecting (as in the fine April 1817 sonnet "On the Sea") the first effects of Keats's simultaneous disenchantment with Hunt and renewed passion for Shakespeare, whom he now saw as his "Presider." Some passages, especially the "Hymn to Pan" in book I, which is his first major ode (the "Ode to Sorrow" in book IV is less distinguished), look forward to the work of 1819. New ground is broken in his use of a narrative medium to express current ideas about human experience, while his poetic creativity is stimulated afresh by his "thronging" literary recollections, now chiefly from George Sandys' translation of *Ovid* and classical reference books "devoured" (as Clarke put it) at school; allusions to Endymion and the moon in the Elizabethans, particularly Shakespeare, Edmund Spenser, and Michael Drayton; and details of magical journeys from *The Arabian Nights* and colorful modern verse narratives including Walter

Savage Landor's *Gebir* (1798) and Robert Southey's two lengthy poems, *Thalaba the Destroyer* (1801) and *The Curse of Kehama* (1810).

Endymion's journeys—he seeks the shining amorous girl of his dream vision on the earth (book I), beneath it (book II), under the sea (book III), and in the air (book IV)—rework the stages of individual development outlined in "Sleep and Poetry." From his carefree existence among his native woods and hills, he passes into melancholy obsession with the difference between the ideal and the actual, and is finally admitted to unshadowed bliss only after learning selfless identification with the pain of others. Since love appears in this poem as the supreme good, its frustration is the type of all pain. Endymion's succoring of Glaucus and the drowned lovers in book III, and his sacrifice of his "dream" for the lovelorn Indian maid in book IV, ensure the transformation of this dusky girl into his fair divinity (in context this has a startling and somewhat perfunctory effect that suggests the author's growing fatigue), who summons him to share with her "an immortality of passion."

The poem follows too many side winds of inspiration to qualify as a sustained allegory, as it is sometimes mistakenly described; but the ordering of the story implies—perhaps as an answer to Shelley's gloomy "Alastor" (1816)—that the ideal is indeed attainable, provided one first enters into and accepts the bliss and bale of everyday life. This suggestion is strengthened by the famous "pleasure-thermometer" passage in *Endymion*, book I (777–842), tracing the gradations of human happiness, which rise from delight in nature and art to the human ties of friendship and, supremely, physical love. The driving force throughout is man's longing for "fellowship with essence," by which he will ultimately

> . . . shine
> Full alchemized, and free of space. . . .
>
> (I. 779–780)

The mystery of an ultimate knowledge, felt but not realizable in words, is conveyed in the "Hymn to Pan," where the god of universal nature is invoked as the "unimaginable lodge / For solitary thinkings" that

> . . . dodge
> Conception to the very bourne of heaven. . . .
>
> (I. 294–295)

The lines anticipate the "silent form" in the "Ode on a Grecian Urn" that teases the poet

> . . . out of thought
> As doth eternity. . . .
>
> (44–45)

Keats's fine preface shows that he judged the immaturity of *Endymion*, which is very noticeable in its boyishly succulent love scenes, more penetratingly than its many unfriendly reviewers in the Tory periodicals, who disliked Keats on principle as a member of the "Cockney" school associated with Leigh Hunt. He found similar weaknesses in "Isabella"—"what I should call were I a reviewer 'A weak-sided poem'"—and in "The Eve of St. Agnes," only "not so glaring," but thought "Lamia" was stronger and had more "fire."

His readers generally take a different view: "Isabella" is flawed but represents an advance from adolescence to adulthood;[2] "The Eve of St. Agnes" imaginatively blends with its sumptuous Elizabethan opulence individual feeling for what has "no joy, nor love, nor light"; while "Lamia," with some highly accomplished versification to its credit, uneasily mingles virtuoso pictorial effects, intense feeling, and would-be sophisticated satire, a mode in which Keats was never at home—as the quasi-Byronic "The Cap and Bells," also of late 1819, unhappily demonstrates at some length.

It can be argued that Keats's need to assimilate the experiences of 1818 and 1819 worked as much against as for his success in narrative poetry. "Isabella," which hints at the possibility of a different kind of achievement, was written before George's departure, Tom's death, and the arrival in his life of Fanny Brawne. It was undertaken in obedience to a "public" impulse—the suggestion in William Hazlitt's February 1818 lecture, "On Dryden and Pope," that modern translations of Giovanni Boccaccio's tales, "as that of Isabella," might win a popular success. It is less poised than its successor, "The Eve of St. Agnes," and matches *Endymion* in its lush love scenes and awkward attempts at naturalistic dialogue. "Those lips, O slippery blisses," says Keats in *Endymion*; and Lorenzo's lips "poesy" with Isabella's "in dewy rhyme." "Goodbye! I'll soon be back" is one of several bathetic touches in the lovers' conversation; and the rodomontade in the stanzas

---

[2]See F. W. Bateson, *English Poetry* (London, 1950), p. 222 *n*.

castigating Isabella's brothers, who kill Lorenzo because he is too poor, is out of keeping with the fine plangency in the rest of the tale.

Yet Keats's modern fellow poet Edward Thomas praised the ottava rima stanzas, with their "adagio" effect, for making "Isabella," appropriately, "a very still poem" and for accommodating, better than his early couplets, Keats's "choiceness of detail." Thomas could have added that this detail is more purposefully employed to focus both the events in the narrative and the feelings they generate. The dead Lorenzo, appearing to Isabella in a dream, mourns his lost love and the small, touching sounds of life in the world she inhabits. The chestnut leaves and "prickly nuts" fall onto his grave, a "sheep-fold bleat" reaches him from beyond the river, he hears "the glossy bees at noon . . . fieldward pass"; but

> . . . those sounds grow strange to me,
> And thou art distant in humanity.
> (st. 39, 311–312)

The "immortality of passion" sought in *Endymion* yields to another order of feeling:

> Thy beauty grows upon me, and I feel
> A greater love through all my essence steal.
> (st. 40, 319–320)

A year later, in "The Eve of St. Agnes," Keats's growing concentration on "the object as in itself it is" seems for most of the story to be at the service of a less universalizing vision. But the hostile setting, which includes Madeline's family, who play Capulet to Porphyro's Montague, the bleak winter and rising storm, and the chill of age and death stiffening the figures of the Beadsman and old Angela, provide an oblique commentary on the stolen night in Madeline's room, where Keats introduces the richest "luxuries" yet, exquisitely indulging the senses with music, delicacies from "silken Samarkand to cedared Lebanon," and a love effortlessly consummated in a dream in which the actual and the ideal "melt" deliciously into one another. This interplay of warmth and cold, color and paleness, love and death, constitutes the "criticism of life" in the poem—this time, it seems (since Madeline escapes with Porphyro to his home "over the southern moors"), with a measured optimism about reaching a longed-for good here and now. But the oppositions suggest a more restless preoccupation with the dif-ference between ideal and actual experience than one might have expected after the touching quietude briefly achieved in "Isabella."

Technically, Keats is no less at home with Spenserian stanzas than with ottava rima, commanding in them the peculiarly rich pictorial details that enliven his improvisation on the "popular superstition" that a girl who goes fasting to bed on St. Agnes' Eve will see her future husband in a dream. The medieval coloring, which is more lavish than in "The Eve of St. Mark," the unfinished poem that William Morris saw as a main inspiration behind the Pre-Raphaelite movement, paradoxically owes much to contemporary rather than earlier writers, especially Sir Walter Scott's *The Lay of the Last Minstrel* (1805), Ann Radcliffe's "Gothick" tales, and Samuel Taylor Coleridge's "Christabel" (1816). It owes something, too, to Keats's recent visits to Chichester Cathedral and the newly established chapel at Stansted. Of course the family feud and the role of Madeline's aged attendant Angela come straight from *Romeo and Juliet*, one of the many plays densely marked in his copy of Shakespeare (now at the Keats House in Hampstead).

It is impossible to represent adequately here the textural richness nourished by these currents of literary and personal experience, but the following is an instance of the contrasts between warmth and encompassing cold that make the poem something more than a pretty piece of medievalism inspired by wishful erotic fantasy. The Beadsman, "meagre, barefoot, wan," opens the poem, returning after prayer along "the chapel aisle":

> The sculptured dead, on each side, seemed to freeze,
> Imprisoned in black, purgatorial rails . . .
> (st. 2, 14–15)

And his death ends it:

> The Beadsman, after thousand aves told,
> For aye unsought for slept among his ashes cold.
> (st. 42, 377–378)

In the interval are the events in Madeline's room, which open with the hidden Porphyro secretly watching her say her prayers and prepare for bed, a description much worked over in the manuscript (the self-criticism revealed by Keats's habits of revision is a subject on its own). The final version, with its suggestions of warmth, youth, and physical immediacy, marvelously counterpoints the aged

Beadsman's solitary devotions and his approaching death:

> Full on this casement shone the wintry moon,
> And threw warm gules on Madeline's fair breast
> As down she knelt for heaven's grace and boon;
> Rose-bloom fell on her hands, together pressed,
> And on her silver cross soft amethyst,
> And on her hair a glory, like a saint.
> She seemed a splendid angel, newly dressed,
> Save wings, for Heaven. Porphyro grew faint;
> She knelt, so pure a thing, so free from mortal taint.
>
> Anon his heart revives; her vespers done,
> Of all its wreathèd pearls her hair she frees;
> Unclasps her warmèd jewels one by one;
> Loosens her fragrant bodice; by degrees
> Her rich attire creeps rustling to her knees.
> Half-hidden, like a mermaid in sea-weed,
> Pensive awhile she dreams awake, and sees,
> In fancy, fair St Agnes in her bed,
> But dares not look behind, or all the charm is fled.
>
> (st. 25–26, 217–234)

As I have said elsewhere, in "La Belle Dame Sans Merci," written on 21 April 1819, and "Lamia," written in September of the same year, when Keats had left London to "wean" himself from his passion for Fanny Brawne, so that he could try to make his way with his writing:

The moderate "wishful" optimism of "The Eve of St. Agnes" is rejected for something much more uncompromising. The "knight-at-arms" awakens "on the cold hill side," and Lycius is destroyed. The lady encountered "in the meads," and the "maiden bright" whom Lycius finds "a young bird's flutter from a wood," both turn out to be fatal enchantresses who spell disaster for their victims and are themselves somehow doomed.[3]

Formally, though, there is no similarity between the two narratives. The earlier, perhaps Keats's most magical and self-sufficient poem, is very short; and its austere ballad stanza, forbidding the indulgence of luxuriant detail, relies on compression and spare figurative imagery for emotional effect. The density of imaginative experience that helped to bring this deceptively simple little poem into being makes it barely easier to comment upon in a short space than *Endymion*. But it can be said at once that, in contrast

with Keats's earlier narratives, where love is a kind of dream that quickens and delights every sense and is constantly threatened by the hard realities of the ordinary world, the enchantment is now itself a threat, and from the beginning carries the seeds of its own destruction. The poem opens, like "The Eve of St. Agnes," with winter images that affect us the more because the absences recall what once existed in a happier season:

> The sedge has withered from the lake,
> And no birds sing!
>
> (st. 1, 3–4)

The "lady" and her enchantment are identified with "winter" even more than with "summer," for her thrallèd knights have caught from her an everlasting cold:

> I saw their starved lips in the gloom
> With horrid warning gapèd wide,
> And I awoke, and found me here
> On the cold hill side.
>
> (st. 11, 41–44)

The echoes in the poem arrive most resonantly, perhaps, from Spenser and Chatterton; but the resemblance to the traditional ballad of True Thomas the Rhymer, victim of another enchantress, makes it almost certain that Keats's preoccupation with the destructiveness of love and the inevitability of death is closely associated with fears for his own poetic destiny. His treatment of the three central characters in the much longer "Lamia" and his general uncertainty of direction in that poem suggest his continued concern with an increasingly unsettling dilemma.

Keats based his new story on an anecdote in Robert Burton's *Anatomy of Melancholy*. Lycius, a student of philosophy and "twenty-five years of age," is beguiled by a beautiful woman who leads him to her house in Corinth with promises of music, song, feasting, and eternal love—the pattern of the Keatsian enchanted dream. They live blissfully until Lycius insists on a public wedding; thereupon the philosopher Apollonius appears among the guests, recognizes the lady as an enchantress, "a serpent, a lamia," and all about her "like Tantalus's gold . . . no substance but mere illusions."

In the source she vanishes "in an instant," together with her house and everything in it. In the poem the destiny of both lovers is tragic. Lamia has the power

[3] "'Isabella,' 'The Eve of St. Agnes' and 'Lamia,'" in K. Muir, ed., *John Keats: A Reassessment* (London, 1958; repr., 1969), p. 56.

"to unperplex bliss from its neighbour pain" (which the "dreamer" certainly cannot do, according to the argument in *The Fall of Hyperion*, where he "vexes mankind"), and is herself the victim as well as the caster of spells. And when she is destroyed, Lycius is destroyed too.

> And Lycius' arms were empty of delight,
> As were his limbs of life, from that same night.
> . . .
> . . . no pulse, or breath they found,
> And, in its marriage robe, the heavy body wound.
> (II. 307–308; 310–311)

Here, then, is the problem posed in the 1819 odes. Where does the "truth" lie? In ideal experience or everyday reality? At the far end of the spectrum from the "dream" is "cold Philosophy," though this is not to be confused with the "wisdom" that Keats elsewhere sees nourished by imaginative response to life and art. Matthew Arnold felt that the romantic poets "did not know enough." This was Keats's worry, too. But to "know enough" might mean exercising processes of ratiocination and abstract thought inimical to the poetic imagination. Keats had seen in 1817 and early in 1818 that "a gradual ripening of the intellectual powers" was essential "for the purposes of great productions," and had felt that the way lay through "application, study and thought"; at the same time he had always found it difficult to see "how any thing can be known for truth by consequitive reasoning." Hence his vivid simile "The Imagination may be compared to Adam's dream—he awoke and found it truth" and his call "O for a Life of Sensations rather than of Thoughts."

Torn between Apollonius' "consequitive reasoning" and the quickening "sensations" of Lamia's enchanted dream, he produced a poem interesting to dissect thematically but compelling imaginative assent only in relatively few phrases and passages. To set against his awkward shifts of tone and his stylistic gaucheries, especially his attempted worldly manner in describing "a real woman" as "a treat" and love as always short-lived,

> Love in a hut, with water and a crust,
> Is—Love, forgive us!—cinders, ashes, dust,
> (II. 1–2)

are Hermes seen as "the star of Lethe"; Lamia described first in her brilliantly marked "gordian shape . . . rainbow sided, touched with miseries" and later in her quasi-Miltonic transmogrification, "convulsed with scarlet pain" as she assumes her human form; the ritualistic and inventive construction of her magic palace; and, expanded from a few hints in Burton, the portrait of Corinth:

> And all her populous streets and temples lewd,
> Muttered, like tempest in the distance brewed,
> . . .
> Men, women, rich and poor, in the cool hours
> Shuffled their sandals o'er the pavement white,
> Companioned or alone; while many a light
> Flared, here and there, from wealthy festivals . . .
> (I. 352–353; 355–358)

The latter makes a first-rate companion piece for the cool and charming account of Bertha's quiet cathedral town in the tantalizingly fragmentary "The Eve of St. Mark":

> The city streets were clean and fair
> From wholesome drench of April rains,
> And, on the western window panes,
> The chilly sunset faintly told
> Of unmatured green valleys cold,
> Of the green thorny bloomless hedge,
> Of rivers new with spring-tide sedge,
> Of primroses by sheltered rills,
> And daisies on the aguish hills.
> Twice holy was the Sabbath-bell;
> The silent streets were crowded well
> With staid and pious companies,
> Warm from their fireside orat'ries,
> And moving with demurest air
> To even-song and vesper prayer.
> Each archèd porch, and entry low
> Was filled with patient folk and slow,
> With whispers hush and shuffling feet,
> While played the organ loud and sweet.
> (4–22)

THE 1819 ODES

CERTAIN anxieties underlying "Lamia" became explicit in lines that Keats wrote for Fanny Brawne on their reunion in October 1819. He mourns his lost liberty and the tyranny of a love that impedes his "winged" Muse, in earlier days

> . . . ever ready . . . to take her course
> Whither I bent her force,
> Unintellectual, yet divine to me.

Divine, I say! What sea-bird o'er the sea
Is a philosopher the while he goes
Winging along where the great water throes?
                              ("To Fanny," 12–17)

But in the interval since "The Eve of St. Agnes" Keats had written his famous odes, which could not be what they are without their "intellectual" components and the interpenetration in them of feeling and thought. With Wordsworth's "Ode: Intimations of Immortality," John Milton's "On the Morning of Christ's Nativity," and Coleridge's "Dejection," these are probably the best-known odes in English, and they have generated a quantity of critical and scholarly discussion so vast that it is impossible now to compute its scale. Yet Keats singled out the weakest, "Ode on Indolence," as the poem he most enjoyed writing in 1819, and pushed the manuscript of the "Ode to a Nightingale" behind some books (whence it was rescued by Charles Brown). Although he copied out or mentioned most of his recent poems in his journal-letters to his brother George in America, only the "Ode to Psyche" and "To Autumn" received comment.

The circumstance adds to the mysteriousness of Keats's achievement in these poems. They display a sudden advance in his mastery of poetic skills and in his use of them to explore, more concentratedly than in the narratives and with a stronger gnomic effect, the relationship between human suffering, the ideal in art and individual aspiration, and the role of the poet, whose representations of the beautiful and enduring "tease us out of thought" because we cannot be sure whether they constitute a vision of truth or a wishful dream. At the heart of the odes is the necessity to accept suffering and the transience of youth, beauty, and love, and to do so without destroying imaginative order and harmony.

Earlier, in the "Epistle to John Hamilton Reynolds," written during March 1818, Keats had wished that "dreams" of poets and painters could take their coloring "From something of material sublime" rather than from gloomy inner conflict and, longing for wisdom, had grieved that he was too untutored to "philosophize" without despondency:

                              . . . It is a flaw
In happiness to see beyond our bourn—
It forces us in summer skies to mourn;
It spoils the singing of the nightingale.
                              (82–85)

A year later, in "Ode to a Nightingale," the singing is not "spoilt"; rather, its intense delight sharpens the poet's pain in the everyday world,

Where youth grows pale, and spectre-thin, and dies,
Where but to think is to be full of sorrow,
                              (26–27)

but that still compels a movement of necessary assent. The mental and emotional processes that prepared the way for these poems were reinforced by a bold series of technical experiments. Keats's youthful odes—"Ode to Apollo" is an instance—gesture toward English Pindarics, but his metrical structure in 1819 is entirely new. He evolved his characteristic stanza from long practice with existing sonnet forms. As we have seen, he had a brilliant early success with the Petrarchan kind. He turned after January 1818 to the Shakespearean, which inspired "When I Have Fears" and the "Bright Star!" sonnet, two of his memorable poems on the Shakespearean themes of love, poetic ambition, and the passage of time.

But in April 1819 he set about discovering "a better sonnet stanza than we have," the Petrarchan having too many "pouncing rhymes" and the Shakespearean being "too elegiac—and the couplet at the end . . . has seldom a pleasing effect." His experiments—they include the unrhymed sonnet "If by Dull Rhymes Our English Must Be Chained . . ." and the understandably often anthologized "To Sleep"—seem not to have satisfied him. Yet they led to his ode stanza's combination of a "Shakespearean" quatrain and a "Petrarchan" sestet and to the form that gave him both discipline and flexibility in a manner removed from the neatly tripping seven-syllable trochaic couplets he had used for his "Fancy" and "Bards of Passion . . ." in the previous December. He gives a hint of his future development, though, in his attractive fragment of an "Ode to May" written earlier that year.

Keats acknowledged his renewed concern with craftsmanship when he copied out the "Ode to Psyche" on 30 April 1819 in a journal-letter, claiming that it was "the first and only [poem] with which I have taken even moderate pains—I have for the most part dash'd off my lines in a hurry—this I have done leisurely—I think it reads more richly for it." This is a matter of debate among readers, though it seems true to say that just as "To Autumn" is more complex than the direct statement of reconciliation and acceptance it is often taken to be, so the undertones in Keats's celebration of Psyche make it more interesting than "a pretty piece of Paganism" (Wordsworth's ill-fitting description of the "Hymn to Pan").

Keats, we know from his letter, understood that Psyche meant the soul. Elsewhere in the same letter he images the world as "the vale of soul-making," and its "pains and troubles" as "necessary to school an intelligence and make it a soul." He must have fastened on the resemblance between Psyche's quest for Eros and Endymion's quest for the goddess in his own story, since both are "schooled" by "pains and troubles" before reaching "an immortality of passion." It is Psyche thus translated whom Keats celebrates, picturing her in his first stanza asleep beside Eros in the lush grass and disappointingly— but unsurprisingly, if we accept the association— reverting to the artificial style of *Endymion* ("soft-conchèd ear," "tender eye-dawn of aurorean love"). Yet it is difficult not to detect in his later stanzas—which recall that she came "too late" to "Olympus' faded hierarchy," and so missed "the happy pieties," the "antique vows," and "the fond believing lyre"—mingled tones of regret for the vanished "simple worship of a day" (the phrase is from the "Ode to May") and belief that to the "fond worshippers" Psyche's destiny would mean less than to the hard-pressed poet of a darker age.

All the same, Keats's "pains" serve his themes less than the pictorial effects and the quasi-liturgical incantatory rhythms and repetitions, sometimes echoing Milton's "On the Morning of Christ's Nativity," which he strove to create from his studiedly loose Pindaric form with its irregular verse paragraphs and varying length of line. In the densely worked last stanza, which describes the "fane" to be built for Psyche in some "untrodden region of my mind," the emphasis finally shifts from "the pale-mouth'd prophet dreaming" and returns to an individual idiom, especially in the lines (deeply admired by John Ruskin) about the "dark-clustering pines" that fledge "the wild-ridged mountains"; the conception of "the wreath'd trellis of a working brain," which combines with medical recollections Keats's habitual sense of the "labyrinthine" and "Daedalian" nature of the creative imagination; and the closing reference to the window open at night "To let the warm love in," an allusion to Eros now openly visiting Psyche and perhaps also, as at least one critic has thought, to his feelings about Fanny Brawne. She was living at this time next door to him in Hampstead, and he would have been able to see her lighted window at night.

In his next two odes, both of May 1819, Keats "schools" his intelligence by posing against the "worlds of pains and sorrows" an object suggesting the possibility of permanence: in the first the nightingale's song, unchanged from age to age and identified with the beauty of the natural world; in the second an ancient Greek urn, fresh as when the artist made it, and on its frieze depicted a world of unchanging youth, love, and "happy piety." His interrogation determines a poetic structure based on the flight from everyday reality and the return to it; but the "Ode on a Grecian Urn," because it is more ostensibly a "dialogue of the mind with itself" about the ambiguous relationship between ideal and actual experience—taken up from its predecessor's final line, "Fled is that music. Do I wake or sleep?"—possesses wider tonal range with less textural richness. (Keats printed it after the "Ode to a Nightingale" in his 1820 volume, perhaps as an intended reply.)

The new ten-line stanza serves these diverse effects well, though Keats afterward dropped the short eighth line in the "Ode to a Nightingale," which was possibly meant to accord with the lyrical movement of the bird's song. The melodic pattern of onomatopoeic effects, worked at with "pains" in the Psyche ode largely for its own sake, now enacts successive states of feeling: "drowsy numbness" (a state often prefacing Keats's moods of creativity) induced by excessive pleasure in the bird's song; longing to escape with the singer from "the weariness, the fever and the fret" into the flower-scented woods; delight in his own lullingly rich evocation of them; and back, through thoughts of death, to the solitary self, grieving at the term set to human happiness and puzzled about the validity of the reverie. Death, at first seemingly a "luxury," becomes a repellent finality from which only the bird can escape to comfort with its "self-same song" generations of suffering men and women, "emperor and clown" alike, and also "perhaps," in an unforgettable image of loss and exile,

> . . . the sad heart of Ruth, when, sick for home,
> She stood in tears amid the alien corn.
>
> (st. 7, 66–67)

The celebrated stanza imagining the woods on an early summer night transmutes with the familiar Keatsian alchemy passages about summer sweetness, renewal, and growth remembered from other poets (particularly Coleridge's "To a Nightingale" of 1798 and Shakespeare's "I Know a Bank Whereon the Wild Thyme Grows") into an individual celebration of nature's "luxuries" now entangled with thoughts of death. It is in an "embalmèd" darkness that the poet guesses "each sweet" and summons in his session of silent thought the "white hawthorn and the pastoral eglantine," the "fast-fading violets," and

> . . . mid-May's eldest child,
> The coming musk-rose, full of dewy wine,
> The murmurous haunt of flies on summer eves.
> (st. 5, 48–50)

This ode questions the validity of the poet's "fancy" and not the quality of the song that inspires it, but Keats's urn arouses feelings the ambivalence of which affects the tone of his celebration, as the effort is made alternately to subdue and to define uncertainty. The movement is between contrasts of activity and stillness, warmth and cold, permanence and transience, with the sestet in each of the five stanzas countering or expanding upon the quatrain, which may itself set forward puzzling contrarieties. The opening quatrain defines the "still" perfection of this Attic objet d'art, but the humanizing terms— "unravished bride of quietness," "foster-child," "sylvan historian"—direct attention to a paradoxical union of age and youth, the human and the artificial, while the breathless questions of the sestet—

> What men or gods are these? What maidens loth?
> What mad pursuit? What struggle to escape?
> (st. 1, 8–9)

—clearly no longer suggest stillness. In the sestet of the second stanza, the figures are neither vital nor reposed, but imprisoned:

> Fair youth beneath the trees, thou canst not leave
> Thy song, nor ever can those trees be bare.
> (st. 2, 15–16)

The ostensibly comforting lines

> She cannot fade, though thou hast not thy bliss,
> For ever wilt thou love and she be fair!
> (st. 2, 19–20)

recall the antithetical real world in the nightingale ode,

> Where Beauty cannot keep her lustrous eyes,
> Or new love pine at them beyond to-morrow,
> (st. 3, 29–30)

and lead into the plaintive invocation, "More happy, happy love" (the epithet is equally insistent in the two earlier odes), which conveys the total absence of happiness in the poet himself. Simultaneously the urn becomes remote:

> All breathing human passion far above,
> That leaves a heart high-sorrowful and cloyed.
> (st. 3, 28–29)

The entire stanza risks a damaging self-indulgence, from which Keats rescues himself by the brilliant innovation in his subsequent sestet, which turns from the urn to the "actual" world from which its figures came, a "little town" where empty streets

> . . . for evermore
> Will silent be; and not a soul to tell
> Why thou art desolate can e'er return,
> (st. 4, 38–40)

a conception alien to the creator of the urn but typical of the poet, who—this time obliquely—leads us back through the terms "empty" and "desolate" to his "sole self." From this he modulates into his attempted final summary, where the urn at first becomes no more than an "Attic shape" covered with "marble"—not "warm" or "panting"—figures. Yet his first delight still lingers with his new "reflective" position, and the entire complex that teases "us out of thought/As doth eternity" finds its only possible expressive outlet in the paradox "Cold pastoral."

This may be seen as the true imaginative climax of the poem. The sestet, with its too-much-discussed closing lines,[4] represents Keats's final effort to subdue his doubts about the urn. He had opened *Endymion* with the line "A thing of beauty is a joy for ever," a conception reintroduced with the urn, again humanized, as "a friend to man" that will console future generations "in midst of other woe/Than ours" with the one message it can offer. Its statement—

> "Beauty is truth, truth beauty"—that is all
> Ye know on earth, and all ye need to know
> (st. 5, 49–50)

—may be right or wrong. Keats does not say. It is the offering of the urn, and his decision to close with it brings a moment of repose.

---

[4]For a summary of the principal arguments, see M. Allott, ed., *The Poems of John Keats*, pp. 537–538.

There is a correspondence with these themes and ideas in the "Ode on Melancholy," where the references to spring and early summer in the second of its three stanzas suggest that it too was written in May. The poem is perhaps the most concentrated expression of Keats's belief in the necessary relationship between joy and sorrow.

> Welcome joy and welcome sorrow,
>   Lethe's weed and Hermes' feather;
> Come today and come tomorrow,
>   I do love you both together!

are the opening lines of his "little song" written in October 1818. Earlier he had described his "pleasure-thermometer" in *Endymion*, book I, as "a first step" to his central theme, "the playing of different Natures with Joy and Sorrow," and had linked his "Ode to Sorrow" in book IV with his "favourite Speculation," set out in a letter of 22 November 1817 to his friend Benjamin Bailey: "I am certain of nothing but of the holiness of the Heart's affections and the truth of Imagination—What the Imagination seizes as beauty must be truth . . . our Passions . . . are all in their sublime, creative of essential Beauty."

Keats's youthful ode is attributed to the forlorn Indian maid. The burden of her song is

> Come then, Sorrow!
> Sweetest Sorrow!
> Like an own babe I nurse thee on my breast.
> I thought to leave thee
> And deceive thee,
> But now of all the world I love thee best
>   (IV. 279–284)

It foreshadows the "Ode on Melancholy" in connecting melancholy with the perception of beauty and its transience. But it has nothing of the later poem's richness or economy. To repeat an earlier summary of mine, Keats's "argument" now runs "Melancholy is not to be found among thoughts of oblivion (stanza 1); it descends suddenly and is linked with beauty and its transience (stanza 2); it is associated with beauty, joy, pleasure and delight and is felt only by those who can experience these intensely (stanza 3)."[5] The three stanzas possess an imaginative consistency and must have "come clear" after Keats had canceled the false start of his original first stanza with its macabre and violent imagery:

> Though you should build a bark of dead men's bones,
> And rear a phantom gibbet for a mast,
> Stitch creeds together for a sail, with groans
> To fill it out, blood-stainèd and aghast. . . .
>   (1–4)

The climax then is that one would still fail

> To find the Melancholy—whether she
> Dreameth in any isle of Lethe dull. . . .
>   (9–10)

The finished poem picks up this allusion in its opening lines,

> No, no, go not to Lethe, neither twist
>   Wolf's-bane, tight-rooted, for its poisonous wine;

and thereafter unfolds images and ideas that are integral to Keats's self-communings of May 1819. He speaks of the death moth as a "mournful Psyche": the former has markings that resemble a human skull, and Psyche—the soul, as we know—was frequently represented as a butterfly. He rejects the drugged relief of oblivion—"shade to shade will come too drowsily / And drown the wakeful anguish of the soul. . . ."—because, as he finds in the nightingale ode, awareness, even if it is awareness of pain, is better than insentience; and, what is more, the "wakeful anguish" fosters imaginative creativity just as the "weeping cloud" of an April shower "fosters the droop-headed flowers all." He senses the close kinship of intense pleasure and intense pain: "aching Pleasure nigh, / Turning to poison while the bee-mouth sips. . . ."

And, finally, from this keen sensitivity to suffering and change, Keats seeks to evolve a statement the imaginative order of which provides its own stay against impermanence. More explicit than elsewhere, and on another level from his young eroticism in *Endymion*, is his use, noticeable in the closing stanza, of sexual imagery as a paradigm for the inextricable relationship between joy and sorrow:

> Aye, in the very temple of Delight
>   Veiled Melancholy has her sovran shrine.
>   (25–26)

As Douglas Bush said,[6] the ensuing lines,

> Though seen of none save him whose strenuous tongue
> Can burst Joy's grape against his palate fine;

---

[5] See M. Allott, ed., p. 358.

[6] *John Keats: His Life and Writings* (London, 1966), p. 147.

His soul shall taste the sadness of her might,
   And be among her cloudy trophies hung,

(27–30)

indicate a recollection of *Troilus and Cressida*, marked by Keats in his copy of Shakespeare:

              . . . what will it be
When that the wat'ry palates taste indeed
Love's thrice-repurèd nectar? Death, I fear me;
Sounding destruction; or some joy too fine,
Too subtle-potent, tun'd too sharp in sweetness,
For the capacity of my ruder powers . . . .

(III. ii. 19–24)

The parallel strengthens the felt presence of sexual elements in the stanza. Moreover, the curve of feeling, familiar from the structure of the other odes and also found in other poems, which takes the poet from languor to intense sensation and out of this to another, sadder, and more anticlimactic state of being, corresponds to the pattern of Keats's moods of poetic creativity.

It is the "languor" alone that Keats celebrates in his "Ode on Indolence." The poem, not surprisingly, lacks the confident order of the other odes, which were written in obedience to a more urgent creative impulse. Keats, it seems, found difficulty even in deciding on the final arrangement of the individual stanzas, which differs in the various manuscripts. Understandably he omitted the ode from his 1820 collection, though he wrote to Sarah Jeffrey on 9 June, "You will judge of my 1819 temper when I tell you that the thing I have most enjoyed this year has been writing an ode to Indolence." Whatever its weaknesses, its first inception represented a stage in the process leading to the "Ode on a Grecian Urn." On 19 March Keats had written in a journal-letter: "This morning I am in a sort of temper indolent and supremely careless. . . . Neither Poetry, nor Ambition, nor Love have any alertness of countenance as they pass by me; they seem rather like three figures on a greek vase—a Man and two women. . . . This is the only happiness. . . ."

Keats must have begun the poem some time after rereading this passage before sending the letter off in May (its closing entry is 3 May); there are throughout references to summer warmth, and the adoption of his special ode stanza suggests that it followed the "Ode to a Nightingale" and the "Ode on a Grecian Urn." The theme runs alongside certain ideas belonging to the "half" of Wordsworth that Keats said he greatly admired (the other "half" he connected with Wordsworth's "egotistical sublime"—at the opposite pole to Shakespearean "negative capability"—and with the "palpable design" of his explicit didacticism).

Keats's earlier unrhymed sonnet, "What the Thrush Said" (of February 1818), restates in his own terms the Wordsworthian theme of "wise passiveness," especially as this is expressed in "The Tables Turned" (1798):

      Books! 'tis a dull and endless strife:
      Come, hear the woodland linnet,

(9–10)

and

          . . . how blithe the throstle sings!
    He, too, is no mean preacher:
    Come forth into the life of things,
    Let Nature be your Teacher.

(13–16)

Keats's thrush sings:

  Oh, fret not after knowledge—I have none,
    And yet my song comes native with the warmth.
  Oh, fret not after knowledge—I have none,
    And yet the evening listens. . . .

(9–12)

His "Ode on Indolence" is less serene. It captures fleetingly the mood of deep passivity in the summer heat,

         . . . Ripe was the drowsy hour;
  The blissful cloud of summer indolence
    Benumbed my eyes; my pulse grew less and less;
  Pain had no sting, and pleasure's wreath no flower

(15–18)

and turns away from the imaginatively quickening delight aroused by the display of energetic feeling celebrated in the "Ode on Melancholy":

      . . . glut thy sorrow on a morning rose,
  Or on the rainbow of the salt sand-wave,
    Or on the wealth of globèd peonies;
  Or if thy mistress some rich anger shows,
    Imprison her soft hand, and let her rave,
      And feed deep, deep upon her peerless eyes.

(st. 2, 15–20)

225

As the "three figures" in "Indolence" pass again before him (one guesses that some time has elapsed between the writing of one part of the poem and another),

> . . . like figures on a marble urn,
> When shifted round to see the other side
>
> (st. 1, 5–6)

he remains, it seems, unmoved:

> The morn was clouded, but no shower fell,
> Though in her lids hung the sweet tears of May;
> The open casement pressed a new-leaved vine,
> Let in the budding warmth and throstle's lay;
>
> . . .
>
> So, ye three Ghosts, adieu! Ye cannot raise
> My head cool-bedded in the flowery grass.
>
> (st. 5–6, 45–48; 51–52)

A belying want of ease nevertheless weakens the rest of the closing stanza, which falls into the irritable manner that often accompanies Keats's attempts at satirical humor:

> For I would not be dieted with praise,
> A pet-lamb in a sentimental farce!
>
> (st. 6, 53–54)

Other instances of stylistic clumsiness affect Keats's discourse about his three visitants—

> Oh, why did ye not melt, and leave my sense
> Unhaunted quite of all but—nothingness?
>
> (st. 2, 19–20)

—and it becomes increasingly plain that a certain bravado mars his "wise passiveness":

> . . . to follow them I burned
> And ached for wings because I knew the three;
> The first was a fair maid, and Love her name;
> The second was Ambition, pale of cheek,
> And ever watchful with fatiguèd eye;
> The last, whom I love more, the more of blame
> Is heaped upon her, maiden most unmeek,
> I knew to be my demon Poesy.
>
> (st. 3, 23–30)

Like the other odes, this one draws on, even if it cannot organize as they do, the feelings generated by Keats's major concerns in 1819. It assembles what are, in effect, a series of direct personal statements, and so sheds some light on important fluctuations of feeling in his "1819 temper." Its pretensions to detachment present a remarkable contrast with his movement in "To Autumn" toward an unprecedentedly calm acceptance of "the object as in itself it is." He wrote this ode at Winchester about 19 September, when he had not yet returned to London and to Fanny Brawne, and was enjoying a brief mood of quietude and self-containment. "I 'kepen in solitarinesse,'" he said peacefully, quoting his own "imitation of the authors in Chaucer's time" from "The Eve of St. Mark." The weather was mild and tranquilizing. He wrote to Reynolds on 21 September:

How beautiful the season is now. How fine the air. A temperate sharpness about it. Really, without joking, chaste weather—Dian skies—I never lik'd stubble-fields so much as now—Aye better than the chilly green of the Spring. Somehow a stubble-plain looks warm—This struck me so much in my sunday's walk that I composed upon it.

There is no flight from and return to actuality, as in the spring odes. "Where are the songs of Spring," he asks. "Aye, where are they?" And answers, "Think not of them, thou has thy music too." He replaces the images of renewal and growth drawn on for the "Ode to a Nightingale" with images of fullness and completion, for it seems now that "ripeness is all." Autumn is in league with the sun,

> To bend with apples the mossed cottage-trees,
> And fill all fruit with ripeness to the core;
> To swell the gourd, and plump the hazel shells
> With a sweet kernel; to set budding more,
> And still more, later flowers for the bees.
>
> (st. 1, 5–9)

But the poem depends for its unusual poise on exactly that sense of process and the movements of time that accompanied the evocation of summer in "Ode to a Nightingale" and that is found in all Keats's major poetry. The difference lies in the manner in which it is brought under command. Keats had reached a moment of stillness at the close of his debate about the Grecian urn by reproducing, with a strong desire to suspend disbelief, what he took to be its individual message of consolation and reassurance. In this poem he celebrates the period of time that lies between high summer and the onset of winter, as Collins in his "Ode to Evening" celebrates the period that lies between day and night. For both poets, the subject subsumes ideas of process and change, while saluting a point of repose within that process.

In Keats the balanced, but still contrary, aspects of his chosen time are felt from the beginning, for this is a season of "mists" as well as "mellow fruitfulness," and throughout the poem words that suggest fullness also convey heaviness and the hint of decay. Summer has "o'erbrimmed" the "clammy cells" of the bees. Autumn, personified in the second stanza, watches "the last oozings" of the cider press and, in the guise of a reaper, "Spares the next swath and all its twinèd flowers," so that one senses, along with munificence, the ineluctable destructiveness of the scythe (for if Autumn is a reaper, so is Time). The third stanza has the line "in a wailful choir the small gnats mourn," of which the touchingly vivid visual and auditory effect owes much to the thought that the gnats are lamenting the shortness of their life and the lateness of the season. As Arnold Davenport put it, "The music of Autumn which ends the poem is a music of living and dying, of staying and departure, of summer-winter."[7]

The success of the poem lies in its equipollent balancing of the contraries. The passage

> And sometimes like a gleaner thou dost keep
> Steady thy laden head across a brook . . .
> (19–20)

forms part of Keats's address to Autumn at the end of the second stanza; and the subject, with the subtle metrical movement of the lines, could be taken as a figure for his own poetic control. F. R. Leavis admired the lines because "In the step from the rime-word 'keep', across . . . the pause enforced by the line-division to 'Steady', the balancing movement of the gleaner is enacted." Douglas Bush, also testifying to the metrical and structural skills of the poem, has spoken of the ordered deploying through the three stanzas of Keats's sense responses to the ripeness and fulfillment of the season: "In the first stanza the sense of fullness and heaviness is given through mainly tactile images; in the second they are mainly visual . . . in the last the images are chiefly auditory." It should be added that in this, the last and for many

readers the finest, of his 1819 odes, Keats worked further on his own metrical innovations, adding an extra line to his ten-line stanza. This gave him still ampler room to "load every rift with ore" at the same time that it imposed an additional discipline in its demand for another rhyming line.

For all this, I do not think we can say that "To Autumn" represents a decisive new turn in Keats's artistic development. Rather, it seems to enact through its subject and style just such a moment of pause and equilibrium in his "1819 temper" as the tranquilizing season he celebrates may introduce into the cycle of the natural year. For a hint of the direction his genius might have taken, we need to look at the successive stages of his work on *Hyperion*.

THE TWO HYPERIONS

THESE incomplete poems belong to a different and weightier order of achievement than the rest of Keats's poetry. If we take into account their germination, planning, composition, and reconstruction, they can be said to span his entire poetic career, from his "Ode to Apollo" in February 1815 to his final reworkings in December 1819, after which he wrote little more poetry of any significance. His first recorded references in 1817 are associated with Endymion, who is united with the goddess of the moon, sister to Apollo, the god of the sun, of healing, and, above all, of music and poetry. "Thy lute-voiced brother will I sing ere long," Keats tells his hero (*Endymion*, IV.774); and he refers in his 1818 preface to "the beautiful mythology of Greece," which he wished "to try once more, before I bid it farewell." The projected poem had its title by 23 January 1818, when Keats advised Haydon, who wanted to use a passage from *Endymion* to illustrate a frontispiece, "Wait for . . . *Hyperion* . . . the nature of *Hyperion* will lead me to treat it in a more naked and grecian Manner . . . the march of passion and endeavour will be undeviating . . . Apollo in *Hyperion* being a foreseeing god will shape his actions like one."

Keats began composition in the autumn, but the juxtaposing of the two names shows that his subject matter was already established as the defeat of the Titans by the new race of Olympian gods, with the old and the new gods of the sun as the figures central-

[7]"A Note on 'To Autumn,'" in K. Muir, ed., *John Keats: A Reassessment*, p. 98.

ly opposed. The law of progress affirmed by Oceanus in the poem,

> . . . 'tis the eternal law
> That first in beauty should be first in might
> (II. 228–229)

and the identification of "beauty" with wisdom and knowledge through suffering, by which Apollo is transfigured and immortalized, continue the arguments about individual development explored in "Sleep and Poetry" and in Keats's letter to Reynolds of 3 May 1818. This presents life as a "Mansion of Many Apartments," beginning with "the infant or thoughtless Chamber" and going on to the "Chamber of Maiden-Thought," which at first is filled with "pleasant wonders" but is "gradually darken'd" as we come to understand "the heart and nature of Man" and the world as a place filled with "Misery and Heartbreak, Pain, Sickness and oppression. . . ." "Knowledge enormous makes a God of me," says Apollo in the presence of Mnemosyne, who has deserted the Titans for his sake,

> . . . agonies
> Creations and destroyings, all at once,
> Pour into the wide hollows of my brain,
> And deify me, as if some blithe wine
> Or bright elixir peerless I had drunk,
> And so become immortal. . . .
> (III. 115–120)

Keats abandoned the first version of the poem at this climax in April 1819, and went on to write his shorter narratives, his experimental sonnets, and the spring odes. His reconstruction, *The Fall of Hyperion*, at which he worked intermittently from July to September, and seemingly again from November to December, stops short at the entry of Apollo's predecessor Hyperion. Of the various reasons offered as an explanation for this second abandonment of the poem, the most important are connected with Keats's attempt to reconstruct it as a vision in which the defeat of the Titans is related by the priestess Moneta, an august reincarnation of Mnemosyne.

The theme of suffering and its effect on the poetic imagination receives a stronger personal emphasis, with the poet assuming Apollo's role as he drinks the magical "elixir" that induces his vision. It is central to the debate in the first canto, which turns on the general question of the poet's value to humanity and the particular question of Keats's poetic achievement. He is admitted to Moneta's shrine as one of those

> . . . to whom the miseries of the world
> Are misery, and will not let them rest,
> (I. 148–149)

but her stern lesson is that this is not enough:

> . . . "Art thou not of the dreamer tribe?
> The poet and the dreamer are distinct,
> Diverse, sheer opposite, antipodes.
> The one pours out a balm upon the world,
> The other vexes it." . . .
> (I. 198–202)

The poet "pours . . . balm" on suffering because of his knowledge and wisdom; the dreamer "vexes" it, adding to it by dwelling on "miseries" without suggesting how to face them. On 21 September Keats told Reynolds that he had given up the poem because "there were too many Miltonic inversions in it— Miltonic verse cannot be written but in an artful or rather artist's humour. I wish to give myself up to other sensations. English ought to be kept up." The same letter records his composition of "To Autumn," his association of Chatterton with the season, and his admiration of him as "the purest writer in the English language."

But clearly there was also the problem of sustaining his exploratory personal statement at the same time as Moneta's "seer's" vision of the past. Above all, there was the intractable fact that in his revised first canto—which takes its direction from the climactic third canto of the original *Hyperion*—Keats had already given vivid dramatic expression to his central themes.

The evolution and expression of these themes in the two versions reflects Keats's imaginative development from the youthful celebrant of "poesy" in "Sleep and Poetry," who yearned to

> . . . die a death
> Of luxury and my young spirit follow
> The morning sunbeams to the great Apollo
> Like a fresh sacrifice . . .
> (58–61)

to the poet acquainted with the "sharp anguish" of death who in *The Fall of Hyperion* records, in his vision of Moneta's unveiled face, the mystery and dignity of suffering:

> . . . Then saw I a wan face,
> Not pined by human sorrows, but bright-blanched
> By an immortal sickness which kills not.
> It works a constant change, which happy death
> Can put no end to; deathwards progressing
> To no death was that visage; it had passed
> The lily and the snow; and beyond these
> I must not think now, though I saw that face.
>
> (I. 256–263)

There are no Miltonic inversions in this blank verse, nor is it ostensibly the work of an "epic" poet, though in 1817 the writing of an epical poem probably would have appeared to be a natural sequel to the long trial run of *Endymion*, which had given Keats practice in sustaining a narrative through which to dramatize ideas important to him. Further, in 1817 he had added to his renewed familiarity with Shakespeare by beginning to read Milton seriously for the first time. "Shakespeare and the paradise Lost every day become greater wonders," he wrote to Benjamin Bailey on 14 August 1819, adding in a letter of 24 August to Reynolds, in a similar context, "The more I know what my diligence may in time probably effect, the more does my heart distend with Pride and Obstinacy."

The following month Keats changed his mind—"I have but lately stood upon my guard against Milton. Life to him would be death to me"—and asked Reynolds to "pick out some lines from *Hyperion* and put a mark X to the false beauty proceeding from art, and one || to the true voice of feeling." That his instinct was true as usual to his current poetic needs is apparent from his handling of the new material in *The Fall of Hyperion*, but his former ardor accounts for strength as well as weakness. His Miltonic constructions are certainly intrusive—"thunder . . . rumbles reluctant"; "came slope upon the threshold of the west"; "gold clouds metropolitan"; "Regal his shape majestic." Yet Keats's "stationing" of his figures owes much to the grouping that he praised in a marginal note to *Paradise Lost*, VII. 420–424: "Milton . . . pursues his imagination to the utmost . . . in no instance . . . more exemplified than in his *stationing* or *statury*. He is not content with simple description, he must station. . . ." His own finest instance provides the first *Hyperion* with its impressive opening:

> Deep in the shady sadness of a vale
> Far sunken from the healthy breath of morn,
> Far from the fiery noon, and eve's one star,
> Sat grey-haired Saturn, quiet as a stone,
> Still as the silence round about his lair. . .
>
> (I. 1–5)

Keats's disposition of the other fallen Titans, situated amid cavernous rocks and "the solid roar/Of thunderous waterfalls and torrents hoarse" in attitudes of anger, grief, and despair, aims, though not with consistent success, for a similar effect, and their ensuing debate obviously derives from the "Stygian council" in Milton's Pandemonium. But inspiration is not imitation, and Keats's poem takes its own course. As always in his work, it is nourished by a wide range of literary and personal experiences. Some of the "Miltonic" grandeur is in fact owed to his enthusiastic response to the scenery in the Lakes and Scotland during his summer walking tour. He wrote then a number of slight poems and many lengthy, vivid letters, among them a description for Tom of Fingal's Cave, which he called "this cathedral of the sea"—"suppose the Giants who rebelled against Jove had taken a whole Mass of black Columns and bound them together like bundles of matches—and then with immense Axes had made a cavern in the body of these columns"—and which he remembered later in his "stationing" of Saturn and Thea in *Hyperion*:

> . . . these two were postured motionless,
> Like natural sculpture in cathedral cavern.
>
> (I. 85–86)

Keats's reading on the tour was confined to the 1814 edition of Dante's *Divine Comedy*, which added its own contribution to the solemnity of the first *Hyperion* and was instrumental in shaping the second, for it stimulated Keats's eager study during the following summer of the original Italian—especially, to judge by the cadences and echoes in *The Fall of Hyperion*, the *Purgatorio*, which certainly affected his own purgatorial "vision" and gave his portrayal of Moneta some of the flavor of the mingled awe and benignity surrounding Dante's Beatrice.

The "shaping force" at work upon these diverse elements is still unequal to a sustained flight, and is at its most disappointing in the handling of the pivotal theme. The Titans are beings of power and identity; their successors, the Olympians, whose qualities are epitomized in Apollo, have no identity and represent Keats's idea of the poetical character as he expressed it in a letter to Richard Woodhouse of 27 October 1818:

... the poetical Character ... that sort distinguished from the wordsworthian or egotistical sublime ... is not itself— it has no self. ... A Poet is the most unpoetical of any thing in existence; because he has no Identity—he is continually ... filling some other Body.

He had written to Benjamin Bailey the previous November: "Men of Genius are great as certain ethereal Chemicals operating on the Mass of neutral intellect ... they have not any individuality, any determined Character. I would call the top and head of those who have a proper self Men of Power."

Keats knew from his classical reading that although Hyperion preceded Apollo as god of the sun, he was endowed with no power over music and poetry. In the first *Hyperion*, although he makes his Titan less consistently magnificent than the gorgeous palace he inhabits (it takes some hints from Wordsworth's cloud palace in *The Excursion*, II. 839–840, and the halls of Eblis in William Beckford's *Vathek*), he succeeds nevertheless in making him unmistakably a "Man of Power."

> He entered, but he entered full of wrath;
> His flaming robes streamed out beyond his heels,
> And gave a roar ...
>   . . .
>   ... On he flared,
> From stately nave to nave, from vault to vault ...
>   (I. 213–215; 217–218)

His self-centered rage is the expression of his threatened "identity":

>   "... Why
> Is my eternal essence thus distraught
> To see and behold these horrors new?
> Saturn is fallen, am I too to fall?
> Am I to leave this haven of my rest,
> This cradle of my glory ..."
>   (I. 231–236)

This invests the figure with at least sufficiently appropriate poetic force; but on the entry of Apollo in canto III, Keats reverts disastrously to the fruity manner of his *Endymion*. Apollo, deified by "knowledge enormous" of the suffering of the world and supposedly endowed with the imaginative power dependent on such knowledge, remains an effeminate figure who "weeps and wonders somewhat too fondly," as Leigh Hunt said in 1820, though Hunt also thought that "His powers gather nobly on him as he proceeds." The "nobility" belongs, in truth, only to the few lines, quoted earlier, that record the accession of his visionary insight. The poem closes with a semierotic description:

> Soon wild commotions shook him, and made flush
> All the immortal fairness of his limbs,
>
>   . . .
>
>   ... So young Apollo anguished;
> His very hair, his golden tresses famed,
> Kept undulation round his eager neck.
>   (III. 124–125; 130–132)

Mnemosyne the while holds up her arms "as one who prophesied," and

>   ... At length
> Apollo shrieked—and lo! from all his limbs
> Celestial ...
>   (III. 134–136)

And there it ends, with the poet seemingly (and understandably) stumped and the entire war of the Titans against the Olympians yet to record. A year later Keats had transformed this material into the intensely imaginative personal statement of the first canto of *The Fall of Hyperion*.

If we try to hold the two versions together in our mind as one poem, it is apparent at once that they represent two totally different kinds of poetic impulse. Keats's themes and his creative temper could never have lent themselves fully to expression through an epic conflict in the high Miltonic style, for which he had tried in his first version. He makes, it is true, a valiant, and far from unsuccessful, effort to dramatize his ideas about suffering and creativity in his Titans, especially when he differentiates between the grief of the fallen Saturn and Thea, whom sorrow has made "more beautiful than Beauty's self"; the rage of "huge Enceladus," whose words boom among his fellows

>   ... like sullen waves
> In the half-glutted hollows of reef-rocks,
>   (II. 305–306)

and the different kinds of pain felt by the stoical Oceanus, who understands the law by which he must perish, and the simpler Clymene, who alone has heard the song of Apollo, felt the "living death" of its melody, and knows what it is to be

> . . . sick
> Of joy and grief at once. . . .
> (II. 288–289)

But Keats's recasting of the material for *The Fall of Hyperion*, whatever the rights and wrongs of moving from a more "objective" to a more "subjective" kind of writing, is entirely consistent with two strong impulses seen at work in his poetry from the beginning. There is the confessional impulse, which found early expression in "Sleep and Poetry," and there is the impulse toward a more oblique expression of important personal themes that shapes in some degree all the narrative poems and the major odes.

Looked at in this way, *The Fall of Hyperion*, with its mixture of earnestness about the importance of the poet's "public" role, its jealous feeling nevertheless for the poet's individual voice, and its projection of personal themes through a fictional situation, not only is seen to build on these impulses but also offers an early example of the tendency toward the fictionalized spiritual autobiography so common in Victorian prose and poetry.

Carlyle, as we said, was born in the same year as Keats, and his *Sartor Resartus* is often regarded as the first major example of the Victorian habit of disguising as a fiction the history of pressing inner conflict. Other examples, dealing especially with the role of the creative writer in his struggle to penetrate the romantic dream, run from Tennyson's "The Lady of Shalott" to Matthew Arnold's *Empedocles on Etna*. It could be said that all these have an early precursor in *The Fall of Hyperion*, and that Keats's "vision" hints at a potential development of the youthful romantic poet into a writer who might have been a particularly eminent Victorian.

THE LETTERS

At about the time of his last attempts to rework *Hyperion*, Keats wrote to his publisher John Taylor, on 17 November 1819:

I have come to a determination not to publish any thing I have now ready written; but for all that to publish a Poem before long and that I hope to make a fine one. As the marvellous is the most enticing and the surest guarantee of harmonious numbers I have been endeavouring to persuade myself to untether Fancy and let her manage for herself—I and myself cannot agree about this at all. Wonders are no wonders to me. I am more at home amongst Men and Women. I would rather read Chaucer than Ariosto—The little dramatic skill I may as yet have however badly it might show in a Drama would I think be sufficient for a Poem—I wish to diffuse the colouring of St Agnes Eve throughout a Poem in which Character and Sentiment would be the figures to such drapery—Two or three such Poems, if God should spare me, written in the course of the next six years, would be a famous *gradus ad Parnassum altissimum* . . . they would nerve me up to the writing of a few fine Plays—my greatest ambition when I do feel ambitious.[8]

This is one of the last major statements about his poetic intentions in Keats's letters, and it demonstrates the shrewdness of his self-knowledge and the consistency of his debate with himself about his poetry since at least late 1816. Behind his wide range of poetic experimentalism is the unchanging impulse to overcome his native longing for an ideal "romantic" world, in order to reach a Shakespearean understanding and acceptance of the world as it is. In June 1819, a few months before his letter to Taylor, he had distinguished Matteo Boiardo from Shakespeare as "a noble Poet of Romance; not a miserable and mighty Poet of the human Heart." His gifts, at the stage we see them, and particularly in his narratives where he tries to present the passions of "Men and Women," are plainly not in keeping with his ambitions. We find Keats less the "Poet of the human Heart" that he wished to be than the poet of the "wonders" he wanted to grow away from. It is hardly surprising that his one play, the melodramatic *Otho the Great*, written in collaboration with Charles Brown and worked on in the months when he was composing "Lamia" and revising *Hyperion*, is not "fine" at all, nor that the quality of the fragmentary *King Stephen* of the same period, which also was designed as a vehicle for his admired Edmund Kean, rests exclusively on its few but by no means unimpressive passages of quasi-Shakespearean blank verse.

As a writer of prose, on the other hand, Keats is

---

[8]Quotations from the letters are from H. E. Rollins, ed., *The Keats Circle: Letters and Papers and More Letters and Poems of the Keats Circle* (Cambridge, Mass., 1965).

often several jumps ahead of his poetic practice. His letters are perhaps the most vivacious expression of lively and unpretending intelligence in English literary history (there is no eye to posterity in them). They mirror from day to day, and sometimes from hour to hour, the rapid movements of his thinking and feeling, his excited gaiety in observing the world around him, and his remarkably knowledgeable, sensitive, and unselfregarding feeling for other people. Few literary figures—few people anywhere—have won so much affection and respect from their associates. Many of his circle—prominently Charles Brown, John Hamilton Reynolds, and Richard Woodhouse—are known to posterity primarily because of his correspondence with them and their own care in preserving copies of his letters and poems (this is one reason there is such a wealth of Keatsian manuscript material in existence). Characteristically, once his brother George had left for America with his wife Georgiana in June 1818, Keats took pains to write long, affectionate, newsy journal-letters, recording daily happenings and copying out with comments many of his recent poems.

Thus his letters provide a magnificent gloss on his poetry; they also help to explain why he has been so fortunate in his modern biographers, who since 1958 have been able to consult them in Hyder Rollins' superb annotated edition. They form, in effect, an integral part of his creative life, and should be required reading for anyone interested in literature, particularly poetry, the poetic process, and the nature of poetic sensibility. If there is immaturity in their volatile expression and flexibility,[9] there is also unusual self-knowledge.

Keats had no doubts about his ultimate goal, only about how to reach it, and recognized that in exploring possibilities he would swing between opposite poles and "take but three steps from feathers to iron." He used this sharp image on 13 March 1818 to Benjamin Bailey, after copying his sonnet "The Human Seasons," which foreshadows the balanced mood, but not the imaginative poise, of "To Autumn." The relaxed, informal prose of his accompanying remarks, with their darting parentheses and sudden flashes of insight, enacts the ebb and flow of his "speculations." "I shall never be a reasoner because I do not care to be in the right," he declares, and persuades his reader through the suggestiveness

rather than the logic of his improvisations on the theme that "Every mental pursuit takes its reality and worth from the ardour of the pursuer—being in itself a nothing." There are

Things real—such as existences of Sun Moon & Stars and passages of Shakespeare—Things semireal such as Love, the Clouds &c which require a greeting of the Spirit to make them wholly exist—and Nothings which are made Great and dignified by an ardent pursuit. . . .

Even "poetry itself," in his "very sceptical" moods, may appear "a mere Jack a lantern to amuse anyone who may be struck with its brilliance."

This letter clearly represents a stage in the continued communings by Keats with himself and his friends that carried him from his ideas about "negative capability" at the end of 1817 to his definition in October 1818 of the "poetical character" and his poignant affirmation of his dramatic ambitions in November 1819. As he walked away from a Christmas pantomime in December 1817, he was caught up in "a disquisition with [Charles] Dilke" and "several things dove-tailed in my mind":

at once it struck me, what quality went to form a Man of Achievement, especially in Literature, & which Shakespeare possessed so enormously—I mean *Negative Capability*, that is when man is capable of being in uncertainties, Mysteries, doubts, without any irritable reaching after fact & reason.

A day or two earlier, while admiring a painting by Benjamin West, Keats had missed in it "the excellence of every Art," which lies "in its intensity, capable of making all disagreeables evaporate, from being in close relationship with Beauty and Truth—examine 'King Lear' and you will find this examplified [*sic*] throughout." He closes his "negative capability" passage with the reflection that he is saying no more than that "with a great poet the sense of Beauty overcomes every other consideration."

A year later his description of "the poetical character" once more emphasizes his openness of response and refusal to tie himself to unexamined axiomatic systems ("Axioms in philosophy are not axioms until they are proved on our pulses," Keats explains in a May 1818 letter to John Reynolds). He is not concerned, he says to Woodhouse in October 1818, with "the wordsworthian or egotistical sublime . . . a thing *per se*," for which he felt mingled ad-

---

[9]And also, one should add, in their engagingly idiosyncratic spelling and punctuation.

miration and distaste. "We hate poetry that has a palpable design upon us," he said in February 1818 when thinking of Wordsworth's "bullying" didacticism. "Poetry should be great and unobtrusive." Yet he was deeply indebted to this elder statesman among contemporary poets, and in the previous month had praised *The Excursion* as one of the few artistic achievements "to rejoice at in this Age." The "poetical character" with which Keats identifies himself in a letter to Woodhouse of 27 October 1818

. . . has no self—it is every thing and nothing—It has no character—it enjoys light and shade; it lives in gusto, be it foul or fair, high or low, rich or poor, mean or elevated—It has as much delight in conceiving an Iago as an Imogen. What shocks the virtuous philosop[h]er, delights the camelion Poet. . . . A Poet is the most unpoetical of any thing in existence; because he has no Identity—he is continually . . . filling some other Body.

The ability to re-create his own experience of "filling some other Body" is at best fitful in Keats's poems, but the experience itself is constantly displayed in his letters. He is aware of it in his letter to Bailey of 22 November 1817 when he speaks of being "annihilated" when in a room full of other "identities," of being "pressed" upon by the identity of Tom or his sister Fanny; and "if a Sparrow come before my Window I take part in its existence and pick about the Gravel." He responds instinctively to the individual temper of his correspondents. Bailey, the friend who studied theology and took orders, prompted his discussion in this November letter, quoted earlier, about the relative value of "consequitive reasoning" and "sensations" as a means of penetrating truth, and led him on to his celebrated reflections about a possible afterlife, where perhaps "we shall enjoy ourselves . . . by having what we called happiness on Earth repeated in a finer tone."

Keats's letters to Reynolds, including the verse epistle written in March 1818 to cheer him when ill, are stimulated by his responsiveness to this close friend's own interests in writing poetry, and read like continuations of their conversations together. His analysis of life as a "Mansion of Many Apartments" (3 May 1818) is designed to draw Reynolds into its reassuring arguments about the uncertainties of youthful years:

We see not the ballance of good and evil. We are in a Mist—We are now in that state—We feel the "burden of the Mystery", To this point was Wordsworth come . . . when he wrote "Tintern Abbey" and . . . his Genius is explorative of those dark Passages. Now if we live, and go on thinking, we too shall explore them. . . .

It was Reynolds, as we saw, whom he asked to distinguish the Miltonisms from "the true voice of feeling" in *Hyperion*.

To John Taylor, his publisher, and Richard Woodhouse, the lawyer who faithfully transcribed numerous letters and poems, and sometimes acted as an intermediary with his publishers, Keats writes, so to speak, more "publicly" and informatively about his artistic progress, setting out for Taylor on 27 February 1818, as a kind of apologia, "axioms" about poetry that he thinks *Endymion* has not met ("Poetry should surprise by a fine excess. . . . Its touches of beauty should never be half way. . . . if Poetry comes not as naturally as the leaves to a tree it had better not come at all. . . ."). He adapts himself quite differently to the Reynolds sisters, whom he quizzes inventively while staying with Bailey at Oxford in September 1817: ". . . here am I among Colleges, Halls, Stalls . . . but you are by the sea . . . argal you bathe—you walk—you say how beautiful—find out resemblances between waves and Camels—rocks and dancing Masters—fireshovels and telescopes—Dolphins and Madonas. . . ."

He writes for his brothers vigorously raffish Regency jokes about his dancing and drinking parties in late 1817 and early 1818, when he was released from his dogged labors on *Endymion* and for a short time could indulge his pleasure in company and his liking for claret; cracks awful puns for them and for Charles Brown, who was waggish in this way and encouraged such jokes (not very happily for his poetry) when Keats was walking with him in Scotland and living with him at Hampstead after Tom's death; and he invents amusing fantasies to entertain his young sister Fanny. For his brothers, again, he particularizes the magnificences of the waterfalls, the changing colors of slate and stone, and the mixed exhilaration and discomfort of climbing the vast heights of Ailsa Craig and Ben Nevis during his walking tour with Brown.

This quickness of sensibility made it impossible for Keats to respond to experience or to compose poetry tranquilly. The word "fever" recurs in his accounts of his active creative moods, which were usually preceded and followed by the "indolence" that he celebrates in his 1819 ode ("Thou art . . . a fever of thyself" is Moneta's scathing reproach in *The Fall of Hyperion*). It appears in another context when finally, in late 1819, he begins to speak, circuitously, about his current feeling for women. A beautiful woman, he tells George and Georgiana Keats, can haunt him "as a tune of Mozart's might do," and if she distracts him from poetry, "that is a fever."

About his feelings for Fanny Brawne he was deeply reticent to everyone except her. His letters to her worried Matthew Arnold, who thought them effeminate (this was the later, settled Arnold, who long ago had made his own troubled accommodations about his feelings for Marguerite). But in the context of everything we know about Keats, these love letters, with the generosity of their total emotional commitment, are exactly what we should expect from him. They are at first passionate, tender, and amusingly inventive. Later, when he was torn apart first by fears for his imaginative freedom and afterward by his appalling despair at having been separated from her through illness and the tragically ill-advised journey to Italy, they become the most ravaging of any personal letters to have appeared in print.

We see everywhere in all these extraordinarily attaching human documents the play of a particular kind of creative sensibility that vitalizes everything it contemplates, and does so by the peculiar immediacy with which it simultaneously senses and reflects upon the objects of its experience. Long before T. S. Eliot's remarks about the "dissociation of sensibility," Arthur Hallam, the subject of Tennyson's *In Memoriam* and himself a young poet (he died at twenty-two), saluted in a brilliant article of 1831 the interplay of "sensation" and "thought" in certain modern poets, notably Keats and Shelley. "The tenderness of Keats," he says, "cannot sustain a lofty flight" and, like Shelley, he is a poet "of sensation." Yet "so vivid was the delight attending the simple exertions of eye and ear, that it became mingled more and more with their trains of active thought, and tended to absorb their whole being in the energy of sense." Had he lived long enough to read more of Keats's letters in Milnes's 1848 edition of the *Life, Letters and Literary Remains*, and also *The Fall of Hyperion* when it appeared a few years later, Hallam would probably have emphasized even more strongly the "reflective" components contributing to that "energy of sense" in Keats. Eliot saw "traces of a struggle towards unification of sensibility" in the second *Hyperion*. We could add that there is evidence of

such a struggle from the beginning, and that Keats in his letters provides a conscious and continuous commentary upon it.

SELECTED BIBLIOGRAPHY

I. BIBLIOGRAPHY. Detailed bibliographical information can also be found in the appropriate volumes of the *New Cambridge Bibliography of English Literature* and the *Oxford History of English Literature*. See also the *Keats-Shelley Journal*, which carries annual bibliographies. *Catalogue of a Loan Exhibition Commemorating the Anniversary of the Death of John Keats (1821-1921) Held at the Public Library, Boston, February 21-March 14, 1921* (Boston, 1921); G. C. Williamson, ed., *The John Keats Memorial Volume* (London, 1921), contains T. J. Wise, "A Bibliography of the Writings of John Keats"; T. J. Wise, comp., *The Ashley Library: A Catalogue of Printed Books, Manuscripts and Letters* (London, 1928), printed for private circulation, contains a description of books and MSS by or relating to Keats; J. R. MacGillivray, *Keats: A Bibliography and Reference Guide, with an Essay on Keats' Reputation* (Toronto, 1949); D. B. Green and E. G. Wilson, eds., *Keats, Shelley, Byron, Hunt and Their Circles: Bibliographies from the Keats-Shelley Journal, July 1, 1950-June 30, 1962* (Lincoln, Nebr., 1964).

II. COLLECTED EDITIONS. *The Poetical Works of Coleridge, Shelley and Keats* (Paris, 1829), the Galignani ed.; *The Poetical Works* (London, 1840), in Smith's Standard Library, the first English collected ed.; *The Poetical Works* (London, 1854), with a memoir by R. M. Milnes (Lord Houghton), the first illustrated ed., with 120 designs by G. Scharf; W. M. Rossetti, ed., *The Poetical Works* (London, 1872), with critical memoir by Rossetti; Lord Houghton, ed., *The Poetical Works* (London, 1876), the Aldine ed.; H. B. Forman, ed., *The Poetical Works and Other Writings*, 4 vols. (London, 1883), vols. III and IV contain Keats's letters; G. Thorn-Drury, ed., *The Poems*, 2 vols. (London, 1896), with intro. by R. Bridges; H. E. Scudder, ed., *The Complete Poetical Works and Letters* (Boston-New York, 1899), the Cambridge ed.; H. B. Forman, ed., *The Complete Works*, 5 vols. (Glasgow, 1900-1901), brings the eds. of 1883 and 1889 up to date with new material and biographical notes; E. de Selincourt, ed., *The Poems* (London, 1905; rev. eds., 1907; 1926), with intro. and notes; H. B. Forman, ed., *The Poetical Works* (London, 1906), also in H. W. Garrod, ed. (London, 1956), with intro. and textual notes; J. M. Murry, ed., *Poems and Verses of John Keats* (London, 1930; rev. ed., 1949), arranged in chronological order; H. W. Garrod, ed., *Poetical Works* (London, 1939; rev. ed., 1958), the Oxford variorum ed.; M. Allott, ed., *The Poems of John Keats* (London, 1970; repr. with revs., London–New York, 1972; rev. paperback ed., 1973), the first complete, chronological, annotated ed.; J. Barnard, ed., *John Keats: The Complete Poems* (London, 1973), useful, inexpensive annotated ed., with poems in chronological order.

III. SELECTED WORKS. R. Monckton Milnes, ed., *Life, Letters and Literary Remains of John Keats*, 2 vols. (London, 1848), prints many poems and letters for the first time, including the tragedy *Otho the Great; The Eve of St. Agnes, and Other Poems* (Boston, 1876), in the Vest-Pocket series of standard and popular authors; *Odes and Sonnets* (Philadelphia, 1888), with illustrations by W. H. Low; *Selections from Keats* (London, 1889), with preface by J. R. Tutin, includes all the poems from the 1820 vol. and a selection from that of 1817; *The Odes of Keats* (Oxford, 1897; facs. ed., Tokyo, 1965), with notes and analyses and a memoir by A. C. Downer; H. B. Forman, ed., *Endymion and the Longer Poems* (London, 1897); H. Ellershaw, ed., *Poetry and Prose* (Oxford, 1922), with essays by C. Lamb, L. Hunt, R. Bridges, and others; C. W. Thomas, ed., *Poems. With Selections from His Letters and from Criticism* (London, 1932), includes criticism by E. de Selincourt, R. Bridges, and A. C. Bradley; J. A. Walsh, ed., *Selected Letters and Poems* (London, 1954); E. C. Blunden, ed., *Selected Poems* (London, 1955); R. Gittings, ed., *Selected Poems and Letters of John Keats* (London, 1967).

IV. SEPARATE WORKS. *Poems* (London, 1817), facs. ed. in Noel Douglas Replicas series (London, 1927); *Endymion: A Poetic Romance* (London, 1818), type-facs. ed. with intro. and notes by E. C. Notcutt (London, 1927), also in T. Saito, ed. (London, 1931), with notes; *Lamia, Isabella, The Eve of St. Agnes, and Other Poems* (London, 1820; facs. ed., 1970); "La Belle Dame Sans Merci," in *Indicator* (10 May 1820), signed "Caviare"; R. M. Milnes, ed., *Another Version of Keats's "Hyperion"* (London, 1857 [?]), repr. of Milnes's contribution to *Miscellanies of the Philobiblion Society*, 3 (1856–1857), the basic text of *The Fall of Hyperion: A Dream* until the discovery of the Woodhouse transcript in 1904; *Hyperion. A Facsimile of Keats's Autograph Manuscript with a Transliteration of the Manuscript of The Fall of Hyperion: A Dream* (London, 1905), with intro. and notes by E. de Selincourt; R. Gittings, ed., *The Odes of Keats and Their Earliest Known Manuscripts* (London, 1970), with intro. and notes by Gittings.

Students should also consult the *Examiner,* the *Indicator, Annals of the Fine Arts, Blackwood's* magazine, and other periodicals of Keats's day.

V. LETTERS. *Letters to Fanny Brawne, 1819–1820* (London, 1878), with intro. and notes by H. B. Forman; J. G. Speed, ed., *Letters* (New York, 1883); S. Colvin, ed., *Letters to His Family and Friends* (London, 1891), excludes letters to Fanny Brawne; H. B. Forman, ed., *Letters* (London, 1895), contains every letter of Keats's known at the time; T. Watts-Dunton, G. Williamson, and H. B. Forman, eds.,

The Keats Letters, Papers and Other Relics Forming the Dilke Bequest (London, 1914); H. B. Forman, ed., *Letters,* 2 vols. (London, 1931; 2nd ed., 1935; 3rd ed., 1947), the ed. of 1935 adds 10 letters; H. E. Rollins, ed., *The Keats Circle: Letters and Papers, 1816–78,* 2 vols. (Cambridge, Mass., 1948); H. E. Rollins, ed., *More Letters and Poems of the Keats Circle* (Cambridge, Mass., 1955), new ed. entitled *The Keats Circle: Letters and Papers and More Letters and Poems of the Keats Circle* (Cambridge, Mass., 1965), contains the 1948 and 1955 eds. in 2 vols.; H. E. Rollins, ed., *The Letters of John Keats, 1814–1821* (London, 1958), the definitive ed.; R. Gittings, ed., *Letters of John Keats* (London, 1970), replaces F. Page's selection in the World's Classics. See also under COLLECTED EDITIONS, SELECTED WORKS, and BIOGRAPHICAL AND CRITICAL STUDIES.

VI. BIOGRAPHICAL AND CRITICAL STUDIES. P. B. Shelley, *Adonais: An Elegy on the Death of John Keats* (London, 1821); L. Hunt, *Lord Byron and Some of His Contemporaries* (London, 1828), contains an account of Keats with criticism of his poetry, also in J. E. Morpurgo, ed. (London, 1949); A. Hallam, "On Some of the Characteristics of Modern Poetry," in *Englishman's* magazine, 1 (August 1831), 616–621, discusses Tennyson, with arresting analysis of Keats as his forerunner, repr. in G. Matthews, ed., *The Critical Heritage* (London, 1971); S. C. Hall, ed., *The Book of Gems,* III (London, 1838), contains comment on Keats by L. Hunt; L. Hunt, *Imagination and Fancy* (London, 1844), also in E. Gosse, ed. (London, 1907); T. Medwin, *The Life of Percy Bysshe Shelley,* 2 vols. (London, 1847), contains comment on Keats, based on information from L. Hunt, Fanny Brawne, and Shelley; R. M. Milnes, ed., *Life, Letters and Literary Remains of John Keats,* 2 vols. (London, 1848), reviewed by A. de Vere in *Edinburgh Review,* 90 (October 1849), 388–433, in a perceptive essay comparing Keats, Shelley, and Tennyson; review repr. in G. Matthews, ed., *The Critical Heritage* (London, 1971); E. S. Dallas, *Poetics: An Essay on Poetry* (London, 1852); T. Taylor, ed., *Life of B. R. Haydon from His Autobiography and Journals,* 3 vols. (London, 1853).

D. Masson, "The Life and Poetry of Keats," in *Macmillan's* magazine, 3 (November 1860), 1–16, an important essay anticipating some aspects of modern criticism of Keats, repr. in G. Matthews, ed., *The Critical Heritage* (London, 1971); M. Arnold, *On the Study of Celtic Literature* (London, 1867), ch. 4 refers to Keats's "natural magic"; see also Arnold's essay "Maurice de Guérin," in his *Essays in Criticism* (London, 1865); J. R. Lowell, ed., *My Study Windows* (London, 1871), in Low's American Copyright Series of American Authors; Sir C. W. Dilke, *The Papers of a Critic,* 2 vols. (London, 1875), the memoir contains letters from Keats and other material; C. C. Clarke and M. C. Clarke, *Recollections of Writers* (London, 1878); F. M. Owen, *John Keats: A Study* (London, 1880); T. H. Ward, ed., *The English Poets: Selections* (London, 1880), with general intro. by M. Arnold, vol. IV contains an essay on Keats by Arnold that was repr. in his *Essays in Criticism*, 2nd ser. (London, 1888); S. Colvin, *Keats* (London, 1887; new ed., 1889), in the English Men of Letters series; W. M. Rossetti, *Life of John Keats* (London, 1887), contains a bibliography by J. P. Anderson; W. Sharp, *The Life and Letters of Joseph Severn* (London, 1892); R. Bridges, *John Keats: A Critical Essay* (London, 1895), privately printed, also in the Muses' Library (London, 1896), repub. in Bridges' *Collected Essays*, IV (London, 1929).

The Bookman, Keats double number (October 1906), contains original material relating to Keats; A. C. Bradley, *Oxford Lectures on Poetry* (London, 1909), contains essay "The Letters of Keats," followed by a comparison of Keats's *Endymion* and Shelley's "Alastor," repr. with intro. by M. R. Ridley (London, 1965); L. Wolff, *John Keats: Sa vie et son oeuvre, 1795–1821* (Paris, 1910); E. Thomas, *Keats* (London, 1916); D. L. Baldwin, ed., *A Concordance to the Poems of John Keats* (Washington, D. C., 1917); S. Colvin, *John Keats: His Life and Poetry, His Friends, Critics and After-Fame* (London, 1917; rev. ed., 1925); Keats House Committee, *John Keats Memorial Volume* (Hampstead, 1921); H. I'A. Fausset, *Keats: A Study in Development* (London, 1922); A. Lowell, *John Keats*, 2 vols. (Boston, 1925); J. M. Murry, *Keats and Shakespeare: A Study of Keats's Poetic Life from 1816 to 1820* (London, 1925); H. W. Garrod, *Keats* (London, 1926); E. Blunden, *Leigh Hunt's Examiner Examined* (London, 1928); G. L. Marsh, ed., *John Hamilton Reynolds, Poetry and Prose* (London, 1928), with intro. and notes by Marsh; C. Spurgeon, *Keats's Shakespeare: A Descriptive Study* (London, 1928), based on Keats's markings and marginalia in his copies of Shakespeare; T. Saito, *Keats's View of Poetry* (London, 1929); L. Wolff, *Keats* (Paris, 1929).

J. M. Murry, *Studies in Keats* (London, 1930), rev. and enl. as *Studies in Keats, New and Old* (London, 1939), as *The Mystery of Keats* (London, 1949), and as *Keats* (London, 1955); M. R. Ridley, *Keats' Craftsmanship: A Study in Poetic Development* (Oxford, 1933); *Keats House and Museum: An Historical and Descriptive Guide* (London, 1934; new ed., 1966; 7th ed., 1974); E. Blunden, *Keats's Publisher: A Memoir of John Taylor* (London, 1936); C. L. Finney, *The Evolution of Keats's Poetry*, 2 vols. (Cambridge, Mass., 1936); T. Saito, *John Keats* (Tokyo, 1936); C. A. Brown, *Life of John Keats* (Oxford, 1937), D. H. Bodurtha and W. B. Pope, eds., with intro. and notes, the first publication of reminiscences by Keats's friend Charles Brown; D. Hewlett, *Adonais: A Life of John Keats* (London, 1937), rev. and enl. as *A Life of John Keats* (London, 1949; 3rd rev. ed., 1970); W. H. White, *Keats as Doctor and Patient* (London, 1938).

E. Blunden, *Romantic Poetry and the Fine Arts* (London, 1942), Warton Lecture on English Poetry for 1942, first printed in *Proceedings of the British Academy*, 28 (1942), 101–118; G. H. Ford, *Keats and the Victorians: A Study of His Influence and Rise to Fame, 1821–1895* (London, 1944); W. J. Bate, *The Stylistic Development of Keats* (New York, 1945); R. H. Fogle, *The Imagery of Keats and Shelley: A Comparative Study* (Chapel Hill, N. C., 1949); L. Trilling, *The Opposing Self: Nine Essays in Criticism* (New York, 1950), contains "The Poet as Hero: Keats in His Letters"; N. F. Ford, *The Prefigurative Imagination of Keats: A Study of the Beauty-Truth Identification and Its Implications* (Stanford, Calif., 1951); J. Richardson, *Fanny Brawne: A Biography* (London, 1952); R. Gittings, *John Keats: The Living Year, 21 September, 1818 to 21 September, 1819* (London, 1954); R. Gittings, *The Mask of Keats: A Study of Problems* (London, 1956); E. C. Pettet, *On the Poetry of Keats* (Cambridge, 1957), includes an extended analysis of *Endymion*; K. Muir, ed., *John Keats: A Reassessment* (London, 1958; repr., 1969), essays by Muir, K. Allott, M. Allott, A. Davenport, R. T. Davies, J. Grundy, and others; D. Perkins, *The Quest for Permanence: The Symbolism of Wordsworth, Shelley and Keats* (Cambridge, Mass., 1959).

J. Bayley, *Keats and Reality* (London, 1962), lively British Academy lecture; W. J. Bate, *John Keats* (Cambridge, Mass., 1963), highly distinguished and indispensable critical biography; J. Richardson, *The Everlasting Spell: A Study of Keats and His Friends* (London, 1963); A. Ward, *John Keats: The Making of a Poet* (London, 1963), biographical study, making suggestive use of the poems to illuminate Keats's character and temperament; W. J. Bate, ed., *Keats: A Collection of Critical Essays* (Englewood Cliffs, N. J., 1964), in Twentieth Century Views series; R. Gittings, *The Keats Inheritance* (London, 1964), on the question of the Keats family's financial position; W. H. Evert, *Aesthetic and Myth in the Poetry of Keats* (Princeton, N. J., 1965); D. Bush, *John Keats: His Life and Writings* (London, 1966), admirably succinct and informative intro. for the Masters of World Literature series; I. Jack, *Keats and the Mirror of Art* (London, 1967), an examination of Keats's cultural milieu, especially the influence of painters and art critics on his poetic development; J. O'Neill, ed., *Critics on Keats* (London, 1967), extracts from important critical works, arranged in chronological order of Keats's writings; R. Gittings, *John Keats* (London, 1968), impressively detailed biographical study; J. Stillinger, ed., *Twentieth Century Interpretations of Keats's Odes: A Collection of Critical Essays* (Englewood Cliffs, N. J., 1968), includes essays by M. H. Abrams, K. Allott, W. J. Bate, C. Brooks, D. Perkins, R. P. Warren, and others; J. Jones, *John Keats's Dream of Truth* (London, 1969), on Keats and "Romantic feeling."

C. I. Patterson, *The Daemonic in the Poetry of John Keats* (London, 1970), argues that the "daemonic" in Keats is a nonmalicious, pre-Christian, Greek conception, and is in conflict with his personal feeling for the actual world; M. Dickstein, *Keats and His Poetry: A Study in Development* (Chicago, 1971), explores the contrarieties in and the development of Keats's imagination through close reading of the texts, especially *Endymion*, the odes, *The Fall of Hyperion*, and some minor poems; T. Hilton, *Keats and His World* (London, 1971), useful pictorial biography; G. Matthews, ed., *Keats: The Critical Heritage* (London, 1971), invaluable collection of early nineteenth-century and Victorian commentaries on Keats; J. Stillinger, *The Hoodwinking of Madeline and Other Essays on Keats's Poems* (Urbana, Ill., 1971), offers an individual view of Keats's "realism"; T. Redpath, *The Young Romantics and Critical Opinion, 1807–1824* (London, 1973); S. M. Sperry, *Keats the Poet* (Princeton, N. J., 1973), discusses the connection between "sensation" and "thought" in Keats; C. Ricks, *Keats and Embarrassment* (Oxford, 1974), vivacious essay on evidence in Keats's poems and letters of his sensitivity to and intelligence about embarrassment; J. Stillinger, *The Texts of Keats's Poems* (Cambridge, Mass., 1974), offers a detailed analysis of textual problems in Keats and suggests principles for establishing a standard text; reviewed by M. Allott in *Times Literary Supplement* (12 December 1975).

Periodicals containing valuable regular contributions about Keats include *Keats–Shelley Journal* (1952–   ) and *Bulletin of the Keats–Shelley Memorial*: vol. I (1910); vol. II, Sir R. Rodd and H. N. Gray, eds. (1913; repub. 1962); vol. III (etc.), D. Hewlett, ed. (1950–   ).

THOMAS CARLYLE

(1795-1881)

Ian Campbell

I

SOME writers are studied because of their contribution to times of change; some, because of the range of their friends and fellow authors (such as the "circle" of Pope or Swift); some, because they lived to old age, and spanned more than one generation; some, because they introduced important new ideas or authors to their contemporaries. Carlyle is studied for all these reasons. He was a central figure of the Victorian age in Britain, and in another sense he was important as the product (in his formative years) of the "golden age" of Scottish letters in both the classical and romantic eras. After leaving the Scottish scene he became a central feature in London, and as essayist, historian, critic, social commentator, and finally "sage" he was indispensable to the Victorian age in both England and Scotland. He infuriated many by the extreme positions he adopted—and clung to with increasing rigidity as he grew older—but to still more he was the "Sage of Chelsea," a moral influence of great power in an era of shifting values and difficult readjustments. He influenced a great many of the famous writers of the nineteenth century, and outlived most of his contemporaries.

II

YET today Carlyle receives little consideration. How can this be? How can a writer, of whom George Eliot said

There is hardly a superior or active mind of this generation that has not been modified by Carlyle's writings; there has hardly been an English book written for the last ten or twelve years that would not have been different if Carlyle had not lived . . .

(*Leader*, 27 October 1855)

be nearly forgotten, his "revival" since World War II on both sides of the Atlantic being the first sign of life in Carlyle studies for some half-century? Several answers could be put forward, none of them all-embracing.

In the first place, Carlyle was very much a figure of his time who wrote for his time. His contribution to the literature and history of Great Britain was something that grew with the man, adjusted delicately to the circumstances, and frequently created its own market by its originality and the excellence of its style. As he lived through a changing Victorian era, Carlyle changed too; when he grew old, and after he died, the pattern of change continued rapidly, and has continued ever since, but Carlyle's message, a sensitive mirror *of* its time, remains frozen *in* its time.

Second, Carlyle's "message" is a moral one, compounded of values drawn from unfashionable sources: Scottish Presbyterian piety and German transcendentalism—a "Gospel of Work" partly derived from these sources, partly evolved from the real hardship of his formative years. As people looked up to Carlyle in his time, so they look down on him today for the "narrowness" of his moralistic view, his stress on order, on piety, on the necessity of Christian observance and Christian work. They point to his private doubts (vividly made public after his death) and his abstinence from churchgoing, and they draw conclusions that little flatter Carlyle in the late twentieth century.

Third, and following from this, is the question of Carlyle's fall from grace on his death in 1881. His literary executor, James Anthony Froude, wrote what is arguably one of the great literary biographies in the English language, studded though it is with undeniable faults of prejudice and scholarly inaccuracy. But he added to this document a project to publish the private papers of Carlyle, nothing being too insignificant to be included. Letters, private jottings, cutting asides in journals, and hastily composed *Reminiscences* with which the lonely Carlyle eased his emotional shock at the death of his father (1832) and his wife (1866), and which betray in their occasional sarcasms the unsteady nature of the writer's nerves—all were published for a reading audience that remembered a great man, recently dead, and were shocked to find he had been—unforgivably—only human. The swing away from hero worship was violent and prolonged; it was compounded by the fact that some of the doctrines of work, and the necessity of getting society back to work—by force if necessary—were identified in the 1930's and 1940's with fascism, which did little to encourage a cool reappraisal of the dead sage.

Many of these causes of offense are past. Since the 1950's scholars have written biographically of both Thomas and Jane Carlyle (1801–1866), for husband and wife (they married in 1826) have to be considered as two remarkable inseparables, never quite at ease together, always miserable apart. Their lives are fascinating, and have been the subject of numerous biographies, novels, and plays. Theirs is almost certainly the outstanding correspondence of the nineteenth century in English literature, and its scholarly editing (a massive project shared between Duke University in North Carolina and Edinburgh University) is slowly revealing the range of their interests, the number of ways in which each contributed to Victorian Britain, and the extraordinary writing talent that each possessed. Besides biography a large number of important critical studies, welcome contributions to bibliography, and republication of Carlyle's works are laying the foundation for reappraisal. Shamefully, there is no modern critical edition of the massive "works" of this most prolific of authors. The standard edition, an incomplete set of thirty volumes, dates from the nineteenth century. Yet the dam is broached: the massive task of revaluing a massive oeuvre has begun and a flood of material is expected.

The present examination begins, inevitably, with Carlyle's life, and it begins in Scotland.

III

ECCLEFECHAN, Carlyle's birthplace (the house is now a national monument), stands on the main route from Glasgow to London. Progress has bypassed what is now a sleepy village, but in 1795 it was an important coach stop, prosperous enough to sustain Carlyle's father in his trade of stonemason. The family knew some hardship, particularly when they turned to farming in the hard postwar years, but little poverty; Carlyle's many brothers and sisters worked on the farm and cheerfully saw Thomas, the eldest, go to university to study, inevitably, for the ministry, the dearest ambition of his intensely religious parents.

Carlyle's parents contributed much to the development of the future sage. Both were strong personalities, and the family shared a gift of words that made them famous. Accustomed to hard work, they expected the same of their servants, and their sarcasms were widely feared. Their eldest son naturally turned out to be fluent, clever, a little unpopular; he hated his schooling but came into his own in the freedom of Edinburgh University, to which he went before he was fourteen. In this he was merely following the trend of his time and his country, for Scottish students were often (to English eyes) very young, and very unprepared for a "general" course in arts and sciences that left them barely ready for the future specializations of a professional career.

Carlyle's studies did little to encourage him to adopt the career his parents had chosen; his private religious doubts grew larger and larger in the freedom of a university, and his voracious reading fueled the fires of disbelief. His formal studies showed him to be a talented mathematician, and this seemed clearly to be his future career. Logic, languages, and science seemed dull to him; when he left in 1814 to earn a living by teaching school and tutoring, his fields were mathematics and classics. His divinity studies were pursued spasmodically, then dropped; his parents, deeply hurt, nobly accepted his decision and the family bond (always important to him) was preserved. He taught, read, and wrote, generally a lonely man, though he was fiercely loyal to a few intimates. His letters already showed a lively, restless intellect.

By the early 1820's Carlyle's apparent restlessness came to a climax, the nature of which is described in the chapter "The Everlasting No" of *Sartor Resartus* (1833–1834), a partly autobiographical work. Deeply hurt by the apparent aimlessness of his life (for though he rejected the church, he could not reject the experiences of his childhood), unsatisfied by mathematical and scientific studies, lonely, apparently with no future prospects, he made the decision to stop the slide, to make a stand in life, to build new values. These form a fantastic amalgam. In part they stem from the Christian values of Carlyle's youth, always in the background of his thought. In part they come from the omnivorous reading that shows clearly in *Sartor*, as throughout his work. In part they are a recasting of the influence of German metaphysical writers, above all Johann Wolfgang von Goethe, a profound influence on the maturing Carlyle. He slowly evolved a personal philosophy, a substitute for lost values. Slowly his life came back to an even keel.

The process was helped, accelerated, by his meeting in 1821 with the attractive and intelligent Jane Baillie Welsh, with whom he fell instantly in love. Their enchanting correspondence charts the progress of a slow and often apparently hopeless romance; finally they married in 1826, and Jane assumed her far from passive role of hostess, companion, inspiration, critic, catalyst. Two happy years in Edinburgh (still ablaze with talent in the age of Walter Scott and the Edinburgh reviewers) were succeeded by six lonely years at a remote hill farm, Craigenputtoch. They were poor, and had to stay there; occasional visits to Edinburgh and to London merely emphasized the loneliness. Yet Carlyle, cut off from the companionship and conversation he craved, wrote and wrote. Marvelous essays date from this period, essays that attracted attention in Paris and New England, that earned him the respect and friendship of men like Ralph Waldo Emerson and John Stuart Mill. *Sartor Resartus*, his first original work (other than translations and commissioned biographies), was slow to find a publisher—it was published serially in a magazine in 1833–1834, as a book in the United States in 1836, and as a book in England in 1838—and slower still to find success.

In 1834 the Carlyles "burned their bridges"; risking their savings for a year or two in London, they moved to 5 (now 24) Cheyne Row, Chelsea (now a national monument). This move, they calculated, would give Carlyle the time he needed to write a major historical work, combining his social and ethical interests (hammered out in Craigenputtoch) with the historical material available in a major center like London. The result was *The French Revolution* (1837), a work of undisputed genius that made Carlyle a celebrity. (It was reviewed by Thackeray in the *Times* and by Mill in the *Westminster*.) He had arrived. The Carlyles began to be visited, to entertain and be entertained; their wit, their conversa-

tional ability, the magnetism of their characters made their home a focus for a brilliant circle; Dickens, Browning, Tennyson, and John Forster were frequent visitors. The Carlyles talked scintillatingly, if overbearingly. Visitors rushed home, Boswell-like, to copy their bons mots for posterity. Jane captivated many admirers (Dickens among the most fervent), and Carlyle built up a large circle of "disciples." They had found their life in London, and though each visited Scotland very frequently, to keep up old contacts and escape from city life, they were now definitely Chelsea people.

Books came regularly from Carlyle's pen. He wrote with difficulty, but copiously. The year 1839 brought *Chartism*; 1841, the published form of his successful lectures *Heroes and Hero-Worship*; 1843, *Past and Present*; 1845, *Oliver Cromwell's Letters and Speeches*; 1850, *Latter-Day Pamphlets*; 1851, *Life of John Sterling*. Immense controversy followed the social criticism of the *Pamphlets* and *Shooting Niagara* in 1867, but in Carlyle's own eyes the major work of this later part of his writing career was his biography of Frederick the Great, an immense six-volume publication completed in 1865.

Tragedy came to Carlyle when he laid down his pen after *Frederick*, to enjoy retirement with Jane, who had been ailing for years. During his absence at Edinburgh in April 1866 (he was being installed as rector of Edinburgh University), Jane died suddenly in London. The effect was sudden, unexpected, disastrous. Carlyle's creative work ceased almost at once; it was (as he wrote on her tomb) as if the light of his life had gone out.

This was not altogether true. He soon found a new outlet for his energies, and to come to terms with his regrets he wrote the greater part of the *Reminiscences* (1866–1867), reliving with pinpoint accuracy, recalling the details from his remarkable memory, the years of his youth, his meeting with Jane, their friends, their years together. It poured out seemingly disjointed; but when he finished, suddenly, the artistic impulse that made him stop was right. He had covered the subject. He had produced, in vivid colors, a candid picture of himself, a picture so private that he wrote on it a prohibition to publish that he half-retracted and that Froude felt free to override. The *Reminiscences* helped to topple Carlyle from his pedestal in the 1880's, but today (along with *The French Revolution*) they form the most attractive introduction to his work and his life. Painful, uneven, crystal-clear in their pictures, they are a unique periscopic view of nineteenth-century Scotland and England.

Carlyle's letter-writing capacity survived his bereavement, a series of strokes that impaired his writing power, and the collapse of his ability to organize serious, large-scale creative work. A lonely but still strong old man, preyed on by the nervous dyspepsia that followed him throughout his adult life, yet retaining much of the ruddy health he had brought from Scotland, Carlyle lived on in Cheyne Row, surrounded by admirers, talking, reading, writing. Even in old age he was impressive, a tall man (just below six feet), active, with a flowing mane of hair. His voice was resonant and his manner impressive; he talked unforgettably. People remembered most vividly his eyes, which were pale blue. On paper, or in the flesh on the lecture platform and in the arena of public debate, Carlyle was an exceptional figure. Yet now he is remembered, his importance is recognized, not for being the Sage of Chelsea, but for what he wrote.

IV

AFTER a literary apprenticeship of translation, short mathematical articles, and commissioned works of minor biography, Carlyle doggedly built up an impressive list of translated *Märchen* or tales, of Goethe's *Wilhelm Meister* (1824), and a life of Friedrich Schiller (1825) that deeply impressed Goethe. He also wrote about German literature, essays that drew critical attention in London and in Edinburgh and earned him a modest reputation. He understood German literature and thought only imperfectly, but his ability to use what he understood in vivid, memorable ways made his work important.

Carlyle's original ideas soon jostled the Germans aside. He first achieved major stature with two seminal essays analyzing the state of the nation, "Signs of the Times" (1829) and "Characteristics" (1831), both in the *Edinburgh Review*. In these the Germans are not forgotten, only absorbed into a totality in which he is striving still for expression, but striking important and characteristic notes. What are these signs of the times, he asks? Ironic, he puts his finger on the pulse of a developing century:

Were we required to characterise this age of ours by any single epithet, we should be tempted to call it, not an Heroical, Devotional, Philosophical, or Moral Age, but, above all others, the Mechanical Age.[1]

("Signs of the Times," vol. II, pp. 316–317)

At once one sees the critic who is to help shape the Victorian period. Elizabeth Gaskell's Milton and Dickens' Coketown are clearly prefigured in this paragraph, later fictitious cities dominated not only by machinery (factories) but—much worse—by overmechanized ways of thinking. For (to return to Carlyle), "Not the external and physical alone is now managed by machinery, but the internal and spiritual also."

Here he comes to bear firmly on the root of the problem of his age. People are mechanical in their attitudes: to education, to religion, to work, to their fellow human beings. They are mechanical in their reliance on systems, on societies, on periodicals, on the "huge subterranean puffing bellows" of a literary world (above all a literary London) that exists for itself, not for any higher conception of life or literature. The sickness spreads throughout society; men "lose faith in individual endeavour, and in natural force, of any kind," and soon struggle "not for internal perfection, but for external combinations and arrangements, for institutions, constitutions—for Mechanism of one sort or another, do they hope and struggle."

Carlyle is not a man to use one word where two or three will do, but his method here achieves its point most successfully. Here, as throughout the essay, he heaps example on example to illustrate how all-embracing and all-pervasive the influence of "mechanism" is on his time and his country. All around he sees "Nature hold on her wondrous, unquestionable course," unnoticed by men myopically absorbed in mechanism. They "have lost their belief in the Invisible, and believe, and hope, and work only in the Visible." Lacking religion or piety, they cease to worship God or virtue, and substitute the ignoble alternative, profit. "Our true Deity is Mechanism."

Carlyle wrote these words on the fringes of industrial Britain, watching a swift and often seemingly irresistible transformation of a whole country and a whole way of life. He was by no means trying to

[1] All quotations are from *The Collected Works of Thomas Carlyle*, 30 vols. (London, 1869–1871), the Library ed.; references, unless otherwise indicated, are to volume and page numbers in this edition. See bibliography for explanation of the subdivision of certain volumes.

halt progress, to turn back the clock. He had seen some of industrial Britain at first hand; he had experienced financial strain during depressed times; and he knew what it is like to be hungry, to live among starving poor, to see no hope.

Doubtless this age also is advancing. Its very unrest, its ceaseless activity, its discontent contains matter of promise. Knowledge, education are opening the eyes of the humblest; are increasing the number of thinking minds without limit.

(*ibid.*, p. 340)

And what do these minds see? Undereducated or uneducated, they are trapped in the limitations of their mechanical society.

This deep, paralysed subjection to physical objects comes not from Nature, but from our own unwise mode of *viewing* Nature.

(*ibid.*, p. 340)

The process can be halted, changed. Carlyle sees promise of regaining "the wisdom, the heroic worth of our forefathers," so that here and there he sees hope of change. Yet the analysis he makes in this early essay clearly presages his later message. Overreliance on mechanism has produced a sick fabric of society, and change is necessary before improvement can take place.

There is a deep-lying struggle in the whole fabric of society; a boundless grinding collision of the New with the Old. The French Revolution, as is now visible enough, was not the parent of this mighty movement, but its offspring.

(*ibid.*, p. 341)

"Signs of the Times" repays prolonged study, because in miniature it contains much of the analysis Carlyle was to offer his society in the early part of his career. Its central point is repeated in *Sartor* (bk. I, ch. 10):

"Happy he who can look through the Clothes of a Man (the woollen, and fleshly, and official Bank-paper and State-paper Clothes) into the Man himself; and discern, it may be, in this or the other Dread Potentate, a more or less incompetent Digestive-apparatus; yet also an inscrutable venerable Mystery, in the meanest Tinker that sees with eyes!"

(vol. I, p. 65)

Sartor is an elaborate essay on this theme, a hoax, the pseudo edition (by an entirely nonexistent editor arranging nonexistent papers invented by Carlyle himself) of the life and writings of Professor Teufelsdröckh (Devil's Dung) of the University of Weissnichtwo (I don't know where); Teufelsdröckh, whose German title boils down to professor of things in general, is a shadowy figure who is little more than a front for the ferment of ideas Carlyle had lived with and had reduced to order. The work, supposedly set in Germany, is saturated with Germanisms; it shows how little the audience knew of Germany that Carlyle could use these preposterous German names for people and places, and know he would deceive all but a small portion of his readers. Behind the innocent deceit there is a serious attempt to use the playful clothes metaphor to open a debate in the reader's mind, for Carlyle's thrust is to upset the easy generalization with a startling novel idea (bk. III, ch. 9):

Nay, farther, art thou not perhaps by this time made aware that all symbols are properly clothes; that all forms whereby Spirit manifests itself to sense, whether outwardly or in the Imagination, are clothes . . . ?

(*ibid.*, p. 260)

The form of *Sartor* is complex, self-repeating, subtly developing Teufelsdröckh's life story simultaneously with his evolving philosophy of clothes and a conviction that the society mirrored in the book (and all too recognizably the society of author and reader) is sick and must soon be completely restructured; it suffers daily from "the boundless grinding collision of the New with the Old." A radical, a pipe-smoking and free-thinking individualist, a lonely man looked up to by his contemporaries who spends most of his time reading and thinking, yet plainly having an explosive message for his times, could he find the formulation for it, Teufelsdröckh is all too obviously Carlyle. Particularly in "Natural Supernaturalism," Carlyle moves far beyond the semi-autobiographical episodes of the "Everlasting No" and the "Everlasting Yea," to which he fought his way, using his old and new knowledge, from the wreckage of his earlier beliefs.

Sartor Resartus is not just autobiography, but a fantastic, involved, pungent message elaborating the analysis of "Signs of the Times" at great length. The personal dilemma and nightmare are real enough:

the machine universe is part of a personal hell, a huge mill "rolling on, in its dead indifference, to grind me limb from limb." There is no doubting the reality of Carlyle's hell here, but neither is there any possibility of doubting the positive message of *Sartor*. The phoenix symbol that dominates the conclusion is clear: we must see an end to rotten society, and build something new, more just, more durable from the ashes. The old and the new collide, the stultifying mechanism of laissez-faire (Carlyle's hated over-mechanical society, where things drift on, where systems work for better or worse, ignoring the personal and human dilemmas they create) and the "cash nexus" (the hated effect of treating people as units, laborers to be bought and sold, then dismissed at will when no longer needed) preventing either reform or—the important formulation in "Signs of the Times"—a proper view of the problem.

This is Carlyle's contribution, even as early as these first important works. He saw the root of the problem, he felt anger at it, he determined to challenge a system. To be published, to be read, he had to find some way to be acceptable to his age; out of this necessity come the irony of "Signs of the Times," the fantastic structure of *Sartor*. They are comic, often baffling, but they are deadly serious.

Behind these early essays lay the shadow of the French Revolution and the Napoleonic wars through which Carlyle grew up, the strain of which caused in part the financial depression he lived through. *The French Revolution*, the first product of the London years, is a magnificent view of the subject. That it is partial, superseded now (despite Carlyle's lifelong fastidiousness over detail, his finical footnoting of all historical writing), and uneven, few would deny. But few would deny that it is magnificent in its re-creation of the vivid, often brutal happenings of that revolution, and striking in the singleness of its analysis, passionately offered to an age that Carlyle saw as threatened, for the same reasons, by the same sickening bloodbath.

The French Revolution was inevitable, in Carlyle's reading. Trained at Edinburgh, where historians were noted for their cool analyses of the origins of revolutions and dynastic change, sustained by the remembered framework of an only half-rejected childhood Presbyterianism, Carlyle looked at the glittering courts of Versailles and the brilliant but atheistic circle of philosophes who adorned the French Enlightenment, and saw clearly the roots of disaster. For in contradicting the existence of the in-visible, the obligations of the Christian, or at least of the transcendental, Carlyle perceived that the political thinkers of pre-Revolutionary France had abdicated their moral duty and achieved a hopelessly mechanical analysis of their age. By living for luxury and ignoring the distresses of the poor, royalty had abdicated its duty. By sustaining this rotten system and fattening itself, the Church had done the same. From thinkers locked in mechanism there was no hope; history moves, inevitably, to the cataclysm of the fall of the Bastille. Such was Carlyle's view.

Against this there is rebellion. Rebellion is a profoundly ambiguous thing to Carlyle, necessary and desirable in one sense, puzzling and sometimes terrifying in another, a "volcanic lava-flood" that obeys few rules and destroys everything in its path. It can be something ugly: "Plots, plots; a plot for murdering the Girondin Deputies; Anarchists and Secret-Royalists plotting, in hellish concert, for that end!" The outcome of the plots appears on the pages of *The French Revolution* in terrible, vivid prose: anarchy, bloodshed, execution, aimless and wanton cruelty, the ungovernable cruelty of the mob starved for food and starved for power—for government, Carlyle would say—for too long.

But "the will of the Supreme Power was established." It is an odd thing to say against the background of the bloodbath of the Revolution, but it sums up part of Carlyle's philosophy. That there was a Supreme Power he never doubted, and belief in that power was a necessary part of the battle against an overmechanical view of life. One must (and here the disciple of Goethe speaks) recognize the existence of a dimension to life beyond the merely visible and scientifically accountable. Whether one calls him God or not, this Power dominates Carlyle's view of history and society. *The French Revolution* is the working out of a view of history showing one bankrupt and ungodly system being replaced by another that is fearful, violent, at best ambiguous. The bloodshed and tyranny could have been avoided had the previous rulers taken their responsibilities seriously. They did not, and anarchy was the result.

In this way the social analysis of the earlier works, the probing of the roots of the disease of a sick contemporary society, enlarges itself to the probing of history as a working out of the results of such sickness. This is to use history as a distorting mirror, a view of our own future in the past. The voice of the historian is ever there, pointing out cause and effect, urging the present to take note and action, wheedling, exhorting, underlining. At its weakest (as often in *Cromwell*) the method is irritating and wearisome; at its strongest it illuminates the past in a fitful, strongly individual, but irresistible way.

Chartism and *Past and Present* bring the focus of Carlyle's critique a little closer to home after this excursion into the past. The abortive Chartist petitions to Parliament of 1838–1848, and the dreadful privations of the working classes that led to these manifestations, stirred Carlyle deeply. He felt that the problems of France in the 1780's were present in Britain in the 1830's:

To us individually this matter appears, and has for many years appeared, to be the most ominous of all practical matters whatever; a matter in regard to which if something be not done, something will *do* itself one day, and in a fashion that will please nobody. The time is verily come for acting in it; how much more for consultation about acting in it, for speech and articulate inquiry about it!

(vol. V, p. 325: *Chartism*, ch. 1)

Carlyle the historian sees the urgency in terms of the timetable of the past: ". . . this Earthly Life," he writes at the beginning of chapter 6 of book II of *Past and Present*, is

not intrinsically a reality at all, but . . . a shadow of realities eternal, infinite; that this Time-world, as an air-image, fearfully *emblematic*, plays and flickers in the grand still mirror of Eternity; and man's little Life has Duties that are great, that are alone great, and go up to Heaven and down to Hell. This, with our poor litanies, we testify, and struggle to testify.

(vol. XIII, p. 84)

These are the monks of St. Edmundsbury, a historical account of whom spurred Carlyle's creative mind to produce *Past and Present*. The title of the book and its form emphasize throughout the contrast between the fixed pieties of the past, conflicting at every turn with the sordid realities of the everyday, and the unfixed questionings of the present, against the background of even more sordid realities. The time for acting and consulting, as he stressed in *Chartism*, has come. The alternative may be bloody and uncontrollable.

It is not enough to let things slide, to carry on with laissez-faire and treating people through the "cash nexus." Workers are human beings; they have the right to be treated as such, and they have the obligation to work. Employers have the right to command, and the obligation to take their post of responsibility seriously, to make the best job of their command for themselves, for their workers, and for society as a whole. A picture of a structured, self-dependent, self-conscious (in a good sense) society emerges, and the monastery of St. Edmundsbury suited this purpose excellently. *Past and Present* revolves around the episode of the election of Father Samson to the head of the monastic community, and it introduces another important idea in the study of Carlyle's "message" (bk. II, ch. 7):

Given the men a People choose, the People itself, in its exact worth and worthlessness, is given. A heroic people chooses heroes, and is happy; a valet or flunkey people chooses sham-heroes, what are called quacks, thinking them heroes, and is not happy.

(*ibid.*, p. 94)

Hero worship, the necessity of putting a strong man at the head of a society by election, then allowing him to command, is an integral part of Carlyle's concept of a healthy, nonmechanical society. Such men are chosen, they rise to the top naturally, by the inscrutable workings of a divinely ordered history. The immensely popular lectures in *Heroes and Hero-Worship* apply this idea to the arts, to society, to warfare, to education, to religion. Time and again Carlyle sees strong men elevated to positions of leadership, to the exercise of duties of responsibility heroically undertaken and carried through. History is the acid test: with its longer perspective it soon sorts out the real heroes from the quacks. Those in the 1930's and 1940's who accused Carlyle of fascism might do well to ponder this: If he were writing today, Carlyle would have pointed to the short and unfruitful period of leadership allowed by the forces of history to some who were taken as heroes.

The strong, structured, ordered society, the world of the monastery after it gained a strong new Abbot Samson, the world ruled by the heroes of history, the world postulated in *Chartism* as possible in a Britain truly reformed, and not merely tinkered with in the agitations of the 1830's toward social justice, is not an easy paradise. If the rulers have obligations, so have the workers.

This law of "No work, no recompense" should first of all be enforced on the *manual* worker, and brought stringently home to him and his numerous class. . . . Let it be enforced there, and rigidly made good. . . . Let the honest working man rejoice that such law, the first of Nature, has been made good on him; and hope that, by and by, all else will be made good.

> (vol. V, p. 342: *Chartism,* ch. 3)

The result? Hard work, of course (something Carlyle himself was never afraid of), but also order. Just order, Carlyle would add, in a wider definition of justice.

As *dis*order, insane by the nature of it, is the hatefulest of things to man, who lives by sanity and order, so injustice is the worst evil, some call it the only evil, in this world. All men submit to toil, to disappointment, to unhappiness; it is their lot here; but in all hearts, inextinguishable by sceptic logic, by sorrow, perversion or despair itself, there is a small still voice intimating that it is not the final lot; that wild, waste, incoherent as it looks, a God presides over it; that it is not an injustice but a justice. . . . If men had lost belief in a God, their only resource against a blind No-God, of Necessity and Mechanism, that held them like a hideous World-Steam-engine . . . would be, with or without hope,—*revolt.*

> (*ibid.,* p. 357: *Chartism,* ch. 5)

All this was written, as has been noted, against the recent backdrop of the French Revolution, which, as Carlyle emphasized in *Heroes,* was "verily a Fact," one "that the world in general would do well everywhere to regard . . . as such."

To have someone to make the analysis for the age is to help people see more clearly the outlines of social trouble actually in progress. But who is to make the analysis for Carlyle himself? Clearly he does much by private reading, by passionate concern. Clearly also, he accepts divine intervention in the form of heroes.

The certainty of Heroes being sent us; our faculty, our necessity, to reverence Heroes when sent: it shines like a polestar through smoke-clouds, dust-clouds, and all manner of down-rushing and conflagration.

> (vol. XII, p. 240: lecture 6, "The Hero as King")

The trouble was that very few of Carlyle's contemporaries earned his respect as heroes. With considerable contempt for the parliamentary politicians of all parties, for church leaders, for political scientists, and above all for the "dismal science" of political economy, he found few he could bring his proud, rapidly moving mind to reverence. Goethe was an exception, significantly one whom Carlyle reverenced from a distance and never met. Personal foibles, quirks of character often repulsed Carlyle from people he had admired at a distance; only his father shone in memory as a magnificent model of Christian acceptance, piety, rigid and uncompromising upholding of standards, and above all insistence on work in an ordered universe. The reminiscences of James Carlyle are an eloquent testimonial to this belief; but, as Carlyle admits in one of his most piercing asides:

. . . he was in Annandale, and it was above fifty years ago. . . . Religion was the pole-star for my father: rude and uncultivated as he otherwise was, it made him and kept him "in all points a man".

> (*Reminiscences* [1972], pp. 9–10)

It is easy to point out how safe it is to admire only those who are dead or hundreds of miles off. In all honesty Carlyle was not trying to advocate a return to rural simplicity, but to make an analysis of an urban industrialized society; and in the idea of work, of religiously inspired obligation, of the appointment and obedience of "heroes" (he saw the latter as controllers of industry, employers of enlightened temperament) he was producing a formula that he believed would put a sick society back on its feet.

To see such an ideal, to convince a generation of it, required rhetoric of a high order. The Carlyle style is a dated one, highly idiosyncratic, complex, repetitive, cumulative. Its roots lie in Scottish speech patterns; in biblical, Shakespearean, Miltonic, and many other literary allusive patterns; in Germanic influences; in preaching tricks—all combined with an attempt, in construction and punctuation, to record on paper the oratory of the preacher and crowd swayer, piling example on example, vivid apostrophe on apostrophe, ridiculing imagined opposition, venerating imagined (or actual) heroes, wearing down the reader's ability to resist complete agreement. Many imitated "Carlylese," but few had the stamina or the wide reading to do it successfully. He captivated a generation with his style, and though many grew tired of it and few today find it more than intermittently successful (many of its best successes are in *The French Revolution*), it is one of his most powerful weapons for reform.

Paradoxically, Carlyle's copious works are full of pleas for silence.

Looking round on the noisy inanity of the world, words with little meaning, actions with little worth, one loves to reflect on the great Empire of *Silence*. The noble silent men, scattered here and there, each in his department; silently thinking, silently working; whom no Morning Newspaper makes mention of! They are the salt of the Earth. A country that has none or few of these is in a bad way. Like a forest which had no *roots*; which had all turned into leaves and boughs;—which must soon wither and be no forest. . . . Silence, the great Empire of Silence: higher than the stars; deeper than the Kingdoms of Death! It alone is great; all else is small.—

    (vol. XII, pp. 264–265: lecture 6, "The Hero as King")

The verbal structure heaps example on example, pleading for silence. Carlyle saw nothing ridiculous in this, nor would he have done after one of his blazing monologues of several hours, holding an audience spellbound in Chelsea. The thousands of surviving letters also fit into the structure; silence, like Christianity, is something society desperately needs. Carlyle the individual has his obligation to work for reform, and to work in this context defies the plea for silence. To work is to talk, to write, to labor for reform. A reformed society will have time for silence, and Carlyle longed for silence and rest, finishing each book with undisguised relief, then retreating to long, solitary holidays in his native Annandale.

The skeleton of his doctrine is now clearly visible. His remaining published works filled out the picture, always bearing in mind the dreadful reality of suffering behind the cold calculations of reform, more and more emphasizing the necessity of duty, obedience, and work, as the problem seemed further and further from solution. Carlyle himself was convinced: he saw less and less reason to cajole his readers, more and more reason to convey to them something of the urgency of the problem, the need to start the work of reformation.

Something of this comes through in the hectoring tone of his editorial handling of Cromwell's letters and speeches, his open admiration for Frederick the Great's silent, peremptory monarchy that may have trampled human rights, but got things done and (like Cromwell's protectorate) imposed order in place of threatened anarchy. The "old dead days and their extinct agitations" come to life in Carlyle's hands, his minute tracing of details, dating, and topography anxiously orchestrating the facts to the end of bringing all to life. Papers are meticulously transcribed, even (in *Cromwell*) a letter of 1645 with each signature copied, a description of the state and location of the manuscript, and its publication details. Irrelevant? Perhaps, but Carlyle is trying to get to the facts behind the confused historical debate, and from the facts to form his own honest picture. Hence, perhaps, his fury with the editors of some of his sources for *Frederick*, "authentic but thrice-stupid mortals" who

cut short our Eye-witness, not so much as telling us his name, some of them not even his date or whereabouts; and so the curtain tumbles down . . . and we are left to grey hubbub, and our own resources at secondhand.

(*The History of Frederick the Great*, vol. VII, bk. XVIII, ch. 8, p. 340: "Battle of Rossbach")

From the authentic materials Cromwell and Frederick are resurrected so far as Carlyle can resurrect them. He devoted patient years to the amassing of materials, he footnoted scrupulously, and though he did get things wrong (he was quite taken in by a series of forged letters that he incorporated into *Cromwell*, and obstinately refused to acknowledge his mistake when they were unmasked), those two works are enduring monuments to more than his energy and the patience of his readers and publishers. They show Carlyle's view of society, his reconstruction of an ordered society in which certain sacrifices are made for the wider goal of achieving "true" order, a divine order, a historically justified process. That Cromwell and Frederick are tyrants and perform necessary cruelties, Carlyle accepts without question. That they contradict human rights he takes to be a necessary corollary of the times, and part of the necessary cure. That they consider themselves empowered to do this he takes to be as unremarkable as their willingness to force themselves to superhuman feats of endurance in ruling, fighting, and working.

There is dangerous material here, material deeply offensive to the liberal thinker. Some contemporaries (notably John Stuart Mill, earlier a very close friend and near disciple of Carlyle) were frankly revolted by this development in their sage, and either left him or openly attacked him in print. Newspaper reviews became equivocal or hostile. Carlyle had an easy way of dealing with hostile reviews: he ignored them. He felt hostility, though, and the loss of friends was a severe blow. Yet his personality impelled him to carry through his work, including his most unpopular work, which concerned democracy and the rights of individuals in the state.

The *Latter-Day Pamphlets*, *Shooting Niagara*, and *The Nigger Question* are the work of a man past middle age, a man who had fought his way to the position in which he is now seen, who expressed an aging man's impatience with hindrances that he saw as unimportant. Carlyle knew what he was doing in employing the term "nigger," though in his day it was not the emotionally loaded word it is in the late twentieth century. The emancipation of blacks had been an emotional topic of debate for decades, and the middle years of the nineteenth century had seen enormous strides toward the freeing and rehabilitation of slaves in North America and the West Indies. Naturally there had been problems and readjustment was a painful process. Carlyle fixed on these painful difficulties as a case where priorities were wrong in his time, and people were too concerned with short-term measures to see their long-term historical importance. The rhetorical weapons he knew so well were trained on this emotional topic, and public outrage followed. Carlyle regarded the former slaves as not yet ready for the full privileges of a Western democratic society—but he did not think much of Western democratic society.

It was Carlyle's way of expressing the idea that was really offensive. He persistently drew the analogy between how the British treat their horses and how they treat their slaves and former slaves. "The fate of all emancipated horses is, sooner or later, inevitable. To have in this habitable Earth no grass to eat,—in Black Jamaica gradually none, as in White Connemara already none." The whole passage (from "The Present Time," in *Latter-Day Pamphlets*) owes a great deal to Jonathan Swift and the fourth book of *Gulliver*, but people were in no mood to see literary irony. More coolly, we acknowledge the bad taste of much that Carlyle writes about the blacks as not yet ready for a full place in society. But more coolly we also look at what he actually says: emancipation brings freedom—to starve, just as in the Ireland of 1850

. . . to roam aimless, wasting the seed-fields of the world; and be hunted home to Chaos, by the due watch-dogs and due hell-dogs, with such horrors of forsaken wretchedness as were never seen before! These things are not sport; they are terribly true, in this country at this hour.

(vol. XIX, p. 33: "The Present Time")

These things are not sport: when in "Model Prisons" Carlyle lambastes the reformers who pro-duce humane cells and working conditions, he does so not from sadistic motives but because he can point to the dreadful slums around, where the noncriminal population has to starve, and pay taxes, to sustain the philanthropy of the model prisons. In the same way hasty philanthropy to the former slaves merely wrecks the fabric of their society (as happened in the sugar industry of the West Indies, badly hit by industrial disputes after emancipation), and threatens European sugar supplies and the long-term economy of the West Indies.

Seeing a mess, Carlyle writes fiercely for intervention. "Supply-and-demand, Leave-it-alone, Voluntary Principle, Time will mend it"—these he lambastes, these lead only to

. . . Anarchy; the choking, sweltering, deadly and killing rule of No-rule; the consecration of cupidity, and braying folly, and dim stupidity and baseness. . . .

(*ibid.*, p. 35)

And what do the "noble men of genius, Heaven's *real* messengers to us," do? They are trained by their educational and social system to "rise in Parliament," to talk, write, do anything but "real kingly *work* to be approved of by the gods!" Dickens' sweeping dismissal of "parliamentary dust-heaps" to which Gradgrind goes to waste his energy in *Hard Times* could not have a clearer ancestry.

"Captainless soldiers," black and white, welter in chaos for lack of government, and the drifting to and fro of government that is perceived in the *Latter-Day Pamphlets* only aggravates the explosive situation in Britain, in Ireland, in the West Indies. Against this Carlyle puts up an extreme case:

Here is work for you; strike into it with manlike, soldierlike obedience and heartiness, according to the methods here prescribed,—wages follow for you without difficulty; all manner of just remuneration, and at length emancipation itself follows. Refuse to strike into it; shirk the heavy labour, disobey the rules,—I will admonish and endeavour to incite you; if in vain, I will flog you; if still in vain, I will at last shoot you. . . .

(*ibid.*, p. 55)

The reason for Carlyle's wavering popularity should now be all too clear. On the one hand is his firsthand experience of rural poverty, his firsthand inspection of starving Ireland, squalid London. On the other is his application of authoritarian models largely from the past, his lack of firsthand experience of the West Indies. On the one hand we acknowledge his unwillingness to turn the clock back, preferring to find a model for the times, something organic. On the other we admit the extreme authoritarian nature of the model he proposes, the difficulty of justifying such an abrogation of individual freedom. But what are the alternatives? Democracy? For this Carlyle reserved special contempt. Votes will not put the ship of state back on course:

Your ship cannot double Cape Horn by its excellent plans of voting . . . the ruffian Winds will blow you ever back again; the inexorable Icebergs, dumb privy-councillors from Chaos, will nudge you with most chaotic "admonition". . . .

(ibid., p. 20)

Too slow, too uncertain, too open to manipulation, too fallible in the hands of a half-educated public, universal suffrage and recognized democracy were hopeless weapons in Carlyle's armory. He cut through the problem to his solution. The alternative to chaos, divinely ordered work (sanctioned, if necessary, with divinely ordered force), was the only way out that Carlyle saw. Whether he was right or wrong the reader now, as then, must judge.

After *Frederick,* and his wife's death, Carlyle was physically incapable of much writing. He published on social questions and on an amateur interest in Scandinavian history; he tried to dictate works to his niece Mary, who had come to live with him in his old age; but the former success would not come back. In private he could still write startling letters, speak with much of the blazing power of his prime; but as a public figure he settled into a passive role as sage, a relic from an age that seemed to be passing, though its problems lived on. One by one his friends and family died, and the lonely old man grew increasingly isolated, though close friends (including Froude) were fiercely loyal to him. When he died, the nation mourned him, rightly, as a figure of major importance. He had refused the offer of a burial place in Westminster Abbey, and was interred without ceremony alongside his parents in Ecclefechan. A statue of him guards his native village and another is on the Chelsea Embankment at the scene of the nightly walks he took with such pleasure by the Thames. His works line library shelves; his life survives the appraisal and reappraisal of controversy; scholarly estimation proceeds.

V

IT is easy to see what Carlyle was not. He was not a man who came from the mainstream of English thought or possessed the education of many of his contemporaries. Perhaps he lacked insight into their ways of thought as a result. He lacked sympathy with their society, and attacked it fiercely as an outsider. He was no liberal thinker in a conventional sense. The Chartist movement filled him with apprehension as well as with sympathy, for anarchy and chaos were terrible things to him. Black slaves thousands of miles off moved him little as human beings; his sympathies lay with them in the future, starving because of short-sighted measures in the present.

He was not a public orator. His lectures were successful to smallish audiences who were profoundly moved by his thoughts on literature and society, but he would not have swayed thousands from platforms, nor excelled in the urbane debate of government. He moved by his writing, his personal influence, his tremendous monologues in a homely setting.

Carlyle was curiously insensitive to many forms of art. Clearly he was a master of the written word in certain styles, and alert to the possibilities of English as a rhetorical tool. Yet he failed to see John Ruskin and William Morris as reformers, for he lacked any insight into their projected fusion of art and moral endeavor. Amazingly insensitive to many varieties of poetry, he repeatedly urged aspiring poets to turn to more serious writing. Quick to see the virtues in some fiction (such as George Eliot's, or much of Dickens'), he uncritically dismissed much more. His pleasure in music moved little beyond the remembered tunes of childhood. Architecture hardly moved him at all, and painting very little except as a record of fact.

Certain literary forms obviously important to his age were beyond Carlyle. He could not achieve the slow, fastidious architecture of Tennyson's *In Memoriam,* the agonized questionings of a mind looking for a faith and honestly chronicling the fits and starts by which some faith, however ambiguously, might be found. He could not project himself into the psychological realities of the past to equal Browning's success in penetrating the moral situation of many of his characters. His humor lacked the finesse and the varieties of Dickens'; he could not see, like Elizabeth Gaskell, the complications of his "message" actually taking root in a society, flourishing among mere mortals with their unpredictable characters and producing unexpected mutations.

Carlyle was intolerant of what he despised or disagreed with. In private life he was charming to those who disagreed (although he would bear them down when he was in the full flow of monologue), and with his friends could meet objection with argument and even modify his opinions. But he had a black-and-white view of things, and his overriding moral purpose made him brush aside debate in favor of putting down with urgency what was needed, in a way best calculated to bring the desired results. Opposition simply encouraged him to more extreme forms of expression, and he lacked objective standards of comparison to keep his expression within bounds.

VI

CARLYLE was undeniably a major force for good in the nineteenth century. He was not alone or unique in having standards, living up to them, honoring the values of his parents, believing in a predominantly Christian ethic for private and public action, upholding the virtues of a Christian society, practicing what he preached in work and reverence (if not in silence). But his very powers of expression made him remarkable, and thousands of his literate contemporaries (particularly the young) saw him as a model, a yardstick for personal endeavor across an immense range of attitudes, from the convinced Christian to the emergent Communist—such as Friedrich Engels, whose *Condition of the Working Class in England: 1844* was inspired by and dedicated to Carlyle. The "Everlasting No" was all too common in an age that had experienced the industrial upheaval of the times, the readjustments of society, reform, Chartism, and trade union struggles for existence and survival against often savage repression. The churches appeared to be reeling from the enlightened skepticism of the previous century, to have lost the struggle in keeping up with their own internal schisms and in building places of worship in the expanding cities (and slums). Terrible debate over evolutionary theories and terrible self-questionings over imperial policy, social justice, and educational theory accompanied the open and often

justly appreciated successes of the Victorian period. Life seemed to be rushing on, and adjustment was difficult for all, particularly for those who had grown up with the Victorian age.

Carlyle was a living example not of a survivor frozen from previous generations, a man who prolonged the values of some forgotten past, but of a man who carried forward some of these values, alertly watched what was going on around him, battled to synthesize for himself some scheme of values, some philosophy that worked for him and that (with modifications) he could advocate to his age. The cry "Work, and despair not" of *Sartor* was echoed, and still had a great influence on the young minds, when Carlyle concluded his rectorial address at Edinburgh in 1866 with a quotation from Goethe, "Wir heissen Euch hoffen" (We bid you hope). The Carlyle who emerges from this brief study is a man born into an age of conflict, of rapid and apparently uncontrollable development, who, as a public figure and successful writer, was to have a major influence in shaping the thinking of the troubled nineteenth century.

SELECTED BIBLIOGRAPHY

I. BIBLIOGRAPHY. I. W. Dyer, *A Bibliography of Thomas Carlyle's Writings and Ana* (Portland, Me., 1928), the standard work but now out of date; G. B. Tennyson, "Thomas Carlyle," in D. J. DeLaura, *Victorian Prose, a Guide to Research* (New York, 1973), covers both Thomas and Jane Carlyle; R. W. Dillon, "A Centenary Bibliography of Carlylean Studies: 1928-1974," in *Bulletin of Bibliography*, 32, no. 4 (October–December 1975), a substantial listing of articles relevant to Carlyle studies, covers 1928–1974; R. L. Tarr, *Bibliography of English-Language Criticism, 1824–1974* (Charlottesville, Va., 1976). Recent publication can be followed in the annual surveys in *Victorian Poetry* and in the selected commentaries published by the Association of Scottish Literary Studies.

II. COLLECTIONS. *The Collected Works of Thomas Carlyle*, 30 vols. (London, 1869–1871), the Library ed.; volumes divided as follows: I, *Sartor Resartus*; II–IV, *The French Revolution*; V, *Life of Schiller*; VI–XI, *Miscellanies* (subdivided into 6 vols. of which vol. II is *Signs of the Times* and vol. V is *Chartism*); XII, *Heroes and Hero-Worship*; XIII, *Past and Present*; XIV–XVIII, *Cromwell's Letters and Speeches*; XIX, *Latter-Day Pamphlets*; XX, *Life of John Sterling*; XXI–XXX, *The History of Frederick the Great* (subdivided into 10 vols. of which vol. X is the *Battle of Rossbach*); H. D. Traill, ed., *The Works of Thomas*

Carlyle, 30 vols. (London, 1896–1899), the Centenary ed.; J. Slater, ed., *The Correspondence of Emerson and Carlyle* (New York, 1964), an excellent partial ed. of the Carlyle-Emerson correspondence; E. W. Marrs, Jr., ed., *The Letters of Thomas Carlyle to His Brother Alexander* (Cambridge, Mass., 1968), the letters of Carlyle and his brother Alexander; C. R. Sanders and K. J. Fielding, gen. eds., *The Collected Letters of Thomas and Jane Welsh Carlyle*, 9 vols. (Durham, N. C., 1970–1980), covering 1812–1837, the Duke-Edinburgh ed. of Thomas' and Jane's letters, which probably, with indexes, will run to 40 vols.; A. Simpson and M. Simpson, eds., *I Too Am Here* (London, 1977), a selection of Jane's letters.

III. SEPARATE WORKS. *Legendre's Elements of Geometry* (London, 1822), trans. and expanded by Carlyle; *Wilhelm Meister's Apprenticeship. A Novel* (London, 1824), a trans. of Goethe's *Wilhelm Meisters Lehrjahre*; *Life of Schiller* (London, 1825); *Specimens of German Romance* (London, 1827), including Goethe's *Wilhelm Meisters Wanderjahre*; *Sartor Resartus* (Boston, 1836; London, 1838; C. F. Harrold, ed., New York, 1937), first published in magazine form, 1833–1834; *The French Revolution* (London, 1837); *Chartism* (London, 1839); *Heroes and Hero-Worship* (London, 1841), highly successful lectures of 1840; *Past and Present* (London, 1843); *Oliver Cromwell's Letters and Speeches* (London, 1845); *Latter-Day Pamphlets* (London, 1850); *Life of John Sterling* (London, 1851), a tribute to a close friend; *The Nigger Question* (London, 1853), uncompromising antiliberal propaganda; *History of Frederick the Great*, 6 vols. (London, 1858–1865), monumental, often dull, his last major work of history; *On the Choice of Books* (London, 1866), his rectorial address at Edinburgh; *Shooting Niagara— And After?* (London, 1867); *The Early Kings of Norway: Portraits of John Knox* (London, 1875); *Reminiscences* (London, 1881), also in Everyman's Library (London,

1972); *The Last Words of Thomas Carlyle* (London, 1892), which includes the novel *Wotton Reinfred*; A. Carlyle, ed., *Historical Sketches of Notable Persons* (London, 1898), which collects several fugitive pieces; *Two Note Books of Thomas Carlyle* (New York, 1898), part of Carlyle's unpublished journal.

IV. BIOGRAPHICAL AND CRITICAL STUDIES. J. A. Froude, *Thomas Carlyle: A History of the First Forty Years of His Life, 1795–1835* (London, 1882), and *Thomas Carlyle: A History of His Life in London, 1834–1881* (London, 1884), 4 vols. that are opinionated, partial, often inaccurate, yet are the best introduction to Carlyle; D. A. Wilson, *Life of Carlyle*, 6 vols. (London–New York, 1923–1934), less inaccurate than Froude but still very fallible, a mine of information carelessly displayed and often untrustworthy; L. Cazamian, *Carlyle* (Paris, 1913), E. K. Brown, trans. (London–New York, 1932); E. Neff, *Carlyle* (London, 1932); C. F. Harrold, *Carlyle and German Thought, 1819–1834* (New Haven, Conn., 1934); J. Holloway, *The Victorian Sage* (London, 1953), concerns Carlyle's social essays and his use of history as commentary on his own time; H. Shine, *Carlyle's Early Reading to 1834* (Lexington, Ky., 1953); T. Holmes, *The Carlyles at Home* (London, 1965); G. B. Tennyson, *Sartor Called Resartus* (Princeton, N. J., 1965); J. Cabau, *Carlyle ou le Prométhée enchaîné* (Paris, 1968); A. J. Lavalley, *Carlyle and the Idea of the Modern* (New Haven, Conn., 1968); George Levine, *The Boundaries of Fiction* (Princeton, N. J., 1968); J. P. Seigel, ed., *Thomas Carlyle: The Critical Heritage* (London, 1971), in the Critical Heritage series, contains an important selection of previous criticism; I. Campbell, *Thomas Carlyle* (London, 1974; New York, 1975); P. Rosenberg, *The Seventh Hero* (New York, 1974); John Clubbe, ed., *Carlyle and His Contemporaries: Essays in Honor of Charles Richard Sanders* (Durham, N. C., 1976); K. J. Fielding and R. L. Tarr, eds., *Carlyle Past and Present* (London, 1976).

THOMAS HOOD

(1799-1845)

Laurence Brander

INTRODUCTION

ON Saturday, 9 July 1842, there was a dinner of the Literary Fund at Greenwich. Charles Dickens persuaded Thomas Hood to come along, and thoughtfully sent his carriage for him. There was a courteous suggestion that Hood should take the chair, but he excused himself on account of his health. Frederick Marryat presided, with Dickens and Richard Monckton Milnes on one hand and Hood on the other. On the Monday evening Hood, in a letter addressed to Mrs. Elliot, his doctor's wife, described his pleasure at being there:

As to myself, I had to make my *second maiden speech*, for Mr. Monckton Milnes proposed my health in terms my modesty might allow me to repeat to *you*; but my memory won't. However, I ascribed the toast to my notoriously bad health, and assured them that their wishes had already improved it—that I felt a brisker circulation—a more genial warmth about the heart, and explained that a certain trembling of my hand was not from palsy, or my old ague, but an inclination in my hand to shake itself with every one present. Whereupon I had to go through the friendly ceremony with as many of the company as were within reach, besides a few more who came express from the other end of the table. *Very* gratifying, wasn't it? Though I cannot go quite so far as Jane, who wants me to have that hand chopped off, bottled, and preserved in spirits. She was sitting up for me, very anxiously, as usual when I go out, because I am so domestic and steady, and was down at the door before I could ring at the gate, to which Boz kindly sent me in his own carriage. Poor girl! What *would* she do if she had a wild husband instead of a tame one?

Eighteen years later we have another recollection of that evening by a young author who sat at the other end of the table, where William Jerdan was vice-chairman to Captain Marryat. William Makepeace Thackeray was reviewing the *Memorials of Thomas Hood* in a Roundabout paper in his *Cornhill* magazine. He recalls that dinner: "The little feast dates back only eighteen years, and yet somehow it seems as distant as a dinner at Mr. Thrale's. There at the end of the room was Hood. Some publishers, I think, were our companions. I quite remember his pale face; he was thin and deaf, and very silent; he scarcely opened his lips during the dinner and he made one pun."

Thackeray proceeds to one of those literary compliments he managed so well. But it was a compliment with a reservation. The *Memorials* had made him look again at *Hood's Own*, that collection of shilling reprints of *The Comic Annual*, and he says:

He wrote these jokes with such ease that he sent manuscripts to the publishers faster than they could acknowledge the receipt thereof. I won't say that they were all good jokes, or that to read a great book full of them is a work at present altogether jocular. Writing to a friend respecting some memoir of him which had been published, Hood says, "You will judge how well the author knows me, when he says my mind is rather serious than comic". At the time when he wrote these words, he evidently undervalued his own serious power, and thought that in punning and broad-grinning lay his chief strength. Is not there something touching in that simplicity and humility of faith? "To make laugh is my calling", says he; "I must jump, I must grin, I must tumble, I must turn language head over heels, and leap through grammar;" and he goes to his work humbly and courageously, and what he has to do that does he with all his might, through sickness, through sorrow, through exile, poverty, fever, depression—there he is, always ready to his work, and with a jewel of genius in his pocket! Why, when he laid down his puns and pranks, put the motley off, and spoke out of his heart, all England and America listened with tears and wonder! Other men have delusions of conceit, and fancy themselves greater than they are and that the world slights them. Here is a man with a power to touch the heart almost unequalled, and he passes days and years in writing, "Young Ben he was a nice young man", and so forth. To say truth, I have been reading in a book of *Hood's Own* until I am perfectly angry. "You great man, you good man, you true genius and poet", I cry out, as I turn page after page. "Do, do make no more of these jokes, but be yourself, and take your station."

("On a Joke I Once Heard from the Late Thomas Hood," *Cornhill*, December 1860)

In another mood, instead of *Hood's Own*, Thackeray might have taken down from his shelves the two volumes of poems that Edward Moxon published in 1846, soon after Hood's death. There, in the opening poems, he would have found sufficient answer to the charge that Hood brought against himself, in his punning way, that he had always been lively Hood for a livelihood. There are the poems that all England and America listened to with tears and wonder, the public poems that expressed the public conscience at the time, at the beginnings in England of a general sense of social responsibility for man's cruelty to man.

Hood is remembered today for these public poems: "The Song of the Shirt," "The Lay of the Labourer," "The Bridge of Sighs." He is remembered by literary people for his great skill in the writing of verses in a wide range of moods. He is likely to recover a reputation with literary people as a periodical writer as soon as the neglect of that fascinating nineteenth-century field of literary work is remedied. Hood began his literary career on the staff of the *London* magazine, founded by John Scott in 1820. He ended as the editor of *Hood's* magazine (1844–1845), with Robert Browning, Dickens, Walter Savage Landor, and Monckton Milnes among his contributors. He had been part owner of the *Athenaeum* and editor of the *New Monthly* magazine. He had produced ten *Comic Annuals* of his own, and before that (1829) had been editor of the *Gem*.

For the literary student Hood's work will be a main study for anyone concerned with popular reading taste in the early nineteenth century, when the annual was a favorite gift, the shilling installment flourished so vigorously, and the magazine came into its own for reading aloud in the family circle. Hood's work belongs to the story of popular publishing for the new, prosperous middle class. For the general reader Hood's work is valuable because he was one of the literary voices of the social conscience of liberal England along with Dickens and Benjamin Disraeli and Elizabeth Gaskell.

LIFE

HOOD was born at 31 The Poultry in the City of London on 23 May 1799. His father came from Dundee and was a bookseller-publisher. The firm of Vernor and Hood was occasionally associated in a big publishing enterprise, such as an edition of Shakespeare, with Longmans. The elder Hood had written two novels, his son tells us; but they are not known, and there is no evidence that they were ever published. His mother was a Miss Sands, of the engraving family. The family moved to Lower Street, Islington, a few years later, and they remained there after the senior Hood died in the autumn of 1811.

Hood then had to leave his expensive school for a humbler one run by an old Scotsman "who had a proper sense of the dignity and importance of his calling, and was content to find a main portion of his reward in the honourable proficiency of his disciples." Very soon Hood's only brother died, and he was left with his mother and four sisters. In these circumstances his schooling could not continue long, and very soon

. . . a friend of the family having taken a fancy to me, proposed to initiate me in those profitable mercantile mysteries which enabled Sir Thomas Gresham to gild his grasshopper, and like another Frank Osbaldistone I found myself planted on a counting house stool, which nevertheless served occasionally for a Pegasus.[1]

Very soon Hood's health broke down. "I was recommended change of air, and in particular the bracing breezes of the north." He has a great deal to say in his *Literary Reminiscences* about his stay in Dundee, but he never speaks of his work. It seems probable that he worked as an engraver; and certainly, when he returned home in the autumn of 1817, he joined his mother's family as an engraver.

Hood's drawings were a feature of his *Comic Annuals*; but they were reproduced as woodcuts, coarse in craftsmanship, and the humor was often harsh and unpleasing. Of his finer work nothing remains, even the etching he called "The Progress of Cant" being apparently lost, though many admirers of Charles Lamb must have sought the original that inspired the description by Lamb in the *New Monthly* magazine.

[1] W. C. Jerrold, ed., *Thomas Hood and Charles Lamb* (London, 1930), p. 56.

Hood became a professional literary man by one of those chances that afterward look like fate. Hood's father taught his business to John Taylor of Taylor and Hessey, and when that firm took over the *London* magazine in 1821, Taylor offered Hood a job as editorial assistant. According to Hood:

In the beginning of the year 1821, a memorable duel, originating in a pen-and-ink quarrel, took place at Chalk Farm, and terminated in the death of Mr. John Scott, the able editor of the *London Magazine*. The melancholy result excited great interest, in which I fully participated, little dreaming that his catastrophe involved any consequences of importance to myself. But on the loss of its conductor, the periodical passed into other hands. The new proprietors were my friends; they sent for me, and after some preliminaries, I was duly installed as a sort of sub-editor of the *London Magazine*.[2]

Accident had brought Hood into his own:

I dreamt articles, thought articles, wrote articles, which were all inserted by the editor, of course with the concurrence of his deputy. The more irksome parts of authorship, such as the correction of the press, were to me labours of love. I received a revise from Mr. Baldwin's Mr. Parker, as if it had been a proof of his regard; forgave him all his slips, and really thought that printers' devils were not so black as they are painted. But my top-gallant glory was in "Our Contributors!" How I used to look forward to Elia! and backward for Hazlitt, and all round for Edward Herbert, and how I used to *look up* to Allan Cunningham! for at that time the *London* had a goodly list of writers—a rare company.[3]

So we see him in the autumn of 1821. His mother had recently died, leaving him in charge of four sisters. Hood worked to keep them. "Perhaps you will ask what I am doing. Why, truly, I am T. Hood, *scripsit et sculpsit.* I am engraving and writing prose and poetry by turns." Here was the energy and exuberance of youth as well as family need. Until the end of the decade he was cheerfully attempting one kind of writing after another, until at the end he had to accept the fact that he must be a comic writer.

His best friend during this time was Charles Lamb, but his closest friend in collaboration and in age was John Hamilton Reynolds, the Edward Herbert of the

London magazine. Reynolds had shown precocious promise as a writer, but is remembered now only as a friend of John Keats. He did much to launch young Hood. The best-known collaboration between them was in Hood's first volume, the *Odes and Addresses to Great People* (1825), famous in its day as the best volume of satirical verse since James Smith's *Rejected Addresses* (1812). Published anonymously, it was good enough to fox one celebrated judge, for Samuel Taylor Coleridge wrote to congratulate Lamb on writing it. The book ran to three editions within eighteen months, and Hood began to be sought out by editors. Even before this reassuring success he married Reynolds' sister Jane on 5 May 1825. The marriage was a happy one—they had a son and a daughter—and it was from this background that Hood became a favorite supplier of reading matter for Victorian families.

Within two years of his marriage, the pattern of Hood's working life was decided. In 1826 he published his first collection of magazine pieces, *Whims and Oddities.* A second collection of *Whims and Oddities* appeared in the following year, and in the same year Longmans published a collection of his serious poems, which, like the lighter pieces in the *Whims,* had nearly all appeared in the magazines. The *Whims* were both successful, but *The Plea of the Midsummer Fairies* was a failure. There is a popular story that Hood bought up the unsold copies to save them from being sold as wrapping paper. Like so many popular stories, it expresses the right idea without accuracy, for the *Plea* was advertised for sale in the *Comic Annual* for 1830. Nevertheless, sales had decided that Hood was going to make his living as a comic writer.

The *Comic Annuals* succeeded the *Whims* and were published from 1830 to 1839. There were imitators, but Hood survived them, and the last two were selling well when the annual generally had fallen out of fashion. They are almost unreadable now. The drawings are crude and the jokes attached to them often cruel enough to offend us. That the verse and prose in them can also be neglected is most easily tested by turning to *Hood's Own,* in which the annuals were reissued in shilling installments. The shilling installment had replaced the annual in the late 1830's: "a one-shilling book is the very thing where a twelve-shilling one would not do," Hood wrote to his publisher. The bound edition of *Hood's Own* is still fairly common (and should be snapped up for the *Literary Reminiscences*), but the *Comic*

---

[2]*Ibid.,* p. 99.
[3]*Ibid.,* p. 100.

Annuals are rare. He published one more *Comic Annual* in 1842 that was more like the *Whims* in being a collection of pieces that had appeared in *New Monthly* magazine. He succeeded Theodore Hook as editor of the *New Monthly* in 1841, and two volumes of his personal contributions were published in 1844 under a title that recalled his earliest collections, *Whimsicalities*.

Hood's life was one long search for money. It was natural, therefore, that he should try the novel. In 1834 he published *Tylney Hall*, which we should judge very poor but which sold well in its day. In 1840 he published *Up the Rhine*, a novel in letter form, which is based on his own experiences in Germany. He was publishing *Our Family* serially in his magazine when he died.

Twice Hood did himself serious financial damage. The facts are shrouded in decent Victorian obscurity, but we know that he got into debt by being involved in the failure of a publishing firm in 1834. Following his hero, Sir Walter Scott, he determined to repay in full rather than slip out legally by declaring himself bankrupt. A little later he again showed a lack of business acumen when Charles Dilke dramatically brought down the price of the *Athenaeum* from eightpence to fourpence. Hood panicked and sold his share. In a few weeks the circulation was trebled. That was not serious, but leaving Henry Colburn and the *New Monthly* to found his own magazine was desperately so, as we shall see.

As debtors so often did in those days, Hood went abroad. He settled in Koblenz, Germany, in 1835. His family joined him, and two years later they moved to Ostend, Belgium. Every step he took was a misfortune. A violent storm when he was crossing the North Sea made him very ill. He probably was already suffering from tuberculosis, and the popular treatment in Germany at that time was to put the patient between cold, wet sheets. Hood survived; but the cold, damp climate of Ostend was almost equally bad for him. When he returned to London in 1840, he had paid his debts but his health was shattered.

He then ran into another familiar financial trouble: he went to law. He had been so bitterly disappointed at his share of the sales of *Up the Rhine* that he sued the publisher. This very nearly ruined him again. The outcome of the case is not told us, but his letters show that he was for a time reduced almost to penury.

Hood was rescued by Colburn, who offered him the editorship of the *New Monthly* magazine after Theodore Hook died. This was excellent, but again Hood showed that he had very little financial sense. His salary was £300, he was paid in addition for his own contributions, and he had an arrangement for a royalty when these contributions were collected in book form. Hood thought he could do better. He broke away from Colburn at the end of 1843 and founded his own magazine in January 1844, so that he could get what he considered his fair share of the profits. Things went wrong from the beginning. He had an unnamed partner with the necessary capital who found a printer. The printer failed them. Hood wanted to get the middleman's profits in addition to the editorial profits, and opened an office for distributing the magazine in Adam Street, Adelphi. The booksellers nearly boycotted the magazine. Eventually Hood got rid of his partner and published through a medical publisher, Renshaw, in the Strand. By this time he was so ill with worry and the inevitable progress of his disease that friends had to take over and run his magazine for him.

In the last days, the spring of 1845, we find Browning and Landor and Monckton Milnes contributing. Everyone rallied round the sick man; and Hood's last exchange of letters was with Prime Minister Robert Peel, who was settling a life pension on Hood's wife. He died on 3 May 1845.

Thackeray wrote his Roundabout paper in 1860, when editions of Hood's works were still being regularly produced and *Hood's Own* was still a best seller. He was reacting to many volumes of reprinted fun, and comic writing had been his business until, unlike Hood, he was lucky enough to escape from it through the success of *Vanity Fair*. Since then, we have had Alfred Ainger's very civilized memoir of 1897 and Walter Jerrold's long biography and critical assessment in 1907. The only particular things of note since then are Jerrold's introduction to the *Literary Reminiscences*, two short papers by Edmund Blunden, which display his unique knowledge and judgment of English writing of those days, and, in 1963, the full-length study by J. C. Reid.

What do we think today of Hood's writings? Before we begin, it may be as well to state the conclusion: that the best of Hood for us is in the opening poems of the 1846 edition. That edition was prepared before he died, and there is some excuse for thinking that he suggested the contents and their order himself. His best longer poem came first, and then the public poems on which his reputation now depends.

THOMAS HOOD

EARLY POEMS

HOOD's decision to become a comic writer was made as a result of his publications in 1827, when he brought out not only the second series of *Whims*, which was a great success, but two volumes of short stories, called *National Tales*, which had no great success, and a volume of serious poems, *The Plea of the Midsummer Fairies*, which was a failure. It is impossible to disagree with the judgment of the time that the 1827 volume of serious verse was very minor. Hood was later to write genuine poetry, but everything here is romantic imitation.

We can see from a close examination of the lyrics in the volume how much Hood had pinned his hopes to its success. A fair number of them had appeared in annuals and in magazines. "Retrospective Review" and the Shakespeare sonnet first appeared in the *Literary Souvenir*; "Ruth" and "The Water Lady," in *Forget-Me-Not*. The "Ode to the Moon" appeared in *Blackwood's*, but the great repository had been the *London* magazine, in which "Fair Ines," "Ode: Autumn," "Hymn to the Sun," "To a Cold Beauty," and four of the sonnets had appeared.

Hood worked over all these poems before they were republished in his volume, but very few are still alive. Some good judges mention the autumn ode along with the great ode by Keats, and certainly the contrasting treatment of the subject is interesting. Keats thinks of the richness of the season, all nature brought to splendid fruition, while Hood's cast of mind makes him see autumn as the late season that leads to wintry death:

> I saw old Autumn in the misty morn
> Stand shadowless like Silence, listening
> To silence, for no lonely bird would sing
> Into his hollow ear from woods forlorn,
> Nor lowly hedge nor solitary thorn. . . .
> (1–5)

Some of the lyrics—"Fair Ines," "Ruth," and "I Remember"—still give the disturbing pleasure that poetry offers, but the book depended on the longer pieces, and they failed.

"The Plea," which opens the volume, is a pretty conceit; and if the reader can suspend disbelief for half an hour, there comes a point in the tale when one is involved and concerned about what is going to happen. The story is simple: the fairies are threatened with extinction by Saturn, alias Father Time.

They plead prettily, as when Time asks Puck who he is:

> "Alas!" quoth Puck, "a little random elf,
> Born in the sport of nature, like a weed,
> For simple sweet enjoyment of myself,
> But for no other purpose, worth, or need;
> And yet withal of a most happy breed. . . ."
> (793–797)

This is quite in vain, and Time grasps his scythe:

> Which frights the elfin progeny so much,
> They huddle in a heap, and trembling stand
> All round Titania . . . .
> (858–860)

In the next stanza comes the deus ex machina in this elfin play: "a timely Apparition," Shakespeare, whose gift of immortality routs Time. The fairies are saved just in time, for

> . . . bold Chanticleer, from farm to farm,
> Challeng'd the dawn creeping o'er eastern land.
> (1122–1123)

The conceit was pretty enough for Lamb to pay tribute to Hood by retelling the story in prose in William Hone's *Table Book*, ending with a rich compliment: "The words of Mercury are harsh after the songs of Apollo." But the epithet "pretty" that has been repeated here is the irresistible one, and "The Plea" is too slight to have any immortality of its own. The stanzas sing most of the way, and are only occasionally jolted by antique words that refuse to sit naturally in the context. They read quickly and carry the neat little fantasy well, but fairy poetry is a very special skill, requiring the virtuosity of Shakespeare or Keats. The attempt wins our admiration, but attempts are not enough. Hood eventually found success in more human sentiments and situations.

The story of Hero and Leander belongs to the last phase of Alexandrian culture before the city fell to the Arabs. It was used with great effect by Christopher Marlowe, who brought the story to life so that every reader feels two young people obsessed and carried away by love. When George Chapman continued Marlowe's unfinished poem in his own contrasting style, the luxury of ornament was there but nothing of Marlowe's passionate power and depth of utterance. Marlowe made disturbing poetry; Chapman finished the story in skillfully ornamented verse.

Hood's poem has none of these qualities, but he did write his own version of the story. In Hood's version it is not a storm and the disappearance of Hero's torch that causes Leander to drown, but a mermaid who forcefully carries Leander down to her grotto without noticing that she has drowned him. There is a moment when this rather bare and tenuous narrative acquires speed and tension, from stanza 51, when the mermaid "compels him to her deep below," but the interest soon fades.

In "Hero and Leander," Hood adapts a classical legend. In "Lycus, the Centaur" he invents one of his own. In "Hero and Leander" he uses the six-line stanza common in Elizabethan lyrics of an elegiac cast and used by Shakespeare in "Venus and Adonis." In "Lycus" he uses the fast-moving anapestic tetrameter in couplet form. In the variety of his meters, he is already showing his virtuosity; and this time he brings it off as he never looked like doing in "Hero," where he attempted the stanza that Shakespeare used for narrative with such deceptive ease.

There seems to be no explanation of the centaur in classical mythology. Hood provides one. Circe tires of the man, and her curse on him, which was going to turn him into a horse, is interrupted, so he lives as half horse, half man. Hood's centaur is a pathetic outcast from human society, unrecognized and insulted by his own son. That is the whole story, told by the centaur himself. It appeared first in the *London* magazine in August 1822, and there are very few changes in the 1827 version.

"The Two Peacocks of Bedfont" appeared in the same magazine in October of the same year, with the following note, which explains the source of the story:

If any man, in his unbelief, should doubt the truth and manner of this occurrence, he may in an easy way be assured thereof to his satisfaction, by going to Bedfont, a journey of some thirteen miles, where, in the churchyard, he may with his own eyes behold the two peacocks. They seem at first sight to be of yew-tree, which they greatly resemble; but on drawing nearer, he will perceive, cut therein, the date 1704—being, without doubt, the year of their transformation.

It seems likely from this that Hood's fertile fancy invented the story after seeing the two peacocks trimmed out of yew in the churchyard hedge. It is mentioned last here because it has a feeling for the Essex and Hertfordshire countryside that Hood developed in his next poem, *The Epping Hunt* (1829), and in his novel *Tylney Hall*, a few years later. The peasant and his wife in "The Two Peacocks" are very like the country folk in the opening scene of *Tylney Hall*. Further, there are glimpses in this story of a quality in Hood's verse craftsmanship that suggests that this greatly gifted young man missed by very little being one of the considerable romantic poets.

In the *Gem* (1829), Hood offered "The Dream of Eugene Aram, the Murderer," the first long poem that is genuinely his own. It has his special quality of macabre horror, and its long six-line ballad stanzas have something of the doom we hear and feel in Coleridge's "The Ancient Mariner." "Eugene Aram" is successful because it is narrative told in unobtrusive language in an apt stanza. He is no longer trying to be a romantic poet. He is content to tell a story as well as he can, and we see at once the skill he had in verse-making. This is also the first poem of any length by Hood in which the mood and the expression are interpenetrated with the sad music of human frailty and death, which is his special contribution to English verse.

> "And still no peace for the restless clay,
>   Will wave or mould allow;
> The horrid thing pursues my soul, —
>   It stands before me now!"
> The fearful Boy look'd up, and saw
>   Huge drops upon his brow.
>
> That very night, while gentle sleep
>   The urchin eyelids kiss'd,
> Two stern-faced men set out from Lynn,
>   Through the cold and heavy mist;
> And Eugene Aram walk'd between,
>   With gyves upon his wrist.
>
>   (205–216)

An interesting contrast can be instituted with Edward Bulwer-Lytton's novel of the same name. Hood's Eugene is a simple country schoolmaster, with an unusual amount of learning, who has committed a murder out of need. Bulwer-Lytton's Eugene is in the tradition of Goethe's *Faust* and the general German literary tradition, which excused murder when it was the result of an immoderate, hydroptic thirst for human learning. Bulwer-Lytton's Eugene is a savant; Hood's, a dominie.

THOMAS HOOD

COMIC VERSE

WHEN Thackeray regretted that Hood had given so much time to the writing of comic pieces, he may have been reacting from the memory of his own early struggles. If he had taken down the 1846 edition of *Poems*, we said, instead of *Hood's Own*, he would have written differently. We can also say that if he had then taken down the *Poems of Wit and Humour*, published in 1847, and gone through *Hood's Own* also, as they did not overlap, looking for Hood's skill and range in the composition of light verse, we might very well have had a memorable appreciation, for Thackeray learned the craft from Hood and learned it very well.

In comic verse the prosodic structure is very plain, and it is usually part of the fun to watch the poet making his words run swiftly and smoothly, giving an impression of gaiety and conveying the sense speedily, without any difficulty. Hood was a master of this sort of thing, and to find anyone who displayed virtuosity in such a wide range of meters, we have to go back to Jonathan Swift. The mention of Swift brings us back to Thackeray, who was really saying that it requires brains to write comic verse, and that it was a pity that so much of Hood's fine brain had to be used in that way.

Hood's first public success was as a writer of comic verse in "The Lion's Head" in the *London* magazine. He confirmed his success in his first volume, written with his brother-in-law Reynolds, the *Odes and Addresses to Great People*. Hood wrote most of these odes and the best of them, and they give a fair sample of his specialty, the pun. The pun is now used in farcical writing; but it ranked better then, the most obvious evidence being Coleridge's much-quoted letter to Charles Lamb when the *Odes* were published: "The puns are nine in ten good—many excellent—the *Newgatory* transcendent."

> I like the pity in your full-brimm'd eye;
>   I like your carriage and your silken grey,
> Your dove-like habits, and your silent preaching;
> But I don't like your Newgatory teaching.
>   ("A Friendly Epistle to Mrs. Fry,
>   *in* Newgate," 101–104)

For typical Hood comic verse, let us look at the ballads "Faithless Sally Brown" and "Faithless Nelly Gray." The press gang seizes Sally's young Ben:

> And Sally she did faint away,
>   Whilst Ben he was brought to.
>
> The Boatswain swore with wicked words,
>   Enough to shock a saint,
> That though she did seem in a fit,
>   'Twas nothing but a feint.
>   (7–12)

The punning exuberance is sustained to the end. Sally proves faithless, Ben dies, and:

> They went and told the sexton, and
>   The sexton toll'd the bell.
>   (67–68)

The story of the other Ben, with an equally faithless sweetheart, Nelly Gray, is even more impudent in its punning:

> Ben Battle was a soldier bold,
>   And used to war's alarms;
> But a cannon-ball took off his legs,
>   So he laid down his arms!
>
> Now as they bore him off the field,
>   Said he, "Let others shoot,
> For here I leave my second leg,
>   And the Forty-second Foot!"
>   (1–8)

The two volumes of the *Whims* were so successful that Hood began collecting material for a third. Meantime, he published separately a punning ballad of inordinate length, *The Epping Hunt*. It celebrated an old London custom to hunt a deer in Epping Forest at Easter time; but the story fails to attract us as William Cowper's "John Gilpin" does, and the puns merely irritate.

The range of Hood's virtuosity in comic verse writing is worth demonstrating, and Swift's play with long lines is recalled here, in "Our Village—by a Villager":

> Our village, that's to say, not Miss Mitford's village,
>   but our village of Bullock Smithy,
> Is come into by an avenue of trees, three oak pollards,
>   two elders, and a withy;
> And in the middle there's a green of about not exceeding
>   an acre and a half;
> It's common to all and fed off by nineteen cows, six ponies,
>   three horses, five asses, two foals, seven pigs,
>   and a calf!
>   (1–4)

He used the "fourteener" with effect in this comment on the election of the professor of poetry at Oxford. Someone is explaining the row going on in a public house:

But Dick's resigned the post, you see, and all them shouts
    and hollers
Is 'cause two other candidates, some sort of larned
    scholars,
Are squabbling to be Chairman of the Glorious Apollers!

Lord knows their names, I'm sure I don't, no more than
    any yokel,
But I never heard of either as connected with the vocal;
Nay, some do say, although of course the public rumour
    varies,
They've no more warble in 'em than a pair of hen canaries.
        ("The University Feud: A Row at the
        Oxford Arms," 30–36)

That criticism, at any rate, could not be made of recent elections. The same effect of garrulity is conveyed in this description of how Mrs. Round cleared the flues of the washing copper with a pound of gunpowder.

Lawk, Mrs. Round! says I, and stares, that quantum is
    improper,
I'm sartin sure it can't not take a pound to sky a copper;
You'll powder both our heads off, so I tells you, with its
    puff,
But she only dried her fingers, and she takes a pinch of
    snuff.
        ("A Report from Below," 42–45)

Hood's comic verse was popular for domestic recitation during the rest of the century; but even the punning ballads are disappearing now from the verbal nourishment of our nurseries, and the remainder of his great corpus of comic verse is quite forgotten.

Let us end with a sample of his tetrameters, the verse that Swift used so well and that normally tests a writer's speed and lightness. The Devil is selling a speaking trumpet to the deaf Dame Eleanor Spearing:

She was deaf as a post, —as said before—
And as deaf as twenty similes more,
Including the adder, that deafest of snakes,
Which never hears the coil it makes.
        ("A Tale of a Trumpet," 32–35)

The Devil invites her to try his speaking trumpet:

"Try it again, Ma'am, only try!"
Was still the voluble Pedlar's cry;
"It's a great privation, there's no dispute,
To live like the dumb unsociable brute,
And hear no more of the *pro* and *con*,
And how's Society's going on,
Than Mumbo Jumbo or Prester John,
And all for want of this *Sine Quâ Non*;" . . .
        (396–403)

Hood is like his native weather: there is more sun in his composition than we often suppose. The contrast between lively Hood for a livelihood and the writer of the famous public poems is a natural situation. No writer could be sensitive to the human condition, as Hood was, without wishing to express its pathos and at the same time spread what gaiety he could. It made him a fulfilled man.

One longer piece requires notice, a moralizing story in verse that is Hood's outstanding contribution to the Victorian family reader. It is "Miss Kilmansegg and Her Precious Leg," which appeared in Colburn's *New Monthly* magazine in September 1840, when Theodore Hook was still editor. It was the third of a series of poems that Hood was contributing under the title "Rhymes for the Times and Reason for the Season." It is typical of the kind of material that magazines then provided for reading aloud in the family circle. It was a satire for the well-to-do about the far-too-well-to-do. It was a lampoon on outrageously vulgar wealth for an acquisitive society to enjoy. It was reprinted, with a few revisions of no importance, in the *Comic Annual* for 1842, accompanied there by the delicious illustrations by John Leech. It is reprinted after the reforming poems in the 1846 collection.

The story is simple. Miss Kilmansegg is the spoiled daughter of a very wealthy London merchant, so:

She was not doom'd for bread to eat
To be put to her hands as well as her feet—
   To carry home linen from mangles—
Or heavy-hearted, and weary-limb'd,
To dance on a rope in a jacket trimm'd
   With as many blows as spangles.
        (126–131)

In this spirit the whole of Miss Kilmansegg's life is described: her christening, her childhood, her education, and her accident. She falls from a bolting horse; her leg has to be amputated; and she insists on having a gold artificial one. It is "As solid as man could make it," and how she ever manages to use such a weighty aid is not explained. Eventually she marries a foreign count; and it is not explained how her father, who knows so much about money and affairs, could let his daughter marry an impostor without any attempt at checking his credentials. The impostor is a drunken gambler who runs through her money and eventually kills her with her own golden leg. It is possible to read the poem for the brio displayed in Hood's management of the verse and the glancing references that sustain the comic lightness.

PROSE

HOOD's prose was good in various kinds, but very little has much interest for us now. He began with paragraphs, often punning, in the editorial page of the *London* magazine. He wrote a collection of short stories, *National Tales*, in a clogged narrative manner, then developed his gift for short pieces in the *Comic Annuals*. His experience of writing prose for the stage with Reynolds cleared and quickened his style.

Then came the first novel, *Tylney Hall*, in 1834. *Fraser's* reviewer described it as "one of the most stupid and ill-written books we ever had the misfortune to meet with. Dull, heavy, twaddling and uninteresting, it is probably worthy of being dedicated to the Duke of Devonshire . . . who resembles in countenance and intellect a middle-aged Merino sheep." Charles Lamb, thanking Hood for his copy, described the book very well: "'Tis a medley, without confusion, of farce, melodrama, pantomime, comedy, tragedy, and what not."

It is a country novel written by a townsman whose ideas of the country were caught from walking in that strangely unreal region, the Epping Forest. The story tells how a Creole repaid the uncle who took him in and brought him up, by plotting that one of his cousins should kill the other so that the Creole would succeed to the estates. The characters are all unreal; but the *Athenaeum* review highlights the one character interesting to us, because it demonstrates Hood's preoccupation with the poor unfortunates of this world a decade before the great public poems. Unlucky Joe is a postilion for whom everything goes wrong, whatever he does and no matter how much he tries; his "helplessness and hopelessness . . . engage our sympathy," as the *Athenaeum* said. Yet even Unlucky Joe is not a character, but only a faint indication of the way in which Hood's sensibility was going to develop. Dickens' judgment of the novel, which he read some years after its publication, will stand for us: "the most extraordinary jumble of impossible extravagance, and especial cleverness I ever saw."

Hood had not learned how to write sustained narrative; and in his next novel, *Up the Rhine* (1840), he wisely avoided the need for it. He chose the letter form and followed Tobias Smollett closely in making his narrator a young man who described the amusing idiosyncrasies of an old man, which were then reflected in the old man's letters. There are all the usual characters, even that great bore, the half-literate servant who cannot spell. *Up the Rhine* sold a first edition of 1,500 in a fortnight and was much reprinted in London and on the Continent, but it did not have the vitality that makes a classic. As before, the animated things are little jokes and anecdotes, and that alone does not give a novel life.

The last novel, *Our Family*, was going to be much better but another cause, ill health, now prevented Hood from achieving much. Only a few chapters were completed. The novel was to be about a doctor and his family in a Lincolnshire village. The good-natured country practitioner has a Dickensian affability, and all is well when he is able to throw a purse of guineas surreptitiously to some poor patients. Hood shows a touch of realism in making the wretchedly poor family squander the guineas on an absurdly elaborate funeral, and in making the villagers turn upon their benefactor with animal hatred and ferocity. No doubt everything would have come right in the end, for there is a very mean rich character who has only to have a change of heart, like Ebenezer Scrooge, to rescue the family; but in the few chapters we have, one calamity follows another without any relief. This seems to have been to the taste of the times, for a decade later Eliza Cook reprinted some of the chapters in her *Journal*.

Two other prose collections must be mentioned that are much better because they arise out of Hood's natural talent. The *Literary Reminiscences* were written at the inspired suggestion of the publisher of *Hood's Own*. A portrait of Hood by George Robert Lewis was being presented in one of the shilling installments, and it was suggested that Hood contribute an autobiography. "I found myself called upon by my publisher, with a finished proof of the engraving in one hand, and a request for an account of myself in the other." Hood was still in Ostend, and still suffering seriously from the "cures" to which he had submitted during the two previous years. It is not surprising, then, that he had various false starts to his *Reminiscences* and got under way only at the fifth attempt, which was also the last installment. "The trouble is that my malady forced me to temporize:—wherefore the kind reader will be pleased to consider the aforesaid chapters but as so many 'false starts,' and that memory has only now got away, to make play as well as she can."

There are some magnificent sketches in that final part. Hood is writing with a slightly mannered sensitivity, giving us living glimpses of Lamb and John Clare and Thomas De Quincey and other contributors to the *London* magazine. While he sketches his friends, he shows us himself. He had refused the suggestion that he write his autobiography, compromising with reminiscences that turned out to be the best sort of autobiography, for we see him at his best as he describes his friends. As in this famous sketch of Lamb:

I was sitting one morning beside our Editor, busily correcting proofs, when a visitor was announced, whose name, grumbled by a low ventriloquial voice, like Tom Pipes calling from the hold through the hatchway, did not resound distinctly on my tympanum. However, the door opened, and in came a stranger,—a figure remarkable at a glance, with a fine head, on a small spare body, supported by two almost immaterial legs. He was clothed in sables, of a bygone fashion, but there was something wanting, or something present about him, that certified he was neither a divine, nor a physician, nor a schoolmaster: from a certain neatness and sobriety in his dress, coupled with his sedate bearing, he might have been taken, but that such a costume would be anomalous, for a *Quaker* in black. He looked still more like (what he really was) a literary Modern Antique, a New-Old Author, a living Anachronism, contemporary at once with Burton the Elder, and Colman the Younger. Meanwhile he advanced with rather a peculiar gait, his walk was plantigrade, and with a cheerful "How d'ye", and one of the blandest, sweetest smiles that ever brightened a manly countenance, held out two fingers to the Editor.

The two gentlemen in black soon fell into discourse; and whilst they conferred, the Lavater principle within me set to work upon the interesting specimen thus presented to its speculations. It was a striking intellectual face, full of wiry lines, physiognomical quips and cranks, that gave it great character. There was much earnestness about the brows, and a deal of speculation in the eyes, which were brown and bright, and "quick in turning"; the nose, a decided one,

though of no established order; and there was a handsome smartness about the mouth. Altogether it was no common face—none of those *willow-pattern* ones, which Nature turns out by thousands at her potteries;—but more like a chance specimen of the Chinese ware, one to the set—unique, antique, quaint. No one who had once seen it, could pretend not to know it again. It was no face to lend its countenance to any confusion of persons in a Comedy of Errors. You might have sworn to it piecemeal,—a separate affidavit for every feature. In short, his face was as original as his figure; his figure as his character; his character as his writings; his writings the most original of the age. After the literary business had been settled, the Editor invited his contributor to dinner, adding "we shall have a hare—"

"And—and—and—and many friends!"

The hesitation in the speech, and the readiness of the allusion, were alike characteristic of the individual, whom his familiars will perchance have recognized already as the delightful Essayist, the capital Critic, the pleasant Wit and Humorist, the delicate-minded and large-hearted Charles Lamb! He was shy like myself with strangers, so that despite my yearnings, our first meeting scarcely amounted to an introduction. We were both at dinner, amongst the hare's many friends, but our acquaintance got no further, in spite of a desperate attempt on my part to attract his notice. His complaint of the Decay of Beggars[4] presented another chance: I wrote on coarse paper, and in ragged English, a letter of thanks to him as if from one of his mendicant clients, but it produced no effect. I had given up all hope, when one night, sitting sick and sad, in my bedroom, racked with the rheumatism, the door was suddenly opened, the well-known quaint figure in black walked in without any formality, and with a cheerful "Well, boy, how are you!" and the bland sweet smile, extended the two fingers. They were eagerly clutched of course, and from that hour we were firm friends.[5]

There is a glimpse of John Clare and Elia walking arm in arm down the Strand after a *London* magazine dinner, Elia in his sables and Clare in his "bright, grass-coloured coat, and yellow waistcoat." "Little wonder," says Hood, that as they went along,

. . . the peasant and Elia, *Sylvanus et Urban*, linked comfortably together; there arose the frequent cry of "Look at Tom and Jerry—there goes Tom and Jerry!" for truly, Clare in his square-cut green coat, and Lamb in his black, were not a little suggestive of Hawthorn and Logic, in the plates to *Life in London*.[6]

[4] Appeared in the *London* magazine for June 1822.
[5] T. Hood, Jr., and F. F. Broderip, eds., *The Works*, 11 vols. (London, 1882–1884), vol. II, pp. 367–369. All references hereinafter are to this edition.
[6] By Pierce Egan, published in monthly parts during 1820–1821.

The sketch of De Quincey shows Hood, as in the Elia sketch, displaying natural sympathy with his subject. In a few sentences we have an impression of De Quincey's learning and his genius:

When it was my frequent and agreeable duty to call on Mr. De Quincey (being an uncommon name to remember, the servant associated it, on the Memoria Technica principle, with a sore throat, and always pronounced it Quinsy), and I have found him at home, quite at home, in the midst of a German Ocean of *Literature*, in a storm,—flooding all the floor, the table and the chairs,—billows of books tossing, tumbling, surging open,—on such occasions I have willingly listened by the hour whilst the Philosopher, standing, with his eyes fixed on one side of the room, seemed to be less speaking than reading from a "handwriting on the wall". Now and then he would diverge, for a Scotch mile or two, to the right or left, till I was tempted to inquire with Peregrine in John Bull (Colman's not Hook's), "Do you never deviate?"—but he always came safely back to the point where he had left, not lost the scent, and thence hunted his topic to the end. But look!—we are in the small hours, and a change comes o'er the spirit of that "old familiar face". A faint hectic tint leaves the cheek, the eyes are a degree dimmer, and each is surrounded by a growing shadow—signs of the waning influence of that Potent Drug whose stupendous Pleasures and enormous Pains have been so eloquently described by the English Opium Eater.
(vol. II, pp. 379–380)

The last prose collection worth looking at is the letters that make the substance of the *Memorials*, which his son and daughter published in 1860. Everyone who has studied Hood closely is persuaded that one day a great cache of his letters will turn up, for he was a habitual letter writer. In a sense, he lived in his letters because he was so often confined to his sickroom. When he exiled himself in Koblenz, he lived in his letters to his family and his friends, and these letters form the bulk of the *Memorials*.

There must have been many more, and we must hope that one day they will be found, for Hood was a sensitive correspondent, thinking more of the person to whom he was writing than of the need for unburdening himself. Most of the letters are domestic, for the family or about the family, but toward the end of the *Memorials* there is a good deal about his writing and the anguish that writing to deadlines was causing him. They are not great letters. For the most part those to his family are written only to amuse and reassure them; those to his doctor report on his health; and those to his engraver are the simple business letters of a writer to his agent. But they make a much better book than any of his prose writings except the *Literary Reminiscences*, for they become a self-portrait of a good man who lived a difficult life with great courage.

LATER POEMS

HOOD's finest poems were written in the last two years of his life. "The Song of the Shirt" appeared in the Christmas number of *Punch* in 1843. The first number of *Hood's* magazine appeared in the following month and opened with "The Haunted House." Very soon it offered "The Elm Tree" and the rest of the public poems, "The Bridge of Sighs," "The Lady's Dream," "The Workhouse Clock," and "The Lay of the Labourer."

"Eugene Aram" opens the 1846 collection and is followed by the poems just named above and the "Ode to Rae Wilson." This placing is significant to the student of Hood, for it shows that he, or whoever decided the order, knew quite well which poems would live. The Rae Wilson ode is not a great poem but, like so many imperfect pieces, tells us more about the poet than do the successful poems that stand on their own and have detached themselves from their writer.

The public poems, those in which Hood exposed the sufferings of some unfortunate group in society, are so special to him that they require separate consideration. There has been nothing quite like them before or since in English poetry. In an obvious sense it is always true that nothing quite like any poet's work has been written before or since, and this is evidently true of the poems that open the 1846 edition.

"Eugene Aram" need be mentioned again only to note that "The Elm Tree" uses the same stanza to give the same mood: the extended ballad stanza to transmit a sense of doom. The earlier ballad tells the doom of one man, and the reader feels that but for the grace of God, the mark of Cain would be on his or her forehead also. The later ballad celebrates the inescapable doom of all humanity. The poem opens with a sense of decay in the forest, that feeling of "dank earth brown and rotten" that appears from one end of Victorian poetry to the other, and that here takes us back to the autumn poems in *The Plea of the Midsummer Fairies*:

> Ay, now the Forest Trees may grieve
> And make a common moan
> Around that patriarchal trunk

So newly overthrown;
And with a murmur recognize
A doom to be their own!
(308–313)

Sound is made to reflect the mood of the poem throughout, and especially in the refrain stanza that appears with slight variations:

But still the sound was in my ear,
A sad and solemn sound,
That sometimes murmur'd overhead,
And sometimes underground—
'Twas in a shady Avenue
Where lofty Elms abound.
(34–39)

The poet has no story to carry on his stanzas, as in "Eugene Aram." He is writing an entirely descriptive poem of sight, sound, and mood, so he varies his stanza occasionally to carry the reader forward:

The Woodman's heart is in his work,
His axe is sharp and good:
With sturdy arm and steady aim
He smites the gaping wood;
From distant rocks
His lusty knocks
Re-echo many a rood.
(195–201)

And again, in a stanza that sums up the whole poem:

But haughty Peer and mighty King
One doom shall overwhelm!
The oaken cell
Shall lodge him well
Whose sceptre ruled a realm—
While he who never knew a home,
Shall find it in the Elm!
(413–419)

"The Haunted House" is a contrasting study in a much more sophisticated meter, that apt conjunction of trimeters and pentameters in which so many moods can be reflected in English verse. The poem opened the first number of *Hood's* magazine, and presumably was inspired by the engraving of Thomas Creswick's painting of a deserted house that provided the frontispiece. Hood liked the picture, and he wrote a poem on the subject. It turned out to be the most skillful set of verses he ever wrote. The

three pentameters are voweled to give the sense of dread and ghostly haunting, while the following trimeter with the double rhyme so quickly arrived at echoes the reverberating hollowness of the empty house. The management of the stanzas is beyond praise, the long, heavy lines and the dull echoing of the double rhymes, with the effective shortening of the last line of the refrain stanza:

O'er all there hung a shadow and a fear;
A sense of mystery the spirit daunted,
And said, as plain as whisper in the ear,
The place is Haunted!
(29–32)

Hood had special gifts for describing rottenness and decay:

The tempest with its spoils had drifted in,
Till each unwholesome stone was darkly spotted,
As thickly as the leopard's dappled skin,
With leaves that rankly rotted.

The air was thick—and in the upper gloom
The bat—or something in its shape—was winging,
And on the wall, as chilly as a tomb,
The Death's Head moth was clinging.
(241–248)

The "Ode to Rae Wilson," which follows the public poems in the 1846 collection, was written for the *Athenaeum* in 1837 at the suggestion of Charles Dilke, the editor. Rae Wilson, a Scottish member of Parliament who spent much of his time in Mediterranean countries for the purpose of comparing their religions unfavorably with his own brand of Calvinism, had attacked Hood more than once for daring to be jolly, and had conducted a running warfare with the *Athenaeum* for some time. Something Wilson had written presented an opportunity, so Dilke wrote to Hood in Ostend, suggesting that Hood finish him off. Hood quickly wrote the sort of ode he wrote in his first collection. It duly appeared in the *Athenaeum* and was never revised. We read it now not at all for the denunciation of Wilson, although his type survives, but for the passages in which Hood tells us about what he believes. Hood hated the hypocrisy and humbug that, satirists assure us, form the basis of English social life and just possibly can be detected here and there in other human societies. Hood, more positively, spoke out for toleration and generosity of mind. Percipiently, he saw the need for the modern virtues that alone will keep modern, congested human societies in existence: altruism, magnanimity, generosity of mind, toleration, call them what we will.

Once or twice in this ode he rises to lyrical utterance on these questions in passages that give us unique glimpses of the character and spirit of the sick man who was going to write some unforgettable public poems. As in this plea for religious tolerance:

> Say, was it to my spirit's gain or loss,
> One bright and balmy morning, as I went
> From Liège's lovely environs to Ghent,
> If hard by the wayside I found a cross,
> That made me breathe a pray'r upon the spot —
> While Nature of herself, as if to trace
> The emblem's use, had trail'd around its base
> The blue significant Forget-Me-Not?
> Methought, the claims of Charity to urge
> More forcibly, along with Faith and Hope,
> The pious choice had pitch'd upon the verge
>   Of a delicious slope,
> Giving the eye much variegated scope; —
> "Look round", it whisper'd, "on that prospect rare,
> Those vales so verdant, and those hills so blue;
> Enjoy the sunny world, so fresh, and fair,
> But"—(how the simple legend pierc'd me thro'!)
>   "Priez pour les Malheureux."
>   (290–307)

One more poem, "Stanzas," may be quoted, for it gathers together in one lyrical utterance Hood's suffering and courage. It appeared as a tailpiece in *Hood's* magazine for February 1845:

> Farewell, Life! My senses swim;
> And the world is growing dim;
> Thronging shadows cloud the light,
> Like the advent of the night, —
> Colder, colder; colder still
> Upward steals a vapour chill—
> Strong the earthy odour grows—
> I smell the Mould above the Rose!
>
> Welcome, Life! the Spirit strives!
> Strength returns, and hope revives;
> Cloudy fears and shapes forlorn
> Fly like shadows at the morn, —
> O'er the earth there comes a bloom—
> Sunny light for sullen gloom,
> Warm perfume for vapour cold—
> I smell the Rose above the Mould!
>   (1–16)

THE PUBLIC POEMS

Every so often Hood, in his last years, when he had returned from Europe with a sharpened eye for matters of public scandal and concern, composed a public poem. The most famous is "The Song of the Shirt," which, like the others, was inspired by an incident in real life. A woman with a starving baby

> . . . was charged at the Lambeth Police Court with pawning her master's goods, for which she had to give two pounds security. Her husband had died by an accident, and left her with two children to support, and she obtained by her needle for the maintenance of herself and her family what her master called the "good living" of seven shillings a week.
> (*Punch*, 4 November 1843)

Hood wrote his poem, and it was rejected by several editors. At last he sent it to Mark Lemon, editor of *Punch*, telling him to throw it into the wastepaper basket if he could not use it. It appeared just before Christmas 1843, and at once became famous.

Hood brought to this poem the experience of twenty years of writing public verses and all the concern that is apt to overcome a thoughtful man who looks at his own society.

> "Work—work—work
> Till the brain begins to swim;
>   Work—work—work
> Till the eyes are heavy and dim!
> Seam, and gusset, and band,
>   Band, and gusset, and seam,
> Till over the buttons I fall asleep,
>   And sew them on in a dream!
>
> "Oh! Men with Sisters dear!
>   Oh! Men! with Mothers and Wives!
> It is not linen you're wearing out,
>   But human creatures' lives!
>   Stitch—stitch—stitch,
>   In poverty, hunger, and dirt,
> Sewing at once, with a double thread,
>   A Shroud as well as a Shirt."
>   (17–32)

The poem is a masterpiece of its kind, and stands alongside the early work of Dickens as evidence of the beginnings of the new virtue that was rising in Europe and now spread to England, the virtue of hating cruelty. William Blake had cried out against cruelty to children, and Robert Burns against the cruelty of man to man; and there is a long tradition in every literature of liberal expostulation, which "The Song of the Shirt" develops.

In the next month, January 1844, the first number of *Hood's* magazine appeared. The editor used it from time to time as a forum or pulpit, much as Dickens and Thackeray did later with their own journals. "The Lady's Dream," which opened the second number of the magazine, is a poem of the two nations. On the one hand,

> The Lady lay in her bed,
>   Her couch so warm and soft,
> But her sleep was restless and broken still;
>
> (1–3)

for she was dreaming of that other great nation, the poor. Hood used the same extension of the ballad stanza as in "Eugene Aram" and "The Elm Tree" to give the same powerful expression of fate and doom, of the crushing inevitability of human suffering:

> "And oh! those maidens young,
>   Who wrought in that dreary room,
> With figures drooping and spectres thin,
>   And cheeks without a bloom;—
> And the Voice that cried, 'For the pomp of pride,
>   We haste to an early tomb!
>
> "'For the pomp and pleasure of Pride,
>   We toil like Afric slaves,
> And only to earn a home at last,
>   Where yonder cypress waves;'—
> And then they pointed—I never saw
>   A ground so full of graves!
>
> "And still the coffins came,
>   With their sorrowful trains and slow;
> Coffin after coffin still,
>   A sad and sickening show;
> From grief exempt, I never had dreamt
>   Of such a World of Woe!
>
> "Of the hearts that daily break,
>   Of the tears that hourly fall,
> Of the many, many troubles of life,
>   That grieve this earthly ball—
> Disease and Hunger, and Pain, and Want,
>   But now I dreamt of them all!
>
> "For the blind and the cripple were there,
>   And the babe that pined for bread,
> And the houseless man, and the widow poor
>   Who begged—to bury the dead;
> The naked, alas, that I might have clad,
>   The famish'd I might have fed."
>
> (25–54)

That was written very soon after "The Song of the Shirt," and the lives of sewing women are still haunting him.

"The Workhouse Clock" opened the April 1844 number. It has the speed that the trimeter and the tetrameter line give to expression in English, and Hood once again gives the quality of nightmare to his theme. He is describing want, the hunger and thirst of the underemployed and underpaid poor who were the spawn of the industrial revolution. A great rabble is rushing through the London streets:

> A very torrent of Man!
> Urged by the sighs of sorrow and wrong,
> Grown at last to a hurricane strong,
> Stop its course who can!
> Stop who can its onward course
> And irresistible moral force;
> O! vain and idle dream!
> For surely as men are all akin,
> Whether of fair or sable skin,
> According to Nature's scheme,
> That Human Movement contains within
> A Blood-Power stronger than Steam.
>
> Onward, onward, with hasty feet,
> They swarm—and westward still—
> Masses born to drink and eat,
> But starving amidst Whitechapel's meat,
> And famishing down Cornhill!
> Through the Poultry—but still unfed—
> Christian Charity, hang your head!
>
> (45–63)

The May number carried "The Bridge of Sighs," the best of his public poems, judged as poetry. This time it did not have pride of place. That had to be given to a "communication" from Charles Dickens, which it followed immediately.

> One more Unfortunate,
> Weary of breath
> Rashly importunate,
> Gone to her death!
>
> (1–4)

The focus of the poem shifts with the speed of compassionate concern from the body of the dead girl to the streets and the river, and then to lamentation:

> Where the lamps quiver
> So far in the river,
> With many a light
> From window and casement,

From garret to basement,
She stood, with amazement,
Houseless by night.

The bleak wind of March
Made her tremble and shiver;
But not the dark arch,
Or the black flowing river:
Mad from life's history,
Glad to death's mystery,
Swift to be hurl'd—
Anywhere, anywhere
Out of the world!

(56–71)

This is what happened, and the poet then turns to the rigidity of death. It is done with double and triple rhymes:

And her eyes, close them,
Staring so blindly!

Dreadfully staring
Thro' muddy impurity,
As when with the daring
Last look of despairing,
Fix'd on futurity.

(88–94)

The poem is a pattern of compassion made on two heavy beats to the line with that great variety in the number and nature of the weak beats that is natural to English. The contrasting quicker double beat of the lines breathes sympathy:

Take her up tenderly,
Lift her with care;
Fashion'd so slenderly,
Young, and so fair!

(80–83)

There was only one more public poem, and it took pride of place in the November 1844 number. This time Hood wanted immediate practical results, for he hoped to influence the home secretary to reduce a savage sentence of transportation on a teen-ager. He did not rely on verse alone, but put his verses in a prose setting that stated the facts and pleaded for justice rather than mercy. We know that Hood was so moved by the cruelty of the case that he kept a framed newspaper cutting about it on the mantelpiece of his study. It is the story of a Huntingdon teen-age peasant, Gifford White:

In the spring of the present year this very unfortunate and very young man was indicted, at the Huntingdon Assizes, for throwing the following letter, addressed externally and internally to the Farmers of Bluntisham, Hunts, into a strawyard:—

"We are determined to set fire to the whole of this place, if you don't set us to work, and burn you in your beds, if there is not an alteration. What do you think the young men are to do if you don't set them to work? They must do something. The fact is, we cannot go on any longer. We must commit robbery, and every thing that is contrary to your wish.
I am,
AN ENEMY."

For this offence, admitted by his plea, the prisoner, aged eighteen, was sentenced, by a judge since deceased, to Transportation for Life!

(vol. IX, p. 238)

Hood is concerned about two things: the outrageous severity of the punishment for a mere threat that had been freely admitted to the police on inquiry, and the inability of a healthy young man to find means to earn his daily bread, the general lack of work that was the cause of the teen-ager's foolish demonstration. It is a subject that still haunts England, especially those who remember the days of the dole during the Great Depression, the hopelessness of the worker for whom there is no work. In the prelude to "The Lay of the Labourer," the villagers are in the beerhouse, and their talk shows their anxiety about work:

"The job up at Bosely is finished," said one of the middle-aged men. "I have enjoyed but three days' work in the last fortnight, and God above knows when I shall get another, even at a shilling a day. And nine mouths to feed, big and little—and nine backs to clothe—with the winter a-settin in—and the rent behind-hand—and never a bed to lie on, and my good woman, poor soul, ready to—"—a choking sound and a hasty gulp of water smothered the rest of the sentence. "There must be something done for us—there Must," he added, with an emphatic slap of his broad, brown, barky hand, that made the glasses jingle and the idle pipes clatter on the board. And every voice in the room echoed "there must," my own involuntarily swelling the chorus.

(vol. IX, pp. 230–231)

On this question of society finding work for its citizens Hood has much to say:

Some time since, a strong inward impulse moved me to paint the destitution of an overtasked class of females, who work, work, work, for wages almost nominal. But deplorable as is their condition, in the low deep, there is, it seems, a lower still—below that gloomy gulf a darker region of human misery,—beneath that Purgatory a Hell—resounding with more doleful wailings and a sharper outcry—the voice of famishing wretches, pleading vainly for work! work! work!—imploring as a blessing, what was laid upon Man as a curse—the labour that wrings sweat from the brow, and bread from the soil![7]

(vol. IX, p. 235)

Later he speaks of the special case of Gifford White:

To me—speaking from my heart, and recording my deliberate opinions on a material that, frail as it is, will long outlast my own fabric,—there is something deeply affecting in the spectacle of a young man, in the prime of health and vigour, offering himself, a voluntary slave, in the Labour-market without a purchaser—eagerly proffering to barter the use of his body, the day-long exertion of his strength, the wear and tear of flesh and blood, bone and muscle, for the common necessaries of life—earnestly craving for bread on the penal conditions prescribed by his Creator—and in vain—in vain!

(vol. IX, pp. 243–244)

At the very end he addresses the home secretary directly:

It is in your power, Sir James Graham, to lay the Ghost that is haunting me. But that is a trifle. By a due intercession with the earthly Fountain of Mercy, you may convert a melancholy Shadow into a happier Reality—a righted man—a much pleasanter image to mingle in our waking visions, as well as in those dreams which, as Hamlet conjectures, may soothe or disturb us in our coffins. Think Sir, of poor Gifford White—inquire into his hard case, and give it your humane consideration, as that of a fellow-man with an immortal soul—a "possible angel"—to be met hereafter face to face.

To me, should this appeal meet with any success, it will be one of the dearest deeds of my pen. I shall not repent a wide deviation from my usual course: or begrudge the pain and trouble caused me by the providential visitings of an importunate Phantom.

(vol. IX, p. 246)

---

[7]Thomas Carlyle was much concerned with the same problem in *Past and Present*, published in the previous year: "In workhouses, pleasantly so-named, because work cannot be done in them. Twelve-hundred-thousand workers in England alone; their cunning right-hand lamed, lying idle in their sorrowful bosom; their hopes, outlook, share of this fair world, shut-in by narrow walls. They sit there, perhaps, as in a kind of horrid enchantment; glad to be imprisoned and enchanted, that they may not perish starved" (ch. 1). The official returns for 1842 showed an unemployment figure of nearly 10 percent.

Hood sent a marked copy of *Hood's* magazine to the home secretary. The only reply he ever received was this: "Sir James Graham presents his compliments to Mr. Hood, and begs to acknowledge the Magazine accompanying his letter of the 30th instant." A classical example of the response of bureaucracy to an imaginative appeal.

This was the last of the public poems. Hood was by this time very ill, but he had an opportunity of summing up his feelings about the poor and unfortunate, and the contrasts between the lives of the rich and of the poor. He was writing to the prime minister to thank him for the pension that had been settled on his wife, and as always in his letters he addressed his correspondent with instinctive propriety. He said he had wanted to dedicate his powers to fighting the disease that was so deeply disturbing English society then. It was the class war, which had been intensified by the industrial revolution:

Certain classes at the poles of Society are already too far asunder; it should be the duty of our writers to draw them nearer by kindly attraction, not to aggravate the existing repulsion, and place a wider moral gulf between Rich and Poor, with Hate on the one side and Fear on the other. But I am too weak for this task, the last I had set myself.

(letter to the Rt. Hon. Sir Robert Peel, 17 February 1845)

It was this greatness in Hood that made Thackeray regret that so many years had been spent in literary clowning. "I must jump, I must grin, I must tumble, I must turn language head overheels, and leap through grammar." During his lifetime this was the Hood most seen; but now we see only the Hood who was, as Thackeray saw so well, a "true genius and poet," a man deeply concerned about the human condition.

SELECTED BIBLIOGRAPHY

I. Collected Works. *Hood's Own, or Laughter from Year to Year* (London, 1839), includes the contents of the *Comic Annuals*, reprinted with additional text and illustrations, notably the *Literary Reminiscences*, also issued in shilling installments (1839)—Hood's son issued a second series in 1861 that was reprinted with the first series in 1882; *Poems*, 2 vols. (London, 1846; 10th ed., 1858), frequently reprinted, later in one volume—this and the following item together form the first collected edition of Hood's verse; *Poems of Wit and Humour* (London, 1847; 19th ed., 1872), frequently reprinted, excludes the verses in *Hood's Own*;

T. Hood, Jr., ed., *The Works*, 7 vols. (London, 1862), with notes by his son, several times reprinted and extended to 10 volumes, also edited with notes by T. Hood, Jr., and F. F. Broderip (his daughter); T. Hood, Jr., and F. F. Broderip, eds., *The Works*, 11 vols. (London, 1882–1884), with notes by the editors, the most useful edition, including the original illustrations and *Memorials*; A. Ainger, ed., *The Poems*, 2 vols. (London, 1897), each volume with a useful introduction; W. C. Jerrold, ed., *The Poems* (London, 1906), with notes by the editor, who also edited the World's Classics edition (London, 1917).

II. SELECTED WORKS. J. Clubbe, ed., *Selected Poems* (Cambridge, Mass., 1970), with introduction and notes.

III. SEPARATE WORKS. *Odes and Addresses to Great People* (London, 1825), verse, in collaboration with J. H. Reynolds—Hood contributed "Mr. Graham," "Mrs. Fry," "Richard Martin," "The Great Unknown," "Joseph Grimaldi," "The Steam Washing Co.," "Captain Parry," "W. Kitchener," and "Mr. Bodkin"; *Whims and Oddities: in Prose and Verse*, 2 series (London, 1826–1827); *National Tales*, 2 vols. (London, 1827), short stories; *The Plea of the Midsummer Fairies* (London, 1827), verse, also contains "Hero and Leander," "Lycus the Centaur," "The Two Peacocks of Bedfont," and other poems; *The Epping Hunt* (London, 1829), verse, illustrated by G. Cruikshank; *The Dream of Eugene Aram* (London, 1831), originally published in the *Gem* (1829); *Tylney Hall*, 3 vols. (London, 1834), novel, republished in Bentley's Standard Novels with a new preface (London, 1840); *Up the Rhine* (London, 1840), novel; *Whimsicalities: A Periodical Gathering*, 2 vols. (London, 1844), a collection of verse and prose pieces from *New Monthly* magazine, illustrated by J. Leech.

IV. MAGAZINES. *London*, vols. 4–8 (1821–1823), Hood assisted J. Taylor, the editor, and was a regular contributor; *Gem, a Literary Annual*, vol. 1 (1829), Hood was editor; *The Comic Annual* (1830–1839, 1842), after the first number and until 1839, written and illustrated by Hood; *New Monthly Magazine and Humourist* (1841–1843), Hood succeeded T. Hook as editor and edited vols. 63–68; *Hood's Magazine and Comic Miscellany*, vols. 1–3 (1844–1845), Hood edited the first three volumes, then was succeeded by F. O. Ward in February 1845—the magazine continued after Hood's death.

V. BIOGRAPHICAL AND CRITICAL STUDIES. R. H. Horne, *A New Spirit of the Age*, vol. II (London, 1844); T. Hood, Jr., and F. F. Broderip, *Memorials of Thomas Hood*, 2 vols. (London, 1860), a biography by Hood's son and daughter based largely on his letters—also a revised edition, with additional material on his early life (London, 1884); D. Masson, "Thomas Hood," in *Macmillan's*, 2 (August 1860), 315–324; W. C. Jerrold, *Thomas Hood: His Life and Times* (London, 1907), the first full biography since *Memorials*; P. E. More, "The Wit of Thomas Hood," in *Shelburne Essays*, vol. VIII (New York, 1910); W. C. Jerrold, ed., *Thomas Hood and Charles Lamb* (London, 1930), a reprint—the only convenient one—of *Literary Reminiscences*, "edited with certain additions"; E. C. Blunden, "Hood's Literary Reminiscences," in *Votive Tablets* (London, 1931), 287–291; L. A. Marchand, *Letters of Thomas Hood* (New Brunswick, N. J., 1945), a few letters from the Dilke Papers in the British Museum, not in *Memorials* and not used by Ainger, with an introduction; E. C. Blunden, "The Poet Hood," in *Review of English Literature*, 1, no. 1 (1960), 26–34; J. C. Reid, *Thomas Hood* (London, 1963), a full-length study; J. Clubbe, *Victorian Forerunner: The Later Career of Thomas Hood* (Durham, N. C., 1968); P. F. Morgan, ed., *The Letters of Thomas Hood* (Toronto, 1971).

THOMAS BABINGTON MACAULAY

(1800-1859)

Kenneth Young

LIFE

FOR Thomas Babington Macaulay, who made history as popular as novels, transmuted journalism into literature, and packed the House of Commons every time he got up to speak, "it was roses, roses, all the way," and the larger stones cast at him were cast only after he was dead. He was born at Rothley Temple, near Leicester, on 25 October 1800. Fame came to him at twenty-five and presented him, parvenu though he dubbed himself, with a barony two years before his death, at Kensington, London, on 28 December 1859.

His father, Zachary Macaulay, who came from a line of Scottish ministers of the Kirk, was, wrote James Stephen, "possessed by one idea and animated by one master passion": the abolition of slavery. He had been bookkeeper and later manager of an estate in Jamaica, and in the 1790's governed a charter company forming a colony in Sierra Leone of liberated slaves who had fought on the British side in the American War of Independence. The experience left Zachary with no illusions; the freedmen were slothful and quarrelsome, egged on by black fanatics who called themselves Methodists. Thomas never forgot his father's tales of Africa; "I am made sick," he said the year before he died, "by the cant and the silly mock reasons of the Abolitionists." He hated slavery from the "bottom of my soul," yet "the nigger driver and the negrophile are two odious things to me."

Thomas Macaulay's mother was the pretty Selina Mills, daughter of a Quaker bookseller in Bristol and an admirable counterpoise to the dour Zachary, "at once so earnest and so monotonous." As her family grew to nine, she made sure that, amid the sermon reading and earnest talk, Thomas and her other children could romp, play hide and seek and blindman's buff, blow horns up and down the stairs, make up ballads, complete one another's verses, and perform charades.

Zachary seldom interfered with the family fun, though he did nag Thomas to curb his ever-wagging tongue, cease displaying his opinions so violently, and be neat and tidy; he also banned the reading of poetry and novels in the daytime: "drinking drams in the morning," he called it. Thomas and his father got on well enough. Nevertheless, according to his sister, Thomas "could not recall an instance in which his father had ever praised him or shown any sense of his abilities." It was to his mother that he was most deeply attached and to whom he owed his equability, his good humor, and his tenderness.

Macaulay's childhood was spent among a group of well-to-do, middle-class, Church of England activists known as the Evangelicals, who lived in large houses with plenty of servants around Clapham Common, a south London suburb. The austere, heavy-browed Zachary was their magus. William Wilberforce; Henry Thornton, member of Parliament; Lord Teignmouth, governor-general of India; and the irascibly brilliant Lord Brougham were their chiefs. Later came the Grants, Stephens, and Venns, from whom sprang a pervasive intellectual aristocracy. Samuel Johnson, long ago on his Scottish tour, had met Thomas' great-uncle Kenneth and had spotted the type: "He set out with a prejudice against prejudice, and wanted to be a smart thinker."

The Clapham Sect, as they came to be known, were, one of them later wrote, "against every form of injustice which either law or custom sanctioned." They sponsored "that patent Christianity which," quipped the Reverend Sydney Smith, "has been for some time manufacturing at Clapham to the prejudice of the old admirable article prepared by the Church." In a later age they would have been agnostic or atheist Fabian socialists; some of their descendants were.

In this Clapham forcing house Macaulay "talked printed words" when he was four, and at eight wrote an epic on Olaus the Great of Norway, a universal history from the Creation to 1800, and hymns innumerable. He had phenomenal powers of assimilation and memory: "He seemed to read through the skin," said one observer. He read more quickly than others skimmed, and skimmed as fast as others could turn the pages. He thirsted for knowledge, and if he had not talked and written from his earliest years, "he would have burst"; his intellect, he later thought, was likely "to absorb the whole man."

Macaulay's parents wisely did not encourage his precocity. They sent him to a private school in Clapham and later to an Evangelical boarding school, Aspenden Hall in Hertfordshire. There he suffered homesickness for his mother—"the sound of your voice, the touch of your hand." Another humanizing influence on the precocious child was a regular holiday visit to his mother's friend, the celebrated Hannah More, one of Samuel Johnson's circle, during which he was taught to cook and allowed to preach to people brought in from the fields. So the light-haired, rather slight boy remained, for all his erudition, "playful as a kitten," sweet-tempered, the perfect elder brother arranging games and during the holidays leading expeditions across Clapham Common.

Macaulay went to Cambridge in his eighteenth year, and the university became the love of his life, exceeded only by his devotion to his young brothers and sisters. His college, Trinity, was to him as Athens to an exiled Greek; and as often as he could in later life, he returned to walk the flagged pathway between his rooms and the wall of the chapel, where he had strolled, conning his books. Clever as he was, he found the curriculum hard. There was the tiresome business of the necessary mathematical tripos: "Oh!" he wrote to his mother, "for words to express my abomination of that science . . . I feel myself becoming a personification of Algebra, a living trigonometrical canon, a walking table of logarithms. The pursuit contemptible, below contempt, or disgusting beyond abhorrence. Oh, to change Cam for Isis!" (Oxford made no such demands on its classical aspirants.) He added, "All my perceptions of elegance and beauty gone, or at least going."

There were compensations. Macaulay won two chancellor's gold medals for poetry, a prize for Latin declamation, a Craven classical scholarship, and, at a second attempt, a fellowship—the most desirable honor, in his eyes, that Cambridge had to give, bringing with it £210 a year for seven years, six dozen audit[1] ales at Christmas, a loaf and two pats of butter every morning, and a good dinner at High

[1]An ale of special quality brewed by the university.

Table for nothing, with almonds and raisins ad lib at dessert.

What he prized no less were the opportunities to talk to such forgotten luminaries as John Moultrie and Charles Austin and Lord Belper, and to spout at the Cambridge Union before Samuel Taylor Coleridge's son, Derwent, and the witty poet (and later a member of Parliament) Winthrop Mackworth Praed, who thus described the voluble young Macaulay:

Then the favourite comes with his trumpet and drums,
And his arms and his metaphors crossed.

(Zachary was later to complain of his son's lese majesty in addressing a gathering attended by a royal duke with his arms crossed.)

Macaulay loved conversation at any hour and engaged in it so long as a door was open or a light burning, supping at midnight on milk punch and roast turkey, drinking tea in floods at three in the morning, pouring out with friends into the dawn and the twittering of birds to chatter down the Madingley Road, debating and debating and learning the "skill of fence"—G. O. Trevelyan's words—"which rendered him the most redoubtable of antagonists." That, in the days of the Regency "bucks," seems to have been the limit of his roistering. There is no record of any drunkenness or debauchery, when both were commonplace. Macaulay had the purposeful drive of the Victorians, even before the queen came to the throne.

After Cambridge he was called to the bar in 1826 and practiced desultorily on the northern circuit. He wrote light verses and other pieces for *Knight's Quarterly* magazine and then a powerful piece on slavery in the West Indies, followed by an essay on John Milton in the August 1825 number of the *Edinburgh Review*, edited by Francis Jeffrey. The effect of this essay, which Macaulay himself later thought "gaudy and ungraceful," was astonishing: "Where," asked Jeffrey, "did you pick up that style?" Overnight he became a celebrity, and invitations to dine fell like confetti on the family breakfast table. Such instant fame from a literary essay, even though it had political connotations, is scarcely credible today.

Periodicals such as the *Edinburgh Review*, the *Quarterly Review*, and *Blackwood's* magazine had great prestige in the early nineteenth century. They existed to satisfy the "irrepressible passion for discussion" of a small, well-educated, influential public, deprived for so long of an open forum because of the censorship necessitated by the war against France and against French revolutionary ideas. These reviews offered "talking points" not only about politics but also about the national heritage of the arts, history, and the law. The leisured classes enjoyed ideas as they enjoyed good food and wines, sport and music, dining out, and, for the men, nights at the club.

The *Edinburgh Review*, for which Macaulay wrote throughout his middle years, was not exclusively Whig: Walter Scott, soundest of Tories, and Robert Southey, a Whig apostate, frequently put life into its often flat and shallow contents. But it was Macaulay's brilliant virtuosity that made the *Edinburgh* a vade mecum for society, procured him a commissionership in bankruptcy at £250 a year, and in 1830 brought election to Parliament for the Whig Lord Lansdowne's "pocket" borough[2] of Calne in Wiltshire. Fortunate as always, Macaulay was just in time to profit from the unreformed franchise, into the coffin of which he put a few nails, and then benefited from its demise.

On 5 April 1830 he made his maiden speech, in a Parliament led by the duke of Wellington, in support of a bill to remove Jewish political disabilities. Across the hurly-burly of the years 1830–1832, when England rioted and nine farm laborers were hanged and others transported, and the middle classes threatened a run on the banks to bring the government to heel, Macaulay's shrill, monotonous alto voice, his words clipped and hissing, poured forth tumultuously in a House of Commons where parties had splintered into caves and factions and schisms, coteries and cliques. Once on his feet, he stopped neither for breath nor for thought, "hauling the subject after him with the strength of a giant, till the hearer is left prostrate and powerless by the whirlwind of ideas and emotions that has swept over him," wrote a reporter, G. H. Francis. The extraordinary thing was that the toneless, breathless Macaulay had every listener on tiptoe, not least when he spoke in support of the Whig reform bills, the passage of which raised storms inside and outside Parliament in these years.

Macaulay, adulated at Holland House and adored in his family circle even though checked by his father, loved the good fellowship and easy equality of the Commons, that best of all clubs, and loved

walking home by daylight after a twelve-hour debate. But money became a problem. His commissionership was swept away and his father's firm of Macaulay and Babington, trading with Africa, suffered severe reverses. Macaulay was reduced to selling the gold medals won at Cambridge.

With a fortunate man all things are fortunate, wrote Theocritus, and the advent of Earl Grey's government enabled Macaulay to become the lawyer member on the Indian Board of Control. In 1834 he accepted a seat on the Supreme Council of India and a munificent salary of £10,000 a year, out of which he believed he could save £30,000 in five years. He had no desire to go to India; he sacrificed a promising political career simply to "save my family," to ensure that after a few years they would all be together again "in a comfortable though modest, home; certain of a good fire, a good joint of meat, and a good glass of wine."

The wrench was poignant. Although Macaulay's mother, that "bright half of human nature," had died in 1831, his brothers and sisters remained the core of his emotional existence, for he never married. Could he live, exiled, without them? His grief was intense when a sister married and set up house on her own: "She is dead to me," he wrote. He appealed to his sister Hannah: "If you will go with me, I will love you better than I love you now, if I can. Whether the period of my exile shall be one of comfort—and after the first shock, even of happiness—depends on you."

Hannah consented and, with joy now, Macaulay set about assembling books—"the *Orlando* in Italian, *Don Quixote* in Spanish, Homer in Greek . . ." —for the voyage, and finding a lady's maid for Hannah. After three months at sea, they landed at Madras to a fifteen-gun salute on 10 June 1834. He wonderingly noted: "The dark faces, with white turbans, and flowing robes: the trees not our trees: the very smell of the atmosphere that of a hothouse. . . ." He soon met one of the dotty Englishmen who even then haunted British possessions overseas. At the British residency in Mysore

I found an Englishman, who, without any preface, accosted me thus: "Pray, Mr. Macaulay, do not you think that Buonaparte was the Beast?" "No, Sir, I cannot say that I do." "Sir, he was the Beast, I can prove it. I have found the number 666 in his name. Why, Sir, if he was not the Beast, who was?" This was a puzzling question, and I am not a little vain of my answer. "Sir," said I, "the House of Commons is the Beast. There are 658 members of the House;

---

[2]A Parliament seat under the control of one person or family.

and these, with their chief officers—the three clerks, the Sergeant and his deputy, the Chaplain, the doorkeeper, and the librarian,—make 666."[3]

From India, Macaulay persuaded governments, under Robert Peel and later William Lamb, Lord Melbourne, that censorship should be lifted from the press and that English residents should lose the privilege of bringing civil appeals before the Calcutta Supreme Court, thus making natives and English equal before the law. The former relaxation laid him open to the vilest calumnies on account of the latter; the mildest of the local periodicals called him cheat, swindler, and charlatan, while the others went so much further that he removed the papers from his sister's sitting room. He himself laughed and stood his ground: "We were enemies of freedom because we would not suffer a small white aristocracy to domineer over millions." India could not have a free government, but at least it should have "a firm and impartial despotism."

Much more controversial was Macaulay's support for teaching Indians in English in the higher branches of learning rather than, as previously, in Sanskrit, Arabic, and Persian. In the past Warren Hastings, no less than Edmund Burke and, after him, Benjamin Disraeli, believed that a true liberalism would encourage Indians to study their own no small store of literature, laws, religions, and philosophy. Macaulay brusquely dismissed all Oriental learning:

There are no books on any subject which deserve to be compared to our own . . . medical doctrines which would disgrace an English farrier, astronomy which would move laughter in the girls at an English boarding-school—history abounding with kings thirty feet high, and reigns 30,000 years long—and geography made up of seas of treacle and seas of butter. . . . I doubt whether the Sanskrit literature be as valuable as that of our Saxon and Norman progenitors.[4]

Such "pistolling ways," as G. E. Saintsbury called them, so sweeping a dismissal of the Orient and all that lay in it, were wrong. No wonder Melbourne was once heard to mutter: "I wish I was as cocksure of any one thing as Macaulay is of everything," or that T. S. Eliot should assert that "The benefits of British rule will soon be lost, but the ill-effects of the disturbance of a native culture by an alien one will remain."

Yet Macaulay may have been right. If Indians were to take responsible positions in the administration—which he did not doubt would eventually become an Indian administration—English and westernization were essential. English was increasingly the language of commerce throughout the East; neither science nor technology could be understood without it. Just as the languages of western Europe had civilized Russia in no more than 120 years, so "I cannot doubt that they will do for the Hindoo what they have done for the Tartar." And, to a point, they have.

The new edict, announced by Governor-General Sir William Bentinck on 7 March 1835, was that "The great object of the British Government ought to be the promotion of European literature and science among the natives of India." Macaulay, as president of the Committee of Public Instruction, set about implementing it, though with an agreeable lack of pomp and purism. Forget logic and rhetoric, he advised: "Give a boy *Robinson Crusoe.*" *Jack the Giant-killer* was better than any book of logic ever written. How ridiculous, he observed, to see Portia represented by a little black boy, or at a school speechday a boy repeating "some blackguard doggerel of George Colman's, about a fat gentleman who was put to bed over an oven. . . . Really, if we can find nothing better worth reciting than this trash, we had better give up English instruction altogether."

Allowing himself little respite even in the rainy season, when most of his colleagues fell sick, Macaulay drafted a code for criminal law that was later adopted and is still the basis, however eroded, of Indian law. He found time for vast reading from Hesiod to Macrobius in the "long, languid leisure of the Calcutta afternoon, while the punkah swung overhead, and the air came heavy and scented through the moistened grass-matting which shrouded the windows." He disliked formal banquets and "the most deplorable twaddle" to be heard there. Like Edward Gibbon he had a poor opinion of parsons; when others worked, "the reverend gentlemen are always within doors in the heat of the day, lying on their backs, regretting breakfast, longing for tiffin, and crying out for lemonade." He thought little of native Indian fruits ("a plantain is very like a rotten pear . . . a yam is an indifferent potato").

Always Macaulay longed to be in England, pining (to adapt his own poem on the old Jacobite) by the Hooghly for his "lovelier" Thames. When Hannah

[3]G. O. Trevelyan, ed., *The Life and Letters* (New York-London, 1876), vol. I, p. 268.
[4]Minute of 2 February 1835, Trevelyan, vol. I, p. 290.

married Charles Trevelyan, Macaulay suffered a "frightening" mental disturbance. It passed and he left India, never to return, in 1838. The Trevelyans went with him, and on board ship he tended their baby daughter an hour or so a day and taught her to talk.

Back in London, work on his long-projected *History of England*, then visualized as extending from the Glorious Revolution of 1688 to the death of George IV in 1830, was postponed. Macaulay was elected a member of Parliament for Edinburgh in 1839, and Melbourne called him to be secretary for war and a member of the cabinet. He was not yet forty. The *Times*, snobbishly averse to the elevation of such a middle-class person, referred to him as "Mr. Babbletongue Macaulay." In cabinet, with his rumpled appearance, strange eyes, and "waterspouts of talk," he was regarded as an oddity, Melbourne remarking that he would prefer to sit in "a room with a chime of bells, ten parrots and Lady Westmorland" than with Macaulay.

His new post was easy. "The House of Commons of 1840 spent upon the Army very little of its own time, or of the nation's money," his nephew G. O. Trevelyan wrote. But Macaulay had to defend the notorious earl of Cardigan, who by purchase commanded a fine cavalry regiment, the 11th Hussars, which he proceeded, as Trevelyan put it, to "drag through a slough of scandal, favouritism, petty tyranny and intrigue," dueling with a lieutenant and flogging a soldier on a Sunday between church services. With his customary skill Macaulay resisted demands for Cardigan's removal from his command, thus leaving him free to quarrel fifteen years later in the Crimea with his brother-in-law, Lord Lucan, and to lead the charge of the Light Brigade into the valley of death.

Macaulay, longing for "liberty and ease, freedom of speech and freedom of pen," had not long to wait; the Whigs resigned in August 1841. "Now I am free. I am independent," he wrote to Macvey Napier, Jeffrey's successor at the *Edinburgh Review*. "I am in Parliament, as honourably seated as a man can be. My family is comfortably off. I have leisure for literature . . . I am sincerely and thoroughly contented." He was to have one more brief spell in office as paymaster-general in Lord John Russell's cabinet. With a break of five years, he remained a member of Parliament for Edinburgh until 1856.

From 1841, Macaulay was nearly a full-time writer. In 1842 appeared his only major poetic col-

lection, *Lays of Ancient Rome*, a sweeping success and soon into a second edition. Next year came the first authorized edition of his *Critical and Historical Essays*, with no less success. Not surprisingly, perhaps, it was Macaulay the member of Parliament who occupied himself with extending the copyright protection on books from twenty-eight to forty-two years from the date of publication; his bill passed to the statute book.

Macaulay's letters to his great friend Thomas Flower Ellis and to his sisters are delightful. Taking a holiday from his labors on his *History of England*, he set out in 1843 for a tour of the Loire Valley, via a train to Brighton: slow and crowded, he tells Hannah, with "a sick lady smelling of aether; a healthy gentleman smelling of brandy; the thermometer at 102 degrees in the shade and I not in the shade."

With his nephew and nieces Macaulay happily dawdled hours away, inventing games and small dramas for them, himself playing a dog stealer or Dando, the clown, at an oyster shop. He also wrote small poems for them to recite:

> There once was a nice little girl,
> With a nice little rosy face.
> She always said "Our Father",
> And she always said her grace.

He took the children on tours of London, to the zoo and to Mme. Tussaud's; he hired a whole railway compartment for a trip to York and Cambridge, and once even to Paris. "How such things twine themselves about our hearts!" he wrote. Traveling was also necessary for his *History of England*. William Makepeace Thackeray said: "He travels a hundred miles to make a line of description," here sketching the ground plan of streets, there timing how long it took to walk around town walls. When Macaulay wandered alone through Whitehall or down by the old houses near the river, he invented conversations between the great people of past times. In the country he usually read as he walked. One afternoon he reread the last five books of the *Iliad* and had to turn aside from a party of walkers, lest they "should see me blubbering for imaginary beings, the creations of a ballad-maker who has been dead 2,700 years."

This eccentric, stumpy man—a book in breeches, Sydney Smith called him—still loved good talk, especially at the social breakfasts, then all the vogue, where verse was declaimed, memory was tested, and repartee sparkled between such as Sydney Smith, Henry Hallam, Charles Greville, and John Cam Hobhouse, and such lords as Carlisle, Lansdowne, and Mahon. Bolt upright in his chair, hands folded over the handle of his walking stick, Macaulay brightened "from the forehead downwards when a burst of humour was coming." Now he seldom talked to win: "truly considerate towards others—so delicately courteous." Thomas Carlyle saw in his face in repose, as he was reading, "homely Norse features that you find everywhere in the Western Isles . . . an honest good sort of fellow, made out of oatmeal." To another observer, "His was the sort of face you might expect above a cobbler's apron."

After protracted labors, rewriting, reading aloud, punctilious proof correction, and author's twitch— "I see everyday more clearly how my performance is below excellence"—the first two volumes of the *History of England* appeared in December 1848, to be greeted by what Macaulay's biographer called "an ebullition of national pride and satisfaction." Daily his publisher, Longman, brought him "triumphant bulletins." The first edition of 3,000 was sold within ten days; the third, by the end of January 1849. By April 1850, 22,000 copies had gone. "I feel no intoxicating effect," he noted in his journal, "but a man may be drunk without knowing it." Walking past a bookshop window, he saw David Hume's *History of England* advertised as "valuable as an introduction to Macaulay," and laughed "so convulsively" that he was taken "for a poor demented gentleman."

Macaulay became rector of Glasgow University; he was offered the Cambridge professorship of modern history by Prince Albert; and he stayed at Windsor: "When we went into the drawing-room, the Queen came to me with great animation, and insisted on my telling her some of my stories, which she had heard at second-hand from George Grey. I certainly made her laugh heartily. She talked on for some time, most courteously and pleasantly."

His affluence made Macaulay royally, if not always discriminatingly, generous. He lived now in a fine villa on Campden Hill, kept four servants, and "set up" his own brougham, in which he drove, "pleased and proud." Did he ever pass the fine house in Regent's Terrace where the wealthy Friedrich Engels was plotting the downfall of England? Certainly when he visited the Great Exhibition of 1851 in Hyde Park, he "saw none of the men of action with whom the Socialists were threatening us." But he was exhilarated by "the boats and little frigates dart-ing across the lake, the flags, the music, the guns." Joseph Paxton's Crystal Palace was "a most gorgeous sight; vast, graceful, beyond the dreams of the Arabian romances. . . . I was quite dazzled and felt as I did on entering St. Peter's." He reveled in the ingenuity of his times.

In 1852 illness struck Macaulay, and the physician Richard Bright told him the action of his heart was deranged. He was never quite well again, suffering from bronchitis and asthma and fits of violent coughing. He contemplated his death with "perfect serenity," regretting only the leaving of those he loved, and declared that he was growing "happier and happier." Six years were left him, and he husbanded his powers to finish the next two volumes of his *History of England*. Despite days when he felt weak and despondent, he delighted in "a work which never presses and never ceases."

Volumes III and IV appeared in December 1855, in an edition of 25,000 copies weighing, Macaulay noted, 56 tons. Their success was enormous, and they were translated into nearly all European languages as well as Persian. In 1857 he became, to universal acclaim, a baron, and in 1858 paid a last visit to Cambridge when—though scarcely able to totter across Clare Bridge—he was made high steward of the borough.

Though he tried to continue his *History of England*, Macaulay found it hard to settle to work, and in his heart knew he would not complete even his volume on Queen Anne's reign. He died without pain in his library, fully dressed and seated in his easy chair, on 28 December 1859. He was buried, as his father was, in Westminster Abbey.

POLITICS

MACAULAY's introduction to practical politics was a cat flung into his face during an election meeting at Cambridge. At Leicester, when he was twenty-six, he worked for a Whig candidate and had to be dissuaded from rushing out to confront a mob, 128 of whom ended up in jail after the yeomanry was called out. Campaigning for himself in newly enfranchised Leeds, he fled from the threat of physical attack when his opponents climbed onto the roof of the coach from which he was addressing a drunken, disorderly crowd; and he allowed himself to refer to his Tory opponent as a "hyena"—in return, no doubt, for being dubbed "an impertinent puppy" by *Blackwood's* magazine.

He was, he said in 1839, a Whig because that party had established "our civil and religious liberties":

To the Whigs of the seventeenth century we owe it that we have a House of Commons. To the Whigs of the nineteenth century we owe it that the House of Commons has been purified. The abolition of the slave trade, the abolition of colonial slavery, the extension of popular education, the mitigation of the rigour of the penal code, all, all were effected by that party; and of that party, I repeat, I am a member.[5]

As for the future, the party

. . . should leave themselves [the public] to their own legitimate duties—by leaving capital to find its most lucrative course, commodities their fair prices, industry and intelligence their natural reward, idleness and folly their natural punishment—by maintaining peace, by defending property, by diminishing the price of law, and by observing strict economy in every department of the state. Let the Government do this—the People will assuredly do the rest.

But what *was* the Whig party of which Macaulay was determined to remain a member? In the late 1820's and 1830's it was as amoebic as the Tory party, all protoplasmic limbs forever waving out to touch and link and unlink with neighboring limbs. Ultra-Tories joined some Whigs in demanding the parliamentary reform that most Tories opposed; Charles Canning, a Tory, supported liberalizing movements abroad as Peel did at home; and Brougham, a Whig, sought to fuse his aristocratic, land-owning party with the Tory commercial classes. Macaulay's political position reflected the amorphous condition of the politics of his time.

He spoke notably in favor of Catholic emancipation—that is, to allow Catholics to sit in Parliament—and to the same end, for the Jews. A Jew could own half of London, but could not sit in the Commons. With great force Macaulay supported the Reform Bills of 1831–1832, the burden of his argument being that if the franchise were not expanded, there would be revolution:

Turn where we may, within, around, the voice of great events is proclaiming to us, Reform, that you may pre-serve. Now, therefore, while everything at home and abroad forebodes ruin to those who persist in a hopeless struggle against the spirit of the age, now, while the crash of the proudest throne of the continent is still resounding in our ears, now, while the roof of a British palace affords an ignominious shelter to the exiled heir of forty kings, now, while we see on every side ancient institutions subverted, and great societies dissolved, now, while the heart of England is still sound, now, while old feelings and old associations retain a power and a charm which may too soon pass away, now, in this your accepted time, now, in this your day of salvation, take counsel, not of prejudice, not of party spirit, not of the ignominious pride of a fatal consistency, but of history, of reason, of the ages which are past, of the signs of this most portentous time. Pronounce in a manner worthy of the expectation with which this great debate has been anticipated, and of the long remembrance which it will leave behind. Renew the youth of the State. Save property, divided against itself. Save the multitude, endangered by its own unpopular power. Save the greatest, and fairest, and most highly civilised community that ever existed, from calamities which may in a few days sweep away all the rich heritage of so many ages of wisdom and glory. The danger is terrible. The time is short. If this bill should be rejected, I pray to God that none of those who concur in rejecting it may ever remember their votes with unavailing remorse, amidst the wreck of laws, the confusion of ranks, the spoliation of property, and the dissolution of social order![6]

Whether Macaulay's speeches affected the issue is debatable. The bills passed because one party leader thought it desirable and the other found it expedient. The acts were more sweeping than is sometimes supposed: a quarter of the borough seats were wiped out, and some great industrial centers were enfranchised, even though only for those occupying houses whose rental value was £10 or more per year, and even though the vote in the counties was still confined to the forty-shilling freeholders (owners of houses that were valued at forty shillings). This was quite enough for Macaulay. No more concessions:

My firm conviction is that, in our country, universal suffrage is incompatible, not with this or that form of Government, but with all forms of Government, and with everything for the sake of which forms of Government exist; that is, incompatible with property and that is consequently incompatible with civilization.[7]

[5]Speech of 29 May 1839 on the Edinburgh election, in Lady Trevelyan, ed., *The Works* (London, 1906–1907), vol. VIII, p.159.

[6]Speech of 2 March 1831 on parliamentary reform, in Trevelyan, vol. VIII, pp. 24–25.
[7]Speech of 3 May 1842 on the People's Charter, in Trevelyan, vol. VIII, p. 221.

Macaulay shared the Radicals' distaste for aristocratic privilege and pretentiousness. He shared the Tory and moderate Whig fears that with universal suffrage, the majority of voters would be poor and ignorant people whose interest, at least in the short term—which is all they would visualize—would be to plunder the rich, whether through taxes, confiscation, or otherwise. This majority, "if they have the power, will commit waste of every sort on the estate of mankind and"—here he talks in the very accent of Burke—"transmit it to posterity impoverished and desolated."

Macaulay spoke for the middle ranks, "that brave, honest and sound-hearted class," who knew that wealth must be accumulated, and that democracy would annihilate capital and reduce the most flourishing countries to "the state of Barbary or the Morea." He laughed off the mouthings of "this small sect of Utilitarians," who demanded votes for all.

Though quibbling about self-interest and motives, and objects of desire, and the greatest happiness of the greatest number, is but a poor employment for a grown man, it certainly hurts the health less than hard drinking, and the fortune less than high play: it is not much more laughable than phrenology, and is immeasurably more humane than cockfighting.

Macaulay was early and late against "one man, one vote." In 1857 he wrote to H. S. Randall:

I have long been convinced that institutions purely democratic must, sooner or later, destroy liberty or civilization, or both. In Europe, where the population is dense, the effect of such institutions would be almost instantaneous. . . . Either the poor would plunder the rich and civilization would perish; or order and prosperity would be saved by a strong military government, and liberty would perish!

Randall was the biographer of Thomas Jefferson, whose country had adopted "universal suffrage." As long as free land was available, Macaulay told him, there would probably be no

. . . fatal calamity, but the day will come when in the State of New York a multitude of people, none of whom has had more than half a breakfast, or expects to have more than half a dinner, will choose a Legislature. Is it possible to doubt what sort of a Legislature will be chosen? . . . There is nothing to stop you. Your Constitution is all sail and no anchor. . . . Your Huns and Vandals will have been engendered within your own country by your own institutions.

Macaulay, in short, was all for liberty and against equality, which he knew could not exist. But there was a dilemma. It was fatal, he thought, to trust unpropertied masses with political power; yet the industrialization, mechanization, and urban development that he admired created wealth, and wealth set off a vast increase in population, a greater inequality in income, and, thus, the danger of explosive mobs. He pictured vividly for members of Parliament the Gordon "No Popery" riots of 1780, proof of the proposition "that the ignorance of the common people makes the property, the limbs, the lives of all classes insecure." These swollen mobs were not of the past only. Over the years they had caused "the riots of Nottingham, the sack of Bristol, all the outrages of Ludd, and Swing, and Rebecca,[8] beautiful and costly machinery broken to pieces in Yorkshire, barns and haystacks blazing in Kent, fences and buildings pulled down in Wales."

Yet it was that "beautiful and costly machinery" that could bring a better future.

If we were to prophesy that in the year 1930 a population of fifty millions, better fed, clad, and lodged than the English of our time, will cover these islands; that Sussex and Huntingdonshire will be wealthier than the wealthiest parts of the West Riding of Yorkshire now are; that cultivation, rich as that of a flower-garden, will be carried up to the very tops of Ben Nevis and Helvellyn; that machines constructed on principles yet undiscovered will be in every house; that there will be no highways but railroad, no travelling but by steam; that our debt, vast as it seems to us, will appear to our grandchildren a trifling encumbrance which might easily be paid off in a year or two—many people would think us insane.

For all his anti-Radicalism, Macaulay's vision here is as materialistic as that of the utilitarians and he is not far from the Benthamite calculus. He thoroughly approved "the Baconian doctrine, Utility and Progress," and with almost Marxist scorn dismissed any other considerations: "Shoes have kept villains from being wet; we doubt whether Seneca ever kept any-

---

[8]The Luddite riots first took place in Nottinghamshire in 1811. They were directed against the introduction of machinery into the textile industry, which caused the dismissal of many craftsmen. Swing was a fictitious captain in whose name intimidating letters were sent to farmers and landowners in southern England during 1830–1831, and their ricks set on fire. The Rebecca riots took place in South Wales in 1843, in protest against the charges levied at tollgates on the public roads, the rioters being mounted and disguised as women. Macaulay's speech was made in 1847.

body from being angry." This is to dismiss morality in favor of materialism.

How, then, to stop the mob from wrecking the future from which they had most to gain? The answer must be to educate them. Macaulay strongly supported the government request in 1847 for a grant of £100,000 for the education of children whose parents could not afford to pay for it. It was the only possible way to avoid the ignorance of the "common people," which was the "principal cause of danger to our property and persons"; the alternative was "guns and bayonets, stocks and whipping posts, treadmills, solitary cells, penal colonies, gibbets." Make men "better and wiser and happier," or make them "infamous and miserable." Obviously Englishmen must prevent "hundreds and thousands of our countrymen from becoming mere Yahoos." Through education the poor man might be persuaded to "find pleasure in the exercise of his intellect, be taught to revere his maker, taught to respect legitimate authority, and taught at the same time to seek the redress of real wrongs by peaceful means."

Macaulay did not ask, with Socrates, whether in fact virtue can be taught, nor did he wonder whether schooling can compensate for social ills. Moreover, a little learning often merely makes mobs craftier, and itself may become the instrument of a subversiveness that is far more dangerous to "property and persons" than the irrationality of mobs. "A proletariat," writes Russell Kirk with the benefit of hindsight, "does not cease to be proletarian because it has been compelled to drowse through state schools—or because the price of corn has decreased five shillings a quarter."

Macaulay's support for state financing of education landed him in the same camp in which the Radicals jostled ultra-Tory paternalists such as Southey. Macaulay had condemned both and was generally against state intervention. The state might be allowed to erect buildings for public purposes, but that must be the end of it. Free, private enterprise was essential: "We firmly believe that £500,000 subscribed by individuals for railroads or canals would produce more advantage to the public than five millions voted by Parliament for the same purpose."

This position was self-contradictory and made Macaulay uneasy. He spoke on 22 May 1846 about a bill to limit the labor of young persons in factories to ten hours a day. The argument against it was that it concerned "one of those matters which settle themselves far better than any Government can settle them." This normally would have been Macaulay's own standpoint, particularly where factory owners, whom he respected and to whom he bore goodwill, were involved. But he saw the dilemma:

I hardly know which is the greater pest to society, a paternal government, that is to say a prying, meddlesome government, which intrudes itself into every part of human life, and which thinks that it can do everything for everybody better than anybody can do anything for himself; or a careless, lounging government, which suffers grievances, such as it could at once remove, to grow and multiply, and which to all complaint and remonstrance has only one answer: "We must let things alone: we must let things take their course: we must let things find their level." There is no more important problem in politics than to ascertain the just mean between these two most pernicious extremes, to draw correctly the line which divides those cases in which it is the duty of the State to interfere from those cases in which it is the duty of the State to abstain from interference.[9]

Difficult indeed! We certainly do not want to go back, Macaulay ruminates, to rulers in "the old time," who were always telling people "how to keep their shops, how to till their fields, how to educate their children, how many dishes to have on their tables, how much a yard to give for the cloth which made their coats." Such rulers were "so much shocked by the cunning and hardheartedness of moneylenders that they made laws against usury; and the consequence was that the borrower, who, if he had been left unprotected, would have got money at ten per cent . . . could hardly, when protected, get it at fifteen per cent!"

Macaulay declares himself strongly attached to the "principle of free trade" and to noninterference with it "on commercial grounds." Yet, he claims, government rightly interferes with trade for the sake of national defense; it fixes rates of pay for cabs plying for hire; it forbids farmers to cultivate tobacco. It stops trade in "licentious books and pictures" on the ground of morality; it may order a man to build a drain to an old house on the grounds of public health. Reluctantly he concludes that it *should* restrict working hours, for who can "doubt that twelve hours a day of labour in a factory is too much for a lad of thirteen?"

---

[9]Speech of 22 May 1846 on the Ten Hours Bill, in Trevelyan, vol. VIII, p. 361.

Moreover, with such hours there could be no leisure; and without leisure there could be no time for Macaulay's pet panacea, education. Minors in any case must be protected. No one, he asserts, doubts that England should, for example, prevent a wealthy youth of thirteen from conveyancing his estate or giving a bond of £50,000. The poor minor is no less the country's concern than the rich one, particularly as the only inheritance of the poor is "the sound mind in the sound body." The first factory act, introduced by Peel's father in 1802, had had none but beneficial results. Long hours over the year would produce less than shorter ones.

Then again, Macaulay reflects, man is more than a "machine for the production of worsted and calico"; he is "fearfully and wonderfully made." Even a fine horse or a sagacious dog is not treated like a spinning jenny; a laborer is no "mere wheel or pulley!" Treat boys and men so, and England will become "a feeble and ignoble race, parents of a more feeble and more ignoble progeny." The great British industrial inventors have usually come from the artisan class—James Hargreaves, Samuel Crompton; that class must be protected, even if only from the point of view of national self-interest:

Never will I believe that what makes a population stronger, and healthier, and wiser, and better, can ultimately make it poorer. You try to frighten us by telling us that, in some German factories, the young work seventeen hours in the twenty-four, that they work so hard that among thousands there is not one who grows to such a stature that he can be admitted into the army; and you ask whether, if we pass this bill, we can possibly hold our own against such competition as this? Sir, I laugh at the thought of such competition. If ever we are forced to yield the foremost place among commercial nations, we shall yield it, not to a race of degenerate dwarfs, but to some people preeminently vigorous in body and in mind.[10]

Macaulay sums up with his customary antitheses and the help of the Book of Common Prayer:

We have regulated that which we should have left to regulate itself. We have left unregulated that which we were bound to regulate. We have given to some branches of industry a protection which has proved their bane. We have withheld from public health and public morals the protection which was their due. We have prevented the labourer from buying his loaf where he could get it cheapest; but we have not prevented him from ruining his body and mind by premature and immoderate toil. I hope that we have seen the last both of a vicious system of interference and of a vicious system of noninterference, and that our poorer countrymen will no longer have reason to attribute their sufferings either to our meddling or to our neglect.[11]

His speeches in the Commons, however splutteringly delivered, riveted his hearers so that they did not notice their repetitiousness. His speech on the Anatomy Bill, as G. M. Young pointed out, has only two central points: the poor are most in danger of being burked (that is, of being killed by a body snatcher), and the poor are the greatest sufferers from bad surgery. Each is restated six times, and the demonstration is rounded off with a picturesque anecdote. But in the course of the short speech Macaulay has touched on the habits of murderers in various countries, the Russian peasants and the czar, mountebanks and barbers, old women and charms, the squaring of the circle and the transit of Venus, Richard of England, Leopold of Austria, and the bricklayer who falls from a ladder. The matter is perfectly fused, the speed exhilarating; and he ends before the listener has rightly discerned where he is going.

Macaulay's phrasing was often memorable and could sting: Radicals "without talents or acquirements sufficient for the management of a vestry," he said, "sometimes become dangerous to great empires." Some of his *trouvailles* have become part of the language: "The gallery in which the reporters sit," he was the first to remark, "has become the fourth estate of the realm." Such apothegms, which are everywhere in his *Essays*, were not the inspiration of the moment. All his speeches were carefully prepared, not in writing, which he thought detracted from their spontaneity, but in his head and, when perfect, were committed to memory. A good speech, he told his sister Margaret, emerged from plan and order, but should sound careless and unconscious.

Macaulay was by all accounts scrupulous in his parliamentary duties and regularly in his seat. To those who elected him he was peremptory and even arrogant, and in those days members of Parliament, once elected, rarely visited their constituencies. They were representatives, not delegates; and Macaulay resented being buttonholed by all those

[10]Trevelyan, vol. VIII, p. 375.

[11]*Ibid.*, p. 376.

who thought they had a right to see him. There were lighter moments. He wrote to his sister: "Colonel Torrens made a tipsy speech about rents and profits, and then staggered away, tumbled down a stairway and was sick as a dog in the Long Gallery."

Through all Macaulay's political thought runs an underlying pragmatism, more typical of the Whigs than of the Radicals and Tories: "I rest my opinion on no general theory of government. I distrust all general theories of government," he once told the Commons, and he praised the leadership of "practical statesmen." It was practical to reform the franchise; impractical (and dangerous) to create a universal franchise. Reform, though, was not merely an ad hoc necessity; it was, on his reading of history, a historical necessity too: "The Great Charters, the assembling of the first House of Commons, the Petition of Right, the Declaration of Right, the Bill now on our table, what are they all but steps in one great progress?" A progress led, of course, by Whigs with their idea of government as "a progressive science." Tories had merely followed on: "The tail is now where the head was some generations ago." He agreed that a Queen Anne Tory is a modern Whig.

He himself, Macaulay always insisted, was a Whig, not a Liberal; he smote Jeremy Bentham for his ideas of "planning," which he at once detected as being illiberal and, if pushed, tyrannical.

You call me a Liberal, but I don't know that in these days I deserve the name. I am opposed to the abolition of standing armies. I am opposed to the abrogation of capital punishment. I am opposed to the destruction of the National Church. In short, I am in favour of wars, hanging, and Church Establishment.

He was a patriotic Englishman, deeply concerned about national defense; toward the end of his life, he read with concentration of every move in the war with Russia in the Crimea. He came to be at one with the Whig Burke's philosophy of conservatism.

ESSAYS

POLITICAL concepts also run through the essays Macaulay regularly wrote for the *Edinburgh Review*, but they are not the reason the public gobbled up edition after edition of his selection of them, *Critical and Historical Essays*, published in 1843. Such early essays as "The West Indies" and "Milton"

(1825), with their forceful Whiggism, appealed to those involved in politics; his firm and optimistic belief that England had progressed and would continue to do so was welcome to an age flexing its industrial and technological muscles. Few would deny the commendation of the reform acts implied in his essay "Mirabeau" (1832), where he wrote that the French aristocracy "would not have reform and they had revolution. They would not endure Turgot and they were forced to endure Robespierre."

These observations were acceptable. What was irresistible, and to an ever-widening public, was Macaulay's vivid, swift narration of men's lives or of historical happenings. His analyses of literary and philosophical works and of complex situations were crystal clear; he never wrote an obscure sentence; he seemed to get to the heart of every matter. His phrases were a joy; his iconoclasm challenging; his reasoning persuasive. He soon had his readers convinced that what he thought, they had long thought —though, admittedly, "ne'er so well expressed."

Macaulay etched on the minds of Victorian and Edwardian readers pictures that would last their lifetimes—of the blind Milton in his small lodging, sitting at the old organ beneath the faded green hangings, "the quick twinkle of his eyes, rolling in vain to find the day"; of Lord Byron's "so sad and dark a story," condemned by "the British public in one of its periodical fits of morality"; of Francis Bacon, weak in character, powerful in mind, whose "humble aim" in his philosophy was "to make imperfect men comfortable"; of Warren Hastings' great qualities, though "to represent him as a man of stainless virtue is to make him ridiculous."

If they recalled anything of the War of the Spanish Succession, or Niccolò Machiavelli, or Horace Walpole, or the then unperformed playwrights of the Restoration, they recalled Macaulay's colorful and cogent representations of them; and it is not too much to say that their stock of general knowledge came to a great extent from that "vast mine, rich with a hundred ores" which Macaulay ascribes to Joseph Addison, but which more fittingly applies to his own lavishly stocked mind.

Immaterial to them—and to us—the numerous refutations of Macaulay's facts, deductions, and dramatic *scenas*; immaterial, too, such criticism as Thomas De Quincey's "Every sentence seems saturated with its separate charge of quicksilver; and paragraph after paragraph roll off in volleys of minute explosions, flashes, raps, and bounces, like the small artillery of a schoolboy, or the *feu-de-joie* of squibs"—immaterial because this is exactly what readers loved.

Click goes Macaulay's camera, and we see, amid the admirers of Fanny Burney and her *Evelina*, Burke, Gibbon, Richard Brinsley Sheridan, one other: the royal duke of Cumberland, who "acknowledged her merit, after his fashion, by biting his lips and wriggling in his chair whenever her name was mentioned"; click again, and here are Madame Schwellenberg, "a hateful old toadeater," and Dr. Charles Burney himself, an excellent musician and man, who "thought going to Court like going to Heaven."

Nevertheless, Macaulay gives a just estimate of Fanny Burney's writings and her place in literary history, no less than in the coruscating "Milton" he calls attention to the prose writings of the poet, then little read, to the sublime "wisdom" of the *Areopagitica*, to "the devotional and lyric rapture" of passages that are "a perfect field of the cloth of gold," beside which "the finest declamations of Burke sink into insignificance"; and he offers the exquisite comparison of Milton's poetry to "the roses and myrtles which bloom unchilled on the verge of the avalanche" in the Alps. Bacon may have been a weak man in Macaulay's eyes, but in his essay on him, as in few later studies, he puts a luminous finger on the real originality of the *Novum Organum* and the *Advancement of Learning*: "The philosophy of Plato began in words and ended in words. . . . The philosophy of Bacon began in observations and ended in arts. . . . An acre in Middlesex is better than a principality in Utopia. The smallest actual good is better than the most magnificent promises of impossibilities."

Where others used abstractions, Macaulay personalized. Socrates and Phaedrus do not merely hold a discussion; they hold it "on that fine summer day under the plane-tree, while the fountains warbled at their feet, and the cicadas chirped overhead." He does not refer to the characters in Restoration plays as licentious and libidinous; they have "foreheads of bronze, hearts like the nether millstone, and tongues set on fire of hell." Warren Hastings does not take up a clerkship; "he is immediately placed at a desk in the Secretary's office." England and France do not become allies; they "pair off together." We are not told that Count Orloff, ablaze with medals, is tall, but that he "brushes the ceiling with his toupee."

Up into the night sky go the fireworks, the rockets, and the Roman candles, at once keeping readers from their beds and lighting up Macaulay's often highly original and complex notions on, for example, the contradictory traits in Machiavelli, exalting liberty at the same time he advocated dissimulation —contradictory only, suggests Macaulay, because of the wide gap in value judgments between northern and southern races. Iago was detested by northern audiences for his wicked plots; an Italian audience might find something to admire in his wit, clarity of mind, and skill in dissimulation.

Here Macaulay stands, long before most historians, on the principle of moral relativism, of not judging men of the past by contemporary standards: "He alone reads history aright, who, observing how powerfully circumstances influence the feelings and opinions of men, how often vices pass into virtues and paradoxes into axioms, learns to distinguish what is accidental and transitory in human nature from what is essential and immutable." In the end, though, Macaulay kowtows to the prejudices of his time: yes, *The Prince* is immoral and offensive.

Although Macaulay sometimes circumspectly shrank from his own originality, he persisted in it. He, Whig progressive that he was, asserted in his "Burleigh" essay that the Tudor despotism was popular and no bad thing. The Tudors had to take heed of public opinion because they had no means of protecting themselves against public hatred. So public favor had to be courted, which meant that the public of the sixteenth century, while lacking "the outward show of freedom," had the reality—they were beyond all doubt a free people. He adds the still-relevant caveat: "Constitutions, charters, petitions of right, declarations of right, representative assemblies, electoral colleges, are not good government; nor do they, even when most elaborately constructed, necessarily produce good government."

His readers also marveled at and enjoyed the extraordinary range of his knowledge. They felt they were being agreeably educated when, discussing dramatists, Macaulay chatted about Islamism and Brahmanism; or, in an essay on a minor poet, wrote of "the practices of puffers, a class of people who have more than once talked the public into the most absurd errors," of the age of private patronage when men of letters spent "their lives in dangling at the heels of the wealthy and powerful"; and when he tossed in, here, a generalization—"Men of real merit will, if they persevere, at last reach the station to which they are entitled"—there, an *aperçu* such as that Alexander Pope "kept up the dignity of the literary character so much better" because at thirty he possessed £6,000–7,000. Yet nowhere is there a sense of his stretching out the long arm. All comes as naturally as can be.

What a variety of arrows Macaulay's quiver contained—some of them quite deadly! Of the three-volume life of Lord Burghley by the Oxford Regius professor of modern history, Dr. Edward Nares, he writes: "Compared with the labour of reading through these volumes, all other labour, the labour of thieves on the treadmill, of children in factories, of negroes in sugar plantations, is an agreeable recreation." He performed another hatchet job on the then popular poet Robert Montgomery, whose writing, says Macaulay, bears the same relation to poetry as a Turkish carpet bears to a picture. Montgomery, he admits, uses words that

. . . when disposed in certain orders and combinations have made, and will again make, good poetry. But, as they now stand, they seem to be put together on principle in such a manner as to give no image of anything "in the heavens above, or in the earth beneath or in the waters under the earth."[12]

His readers wriggled with pleasure when Macaulay deflated a public figure such as the poet laureate, Robert Southey, who from being a republican had turned ultra-Tory. Macaulay begins, smooth as silk, by praising Southey's *Life of Nelson* as "most perfect and most delightful." But this new work, *Sir Thomas More, or Colloquies on the Progress and Prospects of Society*! Tongue in cheek, he gives a précis of it. The laureate is sitting by his fireside, reading his newspaper. An elderly person appears whom he takes to be an American gentleman come to stare at the Lakes and the Lake poets, among whom Southey is numbered.

But Mr. Southey is mistaken:

The visitor informs the hospitable poet that he is not an American but a spirit. Mr. Southey, with more frankness than civility, tells him that he is a very queer one. The stranger holds out his hand. It has neither weight nor substance. Mr. Southey upon this becomes more serious; his hair stands on end; and he adjures the spectre to tell him what he is, and why he comes. The ghost turns out to be Sir Thomas More. The traces of martyrdom, it seems, are

worn in the other world, as stars and ribands are worn in this. Sir Thomas shows the poet a red streak round his neck, brighter than a ruby, and informs him that Cranmer wears a suit of flames in paradise, the right hand glove, we suppose, of peculiar brilliancy.

Sir Thomas pays but a short visit on this occasion, but promises to cultivate the new acquaintance which he has formed, and, after begging that his visit may be kept secret from Mrs. Southey, vanishes into air.[13]

If Southey momentarily survived this sardonic raillery, he tottered when Macaulay summed up his political philosophy—"To stand on a hill, to look at a cottage and a factory, and to see which is prettier"—and fell to the floor when Macaulay stigmatized his paternalism as necessitating "a Lady Bountiful in every parish, a Paul Pry in every house, spying, eavesdropping, relieving, admonishing, spending our money for us, and choosing our opinions for us." It is ironic that Macaulay's none too scrupulous lampooning of Southey's high Toryism should put us in mind of the socialism of the later twentieth century.

Macaulay could wield the broadsword as well as the poniard. J. W. Croker's edition of a five-volume text of James Boswell's *Life of Johnson* is "ill compiled, ill arranged, ill written and ill printed." Croker's notes "swarm with mis-statements . . . scandalous inaccuracy . . . ignorance, heedlessness . . . classical blunders" for which even a schoolboy would expect a flogging. Croker, Tory member of Parliament, and contributor to *Blackwood's*, never forgot an injury: twenty years later he wrote a rancorous review of the first two volumes of Macaulay's *History of England*.

Macaulay had little time either for Boswell—"thoughtless loquacity"—or for Johnson himself, a shocking anti-Whig whom he portrays as grotesque, uncouth, and maladroit. But, observed his sister Margaret, noting her brother's shambling deportment and careless dress, Macaulay and Johnson had similarities: their hatred of cant, their disputatiousness, their indifference to the beauties of nature. And what Macaulay said of Johnson's style was later said, though not quite fairly, of his own. When Johnson spoke, he used simple, energetic, and picturesque words, observes Macaulay, but

When he wrote for publication, he did his sentences out of English into Johnsonese. . . . His letters from the Hebrides

[12]"Mr. Robert Montgomery's Poems," in Trevelyan, vol. V, p. 377.

[13]"Southey's *Colloquies*," in Trevelyan, vol. V, pp. 337–338.

to Mrs. Thrale are the original of that work of which the *Journey to the Hebrides* is the translation; and it is amusing to compare the two versions. "When we were taken up stairs," says Johnson in one of his letters, "a dirty fellow bounced out of the bed on which one of us was to lie." This incident is recorded in the *Journey* as follows: "Out of one of the beds on which we were to repose started up, at our entrance, a man black as a Cyclops from the forge."

Generally, though, the *Essays* are more appreciative than depreciative. Macaulay's "Byron" essay, written in 1831, gives a sympathetic and understanding account of the "great literary revolution" brought about by William Wordsworth—whose later poems he thought a bore—Coleridge, and the rest, and indicates his own predilections firmly: "We prefer a gipsy by Reynolds to his Majesty's head on a signpost, and a Borderer by Scott to a Senator by Addison." He praises "the magnificent imagery and the varied music of Coleridge and Shelley." He declares that the "heart of man is the province of poetry, and of poetry alone." William Cowper was the forerunner of "the great restoration of our literature"—poor, gentle, melancholy Cowper, "whose spirit" (and here Macaulay sinks into bathos) "had been broken by fagging at school." Macaulay recovers to specify what for him was the nature of the "restoration": "Instead of raving about imaginary Chloes and Sylvias, Cowper wrote of Mrs. Unwin's knitting needles." It was the sort of particularizing that Macaulay himself gloried in. But if a lady's knitting needles, why not Simon Lee's "ankles swollen and thick" or "Spade! with which Wilkinson hath tilled his lands"? Answer: the ankles and spade were Wordsworth, whom he disliked, not Cowper, whom he admired.

Surprisingly, it was Byron who, for Macaulay, consummated the poetic "revolution," though he never quite shows how, except in a rather irrelevant witticism alleging that Byron, who lived much abroad, founded "an exoteric Lake school." What, indeed, had the musing Wordsworth and the drug-inspired Coleridge to do with the Regency Byron and his fans, who discarded their neckcloths in imitation of him, practiced at the mirror the curl of the lip and the scowl, and who included many "hopeful undergraduates and medical students who became things of dark imaginings. . . . Whose passions had consumed themselves to dust"; who from their hero's poetry had deduced "two great commandments, to hate your neighbour and to love your neighbour's wife"?

Quite simply, Macaulay did not respond to Wordsworth's transcendentalism; he did respond to the Byronic mixture of man of the world, violent passion, and satire. For Macaulay, Byron excelled in description and meditation.

The wonders of the outer world, the Tagus, with the mighty fleets of England riding on its bosom, the towers of Cintra overhanging the shaggy forest of cork-trees and willows, the glaring marble of Pentelicus, the banks of the Rhine, the glaciers of Clarens, the sweet Lake of Leman, the dell of Egeria with its summer-birds and rustling lizards, the shapeless ruins of Rome overgrown with ivy and wallflowers, the stars, the sea, the mountains![14]

These were the "accessories" to a single personage, whether called Harold or Lara or Manfred, "proud, moody, cynical, with defiance on his brow, and misery in his heart, a scorner of his kind, implacable in revenge, yet capable of deep and strong affection." There was of course also a woman, "all softness and gentleness, loving to caress and to be caressed, but capable of being transformed by passion into a tigress!" But in the end both were the poet: "He was himself the beginning, the middle, and the end, of all his own poetry, the hero of every tale, the chief object in every landscape."

Of this hero, Byron, Macaulay writes: "From maniac laughter to piercing lamentation, there was not a single note of human anguish of which he was not master." Miserable, satiated, withered in heart, defying the power of earth and heaven, scornful of society and at war with it—such was the persona Byron presented. "That he was not such a person is beyond all doubt," Macaulay declares. Of course some of the morbidity may have been real, perhaps stemming "from the nervousness of dissipation." But, asks the realist Macaulay, would someone who so scorned his fellow creatures publish three or four books a year to tell them so? Would he be so elated when his maiden speech in the House of Lords was praised? Sad he doubtless was, but "the interest which his first confessions excited induced him to affect much that he did not feel; and the affectation probably reacted on his feelings."

Time, Macaulay was sure, would sift Byron's poetry, and much would be rejected as worthless; to another age he would be simply a writer, not a personality. But, he concludes, "After the closest

---

[14]"Moore's Life of Lord Byron," in Trevelyan, vol. V, p. 415.

scrutiny, there will still remain much that can only perish with the English language." That, indeed, has happened. Macaulay, though, never explains why he is so sure it will.

An even better example of Macaulay's biographical-critical essays—and almost his last—came a dozen years later: his "Life and Writings of Addison." To Addison he felt bound by "affection," though not, he hastens to add, by "abject idolatry," and there were similarities; both were Whigs, both politicians and ministers as well as writers. They shared a middle-class, professional ancestry. They had "got on."

So naturally a certain idolatry comes through Macaulay's telling of the story of the shy, retiring fellow of Magdalene who became the most influential man of letters in London, as well as undersecretary of state and husband of the dowager countess of Warwick, "unsullied statesman, master of pure English eloquence, consummate painter of life and manners, great satirist, who, without inflicting a wound, effected a great social reform." Macaulay does not ignore Addison's shortcomings; on the other hand, he never even hints that his conduct can be interpreted as sly, coldly self-seeking, and pusillanimous. Nor today would most readers agree that Addison's contributions to the *Tatler, Spectator,* and *Freeholder* show him either as a "great satirist" or a "consummate" guide to the life of his times. But he has certainly been greatly underestimated since the 1930's, and perhaps the greatest tribute to be paid to Macaulay's essay is that it makes the reader's fingers itch to turn the pages of Addison's contributions to the *Spectator* and even of his tragedy, *Cato.*

POEMS

Of Macaulay's verse, and particularly the *Lays of Ancient Rome* (1842), Saintsbury remarked that, though "poetry for the million, nevertheless those who do not recognise the poetic quality in it show that their poetical thermometer is deficient in delicacy and range." The *Lays,* enormously successful in the poet's day and long afterward, sprang out of Macaulay's wide and deep classical reading fused, less obviously, with his love of English ballads, which he bought, almost compulsively, from the bookstalls then a feature of many London streets. "Every half-penny song on which he could

lay his hands, he acquired," says Trevelyan, "if only it was decent and a genuine, undoubted poem of the people."

Macaulay believed, following Jacobus Perizonius and supported by Barthold Niebuhr, that the tales of the birth of Romulus and Remus and the fight of the Horatii and the Curatii, related by Livy, sprang from ballads sung by the very early Romans, and long lost. He sought to re-create them using English ballad meter, and was delighted to discover later that his "Lars Porsena of Clusium," written in what he calls a catalectic dimeter iambic line, had a Latin source of sorts; at least an old grammarian recalled seeing "Dabunt malum Metelli Naevio poetae," which resembled the beat of Macaulay's "saturnian" line. The only parallel he could think of in English was in the nursery rhyme "Four and Twenty Blackbirds":

> The Queen was in her parlour
> Eating bread and honey.

The four *Lays* are supposed to be told by a minstrel living some three or four hundred years before Christ, and himself recalling yet earlier legends. The narrator of "Horatius" looks back about a century and a quarter, and, says Macaulay in a preface, "seems to have been an honest citizen, proud of the military glory of his country, sick of the disputes of factions, and much given to pining after good old times which never really existed"—all of which fitted Macaulay himself, despite his warning about nostalgia in the *History of England.* The *Lays* were intended to bring vividly to the mind's eye what he soberly calls "some information about past times," which everyone "not utterly savage longs for." This aim differed not at all from the primal, private urge that drove Macaulay toward writing the *History.*

The *Lays* move fast, the story line is clear, heroes and villains are immediately distinguishable, and an atmosphere of "long ago" is breathed out imperceptibly, as from a bowl of potpourri. The whole is pulled together, clinched, by the thumping rhythm and rhymes that are inevitable, not ingenious. "The verses are not just easy to remember but almost impossible to forget," said one critic. The colors are primary, the drama as basic as in a child's dreams. Through all rings, triumphant, the trumpet note of high endeavor, "backs against the wall" steadfastness, heroism against odds, the simple patriotism of an uncorrupted people in "the brave days of old":

Then out spake brave Horatius
The Captain of the Gate:
"To every man upon this earth
Death cometh soon or late.
And how can man die better
Than facing fearful odds,
For the ashes of his fathers
And the temples of his Gods".

(217–224)

Macaulay treated other historical subjects, as in "Ivry: A Song of the Huguenots":

Now glory to the Lord of Hosts, From whom all glories are!
And glory to our sovereign Liege, King Henry of Navarre!

(1–2)

He made another sort of drama from an incident in Genesis ("The Marriage of Tirzah and Ahirad"). He left only a fragment of "The Armada" and the brief, echoing "Epitaph on a Jacobite" who, for his "true King," threw away "lands, honours, wealth, sway":

And one dear hope, that was more prized than they.
For him I languished in a foreign clime,
Grey-haired with sorrow in my manhood's prime;
Heard on Lavernia Scargill's whispering trees,
And pined by Arno for my lovelier Tees. . . .

(4–8)

Not surprisingly for one who had been at Trinity and in the House of Commons with Praed, Macaulay wrote "society" or occasional verses, often in letters to his sisters. Here he describes the magnificent dinner given by the banker Isaac Lyon Goldsmid to celebrate the Jewish emancipation act:

I dined with a Jew,
Such Christians are few,
He gave me no ham,
But plenty of lamb,
And three sorts of fishes,
And thirty made dishes.
I drank his champagne
Again and again.

. . .

O Christians whose feasts
Are scarce fit for beasts,
Example take you—
By this worthy old Jew.

The only poem of deeper personal significance is that written the evening of his defeat in Edinburgh during the election of July 1847. It is in the form of a dream of the "fairy queens" attendant on his birth and of one last, mightiest, and best—a "glorious lady, with the eyes of light" who advises him to let go "gain, fashion, pleasure, power": hers is "the world of thought, the world of dream. Mine all the past, and all the future mine." She, the muse of history, perhaps, tells him:

Yes; thou wilt love me with exceeding love;
And I will tenfold all that love repay!

(61–62)

So, indeed, she did.

THE HISTORY

HISTORY was popular reading all over western Europe in the 1830's and 1840's, and those who wrote it could become rich and famous. Apart from Gibbon and Hume, Voltaire and Niebuhr, Macaulay's friend Henry Hallam had a success with his *Constitutional History of England* in 1827, outdone only by Thomas Carlyle's *The French Revolution* ten years later.

Macaulay had long wished to join this happy band. He knew what he wanted to write about: English history from 1688 on, which even to educated people was, he thought, "almost a terra incognita"; and he knew how he wanted to write it. It would be "an amusing narrative . . . which shall for a few days supersede the last fashionable novel on the tables of young ladies." He later corrected this: "I have had the year 2000 and even the year 3000 often in my mind."

He would reclaim from such novelists as Walter Scott that part of the historian's role they had appropriated. The historian, too, should seek

. . . to make the past present, to bring the distant near, to place us in the society of a great man or on the eminence which overlooks the field of a mighty battle . . . to call up our ancestors before us with all their peculiarities of language, manners and garb, to show us over their houses, to seat us at their tables, to rummage their old-fashioned wardrobes, to explain the uses of their ponderous furniture.

The historian also should lay

. . . before us all the springs of motion and all the causes of decay . . . tracing the connection of causes and effects . . . we should not have to look for the wars and votes of the Puritans in Clarendon, and for their phraseology in *Old Mortality*; for one half of King James in Hume, and for the other half in *The Fortunes of Nigel*.[15]

Of course the historian must relate no fact, attribute no expression to his characters that is not authenticated by sufficient testimony. In any case, Macaulay loved facts and *"minute* touches." He felt that almost metaphysical sense of the past and urgent need to share in the thoughts and feelings of men long dead, to handle the very document Oliver Cromwell indited; to tread, as John Keats wrote, "the heath where Druids old have been, where mantles grey have rustled by. . . ." Gibbon, striding the ruins of the Forum and standing on the spot "where Romulus stood, or Tully spoke, or Caesar fell," described it as "intoxication."

Macaulay prepared himself well. He ransacked French and Dutch archives. He turned over thousands of pamphlets and ballads collected from musty shops and street stalls. He worked in libraries at Lambeth, the British Museum, and Edinburgh. At All Souls' he discovered in Narcissus Luttrell's diary such curiosa as that the Jacobites drank treasonable healths by limping around the room with glasses at their lips ("To limp meant L. Louis XIV, I. James, M. Mary of Modena, P. Prince of Wales"). The Tanner, Wharton, and Nairne manuscripts were devoured. He tramped Londonderry with old maps; he saw Glencoe ("the very valley of the shadow of death") and Killiecrankie; and he knew York, Bristol, and Norwich as well as he knew London.

Down it all went into a multitude of notebooks. Printed accounts Macaulay accumulated in his own library; and behind him he had a lifetime of almost incontinent reading—from Homer and Thucydides ("The Great Historian") to Bacon, Burke ("the greatest Englishman since Milton"), Voltaire, Leopold von Ranke, Southey, Niebuhr. Underpinning all was a phenomenal photographic memory.

When Macaulay had the details of an episode clear in his head, the inconsistencies in sources sorted out, and the "humour" upon him,

He would sit down and write off the whole story at a headlong pace . . . securing in black and white each idea, and epithet, and turn of phrase, as it flowed straight from

his busy brain to his rapid fingers. His manuscript, at this stage, to the eyes of anyone but himself, appeared to consist of column after column of dashes and flourishes, in which a straight line, with a half-formed letter at each end, and another in the middle, did duty for a word.[16]

From this rough draft Macaulay would next morning write out in a large hand and with many erasures a full version, seldom doing more than six pages a day because, says Trevelyan, he knew by experience that "This was as much as he could do at his best; and except when he was at his best, he never would work at all." When the thoughts and words ceased to flow fast, he stopped writing. But he never stopped revising. Often he rewrote a chapter for the sake of "a more lucid arrangement." Every word was scrutinized and, if he thought it appropriate, none was rejected because it was unknown to Jonathan Swift and John Dryden. Thus we find such twentieth-century-sounding nouns as "squatters," secrets being "blabbed," buildings being "gutted" (a "coarse metaphor," he admits), and military duties being "shirked"—a word, he says, used by high and low because it is the "only word for the thing." In his journal he was matter-of-fact about his "impotency and despondency" when he found "arrangement and transition" difficult, and frank about "sewing on a grand purple patch."

All that Macaulay intended, he achieved, except that his *History of England from the Accession of James II* scarcely reached the death of William III in 1702, about a century and a half short of the target. And even that last event takes place in the fragmentary and posthumous volume V, put together by his sister. The *History* as it stands is incomplete and inevitably out of balance. Macaulay covers the first two millennia or so of British (rather than English) history, from the discovery of the inhabitants by "the Tyrian mariners, the Phoenicians," to the restoration of Charles II, in a mere 160 pages. The subsequent 1,200 or so pages are given to forty-two years, of which two reigns of some seventeen years take up the bulk of the space. He had sacrificed his grand harmonious design, lengthening his history by shortening its time span.

The unity of the work is best conveyed in the first two volumes. The forward rush gets under way as George Monck and his Scottish army march into England and declare a free parliament. "The bells of all

---

[15]"History," in Trevelyan, vol. V, pp. 157–158.

[16]*The Life and Letters,* vol. II, p. 501.

England rang joyously: the gutters ran with ale; and night after night, the sky five miles round London was reddened by innumerable bonfires." Charles II lands at Dover, the cliffs of which are "covered by thousands of gazers" and, despite the coolness of the troops drawn up on Blackheath, the "restored wanderer" is soon reposing "safe in the palace of his ancestors." Then comes a quieter passage, picking up momentum again as the Cavaliers become violent, the earl of Clarendon falls, the earl of Danby falls, the Papists plot, Louis XIV plots, and the conflict between the crown and Parliament seems about to be brought "to a final issue."

Next comes a halt of 120 pages, during which Macaulay makes social history respectable; then the pounding course resumes, interspersed with quieter moods—the deathbed of Charles II, the sly and slimy hugger-mugger of spies—until with crashing and discordant chords we come to the execution of the duke of Monmouth ("It was ten o'clock. The coach of the lieutenant of the Tower was made ready. . . ."), and the vengeance of George Jeffreys in the West, the Bloody Assizes, and executions everywhere: "a time of misery, and terror," and as the blood and fury ebb, the dissenting spirit is left cowed. There is only the "good" Bishop Thomas Ken to soften the harsh, cruel notes. Then, as the dire autumn of 1685 crawls to its end, come intimations of spring and "the first faint indications of a great turn of fortune."

Hopefully we take up volume II, only to discover that spring is delayed. Still twisted and twisting, James II is at "the height of power and prosperity," his enemies' courage "effectually quelled." We are vouchsafed a temporary glimpse of hope—William of Orange, married to James's daughter Mary. But that glimpse swiftly fades; not for many a long, dissonant page of miseries and faithlessness do we see him again, this time setting sail for England. Optimism grows as gradually as William's advance —almost a saunter, with stumbles—from his landing at Torbay through the West Country to Hungerford, while James makes frantic attempts to get his queen and the Prince of Wales out of the country.

Then, a grand climax: the prince and princess of Orange stand beneath the canopy of state in Inigo Jones's magnificent Banqueting Hall in Whitehall. Lords and Commons move toward them, bow low; William and Mary step a few paces forward, the Declaration of Rights is read in a loud voice, William and Mary accept the crown. A sudden, piercing

. . . shout of joy is heard in the streets below, and is instantly answered by huzzas from many thousands of voices. . . . The heralds and poursuivants were waiting in their gorgeous tabards. All the space as far as Charing Cross was one sea of heads. The kettle drums struck up; the trumpets pealed. . . .[17]

The volume closes calmly, "all passion spent," with Macaulay musing over the peacefulness of the Glorious Revolution, "conducted with strict attention to ancient formalities." With some complacence he contrasts it with the revolutions raging, as he writes in 1848, in the proudest capitals of western Europe, now streaming with "civil blood . . . evil passions . . . the antipathy of class to class, race to race. . . ." And so to the final, firm chord: "For the authority of law, for the security of property, for the peace of our streets, for the happiness of our homes, our gratitude is due under him who raises and pulls down nations at his pleasure, to the Long Parliament, to the Convention and to William of Orange."

Volumes III and IV, which appeared in 1855, some seven years after the first two volumes, are different. The drive toward a glorious consummation is gone. The focus is steadily on William, to whom all the threads of the story lead. Events occur and are dramatically described: the battle of the Boyne, Glencoe, Steinkirk, Landen. The recoinage is remarked and the quarrel about Darien, but all are linked with William. These two volumes and the posthumous one are largely a biography of the king.

Nevertheless, wherever in the whole *History of England* the reader dips, he is likely to go on reading page after page. This is a testimony to Macaulay's art. He knows how to alternate long and short sentences in consonance with what he is describing. Wherever possible, he uses dialogue, and where appropriate, devices from rhetoric such as anaphora and antitheses, usually to sum up: "The liberality of the nation had been made fruitless by the vices of the government." He sometimes uses the dramatist's trick of raising tension by delaying a dénouement.

Macaulay's devices are seldom employed merely to dazzle. The paradox that "We owe more to the weaknesses and meannesses [of James I] than to the wisdom and courage of much better sovereigns" is true. The striking phrase is everywhere: Charles I's great qualities were spoiled by "an incurable propensity to dark and crooked ways," even though his ex-

---

[17]*History of England*, in Trevelyan, vol. II, p. 391.

ecution was "not only a crime but an error." We really see that London mob "hopping and crawling in crowds," and William "carried away in fits from Mary's dying bed." Bishop Gilbert Burnet is "a living dictionary of British affairs." Macaulay is adept, too, at tossing in ideas that may still provoke thought: "It is better that men should be governed by priestcraft than by brute force"; or, at the close of the reign of Charles II, there was "not a single English painter or statuary whose name is now remembered." And speaking of his own time, he says, "The progress of civilization has diminished the physical comforts of a portion of the poorest class."

The *History of England* is also a gallery of portraits, done in primary colors and with the broad strokes of a Pre-Raphaelite. Their literary provenance includes the seventeenth-century "character," harking back to Theophrastus, made popular by Joseph Hall, Sir Thomas Overbury, and John Earle's *Microcosmography*. Sometimes, but not always, Macaulay draws a character as either simon-pure or as the devil lacking only horns.

His Judge Jeffreys, who is heralded as that "wicked judge" whose "depravity" has become proverbial, is unrelievedly horrid. As he condemns men, "Their weeping and imploring seemed to titillate him voluptuously." He sends a woman to be scourged at the cart tail with the instruction: "Scourge her till the blood runs down! It is Christmas, a cold day for madam to strip in! See that you warm her shoulders thoroughly!" Jeffreys is a drunkard, and we are shown him stripped naked, with an equally drunken lord treasurer, attempting to climb a signpost to drink the king's health. He is also a turncoat. He exacts an appalling vengeance throughout the West Country after the rebellion of James Scott, duke of Monmouth, leaving behind him carnage, mourning, and terror. He is cordially welcomed back from his campaign in the West by a delighted James II, who recounts with glee to the aghast foreign ambassadors the horrors Jeffreys had committed. The picture of Jeffreys, as we now know from the researches of G. W. Keeton, is flawed by great exaggeration and as great omissions.[18]

Macaulay leaves James II with scarcely a shred of reputation. Yet Charles II, whom politically and morally he condemned, is done in curiously soft colors. He acts (over the Exclusion Bill) from "a sense of duty, and honour." Careless and profuse as he was

[18]G. W. Keeton, *Lord Chancellor Jeffreys and the Stuart Cause* (London, 1965).

with money for his pleasures, he does spare a sum to form a "little army," the germ of "that great and renowned army which has, in the present century, marched triumphant into Madrid and Paris, into Canton and Candahar." Though Charles's temper could be harsh, he had an easy way of allowing "all persons who had been properly introduced" to "see him dine, sup, dance and play at hazard"—the lion allowing the public to watch him feed—and hear him tell the stories, which indeed he told remarkably well, of his flight from Worcester and the miseries he endured as state prisoner "at the hands of the canting, meddling preachers of Scotland." These sociable habits, Macaulay declares, proved "a far more successful Kingcraft than any that his father or grandfather had practised."

Of course, Charles was a liar, he had more than dubious dealings with the French, he thought that every person was to be bought, that integrity was a trick by which "clever men kept up the price of their abilities," that the loves of God, country, family, friends were synonyms for the love of self. All the same Macaulay had a soft spot for him and devoted every skill he possessed to describe at length the comings and goings around Charles's deathbed. After the illness first shows itself, we see him "chatting and toying" with three women whose charms were the boast and whose vices were the "disgrace, of three nations" while "some amorous verses were warbled." Then he collapses, face black, eyes turning in his head; the duchess of Portsmouth hangs over him "with the familiarity of a wife" in an "agony of grief"; she is forced to retire by the arrival of the queen, who is so affected that she faints and is "carried senseless to her chamber."

Now the Anglican prelates besiege him, fruitlessly; but the duchess, despite her "life of frivolity and vice," retains "all that kindness which is the glory of her sex," and knows that the king in his few serious moments was a Roman Catholic. She sends to find a priest; and in great secrecy, through a back door, an illiterate Benedictine is brought in—a cloak over his sacred vestments, "his shaven crown concealed by a flowing wig." He gives the king communion, but he cannot swallow the bread until water is brought. Next day, after apologizing for being an unconscionable time dying, he dies: "the last glimpse," wrote Macaulay, "of that exquisite urbanity, so often found potent to charm away the resentment of a justly incensed patron."

The reader has the strong impression that he is watching events as they happen. The illusion is created also in the description of Monmouth's trial and death, and of the battle of the Boyne. People seem to move before our eyes: Charles Seymour, sixth duke of Somerset, "looking like what he is, the chief of a dissolute and high-spirited gentry, with the artificial ringlets clustering in fashionable profusion round his shoulders, and a mingled expression of voluptuousness and disdain in his eye and on his lip"; Titus Oates, "legs uneven, the vulgar said, as those of a badger, his forehead low as that of a baboon, his purple cheeks, his monstrous length of chin." Macaulay can create his effect even with groups of people, such as the extreme Puritan known by his gait, his lank hair, the sour solemnity of his face, the upturned whites of his eyes, his nasal twang, and his peculiar dialect.

Macaulay used his gift for personalizing groups of people and bringing dull facts to life with notable power in his celebrated "sociological" chapter 3 in volume I, in which he describes the general state of the country when James II came to the throne. The country was physically different from the one the Victorians knew. In 1685 the wilder parts—Cumberland and Northumberland—were unmapped, the paths a local secret, the forests larger and impenetrable, tenanted by wolves, wild bulls with white manes, wailing wildcats, and troops of huge bustards.

The roads were such that Samuel Pepys and his wife in their coach lost their way between Newbury and Reading. To travel by public coach, Macaulay discovers, cost twopence halfpenny a mile in summer and rather more in winter. He casts his eyes down and sees that the floors of dining rooms were "coloured brown with a wash made of soot and small beer, to hide the dirt." In those days, too, St. James's Square was the receptacle of offal, cinders, and all the dead dogs of Westminster—under the very windows "of the gilded saloons in which the first magnates of the realm, Norfolks, Ormonds, Kents and Pembrokes, gave banquets and balls." He examines the immense variety of coffeehouses—the Londoner's home—and finds that some were frequented by Puritans; Jews, "dark-eyed money changers from Venice and Amsterdam," also had their own special places.

He notes that the average wage for the laboring classes was four shillings a week in agriculture, while those who tended looms received one shilling a day, and a bricklayer two shillings sixpence. The well-paid Macaulay observes with dismay that the famous John Dryden's *Fables* brought him only £250

for the copyright—"less than in our days has sometimes been paid for two articles in a review." Nor does he overlook "the seats of industry": Manchester ("a busy and opulent place," but without a single coach), the forges of Sheffield, and the buttons of Birmingham.

Then, skillfully varying his approach, Macaulay focuses on a person, a type, and breathes life into him or her. The young chaplain attached to the household of

> . . . the coarse and ignorant squire . . . cast up the farrier's bill. He walked ten miles with a message or a parcel. . . . He might fill himself with the corned beef and carrots; but, as soon as the tarts and cheesecakes made their appearance, he quitted his seat and stood aloof till he was summoned to return thanks for the repast, from a great part of which he had been excluded. . . . A waiting woman was generally considered as the most suitable helpmate for a parson . . . the chaplain was the resource of a lady's maid whose reputation had been blown upon.[19]

Macaulay was always immensely interested in inventions and industrial processes, so he praises the Royal Society of London for Improving Natural Knowledge, founded in 1660. Although its new philosophy bred "dreams of wings with which men were to fly from the Tower to the Abbey," Macaulay recognizes that its pottering with hydrostatics, barometers, air pumps, telescopes, and a microscope that "made a fly look as large as a sparrow" were the beginning of a "long series of glorious and salutary reforms. . . . Already a reform of agriculture had been commenced . . . medicine became an experimental and progressive science. . . . One after another phantoms which had haunted the world through ages of darkness fled before the light. Astrology and alchemy became jests. . . ." John Wallis, Edmund Halley, John Flamsteed, and Isaac Newton are singled out as the heirs of the spirit of Francis Bacon experimenting with refrigeration in the snow, a spirit "compounded of audacity and sobriety."

What the whole *History of England* exhales, like an unknown perfume, is the strangeness of our seventeenth-century ancestors. They seem, in Macaulay's pages, to be as foreign as Trobriand Islanders, their emotions volatile as a baby's, their tolerance of horrors enormously high. The Whigs, Macaulay tells us, murmured because William Staf-

---

[19]*History of England*, in Trevelyan, vol. I, pp. 256–257.

ford was allowed to die "without seeing his bowels burned before his face." It seemed proper that the wicked should be drawn and quartered while yet alive. At the same time, the arts of the age were often exquisite, full of sentiment and suffused with pathos. The attitude to death, including one's own, was often casual. The people lived with a sense of eternity stretching before them, so what mattered was not their departure to it, but whether they died in a faith guaranteeing them heaven rather than hell. Hence the overwhelming importance of religious differences.

It is hard to disagree with Macaulay's belief that the English national character has been mollified, that people have become "kinder" and more humane. We now have, he writes, a "sensitive and restless compassion . . . which winces at every lash laid on the back of a drunken soldier" and extends "a powerful protection to the factory child, to the Hindoo widow, to the negro slave." Life had become longer, health better, communications faster.

This process Macaulay sometimes refers to as "betterment" or "improvement," which can scarcely be denied, and sometimes as "progress," which has always been disputed. "Progress to what and from where?" inquired Benjamin Disraeli. "The European talks of progress because by an ingenious application of some scientific acquirements he has established a society which has mistaken comfort for civilization." Or, put another way, it is mistaken to equate progress with happiness.

While from Macaulay's vantage point in history it might seem that people had become more humane and would continue further along that way, he had no smallest prevision of the murderous world wars, the institution of state slavery enforced by torture and murder in the totalitarian states of Europe, the "liberation" of India and Africa to killing and rapine. To us Macaulay's statement that "No man who is correctly informed as to the past will be disposed to take a morose or desponding view of the present" has a sour ring.

THE HISTORY UNDER FIRE

READING the *History of England* is a tremendous experience, but, as Macaulay himself confessed, there are in it "real blemishes as I too well know!"

Some details of the period he was not and could not be aware of, because the documents were not then available—for example, the letters from King William to his friend the prince of Waldeck, or the conversations recorded between the king and the earl of Halifax. Sometimes he simply ignored matters important to his text, such as the "Settlement" Act of 1662, which prevented laborers moving from one parish to another in search of work, or overlooked whole areas of history, such as the growth of English trade with America and other colonies, now recognized as being the most remarkable development in economic history in the latter half of the seventeenth century. While the loss of the American colonies interested him greatly (see his essay on William Pitt), their acquisition went unnoted; and the only colonies to which he devoted attention are India and Ireland.

Macaulay's account of William's landing in England is partly vitiated by his omitting the numbers in the opposing forces, thereby rendering the military situation unintelligible. Sufficiently precise figures were given in the sources he used. Sometimes he leaves out material facts, occasionally using the least trustworthy sources, with no worthier motive than to make a better story.

For James II, Macaulay had twice the number of sources available to his predecessor Hume. He tries to evaluate them, but not systematically or with the critical, minute analysis that his near contemporary, Leopold von Ranke, practiced. Nor does he always cite his sources with care: quoting from John Evelyn's diary, he gives the date of the entry, while quoting from Luttrell's "Brief Historical Relation," he does not. Airily he directs us to James Harrington's vast *Oceana*, without indicating the exact locus; blandly he refers to one of his sources as "nauseous balderdash, but I have been forced to descend even lower, if possible, in search of materials." A spate of close, accurate annotation of Paul de Barillon d'Amoncourt and Gilbert Burnet is followed by an apparently dogmatic claim without reference to any authority at all.

Macaulay could be very stubborn in his inaccuracy. He was totally wrong about William Penn, even to confusing him with an unrelated George Penn. When this was pointed out in time for a second edition, he refused to correct: he had formed his conception of Penn early on and was adamant in conserving it, even haranguing into silence a group of Quakers who visited him to protest. Did he pass too lightly over Continental politics? "I am writing a History of *England*," was his haughty reply.

The figures for executions and transportations at the "Bloody" Assizes are exaggerated. Macaulay says 300 were executed; the real figure was less than 150. He pictures Jeffreys as a devil from whom only the horns, the fork, and the tail are missing. He does so by extracting spicy items from gossipy pamphlets of doubtful veracity, such as those of John Tutchin, himself sent to prison by Jeffreys. He even puts words into Jeffreys' mouth. The punishments imposed, he suggests, were Jeffreys' inventions, such as whipping at the cart tail; in fact, they were still lawful in Macaulay's early years. He overlooks the fact that the strict rules governing the admissibility of evidence had not then been promulgated, and that the lack of provision in the law for legal representation in cases of treason and felony positively compelled judges to take an active part in examining witnesses.

Then there was John Churchill, duke of Marlborough, who, Macaulay tells us, "to those who can look steadily through the dazzling blaze of genius and glory," is really "a prodigy of turpitude." This is a distortion. That Marlborough was not always high-minded and was capable of deceit, that he entered into treasonable communication with James II, that he had a sexual liaison with the duchess of Cleveland, is true; but he was something else as well (as Macaulay elsewhere recognized). In the *History* he is cast in the role of villain, and nothing should turn aside the shower of barbs Macaulay designed for him: "insatiable of riches . . . at twenty he made money of his beauty and vigour; at sixty he made money of his genius and glory"; "thrifty in his very vices"; master of a "hundred villainies." C. H. Firth believed that Macaulay's refusal to see the nobler side of Marlborough—which of course he might have shown in the unwritten volumes of the *History*—was due to his suspicion that Marlborough plotted to overthrow King William, put Anne in his place, and so become director of the civil and military government. No evidence for such a plot exists.

A more general criticism is that Macaulay's characters rarely change and grow, that they are composed of antitheses simulating the complexity of human beings, rather than drawn from observation. Or, as Lord Morley put it, "He did not find his way to the indwelling man of many of his figures." Macaulay describes, no one better, "the *spectacle* of a character," wrote Walter Bagehot; of the depths of the psyche there is no hint. Nor, as W. J. Dawson wrote, does he show any sense of the mystery of living, whence we came and why we all, heroes and villains alike, tread the road to death. The eternal silence of these infinite spaces terrified Blaise Pascal; Macaulay had never noticed them. Life to him was a brilliant pageant; it did not occur to him that "We are such stuff as dreams are made on."

Even the tumultuous onward drive of the *History of England*, enjoyed by most readers, was objected to by Carlyle, who said Macaulay "is all very well for a time, but one wouldn't live under Niagara." Again, Macaulay knew from the inside how politics worked: he was one of the many Victorian historians—George Grote, John Acton, William Lecky, James Bryce—who were in Parliament and public life. Yet John Morley, a member of Parliament and former minister, wrote that the way Macaulay described the workings of politics was not the "way in which things happen."

It was James Augustus Cotter Morison in 1882 who first fired the big gun, the trigger of which subsequently became worn with pressing, against Macaulay, the charge being that as a Whig he interpreted all his history from a party point of view. Macaulay, according to Morison, compared all past history "to its disparagement with the present . . . to show how vastly the period of which he treats has been outstripped by the period in which he lives . . . a matter utterly indifferent to scientific history." In short, Macaulay was biased.

Macaulay was not a Whig historian in the sense that Samuel Johnson, a Tory, said of his early parliamentary reporting, "I always saw to it that the Whig dogs had the worst of it." Often in Macaulay the Tory dogs, such as Bishop Ken or Jeremy Collier, had the best of it, and he wrote in volume I, chapter 1, of the *History* that "The truth is that, though both parties have often seriously erred, England could have spared neither. . . . The difference between the two great sections of English politicians has always been a difference rather of degree than of principle." All the same, he extenuates in William what he deplores in James, and is more aware of moral defects in a Tory than in a Whig. He is certain that the Whigs wrested the prerogatives of the crown for the people, destroyed the Star Chamber, carried the Habeas Corpus Act, effected the Glorious Revolution of 1688: in short, to them Britons owe it that they have a House of Commons.

That Macaulay's Whig interpretation of history was no more than one possible interpretation was demonstrated by Herbert Butterfield in 1931. C. H. Firth, in his *Commentary on Macaulay's History* (1938), offered a Tory reply: The vaunted Whig "progress" was not always in the right direction; the Whigs, by attempting in 1640 to overthrow the existing government of the Church of England and to substitute a Presbyterian system, caused the first Civil War, and by their aggressive intolerance to all who were not Presbyterians caused the second Civil War in 1648. The Whigs' intolerance made a settlement in Ireland impossible; their fanatical hatred of Catholicism and their attempt to place a pretender on the English throne caused the futile struggle over the Exclusion Bill and the yet more futile Monmouth rebellion, and so on.

Today it is all "old hat." Popular history is propagandist to a degree Macaulay never dreamed of, and Voltaire's cynical view prevails, that history is "a pack of tricks we play on the dead." Serious history, on the other hand, has become a matter of econometrics and the computer. Macaulay's "the people thought" and "a majority favoured" are replaced by detailed answers as to "how many people" and "what actual percentage." The change is helpful, but it does not obviate our need for a historian who can tell a tale "which holdeth children from play and old men from the chimney corner."

The need is increasingly recognized. A. J. P. Taylor, condemning as unforgivable in a historian "tired metaphors and flabby sentences," boldly asserts:

Although history may claim to be a branch of science or of politics or of sociology, it is primarily communication, a form of literature. No historian is worth his salt who has not felt some twinge of Macaulay's ambition—to replace the latest novel on the lady's dressing table. It is to the credit of English history at the present time that some historians have felt this ambition and a few have even accomplished it.[20]

Not least, of course, Taylor himself.

Even Macaulay's concentration on politics and government as the core of history, so often derided in the socioeconomic 1930's, is upheld by such as Sir George Clark, on the ground that "It is in public institutions that men express their will to control events," and by others because government is the "synthesizing element" from which most other

things flow, even the "cultural qualities of an age." Macaulay's idea of progress, to which two world wars seemed adequate refutation, is now defended. J. H. Plumb sees the idea as providing historians with an escape from stultifying fact grubbing and myth destruction. We *have* progressed: this is a "great human truth, and if we accept it and explore its consequences history would not only be an infinitely richer education but also play a much more effective part in the culture of Western society."

So the critical winds seem to be blowing in Macaulay's favor again. Undoubtedly the *History of England* is still the best introduction to the brief period it covers; and most of the errors and lacunae could be put right by means of thorough annotation.[21] The book is worth it. As Lord Acton told Mary Gladstone, "Read him, therefore, to find out how it comes that the most unsympathetic of critics [that is, Acton] can think him very nearly the greatest of English writers."

SELECTED BIBLIOGRAPHY

I. Collected Works. Lady Trevelyan, ed., *The Works*, 8 vols. (London, 1866); *The Works*, 12 vols. (London, 1898), the Albany ed.; Lady Trevelyan, ed., *The Works*, 9 vols. (London, 1906–1907), vols. IV–VIII are *The History of England*, T. F. Henderson, ed.

II. Selected Works. *Selections from the Essays and Speeches*, 2 vols. (London, 1856); T. F. Ellis, ed., *The Miscellaneous Writings*, 2 vols. (London, 1860), best repr. is Everyman's Library, 2 vols. (London, 1910), contains his contributions to *Knight's Quarterly* (1823–1824) and the five biographies written for the English ed. of the *Encyclopaedia Britannica* (1854–1859); G. O. Trevelyan, ed., *Selections from the Writings* (London, 1876); E. V. Downs and G. L. Davis, eds., *Selections* (London, 1930); W. H. French and G. D. Sanders, eds., *The Reader's Macaulay: A Selection from His Essays, Letters and History of England* (New York, 1936); C. D. Dharker, comp., *Lord Macaulay's Legislative Minutes* (Madras, 1946); G. M. Young, ed., *Macaulay: Prose and Poetry* (London, 1953).

III. Separate Works. *Pompeii* (Cambridge, 1819), awarded the chancellor's gold medal for English verse, 1819; *Evening* (Cambridge, 1821), awarded the chancellor's gold medal for English verse, 1821; *Lays of Ancient*

---

[20]A. Marwick, *The Nature of History* (London, 1970).

[21]There was such an annotation by T. F. Henderson, but published in 1906–1907 and therefore not including much later material.

Rome (London, 1842), the 1848 ed. also includes "Ivry" and "The Armada," also in G. M. Trevelyan, ed. (London, 1928), the World's Classics; *Critical and Historical Essays Contributed to the Edinburgh Review*, 3 vols. (London, 1843), frequently repr., in F. C. Montague, ed., 3 vols. (London, 1903), the standard, Everyman's Library, 2 vols. (London, 1907), and the Oxford ed., 2 vols. (London, 1913); *The History of England from the Accession of James II*, 5 vols. (London, 1848–1861), also in 8 vols. with a memoir by H. H. Milman (London, 1858–1862), in Everyman's Library, 3 vols. (London, 1906), C. H. Firth, ed., 6 vols. (London, 1913–1915), and T. F. Henderson, ed., 5 vols. (London, 1931), the World's Classics; *Speeches, Parliamentary and Miscellaneous*, 2 vols. (London, 1854); *The Indian Civil Service: Report to the Rt Hon. Sir C. Wood, Bart, by T. B. Macaulay, Lord Ashburton, The Revd. H. Melvill, B. Jowett and the Speaker of the House of Commons* (London, 1855); G. Woodrow, ed., *The Indian Education Minutes Now First Collected from Records in the Department of Public Instructions* (Calcutta, 1862); G. M. Young, ed., *Speeches* (London, 1935), the World's Classics; J. Pinney, ed., *The Letters of Macaulay*, 6 vols. (London, 1974–   ), with valuable intro. and notes.

IV. BIOGRAPHICAL AND CRITICAL STUDIES. C. Babington, *Mr. Macaulay's Character of the Clergy in the Latter Part of the Seventeenth Century Considered* (Cambridge, 1849); W. H. Dixon, *William Penn: An Historical Biography* (London, 1851), doubts Macaulay's portrait of Penn, with apparent justification; J. Paget, *An Inquiry into the Evidence Relating to the Charges Brought by Lord Macaulay Against William Penn* (Edinburgh, 1858); J. Paget, *The New "Examen", or an Inquiry into the Evidence Relating to Certain Passages in Lord Macaulay's History* (Edinburgh–London, 1861), repr. with intro. by W. Churchill (London, 1934); F. Arnold, *The Public Life of Lord Macaulay* (London, 1862); H. H. Milman, *A Memoir of Lord Macaulay* (London, 1862); J. H. Stirling, *Jerrold, Tennyson and Macaulay* (Edinburgh, 1868); H. Martineau, *Biographical Sketches* (London, 1869); J. Morley, *Critical Miscellanies* (London, 1871–1877), vol. II; G. O. Trevelyan, ed., *The Life and Letters*, 2 vols. (New York–London, 1876), by Macaulay's nephew, still the best complete biography, also contains extracts from the journals—also in the World's Classics, 2 vols. (London, 1932); L. Stephen, *Hours in a Library*, 3rd ser. (London, 1874–1879); W. Bagehot, *Literary Studies*, R. H. Hutton, ed., 2 vols. (London, 1879), also in G. Sampson, ed. (London, 1911), in Everyman's Library; W. E. Gladstone, *Gleanings of Past Years, 1843–78*, 7 vols. (London, 1879); A. S. G. Canning, *Lord Macaulay, Essayist and Historian* (London,

1882; rev. and enl. ed., 1913); J. C. Morison, *Macaulay* (London, 1882), in the English Men of Letters series; F. Harrison, *Studies in Early Victorian Literature* (London, 1895), contains "Macaulay's Place in Literature"; W. J. Dawson, *The Makers of Modern Prose* (London, 1899), two chs. on Macaulay give the general critical attitude toward him at the turn of the century.

R. C. Jebb, *Macaulay: A Lecture* (Cambridge, 1900); W. M. Thackeray, *Stray Papers* (London, 1901), contains "Mr. Macaulay's Essays"; Lord Avebury, *Essays and Addresses, 1900–1903* (London, 1903); P. Clark, *Index to Trevelyan's Life and Letters of Lord Macaulay* (London, 1907); G. O. Trevelyan, comp., *The Marginal Notes of Lord Macaulay* (London, 1907); G. M. Trevelyan, *Clio: A Muse* (London, 1913); S. C. Roberts, *Lord Macaulay: The Pre-eminent Victorian* (London, 1927), English Association pamphlet no. 67, repr. in Roberts' *An Eighteenth-Century Gentleman and Other Essays* (London, 1930); A. J. Balfour, *Chapters of Autobiography* (London, 1930); H. Butterfield, *The Whig Interpretation of History* (London, 1931); A. Bryant, *Macaulay* (London, 1932); C. H. Firth, *A Commentary on Macaulay's History of England* (London, 1938), very fair consideration of the criticisms of Macaulay's historical accuracy, voiced before his death and subsequently by J. Paget—Firth's lectures were given before 1914, so he was unable to consider criticisms made by W. Churchill in *Marlborough, His Life and Times* (London, 1933–1934); E. Stokes, *The English Utilitarians and India* (Oxford, 1959); M. A. Thomson, *Macaulay* (London, 1959), no. 42 in the Historical Association's general series; D. Knowles, *Lord Macaulay 1800–1859* (Cambridge, 1960); A. N. L. Munby, *Macaulay's Library* (Glasgow, 1966), the David Murray Foundation Lecture, given at the University of Glasgow, 9 March 1965; A. Marwick, *The Nature of History* (London, 1970), useful references to Macaulay in a historiographical context; J. Clive, *Thomas Babington Macaulay. The Shaping of the Historian* (London, 1973), excellent study, but ends before the *History* was begun; J. Millgate, *Macaulay* (London, 1973), has the best bibliography, in Routledge's Author's Guide series; P. Gay, *Style in History* (London, 1975), contains a stimulating essay, "Macaulay, Intellectual Voluptuary."

The Macaulay MS diaries from which Trevelyan quoted selectively are in the library of Trinity College, Cambridge. The British Library has collections of MSS about Macaulay's friends, such as Macvey Napier, Lord and Lady Holland, and others. Macaulay family material is at the Huntington Library in San Marino, Calif.; London University Library has smaller collections of such material.

BENJAMIN DISRAELI

(1804-1881)

Paul Bloomfield

Who breaks his birth's invidious bar
And grasps the skirts of happy chance
And breasts the blows of circumstance
And grapples with his evil star

Who makes by force his merit known
And lives to clutch the golden keys
To mould a mighty state's decrees
And shape the whisper of the Throne
(Tennyson, *In Memoriam*)

I

"DISRAELI, BENJAMIN; Earl of Beaconsfield (1804-1881), statesman and man of letters." This is how the *Dictionary of National Biography* introduces him. "Without a study of his books," wrote W. F. Monypenny, "it is impossible to understand his life." Ought we to understand his life? He was prime minister of Great Britain at the height of its nineteenth-century power and influence, a dominating figure in British politics for a generation. That he, with his handicap of "race," social obscurity, and modest means, should have attained such a position constitutes a claim to attention. He had plenty of it in his own day, and has continued to get it from politicians, historians, and biographers. Neither then nor since have strictures on his labors or his personality been wanting. It is all the more interesting to find Lytton Strachey, that sedentary genius—so many of whose comments on the man verge on the derisory—pulling himself up in good time. Disraeli, he said, "was formidable—one of the most formidable men who ever lived" ("Dizzy," in the *Woman's Leader*, 16 July 1920).

Formidable as a man and a statesman; but what concerns us here is whether, besides being formidable, he is, as a novelist, readable. He *is* readable, partly for the reason given by G. W. E. Russell, of the great Whig family opposed to Disraeli and his Tories. According to Russell, "By far the acutest observer of our national life in the nineteenth century was Lord Beaconsfield, who combined the shrewdness of his race with unique opportunities of observation." What was unique about those opportunities was that he had to make them himself. And, even more remarkable, he announced his ambitions in his early novels while in process of achieving them. We can transpose Monypenny and say: "Without a study of his life it is impossible to understand his books"—though not impossible to be highly entertained by them.

Disraeli, born in London on 21 December 1804, was the second child and eldest son—he had a sister and two younger brothers—of a well-to-do Jewish man of letters, Isaac D'Israeli (this was how he spelled his name), of a Sephardic family that settled in England in 1748. In that year Isaac's father, Benjamin Israeli (*sic*), came over from Cento, near Ferrara, Italy, at the age of eighteen, probably to find a good market for his straw bonnets. An amiable agnostic who ceased to be a practicing Jew without becoming a Christian, Isaac took a Gentile friend's advice and in 1817 arranged for his children to be received into the Church of England. Benjamin became a Christian without for a moment feeling that he had ceased to be a Jew. At least now he was not disqualified from public office, supposing he ever aspired to one. It was not his "race" that disfranchised an English Jew. Like Quakers and Roman Catholics, Orthodox Jews had no vote. The three groups were excluded from Parliament until 1828, 1829, and 1858, respectively.

Disraeli got on well with his father but not with his mother, whose coldness to him is reflected in the stepmother's character in *Contarini Fleming*. Mrs. Disraeli did not think highly of his powers: "tho' a clever boy—no prodigy . . . ," and she didn't begin to believe otherwise until as late as 1847. It was quite different with his sister Sarah—the first of the women, as he constantly insisted, who played such a benign part in his life.

The schools Disraeli attended were quite good, without being fashionable. At Higham Hall in Essex, he developed an emotional affection for another boy. He was thinking of it when he—who sexually was perfectly "normal"—wrote in *Contarini:*

Oh! days of rare and pure felicity, when Musaeus and myself with our arms around each others' necks wandered together. . . . I lavished upon him all the fanciful love that I had long stored up; and the mighty passions that yet lay dormant in my obscure soul now first began to stir in their glimmering abyss.[1]

(ch. VII, p. 25)

Disraeli never went to a university, instead putting in a year of hard reading by himself, an effort to which he alludes in *Vivian Grey* and *Contarini Fleming.* In them, as in most of his novels, he is recollecting his own life story when he is not anticipating it. In 1821 he was articled to a solicitor, but three years later he abandoned the law. He had begun to write; and so, of course, had scores of his contemporaries.

Thus in 1824, at the age of twenty, Disraeli, a converted Jew of middle-class family, with no influential connections—at any rate no political ones—no great school behind him, no university degree, might have seemed one of the young men least likely to attain the highest office in the land. And in fact, when he became prime minister for the first time in 1868, he was breaking some records. Never had there been a cabinet minister, let alone a prime minister, who was not of aristocratic family, or very wealthy, or educated at one of the great public schools such as Eton, Westminster, or Harrow, or who had not had two or all three of those advantages. Neither had there ever been (nor has there been since) a prime minister who had begun and ended his career by writing novels.

This much, then, is certain: the young Disraeli could take nothing for granted. Lacking all hereditary requisites for success in public life—except, as he would have said, one very significant one, his Jewish antecedents—he was going to have to think out his aims and his principles for himself. Luckily he did much of the thinking aloud, so to speak; he gave it expression in his books. The gift that enabled him

to do so was not his only one. Though he had not first seen the light from what he would have called a "patrician" cradle, his heredity assured him of courage, imagination, brains, and charm. Even before starting his self-questionings—what was he to aim at in life?—and his probings into the nature and functions of the political parties and the churches, he had taken his stand on two convictions from which he never budged. They were faith in what he rather misleadingly called "race," and an absolute assurance that he was cut out for great things. By "race" he meant good breeding, but by "Jewish race" (which is not a true category) he meant something more esoteric. "We belong to a race," he said in his old age to a Jewish boy, "which knows how to do everything except to fail." As for the importance of personality, he once said: "It is the fashion of the present age to underrate the influence of individual character. For myself, I have ever rejected this consolation of mediocrity. I believe that everything that is great has been accomplished by great men."

II

DISRAELI's writing career began in 1826 with the appearance of the first two volumes of *Vivian Grey.* This novel of fashionable life and political machinations caused a stir because the publisher, Henry Colburn, had hinted that its anonymous author had put many prominent persons into it under thin disguises.

Colburn was an expert at publicity, and bent on making the most of the vogue for "society" novels started by R. P. Ward's *Tremaine.* In later years Disraeli was understandably ashamed of the slapdash writing and the nonsense he had put into *Vivian Grey, The Young Duke,* and *Henrietta Temple.* With one exception these have been reprinted since 1853 only in the expurgated form he gave them in his own edition of that year. The exception is Lucien Wolf's 1904 reprint of the original *Vivian Grey.*

All the same, though this first novel is far from being a precocious masterpiece, like Dickens' *Pickwick,* it has precocity—a youthful verve and forwardness and boldness of imagination. In fact Disraeli knew hardly any prominent persons except his father's literary friends and the friends of the second of the women in his life, the vivacious Sarah Austen, a solicitor's wife, who had made a fair copy of the book and persuaded Colburn to publish it. It was not

[1]Quotations from the works are from P. Guedalla, ed., *The Novels and Tales,* 12 vols. (London, 1926-1927).

long though, before he found his way into the intellectual demimonde, where the two reigning hostesses were those brilliant and much-wronged women Caroline Norton and Marguerite, Lady Blessington. When in due course he graduated into the grand monde of society, he did not neglect them; he remained their affectionate champion and devotee. If his relationship with Sarah Austen became embarrassed, it was because her husband, at first a generous patron, lost faith in him and made difficulties (as one can understand without altogether sympathizing) over a loan of money. Sarah Austen herself was not alienated; she evidently had a soft spot in her heart for Disraeli, to say the least.

A huge and bubbling book with an engaging brashness, *Vivian Grey* has several points of interest. In it Disraeli gives his readers a kind of prospectus of his intentions. An ambitious young man, Vivian Grey, finds a patron in the marquess of Carabas—a caricature of John Murray, second of his name in the famous firm of publishers. For Carabas, Vivian organizes a party—including a Lord Beaconsfield, "a very worthy gentleman, but between ourselves a damned fool." In the 1820's generous-minded young men with a social conscience were dissatisfied with both the Tory and the Whig leaderships, and were either radicals or bent on reforming the existing parties. Reforming the Tory party became one of Disraeli's self-imposed tasks; meanwhile, here is Vivian Grey throwing himself into the battle. Lord Carabas reads from the *Morning Post:*

"We are informed that some alteration in the composition of the present administration is in contemplation; Lord Past Century, it is said, will retire; Mr. Liberal Principles will have the———; and Mr. Charlatan Gas the———. . . ."

It would have been impossible for a hawk to watch its quarry with eyes of a more fixed and anxious earnestness than did Vivian Grey the Marquess of Carabas as his Lordship's eyes wandered over the paragraph.

(bk. II, ch. 2)

No, indeed!—for politics was Vivian Grey's ruling passion, as it was to become his creator's. "I wish to act what I write," Disraeli confessed some years later. "My works are the embodiment of my feelings. In *Vivian Grey* I have portrayed my real ambition." But in it he portrayed some of his other predispositions as well. An offhand Byronic cynicism about the socially great combined with a taste for high life and for the good things of life, including good food; respect for the learned and the wise, as here represented by Vivian's father, a portrait of Disraeli's own father; and deference to the role played by women in affairs of state through their hold on the male dramatis personae.

Disraeli's imagination was always haunted, his books show, by certain archetypal figures. There was an Apollonian youth, with a touch of Mercury, who as time went on softened, it may seem incongruously, into a kind of Candide. With Disraeli's own increase in self-confidence and power, Vivian Grey, Contarini Fleming, and Coningsby gave way to Tancred, Lothair, and Endymion (all six the eponymous heroes of as many novels). Since this metamorphosis was correlated with his own transformation from an obscure young man into a prime minister, the psychological analysis is easy. In his own words, "Everybody has a right to be conceited until he is successful."

If the archetypal hero gradually became toned down, it was the other way around with the mentor or sage, for the progress from Mr. Grey to the Sidonia of later novels was steeply upward. Luckily for Disraeli's readers, his archetypal woman bears not the remotest resemblance to the insipid or arch maidens who infest English nineteenth-century fiction. She is strong: a young Diotima or prophetess, an Egeria. Exceptionally, in *Vivian Grey* the leading woman is a bad woman.

When it came out, as of course it soon did, that the author of *Vivian Grey* was nobody in particular, and that besides Carabas-Murray he had only taken off a few obvious public characters (Lord Past Century was the earl of Eldon, the duke of Waterloo was the duke of Wellington, Cleveland was J. G. Lockhart), a storm broke over Disraeli's head. This afflicted him sufficiently for him to make a similar bother give a turn for the worse to the fortunes of his hero in *Contarini Fleming*, published six years later. Perhaps the apparent setback had something to do with his bad health in 1827; yet by the spring of the following year, he had the resilience to produce an amusing satire, *The Voyage of Captain Popanilla*.

It is not enough to say of this little book, which is stylized in the Voltairean manner, that it ridicules the utilitarians, since it also sheds light on the author's intellectual evolution. He was one of the first in the field against those well-meaning (and indeed effective) theorists. The loud, idiosyncratic booming of Thomas Carlyle had not yet been heard, and *Hard*

Times was still to come. In any case Dickens, for all his incomparable genius, was such a child when it came to social theory and administration that G. M. Young was justified in calling his political satire "tedious and ignorant." Carlyle, like Disraeli, believed in immaterial values, personality, and the need for strong leadership; but even his best friends recognized that he could not be trusted with the management of so much as a magazine. Disraeli, on the other hand, was born to manage the affairs of a nation and an empire.

Popanilla, native of Fantaisie, a utopian island in the Indian Ocean, finds a box packed with Benthamite literature washed up on the beach. He reads it, is converted, and at once sets out to proselytize his king and fellow countrymen. He explains to them:

that man was not born for himself but for society; that the interests of the body are alone to be considered, and not those of the individual; and that a nation might be extremely happy, extremely powerful, and extremely rich, although every member of it might at the same time be miserable, dependent and in debt.

(ch. 4, p. 15)

Though this is an echo of Pangloss' axiom in Voltaire's *Candide* that "les malheurs particuliers font le bien général," the time was ripe for the warning to be repeated. In more than one great nation of the twentieth century, the utilitarian principles, stiffened by Marxism, have swept the board. In Victorian England the compromise worked out between Liberal laissez-faire and Disraelian humanist Toryism allowed the individual, and still allows him or her, to preserve freedom of thought and contract as well as idiosyncrasies. How the king and people of Fantaisie rid themselves of Popanilla by sending him on an embassy to Hubbabub (London), capital of Vraibleusia (Trueblueland, or England), and the account of what he sees and does there, all go to make an amusing enough political essay, even if it creaks a little in places. The main point is that we find Disraeli coming out as an energetic defender of those personal values that, he realized, were being threatened as much by the new industrial civilization as by the Benthamite philosophy.

Popanilla was fun but it buttered no beans, and the author, partly owing to some rash speculations, was in debt; he badly needed money. He therefore wrote a second novel of fashionable life, *The Young Duke* (1831). His father was puzzled: "What does

Ben know of Dukes?" What Ben knew was that there was a public for descriptions of high life, just as there is one today for paragraphs about the private affairs and goings-on of film stars. And although he afterward said, "Until my return from the East on the eve of the 1832 election I had lived a very secluded life and mixed not at all with the world," he was already acquainted with some of the most brilliant young men of family in his own generation. The famous little dinner he attended at Edward George Bulwer-Lytton's house, alluded to nearly fifty years later in *Endymion,* took place while he was writing *The Young Duke.* Present also were Henry Bulwer, Lord Clarendon's nephew Charles Villiers, and Alexander Cockburn, a future lord chief justice of England. Henry Bulwer afterward recorded that "If on leaving the table we . . . had been asked which was the cleverest of the party we should have been obliged to say 'the man in the green velvet trousers.'"

Disraeli only overdressed *as if* he were decadent, but his young duke in the novel is presented as truly decadent and spoiled—"Let me die eating ortolans to the sound of soft music" is the least noxious kind of sentiment uttered by him before his reform. If Disraeli was not yet perfectly informed about the gilded life, he could always invent—and so he freely did, as novelists do. The duke of St. James, like most of Disraeli's heroes, was destined to be redeemed—whether from weltschmerz or political heresy or, as in this case, his bad habits—by a good woman. The heroine this time was a Roman Catholic, Mary Dacre, which was significant not only because it reflected the author's approval of Catholic emancipation but also because he, a tolerant Christianized Jew, was coming more and more to feel that since man is a religious being, the churches had as much an imperative duty to help preserve culture as they formerly had a preeminent part in creating it.

Another regular Disraelian feature of the book is the introduction of living personalities, here given ultratopicality by a brisk and trenchant commentary on parliamentary debate. ("I hear that Mr Babington Macaulay is to be returned. If he speak half as well as he writes the House will be in fashion again.") Among the author's asides there is one that Monypenny calls "a truly astonishing bit of prescient impertinence":

One thing is quite clear,—that a man may speak very well in the House of Commons and fail very completely in the House of Lords. There are two distinct styles requisite: I intend in the course of my career, if I have time, to give a specimen of both. In the Lower House, *Don Juan* may perhaps be our model; in the Upper House, *Paradise Lost.*

(bk. IV, ch. 6)

And so, while nobody has ever suggested that this lively book is one of Disraeli's masterpieces, there is nothing of feuilleton flatulence about it. On the £500 his publisher advanced him, Disraeli set out, accompanied by his sister's fiancé, William Meredith, on a tour of the Mediterranean and the Middle East.

III

THE pair visited Spain, Malta, Corfu, Albania, Greece, Cyprus, Turkey, Palestine, and Egypt. Disraeli, to judge by his own and other people's accounts, seemed to be impersonating one of the more colorful heroes of his early novels. The exoticism of his clothes made people wonder whether this Englishman was wearing fancy dress, and his deliberately mannered behavior did not always go down quite as well with other Englishmen as he thought it was doing. Soon after the two travelers had been joined at Malta by their friend James Clay and his servant, Disraeli wrote, in one of his many lively letters to his family:

To govern men, you must either excel them in their accomplishments, or despise them. Clay does one; I do the other . . . Yesterday in the racket court, sitting in the gallery among strangers, the ball entered, and lightly struck me, and fell at my feet. I picked it up, and observing a young rifleman excessively stiff, I humbly requested him to forward its passage into the court, as I really had never thrown a ball in my life.[2]

(25 August 1830)

Clay's servant, by the way, was Giovanni Battista Falcieri, known to fame as Tita: "Byron died in his arms, and his moustachios touch the earth." At the end of the tour, Disraeli took Tita over, kept him employed and content until his death more than forty years later, and then had no difficulty in persuading Queen Victoria to pension his widow.

By the time Disraeli had spent a week in Jerusalem, it would be less true to say that the East was casting its spell on him than that he found there something

he was more or less consciously looking for: a sense of mystic communion with the genius of his ancestors. Characteristically, he was not satisfied to store up his impressions, but replanned *Alroy,* a book he had in mind for some years; conceived a second, *Contarini Fleming;* and set to work on both of them. As if this was not enough, he also made up his mind to stand for Parliament at the first opportunity. He returned to England in October 1831, in excellent health but distressed of spirits; Meredith had died of cholera in Cairo. Sarah Disraeli lived out her life unmarried, devoting herself to her brother. "Until his marriage," says Robert Blake, "she played as important a part in his personal life as anyone, by her constant and judicious admiration and encouragement." She died in 1859.

Contarini Fleming: A Psychological Auto-biography (1832) is an Aladdin's cave of so much strangely assorted treasure that one can equally understand why the poet Heinrich Heine praised it for its "Gothic richness" and why it is less often reprinted than the tidier and more topical *Sybil* or *Lothair.* These latter are also, in a sense, better books, though Disraeli himself did not think so: he regarded *Contarini* "as the perfection of English prose and a chef d'oeuvre." (His boasting usually had something of Oscar Wilde's flippancy—as when he said to a lady who asked him if he had read such-and-such a novel: "Madam, when I want to read a good novel I write one.") *Contarini* is no exception to the rule by which the creatures of Disraeli's imagination move on the highest social levels, preferably close to the throne where there is one. (In *Endymion* the hero's sister is actually promoted to one of those exalted seats.)

Young Fleming, with his noble Saxon father and noble Venetian mother—reflecting, respectively, Disraeli's ideas about his own nurture and nature—oscillates more violently between art and action than the author himself ever did. The object of the sort of action Disraeli had in mind was to get power; and power, as he already knew both from what he had observed of the world and from introspection, was liable to corrupt. He had the frankness to correlate Contarini's rise in the political world with a progressive, though not permanent, deterioration of character; I realize, he seems to say, that this is what can easily happen to an ambitious, able young man. But at the height of his success, Contarini has misgivings. Alone at a window, watching the sun set over a distant horizon: "I felt indeed a disgust for all the worldliness on which I had been late pondering. And

---

[2]See *Home Letters* (1830–1831), which is included in A. Birrell, ed., *Letters, 1830–1852* (London, 1928).

there arose in my mind a desire to create things beautiful as that golden sun and that glittering star."

The publication of an indiscreet book, *Manstein* —Contarini's *Vivian Grey*, so to speak—precipitates him into the course for which he, unlike Disraeli, has the greater temperamental inclination. He opts for art—in spite of his father's prophecy, "My son, you will be Prime Minister. . .," and in spite of much advice from the usual sage, this time an artist called Winter, who oddly enough counsels action: "Act without ceasing, and you will no longer talk of the vanity of life." There is no doubt that good advice—both offering it and seeking it—is an ancient and perennial Jewish addiction, though when it comes to taking it, there is little to distinguish Jew from Gentile. Though at times, especially when Sidonia is being oracular in the later novels, we may become restive, Disraeli's sense of humor is seldom eclipsed for long. "Talk to women," Baron Fleming advises his son, "talk to women as much as you can. This is the best school. This is the way to gain fluency, because you need not care what you say, and had better not be sensible."

Greater works than *Contarini Fleming* have been patchy, scarred rather than marred by melodrama, bathos, or irrelevances; but with something of all three of these flaws, it is an interesting variation on the theme that character is fate—"destiny is our will," Contarini proclaims, "and our will is our nature." It is a revealing book, as it was meant to be, though it is strange that Disraeli should have bracketed *Alroy*, which came out in the following year, with *Vivian Grey* and *Contarini Fleming*, saying (in the diary he kept between 1833 and 1836, at the time of his love affairs), "This trilogy is the secret history of my feelings—I shall write no more about myself." He was better than his word, and went on writing about himself to within a few days of his death. We must believe he was sincere when he said at the time that *Alroy* was his "ideal ambition"; but if ever he dreamed of starting or leading a Zionist movement, it was not for long. The whole trend of his thinking was in quite another direction. It might have been otherwise today.

Alroy, a romanticized history of a twelfth-century Jewish impostor under the Seljuks, whom Disraeli turned into a second Judas Maccabeus and martyr for his faith, must not be underrated, though it is overly rhetorical and a dead end, for Disraeli soon came round to the view that Judaism was fermenting Christianity and Christianity was leavened Judaism.

There is more to interest us in the two jeux d'esprit he produced at about the same time, intellectual whimsies in the manner of the Greek satirist Lucian: *Ixion in Heaven* and *The Infernal Marriage*. In these two short, lively, irreverent pieces, he served notice that although he aspired to the highest rank and dignities, he was not taking the socially great at the valuation they liked those outside their charmed circle to put on them. Young Ixion, having been admitted to heaven by Jupiter, throws his weight about with Disraelian aplomb. Invited to write something in Minerva's album, he makes this contribution:

I have seen the world, and more than the world; I have studied the heart of man, and now I consort with Immortals. The fruit of my tree of knowledge is plucked, and it is this, ADVENTURES ARE TO THE ADVENTUROUS.
Written in the Album of Minerva, by
IXION IN HEAVEN
(p. 129)

"Adventures are to the adventurous": these words might have been Disraeli's motto. He had already used them in *Alroy*, and Sidonia was to repeat them, with as much gravity as if the sentiment had been quite original, in *Tancred*.

The Infernal Marriage is the marriage between Pluto and Proserpine, made, like the Ixion story, an occasion for much brilliant pastiche and nonsense, in a form that no one but a born literary artificer would have dreamed of choosing. There are more allusions to current politics than in *Ixion*, more recognizable caricatures of well-known people, and the Titans are the Tories, the Olympians, the Whigs. The juxtaposition of classic formulas and colloquialisms is sometimes very funny. Earlier than this (and he was still only thirty) Disraeli had been pouring out, and all his life continued to pour out, aphorisms, not all of equal neatness but some that deserve a place in the anthologies—like this one from Tiresias (the duke of Wellington) in *The Infernal Marriage*: "Next to knowing when to seize an opportunity, the most important thing in life is to know when to forego an advantage." This is the wisdom of the animal kingdom, divined by Disraeli years before Konrad Lorenz came along with his injunction to imitate the wolf and the greylag goose. And when a young Titan, Rhoetus—who but Disraeli himself?—says to one of his companions "that for his part he was convinced that the only way to beat the Olympians was to turn them to ridicule," we, wise after the event, perceive that a draft from the upper air had eddied down into the realm of twilight.

It was going to take more than ridicule to beat the Olympians—to unseat the Whigs. In 1830, while Disraeli was on his travels, they had come into power after an interminably long Tory innings. In 1832, the year of their great Reform Bill, when Disraeli first tried and failed to enter Parliament, he met a Mr. Wyndham Lewis, member for Maidstone, with his wife, "a pretty little woman," he wrote to his sister, "a flirt and a rattle." It could not have entered his head that Mary Anne Lewis, married and twelve years older than he, would one day become his wife and live with him for nearly thirty-five years in a state of model domesticity that was to be almost the only thing about him that his future rival, William Gladstone, ever approved of. For the moment Disraeli was skeptical about love marriages, and indeed was not thinking of marriage for himself at all. "All my friends who have married for love or beauty," he noted, "either beat their wives or live apart from them. I may commit many follies, but I never intend to marry for love, which I am sure is a guarantee of infelicity."

Politics was absorbing Disraeli more and more. Meeting Lord Melbourne at Caroline Norton's in 1834, he solemnly informed him: "I want to be Prime Minister." Even if the worldly Melbourne had not been impressed, he was too much a gentleman to laugh this off. But he shook his head. "Nobody can compete with Stanley," he said. "Stanley will be the next Prime Minister, you will see." Melbourne lived long enough to be moved, by what he saw of Disraeli's progress, to exclaim: "My God—I believe the fellow will do it yet!"

Disraeli's political journalism of 1835 is consistent with those parts of his later novels in which he gave imaginative expression to his social ideals; he was to become, after all, the creator of the "political novel," and with him life, journalism, politics, literature were all of a piece—his story is singularly free from digressions. In the *Letters of Runnymede* (1836), contributed to the *Times*, and in a book, *Vindication of the English Constitution* (1835), which he dedicated to his powerful new friend, the American-born Lord Chancellor John Lyndhurst, he is less convincing when damning the Whigs than when defending the old, or recommending the new, Toryism (his own brand of it).

For "beating the Olympians," Rhoetus in Disraeli's person was inclined to use strong language rather than ridicule. Even if there was something in

his charge that the great Whig families had crystallized into "a Venetian Oligarchy," that "Oligarchy" had been in process, first, of establishing the Hanoverian kings firmly on that throne for the mystique of which Disraeli had so much piety, and second, of saving England from revolution by bowing to the demand for political reform. More lately its members had identified themselves with Disraeli's bêtes noires, the utilitarians, because they realized that without what we should describe as bureaucratic measures, there was no hope of dealing with a situation of unprecedented complexity. England was the first country to experience an industrial revolution; its death rate was down and its birth rate up, and nearly everywhere people were on the move pell-mell from the rural districts to the new towns. There was, though, some substance in Disraeli's fears that if bureaucracy got out of hand, it would take the geniality out of people's dealings with one another. Everybody could see that society was being transformed: let it not be into a soulless mechanism. "He demanded," as V. S. Pritchett has well said, "the glory of a dogma, the sensation of re-birth, the emotion of a new era." Dogma and the concept of rebirth are associated with religion. Sure enough, in the *Vindication*, as in his later novels, he insisted that it was the duty of the clergy to resist materialism with more energy than they seemed to be doing.

Meanwhile, there were love affairs. About 1832, Disraeli seems to have been having a liaison with Clara, wife of a Dr. Bolton who practiced in the West End. But in 1833 he really fell in love with the emotional Henrietta, Lady Sykes, whose complaisant husband, Sir Francis, took on the equally complaisant doctor's Clara. In August 1836, Disraeli wrote in his diary: "Parted for ever from Henrietta." If marrying for love was "a guarantee of infelicity," an affair of that kind, continued too long, might be fatal both to happiness and to worldly prospects. All the more so since his mistress, though affectionate, was neither stable nor adequately provided for by her husband, the father of her four children. Disraeli broke with her when he found she had been unfaithful to him with the painter Daniel Maclise, and sublimated the pain of parting in a novel, *Henrietta Temple: A Love Story* (1837).

In this book, and in his next one, *Venetia* (1837), Disraeli was dealing, as he put it, with "feelings more enduring than public passions." But this is not to say that *Henrietta Temple* is memorable for its love interest alone, feelingly though this is developed. Every day of his life Disraeli's circle of acquaintance among influential people had been widening, so that by now his father would have acknowledged that he even knew something about dukes; and his travels had given him an insight into the manners and customs of the British official overseas. For this novel he drew freely on his enlarged experience. The hero, Ferdinand Armine, is at Malta with his regiment; he is poor but (of course) of "good" family, and—once more "of course"—in need of a good woman to redeem him from his bad habits (preferably also from his penury). Since he makes up to the first good woman who comes his way, his cousin Katherine, because she is an heiress and not because he loves her, he seems to be going—from a moral point of view—from bad to worse. Then Henrietta comes on the scene, and Ferdinand and she really fall in love. The skein of the plot is disentangled by the diplomacy of the benevolent Count Alcibiades de Mirabel, a portrait—too flattering to be a true likeness—of Disraeli's friend Alfred, Count d'Orsay. Among other recognizable characters is Lady Bellair, in life the eccentric old hostess and lion hunter Lady Cork, to whom in her girlhood Samuel Johnson had said, "Dearest, you're a dunce," and who, when approaching her ninetieth birthday, had called *The Infernal Marriage* "the finest book ever written." Isaac D'Israeli also thought well of it—indeed, he considered it and *Ixion* to be his son's most original contributions to literature. (When Isaac died in 1848, only *Lothair* and *Endymion* were still to be written.)

If what Disraeli's public got there and then, besides an impassioned love story, was something of a roman à clef, what posterity gets is the love story and some social history. Though his first full-bodied political novel, *Coningsby*, was still to come, a small infusion of the essence of his political philosophy had been perceptible in *Vivian Grey*, and the doses were being gradually increased. Curiously enough, where English literature is concerned, Disraeli is the outstanding apologist of the principle of noblesse oblige. He made it abundantly clear from the start that he already suspected how much extravagance, insensibility, jobbery, chichi, and scandal there was in the highest circles; but he believed, and he continued all his life to believe—and he found ample evidence to support him—that the British ruling class in every generation produced men prepared to rule, and to do so disinterestedly and capably, without regard to their comfort, health, or domestic enjoyments. Disraeli was not deceived by titles ("Dukes can be made!" he once exclaimed angrily

when a duke kept him waiting), but expected to find good breeding among the well-bred. And with the enlightened prejudice of a eugenicist, he put nature before nurture—thus in *Contarini Fleming* he had made Winter say: "Nature is more powerful than education." It never surprised him to find natural ability in a poor Jew or an underpaid mill hand. If in *Henrietta Temple* the human decencies, together with charm and sagacity, are conspicuously embodied in Lord Montfort, heir to a dukedom, it is because this is relevant to the story Disraeli wanted to tell, as well as compatible with his romantic feeling for the English aristocracy.

About a year later, in May 1837, six months before the beginning of his great parliamentary career, Disraeli published *Venetia: Or the Poet's Daughter*. This is the least self-regarding of his early novels, even if there is some identification of himself both with Lord Cadurcis and Marmion Herbert, who stand, respectively, for Lord Byron and Percy Shelley. Writing under the shadow of debt, bad health, and doubts about his chances of a political future, he threw himself imaginatively into the strange drama of the lives of the two poets. Byron's child Allegra becomes Marmion Herbert's Venetia, and Disraeli gives us one of the earliest sympathetic studies of a child growing up in a broken home. His setting their story back by more than half a century is awkwardly done, and Marmion-Shelley is hardly convincing as an American rebel commander. On the credit side there is the fact that English society had soon forgiven Byron for breaking certain rules (it is better to speak of rules than conventions, for the "great world" was not very conventional), but Shelley, more neurotic, more of what today we should call an ideologist, was still under a cloud—though some of the Cambridge "Apostles" had begun his defense. Is it strange that on the eve of important developments in his own career, the "formidable" Disraeli should have concerned himself with the poet's rehabilitation? By no means, for Shelley had been a prophet; and it was in a prophetic or messianic role that Disraeli saw himself. And of course as a kind of commander or leader of men, as well.

IV

For eleven years he had been writing hard. The next seven made the first long break in his output. When the young Queen Victoria's first Parliament met in

November 1837, Disraeli took his seat as one of the Tory members for Maidstone. He owed his election to his fellow member, Wyndham Lewis. On 7 December he made his maiden speech, an apparent failure, ending it with the famous words "I sit down now, but the time will come when you will hear me." In March 1838, Wyndham Lewis died, and the following year Disraeli married his widow, a woman of forty-six with an income of £4,000 a year. It is enough to say that posterity has been disarmed by her summing up of the affair long after: "Dizzy married me for my money, but if he had the chance again he would marry me for love." Mary Anne was eminently middle class; there were some grandes dames (like Lady Jersey) who began by showing disdain for her—but Disraeli felt quite sure they would come round, and they did.

So quickly after this did Disraeli make his political reputation that when, in 1841, the Tories came in, under the eminent Sir Robert Peel, he stood an excellent chance of high office. Peel was ready to offer him an appointment, but young Lord Stanley objected. Stanley, of whom Melbourne and almost everyone else in politics still thought so highly, was arrogant and opinionated. He despised Disraeli, and told Peel that "If that scoundrel were taken in [to the ministry] he would not remain himself." The ironies of what followed are remarkable. Peel soon lost both Stanley and Disraeli through his decision to repeal the duty on imported grain; this forced Stanley to cooperate with Disraeli and, when later his health began to fail, to hand over to "that scoundrel" the reins of power.

Meanwhile, in the decade 1841–1851, there was Disraeli, first abandoned by his chief and then in opposition to him, and on bad terms with Stanley, the supposed hope of the orthodox Tories. The outlook had grown dark again. As usual, under such circumstances, Disraeli sat down and began to write, only this time there was a difference. It may be, as Monypenny says, that his exclusion from office in 1841 "led to . . . the creation of the political novel." But though out of office, the novelist was not out of politics. He was going one better than *Contarini Fleming*. For Disraeli it was to be both art *and* action.

Between 1841 and 1852, when he became chancellor of the exchequer for the first time under Stanley, Disraeli wrote four books, three of them novels that can more truly be called a trilogy than can the earlier series of *Vivian Grey*, *Contarini Fleming*, and *Alroy*; they were *Coningsby*, *Sybil*, and *Tancred*. Then came a political biography, a life of Lord George Bentinck. We must attribute the temptation to think of *Coningsby* as the most Disraelian novel of them all to the enthusiasm the author put into it, and to the skill with which he mixed all the ingredients at his disposal.

Coningsby appeared in 1844. Disraeli devoted more than half his preface to the fifth edition (1849) to his cherished thesis that Toryism is indissolubly linked with the Church of England, and the Church of England with its Mosaic and Judeo-Christian inspiration:

In vindicating the right of the Church of Christ to be the perpetual regenerator of man, the writer thought that the time had arrived when some attempt should be made to do justice to the race which had founded Christianity.

The setting of the book is contemporary social and political life; many well-known characters are introduced, some disguised and others under their own names; there is the first appearance of the most celebrated of the Disraelian sages, Sidonia; and the whole is not only a commentary, often sparkling, but also a forecast: *Coningsby; or, The New Generation* is the manifesto of "Young England." The future, as Disraeli meant it to be, is announced with topical emphasis, and the public had no difficulty in recognizing his friends and followers in Coningsby himself (the Hon. George Smythe), Lord Henry Sydney (Lord John Manners), and Sir Charles Buckhurst (Alexander Cochran). It was a very small pressure group, but its members sat in Parliament, where they helped to make Disraeli's weight felt, if not their own.

What was it they stood for? We can infer a good deal of it from a sentence in *Coningsby* telling us what they disapproved of: "a crown robbed of its prerogative, a Church extended to a Commission and an aristocracy that does not lead." They believed it would be a mistake to abandon protection of home-grown grain, because this would mean a dangerous one-sided development of the national economy. Disraeli distinguished sharply between wealth and welfare, convinced there was now too much concentration on industry and making money. He and his disciples (in and out of *Coningsby*) wanted the country to be less of a machine, more of a living organism. Whatever a man's social status, his individuality must be respected. When Coningsby first meets the great Sidonia, he asks him a question:

"But what is an individual", Coningsby exclaimed, "against a vast public opinion?" "Divine", said the stranger. "God made man in His own image, but the Public is made by Newspapers, Members of Parliament, Excise Officers, Poor Law Guardians."

(bk. III, ch. 1)

Reading the book, we are inducted into the mysteries of a ruling-class young man's political, social, and sentimental education in the England of the 1830's. And through what a wonderful portrait gallery of men and women in all walks of life our voluble, brilliant, well-informed guide conducts us! From the good and the beautiful to that mischievous old epicurean, Coningsby's grandfather, Lord Monmouth; his agent, the time-serving Rigby; and the lesser wire-pulling types, Mr. Tadpole and Mr. Taper, whose names have passed into English idiom. Monmouth, taken like William Makepeace Thackeray's Lord Steyne in *Vanity Fair* from the bon vivant marquess of Hertford (who was dead), comes off better than Rigby, who was the politician John Croker, an antagonist of Disraeli's (and still alive). Though Thackeray, in perhaps the most perfect of English novels, makes a memorable character of Lord Hertford, Disraeli's version plausibly suggests more of the kind of motives, besides lasciviousness, that would have explained his nature and behavior.

The long-windedness of certain passages at the beginning and in the middle of *Coningsby* is due to the characters' having too much to say, not to the author's having too little. But when the plot gets under way, it grips. Coningsby, a young man of high principles, is caught between his love for Edith, daughter of the estimable industrialist Millbank, and his duty to and affection for his unscrupulous grandfather, Millbank's relentless enemy. In the course of making everything end happily, Disraeli uses some shock tactics; on the other hand, he often proves that he knows very well that critical events are apt to be the result of what may seem trifles:

There is no end to the influence of woman on our life. It is at the bottom of everything that happens to us. And so it was that, in spite of all the combinations of Lucretia [Monmouth's wife] and Mr Rigby, and the mortification of Lord Monmouth, the favourable impression he casually made on a couple of French actresses occasioned Coningsby, before a month had elapsed since his memorable interview at Monmouth House, to receive an invitation again to dine with his grandfather.

(bk. VIII, ch. 7)

No less severe a critic than Leslie Stephen said of *Coningsby* that "It wants little but a greater absence of purpose to be a first-rate novel." *Sybil: or The Two Nations*, which came out the following year (1845) and was dedicated to "a perfect Wife," has even more purpose—and it is a finer book, still the most often read of Disraeli's works and perhaps the second-best thing he did. In *Coningsby* it is noticeable that although Mr. Millbank is a factory owner, the industrial background, the life of the factory workers, is hardly even sketched. If he had wanted to, Disraeli could have filled in the picture, as he did in *Sybil*, for since his entry into Parliament he had been absorbed by social problems, and in the early 1840's—the "Hungry Forties"—had paid visits to the industrial North to see conditions there with his own eyes. Already in 1839 he had puzzled both sides of the House of Commons by coming out in sympathy with the Chartists, those radicals, mainly working-class, who were pressing for constitutional reform. In *Sybil*, on the same occasion the aristocratic hero, Charles Egremont, makes a speech in the House very like Disraeli's own:

"It was a very remarkable speech of Egremont," said the grey-headed gentleman. "I wonder what he wants."

"I think he must be going to turn Radical," said the Warwickshire peer.

"Why, the whole speech was against Radicalism," said Mr Egerton.

"Ah, then he is going to turn Whig, I suppose."

"He is an ultra anti-Whig," said Egerton.

"Then what the deuce is he?" said Mr Berners.

"Not a Conservative, certainly, for Lady St Julians does nothing but abuse him."

. . .

"That speech of Egremont was the most really democratic speech that I ever read," said the grey-headed gentleman.

(bk. V, ch. 1)

"Democratic" is a much-abused word, but nobody can read *Sybil* and not acknowledge that Disraeli's indignation at social injustice was passionately felt. The first novel of its kind, it presented the rich with an authentic and devastating picture of the life led by the poor—starving weavers, ironworkers sunk in squalor, harassed peasants breaking up the newfangled machinery that they blamed for their misfortunes. Two years earlier, in *Past and Present*, Thomas Carlyle had expressed something like Disraeli's opinions—a book that might have caused popular disturbances, Richard Monckton Milnes thought, if Carlyle had written it in plain English and it had been widely read. Oddly enough, Carlyle regarded Disraeli as "an absurd monkey dancing on John Bull's chest." He lived to see him as prime minister thirty years later, passing laws that might have been drawn up by Coningsby and Egremont—with some help from the author of *Past and Present*.

The rich and the poor were "the Two Nations." To mark the contrasts between them, Disraeli opens *Sybil* at the Jockey Club in London, where "in a golden saloon that . . . in its splendour would not have disgraced Versailles," the idler rich are placing bets for the Derby of 1837. Then he quickly translates us to a very different spot.

> This town of Marney was a metropolis of agricultural labour, for the proprietors of the neighbourhood having for the last half-century acted on the system of destroying the cottages on their estates, in order to become exempted from the maintenance of the population, the expelled people had flocked to Marney, where, during the war, a manufacturer had afforded them some relief. . . .
>
> (bk. II, ch. 3)

But the factory wheels had long stopped turning.

The local magnate is the callous Lord Marney; his brother Charles Egremont is another sort, and the hero of the book. Looking for deliverance from his perplexities, he meets Sybil, the daughter of a Roman Catholic mill manager, and she confirms him in his popular sympathies. But he follows her neither into Catholicism nor into Chartism. Disraeli, after all, was never a Jacobin, so for Egremont, as for him, the watchword once again is noblesse oblige. If this is not socialism, neither is it a plea for preserving class distinctions. In *Coningsby* we read of Sydney's ducal mother that she had "that perfect good breeding which is the result of nature and not of education, for it may be found in a cottage and may be missed in a palace." Disraeli, in fact, equates good breeding with good nature, and good nature with an upright character—the product of what, if not of good breeding? He never altogether admits that people are often the creatures of their conditions. Yet, from the propaganda he made in *Sybil*, and from what he did when he became prime minister, we can see how important he knew it was to improve conditions.

The contrasts of *Sybil*, the warning conveyed in the vivid scenes of riot and violence (which England was to be spared in 1848, the year of revolutions),

the threads of idealism running through the book, and much bracing dialogue add up to something impressive. The whole is, as a work of fiction should be, greater than the sum of the parts.

If it had not been for the political crisis of 1846 over the repeal of the corn laws, *Tancred* would have come out even harder on the heels of *Sybil* than it did. This last volume of the trilogy was published in 1847; after examining the political scene and the condition of the people, Disraeli had turned to the most fundamental problem of all, that of belief. "I do not believe in belief," said E. M. Forster in 1939. This was honest of him; but Disraeli's exclamation seventy-five years earlier, "Man is a being born to believe," was on the mark. When in 1864 he told an Oxford audience "I am on the side of the Angels," he was not setting up as a fundamentalist, but repeating that he believed in belief—believed, that is, that man, whatever his ancestry, is a spiritual being.

Tancred: or, The New Crusade is a curious book, even for a book by Disraeli. English literature does not abound in heroes who are seeking the truth. Such a one is Tancred, Lord Montacute, a young nobleman with every advantage in life, except that he does not know what to believe. He astonishes his sympathetic parents, the duke and duchess of Bellamont, by telling them he feels he ought to make a pilgrimage to the Holy Sepulchre, as a crusading forebear of his had done six centuries earlier:

> "I, too, would kneel at that tomb; I too, surrounded by the holy hills and sacred groves of Jerusalem, would relieve my spirit from the bale that bows it down; would lift my voice to heaven, and ask, What is DUTY, and what is FAITH? What ought I to DO, and what ought I to BELIEVE?"
>
> (bk. II, ch. 1)

Lady Bellamont would not have minded his going to Holland—"a Protestant country, and there are no vermin." But Jerusalem! A bishop is called in, to try to head off the eccentric young man from his purpose. Is there no religious inspiration to be found in England? He says complacently to Tancred:

> "We shall soon see a bishop at Manchester."
> "But I want to see an angel at Manchester."
> "An angel!"
> "Why not? Why should there not be heavenly messengers when heavenly messages are most wanted?"
>
> (bk. II, ch. 4)

So, the bishop having failed, the Bellamonts resort to a man of the world, Lord Eskdale. By luring Tancred into "society," where he meets the fetching Lady Constance, Eskdale almost succeeds. But Lady Constance has "guanoed [fertilized] her mind" by reading French novels and some modern science. She presses on Tancred a book on evolution that explains "everything":

First there was nothing, then there was something; then, I forget the next, I think there were shells, then fishes; then we came; let me see; did we come next? Never mind; we came at last. And the next change there will be something very superior to us, something with wings. Ah! that's it: we were fishes, and I believe we shall be crows. But you must read it.

(bk. II, ch. 9)

"I was a fish, and I shall be a crow. . . . What a spiritual mistress!" Tancred says to himself—and gets ready for his pilgrimage. Disraeli's satire here shows him at once abreast of the times and allergic to some of the inferences that were going to be hastily made from Charles Darwin's *Origin of Species* when it came out twelve years after *Tancred*. But on the eve of leaving England, Tancred agrees to consult one more oracle, none other than Sidonia. "It appears to me, Lord Montacute," this eminent Jewish banker says to him, "that what you want is to penetrate the great Asian mystery." If A. J. P. Taylor is right, and "Disraeli increased the obstacles in his path for the pleasure of overcoming them," then to introduce this theme of an "Asian mystery" was for once a miscalculation, for he never heard the end of it in his lifetime. And Taylor has declared that the reason why he never revealed the mystery was that there was nothing to reveal.

But there is really no doubt what the mystery was that Tancred set out to "penetrate" in the second and longer part of the book. Disraeli believed in "a divine reality substantial to the world of things and lives and minds" (Aldous Huxley's words), and it was this perennial philosophy that he hoped to convey in *Tancred*. In one view his mistake was to overemphasize the role of the Jewish people as the depository of divine revelation, though it is hardly for the stricter sort of Christians to find fault with this. On aesthetic grounds, though, they might recoil from Tancred's ardors and exaltations—and from the anticlimax of the end: "The Duke and Duchess of Bellamont have arrived in Jerusalem."

It happened that the year after *Tancred* was published, Sidonia's original, Baron Lionel de Rothschild, was elected member of Parliament for the City of London. He was not allowed to sit because, as a Jew, he could not take his oath "on the true faith of a Christian." The City voters went on obstinately reelecting him until the matter was at last put right under the second Derby-Disraeli administration in 1858. Disraeli had carried on the fight in the House of Commons, where most members were not very pleased when he reminded them—as he was to remind his readers in the preface to the fifth edition of *Coningsby:*

All the early Christians were Jews. The Christian religion was first preached by men who had been Jews till they were converted; every man in the early ages of the Church by whose power, or zeal, or genius the Christian faith was propagated, was a Jew.

This during the debate in December 1847 on Russell's motion to remove Jewish disabilities. The bill was passed by the Commons, but the Lords threw it out. Emancipation for the Jews was not to come until 1858.

Then, in chapter 24 of his life of his dead friend, the protectionist Lord George Bentinck (1852), Disraeli faced about and asked the Jews to consider it an honor that "the Queen of Heaven" should be a Jewess, and "that the redemption of the human race has been effected by a child of Israel": he was again preaching that Christianity is perfected Judaism. But the children of Israel were no more edified than the members of Parliament had been.

Anyhow, Rothschild was at last safely in the House of Commons. The funny part of it is that during his fifteen years there, 1858 to 1873, he sat not uttering a word.

V

AFTER the life of Bentinck there was a break of nearly twenty years in Disraeli's literary production. The time for action had come. In 1852 he was chancellor of the exchequer under Stanley, now earl of Derby, and Queen Victoria told her uncle: "Mr Disraeli (*alias* Dizzy) writes very curious reports to me . . . much in the style of his books." Twenty-five years later such reports had become one of her chief pleasures in life, and their author was her intimate friend. Disraeli was in office again with Derby in 1866; their Reform Bill of 1867 gave urban working-class men the vote; in 1868, Derby retired and Disraeli was for the first time prime minister. "By God!" Melbourne would have exclaimed if he had been alive. "The fellow has done it!"

Some months later the government fell. Cheerfully the Tory leader, who was now sixty-five, sat down and wrote a novel, *Lothair*, which appeared twenty-three years after *Tancred*. The idea for the story was put into Disraeli's head by the conversion to Catholicism of the wealthy young marquess of Bute, so the Lothair of the book is again a youth of high degree, like Tancred, wondering "what I ought to DO, and what I ought to BELIEVE." Cardinal Grandison is Henry Manning—who, Disraeli had reason to feel, had let him down over his Irish church policy. Some of the satire in the book is extremely amusing, but nobody can be blind to the earnestness of the author's concern with faith and with principle.

Unlike Tancred, Lothair does not at first strike out on a line of his own; indeed, he is, or appears to be, so malleable that Leslie Stephen said he was "unpleasantly like a fool." But the fools of life or fiction are not necessarily unpleasant, nor does it much matter if Lothair was susceptible. On the contrary, it would have been fatal if he had not been, since the plot and purpose of the book require him to respond to three young women representing three attitudes to duty and belief, and in the end to point Disraeli's moral by getting himself tied up with the right one. Robert Blake agrees with G. W. E. Russell in thinking *Lothair* to be Disraeli's masterpiece—as well they might, considering, among other things, his skill in creating the three heroines. These were the apostle of international revolution, the beautiful and passionately committed Theodora Campian; the charming and pious Roman Catholic, Clare Arundel; and Lady Corisande. The superb duke, her father, is believed to have been modeled on the handsome marquess of Abercorn, whom Disraeli had raised to a dukedom in 1868. When Lothair has nearly lost his life at Mentana, fighting for Garibaldi against the successful French defenders of Rome, it is Clare who nurses him back to health. But when he sees the "official" papal account of what happened, he is startled. He expostulates with Cardinal Grandison:

"Good God!" exclaimed Lothair. "Why! take the very first allegation, that I fell at Mentana fighting in the ranks of the Holy Father. Everyone knows that I fell fighting against him, and that I was almost slain by one of his chassepots. It is notorious. . . ."

. . .

"I know there are two narratives of your relations with the battle of Mentana," observed the Cardinal quietly. "The one accepted as authentic is that which appears in this journal; the other account, which can only be traced to yourself, bears no doubt a somewhat different character, but . . . it is in the highest degree improbable. . . ." "I think," said Lothair, with a kindling eye and a burning cheek, "that I am the best judge of what I did at Mentana."

"Well, well," said the Cardinal with dulcet calmness, "you naturally think so, but you must remember you have been very ill, my dear young friend, and labouring under much excitement."

(ch. 68)

Though Disraeli gives Lady Corisande the least striking personality of the three young women, he has the art to make it seem inevitable that she should be Lothair's fate. She is in the disciplined English tradition, Anglican, and moderate—three very good things to be, according to his mature opinion, in a dangerous world. Europe seemed to have passed into an age of conspiracy. The agitations of those rival dissentients, Giuseppe Mazzini and Giuseppe Garibaldi, were nothing to what might be expected if Karl Marx or his rival, the anarchist Mikhail Bakunin, had his way. Together with all the regular Disraelian features, *Lothair* offers a disturbing picture of movements of which the author saw the unfolding pattern in clearer focus than most people in England.

Gladstone had another four years in power. It was at a Gladstone reception that Disraeli hit off their mutual antipathy in a remark as tactful as it is witty. When one of the Gladstone girls asked him to identify a foreign grandee for her, he answered: "That, my dear young lady, is the most dangerous statesman in Europe—except, as your father would say, myself . . . or, as I should prefer to put it, your father."

In 1874 came Disraeli's great chance. One must pause and ask: Chance of what? What were his political principles and aims?

Only a little reflection will prepare a student of history for finding a world of difference between political thought and political thinking. Consider Ernest Walker's admirably succinct *Political Thought in England, 1848–1914*. In the index we find twenty-four references to Jeremy Bentham (1748–1832) and many more than that to Herbert Spencer

(1820–1903), whereas for Disraeli and Gladstone (1809–1898) there are only two each. Yet it was these two practitioners, as one might put it, who dominated the English political scene more consistently than anyone else in the second half of the nineteenth century. Philosophizing is one thing, governing is another. England in Disraeli's lifetime was undergoing quicker and more unforeseen change than any other country before the Industrial Revolution, of which England was the pioneer. When he was born, in 1804, the population was about eight million; it had trebled by the year of his death. Railways and steamships were transforming communications in the 1860's. Illiteracy was not seriously tackled until 1870. And there were the problems of foreign policy—the rise of Prussia and the indirect threat from Russia, against whom England fought in the Crimean War (1853–1856). Then, near the end of Disraeli's life, there was the Eastern Question.

However, governing is not merely pragmatical and, short of an ideology, a statesman deserving this title will have his ideals or principles, which need not be (and in Disraeli's case certainly were not) "my party right or wrong." He did not get his seat in the House of Commons until he had stood and been defeated four times—the first three times as a Radical. Before long, as a Tory, he was fighting his chief, Robert Peel, over the repeal of the Corn Laws; this was not how a young politician showed himself a careerist. Indeed, Disraeli was a man of conscience much as the great Lord Halifax (1633–1695), nicknamed "the Trimmer" by his adversaries, had been. Britain did not have the same kind of party government in Halifax's day that began in 1721, when Robert Walpole was prime minister; but parties and, inevitably, a ruling party are an old story. Halifax gloried in his nickname, since his trimming was aimed at keeping or arriving at fair compromises. Disraeli, possessing a sense of the past that was as realistic as it was romantic and, at the same time (as he so vividly showed in *Sybil*), an acute awareness of the need for social reform in the industrial age, did not wish to see the baby thrown out with the bathwater. What was good in England, such as an established church and a class of landed gentry with a sense of responsibility for their less privileged fellow citizens, was not to be impetuously reformed away. In *Coningsby* he had written that his idea of a sound Conservative government was "Tory men and Whig measures," and when he said in 1867 that he had "dished the Whigs" he only meant that he (serving under Lord Stanley) had contrived to do what Gladstone (serving under Russell) would have done if the Whigs had not been ousted two years earlier. Nevertheless, on succeeding Stanley in 1868 he was only able to stay in office for a few months. He was not back until 1874, for his one long, and final, term as prime minister.

In the next six fruitful years he sponsored a good deal of domestic legislation. His laws benefited sailors, shop assistants, the trade union movement, and, by a public health act, the nation as a whole. This is not to say that buying the Suez Canal company shares in 1875, with the Rothschilds' help, or making Queen Victoria empress of India did not have their significance. And there was the congress of Berlin in 1878, where Bismarck, who was much impressed, said: "The old Jew—that's the man!" Disraeli himself said he had brought back "Peace with Honour." His reports to his Royal Mistress were not too stuffily official. On 13 June 1878 he wrote to her:

At two o'clock the Congress met in the Radetsky Palace—a noble hall just restored and becoming all the golden coats and glittering stars that filled it. Ld. B. believes that every day is not to be so ceremonious and costumish. P. Bismarck, a giant, 6 feet 2 at least, and proportionately huge, was chosen President. In the course of the morn, P. Gortchakoff, a shrivelled old man, was leaning on the arm of his gigantic rival, and, P. Bismarck being seized with a sudden fit of rheumatism, both fell to the ground. Unhappily, P. Bismarck's dog, seeing his master apparently struggling with an opponent, sprang to the rescue. It is said that P. Gortchakoff was not maimed or bitten through the energetic efforts of his companion.

What had all the wrangling at Berlin been about? The massacring of Bulgarians by the unpredictable Turks had given Russia a chance to intervene in a cause that was naturally as much political as humanitarian. In March 1878, a Russian army reached Constantinople, and the defeated sultan was forced to sign the Treaty of San Stefano, which was unacceptable to the other Great Powers—especially to the British, who had imperial responsibilities in the East. Disraeli threatened the Russians with war unless they submitted the treaty to a European congress. The essentials of a compromise were reached by him and the Russian war minister even before the congress met at Berlin to replace the treaty.

"Peace with Honour"? There were some doubts

about this from the start. A little dog-Latin rhyme became popular:

> Ubi sunt provinciae
> Quas est laus pacasse?
> Totae, totae sunt partitae—
> Has tulerunt Muscoviti
> Illas Count Andrasse.

Meaning that, apart from Russia's own gains, Austria had gotten Bosnia and Herzegovina as her share of the spoils when the Turkish frontiers had been thrust back by the treaty—but not as far back as the Bosphorus. This and the Turks' thanksoffering of the island of Cyprus to Britain were Disraeli's achievements. And, indeed, the avoidance of a great war.

Less than two years later, in April 1880, Disraeli's ministry fell. He was seventy-five, afflicted with gout, bronchitis, and asthma—and yet, by August he had put the finishing touches to his last complete novel, *Endymion*. He dedicated it to the charming grandmother, Lady Bradford, with whom he was conducting a romantic and rather uninhibited flirtation. "I owe everything to woman," he had once written to her. This was not correct, but as G. E. Buckle says, "of Endymion, the hero of his last novel, it is true."

In the story Endymion, with the help of his sister, his wife, and other devoted women, becomes prime minister at the age of forty—as Disraeli wished he could have done. As in his other political novels, the treatment of situations and the elucidation of ideas have priority, while the dialogues between the secondary figures—taken from life by that shrewd observer—contribute an extraordinary vivaciousness besides offering what to readers then was a spice of gossip, and to readers now is living history. *Endymion* has more portraits than any of its predecessors, a tremendous gallery of them, British and foreign. Disraeli once told Sir Charles Dilke that *he* had been the model for Endymion. Manning reappears: as the archbishop of Tyre this time—a more friendly figure than "Grandison" (by now Manning had quarreled with Gladstone). Samuel Wilberforce is the bishop, and Dickens is Gushy. Thackeray (St. Barbe) is unjustly treated; he was no more just a snob than Dizzy himself was just an oriental snake charmer.

More than fifty years had passed since Vivian Grey had made his bold bid for a worldly success that in the end had eluded him, perhaps because his worldly wisdom, like his creator's at the time, had left so much to be desired. *Endymion*, on the other hand, is pervaded by "the experience of the states-man who had taken his full share in the direction of great affairs." It is a more tolerant book than *Lothair* or the Young England trilogy, and less idealistic—except that Disraeli showed he had never lost his confidence in youth, as he had also proved when in power by going out of his way to help promising young men.

How does one sum Disraeli up as a writer? George Saintsbury, who admired his novels, said nobody had ever quite known how to classify them. Indeed, according to Lord David Cecil, "For all their brilliance, they are not strictly speaking novels." (What, "strictly speaking," *is* a novel, then?) And, according to Leslie Stephen, "He was not exactly a humourist, but something for which the rough nomenclature of critics has not yet provided a distinctive name." However, we have already noted that Stephen looked on *Sybil* as all but a first-rate novel. Lord Blake concedes that much Disraelian conversation is uttered by persons who are "humours," like the people in those fascinating stories by Thomas Love Peacock; "but, if neither Disraeli nor Peacock wrote novels in the usual sense of the word, what they wrote was more like the novel than anything else." And anyhow, "humours," or what E. M. Forster called "flat" characters, may be so because they are caricatures (see for instance Dickens), and since there is a general disposition among perhaps most human beings to caricature themselves, the loss to realism is not compensated. Anthony Trollope detested the whole body of his work, and spoke of it as if it consisted entirely of stories about people whose way of life he disapproved of, ignoring the salient fact that, as V. S. Pritchett put it in his essay on Disraeli in *The Living Novel* (1946): "The novels of Disraeli tell us everything." Given his talents and temperament, and the circumstances of his career, Disraeli was certainly in a position to tell us a great deal. It is not a reproach if he runs on more about some things (high society and politics) and less about others than we get from more introvert authors who had not kept such a varied company nor been so interested in the social mechanism. Trollope might have found writing his political novels a severer task if Disraeli had not blazed the trail for him.

Of Disraeli's poems, early and rather derivative work, there is perhaps no need to say much here; *The Revolutionary Epick* is indeterminate, and though *Alarcos*, dramatized, had a certain succès d'estime at the time, it is not a thriller we are likely to see revived.

Of his prose fiction one can pronounce, uncontroversially, that, like his career, it is unique. He knew as well as anyone what was peculiar about his books. Hadn't he in earlier days said of *Henrietta Temple* and *Venetia* that they "dealt with feelings more enduring than public passions"? It was nevertheless on public passions that he had concentrated—on them and on faith and principle (neither of them commonly the main course in a work of fiction). In a word, from the common reader's point of view, the tone of Disraeli's novels is provokingly—or for a change agreeably—far removed from, say, the atmosphere of intimate tensions prevailing in *Wuthering Heights*, which is also unique and, of course, a work of genius.

Lord Blake has summed up Disraeli's dual achievement as writer and statesman, as follows:

Disraeli was in many ways a very unVictorian figure. . . . Disraeli was a sceptic and a romantic. Optimistic and cheerful about his own career, which he saw as a colourful adventure story, he was less optimistic about the extent to which human endeavour could improve the lot of humanity. His views were the opposite to those of Macaulay. The spirit of strenuous moral effort, belief in progress, faith in the efficacy of representative institutions, confidence in material prosperity, struck no echo in his mind. "Progress to what and from where? The European talks of progress, because by an ingenious application of some scientific acquirements he has established a society which mistakes comfort for civilization."

This scepticism makes Disraeli a less "dated" figure than almost any other contemporary politician. . . . It is hard to imagine Gladstone living in any other period, whereas it is quite easy to envisage Disraeli living either today or in the era of Lord North. It is this timelessness which gives his best novels their lasting fascination and makes his wit as good now as it was a hundred years ago. . . . No Prime Minister has received and deserved more space in the dictionary of quotations. He also had a rare detachment and an extraordinary ability to survey the scene from outside and to wonder what it was all about.[3]

VI

ONCE *Endymion* was out, Disraeli went to it again. He had written nine chapters of yet another novel when the pen almost literally dropped from his hand at the end of the first paragraph of chapter 10. The unfinished book (which can be read in an appendix to volume V of Monypenny and Buckle's *Life*) had the old satirical touch; it was to be about a man

[3]R. Blake, *Disraeli* (London, 1966).

called Falconet, a thinly disguised Gladstone, and about the spirit of revolution that had come into the world—and to which Falconet may have been going to succumb.

But the cold January of 1881 proved fatal to the earl of Beaconsfield (as he had become in 1876). "I beg you will be very good and obey the doctors," the queen wrote to him; but his time was up and, on 19 April, he died in London. He comes to life again like no other statesman when we open one of his books. When we shut it, it is with an encouraging (not, as it could be, an alarming) sense of the truth of Alroy's affirmation: "By what Man has done we learn what Man can do, and gauge the power and prospects of our race."

VII

COULD Disraeli have earned his living by writing novels? By writing, probably, if he had set his mind to it; not at first by novels only. As things were, he did not get much for his early works; and it was not until he was forty that the tide turned with *Coningsby* (1844). He made about £2,000 each from *Coningsby* and *Sybil* (1845), and a little less from *Tancred* (1847), so this trilogy brought him nearly £34,000 within five years, in terms of today's value of the pound. This was not bad going, considering that his real political prominence dated only from 1852. In 1870 came *Lothair*, from which he made in all £10,000 (today £120,000), and of course by this time he was famous. It is interesting to note that halfway between *Lothair* and *Endymion*, Trollope published *The Way We Live* (1875), made into a television film by the BBC; it was one of his best sellers and earned him £6,000.

Longman had offered £7,500 for *Endymion*, but Disraeli's private secretary, Lord Rowton (Montagu Lowry Corry), persuaded him to raise the figure to £10,000. When the book did not seem to be catching on, Disraeli very decently offered to cancel the agreement. Longman as generously refused to accept. Then the cheap edition of 1881 sold well—a happy ending for both parties.

SELECTED BIBLIOGRAPHY

I. BIBLIOGRAPHY. M. Sadleir, *Excursions in Victorian Bibliography* (London, 1922), contains a bibliography of Disraeli; R. Blake, *Disraeli* (London, 1966), contains the best bibliography of Disraeli; R. W. Stewart, ed., *Disraeli: A List of Writings by Him and Writings About Him* (Metuchen, N. J., 1972), with notes.

II. COLLECTED WORKS. *Collected Edition of the Novels and Tales*, 10 vols. (London, 1870–1871); *Novels and Tales*, 11 vols. (London, 1881), the Hughenden ed.; P. Guedalla, ed., *The Novels and Tales*, 12 vols. (London, 1926–1927), with intro. by Guedalla; *The Novels*, 11 vols. (London, 1927–1928). *Note:* For MS collections see R. Blake's *Disraeli* (see BIBLIOGRAPHY above), p. 781.

III. NOVELS. *Vivian Grey*, vols. I–II (London, 1826), vols. III–V (London, 1827), also in L. Wolf, ed., 2 vols. (London, 1904); *The Voyage of Captain Popanilla* (London, 1828), also with *Alroy* in W. S. Northcote, ed. (London, 1906); *The Young Duke*, 3 vols. (London, 1831), also in W. S. Northcote, ed. (London, 1906); *Contarini Fleming: A Psychological Auto-biography*, 4 vols. (London, 1832), also in W. S. Northcote, ed. (London, 1905); *The Wondrous Tale of Alroy* and *The Rise of Iskander*, 3 vols. (London, 1833), also with *Popanilla* in W. S. Northcote, ed. (London, 1906); *Henrietta Temple: A Love Story*, 3 vols. (London, 1837), also in W. S. Northcote, ed. (London, 1906); *Venetia: Or the Poet's Daughter*, 3 vols. (London, 1837), also in W. S. Northcote, ed. (London, 1905); *Coningsby; or, The New Generation*, 3 vols. (London, 1844), also in L. N. Langdon-Davies, ed. (London, 1911) and in A. Maurois, ed. (London, 1931), the World's Classics ed.; and see *Anti-Coningsby: or The Generation Grown Old* (London, 1844) and *Strictures on Coningsby* (London, 1844); *Sybil: or The Two Nations*, 3 vols. (London, 1845), also in W. S. Northcote, ed. (London, 1905), W. Sichel, ed. (London, 1925), the World's Classics ed. (London, 1925), V. Cohen, ed. (London, 1934), and T. Brown, ed. (Harmondsworth, 1954), with intro. by R. A. Butler, the Penguin English Library ed.; *Tancred: or, The New Crusade*, 3 vols. (London, 1847), also in W. S. Northcote, ed. (London, 1905); *Ixion in Heaven, The Infernal Marriage, Popanilla, Count Alarcos* (London, 1853), also in W. S. Northcote, ed. (London, 1906), *Ixion in Heaven* and *The Infernal Marriage* repr. separately in 1925 and 1929 respectively, *Ixion in Heaven* repr. in 1927 with W. E. Aytoun's burlesque *Endymion; or, A Family Party on Olympus* and with a preface by E. Partridge; *Lothair*, 3 vols. (London, 1870); *Endymion*, 3 vols. (London, 1880); *Tales and Sketches* (London, 1891), with a prefatory memoir by J. L. Robertson.

IV. VERSE. *The Revolutionary Epick*, 2 vols. (London, 1834; rev. ed., 1864), also with other poems in W. D. Adams, ed. (London, 1904); *The Tragedy of Count Alarcos* (London, 1839), also with *Ixion in Heaven* and *Alroy* in W. S. Northcote, ed. (London, 1906); *The Dunciad of Today: A Satire; and, The Modern Aesop* (London, 1928), with an intro. by M. Sadleir.

V. POLITICAL WRITINGS. *Lord George Bentinck: A Political Biography* (London, 1852), also in C. Whibley, ed. (London, 1905); W. Hutcheon, ed., *Whigs and Whiggism: Political Writings* (London, 1913), includes the following treatises first published separately as dated: *What Is He?* (1833); *The Crisis Examined* (1834); *Vindication of the English Constitution* (1835); *Letters of Runnymede* (1836); *The Spirit of Whiggism* (1836). *Note:* The most complete list of Disraeli's political and other writings is that compiled by R. W. Stewart and printed as Appendix II in R. Blake's *Disraeli* (see BIBLIOGRAPHY above).

VI. LETTERS. A. Birrell, ed., *Letters, 1830–1852* (London, 1928), includes *Home Letters* (1830–1831) and *Disraeli's Correspondence with His Sister* (1886), both originally ed. by R. Disraeli and first repr. together as *Lord Beaconsfield's Letters 1830–52* (London, 1887); Lord Zetland, ed., *Letters to Lady Bradford and Lady Chesterfield*, 2 vols. (London, 1929); *Letters to Frances Anne, Marchioness of Londonderry, 1837–61* (London, 1938).

VII. SPEECHES. *Church and Queen. Five Speeches, 1860–1864* (London, 1865); M. Corry, ed., *Speeches on Parliamentary Reform, 1848–66* (London, 1867); J. F. Bulley, ed., *Speeches on the Conservative Policy of the Last Thirty Years* (London, 1870); *Selected Speeches*, 2 vols. (London, 1882), with notes by T. E. Lebbel; H. W. J. Edwards, ed., *The Radical Tory. Disraeli's Political Development. Illustrated from His Original Writings and Speeches* (London, 1937).

VIII. BIOGRAPHICAL AND CRITICAL STUDIES. J. Manners [Duchess of Rutland], *Some Personal Recollections of the Later Years of the Earl of Beaconsfield* (London, 1881); T. P. O'Connor, *Lord Beaconsfield* (London, 1884); J. A. Froude, *Lord Beaconsfield* (London, 1890); H. Lake, *Personal Reminiscences of Beaconsfield* (London, 1891); W. Meynell, *Disraeli. An Unconventional Biography* (London, 1903; rev. ed., 1927); W. Sichel, *Disraeli* (London, 1904); W. F. Monypenny and G. E. Buckle, *The Life of Benjamin Disraeli, Earl of Beaconsfield*, 6 vols. (London, 1910–1920; rev. ed., 2 vols., 1929), indispensable; D. C. Somervell, *Disraeli and Gladstone* (London, 1925); E. G. Clarke, *Benjamin Disraeli 1804–81* (London, 1926); A Maurois, *La Vie de Disraeli* (Paris, 1927; English trans., London, 1928); D. L. Murray, *Disraeli* (London, 1927); E. Thane, *Young Mr. Disraeli* (New York, 1936); R. G. Stapledon, *Disraeli and the New Age* (London, 1943); A. Powell, *Novels of High Society* (London, 1947); M. Masefield, *Peacocks and Primroses, a Survey of Disraeli's Novels* (London, 1953); K. Tillotson, *Novels of the Eighteen-Forties* (London, 1954); B. R. Jerman, *The Young Disraeli* (Princeton, N. J., 1961), contains some new material; R. W. Seton-Watson, *Disraeli, Gladstone and the Eastern Question* (London, 1962); R. Blake, *Disraeli* (London, 1966), in certain respects supersedes even Monypenny and Buckle; D. Cowling, *Disraeli, Gladstone and Revolution: 1867* (London, 1967); D. Feuchtwanger,

Disraeli, Democracy and the Tory Party (London, 1968); R. W. Stewart, ed., *Disraeli's Novels Reviewed (1826–1968)* (London, 1975); D. Sultana, *Disraeli in Spain, Malta and Albania (1830–1832)* (London, 1976); J. R. Vincent, ed., *Disraeli, Derby and the Conservative Party: The Political Journals of Lord Stanley (1849–1869)* (London, 1977); T. Aronson, *Queen Victoria and Disraeli* (London, 1977); C. Hibbert, *Disraeli and His World* (London–New York, 1978); R. Schwarz, *Disraeli's Fiction* (London, 1979).

ELIZABETH BARRETT BROWNING

(1806-1861)

Alethea Hayter

I

When Wordsworth died, just halfway through the nineteenth century, and a successor for him as poet laureate had to be found, the claims of Elizabeth Barrett Browning to succeed him were seriously canvassed. It was suggested that a female poet laureate would be particularly suitable when a woman was on the throne of England, but the influential *Athenaeum* flatly stated that in any case no living poet of either sex had a higher claim than Mrs. Browning's. This seems to us a startling pronouncement to have been made on the same day—1 June 1850—on which *In Memoriam* was published. Tennyson in fact got the laureateship, to Mrs. Browning's satisfaction, though she had thought Leigh Hunt ought to have it; not even she had thought of Browning as a possible candidate.

The suggestion that a female sovereign should have a female poet laureate seemed foolish enough to Mrs. Browning. She thought of herself as a poet, not a poetess; she considered that poetry should be judged by its merits, not by the sex of its writers. "When I talk of women, I do not speak of them . . . according to a separate, peculiar, and womanly standard, but according to the common standard of human nature," she said. But it has never been possible for critics to disentangle Mrs. Browning from her sex. She was always being classed by her contemporaries as the top woman poet (generally bracketed with Sappho), not simply as a good, or very good, or fairly good poet. No such woman writer would probably come again for a millennium, wrote Sydney Dobell unprophetically in 1850; but he went on to say that no woman writer, not even Mrs. Browning, would ever write a great poem. "She was a woman of real genius, I know; but what is the upshot of it all? She and her sex had better mind the kitchen and the children," said Edward FitzGerald. Elizabeth Barrett Browning was as much obscured as

a poet by her sex and her personal legend as Byron was by his. It is therefore difficult to assess her achievement as objectively as that of other nineteenth-century poets such as Coventry Patmore, or Arthur Hugh Clough, or George Meredith, with whom she might reasonably be classed; but she has in fact much more in common with them than with Christina Rossetti or Emily Brontë.

II

Elizabeth Barrett was born on 6 March 1806 at Coxhoe Hall in Durham. She was the eldest of the twelve children of Edward Moulton Barrett and his wife Mary. When she was three years old, the family moved to Hope End in Herefordshire, and she spent the next twenty-three years of her life in this minareted country house overlooking a lake and deep in a wooded park. Here she produced her juvenilia: *The Battle of Marathon*, an epic poem written when she was thirteen and privately printed by her father in 1820; *An Essay on Mind, with Other Poems*, published in 1826; a number of poems published in magazines; and a good deal of verse, including one long poem, "The Development of Genius," which remained unpublished in her lifetime. Encouraged by two neighbors, the scholars Hugh Stuart Boyd and Uvedale Price, she made a thorough study of classical and Byzantine Greek literature, and of prosody. Apart from a severe but unidentified illness in 1821, she led a normal social and family life during all these years.

In 1832 financial losses forced her father to sell Hope End and move with his children (his wife had died in 1828) first to Sidmouth, in Devonshire, and then in 1835 to London. In 1833, Elizabeth Barrett published a volume containing a translation of the *Prometheus Bound* of Aeschylus, and some short poems, but neither this nor her earlier volumes (all published anonymously) attracted much notice. Her first real success was achieved with *The Seraphim, and Other Poems*, published in 1838 under her own name, which was given long and mainly favorable reviews in the leading journals.

The literary scene on which Elizabeth Barrett entered in the late 1830's was comparatively empty —an undistinguished pause between two great periods of creative writing. Wordsworth, Leigh Hunt, and Walter Savage Landor were the patriarchs of the day, but their best work was past; Tennyson, Browning, Dickens, Carlyle had published their first works, but their great achievement and fame were still to come; Thackeray, Ruskin, and the Brontës were still just below the literary horizon. The admired writers of the day were Field Talfourd, Harriet Martineau, Harrison Ainsworth, Mary Russell Mitford, Thomas Hood, Edward Bulwer-Lytton, Barry Cornwall, Felicia Hemans, Letitia Landon, and Sheridan Knowles. Among these writers Elizabeth Barrett began to make friends and a place for herself. Her ill health and her family circumstances prevented her from going out much into the social life of London, but she embarked on exchanges of letters with literary figures which were to influence both her writing and her life. Among her correspondents were Wordsworth, Edgar Allan Poe, Carlyle, Harriet Martineau, Mary Russell Mitford (who gave her Flush, her spaniel), John Kenyon, R. H. Horne, and the painter Benjamin Robert Haydon. They exchanged criticisms and appreciations of each other's work, discussed other writers of the day and the ethics and techniques of their profession; Elizabeth Barrett was at last enjoying the stimulus of intellectual equality which had been missing from her secluded childhood and adolescence.

In 1837 her health broke down, her lungs were affected, and she was sent from London to the milder climate of Torquay. Her family took it in turns to stay with her there; and while her eldest brother Edward, nicknamed Bro, was prolonging his stay at Torquay at her entreaty, he went out sailing and was drowned. His sister's lasting grief altered and in some ways strengthened her character.

She came back to London in 1841, still very much of an invalid, and plunged into literary work—book reviews, articles, translations, contributions to symposia. This productive period culminated in the two-volume *Poems* of 1844, the most popular of all her works until *Aurora Leigh* with both the critics and

the public. One poem in this collection, "Lady Geraldine's Courtship," referred favorably to the work of Robert Browning, and he wrote to Elizabeth Barrett to thank her. So began, on 10 January 1845, a correspondence which led to their first meeting four months later. On the day after he had first seen Elizabeth Barrett, Browning sent her a declaration of love, which disturbed her so much that he had to disclaim it before she would consent to receive him again; and it was only gradually, with devoted patience, that he was able to convince her of the reality of his love, to make her avow hers, and to get her consent to an engagement. For a whole year they wrote to each other almost daily, sometimes twice a day, and he called on her every few days. More frequent visits would have aroused suspicion. Mr. Barrett's immovable objection to the marriage of any of his children enforced secrecy on Browning and Elizabeth Barrett until they had left for Italy, a week after their marriage on 12 September 1846.

After some months in Pisa, the Brownings moved to Florence, which was to be their base for the rest of Mrs. Browning's life; from 1848 they kept a permanent residence there, Casa Guidi, though they were often away from it for many months at a time, on visits to Rome, to Lucca, to Siena. In 1849 the poets' only child, a son christened Wiedeman, but afterward nicknamed Pennini or Pen, was born. The Brownings visited London four times during the 1850's, and renewed their friendships in its literary world. They also spent two winters in Paris, where they got to know many French writers, and were witnesses of some of the most striking events in the rise to power of Napoleon III. Mrs. Browning became increasingly absorbed in European politics, particularly the political development of Italy and France, and this preoccupation was reflected in the poetry which she wrote in the last ten years of her life. She also became deeply, almost obsessively, interested in spiritualism, though her credulity was tempered by occasional flashes of common sense.

In the 1840's and 1850's Elizabeth Barrett Browning's poetic reputation was at its height, and made her a serious candidate for the poet laureateship. The four books of poetry which she published between 1846 and 1861 were: the first collected edition of her poetry, published in 1850 and including, as well as the best of the 1838 and 1844 poems, some new lyrics and the celebrated "Sonnets from the Portuguese," addressed to her husband; *Casa Guidi Windows*, a partly political poem about Italy, which appeared in

1851; *Aurora Leigh*, a modern epic or "novel in verse," as she called it, which was published in 1857 and won immense acclaim; and *Poems Before Congress* (1860), again political in inspiration and deservedly less popular than any other work of her maturity. This was the last book which she published in her lifetime. Her health, which had greatly improved with the happiness and the change of climate which her marriage and her move to Italy brought her, weakened again after she had reached the peak of her achievement in *Aurora Leigh*, and she died in Florence on 29 June 1861.

Last Poems, containing some of her most famous lyrics, was published posthumously in 1862. Since then many of her unpublished poems, especially her juvenilia, have appeared in small collections, and many volumes of her letters have been published in England and in America, where most of the surviving original letters are now. The most famous of these volumes of correspondence is her exchange of love letters with Robert Browning, a unique interplay of genius and passion. The best of the other collections of Elizabeth Barrett Browning's letters are those to R. H. Horne, Mary Russell Mitford, and Benjamin Robert Haydon, full of comment on contemporary literature, art, and social problems; the letters to H. S. Boyd, chiefly concerned with Greek scholarship and metrical experiments; and the letters to her sister Henrietta and her brother George, which give a picture of her family and daily life. The best selection from her general correspondence is still Frederic Kenyon's two-volume one, published in 1897, though it necessarily omits a good deal of interesting biographical material which has appeared since then.

Even the baldest statement of the main events in Elizabeth Barrett Browning's life reveals an exceptional character and destiny. She was a fortunate woman. She had a happy childhood and, even after she grew up, a family life in which she never lacked affection, companionship, and admiration for her talents, however much she was deprived of sympathetic understanding and of freedom. She experienced keen pleasure from the study of languages and literature, and had the leisure to indulge the taste fully. In middle life, when she seemed a confirmed invalid, she met and married a great poet who devotedly loved her. She had a charming and intelligent child; she lived in the most beautiful cities of Italy; she never experienced any real want of money; she had many devoted friends, who included most of the

great writers of the day. She was convinced that she herself was born to be a poet, she was intensely happy writing poetry, and she had splendid success with her poems when they were published. She died without pain or lingering.

Her good fortune was due to the strength and integrity of her character as much as to her innate talents and her social and economic advantages. She had to overcome crippling ill health, the loss of a dearly loved brother, and the unforgiving tyranny and hardness of her father. To achieve this, and to make such a success of her personal and professional life, required a toughness of will, a generosity of heart, a healthiness of mind which have not always been recognized in Elizabeth Barrett Browning, whose willpower and fierce mental energy have been somewhat obscured by her legend of invalidism and ringlets.

III

"A genuine poetess of no common order," said the *Examiner* of Elizabeth Barrett when reviewing *The Seraphim, and Other Poems*, which was published in 1838 and widely praised. The title poem, a lyrical drama on the Crucifixion as seen through the eyes of two mourning archangels, is an ambitious, uneven work full of imagination, of mystical visions of the red primeval heats of creation still forever burning from the heavenly Throne and casting fiery shadows on the crystal sea; of the whole hierarchy of Heaven attendant on the hill of Golgotha:

> Beneath us sinks the pomp angelical,
> Cherub and seraph, powers and virtues, all,
> The roar of whose descent has died
> To a still sound, as thunder into rain.
> Immeasurable space spreads magnified
> With that thick life, along the plane
> The worlds slid out on.[1]
> (*The Seraphim*, pt.I, 18–24)

The volume also contained several shorter poems, such as "The Deserted Garden," "The Sleep," and "Cowper's Grave," which have always been popular with the anthologists. In this volume, too, appeared the first of the ballads which Elizabeth Barrett

[1]All quotations from the poetry are from the *Poetical Works, with Two Prose Essays* (London, 1920).

Browning's contemporaries loved best of all her works. Poems such as "The Romaunt of Margret," "Isobel's Child," and "The Lay of the Brown Rosary" (the last was published in 1844), in which the challenge between Love and Death is played out over and over again, with Death always triumphing, have a haunting Gothic strangeness and necromancy which is a persistent mood in nineteenth-century English poetry; from "Christabel" and "La Belle Dame sans Merci" and "The Lady of Shalott," it runs through Mrs. Browning's ballads, and on from them to influence Dante Gabriel Rossetti's "Sister Helen" and William Morris' "The Blue Closet."

Most of Elizabeth Barrett Browning's religious poetry also dates from the volume of 1838: not only "The Seraphim" but also such lyrics as "The Soul's Travelling," "The Virgin Mary to the Child Jesus," and "Cowper's Grave," in which she meditated on mystical experiences and on the problem of reconciling belief in Divine Love with the suffering and the evils of the world—the problem which tormented so many of her contemporaries, above all Tennyson as he wrote *In Memoriam*. Most of these early religious poems of Mrs. Browning's, though intense in feeling, are diffuse and undisciplined in expression; but in a few of the lyrics written at this time she achieved an economy of words which startles the reader by its fineness, as in "My Doves," her poem about the imprisonment of city streets and the longing for escape. Most of the poem is musically sweet, rather than strong, as when she describes the cooing of the doves who share her imprisonment:

> . . . Of living loves
> Theirs hath the calmest fashion,
> Their living voice the likest moves
> To lifeless intonation,
> The lovely monotone of springs,
> And winds, and such insensate things.
>
> (st. 4)

Then she surprises the reader with the unadorned fitness of her conclusion, in which, renouncing the hope of airy shores and silent, dewy fields, she says:

> My spirit and my God shall be
> My seaward hill, my boundless sea.
>
> (st. 14)

This concentration is rare in her work; she achieved it in "A Sabbath Morning at Sea," in "A Seaside Walk," in snatches of "The Poet's Vow" and "Night

and the Merry Man," but most completely in "A Reed":

> I am no trumpet, but a reed;
> Go, tell the fishers, as they spread
> Their nets along the river's edge,
> I will not tear their nets at all,
> Nor pierce their hands, if they should fall:
> Then let them leave me in the sedge.
>
> (st. 3)

Elizabeth Barrett's next volumes of poems, published in 1844, showed a development and hardening of her character and style. Illness, bereavement, approaching middle age had made her less dreamy and more confident, even aggressive in her mannerisms. The 1844 volumes include her most advanced prosodic experiments, some of which seemed barbarous innovations to her contemporaries, but have many parallels in mid-twentieth-century poetry. Her political and social opinions were also growing more definite. Two poems in the 1844 volumes, "The Cry of the Children" and "The Cry of the Human," were militant attacks on the employment of child labor in factories, and on the protectionists who kept up the price of bread; the poems were widely commented on, and influenced public opinion in favor of reform. There is more intellect, and a more individual character, in the 1844 *Poems* than in Elizabeth Barrett Browning's earlier works, and the volumes had a considerable success with the critics and the public; but in a good many of them there is a note of wildness and exaggeration which has caused subsequent literary historians to class Mrs. Browning with the poets who were nicknamed the Spasmodic School, and were attacked for their overstrained hyperbole, subjectivism, and lack of discipline. Two of the longer poems in Elizabeth Barrett's 1844 volumes—"A Drama of Exile," a strange, cloudy work on the expulsion of Adam and Eve from Paradise, and "A Rhapsody of Life's Progress"—do almost justify her classification as a Spasmodic. But these same uneven volumes also contain some of her finest and most disciplined sonnets. Some, like "Futurity" or the lapidary "Grief," commemorate her brother's death and her struggle to accept her loss of him; some, like "The Soul's Expression" and "The Prisoner," are analyses of the workings of poetic inspiration:

> I count the dismal time by months and years,
> Since last I felt the green sward under foot,

And the great breath of all things summer-mute
Met mine upon my lips. Now earth appears
As strange to me as dreams of distant spheres,
Or thoughts of Heaven we weep at. Nature's lute
Sounds on behind this door so closely shut,
A strange, wild music to the prisoner's ears,
Dilated by the distance, till the brain
Grows dim with fancies which it feels too fine:
While ever, with a visionary pain,
Past the precluded senses, sweep and shine
Streams, forests, glades,—and many a golden train
Of sunlit hills, transfigured to Divine.

("The Prisoner")

One poem in the 1844 volumes, "Catarina to Camoens," was a particular favorite with Robert Browning; he identified Elizabeth Barrett with the Portuguese girl Catarina, the beloved of the poet Camoens, and when his wife's sonnets to him were eventually published, the Brownings chose to call them "Sonnets from the Portuguese," an ambiguous title which was a disguise from the world but full of secret meaning for the Brownings themselves. These sonnets were published in 1850, four years after the Brownings' marriage, in the first collected edition of Mrs. Browning's works. The "Sonnets from the Portuguese" are her best-known poems, but not her best. The dramatic story of her marriage has given the sonnets something of the fascination of a roman à clef; but considered simply as poetry, they are uneven and sometimes embarrassing. Individual lines are strong and shapely:

Beholding, besides love, the end of love,
Hearing oblivion beyond memory;
As one who sits and gazes from above,
Over the rivers to the bitter sea.

(Sonnet xv)

or

Yet love, mere love, is beautiful indeed
And worthy of acceptation. Fire is bright,
Let temple burn, or flax. An equal light
Leaps in the flame from cedar-plank or weed. . . .

(Sonnet x)

And there are some whole sonnets, notably xxii and xliii, which sustain an unforced strength of music. But it is impossible to say of the "Sonnets from the Portuguese" as a whole, as one can say of the greatest sonnet sequences, that their beauty and

interest are self-sufficing, independently of their personal reference. The abiding attraction of these sonnets is the psychological interest of tracing the evolution in love of a thirty-nine-year-old invalid, who at first cannot believe that a brilliant poet, six years younger than herself, can really love her and want to marry her; then, when she begins to believe it, is held back by conscientious scruples at burdening him with her melancholy and ill health; then is brought to confess her own passion, and to see that he knows what he needs, and loves her for what she really is; then grows happy, and luxuriates in the tokens and catchwords and secrets of acknowledged lovers; and at last looks forward to a lifetime, an eternity, of enduring love.

Elizabeth Barrett Browning's marked individuality of style and personality makes all her poetry distinctive, but she was at various times much influenced by other poets. Pope was her model in her juvenilia; Thomas Campbell, Byron, Wordsworth lent forms and themes to her early lyrics; and after her marriage to Browning, she acquired something of his powers of vivid, ironic characterization and comment, an element in her poetry which had been latent since her earliest work but first came to the surface, under Browning's influence, in *Casa Guidi Windows*, published in 1851. This poem, written in a modified terza rima, is a reflection on recent political events in Florence and on the character and destiny of the Italians, about whom she is sympathetic but unsentimental:

We chalked the walls with bloody caveats
Against all tyrants. If we did not fight
Exactly, we fired muskets up the air
To show that victory was ours of right.
We met, had free discussions everywhere
(Except perhaps i' the Chambers) day and night.
We proved the poor should be employed . . . that's fair,—
And yet the rich not worked for anywise,—
Pay certified, yet payers abrogated,—
Full work secured, yet liabilities
To over-work excluded. . . .

(part II, 153–163)

Six years later, in 1857, she published her masterpiece, *Aurora Leigh*. This immense nine-book poem, longer than *Paradise Lost*, contains the finest passages that Elizabeth Barrett Browning ever wrote; but they are imbedded in an implausible story of a woman poet, a philanthropist who loves her, and a series of misunderstandings and catastrophes which keep them apart until the happy ending. The poem traces the parallel careers of Aurora Leigh, the successful but lonely and dissatisfied poet, convinced that man's salvation must come through the inspired individual, and her cousin Romney Leigh, the social reformer, who believes in progress organized for the people as a whole. He sets up a phalanstery on his ancestral estate, and decides to marry a poor seamstress as a precedent for a classless society. Romney's schemes fail—his bride is tricked away before the wedding, and entrapped into a brothel; the destitute people for whom he set up his phalanstery destroy it; and he loses his sight in the holocaust. When he and Aurora are finally reunited, they conclude that both were partly wrong: he had failed to recognize that to raise men's bodies, one must first raise their souls; she had not seen that one must work with, as well as for, humanity.

Mrs. Browning took various elements of the story of *Aurora Leigh* from Charlotte Brontë, George Sand, and other novelists; but the best way to appreciate the poem is to disregard its story, and to read it—like Wordsworth's *Prelude*, which is perhaps its nearest affinity—not for the narrative, but for the reflections occasioned by the events in the narrative, for the glimpses of distant mountains, for the moments of intense feeling. Elizabeth Barrett Browning said that *Aurora Leigh* contained her highest convictions on life and art, and in it she was above all concerned with the poet's responsibilities, his call to be a witness to the values of humanity. She was an early propagandist for *la littérature engagée*, maintaining that the sole work of poets is

> . . . to represent the age,
> Their age, not Charlemagne's,—this live throbbing age,
> That brawls, cheats, maddens, calculates, aspires,
> And spends more passion, more heroic heat,
> Betwixt the mirrors of its drawing-rooms,
> Than Roland with his knights at Roncesvalles.
> To flinch from modern varnish, coat or flounce,
> Cry out for togas and the picturesque
> Is fatal,—foolish too. King Arthur's self
> Was commonplace to Lady Guenevere;
> And Camelot to minstrels seemed as flat
> As Fleet Street to our poets.
>
> (*Aurora Leigh*, bk. V, 203–214)

Aurora Leigh is rich in unusual and glowing imagery, mature and often witty in its comments on contemporary society, compassionate over injus-

tices and the sufferings of the poor, and written in a vigorous and agile blank verse. It had a great and immediate success, though some readers were shocked by its frank sexual references to prostitution and even to rape. Mrs. Browning was not a prude; she thought that social evils were more likely to be abolished by plain speaking about them than by pretending they did not exist.

The last volume of poems which Mrs. Browning published in her lifetime, *Poems Before Congress*, which appeared in 1860, was a disappointment. It was a small collection of mainly political poems about France and Italy, too much imbued with her obsessive and often faulty judgments on contemporary political events and personalities. A year after her death, a further small volume, *Last Poems*, was published; it contained two lyrics, "A Musical Instrument" and "The North and the South," which have found their way into many anthologies, and one remarkable poem, "Bianca Among the Nightingales," which has a story and a refrain like some of the ballads of her youth, but a passion and a sophistication which are quite new.

"*Last Poems* is the last title which anyone could desire to read on a book which bears the name of Elizabeth Barrett Browning," began the *Athenaeum* review of her posthumous volume, and it went on to call her "the greatest English poetess that has ever lived" and to say that she had "the heart of a lion, the soul of a martyr, and the voice of a battle-trumpet. Hers was a great genius, nurtured alike on study of the ancients and instinct for the moderns." Now, more than a century later, no one would claim "great genius" for Elizabeth Barrett Browning, but there are qualities in her poetry which still have power to move and interest us.

IV

PERHAPS the best approach to the poetry of Elizabeth Barrett Browning is to note first the thorough training and preparation she underwent in the techniques of her profession. It was a profession to her; she worked full-time, all her adult life, at the business of poetry, and she took seriously the skills and the responsibilities of her trade. In writing of its responsibilities, she sometimes lapsed into a shrill didacticism; but at its best her vocation emerges as a genuine poetic impulse to show life, and enable others to see it, as it really is, unobscured by prejudice, self-interest, or self-deception. Poets, she said, are "the only truth-tellers still left to God"; and they must speak out against tyranny, against unjust wars, against the exploitation of women and children, against want and slavery, against complacency and ignorance. They must make human beings think for themselves, must help them to be honest about their emotions, must teach them to outgrow narrow nationalism and sectarianism.

But if poets are to have the power to move men's minds in this way, they must learn the skills which give such power to poetry. She herself gave much time and study to the science of versification; she experimented in many different meters, and was a pioneer in the use of assonantal double rhymes. Her very thorough reading of English poetry, from the earliest to the latest, had convinced her that not enough use was made of the possibilities of rhyme. Double rhymes were almost entirely confined to comic poetry; in any case, regular double rhymes were rare in English. Her innovation was to introduce such assonantal double rhymes as "trident/silent" and "benches/influences," or still more extreme ones, matching neither in vowel nor in consonant, such as "angels/candles" or "burden/disregarding." These are commonplaces in English poetry of the 1930's and 1940's; but in Mrs. Browning's day, and for half a century afterward, they were considered utterly lawless. Her metrical experiments were less extreme. She used a very wide variety of meters, from the most regular rhymed couplets and Petrarchan sonnets to the loosest accentual verse, approximating to sprung rhythm.

Her prosodic experiments were often more daring than successful, but they were the result of much exploration of classical and Byzantine Greek literature and of early English poetry. She published a modernized version of a Chaucer poem, and translations of Aeschylus, Theocritus, Apuleius, Nonnus, and Anacreon; she also wrote a critical study, illustrated by many translations, of Byzantine poetry from the fourth to the fourteenth centuries. Greek was the language she loved best; but she also knew Latin, French, Italian, and some German, Spanish, and Hebrew, and was so widely read in the literature of these languages that she could trace an image from Lucretius through Saint Basil to Tasso, and draw a parallel between *The Choephoroe* and *Macbeth*, or between an ode of Anacreon and *Romeo and Juliet*. Some of the best-known passages in her poetry are her roll calls of other poets: in *An Essay on Mind*; in "A Vision of Poets," where she dashes off some notable sketches, such as

> . . . bold
>
> Electric Pindar, quick as fear,
> With race-dust on his cheeks, and clear
> Slant startled eyes that seem to hear
>
> The chariot rounding the last goal,
> To hurtle past it in his soul.
>
> (st. 104–106)

and

> Lucretius—nobler than his mood;
> Who dropped his plummet down the broad
> Deep universe, and said "No God",
>
> Finding no bottom: he denied
> Divinely the divine, . . .
>
> (st. 112–113)

and in *Aurora Leigh*, where she analyzes the young poet's reactions to his predecessors, how he loves and imitates them and then finds his own inspiration, and how sometimes there comes a poet like Keats, to whom none of the generalizations about young poets apply; and then she wrote the lines on Keats with which Edmund Blunden chose to sum up Keats's achievement:

> the life of a long life
> Distilled to a mere drop, falling like a tear
> Upon the world's cold cheek to make it burn
> For ever.
>
> (*Aurora Leigh*, bk. I, 1007–1010)

Mrs. Browning's knowledge of comparative literature gave her an acute ear for style and the boldness to refute, on internal stylistic evidence and in an astonishing metaphor, the theory of the multiple authorship of Homer. She possessed a handsome edition of Friedrich Wolf's *Prolegomena ad Homerum*, on thick, white paper with wide margins, and she wrote these memorably indignant lines about "the kissing Judas, Wolf":

> Who builds us such a royal book as this
> To honour a chief-poet, folio-built,
> And writes above, "The house of Nobody!",
> Who floats in cream, as rich as any sucked
> From Juno's breasts, the broad Homeric lines,

And, while with their spondaic prodigious mouths
They lap the lucent margins as babe-gods,
Proclaims them bastards. Wolf's an atheist;
And if the Iliad fell out, as he says,
By mere fortuitous concourse of old songs,
Conclude as much too for the universe.
                    (*Aurora Leigh*, bk. V, 1149–1159)

The metaphor of the printed lines sucking the milk of the white page margins is a good example of another of Elizabeth Barrett Browning's special poetic qualities—her command of striking and original imagery. The richness of her imagination is all the more surprising in view of how few opportunities she had to observe either mankind or nature. She spent the first twenty-six years of her life in the seclusion of a remote countryside, and most of the next fourteen years shut up in a London house, meeting very few strangers and ill in bed for whole years. But she made the fullest use of what experience she had—of the conversation and letters of her literary friends, of her long explorations and adventures of the mind between the covers of books, even of her own ill health and its accompaniments. There is in her work a whole image cluster derived from her illness—from insomnia, from states of trance, from night silences and transfigurations, from opium visions, from fainting, from the vibrations of a galloping pulse. These made the landscape of her mind; they were to her what external nature was to Wordsworth or Tennyson. She lived in the country as a child, and she traveled widely after her marriage, but it was mostly from one sofa to another. She led an indoor life, and she writes like an indoor poet. Her descriptions of nature often have the freshness of delighted surprise; trees and hills and fresh air were to her not a necessity but a delicious occasional stimulus, like going to the theater. The spaciousness and dewy greenness of some of her landscape descriptions:

      The mythic oaks and elm-trees standing out
      Self-poised upon their prodigy of shade
                    (*Aurora Leigh*, bk. I, 1089–1090)

remind one of the close, dark room in which they were written. What she actually saw from the window of her room was the texture of the London skies—in winter "wrapped like a mummy in a yellow mist," in summer "a thick mist lacquered over with light"; the sunsets which "startle the slant roofs and chimney pots/With splashes of fierce colour"; and the classic Dickensian spectacle, watching

      the great tawny weltering fog
      Involve the passive city, strangle it
      Alive, and draw it off into the void,
      Spires, bridges, streets, and squares, as if a sponge
      Had wiped out London,
                    (*Aurora Leigh*, bk. III, 180–184)

surely a deliberate and ironic echo of Wordsworth's

      Ships, towers, domes, theatres and temples lie
      All bright and glittering in the smokeless air.

Mrs. Browning's semantic studies often gave a special turn to her imagery, an interlocking, punning ambiguity, as in her description of a man trying to rid himself of the ghost of a dead love:

      He locks thee out at night into the cold
      Away from butting with thy horny eyes
      Against his crystal dreams,
                    (*Aurora Leigh*, bk. V, 1104–1106)

where the adjective "horny" is used in a double sense: the eyes of the little ghost are horns to butt against a fragile complacency, but also dim horn windows through which an icy memory peers in. Mrs. Browning concentrates and interweaves her images so closely that they sometimes defy analysis, and yet have a fierce impact:

      Ten nights and days we voyaged on the deep;
      Ten nights and days without the common face
      Of any day or night; the moon and sun
      Cut off from the green reconciling earth,
      To starve into a blind ferocity
      And glare unnatural; the very sky
      (Dropping its bell-net down upon the sea
      As if no human heart should 'scape alive)
      Bedraggled with the desolating salt.
                    (*Aurora Leigh*, bk. I, 239–247)

This passage describes how the orphan child, carried away from her home on a miserable voyage to a sad destination, sees all nature turned into the famished wild beasts of some cosmic circus, glaring through the net which has become man's prison, not his protection.

Another of Elizabeth Barrett Browning's special qualities, at once a virtue and a vice, is her great variety. She could plunge from heights of beauty to depths of bathos, sometimes within the same poem. But not all her good work is in one manner, and all her bad in another; even her best work is in several different manners. She could write with classic economy, as in her sonnet on hopeless grief:

> Most like a monumental statue set
> In everlasting watch and moveless woe,
> Till itself crumble to the dust beneath.
> Touch it: the marble eyelids are not wet;
> If it could weep, it could arise and go
>   ("Grief")

or in her description of Michelangelo's statue of Lorenzo de' Medici:

> With everlasting shadow on his face,
> While the slow dawns and twilights disapprove
> The ashes of his long-established race,
> Which never more shall clog the feet of men.
>   (*Casa Guidi Windows*, pt. I, 94–97)

Both these passages are inspired by sculpture, which was always one of Mrs. Browning's most potent images; to her, as to Wordsworth, a statue was a "marble index" of long voyages of the mind. But though she could write marmoreally, much of her most vivid poetry is more like a modern sculptor's conglomeration of *objets trouvés*—mechanisms and reptilian forms welded together in flowing or glutinous structures—as in some passages from *Aurora Leigh*:

> This social Sphinx
> Who sits between the sepulchre and the stews,
> Makes mock and mow against the crystal heavens,
> And bullies God
>   (bk. IV, 1184–1187)

or

>   That June-day
> Too deeply sunk in craterous sunsets, now
> For you or me to dig it up alive,—
> To pluck it out all bleeding with spent flame
> At the roots, before those moralizing stars
> We have got instead
>   (bk. VIII, 489–494)

a passage which may recall to readers the poetry of Christopher Fry, rather than of any nineteenth-century writer.

Mrs. Browning's learning and many interests, enriched by the influence of her husband's still greater erudition, give her poetry a very wide reference. Religion, philosophy, politics, social reform, education, classical literature, and scientific discovery all gave impulse to her poetic inspiration. Indignant at the chicanery of the great powers who concluded the Peace of Villafranca, she dreams of

>   the grand solution
> Of earth's municipal, insular schisms,
> Statesmen draping self-love's conclusion
> In cheap, vernacular patriotisms,
> Unable to give up Judaea for Jesus.
>   ("Italy and the World," st. 8)

She draws a vivid image from the excavations at Pompeii, from Alexander's project to carve Mount Athos into a colossal statue, from the holy ox of Memphis, from the mixture of gall and potash on a painter's palette, from the valves of a dissected hyacinth bulb. She reads Lyell's *Principles of Geology* and Chambers' *Vestiges of the Natural History of Creation*, and is prompted to the reflection that

> Good love, howe'er ill-placed,
> Is better for a man's soul in the end,
> Than if he loved ill what deserves love well.
> A pagan, kissing for a step of Pan
> The wild-goat's hoof-print on the loamy down,
> Exceeds our modern thinker who turns back
> The strata . . . granite, limestone, coal and clay,
> Concluding coldly with "Here's law! where's God?"
>   (*Aurora Leigh*, bk. V, 1113–1120)

Often the imagery in her poetry can be traced back to references in her letters. These are now more read than her poetry, and would be more popular still if they were easily accessible in an up-to-date chronological arrangement. They are a barometer of the intelligent liberal public opinion of her times. Was it true that Newman had gone over to Rome? How long would it be before manhood suffrage was universal? Was Florence Nightingale really making the best use of her powers by being a hospital nurse? Could not prosperous Britain afford schools for all her children? In a letter of 7 April 1846, she argues with Browning over the ethics of dueling. He has agreed with her in condemning capital punishment, and in opposing war, yet he maintains that "honourable men are bound to keep their honours clean at the expense of so much gunpowder and so much risk of life—*that* must be, ought to be—let judicial deaths and military glory be abolished never so!" For her part, setting aside Christian principle, and on merely rational gounds, she

cannot conceive of any *possible combination of circumstances* which could—I will *not* say *justify*, but even *excuse*, an honourable man's having recourse to the duellist's pistol, either on his own account or another's . . . His honour! Who believes in such an honour—liable to such amends, and capable of such recovery! *You* cannot, I think—in the secret of your mind. Or if *you can—you*, who are a teacher of the world—poor world—it is more desperately wrong than I thought.[2]

(vol. II, p. 41)

When one finds Browning defending the principle of dueling as late as 1846, Pushkin's death in a duel only nine years earlier seems less strange.

Elizabeth Barrett Browning knew, in person or by correspondence, nearly all the eminent writers of her day, and read all the new books of any merit as they came out; and in her letters one can trace the rise and fall of reputations, the literary mysteries and controversies of the day. Could the author of *Adam Bede* really be a woman? How could anyone think Casimir Delavigne's poetry superior to Lamartine's, or Monckton Milnes's to Browning's? Could it possibly be true that *Jane Eyre* was by the governess of Thackeray's daughters? New names begin to rise in her literary firmament—Trollope's *Framley Parsonage* is "really superb"; she is "thunder-struck" by *Madame Bovary*; she had no idea that Thackeray had such intellectual force as *Vanity Fair* revealed; Matthew Arnold and Clough seem to her full of promise. In her letters one can also chart the rising temperature of her own fame; fan letters addressed to her simply as

Miss Elizabeth Barrett
Poetess
London

find their way to her in Wimpole Street; the terrible arbiters of the *Quarterly Review* and the *Examiner* begin to treat her with respect; her fellow poets write

to congratulate her. But how was she to reply to a letter from Edgar Allan Poe hailing her as "the noblest of her sex"? Perhaps she might say, "Sir, you are the most discerning of yours."

This little joke, mocking herself as well as others, is typical of the personal style which makes Mrs. Browning's letters, over and above the interest of many of their topics, so delightful. She had trained herself to write letters naturally, as though she were talking; they were indeed her only means of conversation for much of her life, when she was imprisoned by ill health. And she had a rare ear and memory for the few face-to-face conversations which she did have, such as the misadventure of the Leeds poetess and the dropped H, which she recounted to Browning in a letter of 6 May 1846.

Ellen Heaton had come to call, and had told Miss Barrett that "the poetess proper of the city of Leeds was '*Mrs A*'":

"*Mrs A*?" said I with an enquiring innocence. "Oh" she went on, (divining sarcasm in every breath I drew) "oh! I dare say, *you* wouldn't admit her to be a real poetess. But as she lives in Leeds and writes verses, we call her our poetess! and then, really, Mrs A is a charming woman. She was a Miss Roberts—and her 'Spirit of the Woods', and of the 'Flowers' has been admired, I assure you". Well, in a moment I seemed to remember something,—because only a few months since, surely I had a letter from somebody who was once a spirit of the Woods or ghost of the Flowers. Still, I could not make out *Mrs A*! "Certainly" I confessed modestly, "I never did hear of a Mrs A.—and yet, and yet—" A most glorious confusion I was in, when suddenly my visitor thought of spelling the name. "H-E-Y" said she. Now conceive that! The Mrs Hey who came by solution, had both written to me and sent me a book on the Lakes quite lately "by the author of the Spirit of the Woods". *There* was the explanation! And my Leeds visitor will go back and say that I denied all knowledge of the charming Mrs A. the Leeds poetess, and that it was with the greatest difficulty I could be brought to recognize her existence. Oh, the arrogance and ingratitude of me!

(vol. I, pp. 133–134)

This anecdote brings out the personality of Elizabeth Barrett—her ability to see herself as others saw her, her compassionate fear to wound competing with her irresistible sense of the absurd; a complex of qualities that made Henry James say, "There is scarce a scrap of a letter of Mrs Browning's in which a nameless intellectual, if it be not rather a moral, grace . . . does not make itself felt." Elizabeth Barrett

[2]Quotations from the letters to Browning are from *Letters of Robert Browning and Elizabeth Barrett, 1845-46*, 2 vols. (London, 1899).

Browning's personality, as expressed in her writing, could be maudlin and overexcited; at other times she could be astringent and satirical; but she was not mean or sly. She had that magnanimity which, though it cannot be a substitute for talent, adds a grace to it. She was magnanimous in her freedom from all religious, national, class, or sex prejudices, and magnanimous in her personal relationships. The greatest wrong she ever had to suffer was the selfish tyranny of her father, and here is what she said of it:

After all, he is the victim. He isolates himself—and now and then he feels it . . . the cold dead silence all round, which is the effect of an incredible system. If he were not stronger than most men, he could not bear it as he does.

(vol. I, p. 436)

The complement to Elizabeth Barrett Browning's magnanimity, the final quality which distinguishes her poetry—and makes her resemble an Elizabethan poet such as Webster, or a modern one such as Dylan Thomas—is her outrageousness, the fearless unconcern with which she shouts and shocks and exaggerates. In real life she was a quiet-voiced, gentle woman, a good listener rather than a good talker, but on paper she would say anything. Christian as she was, she would compare a waltz to the Mass, the unification of Italy to the Resurrection; no squeamishness prevented her from using scalps and tortures and rotting corpses as symbols; no prudery deterred her from talking of the smell of brothels. Like her prosodic experiments, these were deliberate attempts to create a new kind of poetic language which would startle the reader into full participation. She often overdosed her poetry, and produced a lassitude rather than a stimulus in the reader. Her poems are not tasteful or aristocratic, and will never be appreciated by those who value restraint as a necessary element in good poetry. In thinking of her work, one is reminded of Roy Campbell's memorable lines:

You praise the firm restraint with which they write—
I'm with you there, of course;
They use the snaffle and the curb all right,
But where's the bloody horse?

Elizabeth Barrett Browning was not very handy with the snaffle or the curb, but the horse was there—a snorting and muscular charger, very liable to do a bolt.

V

In 1856 Ruskin said that Elizabeth Barrett Browning's poetry was "unsurpassed by anything but Shakespeare." In 1932, Virginia Woolf said that the only place in literature assigned to Mrs. Browning was with Eliza Cook and Alexander Smith and other totally forgotten poets. Today, more than a century after Elizabeth Barrett Browning's death, her true worth as a poet is still unfixed between these extremes of critical inflation and deflation. Her poetry is very much out of favor with the academic critics and historians of literature. You will not find it in the syllabuses of British university courses in English literature, nor in the latest anthologies. There is not a single poem of hers in John Hayward's *Penguin Book of English Verse*, and Helen Gardner's *New Oxford Book of English Verse* includes only a few of the "Sonnets from the Portuguese." Not every public library in Britain has a copy of her works; and where copies do exist, they are not very often borrowed. No edition of the collected works is in print in Britain, though new editions of "Sonnets from the Portuguese" appear from time to time. Elizabeth Barrett Browning's memory is kept alive at present more by the plays, films, and musical comedies concerned with her private life than by readers of her poetry.

It is still too soon to say whether her fame as a poet will ever return. She may have to wait 200 years, as Ford and Webster did, till Charles Lamb brought them back to life. English literary taste moves in a circle, from extravagance to elegance and round again. It is possible that Elizabeth Barrett Browning's poetry will have a revival of favor at some future time when taste has followed its wonted cycle, and the terms "Gothic" and "enthusiastic" have once again become terms of praise, not of abuse.

SELECTED BIBLIOGRAPHY

I. Bibliography. T. J. Wise, *Bibliography of the Writings in Prose and Verse of E. B. Browning* (London, 1918), includes texts of some letters not published elsewhere, but lists as authentic Wise's forged "Reading, 1847" edition of "Sonnets"; T. J. Wise, *A Browning Library. A Catalogue of Printed Books, Manuscripts etc. of R. and E. B. Browning* (London, 1929), the catalog of Wise's Browning collection, now in the British Museum; T. G. Ehrsam and R. H. Deily, *Bibliographies of Twelve Vic-*

torian Authors (New York, 1936), supplement by J. G. Fucilla in *Modern Philology*, 37 (1939), 89–96; G. B. Taplin, *The Life of Elizabeth Barrett Browning* (London, 1957), contains a list of principal manuscript sources and of contributions to annuals, almanacs, periodicals, and series; W. J. Barnes, *The Browning Collection at the University of Texas* (Austin, Tex., 1966); P. Kelley and R. Hudson, *The Brownings' Correspondence: A Checklist* (New York, 1978).

II. COLLECTED WORKS. *Poems*, new ed., 2 vols. (London, 1850; 3 vols., 1856; 4 vols., 1864), the 1844 *Poems* with the addition of "Sonnets from the Portuguese" (here first published; the "Reading, 1847" edition is a forgery), a revision of *Prometheus Bound*, and 35 other sonnets and lyrics not previously published in book form; *Poems*, 5 vols. (London, 1866), 6 vols. (1889), with a prefatory note by R. Browning; *The Poems* (London, 1893), with a memoir by Mrs. D. Ogilvy; F. G. Kenyon, ed., *The Poetical Works* (London, 1897); *The Poetical Works* (Oxford, 1904), first ed. in the Oxford Standard Authors series; *Complete Poetical Works of Elizabeth Barrett Browning*, 2 vols. (New York, 1919), with intro. by L. Whiting; *Poetical Works, with Two Prose Essays* (London, 1920).

III. SELECTED WORKS. *A Selection from the Poetry*, 2nd series (London, 1866–1880), with a prefatory note by R. Browning; *Poems* (London, 1903), with intro. by A. Meynell; E. Lee, ed., *Selected Poems* (Boston, 1904), with intro. and notes by Lee; *Poems* (London, 1912), the World's Classics ed.; *Poems* (London, 1948), selected and with intro. by S. J. Looker; C. Kaplan, ed., *Aurora Leigh and Other Poems* (London, 1978).

IV. SEPARATE WORKS. *The Battle of Marathon, a Poem* (London, 1820), published anonymously; *An Essay on Mind, with Other Poems* (London, 1826), published anonymously; *Prometheus Bound, Translated from the Greek of Aeschylus, and Miscellaneous Poems* (London, 1833), also with intro. by A. Meynell (London, 1896); *The Seraphim, and Other Poems* (London, 1838); *The Poems of Geoffrey Chaucer Modernized* (London, 1841), to which she contributed a modernized version of "Queen Annelida and False Arcite"; R. H. Horne, ed., *A New Spirit of the Age* (London, 1844), to which she contributed a number of essays and parts of essays; *Poems*, 2 vols. (London, 1844), the ed. used as the basis for subsequent eds. of her collected works produced in her lifetime and immediately after her death—new ed. (1850) included much new material; also 3rd ed. (1853); 4th ed. (incorporating *Casa Guidi Windows*), 3 vols. (1856); 5th ed. (1862); 6th ed. (incorporating *Aurora Leigh*) (1864); 7th ed. (1866); *Casa Guidi Windows, A Poem* (London, 1851); *Aurora Leigh* (London, 1857), also with intro. by A. C. Swinburne (London, 1898); *Poems Before Congress* (London, 1860), repr. as *Napoleon III in Italy and Other Poems* (New York, 1860).

Last Poems (London, 1862); *The Greek Christian Poets and the English Poets* (London, 1863), articles repr. from the *Athenaeum* (1842), *English Poets* being a review of an anthology titled *The Book of the Poets*; *Psyche Apocalypté, a Lyrical Drama* (London, 1876), written with R. H. Horne, an earlier draft printed in *Hitherto Unpublished Poems* (see below); *The Enchantress, and Other Poems* (London, 1913); E. Gosse, ed., *Epistle to a Canary* (London, 1913); *Leila, a Tale* (London, 1913); H. B. Forman, ed., *Hitherto Unpublished Poems and Stories, with an Unedited Autobiography*, 2 vols. (Boston, 1914); F. G. Kenyon, ed., *New Poems by Robert Browning and Elizabeth Barrett Browning* (London, 1914); H. B. Forman, ed., *The Poet's Enchiridion* (Boston, 1914); F. Ratchford, ed., *Sonnets from the Portuguese* (New York, 1950), centennial variorum ed., with intro. by Ratchford and notes by D. Fulton—the 1856 text as finally rev. by E. B. Browning, but with variant readings from MS texts in the British Museum, Morgan Library, and Houghton Library.

V. LETTERS AND DIARIES. S. R. T. Mayer, ed., *Letters Addressed to Richard Hengist Horne*, 2 vols. (London, 1877); *Kind Words from a Sickroom: [Four] Letters Addressed to Allan Park Paton* (Greenock, 1891), privately printed; F. G. Kenyon, ed., *Letters of Elizabeth Barrett Browning*, 2 vols. (London, 1897), with biographical additions by Kenyon; *Letters of Robert Browning and Elizabeth Barrett, 1845-46*, 2 vols. (London, 1899); P. Lubbock, *Elizabeth Barrett Browning in Her Letters* (London, 1906), a selection of the letters with critical commentary; *The Religious Opinions of Elizabeth Barrett Browning: Three Letters Addressed to William Merry* (London, 1906), originally printed privately (1896); *The Art of Scansion: Letter to Uvedale Price* (London, 1916), with intro. by A. Meynell; *Letters Reprinted by T. J. Wise* (London, 1916; 1919); T. J. Wise, ed., *Letters to Robert Browning and Other Correspondents* (London, 1916), privately printed; L. Huxley, ed., *Elizabeth Barrett Browning: Letters to Her Sister 1846-1859* (London, 1929); *Twenty-Two Unpublished Letters of Elizabeth Barrett Browning and Robert Browning, Addressed to Henrietta and Arabella Moulton-Barrett* (New York, 1935); W. R. Benét, ed., *From Robert and Elizabeth Browning: A Further Selection of the Barrett-Browning Family Correspondence* (London, 1936); M. H. Shackford, ed., *Letters to Benjamin Robert Haydon* (New York, 1939).

B. Weaver, ed., *Twenty Unpublished Letters to Hugh Stuart Boyd* (London, 1950); B. Miller, ed., *Elizabeth Barrett to Miss Mitford: Letters to Mary Russell Mitford* (London, 1954), with intro. by Miller; S. Musgrove, ed., *Unpublished Letters of Thomas De Quincey and Elizabeth Barrett Browning* (Auckland, 1954); B. P. McCarthy, ed., *Elizabeth Barrett to Mr. Boyd: Unpublished Letters to Hugh Stuart Boyd* (London, 1955), with intro. by McCarthy; P. Landis and R. E. Freeman, eds., *Letters of the Brownings to George Barrett* (Urbana, Ill., 1958); G. R. Hudson, ed., *Browning and His American Friends: Letters Between the Brownings, the Storys and James Russell Lowell, 1841-1890* (London, 1965); V. E. Stack, ed., *The*

Love Letters of Robert Browning and Elizabeth Barrett (London, 1969), selected and with intro. by Stack; E. Kintner, ed., *The Letters of Robert Browning and Elizabeth Barrett, 1845–1846*, 2 vols. (Cambridge, Mass., 1969); W. B. Pope, ed., *Invisible Friends: The Correspondence of Elizabeth Barrett Browning and Benjamin Robert Haydon* (Cambridge, Mass., 1972); E. Berridge, ed., *The Barretts at Hope End: The Early Diary of Elizabeth Barrett Browning* (London, 1974); P. N. Heydon and P. Kelley, eds., *Elizabeth Barrett Browning's Letters to Mrs. David Ogilvy* (London, 1974).

VI. Biographical and Critical Studies. R. H. Horne, ed., *A New Spirit of the Age* (London, 1844), contains a chapter on "Miss E. B. Barrett and Mrs. Norton"; H. A. Taine, *Notes sur l'Angleterre* (Paris, 1872), includes a brief but important study of E. B. Browning's poetry; P. Bayne, *Two Great Englishwomen: Mrs. Browning and Charlotte Brontë* (London, 1881), critical study with a useful analysis of *The Seraphim* and "A Drama of Exile"; C. des Guerrois, *Étude sur Mistress Elizabeth Browning* (Paris, 1885), analysis of her aesthetic theory and trans. of some of the poems; G. Sarrazin, *Poètes modernes de l'Angleterre* (Paris, 1885), critical study; J. H. Ingram, *Elizabeth Barrett Browning* (London, 1888), the first biography, inaccurate as to some dates and facts, but sensible on poetry; E. C. Stedman and G. E. Woodbury, eds., *Works of Edgar Allan Poe* (Chicago, 1895), vol. VI contains an 1845 essay, "Miss Barrett's *A Drama of Exile, and Other Poems*"; A. Meynell, intro. to *Prometheus Bound..., and Other Poems* (London, 1896), her first trans., first published in 1833; A. C. Swinburne, intro. to *Aurora Leigh* (London, 1898); H. James, *William Wetmore Story and His Friends* (Edinburgh, 1903), includes some short but penetrating references to E. B. Browning; E. P. Gould, *The Brownings and America* (Boston, 1904), contains a survey of American reviews of her poetry; G. M. Merlette, *La vie et l'oeuvre d'E. B. Browning* (Paris, 1905), contains summaries and analyses of all principal poems and a study of prosodic experiments.

L. Whiting, *The Brownings, Their Life and Art* (London, 1911), the first authoritative biography, includes many facts obtained from the Brownings' son; G. M. Trevelyan, *English Songs of Italian Freedom* (London, 1911), assesses her influence on political opinion; R. B. Nicati, *Femme et poète: Elisabeth Browning* (Paris, 1912), critical study which includes analysis of her religion; B. Viterbi, *Elisabetta Barrett Browning* (Bergamo, 1913), biography; G. M. Trevelyan, *Englishmen and Italians: Some Aspects of Their Relations Past and Present* (London, 1919), assesses her influence on political opinion; O. Burdett, *The Brownings* (London, 1928), critical study; L. S. Boas, *Elizabeth Barrett Browning* (London, 1930), biography; V. Woolf, *The Common Reader*, 2nd ser. (London, 1932), the most

important critical study by a twentieth-century creative writer; V. Woolf, *Flush* (London, 1933), ostensibly a biography of E. B. Browning's dog, but contains biographical material on her; J. Carter and G. Pollard, *An Enquiry into the Nature of Certain Nineteenth Century Pamphlets* (London, 1934), exposes the 1847 edition of *Sonnets from the Portuguese* as a forgery; M. H. Shackford, *Elizabeth Barrett Browning: R. H. Horne: Two Studies* (Wellesley, Mass., 1935), critical study; J. A. Marks, *The Family of the Barrett* (New York, 1938), history of the Barrett family in Jamaica, with a section on E. B. Browning's opium addiction.

F. Winwar, *The Immortal Lovers* (London, 1950), biography; D. Hewlett, *Elizabeth Barrett Browning* (London, 1953), biography and critical study; A. Maurois, *Robert et Elizabeth Browning* (Paris, 1955), the best representative of the disillusioned view of the Brownings' story; G. A. Treves, *The Golden Ring: The Anglo-Florentines* (London, 1956), section on the Brownings' lives and friends in Florence; G. B. Taplin, *The Life of Elizabeth Barrett Browning* (London, 1957), biography incorporating much new material, valuable bibliography; J. M. S. Tompkins, *Aurora Leigh* (London, 1961), the Fawcett Lecture, analyzes E. B. Browning's ideas on women as writers; A. Hayter, *Mrs. Browning: A Poet's Work and Its Setting* (London, 1963), critical study; A. Hayter, *A Sultry Month: Scenes of London Literary Life in 1846* (London, 1964); A. Hayter, *Opium and the Romantic Imagination* (London, 1968), contains ch. on E. B. Browning as an opium taker; G. Pickering, *Creative Malady* (London, 1974), also discusses E. B. Browning as an opium taker; R. Mander, *Mrs. Browning: The Story of Elizabeth Barrett* (London, 1980).

Important material on E. B. Browning is contained in Robert Browning's letters and in biographies of him: Lady Ritchie (Anne Isabella Thackeray), *Records of Tennyson, Ruskin and Browning* (London, 1892); G. K. Chesterton, *Robert Browning* (London, 1903); Mrs. S. Orr, *Life and Letters of Robert Browning* (London, 1908); W. H. Griffin and H. C. Minchin, *Life of Robert Browning* (London, 1910); T. L. Hood, ed., *Letters of Robert Browning* (London, 1933); R. Curle, ed., *Robert Browning and Julia Wedgwood. A Broken Friendship as Revealed in Their Letters* (London, 1937); E. C. McAleer, ed., *Dearest Isa. Robert Browning's Letters to Isabella Blagden* (Austin, Tex., 1951); W. C. de Vane and K. L. Knickerbocker, eds., *New Letters of Robert Browning* (London, 1951); B. Miller, *Robert Browning, a Portrait* (London, 1953); H. C. Duffin, *Amphibian: A Reconsideration of Browning* (London, 1956); M. Ward, *Robert Browning and His World; the Private Face* (London, 1968); W. Irvine and P. Honan, *The Book, the Ring and the Poet: A Biography of Robert Browning* (London, 1975).

ALFRED TENNYSON

(1809-1892)

Brian Southam

I

FOR many years the prevailing image of Tennyson has been of one of the great corruptors of English poetry, of a writer with a style so meretricious and insidiously molding that he misshaped the taste of generations of readers and the practice of generations of poets. A succession of influential critics, from Matthew Arnold to F. R. Leavis (and their many disciples), have condemned Tennyson as a second-rater, as an artist of Tennysonian verse—polished, melodious, and decorative; and in this artistry marooned, isolated from the central vitality of English poetry, cut off from the resources of the living language as Keats, immediately before him, was not. In this perspective the creative effort of Yeats, Eliot, and Pound, at the beginning of the century, is seen as a disinfection of poetic language and style, a breaking away from the Tennysonian embrace and the foundation of the modern movement as a counterforce to the Victorian poetic: the old style characteristically escapist, weakly romantic, medievalizing, moralizing, sentimental, simple, and unsubtle in its thought and feeling, the new style characteristically intelligent, unromantic, subtle, and complex in its tones and irony, realistic in its approach to human experience, seeking not to escape but to confront.

Broadly, this is an acceptable theory of action and reaction. Tennyson's popular style was indeed swamping; it formed public taste and set a standard by which poetry was to be judged; and a great deal of his writing can be described as Tennysonian, the heavy hand against which the modern poets turned in protest, just as there was a widespread reaction against Victorianism in general. Tennyson suffered particularly as the representative Victorian poet. His rejection was part of a historical process. But the continuing prejudice against Tennyson is as indefensible as the romantics' rejection of Pope and Dryden.

Difference is not inferiority. Although there is a good deal of Tennyson that is pompous, banal, grotesquely sentimental, and in many other ways laughably or unpleasantly Victorian, there is a sufficient body of his finest work to place him among the great poets of English literature. The refreshing challenge for anyone coming to Tennyson in the 1980's is precisely in this question, for there is no commonly accepted view of his achievement. Many critics see him as a minor poet of a minor period, of historical interest only. Others see him as an early symbolist poet, with modern affinities, a writer whose work repays the closest attention and responds to the kind of detailed analysis that we put to poetry of richness and complexity.[1]

Whatever we or posterity may decide on these questions, as a cultural and intellectual figure Tennyson occupies a unique position in English history. No writer has ever dominated his age so completely as Tennyson dominated Victorian England; no poet has ever been so completely a national poet. His writing entered the consciousness of the age. As Henry James said in 1875, his verse had become "part of the civilization of his day." To illustrate the true quality of faith, George Eliot quoted from the opening to *In Memoriam*; to discuss the capacities of women, she quoted from *The Princess*. Tennyson, she wrote in 1885, voiced "the struggles and the far reaching thoughts of this nineteenth century"; *In Memoriam* "enshrines the highest tendency of this age." Matthew Arnold prophesied that in a time of science and spiritual doubt, poetry would come to take the place of religion. How close the poetry of

---

[1]See particularly M. McLuhan, "Tennyson and Picturesque Poetry" (1951) and "Tennyson and the Romantic Epic" (1959); C. Brooks, *The Well-Wrought Urn* (1947); F. W. Bateson, *English Poetry* (1950); G. Hough, "Tears, Idle Tears" (1951); L. Spitzer, "'Tears, Idle Tears' Again" (1952). All are reprinted in J. Killham, ed., *Critical Essays on the Poetry of Tennyson* (London, 1960).

Tennyson came to fulfilling that prophecy we can judge from the words of the historian J. A. Froude:

Your father in my estimate stands and will stand far away by the side of Shakespeare above all other English Poets, with this relative superiority even to Shakespeare, that he speaks the thoughts and speaks *to* the perplexities and misgivings of his own age.

Froude was writing to Hallam Tennyson in 1894, when the biographer-son was compiling the monumental *Memoir.* But this is something more than obituary homage; the comparison with Shakespeare was not mere lip service; nor was Froude a critical simpleton (as anyone can see from his discussion of Shakespeare in "The Science of History").[2] What he says here is an assertion of Tennyson's hold upon the Victorian mind.

Tennyson's domination of the later nineteenth century is partly to be explained by the prosaic fact of his longevity. His career extended over seventy-five years, from childhood until his death in 1892, and he was a known poet, through his published work, from 1830 onward. He began in the shadow of the great romantics and lived to be the older contemporary of Hardy and Yeats. He came to an open field. The earlier generation was dead: Keats in 1821, Shelley in 1822, Byron in 1824; Scott, turned novelist, in 1832; Coleridge, turned philosopher, in 1834. Only Wordsworth survived, the young Wordsworth dead, until 1850, when he was succeeded as poet laureate by Tennyson, the then supreme poet of *In Memoriam.* In these terms Tennyson opened a fresh, post-romantic period in English poetry, a period further defined by historical events, notably the Reform Bill of 1832, the first real step toward modern parliamentary democracy, and the accession of Queen Victoria in 1837. Victorian England developed an unmistakable character. Its sustaining dynamic was the idea of Progress—full-blooded material progress in the growth of industry and trade; social progress in concern for the poor; nervous political progress in the direction of responsible democracy; fearful scientific progress toward the facts of creation and evolution; moral progress, as it was seen, in the ideals of purity and of family life, of paternalism, motherhood, and domesticity; religious progress, again, as it was seen, in the pietism of the Anglican church. There was also a higher, more speculative ideal of progress arising out of the grandiose vision of man's nature and destiny formulated by Thomas Carlyle, the "thinker" of the century, in "Signs of the Times" (*Edinburgh Review*, June 1829):

We have a faith in the imperishable dignity of man; in the high vocation to which throughout his earthly history, he had been appointed. . . . Doubtless this age also is advancing. Its very unrest, its ceaseless activity, its discontent contains matter of promise. Knowledge, education are opening the eyes of the humblest; are increasing the number of thinking minds without limit. This is as it should be; for not in turning back, not in resisting, but only in resolutely struggling forward, does our life consist.

Whether Tennyson read these words, we have no direct evidence. But only four years later, he was using this same cluster of ideas about man's "imperishable dignity" and the "unrest" and "ceaseless activity" of the age in the dramatic monologue "Ulysses," where the aged hero of Homer and Dante becomes a mouthpiece for the nineteenth century, rallying his shipmates with a Carlylean cry:

One equal temper of heroic hearts,
Made weak by time and fate, but strong in will
To strive, to seek, to find, and not to yield.[3]
                                                                    (68–70)

In this poem, as in many others, Tennyson shows himself to be emphatically a modern poet, immersed in the circumstances of the age, its currents of thought and feeling, its way of life. Sometimes his involvement was in the line of duty. As poet laureate he was required to provide verses for the comings and goings of the royal family, and celebratory pieces for great events, such as the funeral of the duke of Wellington and the opening of the International Exhibition of 1862 (where he faced the technical problem of composing an ode suitable for a choir of four thousand). He met these demands with style and a sure sense of rhetoric and public verse.

Outside his official capacity Tennyson came to see himself as a kind of national watchdog. Early in 1852, for example, he thought that the government was not sufficiently alert to the threat of invasion from France. So he fired off a series of squibs to the

[2]In *Short Studies of Great Subjects* (London, 1867).

[3]All quotations of poetry are from C. Ricks, ed., *The Poems of Tennyson* (London, 1969).

press, calling on the ministers to wake up and rousing the country to arms. The archenemies were the "vile" Napoleon III and "bastard Christianity," his term for Roman Catholicism, to be opposed by the stout English virtues of traditional liberty and the strength of national character. In 1854–1855, sections of *Maud* were written against the "peace-at-any-price" party in the Crimean War; and other sections of the poem were directed against contemporary scandals—the adulteration of food, the condition of the poor in the industrial cities, the worship of money (then vilified as Mammonism). Later in the century, in "Politics," he encouraged the former prime minister, Gladstone, to take back the reins of government with a firm hand; this was in 1889, at the end of a troublesome decade which had seen the Irish home rule issue and the Reform Bill of 1884. Occasionally these poems rise above doggerel and survive for some quality of verse. "The Charge of the Light Brigade" is one such poem. It sprang from a report in the *Times* for 2 December 1854; was written, said Tennyson, "in a few minutes"; and appeared in the *Examiner* seven days later.

Tennyson was also determinedly up-to-date in his science and scholarship. The twentieth-century nightmare is the horror of the nuclear age. The nineteenth-century nightmare was the discovery of man's place in the universe, the discrediting of the biblical story of creation, the realization of man's animal origin. These were some of the questions that Tennyson faced in *In Memoriam*, bringing to his poetic task the latest state of scientific knowledge. Readers in the 1850's were reassured that their poet laureate was no warbling songster but a poet-philosopher whose trains of thought involved cold fact and hard speculation—the cataclysmic theory of creation and its refutation in Sir Charles Lyell's countertheory of uniformitarian creation, the nebular hypothesis of the origin of the stars, the biological theory of mutability. What they read in Elegy CXXIII was not a string of poetic images but an account of the earth's past and future which they could substantiate in the textbooks of geology; reading in "Locksley Hall," in 1842, of the weighing of the sun, they would think of the astronomer Baily, who had been attempting that calculation since 1838.

In *In Memoriam* Tennyson set out to provide the nineteenth century with a moral interpretation of the universe, the meaning of life, and the nature of faith in a scientific world. In "Locksley Hall," he shows the impact of science and technology upon the imagination of contemporary man. The prospect of the future brings an uneasy excitement:

For I dipt into the future, far as human eye could see,
Saw the Vision of the world, and all the wonder that would be;

Saw the heavens fill with commerce, argosies of magic sails,
Pilots of the purple twilight, dropping down with costly bales;

Heard the heavens fill with shouting, and there rain'd a ghastly dew

From the nations' airy navies grappling in the central blue. . . .

(119–124)

This is the lesson of history, of man morally incapable of controlling his inventions. But the pattern takes a new turn. War is quelled in "the Federation of the world," "the Parliament of man."

In *The Princess* the scientific-technological vision is domesticated, playfully, to a fete day in the Kentish countryside of the 1840's:

and somewhat lower down
A man with knobs and wires and vials fired
A cannon: Echo answer'd in her sleep
From hollow fields: and here were telescopes
For azure views; and there a group of girls
In circle waited, whom the electric shock
Dislink'd with shrieks and laughter: round the lake
A little clock-work steamer paddling plied
And shook the lilies: perch'd about the knolls
A dozen angry models jetted steam:
A petty railway ran: a fire-balloon
Rose gem-like up before the dusky groves
And dropt a fairy parachute and past:
And there thro' twenty posts of telegraph
They flash'd a saucy message to and fro
Between the mimic stations; so that sport
Went hand in hand with Science, otherwhere
Pure sport: a herd of boys with clamour bowl'd
And stump'd the wicket; babies roll'd about
Like tumbled fruit in grass; and men and maids
Arranged a country dance, and flew thro' light
And shadow, while the twangling violin
Struck up with Soldier-laddie, and overhead
The broad ambrosial aisles of lofty lime
Made noise with bees and breeze from end to end.

(prologue, 64–88)

This is Tennyson's social vision of midcentury life, in the mixing of the classes, the squire among his tenants and their families; in the mingling of the countryfolk with the workingmen of the nearby town. Past, present, and future join hands in the encounter between newfangled science and the world of country sports, songs, and dances. This is the Victorian holiday Arcadia of harmony between man and man, between man and his inventions, and, in the closing lines, of an attendant harmony in nature.

Tennyson's distinctive Victorianism is most clearly shown in a large group of descriptive-narrative poems which he called his "English Idyls."[4] He borrowed the term from the Greek idyll, a type of pastoral poem presenting a scene or event in country life. He knew the form well from his reading of Theocritus and the Latin imitation in Vergil. Nothing quite like it had ever existed in English poetry. Perhaps the closest equivalent was in Crabbe and Wordsworth, telling of "man's inhumanity to man," the harsh realities of country poverty and despotism, and of the human and spiritual values of life in simple communities close to nature. In Tennyson these realities and intuitions are Victorianized. Nature is picturesque, ruralized; man is domesticated, his spiritual and emotional life cozily bounded by the pieties of the cradle, the family hearth, and the parish church. Inhumanity, where it occurs, is often in the shape of the seducer or the oppressive snob. The scenes and stories are carried in poetry of extraordinary descriptive power, such as this passage from "The Gardener's Daughter":

> Not wholly in the busy world, nor quite
> Beyond it, blooms the garden that I love.
> News from the humming city comes to it
> In sound of funeral or of marriage bells;
> And, sitting muffled in dark leaves, you hear
> The windy clanging of the minster clock;
> Although between it and the garden lies
> A league of grass, wash'd by a slow broad stream,
> That, stirr'd with languid pulses of the oar,
> Waves all its lazy lilies, and creeps on,
> Barge-laden, to three arches of a bridge
> Crown'd with the minster-towers.
>   The fields between
> Are dewy-fresh, browsed by deep-udder'd kine,
> And all about the large lime feathers low,
> The lime a summer home of murmurous wings.
>   (33–48)

Here language is pushed to its fullest expressive reach. The weight and density and richness of the water meadows and the "deep-udder'd kine" are car-

ried toward and over us in the embracing onomatopoeia; it is a highly sensuous verbal gesture the effect of which we can compare with another kind of virtuosity in this delicate atmospheric image from "The Miller's Daughter":

> I loved the brimming wave that swam
>   Through quiet meadows round the mill,
> The sleepy pool above the dam,
>   The pool beneath it never still,
> The meal-sacks on the whitened floor,
>   The dark round of the dripping wheel,
> The very air about the door
>   Made misty with the floating meal.
>   (97–104)

This stanza, like so many passages in Tennyson, can be read quite on its own as a beautiful vignette.

This style of pictorialism, applied to English country life and the English scene, was a feature of Tennyson's poetry that shaped nineteenth-century sensibility, although his own practice was shaped in turn—very directly so—in response to advice and criticism of individual poems. We can follow this process closely in the revisions he effected to certain pieces in the volumes of 1830 and 1833. When they were reprinted in *Poems* (1842), many were changed verbally and metrically, sometimes much for the worse, as with "The Miller's Daughter." The narrator is a man country-born and bred. In the 1833 version he is given a touching simplicity of style, a rustic quaintness of diction and phrasing. In the 1842 version this quality is lost. The language is decorated, poeticized; and the story of the fresh and innocent joy of first love is overlaid with what we come to recognize as a typically Victorian celebration of filial ties and domesticity. One such addition is the stanza in which the young man, a squire's son, seeks the consent of his widowed mother:

> And slowly was my mother brought
>   To yield consent to my desire:
> She wished me happy, but she thought
>   I might have looked a little higher;
> And I was young—too young to wed:
>   "Yet must I love her for your sake;
> Go fetch your Alice here," she said:
>   Her eyelid quivered as she spake.
>   (137–144)

It is probably fair to say that an important side to Tennyson's Victorianism was his willingness to con-

[4]Including "The Gardener's Daughter," "Audley Court," "Edwin Morris," "The Miller's Daughter," and many other poems.

form to popular taste, to write a style of poetry that was easily understood and enjoyed, both in its poetic technique and in themes and subject matter which fell within the popular notion of what poetry should be about. To a degree he was able to create and extend these limits by the force of his own writing. One excursion was into dialect poetry, rude eccentricity, perhaps, for a poet of such refined art. Whether the motive was experiment or a nostalgic return to the language of his Lincolnshire childhood (the thick twang of which he never lost) the poems themselves[5] are masterpieces of characterization and irony, Chaucerian in their gusto, their wit, their observation, and their penetration of human nature. They are portraits that Browning would have envied and Dickens enjoyed.

Tennyson's major innovation was to bring to English poetry a very remarkable and sophisticated experience of classical literature, something quite apart from his English-Vergilianism, the characteristics of which are neatly itemized in his official tribute, "To Virgil," written in 1883. He refers there to some of the qualities he most admired in the Roman poet and which he tried to imitate in his own choice of subject matter and in the musicality of his diction: Vergil the "Landscape-lover," the "lord of language," of "many a golden phrase," "majestic in thy sadness," "Wielder of the stateliest measure ever moulded by the lips of man." Much of Tennyson's poetry is decoratively and melodiously Vergilian in these ways. But not his best and most interesting work. There the Vergilian element is often assimilated in a larger, more complex classical presence, to be manipulated as a device of style and meaning, as it is in Elegy IX of *In Memoriam*, where the classical-Augustan surface is a deliberate aestheticism, a contrived face of art, which is destroyed by the sudden breakthrough of emotion, the encroachment of grief. Sometimes the classical presence excludes Vergil altogether for the social tones, the ease, and urbanity of Horace; and the voice we hear again and again in many of the finest lyrics is the voice of Catullus—not Catullus imitated or merely alluded to, but received and controlled in Tennyson's experience, as it is in Elegy LIX, Tennyson's formal and nonetheless beautiful version of the famous song of Catullus, "Vivamus, mea Lesbia, atque amemus," a

favorite among English poets (as we see in Marlowe's "The Passionate Shepherd to his Love," Jonson's "To Celia," Donne's "The Baite"):

> O Sorrow, wilt thou live with me
> No casual mistress, but a wife,
> My bosom-friend and half of life;
> As I confess it needs must be;
>
> O Sorrow, wilt thou rule my blood,
> Be sometimes lovely like a bride,
> And put thy harsher moods aside,
> If thou wilt have me wise and good.
>
> My centred passion cannot move.
> Nor will it lessen from to-day;
> But I'll have leave at times to play
> As with the creature of my love;
>
> And set thee forth, for thou art mine,
> With so much hope for years to come,
> That, howsoe'er I know thee, some
> Could hardly tell what name were thine.
>
> (1–16)

Each poet has his distinctive version. Marlowe's shepherd sings a seductive account of the pleasures they will "prove" together. Jonson's lover is a logic-chopping seducer—love stolen is no sin, only stolen love discovered. Donne is seductive in metaphysical style, in paradoxical hyperbole. This witty and sophisticated tradition is the ironic context, part of the meaning of Tennyson's poem, which has its own internal wit, sad and sardonic, turning the not-a-mistress-but-a-wife joke through the tones of resignation, pleading, stoic fatalism, and fearful wonder as the poet woos Sorrow, the classical muse Melpomene.

The allusive subtlety and literary sophistication of this poem are new in nineteenth-century literature. Ezra Pound thought that he was the discoverer of Catullus for the modern world, the Latin poet he most admired and judged untranslatable. But would he have been quite so contemptuous of Tennyson if he had taken account of Elegy LIX, or "Frater Ave atque Vale," or "Prefatory Poem to my Brother's Sonnets," or "Hendecasyllabics," a brilliant pastiche of Catullus' favorite meter in which Tennyson slyly rebuked the reviewers for their inability to attune to his poetic effects?

> O you chorus of indolent reviewers,
> Irresponsible, indolent reviewers,

---

[5]"Northern Farmer, Old Style" (written 1861), "Northern Farmer, New Style" (1865), "The Spinster Sweet-Arts" (1884), "The Church-warden and the Curate" (1890).

Look, I come to the test, a tiny poem
All composed in a metre of Catullus,
All in quantity, careful of my motion,
Like the skater on ice that hardly bears him,
Lest I fall unawares before the people,
Waking laughter in indolent reviewers.
Should I flounder awhile without a tumble
Thro' this metrification of Catullus,
They should speak to me not without a welcome,
All that chorus of indolent reviewers.
Hard, hard, hard is it, only not to tumble,
So fantastical is the dainty metre.
Wherefore slight me not wholly, nor believe me
Too presumptuous, indolent reviewers.
O blatant Magazines, regard me rather—
Since I blush to belaud myself a moment—
As some rare little rose, a piece of inmost
Horticultural art, or half coquette-like
Maiden, not to be greeted unbenignly.

This is no more than a skit. But, playful as it is, it illustrates as well as any of the lyrics or any of the classical monologues—"Ulysses," "Tithonus," "Tiresias," or "Demeter and Persephone"—that Tennyson's essential classicism is in his view of the poem as a work of art, with form as its distinguishing characteristic. It is this concern that sets him apart from the romantic poets and from the beginnings of the modern movement.

II

TENNYSON's poetry can be divided chronologically into three distinct groups: the poetry written before the death of Arthur Hallam in September 1833; the poetry written from the autumn of 1833 to the publication of *Maud* in 1855, including *The Princess* and *In Memoriam*; and the later writing, including his largest and most ambitious work, the *Idylls of the King*, the first section of which appeared in 1859 and which was virtually complete by 1872. Reading the works in this order, we can watch the poet's emergence from the imitative and derivative stage of his earliest childhood writing; and, in the late 1820's and early 1830's, the development of his own special kind of art poetry, the pictorializing treatment of scenes and situations and the highly expressive technique in the handling of language and verse form. The death of Arthur Hallam, his closest friend, in September 1833 was the immediate inspiration for his finest work in the 1830's and 1840's, leading to the collec-

tion of the elegies and their publication together in *In Memoriam* (1850). *Maud* marks a turning point in his career. It is a poem of great emotional violence and remarkable originality of form—as Tennyson described it, a lyric "Monodrama"—a strange work as original and unprecedented in English literature as *The Waste Land.* At the time the critics rejected *Maud* as a mistake, tainted by morbidity, a work of spasms. Thereafter Tennyson's creative drive was slackened, his fieriness burned out. A harsher, pessimistic note sounds increasingly in his public poetry, a disenchantment with materialism, a fear of overwhelming social and moral chaos following in the train of democracy, fear of contamination from the new freedoms in literature and art. In 1886, in "Locksley Hall Sixty Years After," he delivered his report on the state of Victorian civilization, a ranting diatribe against modern man and his creations: risen "from out the beast," to bestialism he is returning via atheism, radicalism, and the sewer realism of Zola. The idyllic serenity of pastoral England is blotted out by the canker of industrialism and its city-infernos of human degradation. All he could conjure against this was the countervision of the *Idylls*, an attempt to recreate the Arthurian story as a moral and spiritual allegory; and the series of historical plays—*Queen Mary, Harold, Becket,* and *The Foresters*—published between 1875 and 1892, in which he set out to portray periods of crisis in the struggle between right and might in what he called "the making of England." His ambition was to complement the history plays of Shakespeare. But Tennyson's grasp of drama and character was feeble, his sense of history incomplete; and his imagination and lyrical genius were never at home in these surroundings.[6]

The poetry of Tennyson's middle and later years is unmistakably the work of an aging man, finally of an old man—world-weary, reflective, disillusioned, sometimes wise and humane, an ancient sage, sometimes peppery and intolerant, a castigating Timon, sometimes just silly. Yet from the 1830's onward until the end of his life, Tennyson's poetry reveals a curious lack of development. The language, imagery, form, and imaginative vision of the best of the later poetry are not essentially different from the best of the middle years, and this in turn from the best of the early poetry. There is not, for example,

[6]G. W. Knight has argued strongly for the power of these plays in *The Golden Labyrinth* (London, 1962).

the line of radical development that we find in Yeats: the Tennysonianism of his earliest poetry and the Celtic Twilight of the 1880's and 1890's are followed by a purging sharpness and clarity which give way to the rich symbolism of the Byzantium poems, followed in turn by the Crazy Jane poetry and the masks and gnomism of the later 1930's. This development was partly a consequence of the literary situation. Whatever his own impulse toward change, Yeats had change thrust upon him by Eliot and Pound and by the twentieth-century demand for a new poetry, whereas Tennyson's public, by contrast, clung to the style and taste that the poet had himself created and which remained the poetic norm, at a popular level, until the end of the century. This historical, circumstantial explanation is of some value. But the inertia in Tennyson is more than stylistic; its center is in a strange recessive quality of his imagination which we come to recognize in his poetry in the recurrence of certain situations and moods around the experience of doubt, horror, isolation, and loss, of friends absent or dead, of loved ones yearned for, of scenes and events recalled from long ago.

This is naturally the poetry of old age—of "To the Rev. W. H. Brookfield" (1874), of "Vastness" and "To Mary Boyle" (1888), of "The Roses on the Terrace" and "Merlin and the Gleam" (1889), of "The Silent Voices" (1892). Yet this valetudinarian experience is also a feature of Tennyson's early poetry. Declarations of loneliness and deep melancholy are a phase of adolescence and a favorite stance of the Romantic Agony. But there is a note of genuine imaginative morbidity in "The Outcast," in "In Deep and Solemn Dreams," and in the "Ode to Memory," which date from 1826; and among the trivia of the *Poems* (1830 and 1833), the individual poetic voice sounds darkly in the "Mariana" poems, "Song," "The Kraken," "The Dying Swan," and "The Lady of Shalott," where the themes of death, abandonment, and isolation are so closely, sometimes obsessively, explored. So dramatically convincing is the note of depression and desperation in "The Two Voices" that critics have always accepted at face value the statement of Hallam Tennyson that the poem "was begun under the cloud" of his father's "overwhelming sorrow after the death of Arthur Hallam." In fact, the poem, then known as "Thoughts of a Suicide," was largely in existence by June 1833. Similar questions of style make it impossible to decide whether "Youth" and "From Sorrow Sorrow

Yet Is Born," both written in 1833, date from before or after Hallam's death.

Insofar as there can be any clue to the peculiar cast of Tennyson's imaginative temper, it is probably in the renowned "black-bloodedness" of the family, a hereditary melancholia, and in the circumstances of his home life at Somersby. His father was neurotic and took to drink to escape the fits of depression which overwhelmed him increasingly into the 1820's and drove him to homicidal violence. Tennyson recalled how as a child he used to run from the rectory on such occasions, throwing himself down among the gravestones in the churchyard, praying for a release in death. We can only conjecture about the impact of these experiences upon his creative imagination. What Tennyson does discuss about his childhood is "the passion of the past," a phrase which he used to describe the inspiration for "Tears, Idle Tears," and it is this "passion" which provides our best understanding of the recessive quality of his imagination, of which the melancholic and morbid aspects are only a part:

It is what I have always felt even from a boy, and what as a boy I called "the passion of the past". And it is so always with me now; it is the distance that charms me in the landscape, the picture and the past, and not the immediate to-day in which I move.

The poetic elaboration of this idea comes in "The Ancient Sage," written in 1885:

> Today? but what of yesterday? for oft
> On me, when boy, there came what then I called,
> Who knew no books and no philosophies,
> In my boy-phrase 'The Passion of the Past'.
> The first gray streak of earliest summer-dawn,
> The last long stripe of waning crimson gloom,
> As if the late and early were but one—
> A height, a broken grange, a grove, a flower
> Had murmurs "Lost and gone and lost and gone!"
> A breath, a whisper—some divine farewell—
> Desolate sweetness—far and far away—
> What had he loved, what had he lost, the boy?
> I know not and I speak of what has been.
>   (216–228)

Tennyson's "for oft" is a playful echo of the "For oft" that opens Wordsworth's remembered vision of the "golden daffodils." But there is no pretension to a mystical or philosophical interpretation, no move to penetrate the nature of the experience. He remains

content to contemplate its reminders and images—of
half-light, of solitariness, remoteness, and neglect—
and to ascribe to them a strange evocative power, as
of something loved and lost, which he cannot and
will not explain. Three years later, in 1888, Tennyson wrote "Far—Far—Away," a poem which contemplates, with similar delicacy, the "strange
charm" that these three words held for him since
childhood, a charm inexpressible (he says) in poetry,
its meaning only to be guessed at:

> What vague world-whisper, mystic pain or joy,
> Through those three words would haunt him
>   when a boy,
>   Far—far—away?
>
>   (7–9)

In "Tears, Idle Tears," Tennyson defined "the passion of the past" more precisely: its origin and compelling force are located not in childhood but in the
adult experience of unassuageable love:

> Dear as remember'd kisses after death,
> And sweet as those by hopeless fancy feign'd
> On lips that are for others; deep as love,
> Deep as first love, and wild with all regret;
> O Death in Life, the days that are no more.
>
>   (16–20)

This poem was written in 1845, and "the days that
are no more" is almost certainly a reference to his
years of friendship with Arthur Hallam, the "Death
in Life" a reference to the years after Hallam's death.

The memory of Hallam remained a haunting, obsessive presence for the remainder of Tennyson's life,
a focal point for all his sadness and passion, his feelings of yearning, desolation, and loss, the emotional
experiences at the heart of his finest work. The
Hallam origin can be surprising. For example, it is a
recent discovery that the lyric "Oh! That 'Twere
Possible," the nucleus around which *Maud* was built
in 1854–1855, was first written, in a slightly shorter
version, in the winter of 1833–1834. We can see in the
opening stanzas that only a matter of weeks or
months after his death, Hallam, in Tennyson's
imagination, had already been transformed into a
symbolic figure, here an androgynous lover:

> Oh! that 'twere possible,
> After long grief and pain,
> To find the arms of my true-love
> Round me once again!

> When I was wont to meet her
> In the silent woody places
> Of the land that gave me birth,
> We stood tranced in long embraces,
> Mixt with kisses sweeter, sweeter,
> Than any thing on earth.
>
>   (1–10)

Hallam's death was a precipitating experience rather
than an experience in itself. Tennyson's rhetoric of
affection, sometimes strongly sexual, can be properly interpreted only if we understand that the Hallam
of the poet's imagination was invested with many
roles—wife, lover, consoler, savior, muse. In "Vastness," written almost sixty years later, Tennyson
reviewed the history of man's existence, the unending succession of revolution and change—"what is
all of it worth?"

> What the philosophies, all the sciences, poesy, varying
>   voices of prayer?
> All that is noblest, all that is basest, all that is filthy with all
>   that is fair?
>
> What is it all, if we all of us end but in being our own
>   corpse-coffins at last,
> Swallow'd in Vastness, lost in Silence, drown'd in the deeps
>   of a meaningless Past?
>
> What but a murmur of gnats in the gloom, or a moment's
>   anger of bees in their hive?—
>   . . .
> Peace, let it be! for I loved him, and love him for ever: the
>   dead are not dead but alive.
>
>   (31–36)

For Tennyson, so many years later, the simple affirmation of continuing love is offered as a sufficient
and final answer; pathetically, we may think. It was
the only answer he could give, a flat, assertive statement. His deepest experiences of Hallam are in the
"dark house" sections of *In Memoriam* (VII, XCIX),
in the "Valley of Cauteretz," most powerfully of all
in "Cold and clear-cut face" in *Maud*, a single, sustained lyric sentence projecting the haunted mind,
the psychological reality of a nightmare vision, unequaled in English literature from Shakespeare's
Pericles to Eliot's *Marina:*

> Cold and clear-cut face, why come you so cruelly meek,
> Breaking a slumber in which all spleenful folly was
>   drown'd,
> Pale with the golden beam of an eyelash dead on the cheek,

Passionless, pale, cold face, star-sweet on a gloom
    profound;
Womanlike, taking revenge too deep for a transient wrong
Done but in thought to your beauty, and ever as pale as
    before
Growing and fading and growing upon me without a
    sound,
Luminous, gemlike, ghostlike, deathlike, half the night
    long
Growing and fading and growing, till I could bear it no
    more,
But arose, and all by myself in my own dark garden
    ground,
Listening now to the tide in its broad-flung shipwrecking
    roar,
Now to the scream of a madden'd beach dragg'd down by
    the wave,
Walk'd in a wintry wind by a ghastly glimmer, and found
The shining daffodil dead, and Orion low in his grave.

                                   (88–101)

III

ON the evidence of Tennyson's early poetry, up to 1833, it would have been inconceivable to predict the emergence of a great national poet. The quality of imagination is introspective and withdrawn; the poems themselves, highly aesthetic. They announce a writer devoted to exploring language as the medium of art and the forms of poetry as the forms of art distancing and art stylization, with the single poem as an art object, shaped and constructed, to be admired for its formal qualities of shapeliness and poise. *Poems* (1830) also reveals a writer whose sense of his poetic identity is very uncertain. There is an extraordinary unevenness in the collection, with a number of laughable album verses (today's ladies' magazine doggerel), trivially sentimental. At Cambridge he was surrounded by a group of high-minded idealists, the Apostles, who believed (according to one of their members) that it was their mission "to enlighten the world upon things intellectual and spiritual" and "to interpret the oracles of transcendental wisdom to the world of Philistines." Hallam was the born leader, Tennyson the poetic spokesman; and it is easy to understand the kind of pressure to which he was subjected. A neat illustration of this is in "The Palace of Art," his first important discussion of the artist's outward responsibility, his duty toward society.

According to Tennyson himself, the poem was written in response to the challenging remark of a fellow Apostle—"Tennyson, we cannot live in Art." Tennyson's poetic answer is on this same level of platitude: of course, it tells us, we cannot live alone, away from mankind, within our own world of created beauty. The soul that tries to do this is tormented by its conscience and quits the art palace for the humility and down-to-earthness of a country cottage. The art/life question left Tennyson's imagination untouched. The formal argument of the poem exerts no apparent control over its structure, which is largely a succession of isolated pictorial images, projecting the soul's fantasies as individual scenes. Some of these are symbolic landscapes in miniature:

> One seemed all dark and red—a tract of sand,
> And some one pacing there alone,
> Who paced for ever in a glimmering land,
> Lit with a low large moon.
>
>   . . .
>
> A still salt pool, locked in with bars of sand,
> Left on the shore; that hears all night
> The plunging seas draw backwards from the land
> Their moon-led waters white.
>
>   (65–68; 249–252)

This is the neurotic vision of "Mariana," the psychological setting of "Mariana in the South," with the strange, uncanny horror of isolation and abandonment. But the poem's structure is elaborative, not defining; the images might have been continued endlessly; and Tennyson's real answer is implicit in the poem's failure—the artist cannot work by slogans, and imagination will have its say, whatever the artist intends.

His positive response to the art/life question is in "The Lady of Shalott," written, unsolicited, at about the same time, in 1831–1832. The allegory is simple and lucid. It stresses the "magic" of art, and its necessity. The "fairy" lady weaves the "magic" sights from her mirror into a "magic" tapestry. But at last she grows weary of mirror images. Her attention is seized by the brilliant figure of Sir Lancelot. She leaves the tapestry and the mirror to look at him directly. These objects break and she suffers the "curse." She surrenders herself to the swollen river and the stormy night and is carried down to Camelot singing into death. The meaning of this fable is clear. The artist has no choice. He follows his calling, and fate decides the rest. His moral stance is not dedication but submission. His artistic stance is reverence for the magic and mystery of his art. The artist is both the magician and the enchanted, the wielder of the magic power and its subject. The poem asserts this in the fable and in its own poetic magic—the power of its images, its insistent and subtly varied rhythms, its intricately shaped stanzas and patterned lines, its sharp pictorialism, its brilliance of detail. It effects the verbal illusion of a new art experience, of a Pre-Raphaelite tapestry-enamel finely and glowingly colored. It is Tennyson's "Kubla Khan," the creation of the possessed, visionary poet, working his spell of words with such insinuating memorability.

As a quality of poetry and of the poetic imagination, the "magic" of art was a familiar idea to the romantic poets and their critics. Matthew Arnold found "natural magic" to the highest degree in Shakespeare and Keats. The "something magic" Tennyson himself found in Keats belonged, he said, to "the innermost soul of poetry." In turn, Whitman was to find a magic in Tennyson, in his "finest verbalism," in his evocation of the "latent charm of mere words, cunning collocutions, and in the voice ringing them." To appeal to magic and the spell of words in the 1980's may seem like critical antiquarianism. But no amount of technical analysis of sound effects and rhythms can explain the mysterious process whereby certain kinds of poetry are able to engage us, as "The Lady of Shalott" has engaged generations of readers. Its effects are the effects of art. Its figures, scenes, and events are pictorialized. It is a story from the legendary past and, stylized picturesquely, is kept there. There is nothing familiar, no human motivation, nothing for the reader to identify with or to understand in terms of his own experience or any imaginable experience other than the experience of the artist and his art. Perhaps this very exclusiveness and concentration are the secrets of its power, its symbolism so compelling that the allegory and fable assume the universality of myth. Certainly the poem carries Tennyson's personal myth of the artist's isolation, his loneliness and vulnerability, his "magic" of creation, his surrender to its working, his fatalism, his submission to necessity, to Camelot's river of life, which is for him the dark river of dissolution.

The imaginative reality of these experiences became fact with the death of Arthur Hallam. This was the tragedy, according to Hallam Tennyson, which "for a while blotted out all joy from his life, and made him long for death." Tennyson's immediate grief was poured into "Speak to Me,"

"Hark! the Dog's Howl," "Whispers," "On a Mourner," "Oh! That 'Twere Possible," and the earliest of the elegies. These are subjective, emotional utterances, the private poetry of desolation and mourning. At the same time he was searching for ways in which to answer his private needs, to carry his personal vision, in poetry addressed outward to the public at large, thereby attempting to fulfill his Apostolic sense of duty within the resources and compulsions of his own poetic character.

His first invention was a special form of dramatic monologue or dramatic narrative, adapting some classical or legendary situation, reinterpreted obliquely in terms of his own predicament. This group includes "Ulysses," "Morte d'Arthur," "Tiresias," "Tithon" (and possibly "St. Simeon Stylites," which was completed by November 1833, but may have been commenced before Hallam's death). The first two poems carry a message for the age. The Carlylean aspect of "Ulysses" has been referred to earlier. For Tennyson personally, the poem was an act of survival. Written at a time of depression and annihilating grief it gave his feeling, he said, "about the need of going forward and braving the struggle of life." This resolve is echoed in Ulysses' rallying cry to his fellow adventurers:

> One equal temper of heroic hearts,
> Made weak by time and fate, but strong in will
> To strive, to seek, to find, and not to yield.
>
> (68–70)

But there is a discrepancy between this declared moral stance and the character of the poem itself, which is curiously unresolved and undetermined. Its rhythms are long and swelling, lyrical in their larger movement, its imagery expansive and dissolving:

> The long day wanes: the slow moon climbs: the deep
> Moans round with many voices. Come, my friends,
> 'Tis not too late to seek a newer world.
> Push off, and sitting well in order smite
> The sounding furrows; for my purpose holds
> To sail beyond the sunset, and the baths
> Of all the western stars, until I die.
> It may be that the gulfs will wash us down:
> It may be we shall touch the Happy Isles,
> And see the great Achilles, whom we knew.
> Tho' much is taken, much abides; and tho'
> We are not now that strength which in old days
> Moved earth and heaven; that which we are, we are;
>
> (55–67)

332

The one distinct objective is Achilles-Hallam, the comrade in arms who died at Troy. But this aim is far distant. The pervasive experience is the voyager's extinction into eternity, his glorious dissolution "beyond the sunset":

> Yet all experience is an arch wherethro'
> Gleams that untravell'd world, whose margin fades
> For ever and for ever when I move.
>
> . . .
>
> And this gray spirit yearning in desire
> To follow knowledge like a sinking star,
> Beyond the utmost bound of human thought.
>
> (19–21; 30–32)

The discrepancy is between defiance and surrender, between the rousing moral and the poetic counterpull, between the blunt, prosaic, robust good sense of Ulysses' final words and the large, vague, romantic mirage toward which he will endlessly sail, endlessly hopeful. The Homer-Dante Ulysses is Tennysonianized. The poem becomes a metaphor for the poet's own voyage of self-discovery. He knows what, responsibly, he should be doing, what moral sinews should be flexed. Yet his deepest need is not for exhortation or exercise but for consolation.

The allegorical circumstances of "Morte d'Arthur" are very exact. King Arthur-Arthur Hallam is dying; the Round Table-Apostolic brotherhood is breaking up; Sir Bedivere's questions are Tennyson's own. What is left in the world when the leader is gone? What hope remains when fellowship is destroyed? Arthur's answer is Tennyson's poetic rationalization:

> The old order changeth, yielding place to new,
> And God fulfils Himself in many ways,
> Lest one good custom should corrupt the world.
>
> . . .
>
> Pray for my soul. More things are wrought by prayer
> Than this world dreams of. Wherefore, let thy voice
> Rise like a fountain for me night and day.
> For what are men better than sheep or goats
> That nourish a blind life within the brain,
> If, knowing God, they lift not hands of prayer
> Both for themselves and those who call them friend?
>
> (240–242; 247–253)

In delivering these words Tennyson was addressing his contemporaries as well as seeking a shred of comfort for himself. In an age of intellectual doubt and oppressive materialism, what were to be the guiding values? To these questions "Morte d'Arthur" returns no precise answer, only a general sense of good advice in the air and a readiness to believe. Tennyson's own uncertainty, and his limited means of assuaging it, are sounded in Arthur's final, puzzled, consolatory farewell. The visionary promise of Avilion, in all its poetic beauty, is offered as the one substantial comfort:

> But now farewell. I am going a long way
> With these thou seest—if indeed I go—
> (For all my mind is clouded with a doubt)
> To the island-valley of Avilion;
> Where falls not hail, or rain, or any snow,
> Nor ever wind blows loudly; but it lies
> Deep-meadow'd, happy, fair with orchard-lawns
> And bowery hollows crown'd with summer sea,
> Where I will heal me of my grievous wound.
>
> (256–264)

The interest of these poems is their statement of dilemma and, equally, their acceptance of dilemma as a condition of experience. Tennyson acknowledges his need for inspiration, whether in the heroics of the Carlylean message or in the Christian-Stoic resignation of Arthurian pulpit oratory. Yet he was too good a poet, too faithful to his weaker, more pathetic self, to deny his need for consolation, for an un-Christian, unmoral, unrespectable escape into fantasy and myth, into the wan, wistful illusion of Hallam's immortality.

Whereas both "Ulysses" and "Morte d'Arthur" carried a prominent and acceptable public message, and duly appeared in the next collection, *Poems* (1842), the other two poems of this group were held back: "Tithon" until 1860, when it was published, in a revised and lengthened form, as "Tithonus," and "Tiresias," also revised, until 1885. They are not notably inferior poems, and Tennyson's reluctance to make them public in 1842 was almost certainly on account of their lack of a theme more positive than the burden of existence, the appeal of death, and, for Tiresias, the longing for ennoblement in the heroic realms of the afterlife. Possibly Tennyson judged these dramatizations to be too indulgent, too confessional; and his great imaginative effort in the later 1830's, in "Locksley Hall" (written 1837–1838) and *The Princess* (begun by 1839), until *In Memoriam* and *Maud*, was the attempt to write poetry more securely distanced, to create verse structures in which he could develop a more optimistic countervision to the dilemma of "Ulysses" and "Morte d'Arthur" and to the inert withdrawal of "Tithon" and "Tiresias." Tennyson's task was to reconcile his Apostolic sense of duty with his interior nature as the poet of Shalott; and the creative cost of this ambition is clearly marked in the poetry of these years.

During the 1840's, especially after the success of *Poems* (1842), Tennyson's friends and reviewers (sometimes, significantly, the same people) urged him to change course, to engage with one of the great subjects of modern life, something with a human touch. His answer was *The Princess*, published in 1847. Since 1839, possibly earlier, he had been interested in the idea of a poem on women's education, a topic then much in the air. This was to provide the core of the work. Tennyson enlarged on this social theme, taking in the high Victorian notion of womanhood, its proper rights and duties. At a more profound level he considered the false ambitions and delusive ideals that can lure woman along the unnatural path of sexual and intellectual solitude, and within this moral theme, he explored the emotional implications of such separation. Described in this way, *The Princess* is neat and schematic. But for all the poem's ideas, and its seriousness of theme, and, on occasion, its seriousness of treatment, it reveals Tennyson's uneasiness, his inability to dramatize a public theme which touched him so deeply. His recourse is to a mock archaic style, quaint and fanciful, an evasive playfulness, a deprecatory whimsicality.

The modern social picture in the prologue and the conclusion is playful and naively idyllic, unpretentiously so. The message is universal harmony—between the classes, the sexes, mankind and science and nature, and a harmony of all creation with "the Heaven of Heavens." But the assertion is rhetorical; the poem itself is grossly unharmonious—stylistically and imaginatively it remains, as it is subtitled, *A Medley*. In effect it merely serves as a showcase for some of the great lyrics—"Tears, Idle Tears," "Ask Me No More," "Now Sleeps the Crimson Petal."

Tennyson's most ambitious structure and most embracing countervision was achieved in the formation of *In Memoriam*. When he wrote the first elegies in the winter of 1833–1834, it was with no thought of publication or any larger design. But the poems in this common stanza form accumulated until, eventually, in the 1840's, Tennyson introduced narrative-chronological sections and arranged the poems sequentially, so that they recounted a spiritual biography: the first prostration of grief, the onset of

religious doubt and hopelessness, checked by the intimation of a new and tempered faith, leading to a happy sense of God's purpose. The poem's crown is the epilogue, an epithalamium in which there is the fullest exposition of Tennyson's grand myth of consolation and comfort, involving Hallam, nature, and mankind in a triumphant single vision. He looks forward to the child of the marriage, destined to bring the human race one step closer to its highest state. The mood is serene and joyful, with the *Princess*-like harmonies of man, nature, and the universe beyond. Tennyson's prophetic myth is constructed from contemporary evolutionary thought adjusted to the romantic idealism of the age; and both these elements joined to his private fantasy of Hallam as forerunner of the "noble type," the link between later nineteenth-century man and his evolved form as "the crowning race."

The epilogue is a tour de force, a beautiful and suave conclusion to the poem's line of argument. But it has no more than a formal connection with the center of experience of the finest elegies, the poems that arise from Hallam. *In Memoriam* is a construct, an exploitation of the early elegies for the sake of Tennyson's ambition to deliver the great philosophical poem of the age and his need to ameliorate the Hallam experience, just as in *The Princess* the central core of emotion is separated off in the lyrics, contained in a Chinese-box extravaganza.

Tennyson's other recourse, in "Locksley Hall" and *Maud*, was not the escape from personality but its indulgence; not the measured, composed voice of the lyrical seer, nor the indirection of the virtuoso, with his "medley" of artful tones and styles, but the dense psychological and temperamental expression of confused or disordered minds, a thin ventriloquial disguise for the poet's own violence of feeling. Tennyson insisted that "Locksley Hall" was a "dramatic impersonation," not autobiography, a denial repeated more vehemently with *Maud*. But there are striking similarities in the circumstances of both heroes, with a common background story of tyrannical relations, frustrated love, and the power of money; and recent studies of these poems put it beyond doubt that Tennyson was writing out of his own bitterness and frustration in love, his poverty, and the feud with another, snobbishly superior, branch of the family.

Tennyson himself gave a very tepid account of "Locksley Hall": that it "represents young life, its good side, its deficiencies, and its yearnings"; and it was probably in this spirit that he included it in *Poems* (1842) as a young Victorian's view of the years ahead, of accelerating change and the promise of a new age of science and invention. What comes across, however, is not a representative point of view, not a neutrally Victorian response to the future, but the portrait of a disturbed mind, of someone dizzied and terrified by the vistas of change, yet cursing and rejecting the past embodied in the hall, whose name carries this symbolic, "locked" meaning:

Howsoever these things be, a long farewell to Locksley
    Hall!
Now for me the woods may wither, now for me the roof-
    tree fall.
Comes a vapour from the margin, blackening over heath
    and holt,
Cramming all the blast before it, in its breast a thunderbolt.
Let it fall on Locksley Hall, with rain or hail, or fire or
    snow;
For the mighty wind arises, roaring seaward, and I go.
                              (189–194)

As in the opening section of *Maud*, we are faced here with an unaccountable violence, a fantasy of rejection and denial for which there is no explanation either in the circumstances of the poem or in the character of the speaker. We have the impression of something left unsaid or imperfectly rendered, of effect without cause. In *Maud*, Tennyson allowed himself greater license in the persona of a madman; artistically, a dangerous license, for verisimilitude could justify the fragmentation of experience, the disassociation of thought and feeling, the lurchings and incoherences and wildness of a mind out of control—ironically so, since the poem itself is an outstanding exhibition of lyrical virtuosity and technical command over a great range of feeling and tone, from the fine ironies of "She came to the village church" (I.viii) to the sensuous lyricism of "I have led her home" (I.xviii) and the intense psychological realism of "Cold and clear-cut face" (I.iii) and "I heard no sound" (I.xiv. 516–526). One would guess that these sections of the poem, together with "Come into the garden" and several others, belong to the Hallam experience (remembering that the poem's starting point was "Oh! that 'twere possible") and to Tennyson's positive emotional life of the 1830's. The sections of madness come from another part of his experience altogether, from his hurt and pain, from the bitterness and injury of those years, feelings

which rankled and which he was unable to exploit creatively, other than in the madman's ravings:

And the vitriol madness flushes up in the ruffian's head,
Till the filthy by-lane rings to the yell of the trampled wife,
And chalk and alum and plaster are sold to the poor for
    bread,
And the spirit of murder works in the very means of life,

And Sleep must lie down arm'd, for the villainous
    centre-bits
Grind on the wakeful ear in the hush of the moonless
    nights,
While another is cheating the sick of a few last gasps, as
    he sits
To pestle a poison'd poison behind his crimson lights.

When a Mammonite mother kills her babe for a burial fee,
And Timour-Mammon grins on a pile of children's bones,
Is it peace or war? better, war! loud war by land and by
    sea,
War with a thousand battles, and shaking a hundred
    thrones.
                         (I.i. 36–47)

Of course, this is not Tennyson in person. But in a strange sense it is. The images of horror are figments of a demented mind; yet they have a rational, external, historical existence. The adulteration of bread was a current scandal much written about in the period 1851–1855. The "Mammonite" mother was a horrible reality. Children had indeed been murdered for the sake of the "burial fee" of £3 or £4. It is impossible to judge where Tennyson's revulsion ends and the dramatic character of the madman begins. In those closing lines war is a symptomatic image of the hero's own divided, disruptive personality. Yet in the concluding sections of the poem, when the hero has emerged into sanity, war is presented as the ennobling cause, the great destiny which will raise and unify the nation:

For the peace, that I deem'd no peace, is over and done,
And now by the side of the Black and the Baltic deep,
And deathful-grinning mouths of the fortress, flames
The blood-red blossom of war with a heart of fire.

Let it flame or fade, and the war roll down like a wind,
We have proved we have hearts in a cause, we are noble
    still,
And myself have awaked, as it seems, to the better mind;
It is better to fight for the good than to rail at the ill;
I have felt with my native land, I am one with my kind,
I embrace the purpose of God, and the doom assign'd.
                  (III.iv–v. 50–59)

There is nothing remarkable in the fact of Tennyson's warmongering; it is exactly in character with his newspaper squibs of 1852; and he was an opponent of those who wanted peace in the Crimea. What is remarkable is the apparent ease and confidence with which this rousing finale is delivered, so alike in style and manner to the endings of *The Princess* and *In Memoriam*, but to what different harmonies! There the vision was idyllic and spiritual; here it is the glorification of war as a moral force, as the destiny to uplift society and assert the nation's strength, and to join the individual to this great common purpose. This is Tennyson's secular, propagandizing, energizing countervision, to ward off the Hallam experience, to deny the poet of Shalott, to fulfill the Apostolic mission. We must admire the synthesizing power of the verse in answering these complex demands; but we can only regret the imaginative necessity that drove Tennyson to seek a solution so unworthily and triumphantly expedient.

Maud was an act of catharsis. Whatever the personal and imaginative pressures that drove him to this strange, inventive creation, there was no return after this to the anguish and yearning for Hallam or to the powerful eroticism of the lyrics. The lyrical vein continues, much subdued, in poems of friendship—"To Mary Boyle," "To E. Fitzgerald," "To the Master of Balliol," "June Bracken and Heather," "The Roses on the Terrace." These Horatian lyrics are graceful, charming, and witty. But the impulse is low-powered. We see this too in the elegiac poems and the reminiscences of Hallam—"In the Garden at Swainston," *In Memoriam* XXXIX (written in 1868), "Prefatory Poem to my Brother's Sonnets," "Frater Ave atque Vale"—beautiful and moving tributes from which the anguish and poignance have gone.

For the public of the 1850's, *Maud* was an aberration. Tennyson redeemed himself, became once again the poet of *In Memoriam*—and, more than that, a modern Vergil, a great national poet—in the *Idylls of the King*. Tennyson regarded the story of Arthur as "the greatest of all poetical subjects" and Malory's version the best of the existing accounts, full of "very fine things but all strung together without Art." The Arthurian stories had fascinated him since childhood and he planned and hesitated for over twenty years, from about 1833 to the mid-1850's, before seriously embarking upon the poem entire, of which "Morte d'Arthur" had appeared as a separate piece in 1842. Eventually, the *Idylls* came out in four volumes between 1859 and 1885, when they were first collected and placed in their final order.

The "Art" which he applied to his sources, principally to Malory, was characteristically Tennysonian. The cycle of stories is drawn upon to provide the raw material for a group of pictorialized scenes and events, each one isolated and presented rather like a stage tableau, showing a step in the rise and fall of Arthurian society, from Arthur's "Coming" to his "Passing." The moral allegory is pronounced: this is what happens to the ideals of chivalry and Christian heroism—brotherhood degenerates into enmity, love into lust, honor into pride, courage into brutality, vision into delusion. This is the cost of man's all-too-human humanity.

Tennyson is successful in the *Idylls* where we would expect him to be—in the descriptive writing, in establishing atmosphere and mood and the reality of particular disturbed states of mind and feeling. His failure is in the treatment of the figures. On the one hand, he was unable to distance and stylize them allegorically, in the accomplished manner of Chaucer or Spenser; on the other hand, he was unable to bring them to life naturally and realistically (as he did successfully in the Lincolnshire poems); nor could he even manage the halfway dramatization that Wordsworth discovered as the perfect medium for his beggars, leech gatherers, shepherds, and other countryfolk who have both a symbolic and a natural role. It was not simply a technical deficiency but a failing in dramatic sense, which is really an absence of human sympathy. This comes across very sharply, for example, in the confrontation between Arthur and Guinevere. After listening to his wife's plea for forgiveness for her unfaithfulness with Lancelot, Arthur delivers a reprimand two hundred lines long, veering between his allegorical function as the conscience of society:

> Yet must I leave thee, woman, to thy shame.
> I hold that man the worst of public foes
> Who either for his own or children's sake,
> To save his blood from scandal, lets the wife
> Whom he knows false, abide and rule the house:
> ("Guinevere," 508–512)

and his part in the human drama:

> I cannot touch thy lips, they are not mine,
> But Lancelot's: nay, they never were the King's.
> I cannot take thy hand; that too is flesh,
> And in the flesh thou hast sinn'd; and mine own flesh,

Here looking down on thine polluted, cries
"I loathe thee":

(548–553)

Arthur sounds no better than an outraged husband
in a Victorian melodrama—shades of Mr. Collins! If
we try to localize the problem, it is in Tennyson's
decision to purify the legendary Arthur, to transform him into a being sent by God and returning to
Him unsullied by his earthly passage. Tennyson was
proud to point out this purification in a dedicatory
poem "To the Queen," published in the 1872 edition,
in which he underlined the fact that his Arthur was
not Malory's "Touched by the adulterous finger of a
time/That hovered between war and wantonness, /
And crownings and dethronements," and later he inserted a line exactly describing Arthur's allegorical
character: "Ideal manhood closed in real man."

To be precise, Tennyson's crucial act of censorship
was to ignore the stories of Arthur's adulterous conception and of his unwitting incestuous relationship
with his half sister, of which the offspring is Modred.
These elements in the Arthurian story constitute the
doom of the house, the cruel and tragic destiny,
which any Greek dramatist would have lighted upon
as a fable as strong and significant as that of
Oedipus. Whether or not we judge this to be a fair
analogy,[7] the *Idylls* face us squarely with the question of Tennyson's later achievement, its scope and
limitations, its timelessness in placing the poet as a
teller of old tales, its peculiar Victorianism in the
adaptation of the tale and the style of its telling.

SELECTED BIBLIOGRAPHY

I. BIBLIOGRAPHY. Detailed bibliographical information
can also be found in the *New Cambridge Bibliography of
English Literature*, vol. III (Cambridge, 1969). T. J. Wise,
A Bibliography of the Writings of Alfred, Lord Tennyson
(London, 1908), privately printed, the most detailed,
analytical bibliography, includes Wise's forged eds.; F. E.
Faverty, ed., *The Victorian Poets: A Guide to Research*
(Cambridge, Mass., 1956; rev. ed., 1968), contains a sound
account of modern research and criticism by P. F. Baum,
the latter contains an updated account by E. D. H. Johnson; C. Tennyson and C. Fall, *Alfred Tennyson: An Annotated Bibliography* (Athens, Ga., 1967), the only

[7]Swinburne's discussion of this point in *Under the Microscope*
(London, 1872) is the most sustained criticism of Tennyson as a
poet reduced by his own notion of morality.

classified bibliography, useful but with many inexplicable
omissions; A. E. Dyson, ed., *English Poetry: Select
Bibliographies* (Oxford, 1971), contains the best descriptive and critical bibliography of the works of Tennyson,
comp. by J. D. Hunt.

II. REFERENCE WORKS. A. E. Baker, *A Concordance to
the Poetical and Dramatic Works of Alfred, Lord Tennyson* (London, 1914; supp. 1931; reiss. 1966); A. E.
Baker, *A Tennyson Dictionary* (London, 1916); G. O.
Marshall, *A Tennyson Handbook* (New York, 1963).

III. COLLECTED WORKS. *Poetical Works*, 4 vols. (Leipzig,
1860); *Works*, 10 vols. (London, 1870), the Pocket Volume
(Miniature) ed., augmented by one vol. in 1873 and two
more in 1877; A. C. Loffelt, ed., *Complete Works* (Rotter-
dam, 1871); *Works*, 6 vols. (London, 1872–1873; reiss.
1877), the Imperial Library ed.; *Works*, 12 vols. (London,
1874–1877), the Cabinet ed., augmented by an additional
vol. (1881); *Works*, 7 vols. (London, 1874–1881), the
Author's ed.; *Works* (London, 1878), the Crown ed.;
Works (London, 1884), the Macmillan ed., often repr.;
Works (London, 1894), the standard complete one-vol. ed.
of the poems and plays, also issued in the Oxford Standard
Authors series as *Tennyson: Poems and Plays* (London,
1965); *Life and Works of Alfred, Lord Tennyson*, 12 vols.
(London, 1898–1899), the Edition de Luxe, the "Life" by
Hallam, second Baron Tennyson; Hallam, Lord Tennyson, ed., *Poems, Annotated by Alfred, Lord Tennyson*, 9
vols. (London, 1907–1908), the Eversley ed.; C. Ricks, ed.,
The Poems of Tennyson (London, 1969), supersedes all
previous "complete" eds. of the poetry, presenting all the
known poems, published and unpublished, omitting only
MS material still under restriction, has full textual,
historical, and bibliographical notes and can properly be
regarded as the basic document in any study of Tennyson.

IV. SELECTED WORKS. F. T. Palgrave, ed., *Lyrical Poems*
(London, 1885), in the Golden Treasury series, important
because Tennyson advised Palgrave on the selection; J. C.
Collins, ed., *The Early Poems* (London, 1900); H. J. C.
Grierson, ed., *Poems* (London, 1907); B. C. Mulliner, ed.,
Shorter Poems and Lyrics, 1833–42, 2 vols. (Oxford,
1909); J. C. Thompson, ed., *Suppressed Poems, 1830–68*
(London, 1910); T. S. Eliot, ed., *Poems* (Edinburgh, 1936);
W. H. Auden, ed., *A Selection from the Poems* (New York,
1944); D. Bush, ed., *Tennyson: Selected Poetry* (New
York, 1951); C. Tennyson, ed., *Poems* (London, 1954); M.
McLuhan, ed., *Selected Poetry* (London, 1956); J. H.
Buckley, ed., *Poems* (Cambridge, Mass., 1958); B. C.
Southam, ed., *Selected Poems* (London, 1964), the only
ed. apart from the complete one by Ricks to place the
poems in order of composition and to attempt comprehen-
sive historical and explanatory notes; D. Cecil, ed., *A
Choice of Verse* (London, 1971); J. D. Jump, ed., *In
Memoriam, Maud and Other Poems* (London, 1975), the
Everyman ed.

V. SEPARATE WORKS. *Poems by Two Brothers* (London–Louth, 1827), by Alfred and Charles, with three or four pieces by Frederick; 2nd ed., H. Tennyson, ed. (London, 1893); *Timbuctoo* (Cambridge, 1829), in *Prolusiones Academicae; Poems, Chiefly Lyrical* (London, 1830); *The Lover's Tale* (London, 1833; 1st authorized ed., London, 1879), the former was privately printed; *Poems* (London, 1833); *Poems*, 2 vols. (London, 1842), contains many poems repr., and some rev., from *Poems* of 1830 and 1833; *The Princess: A Medley* (London, 1847; rev. eds., 1850, 1851, 1853); *In Memoriam* (London, 1850), an additional poem in the 4th ed. (London, 1851), and another inserted in 1870; *Ode on the Death of the Duke of Wellington* (London, 1852; rev. ed., 1853); *Maud, and Other Poems* (London, 1855; rev. eds., 1856, 1859); *Idylls of the King* (London, 1859; enl. eds., 1862, 1869, 1872, 1885), early eds. consisted of "Enid," "Vivien," "Elaine," "Guinevere"; *Enoch Arden, and Other Poems* (London, 1864); *The Holy Grail, and Other Poems* (London, 1870); *Gareth and Lynette* (London, 1872); *Queen Mary: A Drama* (London, 1875); *Harold: A Drama* (London, 1877); *Ballads and Other Poems* (London, 1880); *Becket* (London, 1884), drama; *The Cup, and, The Falcon* (London, 1884), dramas; *Tiresias, and Other Poems* (London, 1885); *Locksley Hall Sixty Years After* (London, 1886); *Demeter, and Other Poems* (London, 1889); *The Death of Oenone, Akbar's Dream, and Other Poems* (London, 1892); *The Foresters: Robin Hood and Maid Marian* (London, 1892), drama; C. Tennyson, ed., *The Devil and the Lady* (London, 1930); C. Tennyson, ed., *Unpublished Early Poems* (London, 1931).

VI. LETTERS. H. Tennyson, *Alfred Lord Tennyson: A Memoir*, 2 vols. (London, 1897), vol. I, ch. 10, contains letters 1842–1845, and vol. II, chs. 16 and 23, letters 1862–1864; F. A. Mumby, ed., *Letters of Literary Men* (London, 1906), vol. II, pp. 561–567; L. Pierce, ed., *Alfred Lord Tennyson and William Kirby: Unpublished Correspondence* (Toronto, 1929); M. J. Ellmann, "Unpublished Letters of Tennyson," in *Modern Language Notes*, 65 (1950).

VII. BIOGRAPHICAL AND CRITICAL STUDIES. Some of the following articles are repr. in J. D. Jump, ed., *Tennyson: The Critical Heritage* (London, 1967) or in J. Killham, ed., *Critical Essays on the Poetry of Tennyson* (London, 1960). They are referred to under the titles given in those publications. A. H. Hallam, "Poems, Chiefly Lyrical, 1830," in *Englishman's Magazine*, 1 (August 1831), an unsigned review, repr. in Jump, further discussed in M. McLuhan, "Tennyson and Picturesque Poetry" (see below); G. Eliot, "Maud and Other Poems," in *Westminster Review* (October 1855); W. Bagehot, "Idylls of the King, 1859," in *National Review*, 9 (October 1859), an unsigned review, repr. in Jump; M. Arnold, *On Translating Homer: Last Words* (London, 1862), includes a section on Tennyson's simplicity that is repr. in Jump; H. Taine, *Histoire de la littérature anglaise*, 4 vols. (Paris, 1863–1864), trans. by H. Van Laun

into English, 2 vols. (London, 1871), contains the ch. "Poetry—Tennyson," repr. in Jump; W. Bagehot, "Wordsworth, Tennyson and Browning: Or, Pure, Ornate and Grotesque Art in English Poetry," in *National Review*, n.s. 1 (November 1864), an unsigned article, repr. in Jump, contains a review of Tennyson's *Enoch Arden*, further discussed in M. Dodsworth, "Patterns of Morbidity: Repetition in Tennyson's Poetry," in I. Armstrong, ed. *The Major Victorian Poets* (see below); R. Simpson, "Mr. Tennyson's Poetry," in *North British Review* (January 1871); A. C. Swinburne, *Under the Microscope* (London, 1872), includes comments on *Idylls of the King* that are repr. in Jump; H. James, "Tennyson's Drama," in *Galaxy* (September 1875); A. C. Swinburne, *Miscellanies* (London, 1886), includes the essay "Tennyson and Musset," a reply to Taine (above), extracts repr. in Jump; R. H. Hutton, *Literary Essays* (London, 1888), contains the ch. "Tennyson," replying to Swinburne (above) and repr. in Jump; H. Tennyson, *Materials for a Life of A. T.*, 4 vols. (London, 1896), privately printed, basic source material for the author's later official biography; H. Tennyson, *Alfred Lord Tennyson: A Memoir*, 2 vols. (London, 1897).

A. C. Bradley, *A Commentary on Tennyson's "In Memoriam"* (London, 1901; rev. eds., 1902, 1930); A. Lang, *Alfred Tennyson* (London, 1901); G. K. Chesterton and R. Garnett, *Tennyson* (London, 1903); W. P. Ker, *Tennyson* (Cambridge, 1909), the Leslie Stephen Lecture, Cambridge, 11 November 1909; G. K. Chesterton, *The Victorian Age in Literature* (London–New York, 1913); A. C. Bradley, *The Reaction Against Tennyson* (London, 1917), English Association pamphlet no. 39; H. Nicholson, *Tennyson: Aspects of His Life, Character and Poetry* (London, 1923; 2nd ed., 1925), the most popular and influential account, very readable and convincing as a psychological-literary portrait, but must be read with caution; F. R. Leavis, *New Bearings in English Poetry* (London, 1932; rev. ed., 1950), together with his *Revaluation* and *The Common Pursuit* (below), contains this author's influential views; T. S. Eliot, *Essays Ancient and Modern* (London, 1936), contains the essay "In Memoriam," which is repr. in Killham; F. R. Leavis, *Revaluation: Tradition and Development in English Poetry* (London, 1936); G. M. Young, *Victorian England: Portrait of an Age* (London, 1936); J. N. D. Bush, *Mythology and the Romantic Tradition in English Poetry* (Cambridge, Mass., 1937), Harvard Studies in English no. 18; C. C. Abbott, ed., *Further Letters of Gerard Manley Hopkins* (London, 1938), includes a letter dated 10 September 1864 that discusses Tennyson's language and is repr. in Jump; G. M. Young, *The Age of Tennyson* (London, 1939), the Warton Lecture on English Poetry, 1939, also printed in *Proceedings of the British Academy*, 35 (1939).

W. D. Paden, "Tennyson and the Reviewers, 1827–35," in *University of Kansas Publications, Humanistic Studies*, 6, no. 4 (1940), 15–39; W. D. Paden, *Tennyson in Egypt: A*

Study of the Imagery in His Earlier Work (Lawrence, Kans., 1942); C. Brooks, *The Well-Wrought Urn* (London, 1947), includes the ch. "The Motivation of Tennyson's Weeper," on "Tears, Idle Tears," which is repr. in Killham; P. F. Baum, *Tennyson Sixty Years After* (Chapel Hill, N. C., 1948); C. Tennyson, *Alfred Tennyson* (London, 1949), the standard biography, excellent both historically and interpretatively; F. W. Bateson, *English Poetry: A Critical Introduction* (London, 1950), contains the ch. "Romantic Schizophrenia: Tennyson's 'Tears, Idle Tears'"; A. J. Carr, "Tennyson as a Modern Poet," in *University of Toronto Quarterly*, 19 (1950), repr. in Killham; J. H. Buckley, *The Victorian Temper: A Study in Literary Culture* (Cambridge, Mass., 1951); G. Hough, "Tears, Idle Tears," in *Hopkins Review* (1951), repr. in Killham; M. McLuhan, "Tennyson and Picturesque Poetry," in *Essays in Criticism*, 1 (January 1951), repr. in Killham, relates to Hallam's review (above); E. D. H. Johnson, *The Alien Vision of Victorian Poetry: Sources of the Poetic Imagination in Tennyson, Browning and Arnold* (Princeton, N. J., 1952); F. R. Leavis, *The Common Pursuit* (London, 1952); E. F. Shannon, *Tennyson and the Reviewers: A Study of His Literary Reputation and of the Influence of the Critics upon His Poetry, 1827–1851* (Cambridge, Mass., 1952); L. Spitzer, "'Tears, Idle Tears' Again," in *Hopkins Review* (1952), repr. in Killham, a reply to Hough (above); C. Tennyson, *Six Tennyson Essays* (London, 1954); R. Langbaum, *The Poetry of Experience: The Dramatic Monologue in Modern Literary Tradition* (London, 1957); W. W. Robson, "The Dilemma of Tennyson," in *The Listener*, 13 (June 1957), repr. in Killham; B. Ford, ed., *The Pelican Guide to English Literature*, vol. VI (London, 1958), contains R. Mayhead's "The Poetry of Tennyson"; J. Killham, *Tennyson and the Princess: Reflections of an Age* (London, 1958); M. McLuhan, "Tennyson and the Romantic Epic," in Killham (London, 1960).

J. H. Buckley, *Tennyson: The Growth of a Poet* (Cambridge, Mass.–London, 1960), an important biographical-historical study giving a detailed scholarly and critical account of Tennyson's development; J. Killham, ed., *Critical Essays on the Poetry of Tennyson* (London, 1960), a representative collection of the best modern criticism, repr. studies by T. S. Eliot, G. M. Young, C. Brooks, M. McLuhan, G. Hough, L. Spitzer, A. J. Carr, and W. W. Robson; H. S. Davies, comp., *The Poets and Their Critics: Blake to Browning* (London, 1962), gives extracts of adverse criticism of Tennyson; G. W. Knight, *The Golden Labyrinth: A Study of British Drama* (London, 1962); V. Pitt, *Tennyson Laureate* (London, 1962); J. Richardson, *The Pre-eminent Victorian: A Study of Tennyson* (London, 1962); R. W. Rader, *Tennyson's Maud: The Biographical Genesis* (Berkeley–Los Angeles, 1963), explores the significant relationship of the poet's private life and art; J. B. Steane, *Tennyson* (London, 1966); J. D. Jump, ed., *Tennyson: The Critical Heritage* (London, 1967), reprs. a selection of reviews, essays, and other comments for the period 1831–1891 and discusses the contemporary response and critical reception in an extensive intro., selections include criticism by A. Hallam (reviewing *Poems*, 1830), W. Bagehot, M. Arnold, G. M. Hopkins, A. C. Swinburne, H. Taine, R. H. Hutton, and many others; C. Ricks, "Tennyson's Methods of Composition," in *Proceedings of the British Academy*, 52 (1967); I. Armstrong, ed., *The Major Victorian Poets: Reconsiderations* (London, 1969), includes essays by M. Dodsworth, B. Bergonzi, A. Sinfield, and A. S. Byatt; J. D. Hunt, ed., *Tennyson's "In Memoriam": A Casebook* (London, 1970), a collection of documents and critical essays on the poem; C. Ricks, *Tennyson* (London, 1972); D. J. Palmer, ed., *Tennyson* (London, 1973); F. E. L. Priestley, ed., *Language and Structure in Tennyson's Poetry* (London, 1973); C. Tennyson and H. Dyson, *The Tennysons: Background to Genius* (London, 1974); P. Kincaid, *Tennyson's Major Poems: The Comic and Ironic Patterns* (New Haven, Conn., 1975); A. D. Culler, *The Poetry of Tennyson* (New Haven, Conn., 1977); P. Henderson, *Tennyson: Poet and Prophet* (London, 1978); J. S. Hagen, *Tennyson and His Publishers* (London, 1979); R. Pattison, *Tennyson and Tradition* (Cambridge, Mass., 1980); R. B. Martin, *Tennyson: The Unquiet Heart* (London, 1980).

EDWARD FITZGERALD
(1809-1883)

Joanna Richardson

LIFE

ON 31 March 1809, at Bredfield, some seven miles from Ipswich, Mary Frances FitzGerald Purcell gave birth to her seventh child. Edward, for so she named him, entered a distinguished family. The FitzGeralds, who traced their descent from the dukes of Tuscany and earls of Kildare, were among the most eminent Anglo-Norman families in Ireland. The Purcells had come to England with William the Conqueror. As for Mary Purcell, she was not only well descended, but also blessed with Junoesque beauty and strong character. We are told that she was "a very fine woman, but *a bad Mother*"; and certainly she kept at an Olympian distance from her children. Yet Edward's childhood was far from unhappy. He remembered watching from his nursery window as his father and the squire set out in their pink hunting habits; he remembered eating beef and plum pudding and drinking loyal toasts to mark the first anniversary of Waterloo. He remembered vividly how, when he was seven, the family had gone to live in France, and they had seen the royal hunt near Saint-Germain-en-Laye:

Louis XVIII first, with his *Gardes du Corps,* in blue and silver: then Monsieur (afterwards Charles X) with *his* Guard in green and gold—French horns blowing—"tra, tra, tra" (as Madame de Sévigné says), through the lines of chestnut and limes—in flower. And then *Madame* (of Angoulême) standing up in her carriage, blear-eyed, dressed in white with her waist at her neck—standing up in the carriage at a corner of the wood to curtsey to the English assembled there—my mother among them. This was in 1817 . . . I saw, and see it all.

The Purcells lived in Saint-Germain and Paris until, in 1818, Mary's father died, and she became the owner of several handsome estates and, it was said, the wealthiest commoner in England. She and her husband adopted the name of FitzGerald ("I somehow," wrote Edward, "detest my own scrolloping surname") and returned to Bredfield. Edward was promptly sent to the grammar school at Bury St. Edmunds.

The school was blessed with an enlightened headmaster and an outstanding academic record. Edward proved himself an erratic pupil, but at Bury St. Edmunds he formed devoted friendships with William Bodham Donne (a descendant of John Donne); James Spedding, the future editor of Francis Bacon and "the wisest man I have ever known"; and John Mitchell Kemble, son of the actor Charles Kemble, and brother of Fanny. His schooldays were unusually happy, and in middle age he could still revisit the town to enjoy "a Biscuit and a Pint of Sherry" and to gaze affectionately on the old abbey gate.

In 1826, he matriculated at Trinity College, Cambridge; and the pattern of Bury St. Edmunds was repeated. Again the curriculum took second place. The honors degree meant keen competition, and he chose to read for a pass degree. He read widely, but not, of course, the books prescribed by his tutors; he also formed further intimate friendships, one of them, in his final year, being with William Makepeace Thackeray. Early in 1830 he took a pass degree, and embarked upon his apparently aimless life.

It might be more true to say that FitzGerald's allowance of £300 permitted him to follow his fancies, rather than settle down to a calling; and after a brief visit to Paris, he came home to practice his social theories. "Tell Thackeray," he wrote to a friend, "that he is never to invite me to his house, as I intend never to go. . . . I cannot stand seeing new faces in the polite circles. You must know that I am going to become a great bear: and have got all sorts of Utopian ideas into my head about society."[1]

---

[1]All quotations from the letters are from A. M. Terhune and A. B. Terhune, eds., *Letters of Edward FitzGerald,* 4 vols. (Princeton, N. J., 1980).

At twenty-one FitzGerald adopted his lifelong principle of "plain living and high thinking." In 1833 he adopted a diet in which bread and fruit were the staple foods, and his life took on the "even gray paper character" that it would always retain. Reacting, perhaps, against the luxurious life of his parents, resenting "the espalier of London dinner-table company," he determined to fling out his branches in his own way. He rented lodgings in Soho or Bloomsbury; and his greatest London pleasures were browsing in bookshops, visiting galleries, and enjoying the company of his bachelor friends. When he was not in London, he would roam about the country, visiting friends and relations and places of interest, keeping, he said, "on the windy side of care" and writing letters. "I suppose it must seem strange to you," he wrote to a Cambridge friend, "that I should like writing letters . . . . However, here I see no companions, so I am pleased to talk to my old friend John Allen: which indeed keeps alive my humanity very much." "I have such love of you, and of myself," he added a few days later, "that once every week, at least, I feel spurred on by a sort of gathering up of feelings, to vent myself in a letter upon you. . . . I am sorry to say that I have a very young-lady-like partiality to writing to those that I love."

Among those he loved were Thackeray and Alfred Tennyson; and when he thought of Thackeray, "the cockles of his heart were warmed":

> The chair that Will sat in, I sit in the best;
> The tobacco is sweetest which Willy hath blest;
> And I never found out that my wine tasted ill
> When a tear would drop in it for thinking of Will. . . .[2]

He eagerly followed Thackeray's literary fortunes; he offered to help him in his financial reverses; he wrote him some of his most spirited letters. And even when Thackeray became "a little spoiled by London praise, and some consequent Egotism," FitzGerald still considered him "a very fine fellow." Just before he died, Thackeray was asked which, of all his friends, he had cared for most; he is said to have answered: "Why, dear old Fitz, to be sure."

As for Tennyson, FitzGerald watched his career with critical interest. "Tennyson," he once wrote in anger, "thinks more about his bowels and nerves

than about the Laureate wreath he was bound to inherit. . . . How are we to expect heroic poems from a valetudinary?" But the very criticism indicated affection; and if FitzGerald had small patience with the poet's ills, he still delighted in his company and generously recognized his distinction:

> Alfred Tennyson staid with me at Ambleside. . . . I will say no more of Tennyson than that the more I have seen of him, the more cause I have to think him great. His little humours and grumpinesses were so droll, that I was always laughing. . . . I must however say, further, that I felt what Charles Lamb describes, a sense of depression at times from the overshadowing of a so much more lofty intellect than my own. . . . Perhaps I have received some benefit in the now more distinct consciousness of my dwarfishness. . . .
> (letter to John Allen, 23 May 1835)

The self-effacement and modesty were typical of FitzGerald; and his affection was reciprocated, for Tennyson wrote: "I had no truer friend: he was one of the kindliest of men, and I have never known one of so fine and delicate a wit."

In 1837, FitzGerald took possession of Boulge Cottage, which stood outside the gates of Boulge Hall, the family estate near Bredfield. In this doleful place, with a black retriever, a cat, a housekeeper named Mrs. Faiers, and, in time, a parrot named Beauty Bob, he settled down to a serenity that seemed a pirated copy of the peace of God. To his friends such peace must have seemed astonishing, for the walls of the cottage were as thin as a sixpence, the windows refused to shut, and the thatch was "perforated by lascivious sparrows." But here, wrote FitzGerald, "I sit, read, smoke, and become very wise, and am already quite beyond earthly things."

And so, in his twenties and thirties, the genteel gypsy lived the set life of middle age: "A little more folding of the hands—the same faces—the same fields—the same thoughts occurring at the same turns of road—this is all I have to tell of; nothing at all added—but the summer gone."

It would be wrong to assume that FitzGerald led the life of an indolent recluse. He not only kept in touch with his friends by correspondence and visits; he also read voluminously. He became close friends with the local wits: the Quaker poet Bernard Barton and George Crabbe, vicar of Bredfield and the poet's son. In 1840 he attended Carlyle's lectures on "Heroes and Hero-Worship"; and, two years later, he was introduced to that awesome Scottish author.

---

[2] All quotations of poetry and prose are from G. Bentham, ed., *The Variorum and Definitive Edition of the Poetical and Prose Writings*, 7 vols. (New York, 1902).

The meeting was fortunate: Carlyle, who was working on Oliver Cromwell's letters and speeches, had recently gone to Naseby to identify the Cromwellian battlefield; it so happened that Naseby was part of the large FitzGerald estates, and FitzGerald knew it well. He corrected Carlyle's mistaken conclusions, and set laborers to digging at certain spots where (according to tradition) the main action had been fought; on the fourth day a laborer reported that he had discovered bones. "Clearly enough," cried Carlyle in triumph, "you are upon the very battleground . . . the opening of that burial-heap blazes strangely in my thoughts." Carlyle's work on Cromwell owed much to FitzGerald; and FitzGerald owed to Naseby his friendship with Carlyle, which lasted until the latter's death thirty-nine years later.

It was a Suffolk friend who was destined to draw FitzGerald toward the writing of his masterpiece. Edward Byles Cowell was an Ipswich merchant by force of circumstance; he was a scholar by inclination. Latin, Greek, and French did not satisfy his ardor for languages; he studied Persian, Spanish, Italian, Old Norse, and Sanskrit as well. Although he was hardly nineteen when he met FitzGerald about 1845, he had already established himself as an Oriental scholar with his translations of Persian poetry. In 1847 he married Elizabeth Charlesworth, the daughter of a local clergyman; and FitzGerald, who admired Cowell's intellectual powers, and was deeply attached to his wife, became a frequent visitor at their cottage. In this benevolent atmosphere he began "to nibble at Spanish: at their old Ballads; which are fine things. . . . I have also bounced through a play of Calderón." By the end of 1852, when the Cowells had moved to Oxford, he had translated one of Calderón's plays; the following summer *Six Dramas of Calderón. Freely Translated by Edward FitzGerald* appeared.

One wet Sunday at Oxford, Cowell "suggested Persian to him and guaranteed to teach the grammar in a day. The book was Jones's Grammar, the illustrations to which are nearly all from Hafiz. FitzGerald . . . went on to read Hafiz closely." By October 1853 he was translating Sádi; and for the next eighteen months he studied Persia and Persian poetry. In 1856 he published his version of Jámí's allegory *Salámán and Absál* as a "little monument" to his Persian studies with Cowell. It was also a monument to departing friends, for Cowell sailed that summer to become professor of English history at Presidency College, Calcutta.

The departure of his guide and friend, and of the gently inspiring Elizabeth, was not, for FitzGerald, the only calamity of the year. Early in November, inspired by a wildly mistaken sense of chivalry, he married Lucy, the plain, middle-aged, and strictly conventional daughter of Bernard Barton. There could hardly have been a more ill-assorted couple, and in August 1857 they separated. "If," wrote FitzGerald, "people want to go further for the cause of all this Blunder than the fact of two People of very determined habits and Temper, first trying to change them at close on fifty—they may lay nine-tenths of the Blame on me."

Just before the Cowells left for India in July 1856, FitzGerald and his friend had "read some curious Infidel and Epicurean Tetrastichs by a Persian of the Eleventh Century—as Savage against Destiny etc. as Manfred—but mostly of Epicurean Pathos of this kind—'Drink—for the Moon will often come round to look for us in this Garden and find us not.'" These infidel verses were the *Rubáiyát*, or quatrains, of Omar Khayyám, which Cowell had discovered in a Persian manuscript in the Bodleian Library at Oxford. He had copied the verses for FitzGerald; and, in the spring of 1857, FitzGerald had found that Omar "breathes a sort of Consolation!" About the middle of June, he received a copy of a second Omar manuscript, which Cowell had discovered in Calcutta; and on 14 July 1857, the anniversary of his parting from his friend, as he was walking in his rose-filled Norfolk garden, a translation of a stanza formed in FitzGerald's mind:

> I long for wine! oh Saki of my Soul,
> Prepare thy Song and fill the morning Bowl;
> For this first Summer month that brings the Rose
> Takes many a Sultán with it as it goes.

Within the next six months he had translated many of the *Rubáiyát*. He had become (as he signed himself) Edward FitzOmar. "In truth," he wrote to Cowell, "I take old Omar rather more as my property than yours: he and I are more akin, are we not? You see all [his] Beauty, but you don't feel with him in some respects as I do. . . ." He sent thirty-five of his "less wicked" stanzas to *Fraser's* magazine, warning the editor that the verse might be "rather dangerous among his divines." The editor apparently agreed; and by November 1858 even the patient FitzGerald was moved to action. He retrieved his manuscript, added forty quatrains, and had 250 copies printed and bound in brown paper. He kept forty, and handed the rest to Bernard Quaritch, a London bookseller who specialized in Oriental works. On 9 April 1859 the *Rubáiyát* was advertised as "just published," and review copies were sent to various magazines. FitzGerald's name was not on the title page.

While FitzGerald was absorbed in translating and publishing Omar, the course of his private life had been changing. The death of friends had broken some of his last ties with early manhood, his final ties with inland Suffolk, and he had begun to turn seaward for happiness:

> My chief amusement in Life is Boating, on River and Sea. The Country about here is the Cemetery of so many of my oldest Friends: and the petty race of Squires who have succeeded only use the Earth for an *Investment*: cut down every old Tree: level every Violet Bank: and make the old Country of my Youth hideous to me in my Decline. There are fewer Birds to be heard, as fewer Trees for them to resort to. So I get to the Water: where Friends are not buried nor Pathways stopt up. . . .
>
> (letter to Edward Cowell, 22 May 1861)

FitzGerald haunted Lowestoft, on the Suffolk coast, where, in season, the herring boats unloaded their teeming catches. The sea always kept alive, and the streets of Lowestoft were full of rugged sailors, "the old English stuff," "obstinate Fellows with wonderful Shoulders," "a very fine Race of Men, far superior to those in Regent Street." FitzGerald's admiration of physical vigor—of "Sea Language," as he called it—drew him to the tavern kitchens at Aldeburgh, to smoke, drink grog, and sing with the sailors. The small craft he sailed on the river Deben was replaced by a new boat, specially built, with a crew of two. At last, in 1863, he ordered a forty-three-foot schooner, the *Scandal*, which was his summer home for eight years:

> You must think I have become very nautical, by all this: haul away at ropes, swear, dance Hornpipes, etc. But it is not so: I simply sit in my Boat or Vessel as in a moving Chair, dispensing a little Grog and Shag to those who do the work.

This idyllic existence had to be changed in winter for the monotonous life of his lodgings in Woodbridge, "all the faded tapestry of country town life." Here, in inland Suffolk, FitzGerald whiled away the

weeks by reading, translating, and writing letters. In the spring of 1864, however, he bought a cottage on the northern outskirts of the town; he enlarged it, engaged a couple as caretakers, and furnished it as a summer house for friends and relations. It was characteristic of him that for seven years he persisted in staying in Woodbridge and not becoming the laird of Little Grange.

In 1874, FitzGerald finally took possession of what he called his chateau: Little Grange, where he was to spend the remainder of his life. But a sadness settled over him, and to his friend William Aldis Wright he expressed the wish that the sword would fall:

> If I do not write, it is because I have absolutely nothing to tell you that you have not known for the last twenty years. Here I live still, reading, and being read to, part of my time; walking abroad three or four times a day, or night, in spite of wakening a Bronchitis, which has lodged like the household "Brownie" within; pottering about my Garden (as I have just been doing) and snipping off dead Roses like Miss Tox; and now and then a visit to the neighbouring Seaside, and a splash to Sea in one of the Boats. I never see a new Picture, nor hear a note of Music except when I drum out some old Tune in Winter on an Organ, which might almost be carried about the Streets with a handle to turn, and a Monkey on the top of it. So I go on, living a life far too comfortable as compared with that of better, and wiser men: but ever expecting a reverse in health such as my seventy-five years are subject to. . . .
>
> Tomorrow I am going (for my one annual Visit) to G. Crabbe's. . . .
>
> (letter of 12 June 1883)

In all probability this was FitzGerald's last letter. Next day, 13 June, he left for his annual visit to Merton rectory. On 14 June, Crabbe entered his room to find him "as if sleeping peacefully but quite dead."

Five days later FitzGerald was buried at Boulge. At his feet, in time, they planted a Persian rose tree grown from the tree by the grave of Omar Khayyám.

THE MAN OF LETTERS AND TRANSLATOR

FitzGerald's first published book appeared in 1849, his edition of the *Poems and Letters of Bernard Barton*. His "editorial mind" had reduced the nine volumes of Barton's works to some 200 pages. It was a monument to what FitzGerald called his "Irish accuracy." "Some of the poems I take entire," he told Donne, "some half—some only a few stanzas, and these dovetailed together—with a change of word, or even of a line here and there, to give them logic and fluency . . . I am sure I have distilled many pretty little poems out of long dull ones which the world has discarded." This free adaptation was characteristic of FitzGerald's methods of work, and it would purse a good many academic brows; but he prefaced the book with a memoir of his Quaker friend that was lucid, candid, and charming.

In 1851 (again without his name) he published a more important work: *Euphranor: A Dialogue on Youth.* On one of his visits to Cambridge, FitzGerald had been shocked by "the hard-reading, pale, dwindled students walking along the Observatory road." *Euphranor* is written as a Platonic dialogue between himself, in the character of a Cambridge doctor; Euphranor, a bookish graduate; and three students: one hard-working, one idle, and one the admirable *uomo universale.* It is a criticism of contemporary English education. FitzGerald charges the schools with neglect of the physical exercise and practical training that will fit a man "for the campaign of ordinary Life. . . . At any rate," fit him "not only to shoot the Pheasant and hunt the Fox, but even to sit on the Bench of Magistrates—or even of Parliament—not unprovided with a quotation or two from Horace or Virgil." FitzGerald "had it at heart the Book should be read," and posterity can appreciate its progressive thought and wisdom. *Euphranor* is, for the most part, rather heavy and stilted; but the final description of the May Races at Cambridge won the admiration of Tennyson. It is a fine and musical passage of prose:

We walk'd along the fields by the Church . . . cross'd the Ferry, and mingled with the crowd upon the opposite shore; Townsmen and Gownsmen, with the tassel'd Fellow-commoner sprinkled here and there—Reading men and Sporting men—Fellows, and even Masters of College, not indifferent to the prowess of their respective Crews—all these, conversing on all sorts of topics, from the slang in Bell's *Life* to the last new German Revelation, and moving in everchanging groups down the shore of the river, at whose farther bend was a little knot of Ladies gathered upon a green knoll faced and illuminated by the beams of the setting sun. Beyond which point was at length heard some indistinct shouting, which gradually increased, until "They are off—they are coming!" suspended other conversation among ourselves; and suddenly the head of the first boat turn'd the corner; and then another close

upon it; and then a third; the crews pulling with all their might compacted into perfect rhythm; and the crowd on shore turning round to follow along with them waving hats and caps, and cheering, "Bravo, St. John's!" "Go it, Trinity!"—the high crest and blowing forelock of Phidippus's mare, and he himself shouting encouragement to his crew, conspicuous over all, until the boats reaching us, we also were caught up in the returning tide of spectators, and hurried back toward the goal; where we arrived just in time to see the Ensign of Trinity lowered from its pride of place, and the Eagle of St. John's soaring there instead. Then, waiting a little while to hear how the winner had won, and the loser lost, and watching Phidippus engaged in eager conversation with his defeated brethren, I took Euphranor and Lexilogus under either arm, (Lycion having got into better company elsewhere) and walk'd home with them across the meadow leading to the town, whither the dusky troops of Gownsmen with all their confused voices seem'd as it were evaporating in the twilight, while a Nightingale began to be heard among the flowering Chestnuts of Jesus.
(vol. I, pp. 226–228)

FitzGerald's next work, *Polonius: A Collection of Wise Saws and Modern Instances* (1852), was an anthology of quotations on such topics as honesty, riches and liberty, vanity and charity. He predicted that it would be a losing affair, and the sale was certainly limited.

The following year *Six Dramas of Calderón. Freely Translated by Edward FitzGerald* appeared. The selection was designed to "give a fair idea of Calderón's Spanish Life"; and the translator, with his usual Irish freedom, "while faithfully trying to retain what was fine and efficient; sunk, reduced, altered, and replaced, much that seemed not." The result was a series of plays that savored little of the dictionary: vigor, comedy, and character are evident; and the moments of lyrical and dramatic poetry are not wanting. One recalls the words of Manuel to Pedro in *Gil Perez, the Gallician*:

I must to sea, joining the armament
That sails to plant the banner of the church
Over the golden turrets of the north. . . .
(II.i)

It is a felicitous piece of blank verse. Or, again, one recalls the conversation of Serafina and Alvaro in *The Painter of His Own Dishonour*; it shows a quite remarkable ease of manner:

Serafina . . . My husband's love for me, and mine for him,
My station and my name, all have so changed me,

344

That winds and waves might sooner overturn
Not the oak only,
But the eternal rock on which it grows,
Than you my heart, though sea and sky
      themselves
Join'd in the tempest of your sighs and tears.

Alvaro   But what if I remember other times
When Serafina was no stubborn oak,
Resisting wind and wave, but a fair flower
That open'd to the sun of early love,
And follow'd him along the golden day:
No barren heartless rock,
But a fair temple in whose sanctuary
Love was the idol, daily and nightly fed
With sacrifice of one whole human heart . . .
                              Serafina,
Why talk to me of ages, when the account
Of my misfortune and your cruelty
Measures itself by hours, and not by years!
It was but yesterday you loved me, yes,
Loved me, and (let the metaphor run on)
I never will believe it ever was,
Or is, or ever can be possible
That the fair flower so soon forgot the sun
To which so long she owed and turn'd her
      beauty,
To love the baser mould in which she grew:
Or that the temple could so soon renounce
Her old god, true god too while he was there,
For any cold and sober deity
Which you may venerate, but cannot love. . . .
                                    (II.i)

Only the academic would quibble here about linguistic niceties; but if FitzGerald's friends allowed him his liberty of translation, the critics were less indulgent.

In 1856, undeterred, he published a free version of Jámí's allegory, *Salámán and Absál*. 'It shows," wrote a critic, "some poetic feeling, a diligent use of the dictionary, but a very moderate acquaintance with Persian . . . mistakes are numerous. . . . As a first attempt, however, to make Jámí accessible to the English reader, this little volume is deserving of commendation." FitzGerald's next book was to be a classic.

We have seen how, in the summer of 1856, FitzGerald had discovered the quatrains of Omar Khayyám, and had found them a "kind of Consolation" for his disastrous marriage and profound depression. In the spring of 1857 he had written to Joseph-Héliodore Garcin de Tassy, a French scholar of Persian literature, asking if there were any Omar manuscripts in Paris. In May he confessed to Cowell:

"I think I shall become a bore . . . by all this Translation: but it amuses me without any labour, and I really think I have the faculty of making some things readable which others have hitherto left unreadable." In June he had "put away almost all Books, except Omar Khayyám: which I could not help looking over in a Paddock covered with Buttercups and brushed by a delicious Breeze." He turned some of the quatrains into Latin. That month FitzGerald received a copy of a second Omar manuscript, which Cowell had discovered in Calcutta, and decided "Poor old Omar . . . is the best Persian I have seen." "June over!" he added in July. "A thing I think of with Omar-like sorrow. And the Roses here are blowing—and going—as abundantly as even in Persia. I am still at Geldestone, and still looking at Omar. . . ."

FitzGerald was, in fact, increasingly fascinated by the poem, and by the poet, who seemed to anticipate his own sorrows, doubts, and vexations, his own affection for Epicurean ease. In July a translated stanza crystallized in his mind, and within the next six months he had turned many more into English. The first version of the *Rubáiyát* seems to have filled his mind and heart, and to have grown in a slow, generic fashion, like an original poem, with his own mood and experience.

"Translation" is hardly the word to apply to FitzGerald's *Rubáiyát*, "very unilateral as it is. Many Quatrains," he confessed, "are mashed together: and something lost, I doubt, of Omar's Simplicity which is so much a Virtue in him. But there it is, such as it is." "I suppose," he added, "very few People have ever taken such Pains in Translation as I have: though certainly not to be literal. But at all Cost, a Thing must live: with a transfusion of one's own worse Life if one can't retain the Original's better. Better a live Sparrow than a stuffed Eagle."

It is in this spirit that the *Rubáiyát* of FitzGerald must be judged. It is less a translation than a feat of marvelous poetic transfusion. We shall not find a precise English version of the original, following the Persian line by line. We shall find instead a fusion of the Oxford and Calcutta manuscripts, sometimes shortened, sometimes lengthened, often changed in sequence, and inspired by the strangely sympathetic genius of an English writer who was born some seven centuries after Omar died.

Few remarkable poems in English literature have been published so unobtrusively, or have enjoyed a greater romance in their discovery. FitzGerald gave away a mere three copies. He wrote to Cowell:

I hardly know why I print any of these things, which nobody buys; and I scarce now see the few I give them to. But when one has done one's best, and is sure that that best is better than so many will take pains to do, though far from the best that *might be done*, one likes to make an end of the matter by Print.

(letter of 27 April 1859)

Cowell, a pious man, was shocked at the *Rubáiyát*; the reviewers ignored it. The sales, if any, were almost negligible; and for nearly two years the five-shilling pamphlets lay on Quaritch's shelves. Then, in 1861, they were reduced to a penny and dumped into the bargain box outside his shop; and there they stayed until the editor of the *Saturday Review* happened to browse over a copy, and bought a number of them for his friends.

The *Rubáiyát* had entered the literary world; Dante Gabriel Rossetti told Swinburne of the discovery, and both bought copies. "Next day," recorded Swinburne, "when we returned for more, the price was raised, to the iniquitous and exorbitant sum of twopence. . . . But we were extravagant enough to invest in a few more copies, even at that scandalous price." The Pre-Raphaelites were aglow with enthusiasm. Swinburne soon after took the rhyme scheme and almost the same meter for "Laus Veneris"; he also presented the *Rubáiyát* to Burne-Jones, who copied it for many of his friends. When Burne-Jones showed the poem to Ruskin in 1863, the latter wrote a note "To the Translator of Omar Khayyám"; Burne-Jones was told to deliver it when the anonymous poet was discovered:

My dear and very dear Sir

I do not know in the least who you are, but I do with all my soul pray you to find and translate some more of Omar Khayyám for us: I never did—till this day—read anything so glorious, to my mind, as this poem. . . .

In 1868, FitzGerald published a longer edition of the *Rubáiyát*. He remained anonymous; and when, in 1872, the third edition appeared, he was still "the great Un-nameable." But, by a strange series of chances, Burne-Jones had shown the *Rubáiyát* to a visiting American critic, Charles Eliot Norton; and in October 1869, Norton acclaimed the poem in the *North American Review*. The article created a "little Craze" in the United States; the third and fourth editions of the *Rubáiyát* were printed, and Fanny Kemble's daughter, who knew FitzGerald's other translations, wrote to ask him if he was the author. In her limited Philadelphia circle the mystery was solved.

In 1876, FitzGerald was formally acknowledged as the translator of the *Rubáiyát*; but not until he had died did "the little Craze" for the poem grow across the world. His *Rubáiyát* has been set to music. It has been parodied. There are now at least 180 editions, and translations into Gaelic, German, French, Swedish, Spanish, Sanskrit, Italian, Afrikaans, and Yiddish.

It was said by the enemies of Omar Khayyám that his study of astronomy had only prompted him to disbelief. In fact he was neither an atheist nor an agnostic. He was an honest scholar, a student of Lucretius, who rebelled against the bigotry and dogma of Islam. He satirized those who substituted ritual for worship. And, much concerned with the problem of evil, he challenged the benevolence of a God who ordained both good and evil, yet punished man for sin. He was bewildered by the riddle of life, and he consoled himself (as even the Victorians consoled themselves) with the delights of physical existence.

FitzGerald shared Omar Khayyám's contempt for sanctimony, bigotry, and hypocrisy. A widely read Victorian, he observed the opening skirmishes of the long struggle between modern science and religion (his *Rubáiyát* appeared in the same year as *The Origin of Species*). He was more outspoken than his contemporaries, but he was no more unorthodox than many who confessed their doubts while they sought for faith. Voltaire, the true intellectual eighteenth-century skeptic, had declared that if God did not exist, mankind would have to invent Him. Leconte de Lisle, FitzGerald's contemporary, was a bitter atheist. FitzGerald, an Anglican and a frequent churchgoer, never expressed any doubt of the existence of God; he was skeptical only of Old Testament theology (how, in Darwin's day, could he believe in Adam and Eve?) and life after death. In the eleventh-century *Rubáiyát* he discovered an anticipation of nineteenth-century thought: "a desperate sort of Thing, unfortunately found at the bottom of all thinking Men's minds; but made Music of."

This natural sympathy drew FitzGerald to Omar Khayyám, and drew the Victorians and posterity after him. The *Rubáiyát* expressed, in poetry, the doubts, fears, aspirations, and regrets of the great mass of mankind. FitzGerald wrote when the second edition appeared:

It is the only one of all my Great Works that ever has been asked for, I am persuaded, *because* of the Wickedness, which is now at the heart of so much Goodness! Not that the Persian has anything at all new: but he has dared to say it, as Lucretius did: and now it is put into tolerable English music—That is all.

In his *Rubáiyát*, which were epigrams struck off at intervals during his life, Omar Khayyám had attempted no consistency of belief, no continuity of thought. It was FitzGerald who grouped the quatrains already allied in thought, and imposed consistency—indeed, dramatic unity—upon them. His second and longer version, he explained, "gave Omar's thoughts room to turn in, as also the Day which the poem occupied. He begins with Dawn pretty sober and contemplative: then as he thinks and drinks, grows savage, blasphemous, &c., and then again sobers down into melancholy at nightfall."

FitzGerald's poem opens with the dawn, and with the invocation that Horace, Ronsard, and Herrick before him had sung. *Carpe diem . . . Eheu fugaces. . . .*

> Dreaming when Dawn's Left Hand was in the Sky,
> I heard a Voice within the Tavern cry,
>   "Awake, my Little ones, and fill the Cup
> Before Life's Liquor in its Cup be dry."
>
> Come, fill the Cup, and in the Fire of Spring
> The Winter Garment of Repentance fling:
>   The Bird of Time has but a little way
> To fly—and Lo! the Bird is on the Wing.
> (st. 2-3)

The poet urges us to enjoy material pleasures—the bread, the wine, the poetry, the lover—and not to dismiss the present joy for the mere prospect of paradise. We must, like the rose, spend our treasure in a day; we must remember that even the rich and the mighty must come to dust, and that we shall follow them:

> Ah, my Belovéd, fill the cup that clears
> To-DAY of past Regrets and future Fears—
>   *To-morrow?*—Why, To-morrow I may be
> Myself with Yesterday's Sev'n Thousand Years.
>
>   . . .
>
> Ah, make the most of what we yet may spend,
> Before we too into the Dust descend;
>   Dust into Dust, and under Dust, to lie,
> Sans Wine, sans Song, sans Singer, and—sans End!
> (st. 20; 23)

The sages of the world, for all their wisdom, are turned to dust; and the sum of all their knowledge is uncertainty:

> There was a Door to which I found no Key:
> There was a Veil past which I could not see:
>   Some little Talk awhile of ME and THEE
> There seemed—and then no more of THEE and ME.
>
> Then to the rolling Heav'n itself I cried,
> Asking, "What Lamp had Destiny to guide
>   Her little Children stumbling in the Dark?"
> And—"A blind Understanding!" Heav'n replied.
> (st. 32-33)

As the day lengthens and the poet broods, he is moved to anger by the injustice of predestination and the cruel indifference of God:

> Into this Universe, and *why* not knowing,
> Nor *whence*, like Water willy-nilly flowing:
>   And out of it, as Wind along the Waste,
> I know not *whither*, willy-nilly blowing.
>
> What, without asking, hither hurried *whence?*
> And, without asking, *whither* hurried hence!
>   Another and another Cup to drown
> The Memory of this Impertinence!
> (st. 29-30)

Heaven has sent its children into darkness, with only their blind understanding to guide them; and they can find only an earthly consolation for their misery, a temporal solution to their spiritual and eternal problems. Men are merely pawns in the chess game of destiny, and God in Heaven watches the game, uncaring:

> The Ball no Question makes of Ayes and Noes,
> But Right or Left as strikes the Player goes;
>   And He that toss'd Thee down into the Field,
> *He* knows about it all—HE knows—HE knows!
> (st. 50)

Will God, who set the snares on earth, allow man to be enmeshed, and then impute his fall to transgression? As the poet, with growing fury, reflects on such injustice, he is moved to blasphemy:

> Oh, Thou, who Man of baser Earth didst make,
> And who with Eden didst devise the Snake;
>   For all the Sin wherewith the Face of Man
> Is blacken'd, Man's Forgiveness give—and take!
> (st. 58)

And then, as evening draws on, and the wine is finished, and indignation gives way to sober reflection, the poet returns, at last, to lament the passing of youth and the inevitability of death:

Alas! that Spring should vanish with the Rose!
That Youth's sweet-scented Manuscript should close!
 The Nightingale that in the Branches sang,
Ah, whence, and whither flown again, who knows!

Ah Love! could thou and I with Fate conspire
To grasp this sorry Scheme of Things entire,
 Would we not shatter it to bits—and then
Re-mould it nearer to the Heart's Desire!

(st. 72–73)

The *Rubáiyát*, with its doubts of religion, shocked and fascinated an age of religious upheaval. Its themes remain our constant preoccupations. But, as FitzGerald recognized, it has been the music that has sung the *Rubáiyát* into English literature. We may talk of alliteration, metaphor, and scansion, but such analyses do not explain why so many English people find, suddenly, that they know so much of the poem by heart. Whatever the merits of the original, FitzGerald's *Rubáiyát* is a great English poem; and, as he once wrote, "Only God, who made the Rose smell so, knows why such Poems come from the Heart and go to it."

Nonetheless, if one compares a literal translation with FitzGerald's version, one may appreciate a little of his achievement:

Since no one will be answerable for to-morrow,
Make happy now this distraught heart.
 Drink wine by the light of the moon, for the moon
Will seek much, and not find us.

So goes the exact translation of the Oxford manuscript; and FitzGerald recalls it in his two final stanzas:

Ah, Moon of my Delight who know'st no wane,
The Moon of Heav'n is rising once again:
 How oft hereafter rising shall she look
Through this same Garden after me—in vain!

And when Thyself with shining Foot shall pass
Among the Guests Star-scatter'd on the Grass,
 And in thy joyous Errand reach the Spot
Where I made one—turn down an empty Glass!

(st. 74–75)

"As poor Omar is one I have great fellow feeling with, I would rather vamp him up again with a few Alterations & Additions than anything else." So Fitz-Gerald wrote to his publisher in 1867. He did indeed alter and add to "poor Omar." The first edition had 75 stanzas; the second (for which he referred to a French text of Omar as well), 110; the third and fourth, 101. Nine stanzas appeared in the second edition only; and the sequence was so radically changed from edition to edition that stanza 46 in the first edition became stanza 73 in the second edition and stanza 68 in the third and fourth. Moreover, the stanzas themselves were constantly reformed: the opening stanza was twice altered—and not, one would think, for the better:

Awake! for Morning in the Bowl of Night
Has flung the Stone that puts the Stars to Flight:
 And Lo! the Hunter of the East has caught
The Sultán's Turret in a Noose of Light.

So ran the opening lines in the first edition; in the second version they went:

Wake! For the Sun beyond yon Eastern height
Has chased the Session of the Stars from Night;
 And, to the field of Heav'n ascending, strikes
The Sultán's Turret with a Shaft of Light.

In the third and fourth versions the stanza differed yet again:

Wake! For the Sun who scatter'd into flight
The Stars before him from the Field of Night,
 Drives Night along with them from Heav'n, and strikes
The Sultán's Turret with a Shaft of Light.

These alterations do not always intensify the poetry; and, as FitzGerald pointed out, they do not always make the poem more accurate. Wrote Fitz-Gerald blandly to Quaritch:

I daresay Ed[n] I is better in some respects than 2, but I think not altogether. . . . I dare say Ed[n] I best pleased those who read it first: as first Impressions are apt to be strongest. . . . As to the relative fidelity of the two Versions, there isn't a Pin to choose—not in the opening Stanzas you send.

After the appearance of the *Rubáiyát*, FitzGerald did not appear publicly in print until Quaritch issued the second edition in 1868. But he was not idle during these nine years: his first undertaking after the *Rubáiyát* was to finish his translation of Attár's *Mantik-ut-tair*, or *Parliament of Birds*. This was published only after his death, but it may be considered here as one of his most inspired translations.

The poem is a kind of ornithological *Pilgrim's Progress*. The birds set out on a pilgrimage to the sacred mountain, Káf, in search of Symurgh, a bird of great wisdom. They pass through seven valleys of probation, and many die by the wayside before the thirty faithful survivors stand, at last, before the Throne, and the Voice addresses them:

> "Come you lost Atoms to your Centre draw,
> And *be* the Eternal Mirror that you saw:
> Rays that have wander'd into Darkness wide
> Return, and back into your Sun subside."
>
> (vol. VI, p. 200)

Some of FitzGerald's richest poetry may be found in the *Parliament of Birds*. The characters of the birds are brilliantly distinguished:

> Then came the subtle *Parrot* in a coat
> Greener than Greensward, and about his Throat
> A Collar ran of sub-sulphureous Gold;
> And in his Beak a Sugar-plum he troll'd,
> That all his Words with luscious Lisping ran,
>
> . . .
>
> Then from a Pond, where all day long he kept,
> Waddled the dapper *Duck* demure, adept
> At infinite Ablution, and precise
> In keeping of his Raiment clean and nice.
> And "Sure of all the Race of Birds", said He,
> "None for Religious Purity like Me." . . .
>
> (vol. VI, pp. 149; 159)

As for the philosophy of the poem, it is the very opposite of the *Rubáiyát*. Omar had doubted the benevolence of God; but the *Parliament of Birds*, in a magnificent passage, affirms the divine well-wishing:

> For like a Child sent with a fluttering Light
> To feel his way along a gusty Night
> Man walks the World: again and yet again
> The Lamp shall be by Fits of Passion slain:
> But shall not He who sent him from the Door
> Relight the Lamp once more, and yet once more?
>
> (vol. VI, p. 168)

When he had finished the *Parliament of Birds*, FitzGerald, finding that the earlier ones were liked, translated two more plays by Calderón, including the great *La vida es sueño*, of which his *Such Stuff as Dreams Are Made On* is a radical reconstruction. He collected material for a vocabulary of provincial English, and printed glossaries of Suffolk sea words and phrases. In 1876 he published "an impudent Version of the Agamemnon," which was acclaimed as being "profoundly penetrated with Aeschylean spirit." In 1880 and 1881 his translations of Sophocles were privately distributed, and in 1882, Quaritch published his *Readings in Crabbe*. During his last years FitzGerald was working on selections from John Dryden's *Prefaces* and a dictionary for "my dear Sévigné's" correspondence. This last was completed for him after his death by his niece, Mary Kerrich. His projected biography of Charles Lamb never went further than a brief chronology of the essayist's life.

THE LETTER WRITER

FitzGerald has a double claim to immortality. The translator of Omar Khayyám has, perhaps, received his due; the letter writer remains to be discovered. There is no definitive edition of FitzGerald's correspondence, a strange and unjust omission, for he holds so high a place among the English letter writers that at times he is reminiscent of John Keats. One cannot, it is true, trace the same godlike growth of soul and intellect; yet one can understand why, to FitzGerald, "poor Keats' little finger" was "worth all the body" of Shelley. He found, in Keats, his own best genius magnified. FitzGerald's letters, like the letters of Keats, reveal the living, sensual man, with his griefs and humors and pleasures, the lover of life and nature and literature, the possessor of a sharp and loving visual sense; and sometimes they recall the poet by a sudden turn of phrase, by sheer verbal felicity.

FitzGerald's letter writing was largely dictated by his Irish vitality and his constant solitude. Letters, to him, replaced companionship; they were substitutes for conversation:

> I suppose that people who are engaged in serious ways of life, and are of well filled minds, don't think much about the interchange of letters with any anxiety; but I am an idle fellow, of a very ladylike turn of sentiment: and my friendships are more like loves, I think. Your letter found me reading the Merry Wives of Windsor too: I had been laughing aloud to myself: think of what another coat of happiness came over my former good mood. You are a dear good fellow, and I love you with all my heart and soul.
>
> (letter to John Allen, 9 September 1834)

His zest for life, his warmth of feeling, shone through his correspondence:

Ah! I wish you were here to talk with me now that the warm weather is come at last. Things have been delayed but to be more welcome, and to burst forth twice as thick and beautiful. This is boasting, however, and counting of the chickens before they are hatched: the East winds may again plunge us back into winter: but the sunshine of this morning fills one's pores with jollity, as if one had taken laughing gas. . . .

(letter to John Allen, 21 April 1837)

Country sunshine, flowers and books, gentle domestic ease: these were the elements of FitzGerald's English paradise; and he caught them, as if in amber, in his letters. Irish by birth, he was English at heart. "Well, say as you will," he wrote to a friend in Italy, "there is not, and never was, such a country as Old England. . . . I am sure no travel would carry me to any land so beautiful, as the good sense, justice and liberality of my good countrymen make this. . . ." A paragraph of FitzGerald, at his best, can bring a whole English landscape into view, and brilliantly imply the foreground figure:

Here is a glorious sunshiny day: all the morning I read about Nero in Tacitus lying at full length on a bench in the garden: a nightingale singing, and some red anemones eyeing the sun manfully not far off. A funny mixture all this: Nero and the delicacy of Spring: all very human however. Then at half-past one lunch on Cambridge cream cheese: then a ride over hill and dale; then spudding up some weeds from the grass: and then coming in, I sit down to write to you, my sister winding red worsted from the back of a chair, and the most delightful little girl in the world chattering incessantly. So runs the world away. You think I live in Epicurean ease: but this happens to be a jolly day: one isn't always well, or tolerably good, the weather is not always clear, nor nightingales singing, nor Tacitus full of pleasant atrocity. But such as life is, I believe I have got hold of a good end of it. . . .

(letter to John Allen, 28 April 1839)

The English countryside (the "poor mistaken lilac buds," the "old Robin ruffled up to his thickest") inspired some enchanting description. FitzGerald was never entirely happy away from East Anglia, from the Norfolk and Suffolk landscapes he knew so well: "I get radishes to eat for breakfast of a morning," he wrote from London in 1844; "with them comes a savour of earth that brings all the delicious gardens of the world back into one's soul, and almost draws

tears from one's eyes." London disturbed his usual tranquillity; in a brilliant, spontaneous letter he expressed his nostalgia for the country, and conjured up a mirage of his ramshackle cottage:

When I get back to Boulge, I shall recover my quietude which is now all in a ripple. But it is a shame to talk of such things. . . .
A cloud comes over Charlotte Street and seems as if it were sailing softly on the April wind to fall in a blessed shower upon the lilac buds and thirsty anemones somewhere in Essex; or, who knows?, perhaps at Boulge. Out will run Mrs. Faiers, and with red arms and face of woe haul in the struggling windows of the cottage, and make all tight. Beauty Bob [the parrot] will cast a bird's eye out at the shower, and bless the useful wet. Mr. Loder will observe to the farmer for whom he is doing up a dozen of Queen's Head's, that it will be of great use: and the farmer will agree that his young barleys wanted it much. The German Ocean will dimple with innumerable pin points, and porpoises rolling near the surface sneeze with unusual pellets of fresh water. . . . Oh this wonderful, wonderful world, and we who stand in the middle of it are all in a maze. . . .

(letter to Bernard Barton, 11 April 1844)

FitzGerald returned to his cottage to greet the early summer, and sent a fresh pastoral vignette to Frederic Tennyson, the poet's brother and himself a poet:

I read of mornings; the same old books over and over again, having no command of new ones: walk with my great black dog of an afternoon, and at evening sit with open windows, up to which China roses climb, with my pipe, while the blackbirds and thrushes begin to rustle bedwards in the garden, and the nightingale to have the neighbourhood to herself. We have had such a spring (bating the last ten days) as would have satisfied even you with warmth. And such verdure! white clouds moving over the new fledged tops of oak trees, and acres of grass striving with buttercups. How old to tell of, how new to see!

(letter to Frederic Tennyson, 24 May 1844)

FitzGerald's love of nature never deserted him; thirty-five years later we find him lamenting the lateness of the spring:

Scarce a tinge of Green on the hedgerows; scarce a Bird singing (only once the Nightingale, with a broken Voice), and no flowers in the Garden but the brave old Daffydowndilly, and Hyacinth—which I scarce knew were so hardy. I am quite pleased to find how comfortably they do in my Garden, and look so Chinese gay. Two of my dear Blackbirds have I found dead—of Cold and Hunger, I suppose; but one is even now singing—across that Funeral Bell. This is so, as I write, and tell you—Well: we have Sunshine at last. . . .

(letter to Fanny Kemble, 25 April 1879)

FitzGerald's criticism of art, as one might expect, was keen, affectionate, and at times poetic. His judgment has not always been endorsed: "I got a look at the National Gallery," he declared in 1862, "but the Devotion of one whole Room to Turner seems to me to be a national Absurdity." Yet if FitzGerald strangely failed to appreciate Turner, he could pass stringent judgment on the largely representational art of his time; and he could not, for example, persuade himself "that Frith's veracious Portraitures of people eating Luncheons at Epsom are to be put in the Scale with Raffaelle's impossible Idealisation of the Human made Divine."

FitzGerald prided himself on collecting pictures: he was fascinated by auction rooms and dealers' shops, and haunted by pictures that he wished to buy. He enjoyed varnishing and cleaning his collection (and even cutting down a canvas on occasion). In 1841 he acquired what he thought was a masterpiece, and dashed off his jubilation to Frederic Tennyson:

I have just concluded, with all the throes of imprudent pleasure, the purchase of a large picture by Constable, of which, if I can continue in the mood, I will enclose you a sketch. It is very good: but how you and Morton would abuse it! Yet this, being a sketch, escapes some of Constable's faults, and might escape some of your censures. The trees are not splashed with that white sky-mud, which (according to Constable's theory) the Earth scatters up with her wheels in travelling so briskly round the sun; and there is a dash and felicity in the execution that gives one a thrill of good digestion in one's room, and the thought of which makes one inclined to jump over the children's heads in the streets. But if you could see my great enormous Venetian Picture you would be astonished. Does the thought ever strike you, when looking at pictures in a house, that you are to run and jump at one, and go right through it to the other side, as Harlequins do? A steady portrait especially invites one to do so: the quietude of it ironically tempts one to outrage it: one feels it would close again over the panel, like water, as if nothing had happened. . . .

(letter to Frederic Tennyson, 16 January 1841)

FitzGerald's affection for music, like his affection for art, is reflected in his letters. It is, perhaps,

an amateur's affection, an artist's affection, for he expresses it in strongly visual terms. But it was for literature, and literature of the most diverse kinds, that he felt the most intense enthusiasm. "I don't find myself growing old about Poetry," he wrote when he was forty. "On the contrary." And again: "I believe I love poetry almost as much as ever: but then . . . I have not put away childish things, though a man. . . ."

There was nothing childish in FitzGerald's love of poetry, unless it was its eagerness. He read it, always, with the ardor that breeds true appreciation: he felt it with his heart before his head. He had his natural inclinations: "I have rather a wish," he wrote, "to tie old Wordsworth's volume about his neck and pitch him into one of the deepest holes of his dear Duddon." He found Shelley "too unsubstantial for me." "As for the modern Poetry," he admitted toward the end of his life, "I have cared for none of the last thirty years, not even Tennyson, except in parts: pure, lofty, and noble as he always is. Much less can I endure the *Gurgoyle* school (I call it) begun, I suppose, by V. Hugo. . . ." He was sharply critical even of Tennyson:

If one could have good Lyrics, I think the World wants them as much as ever. Tennyson's are good: but not of the kind wanted. . . I felt that if Tennyson had got on a horse and ridden twenty miles, instead of moaning over his pipe, he would have been cured of his sorrows in half the time. As it is, it is about three years before the Poetic Soul walks itself out of darkness & Despair into Common Sense—Plato w^d not have allowed such querulousness to be published in his Republic, to be sure: and when we think of the Miss Barretts, Brownes, Jewsburys &c who will set to work to feel friends' losses in melodious tears, in imitation of A.T.'s—one must allow Plato was no such prig as some say he was.

(letter to W. B. Donne, 28 February 1845)

FitzGerald's disapproval of modern poetry was not so sweeping as he pretended: when, in 1848, Richard Monckton Milnes published the *Life, Letters, and Literary Remains of John Keats*, FitzGerald was among the first to read it; and he was understandably swept off his feet: "By the by," he ordered Tennyson's brother, "beg, borrow, steal or buy Keats' Letters and Poems, written off-hand at a sitting most of them: I only wonder that they do not make a noise in the world." Thirty years later we find him admonishing Fanny Kemble to read the Monckton Milnes *Life and Letters*, "in which you will find

351

what you may not have guessed from his Poetry (though almost unfathomably deep in that also) the strong, masculine, Sense and Humour, etc., of the man: more akin to Shakespeare, I am tempted to think, in a perfect circle of Poetic Faculties, than any Poet since." Matthew Arnold and Middleton Murry were not alone in endorsing FitzGerald's judgment.

And whatever FitzGerald's strictures, he had a high regard for Tennyson: "One must," he wrote, "have labourers of different kinds in the vineyard of morality. . . . Wordsworth is first in the craft: but Tennyson does no little by raising and filling the brain with noble images and thoughts, which . . . prepare and fit us for the reception of the higher philosophy." He would gladly sit up until the small hours of the morning, heavy with influenza, while Tennyson recited "some of his magic music." But "what astonishes me," he told Elizabeth Cowell, "is Shakespeare: when I look into him it is not a Book, but People talking all round me. . . . Milton seems a Dead-weight compared." He wrote to John Allen:

I have been reading Shakespeare's Sonnets, and I believe I am unprejudiced when I say that I had but half an idea of him, Demigod as he seemed before, till I read them carefully. . . . I have truly been lapped in these Sonnets for some time: they seem all stuck about my heart, like the ballads that used to be on the walls of London.

(letter to John Allen, 27 November 1832)

Yet, when all is said, we do not read the letters of FitzGerald to discover his criticism of the arts; we read them, especially, because they reveal himself: serene, detached, unhurried, slightly wistful, with a humor, a modesty, a poetry of his own that touches the heart. And revelation is not, perhaps, the word to use of FitzGerald; for it has been truly said that "There is a sense of kindly mystery about him, and we don't want to account for him. We are glad to have him as he is." "I think," wrote FitzGerald, "I shall become rather a Bore, for I certainly do write Letters which I should not if I had proper occupation. . . ." His diffidence is part of his charm; to read FitzGerald's letters is, inescapably, to love him.

Of the quoting from FitzGerald there is no end. His sudden poetry, his romantic melancholy, his touching modesty, his Elian, Keatsian humors make his letters constantly alive. True, he discusses the great men of his time; but such portraits remain unimportant beside the authentic picture of himself. FitzGerald is always a man of sensibility; he is rarely self-conscious; he is always sincere. He scribbles (it seems that he talks) on the spur of the moment; he writes, as he once described it, "whatever-about-ly." His thoughts "go floating about in a gossamer way." He is a man of taste and genius who likes "to sail before the wind over the surface of an ever-rolling eloquence." But his letters are not merely fine because they are admirable prose. They are masterly because they come from the heart.

It is difficult to place FitzGerald in English literature. In time (and in certain features) he was eminently Victorian. He was a regular churchgoer; he was bewildered by religious controversy; he was acutely conscious of his duties toward his social inferiors; he urged educational reform; he was (though Irish) intensely patriotic. And yet, so often, as one reads his translations or his letters, one discerns the romantic born out of his time: his *mal du siècle*, his pastoral and exotic interests, his morbidity, his humor and chivalry. FitzGerald was no Victorian philosopher: "It really gives me pain," he wrote, "to hear you or anyone else call me a philosopher. . . . I am none, never was . . . . Some things, such as wealth, rank, respectability, I don't care a straw about . . . ." Such a comment struck at the roots of Victorian society.

FitzGerald, like all great men of letters, cannot be neatly classified. He belongs to, and stands apart from, his age. Robert Browning, in a moment of fury, dismissed him as "the wretched Irish fribble and feather-head"; Tennyson, in the birthday poem addressed to him, acclaimed "Old Fitz" as a divine translator, and the *Rubáiyát* as a golden poem, "a planet to the sun which cast it." FitzGerald, with his usual diffidence, decided: "I have not the strong inward call, nor cruel-sweet pangs of parturition, that proves the birth of anything bigger than a mouse. . . . I am a man of taste, of whom there are hundreds born every year."

FitzGerald's judgment was quashed by his contemporaries; it will always be contradicted by posterity. His *Rubáiyát* is indeed a golden poem; his letters sometimes touch the epistolary heights. When he called himself a man of taste, he had perhaps forgotten his own aphorism: Taste is the feminine of genius.

SELECTED BIBLIOGRAPHY

I. BIBLIOGRAPHY. W. F. Prideaux, *Notes for a Bibliography* (London, 1901); A. G. Potter, *A Bibliography of the*

Rubáiyát of Omar Khayyám (London, 1929); T. G. Ehrsam and R. H. Deily, *Bibliographies of Twelve Victorian Authors* (New York, 1936), supp. for FitzGerald by J. G. Fucilla in *Modern Philology*, 37 (August 1939), p. 90. Useful lists of the eds. of the *Rubáiyát* and of articles about FitzGerald and Omar Khayyám are in Glyde's *Life* (see below).

II. COLLECTED WORKS. *Works*, 2 vols. (New York, 1887); W. A. Wright, ed., *Letters and Literary Remains*, 3 vols. (London, 1889; 7 vols., 1902–1903), enl. ed. includes the 1894, 1895, and 1900 items edited by Wright (below); W. A. Wright, ed., *Letters*, 2 vols. (London, 1894), with 43 new letters; W. A. Wright, ed., *Letters . . . to Fanny Kemble, 1871–83* (London, 1895); W. A. Wright, ed., *Miscellanies* (London, 1900), contains "Omar Khayyám," "Euphranor," "Polonius," "Salámán and Absál," "Memoir of Bernard Barton," "Death of Bernard Barton," and "Death of the Rev. George Crabbe"; W. A. Wright, ed., *More Letters* (London, 1901); G. Bentham, ed., *The Variorum and Definitive Edition of the Poetical and Prose Writings*, 7 vols. (New York, 1902), does not include the correspondence; F. R. Barton, ed., *Some New Letters* (London, 1923); C. Q. Wrentmore, ed., *Letters . . . to Bernard Quaritch 1853–83* (London, 1926); C. B. Johnson and N. C. Hannay, eds., *A FitzGerald Friendship* (London, 1932), includes unpublished letters to W. B. Donne; G. F. Maine, ed., *Rubáiyát of Omar Khayyám, Rendered into English Verse by Edward FitzGerald. Euphranor, a Dialogue on Youth. Salámán and Absál* (London, 1953), with intro. by L. Housman; A. M. Terhune and A. B. Terhune, eds., *Letters of Edward FitzGerald*, 4 vols. (Princeton, N. J., 1980), vol. I: *1830–1850*; vol. II: *1851–1866*; vol. III: *1867–1876*; vol. IV: *1877–1883*.

III. SELECTED WORKS. J. Richardson, ed., *Fitzgerald* (London, 1963), with intro. by Richardson, the Reynard Library series.

IV. SEPARATE WORKS. E. FitzGerald, ed., *Poems and Letters of Bernard Barton* (London, 1849); *Euphranor: A Dialogue on Youth* (London, 1851), prose, also in F. Chapman, ed. (London, 1906); *Polonius: A Collection of Wise Saws and Modern Instances* (London, 1852; new eds., 1903, 1905); *Six Dramas of Calderón. Freely Translated* (London, 1853), also in Everyman's Library (London, 1928); *Salámán and Absál: An Allegory Freely Translated from the Persian of Jámí* (London, 1856), verse, 3rd ed. bound with 4th ed. of *Rubáiyát* (London, 1879), comparative ed. by A. J. Arberry (London, 1956), with intro., based on unpublished letters of FitzGerald and Edward Cowell; *Rubáiyát of Omar Khayyám, the Astronomer Poet of Persia* (London, 1859; rev. eds., 1868, 1872, 1879), variorum ed. by N. H. Dole, 2 vols. (London, 1898), with English, French, German, Italian, and Danish trans., and bibliographies; also concordance by J. R. Tutin, ed. (Lon-

don, 1900); *The Mighty Magician and Such Stuff as Dreams Are Made On* (London, 1865), two plays trans. from Calderón, incorporated with the six previously published, as *Eight Dramas of Calderón* (London, 1906); *The Two Generals. I. Lucius Aemitius Paullus. II. Sir Charles Napier* (London, ca. 1865), verse, privately printed; *Agamemnon, a Tragedy Taken from Aeschylus* (London, 1876), privately printed; *The Downfall and Death of King Oedipus*, 2 pts. (London, 1880–1881), drama, privately printed; *Readings in Crabbe's "Tales of the Hall"* (London, 1882), first privately printed (1879); *Occasional Verses* (London, 1891), privately printed; N. H. Dole, ed., *Salámán and Absál . . . Together with A Bird's-Eye View of Faríd-Uddín Attár's Bird-Parliament* (Boston, 1899); M. E. FitzGerald Kerrich, ed., *Dictionary of Madame de Sévigné*, 2 vols. (London, 1914), prose.

V. BIOGRAPHICAL AND CRITICAL STUDIES. F. H. Groome, *Two Suffolk Friends* (London, 1895), repr. of two intimate articles from *Blackwood's* magazine on FitzGerald and R. C. Groome, the author's father; E. Heron-Allen, *Some Sidelights upon Edward FitzGerald's Poem "The Rubáiyát of Omar Khayyám"* (London, 1898), repr. lecture designed to show that FitzGerald's *Rubáiyát* was not only a remarkable paraphrase but also "a synthetical result of our poet's entire course of Persian studies"; H. Jackson, *Edward FitzGerald and Omar Khayyám: An Essay and a Bibliography* (London, 1899); J. Glyde, *The Life* (London, 1900), with intro. by E. Clodd, a moralizing but worthy book with useful bibliographies; G. Campbell, *Edward and Pamela FitzGerald, Being Some Account of Their Lives Compiled from Letters of Those Who Knew Them* (London, 1904); T. Wright, *The Life*, 2 vols. (London, 1904), a solid and competent account; A. C. Benson, *Edward FitzGerald* (London, 1905), the English Men of Letters series, Benson drew chiefly on Wright's *Life* for his bibliographical data; J. Blyth, *Edward FitzGerald and "Posh": "Herring Merchants"* (London, 1908), includes a number of letters from FitzGerald to Joseph Fletcher ("Posh") not previously published; M. Adams, *Omar's Interpreter. A New Life of Edward FitzGerald* (London, 1909; rev. ed., 1911); M. Adams, *In the Footsteps of Borrow and Fitz-Gerald* (London, 1913); J.-M. H. Thonet, *Étude sur Edward FitzGerald et la littérature persane, d'après les sources originales* (Liège, 1929); A. M. Terhune, *The Life of Edward FitzGerald, Translator of the Rubáiyát of Omar Khayyám* (New Haven, Conn., 1947), the most up-to-date and comprehensive study, contains a good deal of new material, but is dully written; P. de Polnay, *Into an Old Room: A Memoir of FitzGerald* (New York, 1949), by a novelist who lived in FitzGerald's Suffolk home for some years; A. J. Arberry, *Omar Khayyám* (New Haven, Conn., 1952); A. J. Arberry, *The Romance of the Rubáiyát* (New York, 1959).

ROBERT BROWNING
(1812-1889)

Philip Drew

LIFE

I only knew one poet in my life:
And this, or something like it, was his way.

BROWNING wrote these lines in one of his finest poems, "How It Strikes a Contemporary." It is a monologue spoken by a carefree young man, and the whole point of it is his total inability to reconcile the dull humdrum routine of the poet, who lives humbly in the world, with the conventional picture of the excitements of artistic life:

I found no truth in one report at least—
That if you tracked him to his home, down lanes
Beyond the Jewry, and as clean to pace,
You found he ate his supper in a room
Blazing with lights, four Titians on the wall,
And twenty naked girls to change his plate!
Poor man, he lived another kind of life
In that new stuccoed third house by the bridge,
Fresh-painted, rather smart than otherwise!
The whole street might o'erlook him as he sat,
Leg crossing leg, one foot on the dog's back,
Playing a decent cribbage with his maid
(Jacynth, you're sure her name was) o'er the cheese
And fruit, three red halves of starved winter-pears,
Or treat of radishes in April. Nine,
Ten, struck the church clock, straight to bed went he.[1]
(72–87)

Many close observers remarked on the contrast between the ordinariness of Browning's own life, especially in his later years when he lived in London, and the exuberant products of his imagination. Per-haps there has never been a poet whose private life was more carefully insulated from his published works. Therefore, in setting out the simple facts of his career, I do so with a double warning—first, that they are not of especial interest in comparison with the really important events of his life, his poems; and secondly, that Browning himself bitterly denounced any attempt to establish a connection, in either direction, between his personal opinions and the ideas he handled in his poetry.

Robert Browning was born on 7 May 1812 in Camberwell, one of the southeastern suburbs of London. His father, a clerk in the Bank of England who had broad and varied tastes in art and literature, owned a large collection of books (chosen on catholic principles), which Browning was encouraged to read. "My first dawn of life," he wrote later, in *Pauline*, "Passed alone with wisest ancient books/All halo-girt with fancies of my own." There is little doubt that this exceptionally wide but unsystematic reading, especially of plays and works of curious scholarship, laid the foundation for the extraordinary diversity of interests that was to mark his poetry throughout his life. At the same time he was keenly interested in the writing of his contemporaries. In 1826, his father's cousin gave him a volume of Shelley's lyrics, which influenced Browning at once. He declared himself, if only temporarily, a vegetarian and an atheist like Shelley; but the literary effect went far deeper, for the book led Browning to read Keats and the other romantic poets and to recognize that poetry was to be his life's work. In a later poem, "Memorabilia" (1855), he recorded the enduring impression of this first encounter with Shelley:

Ah, did you once see Shelley plain,
    And did he stop and speak to you?
And did you speak to him again?
    How strange it seems, and new!

[1]Quotations from all poems published through 1864 (except "Memorabilia," of which the first edition of 1855 has been used) are from I. Jack, ed., *Browning: Poetical Works, 1833–1864* (London, 1970). All later poems are from A. Birrell, ed., *The Complete Poetical Works*, 2 vols. (New York, 1915).

ROBERT BROWNING

But you were living before that,
 And you are living after,
And the memory I started at—
 My starting moves your laughter!

I crossed a moor with a name of its own
 And a use in the world no doubt,
Yet a hand's-breadth of it shines alone
 'Mid the blank miles round about—

For there I picked up on the heather
 And there I put inside my breast
A moulted feather, an eagle-feather—
 Well, I forget the rest.

Browning's mother, Sarah Anne Wiedemann, was born in Scotland of a German father and Scottish mother. She was a devout Congregationalist, and saw to it that her son's religious education was thorough; otherwise he depended on a local school and his father's tuition in the classics. Since he had been brought up as a Nonconformist, the older English universities were not open to him. (It is perhaps worth noting that he and Keats were the only major poets of the nineteenth century not to be enrolled at either Oxford or Cambridge.) His father was one of the original subscribers to the new foundation on nonsectarian principles of University College, London, and in return for his money he was allowed to claim a place at the college for his son. Browning entered classes in 1828 in German, Latin, and Greek, but left after a very short time. Thereafter he lived at home with his parents, at first in Camberwell and, after 1840, in Hatcham, two or three miles farther out of town. He made a journey to St. Petersburg in 1834 with George de Benkhausen, at that time the Russian consul general, and paid two short visits to Italy in 1838 and 1844.

It was in this period, from 1832 to 1846, that he wrote his early poems, long and short, and most of his plays. His first published work, *Pauline : A Fragment of a Confession* (1833), appeared anonymously. It is ostensibly a dramatic monologue addressed to an imaginary Pauline, but most of its early readers assumed that it was a naked revelation of the poet's own adolescent passions and preoccupations. John Stuart Mill, for instance, wrote scornfully of the poet's exposure and indulgence of his own emotions and his "intense and morbid self-consciousness." There is a persistent tradition that it was Mill's critique which determined Browning never again to write poetry which would leave him open to attacks of this kind. Certainly almost all of his subsequent

works were more objective—either unmistakably in the person of a fictitious character or specifically designed to be performed on the stage.

In 1835, he published *Paracelsus* and in 1840, *Sordello*, both long and elaborate poems dealing with men of extraordinary gifts trying to express in words their strivings with the complexities of the world of the Renaissance. *Paracelsus* was on the whole favorably received, but *Sordello* was generally declared unreadable and became a byword for incomprehensibility. It made exhausting demands on the reader's knowledge of an obscure period of history, employed an immense vocabulary of unusual words, and presumed a readiness to master long sentences of great syntactical difficulty. It is hard to exaggerate the derision with which the poem was greeted or the damaging effect on the young poet's reputation of these two long and unyielding poems. This was especially unfortunate, since *Sordello* in particular contained many passages in which a new poetic voice could be clearly heard:

> "Not any strollings now at even-close
> Down the field-path, Sordello! by thorn-rows
> Alive with lamp-flies, swimming spots of fire
> And dew, outlining the black cypress' spire
> She waits you at, Elys, who heard you first
> Woo her, the snow-month through, but ere she durst
> Answer 't was April. Linden-flower-time-long
> Her eyes were on the ground; 't is July, strong
> Now; and because white dust-clouds overwhelm
> The woodside, here or by the village elm
> That holds the moon, she meets you, somewhat pale,
> But letting you lift up her coarse flax veil
> And whisper (the damp little hand in yours)
> Of love, heart's love, your heart's love that endures
> Till death. . . ."
>
> (III.103–117)

Browning himself perhaps wanted, like Sordello, to talk in "'brother's speech'" "'in half-words, call things by half-names,'" and did not realize how difficult it was for the reader to decipher these intimate communications. Nevertheless, the poem was much talked of, and Browning soon found himself on friendly terms with many of the leading poets, editors, and artists of the day.

Meanwhile, his lively interest in the theater continued, and he was persuaded to write a number of verse dramas, mainly for the famous actor-manager William Charles Macready. Although these plays were not as spectacularly unsuccessful as Browning

355

liked to pretend in later years, not all of them were staged, and those that were did not run for long. Browning enjoyed writing for the theater, because it safeguarded the impersonality of the author and yet gave him an immediate response from the audience, but his strength lay, as he observed himself, in depicting "Action in Character, rather than Character in Action."

Of his eight works written in the form of plays, only *Pippa Passes* (1841) has any real dramatic life. It is ingeniously constructed in four parts, in each of which the singing of the little mill-girl Pippa is of crucial effect, as she passes by on her one day's holiday of the year, unconscious of the part she is playing in the lives of others. Between 1841 and 1846, Browning published under the title *Bells and Pomegranates* a series of eight pamphlets that included all the plays that he had written for the theater. These, like most of his earlier works, were printed at the expense of his family. The third and the seventh pamphlets in the series (1842, 1845) were devoted to short poems. They include "My Last Duchess," "Soliloquy of the Spanish Cloister," "Waring," "The Pied Piper of Hamelin," "How They Brought the Good News from Ghent to Aix (16—)," "Pictor Ignotus, Florence 15—," "The Lost Leader," "Home Thoughts from Abroad," "The Bishop Orders His Tomb at St. Praxed's Church," and "The Flight of the Duchess." They were distinguished by their liveliness and strong feeling and by a firm incisiveness that led a contemporary reviewer to comment, "They look as though already packed up and on their way to posterity," while the poet Walter Savage Landor wrote:

> . . . Since Chaucer was alive and hale
> No man has walked along our road with step
> So active, so inquiring eye, or tongue
> So varied in discourse. . . .

One of Browning's most distinguished admirers was the poet Elizabeth Barrett, who included in her *Poems* (1844) some lines in praise of him. When he wrote to thank her, a voluminous and passionate correspondence followed. They met in May 1845 and soon discovered that they were deeply in love. Miss Barrett, however, had been treated for many years as an incurable invalid. Her father was a dominant and possessive man, profoundly attached to his daughter, who depended equally on his love. She was ordered to Italy for her health; when her father

refused to allow her to travel, Robert and Elizabeth decided to wait no longer. They were married secretly in London in September 1846, and left for Pisa a week later, arriving there safely in spite of Browning's notable incompetence in reading a timetable.

Mrs. Browning was never forgiven by her father, who returned her letters unopened, but in every other way the clandestine marriage was strikingly happy and successful. Elizabeth's health improved in Italy and a son, Robert Wiedemann Browning ("Pen"), was born in 1849. The Brownings spent holidays in France and in England, but regarded Italy as their home, living mainly in Florence in a flat in Casa Guidi (the flat is now owned by the Browning Institute. It has been carefully restored and is open to visitors). At first they lived on a fairly small income, but after Pen's birth, John Kenyon, Mrs. Browning's cousin, made them an allowance of £100 a year; when he died in 1856 he left them £11,000. They lived a pleasant life, not mixing very much in Florentine society, but enjoying the company of English and American writers and artists. Mrs. Browning was an ardent supporter of the unification of Italy, a cause with which Browning sympathized more temperately; but both of them were at one in a love of Italy and the Italians. "Italy was my university," Browning wrote, and one of his most famous poems concludes as follows:

> What I love best in all the world
> Is a castle, precipice-encurled,
> In a gash of the wind-grieved Apennine.
> Or look for me, old fellow of mine,
>
>   . . .
>
> In a sea-side house to the farther South,
> Where the baked cicala die of drouth,
> And one sharp tree—'tis a cypress—stands,
> By the many hundred years red-rusted,
> Rough iron-spiked, ripe fruit-o'ercrusted,
> My sentinel to guard the sands
> To the water's edge. For, what expands
> Before the house, but the great opaque
> Blue breadth of sea without a break?
> While, in the house, for ever crumbles
> Some fragment of the frescoed walls,
> From blisters where a scorpion sprawls.
> A girl bare-footed brings, and tumbles
> Down on the pavement, green-flesh melons,
> And says there's news today—the king
> Was shot at, touched in the liver-wing,
> Goes with his Bourbon arm in a sling:
> —She hopes they have not caught the felons.

Italy, my Italy!
Queen Mary's saying serves for me—
    (When fortune's malice
      Lost her—Calais)—
Open my heart and you will see
Graved inside of it, "Italy".
Such lovers old are I and she:
So it always was, so shall ever be!
        ("'De Gustibus—,'" 14–17; 21–46)

A reviewer in *Chambers Journal* commented tartly in 1863: "He has chosen to make his dwelling in Italy. His preference for that spot is undisguised, and, to Englishmen, almost repulsive."

Not surprisingly, many of Browning's most spirited poems at this time dealt with Italian subjects and scenes, but the first poem of his married life, *Christmas-Eve and Easter-Day* (1850), is firmly based on British themes. After a review of the various modes of religious life open to men at the time, Browning affirms his own decision to continue to worship in the tradition of Protestant dissent. We may perhaps detect here the influence of the circumstances of his own life, for his mother, his earliest guide in religious matters, had recently died, and Elizabeth was herself a devoted churchwoman.

In 1852, Browning was asked to write an introduction to a volume of letters by his early hero Shelley. The letters proved to be spurious, but the introduction survives as Browning's only considerable work in prose and an invaluable introduction to his opinions about the nature of poetry. In one of his letters at about this time, he told his French friend Joseph Milsand, "I am writing—a first step towards popularity for me—lyrics with more music and painting than before, so as to get people to hear and see" (24 February 1853). The sentiment is echoed in a letter to John Forster: "I hope to be listened to this time" (5 June 1854). The result was his best-known and most popular work, *Men and Women* (1855). It contained fifty-one poems, most of which are now to be found dispersed under other headings in complete editions of his works. Some of them are short dramatic pieces, such as "Memorabilia," "Love Among the Ruins," "A Toccata of Galuppi's," "'Childe Roland to the Dark Tower Came,'" and "Two in the Campagna," continuing the vein of his earlier lyrics, but with an even more powerful combination of technical assurance and warmth of feeling. Other poems in the volume are among Browning's most celebrated extended dramatic monologues, such as "Karshish," "Cleon," "Andrea del Sarto," "Fra Lippo Lippi," "A Grammarian's Funeral," and "Bishop Blougram's Apology." In addition, there were a very few poems in which Browning for once spoke about himself and his love for his wife, either obliquely as in "By the Fire-side," or openly as in "One Word More":

Love, you saw me gather men and women,
Live or dead or fashioned by my fancy,
Enter each and all, and use their service,
Speak from every mouth,—the speech, a poem.
Hardly shall I tell my joys and sorrows,
Hopes and fears, belief and disbelieving:
I am mine and yours—the rest be all men's,
Karshish, Cleon, Norbert and the fifty.
Let me speak this once in my true person,
Not as Lippo, Roland or Andrea,
Though the fruit of speech be just this sentence:
Pray you, look on these my men and women,
Take and keep my fifty poems finished;
Where my heart lies, let my brain lie also!
        (XIV. 129–142)

. . .

God be thanked, the meanest of his creatures
Boasts two soul-sides, one to face the world with,
One to show a woman when he loves her!
        (XVII.184–186)

It was a fine collection of poems, fit to stand comparison with any in the nineteenth century; but it did not find a large number of readers, except among young people. The reviews were mainly uncomprehending and unsympathetic, and eight years after it appeared his publisher still had copies unsold. Browning was more than a little disappointed by the reception of his work; his letters at this period show his bitterness and resignation. He took refuge in drawing and modeling in clay and in the society of his friends, but soon a graver concern occupied his days. Mrs. Browning, although she had been remarkably restored by living in Italy, had never been strong, and her health began to fail. She died on 29 June 1861 with her husband at her side. Browning was heartbroken. He at once decided to "go away, break up everything, go to England, and live and work and write." In the autumn he left Florence, never to return, and slowly traveled back to England with his young son.

He undertook to prepare Elizabeth's *Last Poems* for the press, unselfishly pleased as ever that the sales of her work much exceeded those of his own. Gradually he began to accept invitations and to move in society, eventually becoming much in demand as a guest. His next book of poems, *Dramatis Personae* (1864), included some of his most intricate argumentative monologues, such as "A Death in the Desert," "Caliban upon Setebos," and "Mr. Sludge 'the Medium,'" yet it proved unexpectedly popular, a second edition being called for during the same year. This, taken together with the encouraging sales of a collected edition and a volume of selections (both 1863), showed that Browning was at last beginning to overcome the mistrust of the British public. On the death in 1866 of Browning's father, who had lived in Paris since 1852 as a consequence of a mildly scandalous court case, the poet's sister Sarianna came to live with him in Warwick Crescent, London. She kept house for him and was his companion in his many holidays abroad.

In four monthly volumes (1868–1869) Browning published his longest and most ambitious work, *The Ring and the Book*, which is over 21,000 lines in length. He had been working on it at intervals since 1860, and had devised a method of telling the story that allowed him full use of his dramatic and speculative gifts. The execution was equally authoritative. The poem's reception was mixed, but the major reviews were full of praise for its vigor, scope, and originality. Once more the sales were encouraging, with a second edition appearing in 1872.

By this time Browning was established as a prominent and high-spirited member of London society, to the point where many people found his unaffected enjoyment of dinner parties hard to reconcile with any very intense inner life. He spent much of his time in London planning his son's education or trying to help him in his career as an artist, and usually spent the summer with friends in France or Switzerland or Scotland. In one of his poems of the 1870's we can catch a pleasant glimpse of Browning on holiday on the French coast; his simple physical enjoyment is as characteristic as his sharpness and specificity of observation:

> Meek, hitherto un-Murrayed bathing-place,
> Best loved of sea-coast-nook-ful Normandy!
> That, just behind you, is mine own hired house:
> With right of pathway through the field in front,
> No prejudice to all its growth unsheaved
> Of emerald luzern bursting into blue.
> Be sure I keep the path that hugs the wall,
> Of mornings, as I pad from door to gate!
> Yon yellow—what if not wild-mustard flower?—
> Of that, my naked sole makes lawful prize,

> Bruising the acrid aromatics out,
> Till, what they preface, good salt savours sting
> From, first, the sifted sands, then sands in slab,
> Smooth save for pipy wreath-work of the worm:
> (Granite and mussel-shell are ground alike
> To glittering paste,—the live worm troubles yet.)
> Then, dry and moist, the varech[2] limit-line,
> Burnt cinder-black, with brown uncrumpled swathe
> Of berried softness, sea-swoln thrice its size;
> And, lo, the wave protrudes a lip at last,
> And flecks my foot with froth, nor tempts in vain.
> (*Red Cotton Night-Cap Country*, I.20–40)

It was while he was staying in Scotland in 1869 that he proposed marriage to Louisa, Lady Ashburton, a rich and attractive widow, explaining candidly to her that his heart lay buried with his wife in Florence and that for him the real attraction of the match would be the advantages to his son Pen. When Lady Ashburton not unreasonably declined the offer, there followed much recrimination and unpleasant gossip, which distressed Browning more than his rejection.

By now Browning wrote with great fluency and was able to produce with comparatively little effort a series of long poems, some narrative, some dramatic, mainly dealing with subjects of contemporary interest. *Prince Hohenstiel-Schwangau* (1871), for example, described obliquely the career and political philosophy of Napoleon III of France. It was followed by *Fifine at the Fair* (1872), a prolonged monologue by a modern Don Juan about constancy in love in a world of shifting values; *Red Cotton Night-Cap Country, or Turf and Towers* (1873), set in Normandy and based on a recent cause célèbre; *The Inn Album* (1875), based on a story current in the clubs of London; and the two series of *Dramatic Idyls* (1879, 1880). Throughout his life Browning was interested, as an accomplished amateur, in the study of Latin and, even more, of Greek. He wrote in the 1870's a number of long poems on classical themes, including *Balaustion's Adventure* (1871), which contains a version of Euripides' *Alcestis*, and *Aristophanes' Apology* (1875), which contains a version of Euripides' *Herakles*. He also made a translation of *The Agamemnon of Aeschylus* (1877), which is so hard to follow—it was said that it could be understood quite easily with the help of the original Greek—that Browning has been suspected of delib-

[2]seaweed.

erately making it obscure and unattractive in order to score a point in his argument with Matthew Arnold about the nature of poetry.

Browning continued to write with undiminished energy. He produced many collections of shorter poems—*Pacchiarotto and How He Worked in Distemper: With Other Poems* (1876), *Jocoseria* (1883), and *Ferishtah's Fancies* (1884)—and two poems of more than usually close personal interest—*La Saisiaz* (1878), in which the poet moves from an elegy for his friend Anne Egerton Smith to a sustained meditation on the need for belief in life after death, and *Parleyings with Certain People of Importance in Their Day* (1887), in which he conducts imaginary dialogues with dead and forgotten writers and artists whose ideas had influenced him at varying stages of his life and who are ingeniously made to contribute to the discussion of some of the major controversial issues of Victorian England. This series of poems is as near as Browning ever ventured to writing an intellectual autobiography.

Browning and his sister continued to take holidays abroad, visiting Italy after 1878, and Browning eventually bought the Ca' Rezzonico in Venice. While staying there in 1889 he caught a cold and became seriously ill. His last book of poems, *Asolando: Fancies and Facts,* had just been published; he had time to learn that it had been favorably received before he died on 12 December. His popularity had been increasing slowly but steadily since the mid-1860's, and had been denoted by honorary degrees from the University of Oxford, an honorary fellowship of Balliol College, and presentation to the queen. Public recognition of his distinction was fittingly completed by his burial in Westminster Abbey. So much for the facts of a life which, apart from the decisive central episode, is little more than a tale of devotion to a demanding and financially unrewarding profession.

This section must conclude as it began, with a warning that Browning himself strenuously objected to any attempt to establish connections between his life and his poetry, between the public and the private face. As he wrote to his publisher in 1887, "I am so out of sympathy with all this 'biographical matter' connected with works which ought to stand or fall by their own merits quite independent of the writer's life and habits that I prefer leaving my poems to speak for themselves." He expresses the same position pungently in poems such as "House" and "At the 'Mermaid.'" Every biographer of the poet must hear the voice of Browning's Shakespeare demanding indignantly:

> Which of you did I enable
>   Once to slip inside my breast,
> There to catalogue and label
>   What I like least, what love best,
> Hope and fear, believe and doubt of,
>   Seek and shun, respect—deride?
> Who has right to make a rout of
>   Rarities he found inside?
>   ("At the Mermaid,'" V)

We have then to observe particular discretion in relating the poems and the life, bearing constantly in mind the advertisement that Browning put before his first collection of short poems: "Such poems as the following come properly enough, I suppose, under the head of 'Dramatic Pieces', being, though for the most part Lyric in expression, always Dramatic in principle, and so many utterances of so many imaginary persons, not mine."

THE DRAMATIC MONOLOGUE

Browning exploited the dramatic mode at every period of his career, and is the most ambitious and successful writer of the dramatic monologue in English. Indeed it is hardly possible to read Browning at all without some understanding of what the dramatic monologue is and of the different purposes it can be made to serve in the hand of a master.

In its simplest form, the dramatic monologue is a poem purporting to be the words of an imaginary or historical character, not the poet. Nothing is provided by way of context beyond the title and the words of the poem, but from these it is generally possible for the reader to infer the circumstances in which the monologue is delivered, who the listener or listeners are and how they are receiving what they hear, and something of the earlier history of the speaker. Of all this the speaker is aware. But expertly handled, the monologue can also reveal a great deal that the speaker does not realize he is betraying, particularly of course about his own character and motives, his accuracy as a narrator of events, and his trustworthiness as a judge of other people. In this indirect way the reader is put in possession of the material he needs to assess the speaker and thus to come to a conclusion about the issues that are raised in the poem. Since this is a process that continues throughout the monologue, it is difficult to illustrate compactly; examples in which it can be seen operating fairly obviously are the early poems "Porphyria's Lover," "Johannes Agricola in Meditation," "My Last Duchess," and "Soliloquy of the Spanish Cloister," or the much later "A Forgiveness."

Formally, of course, we see the entire action from the point of view of the speaker, but it is nevertheless a mistake to suppose that we are therefore committed entirely to the speaker's position, for, as I have said, we are often able to decide whether his view is comprehensive or in some way limited. A simple and straightforward example of this is "Up at a Villa—Down in the City" (1855); the main point of the poem is that the contrasts drawn by the speaker, with his exaggerated ideas of the only fashionable way to live, are all reversed by the reader, so that the arguments advanced in favor of the town are seen to be superficial, while the speaker's complaints about the countryside only show his blindness to its beauty:

> What of a villa? Though winter be over in March by
> rights,
> 'T is May perhaps ere the snow shall have withered
> well off the heights:
> You've the brown ploughed land before, where the
> oxen steam and wheeze,
> And the hills over-smoked behind by the faint grey
> olive-trees.
>
> (V)

The major monologues, however, do not yield their meaning to a simple reversal of values. Consider, for example, the poem "Cleon" (1855). The speaker is a Greek poet, heir to all the riches of Hellenic civilization, yet unhappy and troubled in his mind. He debates with himself the question of the immortality of the soul and the inevitability of death, which, he says,

> . . . is so horrible.
> I dare at times imagine to my need
> Some future state revealed to us by Zeus,
> Unlimited in capability
> For joy, as this is in desire for joy,
>
> . . .
>
> . . . But no!
> Zeus has not yet revealed it; and alas,
> He must have done so, were it possible!
> (323–327; 333–335)

In the last paragraph of the poem Cleon refers slightingly to an inquiry after the apostle Paul:

> . . . we have heard his fame
> Indeed, if Christus be not one with him—
> I know not, nor am troubled much to know.
> Thou canst not think a mere barbarian Jew
> As Paulus proves to be, one circumcized,
> Hath access to a secret shut from us?
> Thou wrongest our philosophy, O king,
> In stooping to enquire of such an one,
> As if his answer could impose at all!
> He writeth, doth he? well, and he may write.
> O the Jew findeth scholars! certain slaves
> Who touched on this same isle, preached him and Christ;
> And (as I gathered from a bystander)
> Their doctrine could be held by no sane man.
>
> (340–353)

So the monologue concludes. The irony of the poem very plainly resides in the fact that Cleon longs for some promise of personal immortality, yet when he has the opportunity to hear Christian teaching, he dismisses it on hearsay evidence because he cannot bring himself to admit that a Greek has anything to learn from a barbarian. The reader is conscious of Cleon's inadequacy and can use this knowledge to arrive at a judgment of him that is not one of simple moral approval or disapproval but rather an assessment of him and his subject.

A similar technique may be observed in "Karshish," in which an Arab physician refuses to accept the testimony of Lazarus himself because his scientific learning and his intellectual caution forbid him to take miracles seriously, yet he too, as we learn, longs for the all-loving God of Christianity. Thus in these two poems, though they are presented dramatically, with no voice heard but that of Cleon or Karshish, we do not rest content with the experiences they describe. Browning forces us to recognize each speaker's limitations, and is able in this way not only to control our opinions of his character but also to suggest fresh ways of thinking about Christianity, both as it was in the days of the early church and as it is in our own time. We can see that the pride that prevents Cleon from accepting the faith for which his heart is yearning and the intellectual scruples that prevent Karshish from acknowledging the true nature of his strange experiences have their counterparts in the nineteenth century and the twentieth.

It is clear that in many of his monologues, including some of the most notable, Browning is challenging the reader to appraise the value of the first-person narrative and to pronounce it and the speaker to be defective in some way. In others he does not invite the same scrutiny, but is, as far as one can tell, "lending his voice out" in an endeavor to allow a speaker to express a point of view that is not ironically exhibited. Poems such as "'How They Brought the Good News'" and "The Flight of the Duchess" fall into this category, as do "Andrea del Sarto" and "Fra Lippo Lippi." We are provided with no reason to suppose that the speaker's words are not to be taken at face value, even though we know, of course, that we are receiving one man's version of events, which is necessarily incomplete.

Most of Browning's monologues fall, as one would expect, somewhere between these two extremes, either because we can sense an ironic undercurrent but cannot be quite sure whether or not it is directed against the speaker, as in "Pictor Ignotus" and "A Grammarian's Funeral," or because the speaker successfully attacks one set of ideas while revealing at the same time that his own position is even less tenable. Such is "Bishop Blougram's Apology," which is worth a closer examination as an outstanding example of Browning's skill in manipulating the single voice of the speaker to produce dramatic and dialectic effects of great complexity.

A few economical phrases serve to establish the setting: a great dignitary of the Roman Catholic church in Britain has for a whim entertained to dinner an insignificant journalist, Gigadibs, who has written critically of the bishop's religious position. As they sit over their wine, the bishop embarks on a long examination of the nature of faith, which is simultaneously an assault on Gigadibs' skepticism and a defense of his own selected compromises. Blougram is a man of the world with a well-stocked mind and a copious supply of witty and ingenious arguments. Wherever he attacks the sterile reductive arguments of Gigadibs he is victorious, but the reader eventually perceives that for all his worldly charm and intellectual flexibility many, if not all, of the points he puts forward in his own favor are disingenuous or evasive, especially his calculating avowal of belief in popular superstitions and his false public professions of complete freedom from religious doubt.

At the conclusion of the poem, Blougram states with great condescension and complacency his conviction that the only possible alternative to Gigadibs'

mean and sheeplike existence is one of luxury and secular influence like his own. Browning then adds an unexpected *coda* in which the monologue form is abandoned and he simply narrates, without comment, the effect of the bishop's words on Gigadibs, who has given close attention to everything he has heard. Routed from his position of complete unbelief, and convinced by Blougram's blatant dishonesty of the falsity of any compromise, he is seized with "a sudden healthy vehemence," renounces his life in Britain, and decides to lead, with his family, a simple, practical life in Australia, where,

> . . . I hope,
> By this time he has tested his first plough
> And studied his last chapter of St. John.
> (1012–1014)

The whole effect of the monologue is thus to convert Gigadibs from disbelief to Christianity. But the judgment involved is not a simple one, for Blougram is by no means presented as an entirely unsympathetic figure. He is intelligent enough to see the implications of his own arguments, but lacks the courage to take them to their logical conclusion. He can only shelter behind defenses whose hollowness is evident even to himself, although he has at times painful glimpses of a world of belief he can never reach. It is because of this self-frustrated desire for faith that the reader, even while he observes the feebleness of Blougram's sophistries, sympathizes with him, just as he does with Karshish and Cleon. But to say that we feel sympathy for the speaker and at the same time condemn his evasiveness is not to say that the two impulses cancel out, leaving us indifferent. On the contrary, the poem is a powerful affirmation not just of faith but of the need for belief, made even more moving by being put into the mouth of a man who is not himself able to sustain the demands of Christianity.

The purpose of that extended account of "Bishop Blougram's Apology" is to illustrate the point that there are two mistaken ways of reading a dramatic monologue—the first, naive way is to suppose that the words spoken are to be taken at their face value as a literal expression of Browning's own sentiments; the second way, scarcely less naive, is to suppose that the only alternative to the first way is to accept that we can never go behind the words of the monologue and infer Browning's opinion of the speaker. This may sometimes be true, but in general the central performance of the monologue is that of putting the reader in a position to judge the speaker.

The most celebrated example of this is *The Ring and the Book* (1868–1869), a poem of great length based on the proceedings in a late seventeenth-century Italian court case. Book I explains how Browning came across an account of the trial as he strolled through a square in Florence, and book XII concludes the story; but books II–XI are all massive monologues, many of them over 2,000 lines long, each recounting a different version of the same set of events as they appeared to the participants, to their lawyers, and to members of the public. It might seem that such a procedure would produce a relativist poem, in which the reader was handed, bewildered, from one narrator to another, each offering an account of the facts that can be neither proved nor disproved and must therefore lead in the end to a complete suspension of judgment. Yet nothing could be further removed from the experience of reading the poem. As each monologue makes its contribution to the reader's knowledge, a central body of truth is gradually established. The entire structure of *The Ring and the Book* implies that there is an objective truth, variously refracted though it may be, and that this truth, once it is perceived, is available for judging the honesty of each speaker. As Browning says, his object is to enable his readers to come at the true facts: "There's nothing in nor out o' the world/Good except truth" (I.698–699). He insists, however, that it is by the oblique exercise of his art, which is itself the mirror of creation, that the writer must make the truth available:

> So write a book shall mean beyond the facts,
> Suffice the eye and save the soul beside.
>   (XII.866–867)

In conclusion it must be emphasized that the dramatic monologue was not, as some have suggested, a refuge to Browning, a mask behind which he could hide instead of writing poetry in his own person, nor was it a predetermined form that permitted only a limited range of effects. On the contrary, it was in Browning's hands, as I have tried to show, an infinitely flexible mode of expression, allowing him to exercise his mimetic and dramatic gifts to present characters with varying degrees of sympathy or satire; to lay stress on action or on "incidents in the development of a soul"; to handle matters from the past in a way that made them seem live and immedi-

ate or to handle issues of his own day with ironic detachment; and to involve the reader in the active process of discriminating truth from falsehood, of discovering the answer to Browning's constant question—"What say you to the right and wrong of that?"

It is at all times an intimate form, designed to entertain and instruct the reader by allowing him to hear the voices of men and women speaking about the matters that lie closest to their hearts: "what I imagine the man might, if he pleased, say for himself." Browning describes Gigadibs listening patiently "While the great bishop rolled him out a mind/Long crumpled, till creased consciousness lay smooth." When we read the great monologues, we can see that the man who fashioned them had nothing to learn from later novelists about the technique of displaying a stream of consciousness or from psychologists about the devious recesses of the human personality.

BROWNING AND CHRISTIAN TEACHING

BROWNING once defined his own interests with memorable brevity as "Man's thoughts, loves, hates," and of the thoughts none engaged him more constantly than the various attempts to comprehend and explain the relation of God and his creation. Having learned from the previous section that Browning had perfected the art of the dramatic monologue to a point where he could, if he wished, control the reader's response to the speaker and hence to the views he puts forward, we shall realize that once we understand the mechanism of the dramatic monologue, it is possible to construct a general sketch of the values that emerge from the poems as normally receiving the poet's approval. Although the religious and philosophical ideas that Browning was prepared to entertain and endorse changed fairly radically during his life, some central points remain constant. Browning never, for example, handles unkindly those who preserve a simple unquestioning faith in God, even though we may sense that he sometimes envies and sometimes pities their innocence. The most celebrated, indeed notorious, example comes from the play *Pippa Passes*, when the young mill-girl on her annual holiday sings happily as she goes on her way through the town of Asolo in the Trevisan:

The year's at the spring
And day's at the morn;
Morning's at seven;
The hill-side's dew-pearled;
The lark's on the wing;
The snail's on the thorn:
God's in his heaven—
All's right with the world!
                    (I.222–229)

The whole action of the play is designed to show that Pippa is quite unconscious of the evil that is abroad in the town, and even the terms of her happy song are called in question in the concluding scene: "Ah Pippa, morning's rule is moved away,/Dispensed with, never more to be allowed!/Day's turn is over, now arrives the night's." Nevertheless, her artless faith, although it is shown to be naively blind to the darker side of life, is certainly not derided, and at the end of the play her trust in Providence is vindicated by events.

Browning never disparages those who with a clear heart and mind are lucky enough to be able to live by an uncomplicated set of religious or moral ideals, yet his own varieties of religious experience are by no means simple. A convenient place to begin the account is with *Christmas-Eve and Easter-Day* (1850). Technically this double poem can be read as an elaborate structure of monologues and dialogues, but Browning drops frequent hints that the arguments he is handling are not purely fictitious or hypothetical, but rather correspond to episodes in his own history and to positions that were in fact available to him and to his contemporaries. The poem, although dramatic in form, is thus not devoted to the manipulation of imaginary characters but to the clash and conflict of real arguments. The speaker reviews various modes of worship—the dissenting sect in "'Mount Zion' with Love-lane at the back of it," the congregation at St. Peter's, the audience in the lecture hall of a German higher critic—and is tempted to say complacently, "This tolerance is a genial mood," and to pride himself on his broadmindedness. But he is violently shaken out of this "Lazy glow of benevolence, /O'er the various modes of man's belief," and forced to choose "one way, our chief/Best way of worship." He decides to stand fast in the dissenting chapel, as representing the sort of faith in which he has been brought up. It is the most difficult and demanding way of life, lacking the firm supporting dogma of Catholicism and the rational reassurances of the higher criticism.

Thank God, no paradise stands barred
To entry, and I find it hard
To be a Christian, as I said!
                    . . .
. . . But Easter-Day breaks! But
Christ rises! Mercy every way
Is infinite,—and who can say?
                    (XXXIII.1029–1031; 1038–1048)

So the poem ends. The concluding words epitomize its speculative, inquiring, anxious approach to matters of faith, and also the kind of Christian Browning had to be if he was to be a Christian at all—earnest, plain, strenuous, committed but undogmatic. Although the poem gives a not unsympathetic voice to an easier kind of religious life, its tenor is to expose the inadequacy of this looser faith, which ultimately appears to be no more than "a condiment/To heighten flavours with." Yet if the path of primitive Christianity is too hard, or, more pertinently, if it calls for an absolute faith in Christ that can no longer be commanded, Browning must face the teasing question of whether the laxer forms of belief are really any better than outright skepticism. *Christmas-Eve and Easter-Day* provides a masterly exposition of the issues at stake, which were to play their part in Browning's poetry for the rest of his life.

From the volumes of *Men and Women* (1855) I need mention only "Saul," "Cleon," "Karshish," and "Bishop Blougram's Apology" by way of example and illustration. These are all poems that are designed to bring home to the reader the power and hope of the dedicated Christian life and the loving promise of the incarnation:

" . . . O Saul, it shall be
A Face like my face that receives thee; a Man like
    to me,
Thou shalt love and be loved by, for ever: A Hand
    like this hand
Shall throw open the gates of new life to thee! See the
    Christ stand!"
                    ("Saul," XVIII.309–312)

Yet in all of these poems great weight is also given to the difficulties and obstacles that lie in the way of faith. Browning never ceases to engage with this insoluble question. It is true that in his later years he wrote fewer poems that discuss Christian doctrines as such, but the central concerns of Christianity were his concerns also. In this sense Browning, though never neglecting "earth's common surface, rough, smooth, dry or damp," was always a religious poet. It is plain that by 1864, the year of *Dramatis Personae*, it was becoming more difficult for him to rely on biblical testimony as a defense against loss of faith, and correspondingly more difficult to rely on his Christian faith to confirm the value of his ethical insights.

In "A Death in the Desert," for example, a long monologue spoken by John the Evangelist on his deathbed, the central issues are the evidences for Christianity, especially the miracles, and the argument of critics like Ludwig Feuerbach that the love, might, and will of God are merely projections of human qualities. This last, in particular, is an argument that John sees to be sincere and worth answering; in doing so he uses arguments that Browning was to find attractive for many years. John reasons as follows: life is not static but a progression. Knowledge of God is a vital stage in man's progress: it leads him, among other things, to a consideration of his own stature in the universe. Now, however, he has not unreasonably concluded that if he is the only being in whom love, power, and will combine, he is himself the "first, last, and best of things," that is, God. If man reaches this conclusion, nobody can prove to him that he is wrong, but "his life becomes impossible, which is death."

> "How shall ye help this man who knows himself,
> That he must love and would be loved again,
> Yet, owning his own love that proveth Christ,
> Rejecteth Christ through very need of Him?"
>
> (508–511)

If, on the other hand, men will only admit in humility that they cannot know God's nature or their own with certainty, they will find their proper place in the world, for it is man's unique nature that he

> "Finds progress, man's distinctive mark alone,
> Not God's, and not the beasts': God is, they are,
> Man partly is and wholly hopes to be."
>
> (586–588)

Such progress is possible only because of man's ignorance and his consequent desire for knowledge. "He learns/Because he lives, which is to be a man."

It is sometimes objected that the language of "A Death in the Desert" is as drab and as arid as the wasteland in which it is set: it is fairer to say that Browning is working in deliberately neutral tones. Colorful rhetoric would be improper in the mouth of a dying man pondering the meaning of human life, and the issues are too delicately balanced to be settled by a passionate assertion of belief. In any case, Browning had not, at this point in his life, any straightforward solution to offer. To distinguish his own position from that of the higher critics, who were expertly scrutinizing the whole status of Holy Writ, he had to make ever more subtle discriminations. His language is consequently circumspect and hesitant, rather than bold and picturesque. By 1864, this constant questioning and sifting of his faith had left Browning far from the safe harbor of any church. Indeed, even the idea of God's love of man being made manifest in the incarnation of Christ, which had animated so many of his poems, is found much more rarely in his later work. Once Browning began to doubt the fundamental revealed truths of Christianity, he was confronted with two alternative ways of proceeding. To put the case crudely, he could either demythologize Christian doctrine and liberalize it until it no longer required an act of faith to assent to it, or he could analyze man's nature, hoping to discover there some elements of the absolute which would provide a stable principle in life. The difficulty is that Browning was always conscious that the first way might be a hyocritical compromise, as it was for Blougram, while the second might issue in the most blatant self-projection, as it did for the misguided Caliban in the monologue "Caliban upon Setebos."

In moving away from anything that might be termed orthodox Christianity, he moved very far also from any poetic tradition that might have helped him. After 1864, one of his chief technical problems was to discover a strategy for developing a poem of analysis and speculation; his chief achievement was the creation of a large number of long poems that were based not on a story or on a system of belief, but on the exploration of an important and difficult question. The clearest example of this is the fine poem *La Saisiaz* (1878). The occasion of the poem was the sudden death of an old friend of Browning's, Anne Egerton Smith, while she was staying with Browning and his sister near Geneva in a villa called "La Saisiaz." During the summer of 1877, Miss Smith and Browning had followed with great interest a symposium in the *Nineteenth Century* on "The Soul and Future Life," in which various writers discussed the question of the immortality of the soul, for the most part without appeal to revelation.

In the central part of *La Saisiaz* Browning makes his own contribution, as it were, to the debate, meditating on the possibility of establishing eternal life by reasoning from first principles and on the moral implications of the conclusions he reaches. Throughout the poem Browning observes the prior conditions of the symposium and does not rely on Christian evidences. He considers earnestly the critical questions that arise: whether he can convince himself of the immortality of the soul simply from an inspection of his own existence; what the purpose is of gaining experience in this world if it is not to be put to use elsewhere; and how a man would have to behave on earth if he knew for certain that there was a life to come. He explores these and other positions with some acuteness and great honesty, deciding at last that no certainty is available in such matters. All man's soul can do on earth is

> . . . pass probation, prove its powers, and exercise
> Sense and thought on fact, and then, from fact educing
> fit surmise,
> Ask itself, and of itself have solely answer, "Does the
> scope
> Earth affords of fact to judge by warrant future fear
> or hope?"
>
> (521–524)

The argument hinted at here, especially in the use of the terms "probation" and "exercise," is one that Browning made great use of throughout his career. It runs: only if we have limited knowledge can we view this life as one of probation; but only if we view this life as one of probation can we postulate a future life. Thus the imperfections of man's knowledge, far from being a source of despair, become the necessary condition for the immortality of man's soul. "Life is probation and this earth no goal/But starting-point of man." This device, by which human defects are seen to be positively welcome if they guarantee a life of constant striving toward an unattainable perfection, was memorably expressed in "Abt Vogler": "On earth the broken arcs; in the heaven, a perfect round"—and lies behind many later poems such as "Jochanan Hakkadosh," "Rephan," and "Reverie." He applies the idea very movingly to his own life in the poem "Development," remembering how gently his father had introduced him to the world of classical learning through the medium of plays based on Homer. Truth is never easy and sometimes it can be arrived at only through fictions, and yet it has its

own unique value, which no fiction can ever have: "Truth ever, truth only the excellent." The particular religious issue that lies behind the poem is the problem of demythologizing: if you dispense with the historical evidences of Christ's existence in favor of an imaginative conviction of the truth of his ministry, is there any point short of total skepticism at which you can arrest the process?

"Development" appeared in *Asolando* (1890), Browning's last book of poems, in which he gives us the reflections of a man who does not claim to have found a final solution to problems of this kind, but is content to remember that at least he never gave up the fight to discover a position where a man might stand without sacrificing either his honor or his hope. The idea of human responsibility, of the duty to keep trying to do whatever it is right for a man to do, is never absent long from Browning's poems on religious subjects. When the framework of religious observance is stripped away, as it was in the poems of his old age, the responsibility remains and indeed becomes even heavier. Although he grew progressively less able to accept the literal truth of the incarnation and progressively less concerned with forms of worship, he was never less insistent that one of man's chief ends is to think earnestly about his place in creation and his corresponding duties.

A man who is living as he should be, doing his best to use his powers in a world that offers no possibility of absolute attainment, will be distinguished by his activeness and resilience:

> Though I do my best I shall scarce succeed.
> But what if I fail of my purpose here?
> It is but to keep the nerves at strain,
> To dry one's eyes and laugh at a fall,
> And, baffled, get up and begin again,—
> So the chace takes up one's life, that's all.
> ("Life in a Love," 10–15)

To discriminate between beneficial and harmful kinds of human energy, Browning's great touchstone is love. Characters who are in love or who act through love are almost always treated with affection and admiration. Love is the master passion, more powerful than evil and stronger than death:

> Love which endures and doubts and is oppressed
> And cherished, suffering much and much sustained,
> And blind, oft-failing, yet believing love,
> A half-enlightened, often-chequered trust. . . .
> (*Paracelsus*, V.702–705)

Thus, letting love slip, either through laziness or timidity, is unforgivable. Poems such as "Too Late" and "Dîs aliter visum; or, Le Byron de nos Jours" illustrate Browning's general attitude to those who are afraid to accept the challenge of loving, while "The Statue and the Bust" is a more extreme example. On the whole, Browning presents favorably in his poems men and women who act intuitively as the heart dictates: "Let him rush straight, and how shall he go wrong?" the pope asks rhetorically. Conversely, he implies his dislike and contempt for those who behave cautiously and calculatingly, contrasting them unfavorably with those who boldly aim at a high mark even though they know that they cannot hope to reach their target. "Andrea del Sarto," with its carefully subdued register of gray and silver tones, shows how coolly Browning felt toward the man who aspired only to what he was certain he could achieve. In contrast, the scholar in "A Grammarian's Funeral," although to a superficial eye he has retreated from the real business of life, has in fact set his goal so high that it is perfectly plain that it cannot be achieved in this world. Therefore he must rely on a life to come, and his renunciation of the possibility of worldly success is in itself a testimony of faith. He is "still loftier than the world suspects,/Living and dying," and is saved because he has perceived that failure through attempting too much is in itself a kind of heroism. Human successes, by definition, are at best trivial compared with the works of God, but when he fails man is doing what God himself cannot do. "The incomplete,/More than completion, matches the immense." This idea can be found in many different places in Browning's work:

> But what's whole, can increase no more,
>   Is dwarfed and dies, since here's its sphere.
>   ("Dîs aliter visum," XXIX.141–142)

> Manhood—the actual? Nay, praise the potential!
>   . . .
> What *is?* No, what *may* be—sing! that's Man's essential.
>   ("Apollo and the Fates," 211; 213)

> "Man's work is to labour and leaven—
> At best he may—earth here with heaven;
> 'Tis work for work's sake that he's needing:
> Let him work on and on as if speeding
> Work's end, but not dream of succeeding!
> Because if success were intended,
> Why, heaven would begin ere earth ended."
>   ("Of Pacchiarotto," XXL.368–374)

> No, Man's the prerogative—knowledge once gained—
>   To ignore,—find new knowledge to press for, to swerve
> In pursuit of, no, not for a moment: attained—
>   Why, onward through ignorance! Dare and deserve!
> As still to its asymptote speedeth the curve,
> So approximates Man—Thee, who, reachable not,
>   Hast formed him to yearningly follow Thy whole
> Sole and single omniscience. . .
>   ("Fust and His Friends," 421–428)

> And what is our failure here but a triumph's evidence
>   For the fulness of the days? Have we withered or
>   agonized?
> Why else was the pause prolonged but that singing
>   might issue thence?
>   Why rushed the discords in but that harmony should
>   be prized?
>   ("Abt Vogler," XI)

If to this brief summary of positions that Browning presents with favor we add the statement that he never doubted that human freedom was real and that men could if they chose attain a sufficient knowledge of truth, we have sketched in the main constants in Browning's thought. In this abstract formulation they may appear a primitive, perhaps even a barbarous, set of values, but when we encounter them as active forces in the poems they are much less naive. Browning realizes the moral lives of his speakers with singular richness and complexity. He portrays his casuists, for example, with great insight, and endows them generously with intellectual resourcefulness. But behind all the equivocations and all the sophistries, the reader is always aware of the presence of equally subtle moral standards which he will ultimately be expected to use himself to assess the worth of the speaker. I do not think that Browning has anywhere expressed these positive values more straightforwardly than in his essay on Shelley, where he wrote: "I call Shelley a moral man, because he was true, simple-hearted and brave, and because what he acted corresponded to what he knew."

BROWNING AS A POET OF VICTORIAN LIFE

So far I have discussed Browning as though his poems were distinguished by nothing more remarkable than an ingenious narrative technique and an uncompromising but basically uncomplicated view of human responsibility. Yet to many readers the essence of Browning lies quite elsewhere—in the exuberant freedom of his language and in the fertility of his invention of unusual situations and subjects for poems. He chose his topics freely from the classical world, from rabbinical lore, from the Middle Ages and the Renaissance, from the world of the Augustans, and from nineteenth-century life in Europe and America. His speakers are equally diverse in character. The experience of reading Browning is thus infinitely varied—from the pathos of "A Woman's Last Word" to the malicious hypocrisy of "Soliloquy of the Spanish Cloister," from the energetic heroism of "Hervé Riel" to the close argument of "A Death in the Desert," from the coarse jollity of "Holy-Cross Day" to the subtle casuistries of "Fifine at the Fair," from the slow unwinding of "The Inn Album" to the rapid easy narrative of "The Pied Piper of Hamelin," a list that could be extended without difficulty. It is worth remembering that at this time there was continuous and heated debate about the role of the poet in the modern world, and in particular about the proper subject matter of Victorian poetry. Browning, by his example no less than by his essay on Shelley, was a major force on the side of pluralism. He rejected alike any supposed romantic requirement to reveal his own commitment in his poems and any suggestion that the poet had a duty to lose himself in the remote classical impersonality of his subjects. Similarly he resisted with equal vigor those who thought that nineteenth-century life was not suitable material for poetry and those who thought that nothing else was. Browning always celebrates the diversity of human characters and activities:

> He stood and watched the cobbler at his trade,
> The man who slices lemons into drink,
> The coffee-roaster's brazier, and the boys
> That volunteer to help him turn its winch.
> He glanced o'er books on stalls with half an eye,
> And fly-leaf ballads on the vendor's string,
> And broad-edge bold-print posters by the wall.
> He took such cognizance of men and things,
> If any beat a horse, you felt he saw;
> If any cursed a woman, he took note;
> Yet stared at nobody,—you stared at him,
> And found, less to your pleasure than surprise,
> He seemed to know you and expect as much.
> ("How It Strikes a Contemporary," 23–35)

He writes always with his eye on the object, determined to render it fully and specifically:

> The swallow has set her six young on the rail,
>   And looks sea-ward:
> The water's in stripes like a snake, olive-pale
>   To the leeward,—
> On the weather-side, black, spotted white with the wind.
>   . . .
> Our fig-tree, that leaned for the saltness, has furled
>   Her five fingers,
> Each leaf like a hand opened wide to the world
>   Where there lingers
> No glint of the gold, Summer sent for her sake. . .
>   ("James Lee's Wife," III.54–58; 61–65)

> I wonder, does the streamlet ripple still,
>   Outsmoothing galingale and watermint
> Its mat-floor? while at brim, 'twixt sedge and sedge,
> What bubblings past Baccheion, broadened much,
> Pricked by the reed and fretted by the fly,
> Oared by the boatman-spider's pair of arms!
>   (Aristophanes' Apology, 199–204)

>   Never mind! As o'er my punch
> (You away) I sit of evenings,—silence, save for biscuit-
>   crunch,
> Black, unbroken,—thought grows busy, thrids each
>   pathway of old years,
> Notes this forthright, that meander, till the long-past
>   life appears
> Like an outspread map of country plodded through,
>   each mile and rood,
> Once, and well remembered still. . . .
>   ("Clive," 9–14)

In the argument about poetic diction Browning once again stands quite apart from the conventional positions, insisting this time on the poet's right to use in his poetry whatever elements of the language he chooses, however exotic or recondite, however homely or prosaic. The sort of broadminded charity he shows to men and women he exercises also in his choice of words. Thus we find in Browning not simply a very large vocabulary (38,957 words, we are told, as against Shakespeare's 19,957) but a remarkable lexical diversity. He claims for the poet the right of a man in ordinary conversation to choose the suitable word for the occasion, whether it happens to be vulgar ("higgledy piggledy") or technical ("asymptote" or "abductor"), newly coined ("calotypist") or old-fashioned ("thill-horse" or "hacqueton"), familiar ("dirt-cheap") or unfamiliar ("olent" [odorous]), prosaic ("candlestick-maker" or "ginger-pop") or fanciful ("rose-jacynth"). Again, in a randomly chosen group of poems we find such strikingly "unpoetical" nouns as shrub-house, window-pane, weevil, geraniums, slide-bolt, cut-throat, proof-mark, moustache, flap-hat, beer, tar, rocket-plant, rubbish, cheese, blister, slug, trousers, dry-rot, parsley, and many others. The unselfconscious use of exact words simply because they are the ordinary way of referring to the things they name is a distinctive feature of Browning's idiom. It makes no small contribution to the crisp concreteness of description which is one of the characteristic pleasures of reading his poetry, and is to be observed whether he is writing about such unpromising material as geological changes:

> The centre-fire heaves underneath the earth,
> And the earth changes like a human face:
> The molten ore bursts up among the rocks,
> Winds into the stone's heart, outbranches bright
> In hidden mines, spots barren river-beds,
> Crumbles into fine sand where sunbeams bask
>
> (*Paracelsus*, V. 653–658)

or small living creatures:

> . . . this kingdom, limited
> Alone by one old populous green wall
> Tenanted by the ever-busy flies,
> Grey crickets and shy lizards and quick spiders,
> Each family of the silver-threaded moss—
> Which, look through near, this way, and it appears
> A stubble-field or a cane-brake, a marsh
> Of bulrush whitening in the sun . . .
>
> (*Paracelsus*, I.36–43)

or about everyday life in Italy:

> As to-night will be proved to my sorrow,
>   When, supping in state,
> We shall feed our grape-gleaners (two dozen,
>   Three over one plate)
> With lasagne so tempting to swallow
>   In slippery ropes,
> And gourds fried in great purple slices,
>   That colour of popes.
> Meantime, see the grape bunch they've brought you:
>   The rain-water slips
> O'er the heavy blue bloom on each globe
>   Which the wasp to your lips
> Still follows with fretful persistence:
>   Nay, taste, while awake,
> This half of a curd-white smooth cheese-ball
>   That peels, flake by flake,

> Like an onion, each smoother and whiter;
>   Next sip this weak wine
> From the thin green glass flask, with its stopper,
>   A leaf of the vine;
> And end with the prickly-pear's red flesh
>   That leaves thro' its juice
> The stony black seeds on your pearl-teeth.
>   Scirocco is loose!
>
> ("The Englishman in Italy," 93–116)

In addition, Browning makes free use of the contractions that represent the normal elisions of informal speech, especially of course in his dramatic monologues. For example, in "Mr. Sludge the Medium'" we find, "He's the man for muck," "I'd like to know," "I'll try to answer you," "I can't pretend to mind your smiling," and "It don't hurt much." These colloquial licenses are common in Browning: they are one of the more obvious ways in which he deliberately rejects a formal rhetorical structure in favor of a much less ceremonious and balanced way of putting his sentences together, full of loose qualifying phrases. This has the effect of making the speaker seem matter-of-fact and reliable, even though he is using a metrical form.

> Ours is a great wild country:
>   If you climb to our castle's top,
>   I don't see where your eye can stop;
> For when you've passed the cornfield country,
> Where vineyards leave off, flocks are packed,
> And sheep-range leads to cattle-tract,
> And cattle-tract to open-chase,
> And open-chase to the very base
> Of the mountain where, at a funeral pace,
> Round about, solemn and slow,
> One by one, row after row,
> Up and up the pine-trees go,
> So, like black priests up, and so
> Down the other side again
>   To another greater, wilder country,
> That's one vast red drear burnt-up plain,
> Branched through and through with many a vein
> Whence iron's dug, and copper's dealt;
>   Look right, look left, look straight before,—
> Beneath they mine, above they smelt,
>   Copper-ore and iron-ore,
> And forge and furnace mould and melt,
>   And so on, more and ever more,
> Till at the last, for a bounding belt,
>   Comes the salt sand hoar of the great sea-shore,
> —And the whole is our Duke's country.
>
> ("The Flight of the Duchess," II.6–31)

Browning's ability to write verse in current English was put to many other uses. In "Too Late," for example, he preserves the realistic surface of the poem, making the extraordinary situation of the speaker, a man at the point of death addressing the woman that he has loved and lost, at once more credible and pathetic by his deliberate reining in of language. Again, colloquial idiom and contemporary speech patterns can suggest the topicality of a monologue set in a remote time or place, as in "Fra Lippo Lippi," or they can operate as touchstones of the heroic attitude, as in *Prince Hohenstiel-Schwangau, Saviour of Society* (1871). Perhaps the faithfulness of Browning's language to its basis in everyday speech is most strikingly shown in those numerous poems that are a conversation or half a conversation between a man and a woman who are, or have been, in love with one another. Dramatic romances such as "Love Among the Ruins," "Two in the Campagna," "A Light Woman," "James Lee's Wife," "The Worst of It," "Dîs aliter visum," "Youth and Art," and "St. Martin's Summer" are representative of the great range of Browning's love poetry: they all depend to some extent on registering the accents of the speaking voice, so that the emotion, whether of ardent love or regret for love lost, is always tested against the language of the real world. Conventional exaggeration and compliment are exposed at once, and so is the kind of love poetry that depends on substituting for a real woman an abstraction built up of traditionally charming clichés. "The Lost Mistress" is a compact example:

> All's over, then: does truth sound bitter
>   As one at first believes?
> Hark, 't is the sparrows' good-night twitter
>   About your cottage eaves!
>
> And the leaf-buds on the vine are woolly,
>   I noticed that, to-day;
> One day more bursts them open fully
>   —You know the red turns grey.
>
> To-morrow we meet the same then, dearest?
>   May I take your hand in mine?
> Mere friends are we,—well, friends the merest
>   Keep much that I resign:
>
> For each glance of the eye so bright and black,
>   Though I keep with heart's endeavour,—
> Your voice, when you wish the snowdrops back,
>   Though it stay in my soul for ever!—
>
> Yet I will but say what mere friends say,
>   Or only a thought stronger;

> I will hold your hand but as long as all may,
>   Or so very little longer!
>
> (st. I–V)

The falling rhythm and unaffected vocabulary reinforce the poem's impression of powerful feelings held in check reluctantly and with difficulty. Henry James, not in general given to overpraising Browning, puts the case finely when he observes that Browning's "treatment of the special relation between man and woman [is] a complete and splendid picture of the matter, which somehow places it at the same time in the region of conduct and responsibility."

A poet as various as Browning not surprisingly provokes contradictory critical responses. Thus he is sometimes spoken of as one of the most exotic of British poets, always escaping to the past or to Italy, sometimes as the most committed of poets, always engaged with the problems of depicting the multitudinous modern world. *The Ring and the Book*, for instance, may be regarded as deliberately removed in time and place from Browning's own readers or alternatively as the only epic poem in which the chief characters are modern men and women, living in cities and swayed by passions like our own. Similarly, Browning's long poems of the 1870's seemed to some readers contrived and novelettish, while others found them topical and realistic.

Consider the poem *The Inn Album*, which was first published in the *New York Times* in 1875, and was, like its predecessor *Red Cotton Night-Cap Country*, based on a true story of Victorian life. The encounter it describes is the culminating event in the lives of two men and two women, but much of the early part of the poem is spent in recapitulation. This is designed to bring to light the unresolved incident from the past that has drawn these four characters on a summer day to the parlor of a country inn. The narration is full of topical references and the setting is deliberately prosaic:

> Two personages occupy this room
> Shabby-genteel, that's parlour to the inn
> Perched on a view-commanding eminence;
> —Inn which may be a veritable house
> Where somebody once lived and pleased good taste
> Till tourists found his coign of vantage out,
> And fingered blunt the individual mark
> And vulgarized things comfortably smooth.
> On a sprig-pattern-papered wall there brays
> Complaint to sky Sir Edwin's dripping stag;

His couchant coast-guard creature corresponds;
They face the Huguenot and Light o' the World.
Grim o'er the mirror on the mantelpiece,
Varnished and coffined, *Salmo ferox* glares
—Possibly at the List of Wines which, framed
And glazed, hangs somewhat prominent on peg.

(I.26–41)

Since the story is one of meanness and greed and unhappiness and its conclusion brings two unnatural deaths, *The Inn Album* puzzled those of its early readers who approached it with fixed ideas about what poetry should do, but many perceptive critics, including Swinburne, recognized that Browning, without ceasing to write poetry, was staking a claim to a new territory, that of novelists like Balzac. This is perhaps the most helpful parallel to the many poems in which Browning began from an incident or an episode in Victorian life. The amplitude of the nineteenth-century novel, its opportunities for leisurely description and careful analysis of action and motive, its impression of a lavishness that is closer to the prodigality of life than to the economy of art, all these features, which distinguish the novel from the short story, are denied to poetry except in the medium of the long poem. The successes of the nineteenth century in this form were few, and mostly Browning's.

Nor is this an admission that Browning is in some way limited by the period in which he lived and about which he wrote. Like the novelists, he realized his age so thoroughly and completely that it survives in him. If we go to Browning expecting neither romantic nor twentieth-century poetry, but simply Victorian poetry, we shall not come away unrewarded. It is very difficult to set up any other expectations in advance. He is exceptionally versatile in his use of meter and equally prolific in devising new stanza forms, while his fondness for unusual and unorthodox rhymes is well known:

A tune was born in my head last week
Out of the thump-thump and shriek-shriek
  Of the train, as I came by it, up from Manchester;
And when, next week, I take it back again,
My head will sing to the engine's clack again,
  While it only makes my neighbour's haunches stir. . . .

(*Christmas-Eve,* IV.249–254)

Unlike some of his contemporaries, Browning had a robust sense of verbal humor and a keen eye for human absurdities: poems as different in tone and setting as "The Bishop Orders His Tomb at St. Praxed's Church," "Caliban upon Setebos," and "Ned Bratts" are equally rich in well-developed comic detailing. The reader's access to a poem is very often by way of a character whose way of thinking is unfamiliar to the point of being eccentric. Browning frequently chooses for his speaker a man or woman with an extraordinary combination of blindness and sharpness of observation, rather as he was said himself to have one eye very long-sighted and the other very shortsighted. What we notice about his speakers is how clearly they see some things, in the simple sense of keen perception of physical fact, and how blind they are, in a metaphorical sense, to other facts in their world. A poem of Browning's can be relied on for one thing: to exact from the reader this totally distinctive combination of physical response to a series of brilliantly accurate sense perceptions, and inferential response to a succession of inaccurate intellectual formulations. This is not true, it must be admitted, of Browning's holy old men, such as Abt Vogler and Rabbi Ben Ezra and the pope, but it is true in the main, and goes some way to explain the characteristic activeness, almost aggressiveness, of the monologues.

The range of effects that Browning commanded is perhaps most effectively suggested by a passage from *Pippa Passes.* Jules, an artist, is speaking:

But of the stuffs one can be master of,
How I divined their capabilities!
From the soft-rinded smoothening facile chalk
That yields your outline to the air's embrace,
Half-softened by a halo's pearly gloom;
Down to the crisp imperious steel, so sure
To cut its one confided thought clean out
Of all the world. . . .

(II.93–100)

Browning's sympathies were wide enough to include the age of Raphael and the age of Disraeli, without using one as a refuge from the other. On the contrary, more than any other poet of his century, more even than Wordsworth, he labored to bring poetry

Down to the level of our common life,
Close to the beating of our common heart.
(*Aristophanes' Apology*)

William Sharp records the following anecdote: "On another occasion I heard him smilingly add, to someone's vague assertion that in Italy only was there any romance left, 'Ah, well, I should like to include poor old Camberwell.'"

BROWNING'S REPUTATION

As Henry James observed:

Browning is "upon" us, straighter upon us always, somehow, than anyone else of his race . . . as if he came up against us, each time, on the same side of the street and not on the other side, across the way, where we mostly see the poets elegantly walk, and where we greet them without danger of concussion.

Many years earlier, Matthew Arnold had perceived the same immediacy and the same bristling actuality in Browning, but had found them much less congenial. In a letter to Arthur Hugh Clough he wrote, " . . . Browning is a man with a moderate gift passionately desiring movement and fulness, and obtaining but a confused multitudinousness." Although this was written in 1849, and is therefore based on only a small fraction of Browning's work, it does point to a permanent point of critical divergence.

The predominant impression derived from reading Arnold's poetry is that of a man of great sensibility attempting in vain to discover ideal certainties in a utilitarian age with which he is quite out of sympathy. Renunciation, resignation, and patient suffering are the only attitudes he can adopt in a world from which the traditional supports of life have been withdrawn, leaving the individual in isolation. Browning, as I have tried to show, shares Arnold's sense that his is a particularly exploratory and unsettled age. He is not a heedless or blinkered optimist; his constant endeavor is to start with the facts of experience, the "petits faits vrais," and to use them as a basis to proceed to a longer view, which may also be more hopeful:

> Nothing is prominently likeable
> To vulgar eye without a soul behind,
> Which, breaking surface, brings before the ball
> Of sight, a beauty buried everywhere.
> If we have souls, know how to see and use,
> One place performs, like any other place,
> The proper service every place on earth
> Was framed to furnish man with: serves alike
> To give him note that, through the place he sees,

> A place is signified he never saw,
> But, if he lack not soul, may learn to know.
> (*Red Cotton Night-Cap Country*, I.54–64)

It is true that in his less successful poems, Browning's vigor, rapidity, and raciness desert him and we are left with harshness, coarseness, or flatness. He seldom achieves a classic economy of effect—hence Arnold's disapproval.

In Browning's lifetime his reputation was dimmed by that of Tennyson, who began publishing earlier, was established by 1842, and was appointed poet laureate in 1850. In the same year he published *In Memoriam*, a moving and intricate series of poems which furnished all classes of reader with poetic pleasure of one kind or another. Thereafter, Tennyson was accepted as one who voiced the sentiments of his age, and his later volumes commanded an audience comparable with that of a popular novelist. It is true that some Victorian critics complained that Tennyson varied between an official optimism and a private pessimism and never produced the major poem of modern life for which the age stood in wait, but his public remained faithful to him. Browning, on the contrary, was never to attract a mass readership. By the 1860's he had begun to live down the reputation for unintelligibility which had dogged him since *Sordello*, and to receive recognition as a more experimental, more speculative, and more adventurous poet than the laureate. The Browning Society of London, which was founded in 1881, did much to enlist support for him in his later years by discussing papers on his poetry and by providing a series of useful aids to the reading of it. Unluckily, it concentrated on one side of his work and insisted on his value as a philosophical and religious teacher in terms that deterred many people. The prospectus contained the significant sentence "Browning's themes are the development of Souls, the analysis of Minds, Art, Religion, Love, the Relation of Man and Nature to God, of Man to Man and Woman, the Life past, present, and to come." The capital letters were particularly ominous. Edward Berdoe, one of the society's most enthusiastic supporters, wrote, "Browning was not born a mere man, but a Buddha on the highest peak of the Himalayas of thought," while W. G. Kingsland recorded, "Going out from his presence this Sabbath morning, I felt that I had been in the company of a man of God, of a denizen of another sphere, of one who lived in the world, yet was out of it."

To some readers, evidently, Browning was the most profound and philosophical of poets, to others the most dramatic and immediate. This double-sidedness has fascinated and disconcerted his critics and admirers from James to Maisie Ward. If there are, as it is tempting to suppose, two Robert Brownings, one of them is the Browning who has been known and loved for a century and a half, the ventriloquial genius whose greatest poems are "My Last Duchess," "The Bishop Orders His Tomb," and similar condensed dramas. It is of this Browning that Charles Stringham remarked, "He always gives the impression of writing about people who are wearing very expensive fancy dress." The other Browning is much less easy to depict, although he can perhaps be approached by way of Shelley and his insistence on the duty of the poet to be also a prophet. This implies a Browning who valued his dramatic gifts primarily because they enabled him to objectify his arguments. The arguments themselves, however, are what constitute the poem: the endeavor to "get truth and falsehood known and named as such" is the poem's active principle, not the endeavor to reproduce the sound of another man's voice. This is true even of his more obviously grotesque and high-spirited poems. He makes his own reply to critics of his method at the end of *Christmas-Eve:*

> . . . if any blames me,
> Thinking that merely to touch in brevity
>   The topics I dwell on, were unlawful,—
> Or worse, that I trench, with undue levity,
>   On the bounds of the holy and the awful,—
> I praise the heart and pity the head of him,
> And refer myself to THEE, instead of him
> Who head and heart alike discernest,
>   Looking below light speech we utter,
>   When frothy spume and frequent sputter
> Prove that the soul's depths boil in earnest!
> May truth shine out, stand ever before us!
>   (XXII.1343–1354)

Browning's obstinate insistence that poetry is a medium of expression has affected his reception in our own time, when, one might have thought, the surface difficulty that handicapped him during his life would be no deterrent to a modern reader accustomed to tolerating and welcoming in contemporary poets much greater degrees of obscurity and abruptness. Yet Browning is not very well suited by current definitions of poetry, especially those which are implied in the lines "A poem should not mean/ But be." Browning constantly resists any attempt to treat his poems in this way; his voice is insistently heard, saying:

> It is the glory and the good of Art,
> That Art remains the one way possible
> Of speaking Truth.

Browning has always demanded alert, informed reading. Poems such as "A Death in the Desert" or "Caliban upon Setebos" cannot be received in any fullness except by a willing reader prepared to follow the poet's thought, to understand the positions in a debate and evaluate them, and to respond not simply to the patterns of the poem but to the pressures of the argument. In short, Browning must be read not with the easygoing collaboration that is all that many contemporary poets get, and all that they seem to expect, but with the same attention and concentration that we accord to, say, Donne or Marvell.

Since James referred to Browning as "a tremendous and incomparable modern," it has been fashionable to call him the most modern of the Victorian poets, often with the suggestion that he had a direct influence on the poetry of the twentieth century. Edward Lucie-Smith, for example, has drawn attention to Browning's use of an imaginary speaker to some extent detached from the action; his habit of incorporating quotations into his poems with an effect of collage; his display of an impressive erudition, perhaps not all genuine; his free use of proper names and sobriquets; his use of the objects of every day, even of rubbish and miscellaneous refuse, as materials of lists and catalogs; and his willingness to shift abruptly from the sordid to the sublime, achieving particular effects by the juxtaposition. To these devices, which will no doubt be reminiscent of similar features in, for example, Pound and Eliot, one might add other distinctive innovations, in particular the use of a specific oblique objective correlative—an apparently remote and forgotten person or event or scene, which by its very singularity is presented as a unique image of a more immediate general situation. This audacious confidence in his own power to find a previously unimagined point of view on a continuing problem Browning shares with many later poets, though it is perhaps too strong to say that they were influenced by him.

If we are to describe Browning as a modern poet at all, we must do so within limits and with careful qualifications. As I have been at pains to emphasize, he is in many important ways an antimodernist, most obviously in his insistence on the significance of content, not as an accidental motivator of poetic language, but rather as that for which the poem exists. Yet it remains true that when we look at the Victorian age, his is the face that is turned most openly toward us. The firmness and freshness of his language; the inventiveness of his dramatic imagination; his curiosity about the extraordinary workings of the human mind; his resolute inquiry into human purposes and responsibilities; and his refusal to be satisfied either with a traditional formula or with a cynical evasion of the question or with resignation to defeat; all these mark Browning as a modern poet in the only sense that is of importance—as a poet who wrestled for himself with the problems of his art and solved them sufficiently to produce a great series of works of authentic power and originality, and who transmitted to his successors a tradition of poetry as a living and powerful force in the life of urban industrial man.

Browning's lifetime of labor in the service of his art for small reward brings to mind his own description of a dedicated poet:

> I'd like now, yet had haply been afraid,
> To have just looked, when this man came to die,
> And seen who lined the clean gay garret-sides
> And stood about the neat low truckle-bed,
> With the heavenly manner of relieving guard.
> Here had been, mark, the general-in-chief,
> Thro' a whole campaign of the world's life and death,
> Doing the King's work all the dim day long,
> In his old coat and up to knees in mud,
> Smoked like a herring, dining on a crust, —
> And, now the day was won, relieved at once!
> ("How It Strikes a Contemporary," 99–109)

SELECTED BIBLIOGRAPHY

I. BIBLIOGRAPHY. Mrs. S. Orr, *A Handbook to the Works* (London, 1885), an "authorized" handbook, the 6th ed. (1892) and later reprs. contain a bibliography; L. N. Broughton and B. F. Stelter, *A Concordance to the Poems of Robert Browning*, 2 vols. (New York, 1924–1925); L. N. Broughton, C. S. Northrup, and R. Pearsall, *Robert Browning: A Bibliography, 1830–1950* (Ithaca, N. Y., 1953), Cornell Studies in English 39; W. C. DeVane, *A Browning Handbook*, 2nd rev. ed. (New York, 1955), indispensable; F. E. Faverty, ed., *The Victorian Poets: A Guide to Research*, 2nd ed. (Cambridge, Mass., 1968), ch.

on Browning by P. Honan gives a full description of Browning studies up to 1966; A. E. Dyson, ed., *English Poetry, Select Bibliographical Guides* (London, 1971), ch. on Browning by I. Jack, good critical and bibliographical survey; N. B. Crowell, *A Reader's Guide to Robert Browning* (Albuquerque, N. M., 1972), includes bibliographies of Browning scholarship in the period 1945–1969, reading lists, surveys 23 of Browning's short poems; W. S. Peterson, *Robert and Elizabeth Barrett Browning: An Annotated Bibliography, 1951–1970* (New York, 1974), continued in the annual bibliography of *Browning Institute Studies*, the 1971 bibliography was published in vol. I (1973); other annual bibliographies can be found in *Browning Society Notes* and *Studies in Browning and His Circle*.

II. COLLECTED WORKS. *Poems*, 2 vols. (London, 1849); *The Poetical Works*, 3 vols. (London, 1863); *The Poetical Works*, 6 vols. (London, 1868); *The Poetical Works*, 17 vols. (London, 1888–1894), this ed. represents Browning's final arrangement and rev. of his poems; vols. I-XVI ed. by Browning himself, vol. XVII by Dr. Berdoe; C. Porter and H. A. Clarke, eds., *The Complete Works*, 12 vols. (New York, 1898), the Florentine ed., with prefatory essay, biographical intro., and bibliography; A. Birrell, ed., *The Complete Poetical Works*, 2 vols. (New York, 1907), intro. by Birrell, new ed. with additional poems (1915), subsequent rev. reprs.; F. G. Kenyon, ed., *The Works*, 10 vols. (London, 1912), the Centenary ed.; J. Bryson and M. M. Bozman, eds., *Poems and Plays*, 5 vols. (London, 1956–1964), Everyman Library nos. 41, 42, 502, 964, 966; R. A. King, Jr., gen. ed., *The Complete Works* (Athens, Ohio, 1969–   ), Variorum ed., the last vol. to appear was vol. IV (1973); *The Complete Poems*, 3 vols.: R. Altick, ed., *The Ring and the Book* (Harmondsworth, 1971) and J. Pettigrew, ed., *Robert Browning: The Poems*, 2 vols. (Harmondsworth, 1981), Penguin Poets series.

III. SELECTIONS. *Selections* (London, 1863); S. Nowell-Smith, ed., *Browning: Poetry and Prose* (London, 1950; reiss., 1967), the Reynard Library ed.; E. Lucie-Smith, ed., *A Choice of Browning's Verse* (London, 1967), interesting intro. on Browning's use of the dramatic monologue; I. Jack, ed., *Browning: Poetical Works, 1833–1864* (London, 1970), Oxford Standard Authors series; J. F. Loucks, ed., *Robert Browning's Poetry: Authoritative Texts, Criticism* (New York, 1979), texts, criticism, interpretations, essays, etc.

IV. SEPARATE WORKS. *Pauline: A Fragment of a Confession* (London, 1833), also in N. H. Wallis, ed., *Pauline: The Text of 1833 Compared with That of 1867 and 1888* (Philadelphia, 1978), repr. of the 1931 ed., with intro. and notes by Wallis; *Paracelsus* (London, 1835), also in M. L. Lee and K. B. Locock, eds., *Browning's Paracelsus* (London, 1909), useful annotated ed.; *Strafford: An Historical Tragedy* (London, 1837); *Sordello* (London, 1840), also in A. J. Whyte, ed. (London, 1913), helpfully annotated; *Bells and Pomegranates* (London, 1841–1846): no. 1, *Pippa Passes* (1841); no. 2, *King Victor and King Charles* (1842); no. 3,

Dramatic Lyrics (1842); no. 4, *The Return of the Druses. A Tragedy* (1843); no. 5, *A Blot in the Scutcheon. A Tragedy* (1843); no. 6, *Colombe's Birthday. A Play* (1844); no. 7, *Dramatic Romances and Lyrics* (1845); no. 8, *Luria: and a Soul's Tragedy* (1846); each part was published separately in paper wrappers under its own title, the complete series of eight parts was issued in cloth boards under the title *Bells and Pomegranates; Christmas-Eve and Easter-Day. A Poem* (London, 1850); "An Essay on Percy Bysshe Shelley" (London, 1852), written as the introductory essay to the *Letters of Percy Bysshe Shelley*, the book was withdrawn from publication when the letters were found to be spurious, the essay has been frequently repr.; a particularly useful repr. by H. F. B. Brett-Smith, ed. (Oxford, 1921), includes Peacock's *Four Ages of Poetry* and Shelley's *Defense of Poetry; Men and Women*, 2 vols. (London, 1855), also in F. B. Pinion, ed. (London, 1963), the English Classics series, an annotated ed., and P. Turner, ed. (London, 1972), intro., notes, and selected bibliography; *Dramatis Personae* (London, 1864), also in F. B. Pinion, ed., *Robert Browning: Dramatis Personae* (Glasgow, 1969), Collins Annotated Student Texts; *The Ring and the Book*, 4 vols. (London, 1868–1869), also in F. B. Pinion, ed. (London, 1957), the Scholar's Library, an abridgment with intro. and notes, R. Altick, ed. (Harmondsworth, 1971), text of the 1st ed., brief intro., bibliography, and notes; *Balaustion's Adventure* (London, 1871); *Prince Hohenstiel-Schwangau, Saviour of Society* (London, 1871); *Fifine at the Fair* (London, 1872); *Red Cotton Night-Cap Country, or Turf and Towers* (London, 1873); *Aristophanes' Apology Including a Transcript from Euripides, Being the Last Adventure of Balaustion* (London, 1875); *The Inn Album* (London, 1875); *Pacchiarotto and How He Worked in Distemper: With Other Poems* (London, 1876); *The Agamemnon of Aeschylus* (London, 1877), translation; *La Saisiaz: The Two Poets of Croisic* (London, 1878); *Dramatic Idyls* (first series) (London, 1879); *Dramatic Idyls Second Series* (London, 1880); *Jocoseria* (London, 1883); *Ferishtah's Fancies* (London, 1884); *Parleyings with Certain People of Importance in Their Day . . .* (London, 1887); *Asolando: Fancies and Facts* (London, 1890); D. Smalley, ed., *Browning's Essay on Chatterton* (Cambridge, Mass., 1948), convincing attribution to Browning of an article in the *Foreign Quarterly Review*, 29 (July 1842), 465–483.

V. LETTERS. F. G. Kenyon, ed., *Robert Browning and Alfred Domett* [1840–1877] (London, 1906); T. J. Wise, coll., *Letters of Robert Browning* [1830–1889], T. L. Hood, ed. (New Haven, Conn., 1933); R. Curle, ed., *Robert Browning and Julia Wedgwood: A Broken Friendship as Revealed in Their Letters* [1864–1869] (London, 1937); W. C. DeVane and K. L. Knickerbocker, eds., *New Letters of Robert Browning* [1835–1889] (New Haven, Conn., 1950); E. C. McAleer, ed., *Dearest Isa: Robert Browning's Letters to Isabella Blagden* [1857–1872] (Austin, Tex., 1951); P. Landis and R. Freeman, eds., *Letters of the*

Brownings to George Barrett [1861–1889] (Urbana, Ill., 1958); G. R. Hudson, ed., *Browning to His American Friends: Letters Between the Brownings, the Storys and James Russell Lowell, 1841–1890* (London, 1965), with an intro. and notes by Hudson; E. C. McAleer, ed., *Learned Lady: Letters from Robert Browning to Mrs. Thomas Fitz-Gerald, 1876–1889* (Cambridge, Mass., 1966); E. Kintner, ed., *The Letters of Robert Browning and Elizabeth Barrett Barrett, 1845–1846*, 2 vols. (Cambridge, Mass., 1969); P. Kelley and R. Hudson, *The Brownings' Correspondence: A Checklist* (New York, 1978), a comprehensive listing of the Brownings' correspondence; W. S. Peterson, ed., *Browning's Trumpeter, The Correspondence of Robert Browning and Frederick J. Furnivall, 1872–1889* (Washington, D.C., 1979).

VI. BIOGRAPHICAL STUDIES. G. K. Chesterton, *Robert Browning* (London, 1903), lively and perceptive, there are later reprs.; H. James, *William Wetmore Story and His Friends, from Letters, Diaries, and Recollections*, 2 vols. (Boston, 1903), contains an interesting and vivid account of Browning as he appeared to those who knew him; Mrs. S. Orr, *Life and Letters of Robert Browning* (London, 1908), a new, rev. ed. by F. G. Kenyon; B. Miller, *Robert Browning: A Portrait* (London, 1952), a psychological study of Browning that tends to be unsympathetic; M. Ward, *Robert Browning and His World: vol. I, The Private Face* [1812–1861] (London, 1968); vol. II, *Two Robert Brownings?* [1861–1889] (London, 1969), sympathetic to Browning; W. Irvine and P. Honan, *The Book, the Ring, and the Poet: A Biography of Robert Browning* (London, 1975), a comprehensive and fully documented biography with much critical analysis of the poetry; J. Maynard, *Browning's Youth* (Cambridge, Mass., 1977).

VII. CRITICAL STUDIES. A. Symons, *An Introduction to the Study of Browning* (London, 1886); H. Jones, *Browning as a Philosophical and Religious Teacher* (Glasgow, 1891); *The Old Yellow Book* (London, 1911), trans. with an intro. by C. Hodell, Browning's main source for *The Ring and the Book*; A. K. Cook, *A Commentary Upon Browning's "The Ring and the Book"* (London, 1920); W. C. DeVane, *Browning's "Parleyings": The Autobiography of a Mind* (New Haven, Conn., 1927); W. O. Raymond, *The Infinite Moment and Other Essays on Robert Browning* (Toronto, 1950; 2nd ed., 1965); E. D. H. Johnson, *The Alien Vision of Victorian Poetry: Sources of the Poetic Imagination in Tennyson, Browning, and Arnold* (Princeton, N. J., 1952), Princeton Studies in English no. 34, for Browning see pp. 71–143; H. C. Duffin, *Amphibian: A Reconsideration of Browning* (London, 1956); R. Langbaum, *The Poetry of Experience: The Dramatic Monologue in Modern Literary Tradition* (London, 1957); R. A. King, Jr., *The Bow and the Lyre: The Art of Robert Browning* (Ann Arbor, Mich., 1957); P. Honan, *Browning's Characters: A Study in Poetic Technique* (New Haven, Conn., 1961); H. S. Davies, *Browning and the*

Modern Novel (Hull, 1962), the St. John's College, Cambridge, Lecture, 1961–1962; N. B. Crowell, *The Triple Soul: Browning's Theory of Knowledge* (Albuquerque, N.M., 1963); J. H. Miller, *The Disappearance of God: Five Nineteenth Century Writers* (Cambridge, Mass., 1963), interesting section on Browning; W. J. Whitla, *The Central Truth: The Incarnation in Robert Browning's Poetry* (Toronto, 1963); B. Litzinger, *Time's Revenges: Browning's Reputation as a Thinker, 1889–1962* (Knoxville, Tenn., 1964); P. Drew, ed., *Robert Browning: A Collection of Critical Essays* (London, 1966); T. J. Collins, *Robert Browning's Moral-Aesthetic Theory, 1833–1855* (Lincoln, Nebr., 1967); B. Litzinger and K. L. Knickerbocker, eds., *The Browning Critics* (Lexington, Ky., 1967), includes a detailed bibliography, 1951–1965; I. Jack, *Robert Browning* (London, 1968), the Warton Lecture on English Poetry, 1967; N. B. Crowell, *The Convex Glass: The Mind of Robert Browning* (Albuquerque, N. M., 1968); R. A. King, Jr., *The Focusing Artifice: The Poetry of Robert Browning* (Athens, Ohio, 1968); W. D. Shaw, *The Dialectical Temper: The Rhetorical Art of Robert Browning* (Ithaca, N. Y., 1968); B. Melchiori, *Browning's Poetry of Reticence* (Edinburgh, 1968); R. D. Altick and J. F. Loucks, *Browning's Roman Murder Story: A Reading of "The Ring and the Book"* (Chicago, 1968); R. A. King, Jr., ed., *Victorian Poetry: An Issue Commemorative of the Centennial of the Publication of "The Ring and the Book"* (Morgantown, W. Va., 1968), a repr. in book form of *Victorian Poetry*, 6, nos. 3–4 (1968), an interesting collection of essays on *The Ring and the Book*; C. R. Tracy, ed., *Browning's Mind and Art* (Edinburgh, 1968), useful critical anthology; M. R. Sullivan, *Browning's Voices in "The Ring and the Book"* (Toronto, 1969); I. Armstrong, ed., *The Major Victorian Poets: Reconsiderations* (London, 1969), contains four important essays on Browning; B. Litzinger and D. Smalley, eds., *Browning: The Critical Heritage* (London, 1970); P. Drew, *The Poetry of Browning: A Critical Introduction* (London, 1970); D. S. Hair, *Browning's Experiments with Genre* (Edinburgh, 1972); I. Jack, *Browning's Major Poetry* (Oxford, 1973); W. E. Harrold, *The Variance and the Unity: A Study of the Complementary Poems of Robert Browning* (Athens, Ohio, 1973); J. R. Watson, ed., *Browning: "Men and Women" and Other Poems: A Casebook* (London, 1974), useful anthology of critical studies on Browning; I. Armstrong, ed., *Robert Browning: Writers and Their Background* (London, 1974), contains a reader's guide to Browning by P. Keating; E. Cook, *Browning's Lyrics: An Exploration* (Toronto, 1974); C. De L. Ryals, *Browning's Later Poetry, 1871–1889* (Ithaca, N. Y., 1975); B. S. Flowers, *Browning and the Modern Tradition* (London, 1976); B. Brugière, *L'Univers Imaginaire de Robert Browning* (Paris, 1979).